Christian Mehrwald has been working in the area of data warehousing for more than ten years. He introduced SAP Business Intelligence (BI) solutions during the first pilot installations in Germany. Since 2001 he has been a partner at the BI-specialist company, quadox AG located in Walldorf, Germany. He is now working as a senior consultant responsible for projects in the SAP BI area. His main focus is on the planning of large-scale data warehouses and on fine-tuning BI systems.

In addition to his consulting work, Mehrwald trains and coaches new project managers as well as project staff. He has authored several books on SAP BI, published in Germany.

Sabine Morlock is a translator and management assistant. She has been living in Germany and Canada and worked in different roles in the consulting industry and in the financial sector. Sabine currently holds a staff role in a software company and assumes selected translation projects in her spare time.

Data Warehousing with SAP® BW7
BI in SAP NetWeaver® 2004s

First published in 2017 by

INTERLINK BOOKS
An imprint of Interlink Publishing Group, Inc.
46 Crosby Street, Northampton, Massachusetts 01060
www.interlinkbooks.com

Text © Sally Butcher, 2017
Design and layout © Pavilion Books Company Ltd., 2017
Photography © Pavilion Books Company Ltd., 2017
American edition © Interlink Publishing Group, Inc., 2017

Photography by Yuki Sugiura

Library of Congress Cataloging-in-Publication Data available
ISBN 978-1-56656-018-4

3 1703 00634 2309

Printed and bound in China
10 9 8 7 6 5 4 3 2 1

To request our complete 48-page, full-color catalog, please call us toll free at 1-800-238-LINK, visit our website at www.interlinkbooks.com, or send us an e-mail at: info@interlinkbooks.com

When following the recipes, stick to one set of measurements (metric or imperial).

ACKNOWLEDGMENTS

A book is always the sum of many parts, but this one is the sum of more parts than usual, since I have been relying very heavily on my nearest and dearest to keep things going while I have had my head down.

Firstly, let me thank Emily, the commissioning editor, for her continuing support. This is the fourth book I have written under her wing, and she is both scarily efficient and heaps of fun. Thanks also to the rest of the team, especially Kom in PR, and Laura in design.

I was also thrilled once again to work with the totally professional photo shoot crew that is Valerie Berry (on food styling), Yuki Sugiura (for her ace pics), Wei Tang (for her choice of pots and plates and pans), and Dom (for being very sweet).

Thank you to my lovely agent, Veronique, and her assistant Laura for sorting out all the headachey stuff involved in writing a book: they are worth their weight in ibuprofen money.

I also owe a bundle of thanks to my customers/guinea (soy alternative to) pigs, who have been both hugely encouraging and willing to test/try out new recipes.

But the biggest thank you this time goes to my husband and his family for understanding why the light has been on with nobody home for the last few months, and covering my back. You see, Persepolis,* or at least our restaurant within the shop, is very busy (*mash'Allah*), and in theory I do all of the cooking (which I do love, of course). I have been going slightly spare, but everyone has rallied to give me the time I needed to bring the Veggieverse to reality, from mother-in-law making *dolmeh,* down to poor Mr. Shopkeeper working on a hairline-fractured foot to give me more writing time.

Finally, as ever, a huge huggy for my mother for doing and saying all the right motherly things, and emptying my ironing basket regularly.

 And we totally expect to see you here one day. You probably don't need a visa, just an empty tummy and a sense of fun.

Christian Mehrwald • Sabine Morlock

Data Warehousing with SAP® BW7

BI in SAP NetWeaver® 2004s

Architecture, Concepts, and Implementation

Christian Mehrwald, christian.mehrwald@quadox.de
Sabine Morlock, sabine.morlock@hotmail.com

Transtator: Sabine Morlock
Editor: Dr. Michael Barabas
Copyeditor: Judy Flynn
Proofreader: Jimi DeRouen
Layout and Type: Petra Strauch, Just in Print
Cover Design: Helmut Kraus, www.exclam.de
Printed in the USA

First published under the title
„Datawarehousing mit SAP® BW 7 (BI in SAP NetWeaver® 2004s)"
by dpunkt.verlag GmbH, www.dpunkt.de
Heidelberg, Germany

1st English Edition
© 2009
Rocky Nook Inc.
26 West Mission Street Ste 3
Santa Barbara, CA 93101
www.rockynook.com

ISBN 978-1-933952-40-6

Library of Congress Cataloging-in-Publication Data

Mehrwald, Christian.
    [Datawarhousing mit SAP BW7, BI in SAP NetWeaver 2004s. English]
    Data warehousing with SAP BW7 BI in SAP NetWeaver 2004s : architecture, concepts, and
implementation / Christian Mehrwald and Sabine Morlock. -- 1st ed.
        p. cm.
    ISBN 978-1-933952-40-6 (alk. paper)
    1. SAP Business information warehouse. 2. Data warehousing. 3. Management information
systems. 4. Business--Computer programs. I. Morlock, Sabine. II. Title.
    HF5548.4.B875M4413 2009
    005.75'85--dc22
                        2008055168

Distributed by O'Reilly Media
1005 Gravenstein Highway North
Sebastopol, CA 95472

Overview

Table of Content

1 Introduction

Over the last few years, data warehousing has developed into one of the central topics in IT. It is used as a strategic tool to provide information for controlling and decision-making processes. Further, data warehousing provides the basis for other technologies—e.g., in the areas of strategic enterprise management, customer management, and process analysis.

The need for systems to provide and analyze information is as old as information technology itself. Initially, data analysis was understood to be an appendix to operating systems. In the mid-90s, the term *data warehouse* won recognition and turned into a separate area of IT with its own specific concepts since data warehousing systems not only enable the analysis of large volumes of company-wide data but also reduce the complexity of data provision.

Data warehousing systems centrally provide data for controlling and decision-making processes. Technical and functional characteristics make each and every data warehousing system unique.

Data warehousing systems may be classified in two categories:

- Operational administrative systems
- Decision support systems

Operational Administrative Systems

Operational administrative systems (also called *transactional systems*) provide functionality for the enterprise to administer and execute business transactions. The typical tasks of an operational administrative system are order entry, invoicing, inventory management, personnel administration, and payroll. The so-called enterprise resource planning (ERP) systems support not only individual areas but all functions of the enterprise value chain. An example of an EPR system is SAP ERP Central Component (SAP ECC) or its forerunner, SAP R/3. In the following, they are both referred to as SAP ERP.

Since operational administrative systems technically distinguish themselves by showing functions based on individual transactions (orders, booking entries, etc.), they are also called online transaction processing (OLTP) systems.

Decision Support Systems

Given their individual transaction focus, administrative operational systems do not form a suitable basis for complex business decisions. Hence, there is a counterpart—*decision support systems (DSSs).*

A DSS systems are classic reporting and interactive data analysis systems *(online analytical processing,* or *OLAP)* as well as systems used to search for complex coherences and unknown data patterns (data mining).

Figure 1–1

Decision support systems

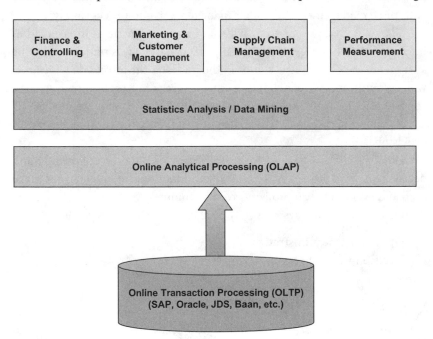

Apart from the tools providing general data analysis functions, there are process-oriented tools specializing in the analysis of particular process data. They are typically used in finance & controlling, marketing & customer management, supply chain management, and performance management (see figure 1–1).

Data Warehouse Systems

Any decision support system requires a data pool on which analytical functions are based. OLTP systems do not form a suitable data pool given their functions and especially their data structures. Usually, DSSs do not have their own data management but may share a data warehouse system with other DSSs.

DSSs are mainly characterized by their data management, which strongly supports the analytical review of the data. The content of a data warehouse is extracted from the OLTP system data and transferred to data models in BW, which are optimized to analyze large databases. It is kept redundantly from source system data.

So, a data warehouse is not a complete decision support system per se but only the basis for such, and it offers the respective interfaces. However, software producers usually couple data warehouse systems at least with an OLAP tool. From this habit, data warehouse systems are often incorrectly called OLAP systems since they only describe sales habits of suppliers.

With SAP Business Information Warehouse (SAP BW), the Business Explorer tool links a complete product suite to decision support systems and they can be part of a BW implementation (e.g., the Data Mining Workbench and large parts of Integrated Planning).

Content

As the title says, this book deals with SAP BW as a data warehouse and as such ignores the BW-integrated decision support tools as far as possible. This is not because these tools may be irrelevant, but an adequate description of such tools would fill a separate book and is beyond the scope of this one.

The book is divided in six sections:

- Architecture
- Data Model
- Analytical Engine
- Extraction and Staging
- BW Design
- BW in Live Operation (also referred to as Productive Operation)

Within the section on architecture, BW installation components and their functions and interrelations are discussed conceptually. The Metadata

Repository, the application platforms of the base system as well as their communication technologies are outlined.

Then, in the next section, the focus is on specific data models in data warehousing in general in order to deduce and explain the specific implementation of the *data model* in SAP BW. We'll discuss performance-relevant aspects of data modeling and give you practical ground rules for modeling.

Between the decision support systems and the data in BW operates the analytical engine. It receives queries, reads the BW data, and considers particular BW data modeling as well as status information from extraction and staging. The respective section describes how the analytical engine works and how it is tuned or monitored.

The section on extraction and staging details how the data flow from source systems to BW can be defined. The description follows a reference architecture that partitions data flow in logical levels in which they are validated, transformed, error-corrected, and integrated. Further, data quality and performance tuning are considered from a staging angle.

The next section is on BW design. In this section we'll discuss typical modifications of the reference architecture, which was discussed in earlier sections. Here, the focus is on partitioning techniques and large-scale architectures.

The section on live operation gives an overview of all regular processes to be executed. And considering organizational as well as technical aspects, I'll explain how automation and monitoring are realized.

The book ends with a comprehensive appendix, dealing with special topics such as currency conversion, transportation, and migration as well as development of metadata content.

I Architecture

A data warehouse architecture usually describes data-warehouse-related components, their functions, and how they cooperate on a conceptually comprehensive level. However, a data warehouse cannot be considered isolated but it is integrated in a system landscape with components other than SAP BW. Chapter 2 describes SAP BW *architecture components* based on a three-layer model; the discussion will center on the particularities of BW architecture, but the components of connected systems will also be considered.

The basic understanding of the underlying application platforms and their communication interfaces is key to building data warehouse architecture with SAP BW, as outlined in chapter 3 on the BW basis system.

Special focus lies not only on data storage but also on data administration and data structures in BW, as described in chapter 4, which is about the Metadata Repository.

2 Architecture Components

As a data warehouse, BW is always used in combination with other system components, which fulfill specific functions in extraction and decision support. When all functional areas of BW as well as the connected systems are combined, BW shows a three-layer architecture:

- Extraction layer
- Data warehouse
- Decision support systems

These three layers are outlined in a separate figure in the fold-out together with their components. They will be described and explained in the following sections.

2.1 Extraction Layer

The extraction layer describes the different functional systems from which SAP BW extracts data as well as the respective extraction procedures.

> The extraction of analysis-relevant data from source systems is a central issue of each data warehousing project. Complex data structures, large volumes of data, and volatility of source system data (e.g., subsequent change of supplied data) may cause extraction to become a very extensive part of BW that you should not underestimate.

With its communication interfaces (see section 3.1), BW uses several powerful tools to access source system data where the type of source system will specify the interface to be used.

Thanks to its own communication interfaces, BW can access the following source systems:

- SAP ERP
- SAP BW systems
- File systems
- Database systems
- XML documents (in SOAP messages)
- Source systems with the Java Database Connectivity (JDBC), OLE DB for OLAP (ODBO), or XML for Analysis (XML/A) interface

Should the BW extraction options not meet requirements, you can use extraction tools from other suppliers (referred to as *third-party ETL tools*).[1]

For third-party ETL tools, BW offers an interface in which it considers the third-party ETL tool to be the source system. Depending on the source system type, these tools use a large variety of extraction methods in alignment with the source system. Note, however, that the BW extraction options have been considerably enhanced in the most recent releases and the use of third-party ETL tools has become almost obsolete.

In the following sections, we'll explain how to access the source system types. You'll find detailed descriptions on how to create an extraction from the source systems or in BW in chapter 14 and 15.

SAP ERP systems In practice, SAP ERP systems are the most relevant type of source system for the BW extraction layer, which explains the extensive extraction options that SAP offers for this source system. The extraction is effected by so-called extractors, which can be installed as plug-ins from version 3.0D of the SAP ERP systems onward.

Extractors offer not only the necessary interfaces and extraction programs to technically enable extraction, but also preconfigured extraction scenarios for the very different modules (called BI content, as described in appendix D).

Preconfigured extraction scenarios can be customized and individual extraction mechanisms can be developed. Technical background information on extraction can be found in section 14.2.

BW systems When you're building large-scale architectures (see chapter 27), the extraction of data from BW systems plays a special role. From a technical point of view, extraction from BW systems is very similar to extraction from SAP ERP systems; in BW, there are also extractors that meet the technical requirements to extract data from BW and to pass it on to other BW systems.

---

1. A current List of certified third-party suppliers can be found in the SAP Service Marketplace.

The communication between BW and a source system always requires a joint communication interface. A limiting factor is the organizational and technical authority over control of the interface, which has to be accepted.

File system

The lowest common denominator of data exchange between heterogeneous systems often is making data available in ASCII files on the file server. There are various disadvantages to this, especially in terms of exchange of metadata and common control information. However, it is often the easiest way for the source system to provide data in a file format.

Since its first release, BW uses a file interface that is well suited for exchanging large volumes of data. The only requirement for a "BW-suitable" file is a flat file structure design; that is, each record in the file needs to show the same composition. Reading of hierarchical data structures is not possible within the standard options of BW.

For several special database systems, BW offers direct access to tables and views on databases with an interface called **DB connect.** Access is not accomplished via a JDBC or comparable interface. Instead, BW functions as a database client to access the database systems, which results in high-performance access.

Database systems

Usage of DB connect requires certain libraries and clients that exist only for database systems that BW can use to store its own data. However, even within this selection, a database system cannot be extracted in every given constellation; especially if BW runs on a UNIX platform, libraries and clients are not available to the various database systems.

Before planning to use DB connect, you should verify that it can be used with the combination of the system platform underlying BW and a database system to be extracted.

To support the so-called "open standards", BW offers a web service. This is the SOAP service, which allows you to supply BW with XML documents. However, the process of doing so is so specific that the SOAP service may hardly be called an open interface.

XML

The protocol of the SOAP service is rather tailored to the Exchange Infrastructure (SAP XI) technology, which has been created for data exchange between heterogeneous systems. It only makes sense to use XML documents for extraction when an XI system is operating between the original source system and the SOAP service. In fact, it is possible to migrate XML data to BW without an XI system. However, the effort to comply with the protocol requirements is so high that the use of the interface is questionable.

In any case, one has to consider that the SOAP service is the slowest of all interfaces (by far!), and ideally, it should be used only to exchange individual records.

JDBC, ODBO, XML/A

Describing the conglomerate of the very different interfaces JDBC, ODBO, and XML/A in one step might seem slightly odd. This grouping results from the change in architecture SAP has realized with the new application platform, the Java™ 2 Platform Enterprise Edition (J2EE) server, whose connection framework allows access to these interfaces via the ***Universal Data Connect (UDC).***[2]

JDBC, ODBO, and XML/A provide access to the J2EE server's connection framework rather than access to the source systems. This is a component of the J2EE engine configuration.

Actually, the J2EE server is a full-fledged application server. Apart from the named interfaces, it may also dispose of components such as Portal, Content Management, and TREX, as well as its own administration environment, the J2EE Visual Administrator. The J2EE server will be addressed in chapter 3, with the description of the BW basis system.

From a BW point of view, the J2EE server is only relevant due to its UDI Java components, and thus—here and in the following—it will be considered only as part of the extraction layer.

2.2   Data Warehouse

The data warehouse layer is the heart of BW and basically covers the Data Manager and the staging engine.

Data Manager

The scope of the Data Manager comprises the administration of specific data structures of SAP BW, the management of data content, and the provision of access to a database.

The *definition of data structures* is achieved in BW on an abstract level in the form of object definitions for master and transactional data (e.g., InfoObjects and InfoCubes). The data structures of the database system where the data will be stored are derived from these object definitions.

---

2.   The terminology differs. The terms *Universal Data Connect (UDC)* and *Universal Data Interchange (UDI)* are used. In this book, I'll use the more common term *Universal Data connect,* or *UD connect,* if UDI does not characterize a special term (e.g., UDI Java components).

Thus, the Data Manager acts as an intermediary between the definition of BW objects in the metadata and the technical storage of data in the related database systems.

The *management of data content* deals with physical access to the databases, and in BW it is the intermediary between the diverse BW functions and the database access. In particular, the Data Manager has to be able to handle the specific data structures of BW.

Database-specific definitions and operations are also included in the scope of the Data Manager; e.g., creation/deletion of indexes, configuration of partitioning, handling of Stored Procedures, and so on.

Thus, *providing external access* is also in the scope of the Data Manager. If BW is used internally to access databases, it is essential that the Data Manager enables analysis tools to access to the BW system.

Access is made using a central interface, the so-called analytical engine, whose task it is to transform and optimize incoming queries in a BW-internal format and also to return result sets. However, the process and quality status of the databases, as well as possibly limited authorizations, have to be considered.

Before the Data Manager can handle any data, the data must have been received and prepared by the extractors of the respective source systems. The preparation is necessary as the source systems usually do not follow any identical conventions regarding data storage (e.g., different use of upper and lower case, handling of leading zeros, different keys to same data) or the data may not have been delivered in the way the BW is supposed to provide it to the user (e.g., calculation of key figures).

Staging engine

Extraction from the source systems and the subsequent controlling and monitoring of data streams is initiated through staging. To accomplish the extraction and processing, the staging uses data structures that are usually temporary but may be filed persistently for quality assurance purposes.

All settings regarding definition, controlling, and monitoring of the Data Manager and the staging engine are filed in a central Metadata Repository, whose structures will be explained in detail in chapter 4.

Data Warehouse administration

In a way, the Easy Access menu serves in SAP BW as a user interface to the Metadata Repository, and it opens right after the SAP graphical user interface (SAPGUI) logon[3] (see figure 2–1).

---

3. The Easy Access menu is an area menu RS00_BW, which can be activated systemwide by using the transaction SSM2.

Figure 2–1

SAP Easy Access menu

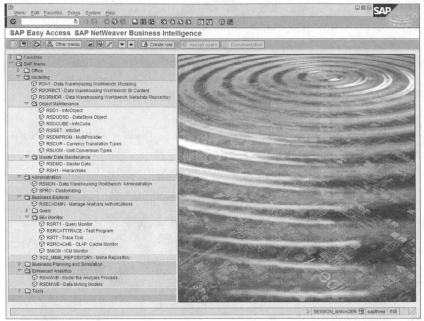

© SAP AG

However, it is wrong to consider the Easy Access menu to be an interface to the Metadata Repository since the Easy Access menu is mainly a structured compilation of menu items that branch out to further BW transactions. There are numerous transactions to control and monitor the system, but there are *also* transactions to maintain the metadata objects in BW.

The transactions can be started either through the menu items of the Easy Access menu or through the direct indication of the transaction in the respective entry field, as shown in figure 2–1 (upper left).

Data Warehousing Workbench

The pivotal part of the BW is the *Data Warehousing Workbench (DWWB)*. It can be accessed from the Easy Access menu, or alternatively through the transaction (see figure 2–2).

The majority of metadata for BW objects is defined in the Data Warehousing Workbench. Furthermore, the DWWB also contains functions to control and monitor administrative processes in the Data Manager and the staging engine.

The majority of explanations in this book refer to settings that are made in the Data Warehousing Workbench.

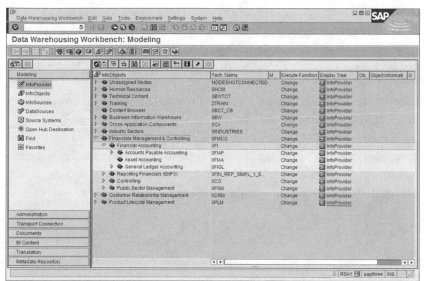

Figure 2–2
Data Warehousing
Workbench

© SAP AG

2.3 Decision Support Systems

The Decision Support layer contains all tools with which data of the BW can be retrieved and prepared to be relevant to decisions. The data is accessed using the MDX processor of the BW, which acts as intermediary between the Data Manager and the query logs of the access interfaces.

The following interfaces can access the BW via the DSS tools:

Interfaces

- The SAP-specific *Business Application Programming Interface (BAPI)*. Up to version 2 of BW, it was the only open interface for DSSs and thus it is the most common interface. SAP's own DSS tools also use BAPI, but they can also access the BW without the BAPIs, which no other DSS tool is allowed to do.
- The HTTP-based BEx-Service to provide websites with HTML code and JavaScript for *Web Queries* and *Web Applications*.
- The HTTP-based *XML/A service* to provide multidimensional data using the platform-independent standardized XML protocol XML/A (XML for Analysis).
- The Microsoft-specific *ODBO interface*[4] to provide multidimensional data based on the COM protocol.

Business Explorer   In addition to the option to supply any DSS tool with data, BW uses a range of its own decision support tools that access BW via interfaces from the outside, exactly as third-party tools do. In BW, these tools are pooled in the product suite *Business Explorer (BEx)*. They contain tools for web- and Excel-based OLAP analysis, preparing and sending formatted reports, developing web-based analytical applications, data mining, running planning applications, and so on.

Until release BW 3.x, the Business Explorer tools could mostly be used independently, but in release 7, some of them can be used only in combination with the NetWeaver 2004s portal. This is the case, for example, for broadcasting or when deploying ad hoc analyses on the Web.

---

4.   ODBO stands for OLE DB for OLAP (Object Linking and Embedding Database for Online Analytical Processing)

3 BW Basis System

SAP NetWeaver 2004s, and thereore also other SAP products (such as BW or ERP), is based on a three-layer client/server platform consisting of database layer, application server, and client.

The application server is the ***SAP Web Application Server,*** which we'll refer to as Web AS. It is a *development and runtime environment* at the same time and has all the components of a typical application server, such as database and communication interfaces, lock management, and job and process control, as well as tools for system administration.

Application server

The execution of processes in SAP BW is based on the runtime environment of Web AS, in which the functionality was developed. It can also be enhanced by proprietary development through its integrated development environment.

For scaling and load balancing, it is possible to use not only one but several application servers to direct dialog and background processes to the application server that has the least load when the process is started.

> The use of several application servers for load balancing is an effective tool to scale operational systems like SAP ERP. With systems such as SAP BW, the bottleneck is usually not the application server but the database server; the use of several application servers for performance tuning often (but not always) fails to produce the desired effects.

Up to this point, Web AS is similar to other application servers. However, from version 6.40[5] onward, Web AS not only had one development and one runtime environment, it had two of each, one for ABAP[6] (**A**dvanced **B**usiness **A**pplication **P**rogramming, originally **A**llgemeiner **B**erichts-

---

5. The versioning of SAP BW and the respective basis system are different. The Web AS in version 6.40 was first released in SAP BW in its BW 3.5 version.
6. In this context, ABAP refers to the programming languages ABAP/4 as well as ABAP objects.

Aufbereitungs-**P**rozessor = general report creation processor) and one for Java programs.

Each of these Web AS components is a self-contained application server, and they can be used technically isolated from each other. Thus, both Web AS components are full application servers that can be run on identical or different physical hardware.

Web AS ABAP   The so-called Web AS ABAP is the actual SAP BW platform. It is an enhanced basis system, comparable to the "old" SAP R/3. So, Web AS ABAP forms the consistent platform for the majority of SAP products.

As in releases prior to 3.5, the data warehouse functions are solely based on WEB AS ABAP; i.e., to run BW 3.5, the Web AS ABAP part needs to be installed, whereas its counterpart, WEB AS Java, is only an optional component of the BW installation.

Web AS Java   From BW 3.5 onward, the Web AS Java is a new component of the BW basis system. It is not an enhancement of Web AS but a completely revised runtime environment or platform, which can be used in coexistence with the existing Web AS ABAP.

The basis for this platform is the J2EE Engine, which is compliant with JMX 1.3 and on which JavaBeans, servlets, JSPs, JNDI, JMS, and Java Mail can be implemented in accordance with the agreed-upon standards.

Database layer   On both platforms, access to data content is encapsulated by a persistence layer that controls all access to the database.

With Web AS ABAP, the persistence layer is the *ABAP Dictionary,* which can be accessed through the SQL dialect Open SQL. Due to its relevance for SAP BW, the ABAP Dictionary will be further explained together with the Metadata Repository in chapter 4.2.

The respective counterpart in Web AS Java is the *Java Database Dictionary,* which can be accessed with Open SQL APIs. However, it is irrelevant for data warehouse application development in SAP BW 3.5.

In both cases, one of the established relational database systems, such as Oracle, MS SQL Server, DB2, Informix, or Max DB (formerly SAP DB or ADABAS D) is used for the actual data management. The Web AS itself stores programs and data structures but not the data content.

Since there is no comprehensive lock mechanism for Web AS ABAP and Web AP Java and individual storing formats are used, the two platforms do not share the same database. Instead, each application server has its own database schema so that the separation of Web AS ABAP and Web AS Java is continued technologically.

Unlike the application layer, the database layer cannot be assigned to several servers,[7] and with high data volume requirements, the database will most likely be the bottleneck in the BW system. When selecting hardware, it is very important to choose the right database server for Web AS ABAP.

There are two hearts beating in Web AS; that is, two application servers. They may coexist, but strictly speaking they do not have much in common because they are using different programming languages and cannot even share a database. Thus, balancing similar tasks on the two servers is impossible—a gradual migration of functionalities from one part of the Web AS to the other is also rather utopian.

Who does what?

The existing data warehouse functionality of SAP BW—and its enhancements—will inevitably remain in the scope of Web AS ABAP. Web AS Java will take over new tasks that typically focus on the data exchange with other systems; after all, with the J2EE Engine, Web AS is to open up to so-called "standards". These are products such as SAP Enterprise Portal, SAP Mobile Infrastructure, Knowledge Management, and SAP Exchange Infrastructure (SAP XI). All products that have been developed on a Web AS Java basis have been bundled with SAP BW in a single product portfolio and have launched as the integration platform *NetWeaver.*

From an SAP BW point of view, the J2EE Engine in Web AS has two purposes: On the one hand, it controls the portal, which is mandatory for several development activities around data analysis; e.g., for ad hoc reporting or the Information Broadcaster. On the other hand, it may control the Universal Data connect (UD connect), which is used to extract data from JDBC, ODBO, and XML/A sources to be handed over to BW (see section 2.1).

Figure 3–1 shows the architecture of the BW basis system.

The description of Web AS ABAP and Web AS Java has established that these two Web AS parts are technologically self-contained system platforms. However, they cannot be called isolated—quite the contrary!

The communication interfaces, which are very important in SAP BW, will be discussed separately in the following chapter.

---

7. An exception is the use of the Real Application Cluster (RAC) in Oracle databases. But even then, the database itself will take on the load balancing on several physical servers and not Web AS.

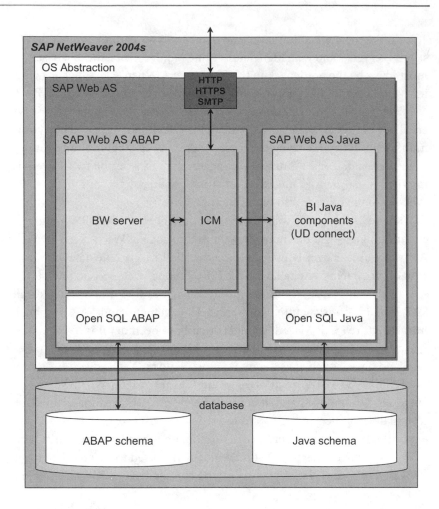

Figure 3–1

BW basis system

3.1 Communication Interfaces

To exchange data with source systems or decision support systems, BW uses a range of communication interfaces. Even though Web AS Java should be used for communication and integration, Web AS ABAP also has communication interfaces. Given the history of this product, the communication interfaces in Web AS ABAP are far more important in practice. Furthermore, Web AS ABAP and Web AS Java not only communicate with other systems but also among themselves.

The basics of the communication technology will be described in this section. A detailed explanation is beyond the scope of this book. For a BW novice, a discussion of the communication interfaces might not be relevant at this point, and it may be used as reference at a later stage.

The fundamental communication technologies of Web AS are as follows:

- Web AS ABAP's *file interface* for communication with heterogeneous systems as well as the *Business Application Programming Interface (BAPI)* to communicate with SAP-compliant systems
- *Internet Communication Framework* to provide web services in Web AS ABAP
- *J2EE Connector Architecture* to develop Java-based interfaces in Web AS Java

At this point, we are not concerned with the data warehouse functions of BW. We are only providing a basic overview, which can be expanded in the following chapters.

3.1.1 File and BAPI

The file interface and BAPI are both technologies that were used in SAP R/3 to communicate with other systems.

In BW, the file interface is used mostly to exchange data with non-SAP systems—e.g., extraction from source systems or migration of edited analysis data in hub and spoke architectures (see chapter 27). *File interface*

In heterogeneous system environments, the file interface often is the lowest common denominator of all systems, and SAP R/3 systems only communicated with each other via file systems prior to release 3.

For systems that are SAP compliant in their communication with SAP BW and SAP ERP systems, SAP designed the Business Application Programming Interface (BAPI). It is a series of interfaces that can be used by SAP itself as well as by third-party suppliers to access SAP systems. The interfaces are defined and open at an application level so that they will remain stable in case of a new BW release by SAP. *BAPI*

Technically, the process of starting a BAPI is a so-called Remote Function Call (RFC). The Remote Function Call is one option you can use to start a function module in a different SAP Web AS ABAP. This can be done from an SAP ERP or BW system or from proprietary programs. The data is transferred via TCP/IP or X.400 as byte flow. *Remote Function Call (RFC)*

Even though starting a BAPI is technically considered a Remote Function Call, the Remote Function Call does not need the open function modules to exchange data. Via RFC, undocumented and nondisclosed function modules can also be started, in the same way as via BW extractors or the DSS tools of BEx. So systems that rely on BAPIs (for certification or otherwise) always have a disadvantage compared to proprietary SAP tools that can bypass BAPIs, if required.

Starting RFCs from SAP ERP systems

For Web AS ABAP and SAP ERP systems, the target system to be communicated with needs to be defined before RFCs can be made. This definition is made once and will be valid systemwide. It contains information on the logon procedure, the target system's IP address, and so on, and will be made via transaction SM59.

The RFC is an extension of the ABAP command CALL FUNCTION. When you add the target system that has been defined earlier, the function module will not be called in the Web AS ABAP or the SAP ERP system where the command is executed, but in the respective target system (see figure 3–2).

Figure 3–2
Function calls via RFC

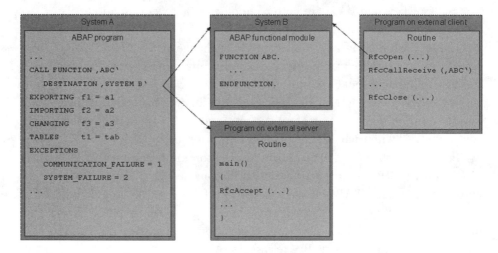

RFCs from proprietary systems

If an RFC is to be made from a proprietary system (or from a tool of a third-party supplier), an RFC library (RFC API) can be used. SAP provides RFC libraries for OS/2, Windows, Windows NT, and all UNIX derivatives released for ERP usage.

RFC connection types

An RFC can be made synchronously as well as asynchronously; it doesn't matter whether the called system is an SAP system or a customer-coded program.

Synchronous means that the call to the RFC component for the called system ends only when the remote function has been executed and terminated with a status code. On asynchronous calls, the status will not be directly returned to the triggering program; i.e., the call is technically terminated as soon as the data is "ready to be sent". If the called system is not available at that time, in SAP BW the basis system will control further attempts to send.

A synchronous call is called transactional RFC (TRFC)[8]; otherwise, the term *RFC* is correct.

Transfer Tools

From a programming point of view (for SAP as well as for customers), the use of file and BAPI interfaces requires much effort if the programs are to use a wide range of communication options (synchronous, asynchronous, file, BAPI).

For this reason, a "toolkit" was built that provides a range of tools that require little programming effort, named *Application Link Enabling (ALE)*.

For the different communication techniques, ALE supports synchronous as well as asynchronous connections and provides monitoring and error correction functions.

For data communication, all information is transferred into so-called *intermediate documents (IDocs)*. This is a type of data container whose structure can be defined individually for the respective communication. Since the use of IDocs requires a given data model (header and data record), IDocs have a bigger overhead than, for example, a communication via RFC where no ALE/IDoc is used.

For this reason, the use of IDocs is unfavorable from a performance point of view. In BW, IDocs are only used to send requirements and confirmations (i.e., for transfers of low data volume).

Since they are so easy to program, IDocs were used for extraction of mass data in previous BW releases. Meanwhile, they have been replaced by RFCs in performance-critical areas, but sporadically they can be used optionally. Since they only serve the purpose of downward compatibility, there is no reason to use IDocs instead of RFCs in new development.

---

8. The TRFC was initially called asynchronous RFC. It was renamed transactional RFC since the asynchronous RFC has a different meaning in R/3.

3.1.2   Internet Communication Framework

There is a central infrastructure for Web AS ABAP and Web AS Java that enables communication via the HTTP, HTTPS, and SMTP protocols: the Internet Communication Framework (ICF) or the Internet Communication Manager (ICM), respectively.

Using ICF or ICM, BW can act as a server and offer HTTP services. Clients can send an HTTP request to BW. These requests are forwarded to the application via the ICM and from the ICM a reply can be returned to the client. This is the case with Web Reporting.

BW can also act as client and send requests to servers offering HTTP services and wait for their reply.

If required, HTTP services can be self-programmed. However, in practice this is rarely required since BW comes with a range of services that can be used both in the area of extraction and in the area of decision support systems. Here are some HTTP services:

- Accessing query data in HTML format via Web Analyzer
- Accessing query data in XML/A format via Open Analysis Interface
- Providing extraction data in XML format via the SOAP service (see chapter 2.1)
- Communicating between web pages and proprietary applications based on Business Server Pages (BSPs)
- Exchanging metadata between different systems in XML format (see appendix C.3)
- Showing metadata related to BW objects in HTML format
- Showing the user-defined documentation of BW objects

In the maintenance of services in the transaction SICF, you can see what services are offered and whether they are active (see figure 3–3).

The handling of a request via ICF is technically realized through a process in Web AS ABAP. There is an individual ABAP class behind each service, which in ICF terminology is referred to as *ICF handler* or *HTTP request handler,* respectively.

ICF handler   The name of the ICF handler can be found in the context menu of the respective service in the transaction SICF under the menu item *Display Service→Handler List.* For the HTTP Service for the Web Analyzer, this would be the ABAP class (= ICF Handler) CL_RSR_WWW_HTTP (see figure 3–4).

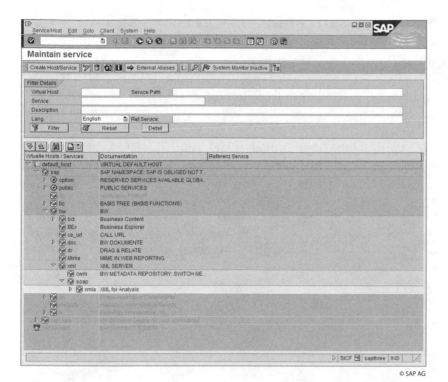

Figure 3–3
*Services of the Internet
Connection Framework*

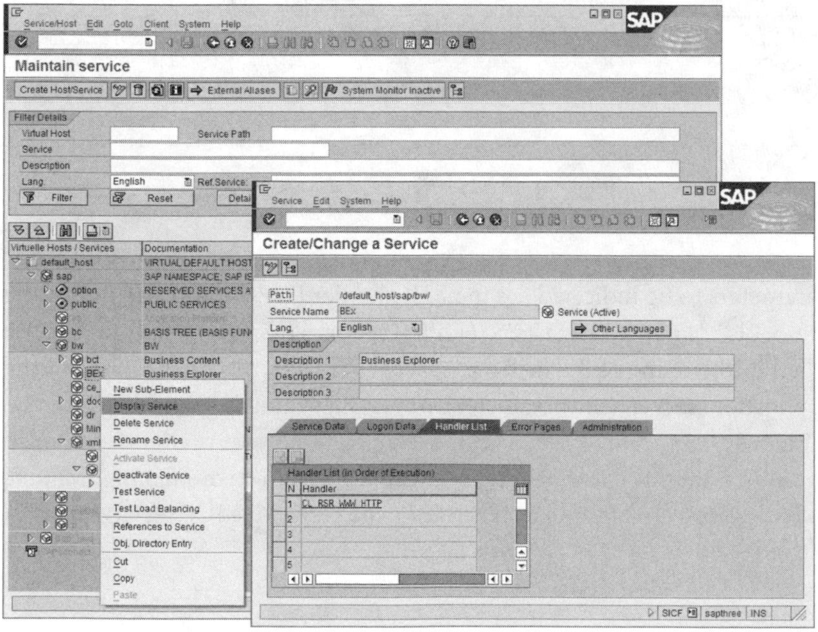

Figure 3–4
ICF services handler

The launch of an HTTP service requires a URL that identifies the server and the ICF handler, and that may transfer to the handler data that is coded within the URL as a query string.

If the service was supplied by SAP in BW, the URL of the HTTP service is always built according to the following schema:

<Protocol>://<Server>:<Port>/sap/bw/<Service>

With the use of the function module RSBB_URL_PREFIX_GET, the URL prefix can be identified. The function module can also be started manually in transaction SE37 (see the example of the URL prefix for the ICF Handler CL_RSR_WW_HTTP in figure 3–5).

Figure 3–5

Identification of the URL prefix for ICF services

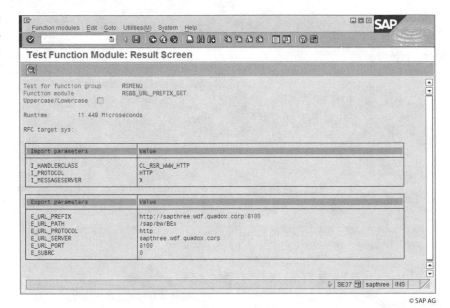

© SAP AG

Parameters to be indicated are the ICF handler (I_HANDLER) and one of the protocols, HTTP or HTTPS (I_PROTOCOL), and you need to specify whether the name of the message server (Parameter X) or the name of the application server (no parameter) or its alias should be coded into the URL.

When the function module is executed (menu item *Function Module →Test→Single Test* in transaction SE37), the respective ICF service must be active.

3.1.3 J2EE Connector Architecture

The J2EE Connector Architecture forms the basis for Web AS Java communication interfaces. This connector framework enables the connection from heterogenous systems to the J2EE platform on the one hand via *Java Connectors* and on the other hand via *Java Resource Adapters.*

Java Connectors are the middleware component (partly platform dependent) of an interface in which communication with the respective application system is implemented.

Java Connectors

The Java Resource Adapters connect Java Connectors and Web AS Java. Their interfaces are compliant with the standard interfaces of the J2EE Connector Architecture.

Java Resource Adapter

Thus, the Java Connectors or the Java Resource Adapter do not have to be supplied in Web AS Java, with delivery of SAP, but may be developed by the suppliers of other systems that are to be connected in the form of J2EE-compliant Java Resource Adapters and Java Connectors.

With the J2EE-compliant standard interface, it is possible to use the access to heterogenous systems in proprietary Java applications since they have access to the interfaces of the Java Resource Adapter.

An essential requirement for the use of the Web AS Java connectivity for BW (i.e., the Web AS ABAP) is communication between Web AS ABAP and Web AS Java.

Communication between Web AS ABAP and Web AS Java

For this purpose, there is a special Java Resource Adapter in Web AS Java: the SAP Java Resource Adapter (SAP JRA). The SAP Java Connector (SAP JCo) is used as a Java connector for this resource adapter; it is a middleware component that enabled communication between Java applications and the Web AS ABAP before Web AS Java was developed.

The SAP JCo supports the communication with the Web AS ABAP both ways (inbound and outbound); i.e., Web AS Java can start ABAP functions via an API and vice versa, and Web AS ABAP can call Java functions via an RFC connection. However, it has to be considered that SAP JRA can take RFC calls (via TCP/IP) but no TRFC calls, IDocs, and certificates.

SAP JCo and SAP JRA are self-contained software components that can be installed as stand-alone components too. However, SAP JRA is always installed as an add-on to SAP JCo, while SAP JCo is automatically installed together with Web AS Java.

In principle, there is not always a Web AS ABAP for each Web AS Java. This means that each Web AS ABAP can basically communicate with several (or no) Web AS Javas and vice versa. To configure the communication between both application platforms, you need to configure a ***JCo RFC Provider*** for Web AS Java and an ***RFC Destination*** for Web AS ABAP (for BW, the J2EE Engine is a system with an SAP-compliant interface).

Configuration of a JCo RFC Providers

The configuration of the JCo RFC Provider is made in the Visual Administrator of the J2EE Engine under the tab *Cluster→Services→ JCo RFC Provider* (see figure 3–6).

Figure 3–6
Configuration of the JCo RFC Provider

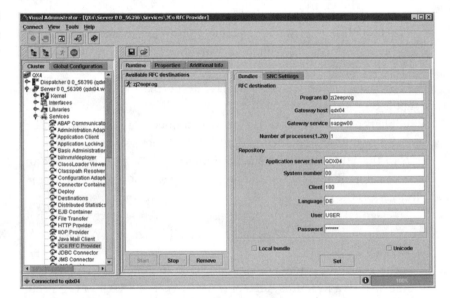

With configuration of the JCo RFC Provider, a number of parameters have to be entered. In the case of the *RFC Destination,* which is to be provided by the J2EE server, these are the settings:

- **Program ID:** An arbitrary but unequivocal ID that clearly identifies the RFC Destination provided by the JCo RFC Provider (i.e., the RFC server program). The indicated program ID will later be used to configure the RFC connection in Web AS ABAP to address the JCo RFC Provider.
- **Gateway host:** The gateway server that processes requests to and from Web AS ABAP. If there is no dedicated gateway server, the Web AS ABAP will fulfill this role.
- **Gateway service:** The gateway service on a gateway server.
- **Number of processes:** The maximum number of running processes to be served via this RFC connection.

With the *Repository* specifications, you need to indicate the logon information for the J2EE server to log onto BW. This is the usual logon information comprising the application server host, the ERP system number, the client, and the language as well as the user and password.

With configuration of the JCo RFC Provider via the *Set* button, the specification regarding the RFC Destination is implicitly reviewed. If the gateway service can be reached by the indicated host, the JCo RFC Provider will be shown in the list of available RFC Destinations and can be started. When the service is started, the RFC Destination can be opened through Web AS ABAP.

You update the respective RFC Destination to call the JCo RFC Provider through Web AS ABAP. This is done with transaction SM59, and the destination must be defined as a new TCP/IP connection (Type T) (see figure 3–7).

Configure RFC Destination to J2EE Engine

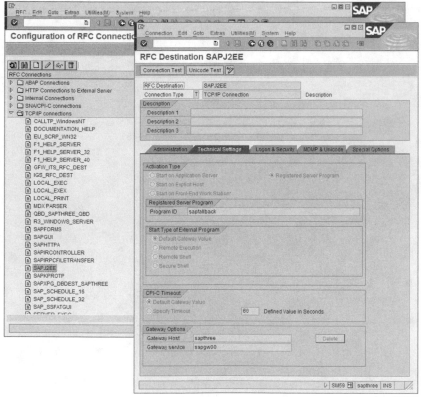

© SAP AG

Figure 3–7
Configuration of the RFC Destination for the J2EE Engine

The start type needs to be the registered server program. For the program ID of the server program, provide the program ID under which the JCo RFC Provider within the J2EE Engine has been defined.

Choose the gateway host and service according to the JCo Provider specification.

4 Metadata Repository

Data warehouse systems will quickly turn into a "black box"[9] if the applied data structures and data streams are not designed transparently. In such a system, correction of errors or modifications is disproportionally more complex and error-prone than in a transparently designed system.

BW responds to this issue with the Metadata Repository, where all objects that are related to the staging engine, the Data Manager, or BW's own decision support tools are centrally stored.

The Metadata Repository usually contains the definitions of objects and settings directly related to the objects. Numerous settings that will be described in this book are not part of the specific object definitions and are not part of the Metadata Repository. Thus, do not assume that you can always find this information in the Metadata Repository.

The objects stored in the Metadata Repository usually fulfill different technical or business functions and can be clustered in three layers:

- Database
- ABAP Dictionary (formerly called Data Dictionary)
- Application (BW objects)

Figure 4–1 shows the three layers in an sample selection of typical objects.

To work in BW, it is crucial that you understand the individual object layers. In the following sections, we will characterize the layers and explain their function within the Metadata Repository.

Please note that the three layers are not administered in a joint Metadata Repository but each in its own Repository.

---

9. This means a system that processes and stores data in an incomprehensible way and thus is similar to a black box, where the interior is invisible and remains unknown.

Figure 4–1
BW object layers

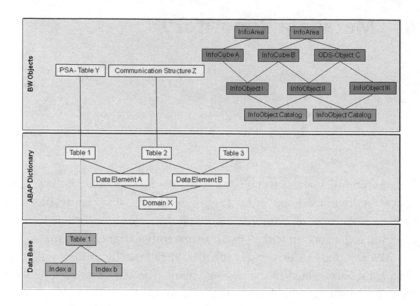

4.1   Database Objects

The physical data storage is done in the database system. There, data is filed with the help of database objects (tables, indexes).

The stored data may be of temporary or persistent nature and may assume different tasks. The database system has its own metadata on the stored structures, but in the case of SAP BW, it has no knowledge of the semantics or business context of the data.

There are two main disadvantages to directly accessing objects of a database system from BW programs:

■ Direct access to the database objects requires that access to applications are designed depending on the database system used. This does not make sense from an administration perspective. It would also require comprehensive database-specific knowledge on the application programmers' part.

■ The database does not provide any semantic information on the data structures and is thus not clear enough for application development.

Due to these disadvantages, the database objects are isolated from direct access by the BW programs. Instead, BW programs have to access the objects in the ABAP Dictionary.

4.2 ABAP Dictionary Objects

The ABAP Dictionary is a form of Metadata Repository for the BW basis system's data structures that apply to all applications system wide. The BW-relevant basic elements are as follows:

- Domains
- Data elements
- Tables

As far as these elements can be displayed in tables in the database, BW programs can access the ABAP Dictionary with the help of a standardized Structured Query Language (SQL) dialect, *Open SQL*. When the ABAP Dictionary is accessed, the basis system translates the Open SQL commands to database-specific commands. Thus, all applications based on the basis system (i.e., all BW programs) are database independent.[10]

The elements of the ABAP Dictionary do not necessarily have to be duplicated in the database. This is the case when the ABAP Dictionary elements contain metadata that does not show any data content (e.g., field structures).

Using transaction SE11, you can display, change, or create the elements of the ABAP Dictionary (see figure 4–2).

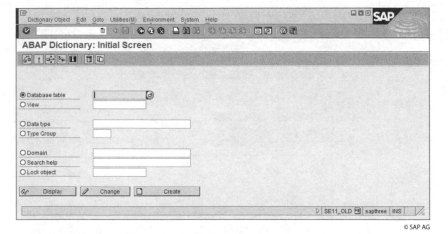

Figure 4–2

Starting the ABAP Dictionary

---

10. In some areas, BW uses special features of individual database systems and this requires particular handling by the ABAP programs depending on the corresponding platform. If necessary, the book will advise accordingly.

In the following sections, the basic elements of the ABAP Dictionary will be explained. In section 4.2.4, the concept of development namespaces will be discussed.

4.2.1 Domains

Domains define the basic business elements of the ABAP Dictionary using a data type and a data length (e.g., customer number, material text, turnover key figure).

For example, a customer number is defined as a 10-digit alphanumerical field by the domain /BIO/OCUSTOMER with the data type CHAR of length 10. All further ABAP Dictionary elements will be based on *domains*.

A particular feature in the definition of domains is the option to store the reference in a check table. Typically, this is a master data table where all values are stored that the domain duplicates in a master data table.

Check tables are especially valuable when entries are validated or the user chooses a value from a selection. Figure 4–3 shows the definition of the domain /BIO/OCUSTOMER (customer number) as CHAR with length 10 and the value table /BIO/MCUSTOMER.

Figure 4–3

Domains in the ABAP Dictionary

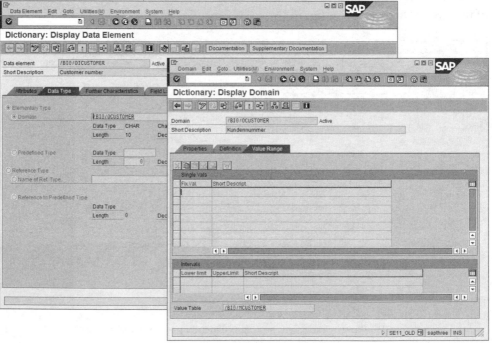

© SAP AG

4.2.2 Data Elements

Data elements are the describing layer over the domains. Each data element refers specifically to a domain, and each domain can be used by several data elements.

A data element contains descriptive data that can be used as a header when displaying field content. Data elements serve to generate a description from the general definition of a basic business element (the domain) that meets the needs of the specific use of the domain.

An example is the domain *customer number*. In sales, the customer number is never used as customer number but as one of the partner roles *customer, regulator,* or *supplier*. To accomplish this use of the domain, three data elements can be defined (customer, regulator, supplier), where each refers to the domain *customer number*.

Figure 4–4 shows the definition of the customer as a data element based on the domain *customer number*.

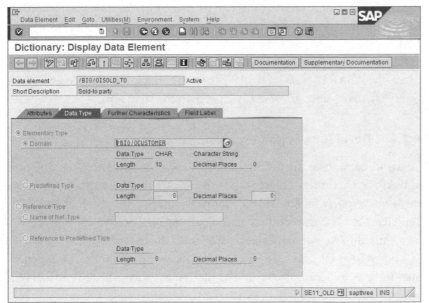

Figure 4–4

Data elements in the ABAP Dictionary

4.2.3 Tables

In the ABAP Dictionary, a structure of several fields is defined in a table. All fields of the structure need to be defined by a data element. Only the field name will be defined in the table. Within the table, the field name needs to be unambiguous. Within a table, a data element can be used repeatedly.

A table is used to bring complex business information into context. One example is the definition of a table to display the customer master data in a combination of customer number, name, phone number, etc.

There are two table types in the ABAP Dictionary:

- Transparent tables
- Structures

Transparent tables

Transparent tables are created in the ABAP Dictionary as well as in the database (the basis system does this automatically during table maintenance). Therefore, transparent tables offer an option to store data in the database system.

Any data stored through BW applications will be stored in database tables that are defined as transparent tables in the ABAP Dictionary.

Structures

Similar to data elements and domains, structures are components of the ABAP Dictionary. Structures can be reused in programs as preconfigured type declarations. BW intensely uses structures for data flow definition.

The advantage of structures is that they are maintained in one central place, the ABAP Dictionary, and any program having to this structure will be able to experience and use any change to the structure.

4.2.4   Development Namespaces

To avoid naming conflicts between proprietary ABAP Dictionary objects and ABAP Dictionary objects supplied by SAP, there are special ***development namespaces*** for all ABAP Dictionary objects. All customer and SAP-supplied objects have to adhere to the naming conventions.

SAP namespace

Thus, all SAP-supplied objects start with the letters A to X.

For ABAP Dictionary elements that are not SAP supplied but generated in SAP standard programs, the namespace /Bxx/ has been reserved, where x stands for the letters A to Z.

For SAP BW, the namespaces /BIO/ and /BIC/ are especially important; they are created during metadata maintenance of BW content objects and customized BW objects (see section 4.3). Thus, the ABAP Dictionary objects related to customized BW objects are also filed in the SAP namespace.

Any customized ABAP Dictionary object starts with Y or Z, but this only applies to objects that are created in the ABAP Dictionary directly.

Standard customer namespace

ABAP Dictionary objects that are generated by BW based on the metadata layer of the BW objects are not stored in the customer namespace even if the respective BW object is a customer-made development.

The definition of SAP and customer namespaces ensures that proprietary development from SAP users do not overlap with the supplied standard programs.

Own customer namespace

Within the customer namespace, it is up to each customer to agree on the use of the namespace for the object development in their organization.

System vendors, however, provide objects where neither the SAP namespace (this would interfere with SAP) nor the customer namespace (this would interfere with the customer) can be used.

Corporations may also face this problem when development is done centrally and locally, e.g., central development from headquarters and country-specific enhancements to globally used development systems.

For this reason, ABAP Dictionary objects can be stored in a so-called customer and partner namespace that is allocated by SAP.[11] It is marked by the prefix /xxxxx/, where xxxxx stands for a 5- (minimum) to 10-digit (maximum) alphanumerical string, starting with a letter, that refers to the respective company (e.g., /QUADOX/).

You request such a customer or partner namespace specifically for selected installations to ensure that the SAP-provided namespace can be used globally on the respective development systems.

4.3 BW Objects

While the Repository elements of the ABAP Dictionary already supply simple semantic information on the stored data and data structures, there are other objects in BW that define all application functions, from the data model and the data flow to monitoring. And for this purpose, they require more detailed semantic information. Here are some samples for such BW objects:

- *InfoObjects* to define business characteristics and key figures
- *BasisCubes* to take analysis-relevant transactional data

---

11. Development namespaces can be requested from SAP free of charge. Details on the application and the installation of namespaces can be found on the SAP Service Marketplace under the reference number 84282.

- *InfoAreas* to group InfoObjects and BasisCubes
- *Transformation rules* to define the data flow
- *Queries* to make analyses

The individual BW objects will be explained in detail in the following sections. To better clarify the tasks of BW objects, we will use the master data InfoObject, which represents business reference parameters (e.g., customers, products), as a sample for BW objects. The InfoObject disposes of master data that needs to be stored in several database tables.

With the InfoObject, information on its reporting behavior is stored. This is not only descriptive information (where a data element would be sufficient), but also information on its aggregation behavior, geocoding, etc. This information will also be stored in tables in the database system.

For this reason, BW objects are complex structures that are created on the Data Warehousing Workbench level with individual characteristics and from which a whole range of objects are usually generated in the ABAP Dictionary.

To make the development of BW objects easier and more transparent, the metadata on each BW object is stored in different versions: active, modified, or delivered.

A version[4]   The A version of metadata on BW objects corresponds with the objects generated for the BW object in the ABAP Dictionary and represents the actively used form of metadata.

M version[5]   With a redevelopment or modification of BW objects, the changes (e.g., adding fields to the master data) will not immediately transfer into the objects generated in the ABAP Dictionary and the programs; instead, they will first be stored as metadata in an M version. This version exists in addition to the A version.

Only when the metadata is activated with the modeling of the BW objects will the changes be transferred from the M to the A version, and then the objects of the ABAP Dictionary and the programs will be generated from the metadata definitions.

D version[6]   BW objects that come with a content system[15] are—with their delivery—not created as an active version in the metadata and the ABAP

---

12. A = Active (active version)
13. M = Modified (modified version)
14. D = Delivered (delivered version of BI content)
15. This refers to the BI content of SAP as well as the customer and partner content that has been provided by proprietary content systems. More detailed information on content development can be found in appendix C.2.

Dictionary. Instead, the metadata of these objects will be stored in a D version. Only when the BW objects of the metadata content are transferred (see appendix C.1.5), will the content of the D version be transferred into the A version and respective objects generated in the ABAP Dictionary and the programs.

The D version will not be deleted when installed, so it can be transferred several times, and transferred BW objects can be modified or deleted without any consequences to the D version.

As described when we explained architecture components, the Data Warehousing Workbench in BW is used as central tool to define metadata. Further, it offers research options for the Metadata Repository (see figure 4–5).

Metadata research

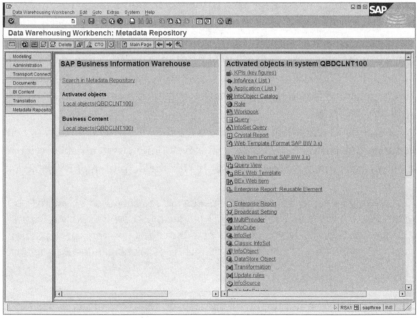

© SAP AG

Figure 4–5

The Metadata Repository

The search function excludes metadata objects of the ABAP Dictionary as well as metadata of the database system. Also, the search function does not consider any object-independent settings. Thus, in a lot of cases, the Metadata Repository of the Data Warehousing Workbench is rather unqualified to give a comprehensive overview on the operation method of the system.

4.3.1   BW Namespaces

BW objects are defined on an application level so that the development namespaces of the ABAP dictionary do not apply (see section 4.2.4). BW's own namespaces are applicable.

BW default namespace

BW default namespaces are used to avoid conflicts between BW objects from SAP (e.g., BI content) and user-defined BW objects.

All BW objects from SAP are marked with the prefix 0 to 9 in the BW default namespace; that is, the name of each BW object that is supplied by SAP or generated by the system will begin with a number from 0 to 9. The name of each customer-defined BW object will have a prefix from A to Z.

For objects of the ABAP Dictionary that are generated from metadata of BW objects, there are ***generation namespaces*** that apply to the respective BW default namespaces. This is the generation namespace /BIO/ for BW objects from SAP and /BIC/ for customer-defined BW objects.

This means, for example, that the InfoObject 0CUSTOMER from the BI content generates a master data table in the ABAP Dictionary with the name /BIO/PCUSTOMER. However, the customer-defined InfoObject ZCUSTOMER generates in the ABAP Dictionary a master data table named /BIC/PZCUSTOMER.

BW partner namespace

As with development namespaces in the ABAP Dictionary, system vendors and customers with central development systems may refer to their own customer/partner namespaces for the definition of BW objects.

> Proprietary customer/partner namespaces are mostly used by system vendors. For corporations with a global IT landscape, they are hardly relevant. Do not be worried if you do not see the need for your own partner namespace in your company. You can keep developing in the BW default namespaces without hesitation.

For this purpose, a development namespace for BW objects as well as a generation namespace has to be requested from SAP and set up in the system (see section 4.2.4).

While the development namespace for BW objects follows regular development namespace conventions, different rules apply to the generation namespace. The name has to be encased with slashes (/) and must not exceed seven characters (slashes included). Also, the namespace has to start with B and otherwise must contain only numbers. A valid generation namespace would be /B10/.

In the transaction RSNSPACE (see figure 4–6), the generation namespace will be assigned to the BW partner namespace and it will apply to the objects in the ABAP Dictionary that are deduced from the metadata of the BW objects.

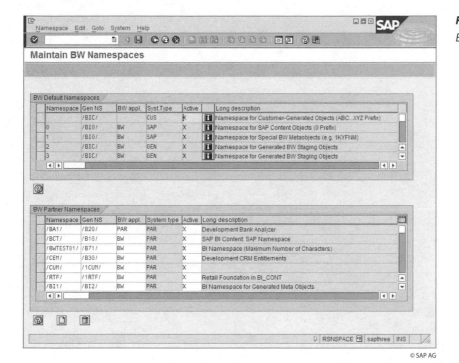

© SAP AG

Figure 4–6
BW namespace maintenance

According to the namespaces defined in the figure, the InfoObject /BQDX/CUST will generate a master data table named /B10/PCUST in the ABAP Dictionary.

II Data Model

The data model is the central topic around storage of data in any data warehouse system. It is based on the business requirements that a user brings to the system.

First, this part addresses data models in general and gives a basic understanding of the different models that are applied in data warehouse systems (chapter 5).

Then, we'll provide detailed explanations of the data models used in BW. A good grasp of these data models is essential to build a BW system (chapter 6).

Further, we'll explain performance-relevant aspects of data modeling. The options described hereafter can only be realized retroactively with a lot of effort, so they should be considered in the initial drafts of the modeling (see chapter 7).

The explanation of the BW data model is supplemented by a range of samples and solution approaches that reflect the typical requirements in daily practice.

The part ends with a description of how BW data models are organized in the Data Warehousing Workbench and how they can be modified (chapter 8).

5   General Data Models

Data modeling always aims at duplicating reality in a data-managed way. The individual models differ regarding closeness to reality, simplicity, and performance. These goals are opposing, so the different models show a different focus on the individual goals and there cannot be any "best-in-class data model". Each model has specific advantages, so a data model can only be designed subject to the business requirements.

In the following sections, we'll address the basics of data model development. Then we'll explain the most common data models for modeling a data warehouse system:

- Transactional structures
- Flat structures
- Star schema
- Snowflake schema

5.1   Basics of Data Modeling

The goal of a data model is to duplicate a certain section of reality. The clear definition of this section characterizes each data warehouse and separates it from other systems such as document management systems or web content systems.

This is not about nonvolatile data that is not (or only slightly) modified from the moment of transfer into the data warehouse and is used for analyses and decision-making purposes, i.e., not for live operation.

One component of data modeling consists of facts that are expressed in quantifiable measures (key figures) and that can be put into a relationship with grouping measures (characteristics, attributes).

5.1.1   Characteristics

Characteristics are reference variables with business context (e.g., customer, products, production sites, general ledger), according to which a reasonable grouping of key figures can be made (revenue per customer, production cost for products A to G, average delivery period per production site, etc.).

5.1.2   Attributes

Attributes are characteristics that depend on other characteristics, such as postal code (depending on customer) and product features (depending on material).

The dependency of attributes to characteristics is disturbed if they change over time—e.g., if the customer address changes or product features change.

While OLTP systems imperatively rely on current attributes, the situation with data warehousing is different since other options can make sense to show attribute changes over the course of time.

The *historiography of attributes* in the data model can be reproduced in three ways:

- **Current view:** Attributes will be shown as they are at the time of reporting. It is irrelevant whether data of the current month of the last year is analyzed.
- **Key date view:** All attributes will be shown as they were on a fixed key date. Usually, the user defines this key date prior to running the analysis.
- **Historic view:** Attributes will be shown as they were in the reference period of the reporting. Data from the previous year will be shown with attributes that were valid in the previous year, while in the same report, data from the last month will be shown with attributes valid in the last month.

These three options for historiography of attributes bring very different requirements to a data model. Depending on the data model, the different historiographies are supported by the master data.

5.1.3 Key Figures

Key figures are quantifiable measures that allow mathematic operations. It only makes sense to use key figures if they can be related to respective reference values (characteristics); e.g., the indication of a sales item always requires information on the time frame, the customer, the product, or something similar.

When data is analyzed, key figures are combined using arithmetic operations (such as addition, average, minimum/maximum values, etc.) or they serve to calculate other key figures (changes in percent, differences, etc.).

With analyses in BW, key figures are always used in combination with characteristics and vice versa. The use of key figures without characteristics, or vice versa, does not make sense from a data warehouse perspective.

5.1.4 Status Tracking

Status tracking describes the mapping of information in the data model almost on record level, e.g., the storing of order data. As with the historiography of attributes, updating order-related data becomes more relevant.

Should the order status (which is dependent on the order number in the data model) change in the OLTP system, then the order status in the data warehouse needs to change too. However, apart from key figures, this information cannot be stored on an aggregated level but needs to be stored at the same detailed level as in the OLTP system.

5.2 Transactional Structures

Transactional structures are used to store data from an OLTP system in a relational database. Above all, these structures are required to store data on an atomic level,[16] to avoid redundancies[17] and for a faster access to individual transaction data.

For this purpose, the data is usually stored in the third normal form, which fulfills these requirements (see figure 5–1).

---

16. The atomic level describes the storage of information on an individual transaction level (e.g., order position).
17. E.g., by keeping up-to-date master data once only.

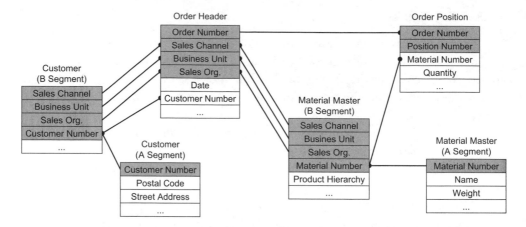

Figure 5–1
Transactional data model

Former OLAP tools accessed the transaction data in the OLTP systems for the analysis since they had no other database available. However, there are two major disadvantages: bad performance and limited business analyses options.

The bad performance of transactional structures comes from the fact that analytical applications usually cannot make use of the individual transactions, but require comprehensive information on several transactions.

However, in a transactional data model, a query on revenue from a company over the last two years would require reading all transactions from the last two years, which could take several hours, days, or even weeks; while this exact itemization is not even required.

Further, the OLTP systems would be burdened with analyses they were not designed for.

Apart from performance problems, the disadvantage of transactional structures is that they only support the current view of attributes.

For these reasons, in modern data warehouse systems, data from OLTP systems is only used to read information once and to transform it into special data models that are more suitable for analytical applications (flat structures, star schema, and snowflake schema).

5.3 Flat Structures

Flat table structures are the "archetype" of OLAP-specific data models. They represent a first step to separate analytical data from operational (transactional) data and thus offer the option to store data in an aggregated form so that, for analyses purposes (depending on the aggregation level), a strongly minimized database can be used[18] (see figure 5–2).

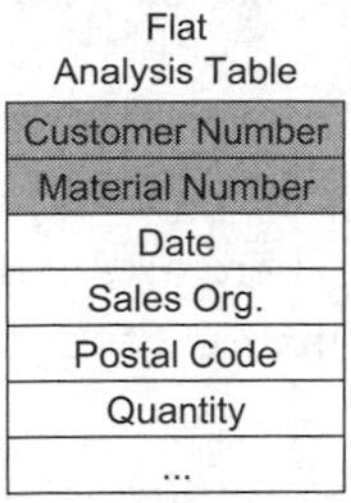

Flat
Analysis Table

| Customer Number |
| Material Number |
| Date |
| Sales Org. |
| Postal Code |
| Quantity |
| ... |

Figure 5–2

Flat data model

While transactional structures are normalized (partly up to the third normal form), flat structures are denormalized on purpose to map the database on an higher aggregation level and in a simpler form. From an analytical perspective, this is an improvement compared to transactional structures. However, because of some disadvantages, they are usually no longer used as a database for OLAP application:

- All characteristics have to be stored as table keys. This causes very long keys, which often result in performance disadvantages in relational database systems.
- The number of table fields is limited by the database system, so not all requirements might be fulfilled.
- Flat structures enable only the historic view of attributes.
- When changes to the data model are made, much effort is required to rebuild the complete table.

In today's data warehouse systems, flat structures are mostly used to exchange data between systems and around staging. Especially for data exchange, the flat structures have an advantage as they do not rely on relational databases and can be stored as (text) files.

In BW, flat structures are used in any area responsible for data exchange (extraction of data from source systems, staging) since this form of data exchange is the easiest and best performing. If required, data is also transformed from the respective data models into flat structures.

Special consideration goes to the key figures that are to be stored in a flat structure. Here, we have to differentiate between two basic models: the **key figure model** and the **account model.**

---

18. Please consider: The amount of key figures stays the same after the aggregation. The aggregation only reduces the level of detail!

The best example for the account model and the key figure model comes with flat structures. However, please consider that any structure—even the models of the star and the snowflake schema described later—need to contain one of these two models.

Key figure model

With the key figure model, there is a field provided for each key figure in the structure of the flat table. Therefore, in the data records all key figures that are related to a key combination of the flat table are stored in the data record.

As a prerequisite for the use of the key figure model, the structure of the respective key figure for each data record must be basically identical. If from a large amount of key figures in each data record only a few are filled, the usage of storage is inefficient and will lead to an unnecessarily high resource waste.

Account model

In this case, the use of the account model will help. The account model provides only one key figure per unit type (currency, amount) and anchors the semantics of the respective key figure in a key field of the table. Thus, a data record of the key figure model that describes four key figures would result in four data records in the account model.

Compared with the key figure model, the account model produces multiple data records, but it scores in terms of flexibility and optimal use of the defined data structure.

In practice, the account model is suitable for controlling purposes where a business can be evaluated from a multitude of different key figures that may hardly be used in other businesses.

For example, figure 5–3 shows the differences between the key figure and the account model where the key figures *revenue* and *price* are always indicated but the key figure *discount* is only indicated sporadically.

Figure 5–3

Key figure model vs. account model

Key Figure Model

Material	Month	Sales	Price	Discount
4711	01.2002	1000.00	2.00	20.00
4711	02.2002	500.00	2.50	
4711	03.2002	675.00	2.25	
4711	04.2002	1250.00	2.00	25.00
4711	05.2002	650.00	2.50	

Account Model

Material	Month	Semantic	KeyFigure
4711	01.2002	Sales	1000.00
4711	01.2002	Price	2.00
4711	01.2002	Discount	20.00
4711	02.2002	Sales	500.00
4711	02.2002	Price	2.50
4711	03.2002	Sales	675.00
4711	03.2002	Price	2.25
4711	04.2002	Sales	1250.00
4711	04.2002	Price	2.00
4711	04.2002	Discount	25.00
4711	05.2002	Sales	650.00
4711	05.2002	Price	2.50

5.4 Star Schema

From an analytical point of view, the star schema offers the same performance characteristics as flat structures, i.e., a historic display of attributes. However, the star schema does not have the disadvantages of flat structures in terms of performance as it is specially aligned to the performance characteristics of relational databases and distributes data to several tables. Here, the data model stays denormalized, as in the flat structure.

The star schema consists of a *central fact table* and several relationally linked *dimension tables*. The relational link between fact table and dimension table is made with the *surrogate keys*.

When graphically displayed, the data model reminds us of a star, which explains the name of this data model (see figure 5–4).

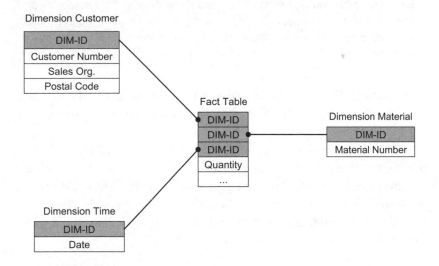

Figure 5–4

Star schema

The fact table includes only key figures and the key fields for the dimensions. This enables the use of keys with few and short fields (usually 4 bytes), which results in better performance of the database.

Access to the fact table is usually made in connection with one or several dimension tables whose key fields are the access key to the fact table. The dimension tables form the ends of the "star". In them, characteristics and attributes for the respective data records of the fact table are stored. Text information ("Miller" for customer 4711) will be stored in the dimensions of a pure star schema.

Fact table

Dimension tables

The connection from the dimension tables to the fact table is made with the use of distinct surrogate keys (explained a bit later). Each of these keys covers a line in the dimension table and one or several lines in the fact table. The key of all dimension tables together identifies one line in the fact table.

Dimension tables are denormalized (like flat structures) and they are built in consideration of technical aspects. Section 6.4 explains how the dimensions in a star schema are built using the example of an expanded star schema of BW.

In practice, dimensions are often named after organizational topics (customer dimension, material dimension, etc.). Here, one often gets the impression that the selection of dimensions is made according to business criteria. This is wrong! The decision as to which dimension is to be created and how the criteria are distributed to the dimensions is only made in consideration of technical aspects. Should the outcome of these technical considerations correspond with the organizational order or dimensions, this is pure coincidence.

Surrogate keys The link from dimension tables to the fact table is made with distinct keys. The key will not be the characteristics value of a dimension; instead, a surrogate key will be chosen.

This makes modeling easier as characteristics and attributes can be distributed freely to the dimensions and even n:m relations within a dimension are possible. This is a prerequisite for the historic display of attributes. Such dimensions are also called *slowly changing dimensions;* here, different combinations of characteristics/attributes are stored in one dimension.

5.5 Snowflake Schema

The snowflake schema is an enhancement of the star schema. It enhances the star schema with master data tables, which allow for attributes to be displayed not only historically but also currently. The basic model of the star schema is kept. However, there is an option added so that attributes can be stored not only in dimensions but also in master data tables that are relationally linked to characteristics in the dimensions.

For example, figure 5–5 shows a postal code that can be added either to the customer dimension (historic display) or to the customer master data (current display).

It is also possible to add the postal code to both tables so that the user can choose between these alternatives in the data analysis. However, this makes the snowflake schema much more complex. Administration requires more effort and it becomes more difficult for the database management system to read the model while maintaining good performance.

Figure 5–5
Snowflake schema

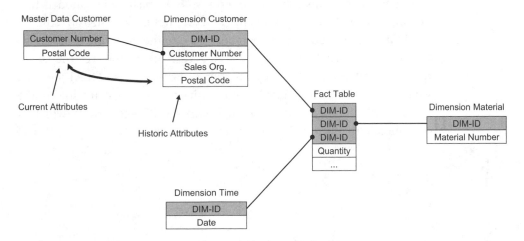

For users, the choice between historic and current display of attributes might be confusing. Please be very aware when using the snowflake schema so that later confusion or a possible rejection of the system will be avoided.

5.6 Summary

The following overview summarizes the most important characteristics of the data models described in this chapter.

Model	Transactional	Flat	Star	Snowflake
Performance	Poor	Good	Very good	Very good
Complexity	High	Low	Medium	High
Historicized	–	✓	✓	✓
Current	✓	–	–	✓
Key date	–	–	–	–

Table 5–1
Overview of general data models

In practice, these data models are used in numerous variations and expansions. BW also uses data models that have been modified to meet special requirements.

Beyond the data models shown, there are numerous other possibilities to store data so that it is kept in an optimized form for analysis. In practice, one often finds in this context the term *MOLAP models,* i.e., models that do not store OLAP data relationally (ROLAP) but multidimensionally.

In implementation, MOLAP models lead to the most different storage forms, and they can hardly be compared to each other. However, they share the particular feature that they can deliver fast results to OLAP queries, whereas changes to the database come with extensive recalculations in the database. SAP delivers such a model with the BI Accelerator, which is described in the section 7.4 on performance tuning.

6   BW Data Model

In the previous chapter, the main data models were described in their purest form. This chapter explains the data model of BW. We'll cover a multitude of different BW objects (see section 4.3) that can be applied to different purposes and that use, combine, and modify different data models for this purpose:

- InfoObjects and their master data concept
- DataStore objects
- BasisCubes

The term *data target* is used as a generic term for these BW objects since they are used to physically load analysis-relevant data. The focus of this chapter is on the explanation of data targets.

The chapter ends with advice on how to store data of the data targets in relation to or depending on a source system.

6.1   InfoObjects

InfoObjects form the basis for the definition of any other data target. All data targets define themselves completely through InfoObjects and can be created only if the required InfoObjects exist.

InfoObjects are defined by a systemwide distinct technical name (e.g., OCUSTOMER), which is supplemented by an additional denomination (e.g., "customer number" for the InfoObject OCUSTOMER).

Apart from the technical name and the denomination, a data type (e.g., CHAR for an alphanumeric data type) and the data length are regulated. These settings are made in the general settings of each InfoObject (see figure 6–1).

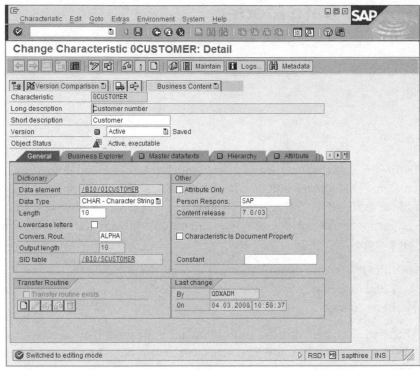

Since all data models in which an InfoObject is used are defined technically in the form of one or several transparent tables in the ABAP Dictionary (see section 4.2.3), a corresponding data element with the respective domain must be defined for each InfoObject in the ABAP Dictionary. As a data element, the InfoObject is used in the elements of the ABAP Dictionary.

The respective data element with the corresponding domain is deduced from the data type and the data length of the InfoObject and follows a naming convention (described) that considers the technical name of the InfoObject (e.g., the data element /BIO/OICUSTOMER and the domain /BIO/OCUSTOMER for the InfoObject OCUSTOMER).

When the metadata of an InfoObject is activated, BW automatically creates the data element and the domain in the ABAP Dictionary. Figure 6–2 shows the connection between the InfoObject and the data element on the InfoObject OCUSTOMER.

If the data type or the data length of an InfoObject is changed, the underlying domain in the ABAP Dictionary will also be adjusted automatically. Should there be transparent tables in the ABAP Dictionary that are filled with data, the tables will be adjusted according to the new settings in the database. This is not possible if the adjustment would result in a loss of information (e.g., shortening of data length).

Figure 6–2
Data element and domain of
an InfoObject

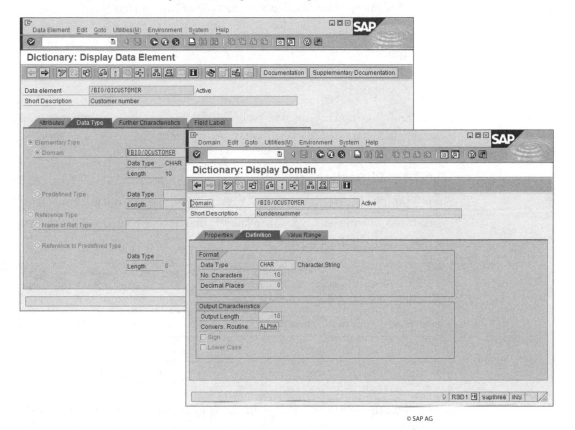

© SAP AG

The following table shows the naming conventions followed for InfoObject names, data elements, and domains.

Naming convention

	Standard InfoObject	**User-Defined InfoObject**
Name of the InfoObject	0tttttttttt	{A-Z}ttttttttt
Name of the data element	/BIO/OItttttttttt	/BIC/OI{A-Z}ttttttttt
Name of the domain	/BIO/0tttttttttt	/BIC/O{A-Z}ttttttttt
Description short	Max. 20 characters	Max. 20 characters
Description long	Max. 60 characters	Max. 60 characters

InfoObject types So far, the options we've discussed for InfoObjects are no different than the options offered by data elements and domains in the ABAP Dictionary. However, InfoObjects store a further range of characteristics in their metadata.

This information is subject to the type of InfoObject:

- Characteristics
- Times
- Units
- Key figures

In the following sections, the named InfoObject types are explained and their characteristics described as far as they are related to the data model.

6.1.1 Characteristics

For InfoObjects that are to be used as a characteristic in the BW data models, the following data types are available that have to be defined in the general settings of the InfoObject:

Data Type	Description	Maximum Length
CHAR	Numbers and letters	Character length 1–60
NUMC	Numbers only	Character length 1–60
DATS	Date	Character length 8
TIMS	Time	Character length 6

Further, the following settings in the InfoObject are relevant to the data model:

- Permission of lowercase letters
- Conversion routine and output length
- SID tables

These settings will be explained in the following sections.

Permission of Lowercase Letters

In the case of characteristics of type CHAR, the question of how to deal with lowercase letters comes up. For example, a customer number could be displayed as 18HB27F or as 18hb27F. It is to be clarified whether identical or different customers are described.

As a result, for each InfoObject, you need to decide whether lowercase letters are permissible or not (see figure 6–3).

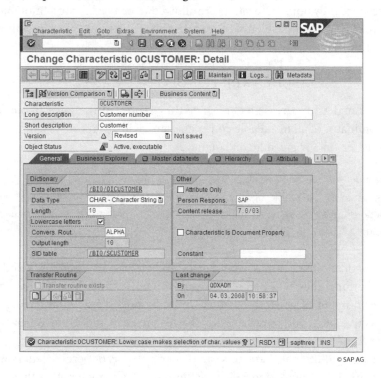

© SAP AG

Figure 6–3
Permission of lowercase letters

Should lowercase letters be allowed, the customer numbers above would be stored in a different form and shown as two different customer numbers in the reports. Further, when selecting customers, users would have to consider both uppercase and lowercase letters, which may turn the permission of lowercase into a problem.

If uppercase letters are permitted for an InfoObject name only, the question is now which letters are considered uppercase. At first glance, the uppercase German Ö clearly seems to be an uppercase letter. According to the known schema, which says that a sign is represented by 8 bits, the same bit sequence that describes an "Ö" in the German code page will become a lowercase "sh" in the Russian code page (to just show one of the many examples).

This problem occurs when character sets are represented by code pages and several code pages are actually used in parallel. Which code page is used depends on the respective logon language. Therefore, there is a danger that, for example, with the German logon language (= German

Uppercase letters when using code pages

code page), an "Ö" will be stored as a characteristic value, but a Russian (= Russian code page) user sees it as a lowercase "sh", which should be impossible since only uppercase letters are allowed to be used for the InfoObject.

To avoid such problems, at least in the BW default settings, initially only the letters

!"%&'()*+,-./:;<=>?_0123456789

ABCDEFGHIJKLMNOPQRSTUVWXYZ

are defined as uppercase letters since they represent the lowest common denominator of all installable code pages and will always represent uppercase letters in any given logon language.

> Usually, BW verifies whether characters are valid only when they are to be written in the SID table of an InfoObject. If you want to verify the validity of a character string in the definition of the data flow, you may use the function module RSKC_CHAVL_CHECK.

In practice, only a limited number of code pages are used (in standard installations, they will be only in English and German), so the use of a larger number of uppercase letters would be possible without having the respective bit strings overlap with the lowercase letters from other code pages.

These additional characters can be permitted as uppercase letters with the help of the transaction RSKC (see figure 6–4). Characteristic values that start with the characters ! and # are never allowed.

Figure 6–4

Permission of uppercase letters as extra characters

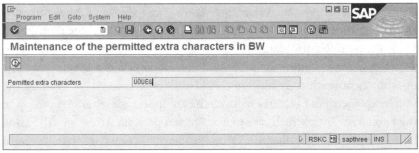

Should the character string ALL_CAPITAL be entered instead of a listing of characters, all these characters considered uppercase letters in the logon language will be valid during the load process. It depends on the logon language of the load process, i.e., the logon language of the background user (see chapter 15.1.1).

> If further languages are subsequently installed, data that has been loaded may no longer be valid after the installation of the language. This will result in an inconsistent database. Thus, please be very careful with the addition of permissible characters and avoid additions completely, if possible.

Especially with Unicode systems, all characters will be represented in all languages by a distinguished bit string of variable length. Therefore, the uppercase German "Ö" will be represented by a bit string that is distinguishable and has nothing to do with the lowercase Russian "sh".

Uppercase letters in Unicode systems

As a consequence, by using the character string ALL_CAPITAL in Unicode BW systems, you permit all uppercase letters of all languages.

Conversion Routine and Output Length

For better internal processing and storing of data, the BW basis system applies an ***internal display.*** For example, times are always stored in the format YYYYMMDD and a cost center always with the leading zeros.

In an ***external display,*** input and output of data different formats are often used, so there has to be a conversion from external into internal display and vice versa. For example, when the cost center 1000 is entered, a conversion into the respective 10-digit value 0000001000 has to be made.

To ensure consistent conversion, BW has conversion routines that are stored in the definition of InfoObjects. Figure 6–1 on page 54 shows the InfoObject OCUSTOMER, where the conversion routine ALPHA is applied.

If no conversion routine is defined for an InfoObject, the external display will be used by internal processing without modification, so, for example, the cost centers 0000001000 and 01000 would be considered two different characteristic values.

With the use of conversion routines, the user's job will be especially facilitated as, for example, a date in both 001.2008 and 012008 format may be entered and both entries will be converted in the internal format 2008001 when the conversion routine PERI7 is stored in the InfoObject.[19]

There are two function modules for each conversion routine:

■ An INPUT module to convert an external format into an internal format
■ An OUTPUT module to convert an internal format into an external format

---

19. This is the case, for example, in the InfoObject OFISCPER (Fiscal Year/Period).

The function modules can be found under the name `CONVERSION_EXIT_xxxxx_INPUT` or `CONVERSION_EXIT_xxxxx_OUTPUT`, where xxxxx is the name of the conversion routine.

For this exceptional rule, BW disposes of special options in the inflow layer in the form of the so-called input conversion to ensure the conformity of characters with the conversion routines ALPHA, NUMCV, and GJAHR.

Conversion routines ALPHA, NUMC, and GJAHR

Conversion routines require special consideration when they cannot convert certain internal values into external values, that is, if there are internal values that will be invalid in the definition of the conversion routine. Primarily, these are the conversion routines ALPHA, NUMCV, and GJAHR.

For example, in a 5-digit InfoObject, you can use the value 1000, which is a CHAR type and has the conversion routine ALPHA. In this case, any external value can never result in the internal value 1000—the entries 01000 and 1000 will both result in the internal value 01000.

This fact is especially relevant when loading. The application of the conversion routine is not mandatory; i.e., values may be characterized as internal values and be processed without validation. Whether a characteristic value is to be considered an internal value or whether it should be subject to a conversion routine is defined in the settings of the input conversion in the inflow layer (see chapter 15.2.3).

As soon as master data has been stored for an InfoObject, the conversion routines ALPHA, NUMCV, and GJAHR can no longer be stored with this InfoObject. Such objects can be replaced only by other InfoObjects that have the right conversion routine in place. In such cases, the so-called remodeling provides support (see chapter 9.2.1).

Conversion routine MATN1

An exception in the conversion routines is the routine MATN1 which is used in the content InfoObject 0MATERIAL. The functioning of this routine is not defined statically but will be set by customizing through the transaction OMSL.

This exception creates problems when data is extracted from other SAP systems where the conversion routine MATN1 is defined differently and the internal display of a material number differs from BW to the SAP source system. Despite the differences, when loading, BW assumes by default that material numbers in the internal format can be processed without a validity check. As a consequence, there will be errors; for example, on posting such data in BasisCubes.

If the transaction OMSL cannot be customized, the solution has to be implemented in the input conversion application.

SID Tables

The description of the star schema showed that dimensions are identified by a dimension key (called DIM ID in BW) and the characteristic values are stored in the dimension. Therefore, characteristics would not require any further identification but would be represented only by their value.

This concept has not been adopted in BW. Instead, in BW all characteristic values are identified by a master data identification number (called SID).

Therefore, unlike with the normal star schema, changes will apply to the whole data model since the true characteristic value will no longer be found in dimension tables but in the attached SID tables of the InfoObjects (see figure 6–5).

Figure 6–5
SID table

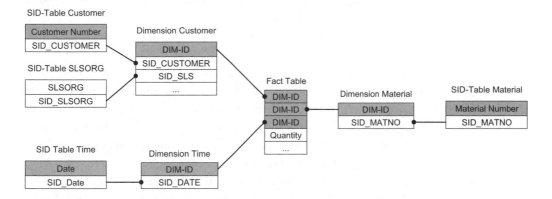

With the introduction of SID tables or the SID, characteristics in BW will be completely decapsulated from BW objects that use them. This enables the SID table to reference a characteristic from several BW objects (see figure 6–6):

Encapsulation of the InfoObject

- InfoCubes
- Hierarchies
- Master data

These object types will be explained in detail in the following sections.

Figure 6–6

SID table: usage in BW objects

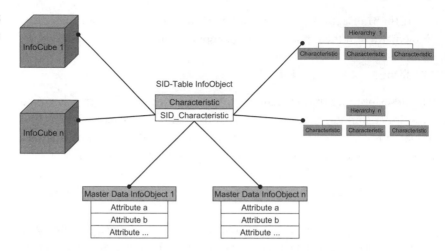

The fact that the SID is always of the type integer (4 bytes in length) may have a positive impact on performance despite its more complex data model because, for example, an 18-digit material number will be stored as only a 4-byte integer value.

Further, the SID offers the option to administer characteristics with a composed primary key.

InfoObjects with composed
primary key (compounding)

For example, this is the case with sales data of the SAP ERP material master (table MVKE). This data is not stored as a material number but is composed from a combination of sales organization, the sales channel, and the material number. These form the primary key of the table MVKE in SAP ERP. In BW language, this means that the material number is **compounded** to the sales organization and the sales channel.

Such a primary key can be considered in SID tables without infringing the SID principle. From the perspective of BW objects that use an InfoObject, this facilitates access to the InfoObject since only the SID table of the InfoObject needs to be accessed.

The compounding of InfoObjects can have negative effects on performance in data preparation and reporting, especially if several InfoObjects are part of the compounding. So, only use compounding if it's justified by the data model. For any other purposes (mapping of attributes, hierarchies, etc.), there are other functions in BW, which are described in the following sections.

The following table is the SID table for the InfoObject OMAT_SALES, which maps the master data of the material master of the Table MVKE in BW.

Field Name	Data Element	Comment
SALESORG	/BIO/OISALESORG	Sales organization
DISTR_CHAN	/BIO/OIDISTR_CHAN	Distribution channel
MAT_SALES	/BIO/OIMAT_SALES	Material number compound with Sales
SID	RSSID	Master Data ID
CHCKFL	RSDCHCKFL	Flag: Value in check tables
DATAFL	RSDDATAFL	Flag: Value in the dimension or available as attribute
INCFL	RSDINCFL	Flag: Value available in all inclusion tables

Since an InfoObject can be used in several other BW objects, the deletion of entries in the master data tables or the SID table is critical when BW objects still refer to these entries. In such cases, the deletion of master data is not permitted.

SID usage list

To keep the BW system informed of whether entries of the SID table are used, two respective flags are protocoled in all SID tables:

- ▪ DATAFL: The SID is used in the dimension of an InfoCube or as attribute in the master data of another InfoObject.
- ▪ INCLFL: The SID is used in the inclusion tables of an external hierarchy.

As soon as an SID is used in an InfoCube, the master data of another InfoObject, or a hierarchy, it will be flagged accordingly (value X) and it will no longer be possible to delete the master data of this SID.

The disadvantage of this concept lies in the fact that flags are set when an SID is used but that they will not be deleted when the SID is no longer in use. This means that once-used master data can be deleted only through time-consuming checks.

The name of the SID table is determined by BW depending on the InfoObject name. The following table shows the name conventions used.

Name convention

	Standard InfoObject	User-Defined InfoObject
Name of the InfoObject	0ttttttttt	{A-Z}ttttttt
Name of the SID Table	/BIO/Sttttttttttt	/BIC/S{A-Z}tttttttt

6.1.2 Time Characteristics

Apart from the characteristics, *times* are relevant for the description of business measurements. Basically, the so-called time characteristics have the same tasks as other characteristics. In BW, however, times are realized as an individual InfoObject type.

So, when you're building a star schema model, you can preconfigure time dimensions, validate the model definition, and provide conversion routines for the definition of the staging (see section 6.1.1).

While individual InfoObjects can be defined with all other types of InfoObjects, you can use only time characteristics that BW supplies with BI content.

The following table shows the time characteristics of the BI content.

InfoObject	Description	Type	Length	Format
0CALDAY	Calendar day	DATS	8	YYYYMMDD
0CALMONTH	Calendar year/month	NUMC	6	YYYYMM
0CALMONTH2	Calendar month	NUMC	2	MM
0CALQUART1	Quarter	NUMC	1	Q
0CAL_QUARTER	Calendar year/quarter	NUMC	5	YYYYQ
0CALWEEK	Calendar year/week	NUMC	6	YYYYWW
0CALYEAR	Calendar year	NUMC	4	YYYY
0FISCPER	Fiscal year/fiscal month	NUMC	7	YYYYMMM
0FISCPER3	Fiscal month	NUMC	3	MMM
0FISCVARNT	Fiscal year variant	CHAR	2	XX
0FISCYEAR	Fiscal year	NUMC	4	YYYY
0HALFYEAR1	Half year	NUMC	1	H
0WEEKDAY1	weekday	NUMC	1	N

If these preset time characteristics basically meet requirements but the name is not suitable, it should be modified in the maintenance of the InfoObject. Renaming of time characteristics of BI content will not be a problem in current operations nor in upcoming release changes.

If totally new time characteristics are to be created, normal characteristics should be created and they should be used as time characteristics. From a content perspective, this will not be a problem, but the advantages of time characteristics (partitioning of compressed fact tables, validation of values and type conversion in staging) can no longer be used.

> The partitioning of a compressed fact table (see section 7.1) will be effected only with true time characteristics from the BI content. You should absolutely avoid using proprietary time characteristics since substantial performance problems can result from the loss of the partitioning options.

6.1.3 Key Figures

As with characteristics/time characteristics, the definition of a data type is the basic setting of the key figure. Since key figures are not measurements but flow or parameter data, the settings are basically different (see figure 6–7).

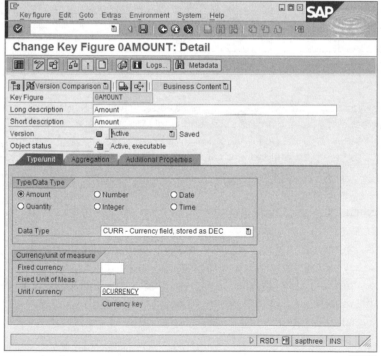

Figure 6–7

Key figure definition: type/unit

The following table shows the possible data types:

Type	Data Type	With Unit	Description
Currency	CURR	✓	Currency field stored as DEC
	FLTP	✓	Floating point number with 8-byte accuracy
Quantity	QUAN	✓	Quantity field, refers to unit field with format UNIT
	FLTP	✓	Floating point number with 8-byte accuracy
Number	DEC		Calculation or amount field with comma and prefix
	FLTP		Floating point number with 8-byte accuracy
Integer	INT4		4-byte integer, whole number with prefix
Date	DEC		Calculation or amount field with comma and prefix
	DATS		Date field (YYYYMMDD), stored as CHAR (8)
Time	DEC		Calculation or amount field with comma and prefix
	TIMS		Time field (hhmmss), stored as CHAR (6)

Key figures of type DATS and TIMS are stored as characteristics fields in the database system and are, as such, unsuitable for arithmetic operations. For this reason, with the definition of the InfoObject, these key figures already have to be stored with the standard aggregation MAXIMUM or MINIMUM (see section 6.1.3).

A special focus with the definition of key figures has to be on the use of units.

Key figures without units

Key figures of the type *number, integer, date,* or *time* do not use units. These key figures are handled in the way described in the previous sections on key figures. They are meant to be added to the fact table of the star schema, and there they can be stored or added up with the use of simple mathematic operations.

The types *date* and *time* are not to be mixed up with the time characteristics! They are not measurements but simple key figures. They can be transferred or added, but they are not suitable for measurement.

For key figures of the type sum or amount, a fixed or variable unit needs to be defined. The definition of units becomes more relevant in the areas of extraction and staging as well as data analysis, where stored key figure values are brought into a relation with a unit or (in the case of currency units) have to be converted into another unit.

Key figures with a fixed unit

If the unit of such a key figure is to be preset (e.g., USD, EUR, etc.), this can be done in the key figure maintenance (see figure 6–8).

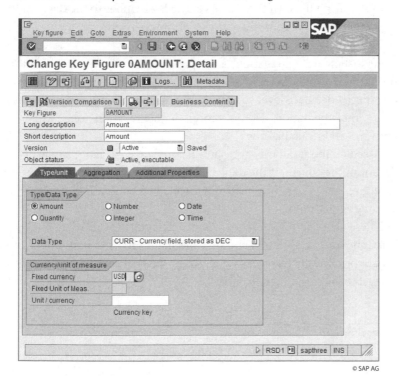

Figure 6–8
Key figures with a fixed unit

© SAP AG

When you preset a unit, the unit will not have to be explicitly stored in the data model since it can be taken from the definition of the key figure.

The use of key figures with a fixed unit might require a conversion prior to storing the data if the supplied data does not work with the same fixed unit. This conversion is possible and is further explained in section 19.3.7.

Key figures with
variable units If a key figure with different units is to be stored in the data model, a fur-ther InfoObject will have to be created with the definition of the key figure, and it stores the respective unit wherever the key figure is stored. For this purpose, a unit InfoObject (e.g., OCURRENCY) can be created (see figure 6–7 on page 65).

If several key figures use the same unit InfoObject, the key figures in the data model will be stored in different data records if they show different units. This has consequences for the data volume, but no matter what, the data is then stored correctly.

Aggregation Behavior of Key Figures

On its way from the OLTP systems via the BasisCubes to the data analysis, transactional data is compressed several times. Therefore, the key figures will be aggregated on a higher compressed detail level.

Standard aggregation   As a standard aggregation, a simple addition or the identification of minimum and maximum values is used. This type of aggregation can be done on the database level so that there will be a simple and high-perfor-mance implementation. Furthermore, the aggregation form will be the basis for further calculations.

Based on the standard aggregations, further aggregations may become relevant in the course of the data analysis. These are complex aggregation procedures that refer to other InfoObjects (exception aggregation) or to currency aggregation.

Figure 6–9
Levels of aggregation
behavior   These aggregations were provided specifically for the data analysis of BasisCubes (see section 6.3) and they are made after the standard aggrega-tion but prior to the transfer of data to the analysis tool. Figure 6–9 shows the levels of aggregation behavior.

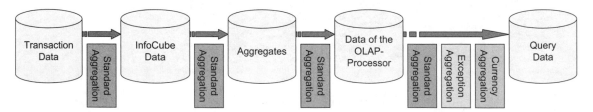

With data targets other than BasisCubes, only the standard aggregation will be made. This results from the fact that BasisCubes are conceptionally designed to be a basis for reporting and are more important than other data targets in serving data analysis.

We'll now describe the options that come with exception aggregation and currency aggregation.

With the help of the exception aggregation, a more complex aggregation of key figures can be effected. Typical examples for an exception aggregation are the calculations of the following items:

Exception aggregation

- Average inventory per month
- Average sales per customer
- Number of orders per month

Such operations only make sense with the indication of another Info-Object, which is used as a reference parameter. Both normal InfoObjects (fact-based aggregation) and time characteristics (timely aggregation) can be used as reference parameters.

The exception aggregation is defined per key figure in the maintenance of InfoObjects (see figure 6–10).

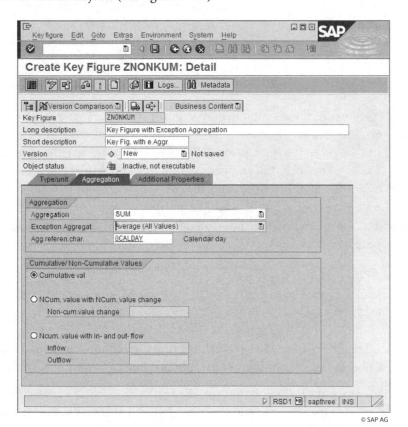

Figure 6–10
Key figures with exception aggregation

When executing an exception aggregation, the analytical engine first makes the standard aggregation and then the exception aggregation for the respective reference characteristic.

Figure 6–11

Aggregation levels of the
analytical engine

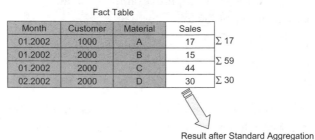

The execution of the exception aggregation is shown in figure 6–11 with the key figure SALES. The key figure has the standard aggregation SUMMA-TION and the exception aggregation AVERAGE with the reference characteristic CUSTOMER. The analytical engine provides this key figure (average sales per customer) monthly for the data analysis.

Exception aggregation with
value change

Value changes are special forms of exception aggregation. These are inventory key figures that are not stored in the data model but only calculated based on value changes stored in the BasisCube.

Contrary to all other key figures, inventory key figures are not physically stored in the data model of the BasisCubes; they are completely calculated from key figures representing value changes.

Depending on the form in which value inflows or outflows are stored in a BasisCube, inventory key figures are separated into two types:

■ **Inventory key figures with value changes:** The inventory key figure is calculated from exactly one other key figure that covers value inflows as well as outflows.

■ **Inventory key figures with value inflows and outflows:** The inventory key figure is calculated from exactly two other key figures. One of these two key figures covers the value inflows and the other the value outflows.

Depending on the type of the given inventory key figure, such key figures have to be identified in the definition of the InfoObject that contains the value changes or the value inflows or outflows (see figure 6–12). The key figures that show the inventory changes must be included in each BasisCube in which the inventory key figure is defined.

© SAP AG

From an inventory perspective, it is irrelevant which type of inventory key figure is used. However, it has to be considered that a separation of inventory changes in inflows and outflows apart from the inventory view allows for an inflow and outflow view since these respective key figures are available in the BasisCube.

Excluding a regular exception aggregation, the inventory key figures definition includes not only a discretionary reference characteristics but

Reference characteristics

also exactly one timely reference characteristic and optionally several fact-based reference characteristics.

As a timely reference characteristic, only the time InfoObject from the time dimension can be chosen. The reference characteristics for an inventory key figure are not defined in the maintenance of the InfoObject (as with regular exception aggregation) but per BasisCube. The definition of reference characteristics is made in the maintenance of BasisCubes under *Extras→Maintain non-cumulative values* (see figure 6–13). This can be done only if the BasisCube does not contain any data.

Figure 6–13

Reference characteristics of non-cumulative value parameters for inventory InfoCube

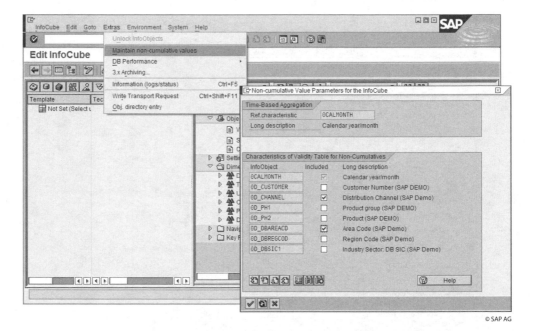

© SAP AG

The cardinality of the reference characteristics significantly affects the complexity of the SQL command, which has to be run for analyses and thus has direct impact on the performance of the data analysis. If possible, please do not use any InfoObject with more than 20 to 30 characteristic values as a reference characteristic.

In addition to defining the reference characteristic, a validation table has to be maintained for the respective BasisCube that describes the time intervals for the possible values of the reference characteristics (e.g., the calculation of the average inventory for plant 2000 and material group 002 from 01/01/2007 until 03/01/2007). This is done with transaction RSDV.

The time intervals need to be maintained in a BasisCube prior to loading the data. If the data is already in a BasisCube, the validation table can be modified with the program RSDG_CUBE_VALT_MODIFY.

After the standard aggregations and the exception aggregation, the currency aggregation will be executed. If a currency conversion is required for the data analysis, this will only be made right before the data transfer to the analysis tool. If a currency conversion does not come with the analysis, the currency aggregation will be omitted.

Currency aggregation

6.1.4 Units

Unit InfoObjects are always used for additional information, such as a value or an amount. Thus, the unit is always a currency or a unit of measure, and the possible values for each unit are always the same (USD, EUR or pieces, kilograms, pallets, etc.).

For this reason, with creation of a unit InfoObject, you need to define only the name and whether it is a unit of measure or a currency (see figure 6–14).

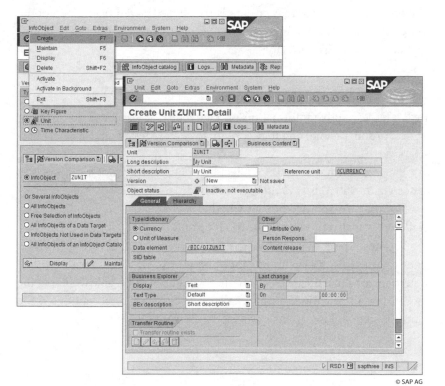

Figure 6–14

Creation of units—InfoObject

© SAP AG

Technically, behind all units are the InfoObjects 0CURRENCY or 0UNIT. They set the available unit and all units refer to them (more information on referencing of InfoObjects in section 6.2.4).

6.2   Master Data

In BW, the concept of *master data* refers to the current and key date display of attributes of characteristics. This term has already been mentioned repeatedly with the description of SID tables and will now be explained in detail.

Master data is an extended form of using characteristic InfoObjects, and it can be compared to storing master data in an SAP ERP system.

Master data contains the following elements:

- Texts of a characteristic
- Master data (attributes) of a characteristic
- External hierarchies

The data content of the master data is usually extracted from operational source systems (e.g., names and attributes of customers), but they can also be maintained in BW directly.

6.2.1   Texts

Texts are descriptive information on characteristic values (e.g., customer names, product name) and may contain lowercase letters and special characters.

The text settings of an InfoObject are made in the InfoObject maintenance via the tab *Master data/texts* (see figure 6–15).

Not only do you need to set whether a characteristic is to have texts available, you also need to define the type of texts.

Text length   You need to set the length of the text information (short text, medium text, long text). Consideration should be given as to whether the source system from which the text information will be loaded is able to supply the chosen text information. It only makes sense to choose all options if the source system holds all texts in short, medium, and long forms.

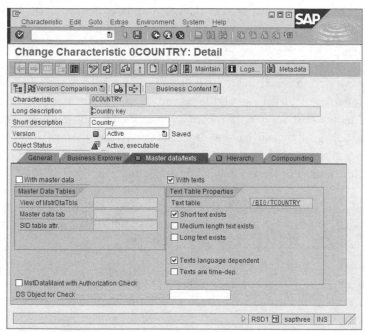

Figure 6–15
Text table properties

	Text Length
Short Text	20 characters
Medium Text	40 characters
Long Text	60 characters

Further, you need to decide whether text information will be language dependent. If it is, a key field for language will also be created in the text table of the InfoObject. As with text length, it only makes sense to store texts as language dependent if the source system from which the texts are read can supply the texts in several languages.

Since the number of data records may multiply with each additionally stored language in a text table, the language dependency should be chosen only if it actually adds value to the reporting.

Language dependency

The BI content defines numerous InfoObjects (e.g., customer) with language-dependent texts. Please consider whether you need this setting or whether it can be undone.

Time dependency Since texts are stored like master data and updated regularly, they always show the current values in a data analysis. Should texts be displayed key date related (see section 5.1.2), this can be done using time-dependent texts.

If this option is activated, a validity period is added to the text table as additional key field. A new validity period comes every time the data loads and thus the number of data records in a text table can multiply quickly. Since such growth will have a negative impact on performance, time-dependent text tables should be used only for small text tables and only if they truly add value from a data analysis perspective.

The key date for texts does not refer to the change date of the texts in the operational system but to the date of the loading into BW. Thus, an ex post creation of key date related texts is not possible.

Naming convention Based on the InfoObject name, a transparent table for text information will automatically be created with the activation of the metadata of an Info-Object.

Figure 6–16
Text tables in the ABAP
Dictionary

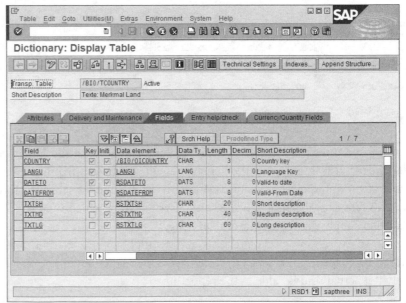

© SAP AG

	Standard InfoObject	**User-Defined InfoObject**
Name of the InfoObject	0ttttttttt	{A-Z}ttttttt
Name of the Text Table	/BIO/Tttttttttt	/BIC/T{A-Z}ttttttttt

The table structure results from the type of text information. A text table with all options (all text lengths, language dependency, and time dependency) would be defined for the InfoObject OCOUNTRY in the ABAP Dictionary as shown in figure 6–16.

6.2.2 Master Data of a Characteristic

The master data of a characteristic (in this context also referred to as a basis characteristic) is basic information (attributes) on characteristic values. Contrary to texts, these attributes can not only be used as descriptive information, they can also be used as independent elements of the data analysis through which one can select and navigate.

As with the settings for texts of an InfoObject, the settings for master data in the InfoObject maintenance are made via the tab *Master data/texts* (see figure 6–17).

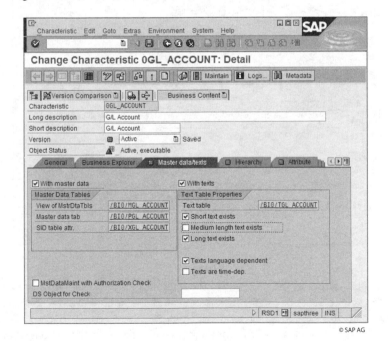

Figure 6–17

Master data properties

During InfoObject maintenance, a number of transparent tables are created, and they are responsible for the storage and administration of master
data. The structure of these tables depends on the InfoObject settings. Relevant are the settings on the following:

- Compounding
- Time-constant attributes
- Time-dependent attributes
- Navigation attribute

Compounding We already mentioned compounding when we discussed the SID table as
possibly displaying a compound primary key.

With the definition of compounding, the compounded InfoObject will
be added to all relevant master data tables of an InfoObject as a primary
key field. Compounding is defined in the InfoObject maintenance in the
Compounding tab (see figure 6–18).

Figure 6–18
Compounding of InfoObjects

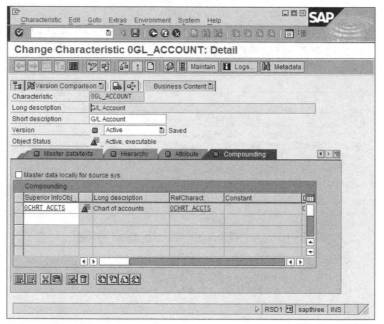

© SAP AG

A useful feature of compounding is the option to locally create master data
in the source system. If this option is activated, the source system ID will be
added to the compounding and automatically be filled at loading. This
makes sense if master data is loaded for the same characteristic from different source systems and these source systems offer the same characteristic
values even though different objects are described.

The attributes of an InfoObject define the information that the master data will offer in addition to the InfoObject. This information is primarily used as display options (e.g., show a postal code together with the customer number), and it is not suited to be used as a filter in analyses or to enable drill down to these attributes (comparable to texts). For these reasons, these attributes are called *display attributes*.

Time-constant attributes

Since the attribute data is always available to the InfoObject in the current form and does not have any dependency on the time axis, it is *time constant*.

Attributes are other existing InfoObjects that are assigned to the master data InfoObject (see figure 6–19). Each InfoObject that holds master data can take on further InfoObjects and thus be used as master data InfoObject.

It may be possible that the assigned attribute is an InfoObject that itself owns attributes. Thus, these attributes may also be used as attributes of the master data InfoObject in order to create deeply nested attribute dependencies. However, this applies only to display but not to navigation attributes (see below).

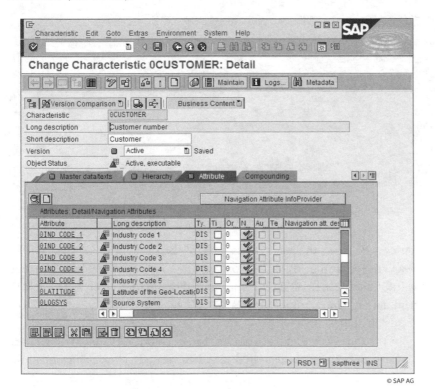

Figure 6–19
Display attributes of an InfoObject

© SAP AG

The master data table of an InfoObject is automatically created with the activation of the metadata of the InfoObject and follows the naming convention described in the following table.

	Standard InfoObject	User-Defined InfoObject
Name of the InfoObject	`0tttttttttt`	`{A-Z}ttttttt`
Master Data Table (time-constant)	`/BI0/Ptttttttttt`	`/BIC/P{A-Z}ttttttt`

Figure 6–20

Structure of time-constant master data tables

The time-constant display attributes of an InfoObject are stored in plain form (i.e., in the form of their actual value and not in the form of an SID) in the time-constant master data table of the InfoObject.

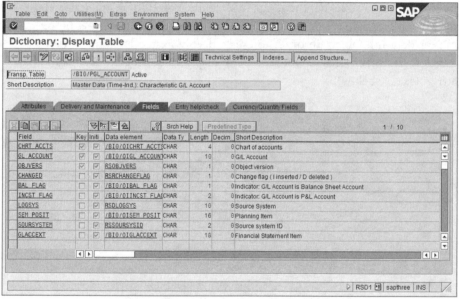

© SAP AG

Figure 6–20 shows the master data table of the InfoObject `0GL_ACCOUNT` as it was created in the ABAP Dictionary. The master data table shows that the InfoObject `0CHRT_ACCTS` is compounded to the InfoObject `0GL_ACCOUNT` (primary key) and the InfoObjects `0BAL_FLAG`, `0[sic]INCST_FLAG`, etc., are used as attributes.

Time-dependent attributes

In the same way that texts can be stored as time dependent, attributes also have the option to be stored key date related. The settings on time dependency for attributes are made in the InfoObject maintenance via *Detail/Navigation Attributes* with activation of the option *Time-dependent* for the respective attribute.

Unlike with texts, the time dependency of attributes is not set for all attributes but can be individually defined for each attribute (see figure 6–21).

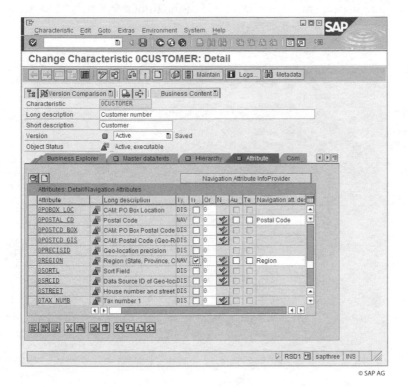

Figure 6–21
Time dependency of attributes

Apart from the master data table for time-constant attributes described earlier, there is another master data table to set the individual time dependency for time-dependent attributes.

	Standard InfoObject	User-Defined InfoObject
Name of the InfoObject	Ottttttttttt	{A-Z}ttttttt
Master Data Table (time-dependent)	/BIO/Qtttttttttt	/BIC/Q{A-Z}ttttttttt

Depending on whether an attribute has been defined as time-constant or time-dependent, it will be listed in either one or the other master data table.

As with the table for time-constant characteristics, the attributes are stored in plain text but with reference to a time period. Figure 6–22 shows the time-dependent master data table of the InfoObject ZMASTRDTA, which contains the InfoObject 0PLANT.

Figure 6–22

Structure of time-dependent master data tables

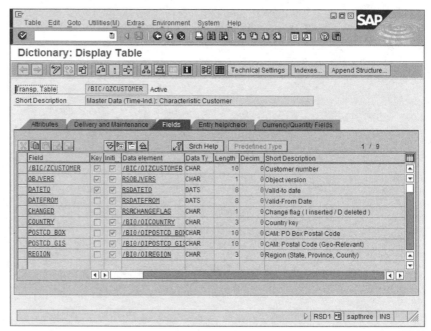

© SAP AG

The two master data tables for time-dependent and time-constant attributes are not read by BW directly but through a view.[20] BW automatically creates this view to facilitate read access from a programming perspective (also for access from self-programmed ABAP programs).

	Standard InfoObject	User-Defined InfoObject
Name of the InfoObject	0ttttttttttt	{A-Z}ttttttttt
Master Data Table View	/BIO/Mttttttttttt	/BIC/M{A-Z}ttttttttt

---

20. A view is a virtual table. Its data comes from a relational connection to one or several transparent tables.

Regular display attributes cannot be used to navigate or to filter queries. For this purpose, attributes can be defined as navigation attributes.

Navigation attributes

Since navigation through the master data tables in which attributes are stored in plain text would not efficient, the attributes that are defined as navigation attributes are stored in additional master data tables. Here, the attribute content is stored in the form of its SID.

Both time-constant and time-dependent attributes can be defined as navigation attributes. Accordingly, there are two master data tables with SID values.

	Standard InfoObject	User-Defined InfoObject
Name of the InfoObject	`0tttttttttt`	`{A-Z}ttttttt`
Master Data SID (time-constant navigation attributes)	`/BIO/Xtttttttttt`	`/BIC/X{A-Z}ttttttt`
Master Data SID (time-dependent navigation attributes)	`/BIO/Ytttttttttt`	`/BIC/Y{A-Z}ttttttt`

As explained previously navigation attributes do not have any disadvantages, from a data model perspective, compared to display attributes. However, during loading, master data goes through check routines on the SID entries of navigation attributes that are not required for display attributes. Thus, navigation attributes may have a negative impact on performance during staging.

6.2.3 Explicit Display Attributes

The option to define an InfoObjects as an attribute only is a special case. Such InfoObjects cannot be added to dimension tables and defined as navigation attributes for other InfoObjects; they can be used only as display attributes of other InfoObjects.

Explicit display attributes of an InfoObject are stored in the table only for time-constant or time-dependent attributes and not in those for navigation attributes. When the master data of an InfoObject is loaded, the SID values for its navigation attributes have to be defined but not the values for its explicit display attributes, which has a positive effect on loading performance.

6.2.4   Referencing Characteristics

With the creation of a characteristic, there is an option to create it with reference to another characteristic. In this case, the referencing characteristic is subject to the technical settings of the reference characteristic. This applies to attributes, master data, texts, hierarchies, data type, length, compounding, lowercase letters, and conversion routines.

It has to be considered that the technical settings will not be copied into a new characteristic but that the InfoObject physically uses the same data element, the same SID table, and other tables as the reference InfoObject. This results in the fact, for example, that after the master data for a reference characteristic is loaded, that same master data will automatically be available to the referencing characteristic.

The referencing characteristic is only independent from the reference characteristic in terms of business semantics. This applies to the description, display, selection of text length, authorization relevance, assignment of constants in the staging, and naming of attributes.

Partner roles   A typical example of the use of a reference characteristic is partner roles. A partner role says that, for example, in a customer order, not only the sold-to party but also the invoice recipient (regulator) and the goods recipient are entered. These partner roles may be identical but show different values; however, they always represent a customer number.

Without referencing characteristics, three InfoObjects (sold-to party, regulator, goods recipient) would have to be created and supplied with the same master data. This does not make sense since all three partner roles are based on the same customer master record.

For this reason, with the BI content (e.g., an InfoObject), 0CUSTOMER is supplied, which has a reference characteristic function. Master data, texts, and hierarchies are loaded into BW only for this InfoObject. Besides, there are further InfoObjects for the partner roles that refer to 0CUSTOMER and thus use its values, attributes, and texts. Figure 6–23 shows the InfoObject 0CUSTOMER being referenced from the content InfoObject 0SOLD_TO.

6.2.5   External Hierarchies

A hierarchy is a formation and summarization of the characteristic values of a characteristic based on defined criteria. The criteria are always defined with reference to exactly one InfoObject.

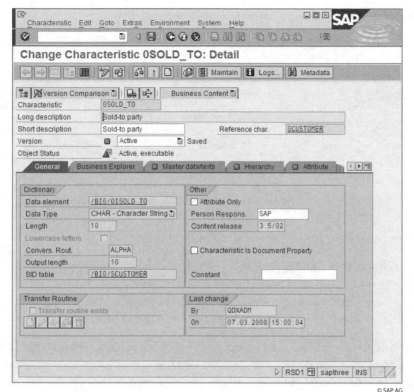

Figure 6–23
Referencing to InfoObjects

Each hierarchy consists of exactly one highest hierarchy node (the *root node*) and further nodes below that define the branching of the hierarchy. Within the hierarchy, the different values of the characteristics are contained so that for reporting purposes, the characteristic values of the structure that defines the hierarchy can be grouped.

External hierarchies offer outstanding options to manually define hierarchies flexibly and quickly. In regard to performance, the use of external hierarchies has some disadvantages. However, there are other options to map hierarchical structures. Please refer to section 8.3 on modeling of hierarchies.

Depending on how far away the node is from the root node, one speaks of *hierarchy levels*. Figure 6–24, for example, shows a possible hierarchy for the InfoObject 0MATERIAL.

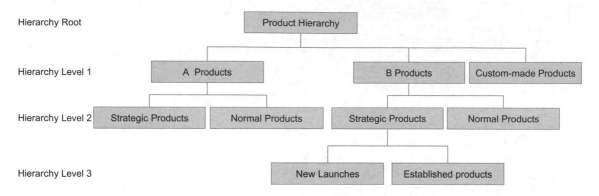

Product Hierarchy from a Product Manager's Point of View

Figure 6–24

Setup of an external hierarchy

There are two types of hierarchy nodes:

- **Nodes that cannot be posted to:** These define the structure of the hierarchy and are kind of a shell for the characteristic values.
- **Nodes that can be posted to:** These are the characteristic values of the InfoObject that has been created for the external hierarchy.

During data analysis, the key figure values of all characteristics that are assigned to one node are aggregated to this node. This enables the creation of nodes to be posted to under nodes that cannot be posted to and vice versa.

Nodes that cannot be posted to

The nodes that cannot be posted to in a hierarchy can be designed at random and they may be distinguished or ambivalent in their description. Also, their branching may be unequally deep (unbalanced). Thus, the structure of the external hierarchy can completely follow the business requirements without being subject to any technical limitations.

There are two types of nodes that cannot be posted to:

- Text nodes
- Foreign characteristic nodes

Text nodes

Text nodes are the simplest form of nodes that cannot be posted to. A text node is only defined by a discretionary node name and a discretionary description.

The values for the node name or its labeling do not refer to any other InfoObject and can be designed and nested completely at will. Figure 6–25 is an example of the definition of a hierarchy structure with the use of text nodes.

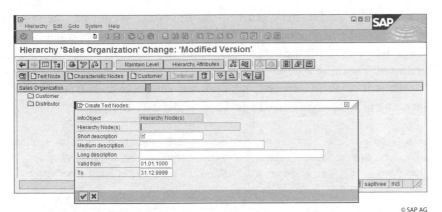

Figure 6–25
Text nodes of a hierarchy

© SAP AG

Usually, text nodes are used to describe a hierarchy structure. However, there is an option to post text content from other InfoObjects in the nodes instead of the statistic denominations. When using the hierarchy, these contents will be referred to from the text tables of the InfoObjects and thus they are always current, even though their denomination might change.

Foreign characteristic nodes

For this purpose, when you're performing hierarchy maintenance, you use the so-called *foreign characteristic nodes*. When you're using this node type, the designated InfoObject and a characteristic value have to be defined for each hierarchy node.

Nodes that can be posted to show the classification of the characteristic values of an InfoObject within the structure of its hierarchy. Thus, the classification of the characteristic values in the hierarchy structure determines the characteristic values that form the total of a hierarchy node.

Nodes that can be posted to

Nodes that can be posted to may form the lowest level of a branch in the hierarchy. This is called a *hierarchical leaf*. It is also possible to create further nodes (nodes that can be posted to, text nodes, foreign characteristic nodes) below nodes that can be posted to.

Hierarchical intervals are a special form of nodes that can be posted to. An exact characteristic value needs to be given to define nodes that can be posted to, but with a hierarchical interval, a number range of characteristic values may be defined.

Hierarchical intervals

This really makes sense when characteristic values are defined by number ranges that come with hierarchy nodes. Under these circumstances, it is even possible to arrange for a classification of master data that has not been created yet. Thus, there has to be no hierarchy modification with the new creation of master data.

Version dependency

If required, a hierarchy can be used in several versions at the same time. Then, the maintenance of the hierarchy structure is always done in the active version. For the data analysis, only the active version of the hierarchy will be available.

The use of version-dependent hierarchies can make sense if tasks[21] like planning or simulation are to be realized by the data analysis.

> To store versions, no version-dependent tables or such are generated. All versions are stored together in the same tables so that the use of several versions may cause performance problems, especially in large hierarchies.

Time dependency

The business need for time dependency of master data also derives the time dependency for hierarchies. The time dependency of hierarchies is comparable to the time dependency of master data and thus shows a clear difference to version dependency: All key dates are available at the same time in reporting. No activation of key dates is required, as is the case with versions.

For time dependency, you can choose between the time dependency of the overall hierarchy and the time dependency of the hierarchy structure.

Time dependency of the overall hierarchy

If the overall hierarchy is time dependent, this dependency will be transferred from the root node to all hierarchy nodes below. Depending on the key date, completely separated hierarchies can be used.

Time dependency of the hierarchy structure

A time-dependent hierarchy structure is defined per node (nodes that can and cannot be posted to) for the time period at which it is to be placed at a defined spot in the hierarchy. This type of time dependency is well suited for basically stable hierarchies where in the course of time only little modification is made.

External hierarchies in the data model

The names of external hierarchies have the prefix *external* because they are detached from the master data of an InfoObject; i.e., they can be maintained separately from the master data of the InfoObject. However, external hierarchies refer to exactly one InfoObject.

Each InfoObject with master data may have several external hierarchies. The properties of all external hierarchies of an InfoObject are defined in the InfoObject maintenance. These properties define the following:

---

21. There are no functions in BW that have been developed for planning or simulation only. With some limitations, the existing functions may be used for such tasks; however, they do not replace products such as SEM, SCM, or APO, which are used to assume explicit planning and simulation tasks.

- Whether an InfoObject is to have external hierarchies at all
- Whether the hierarchies are version dependent
- Whether the overall hierarchy or the hierarchy structures are time dependent
- Whether intervals are to be allowed in the hierarchy

Figure 6–26 shows the definition of hierarchy properties in the InfoObject maintenance.

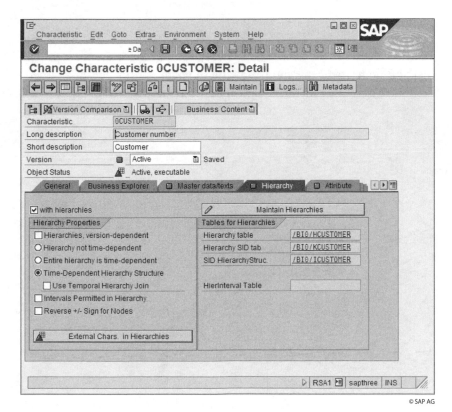

Figure 6–26

Hierarchy properties of InfoObjects

© SAP AG

The fact that hierarchy properties are defined in the InfoObject maintenance means that the properties of all external hierarchies of an InfoObject are identical. For example, it is not possible to create an external hierarchy for an InfoObject where the *overall structure* is time dependent and a separate one where the *hierarchy structure* is time dependent.

External hierarchies can be created for basic characteristics but not for referencing characteristics. Since referencing characteristics use the same master data tables as their reference characteristics, external hierarchies may be used for all reference characteristics. For example, when you're creating a customer hierarchy, the hierarchy will only have to be created for the customer (0CUSTOMER). The same hierarchy will then be available to the referencing characteristics (sold-to party, regulator, and supplier).

6.2.6   Summary

Figure 6–27

Table structure of master data

The data model of the master data is very complex. However, it is crucial that you understand this model for the modeling of further data targets. For this reason, the coherencies are once more summarized in figure 6–27.

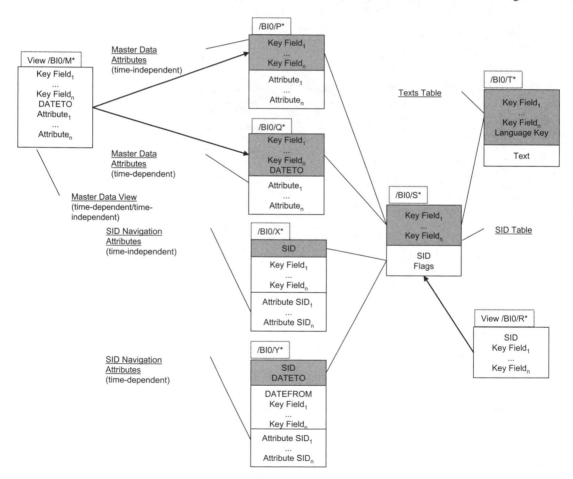

The following overview summarizes the naming conventions of tables that are used to store master data:

Naming convention

	Standard InfoObject	User-Defined InfoObject
Name of the InfoObject	Ottttttttttt	{A-Z}tttttttt
Text Table	/BIO/Tttttttttttt	/BIC/T{A-Z}tttttttt
Master Data Table (time-constant)	/BIO/Pttttttttttt	/BIC/P{A-Z}tttttttt
Master Data SID (time-constant navigation attributes)	/BIO/Xttttttttttt	/BIC/X{A-Z}tttttttt
Master Data Table (time-dependent)	/BIO/Qttttttttttt	/BIC/Q{A-Z}tttttttt
Master Data SID (time-dependent navigation attributes)	/BIO/Yttttttttttt	/BIC/Y{A-Z}tttttttt
Master Data Table View	/BIO/Mttttttttttt	/BIC/M{A-Z}tttttttt
Hierarchy Table	/BIO/Httttttttttt	/BIC/H{A-Z}tttttttt
Conversion Hierarchy Values to SID Values	/BIO/Kttttttttttt	/BIC/K{A-Z}tttttttt
Structure of Hierarchy Nodes	/BIO/Ittttttttttt	/BIC/I{A-Z}tttttttt
Hierarchy Intervals	/BIO/Jttttttttttt	/BIC/J{A-Z}tttttttt

The tables listed will only be created completely for an InfoObject if all options of the master data are used (master data and texts available, navigation attributes in time-constant and time-dependent form available). Depending on the settings of the InfoObject, individual tables might not be required and will thus not be created in the ABAP Dictionary.

6.3 DataStore Objects

The previous explanations of the data model referred to the areas of data definition (InfoObjects for characteristics and key figures) as well as master data, i.e., the master data containing the data area of a data model.

Similar to the flat structures that were described previously, DataStore objects group characteristics and key figures in a table.

Thus, DataStore objects can be used to store transactional data, which often is the predestined application area of DataStore objects. Given their simple structure, DataStore objects basically may contain any other information, such as controlling data, protocols, etc.

BW offers three different types of DataStore objects:

- DataStore objects for direct update
- DataStore objects without delta creation (write-optimized DataStore objects)
- DataStore objects with delta creation (standard DataStore objects)

The standard DataStore objects come with comprehensive functions for staging, which will be explained in chapter 17.

DataStore objects can be used for data analysis, but they are very ill-suited from a performance perspective. Use the DataStore objects for any given purpose but avoid the use of DataStore objects for data analysis.

Naming convention In any case, DataStore objects always represent a table structure that creates corresponding table definitions in the ABAP Dictionary (see section 4.2.3).

The following table shows the naming convention in the ABAP Dictionary for the transparent table that will contain data.

	Content DataStore Object	User-Defined DataStore Object
DataStore Object	0tttttt	{A-Z}ttttt
Table in the ABAP Dictionary	/BIO/Attttt00	/BIC/A{A-Z}ttttt00

In section 17.1.2, further naming conventions will be displayed that are required to identify delta information in standard DataStore objects.

Definition of DataStore Object types The DataStore Object type is defined in the settings of the DataStore Object maintenance (see figure 6–28).

DataStore Object for direct update The most simple form of DataStore Object is the ***DataStore object for direct update*** (referred to as transactional ODS object in BW 3.x). DataStore objects for direct update do not have staging functions, they cannot be used for reporting[22] purposes, and they are primarily to be considered

a better form of transparent table (see section 4.2), which are part of the
BW metadata but do not have any serious tasks in BW.

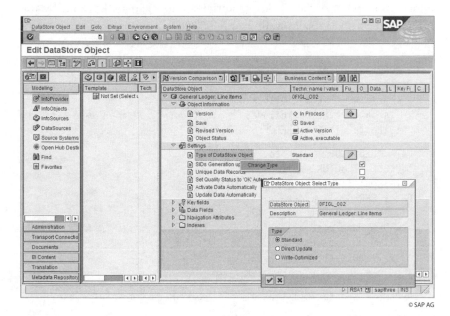

Figure 6–28
*Definition of the DataStore
object type*

Instead, DataStore objects for direct update are used as data targets for
analysis processes of the Analysis Process Designer and the Data Mining
Workbench (transactions RSANWB or RSDMWB, respectively) and can be used
in proprietary programs. In this way, DataStore objects for direct update
serve as data containers for various data that is generated in various ways
and may be processed in various ways too.

The content of DataStore objects for direct update (and only of this
type!) can be generated, modified, and read with proprietary programs in
a user-defined way. A more elegant access can be realized with the use of
the following RFC-enabled function modules that can be accessed across
system boundaries and that come with lock management:

- RSDRI_ODSO_INSERT_RFC
- RSDRI_ODSO_UPDATE_RFC
- RSDRI_ODSO_MODIFY_RFC
- RSDRI_ODSO_DELETE_RFC

---

22. Transactional ODS objects can be used for analysis if they are analyzed with the use
of an InfoSet (see section 11.2).

The following example writes data records in a DataStore Object for direct update (Q_DSTORE), which is defined by the InfoObjects OCUSTOMER (customer number) and OMATERIAL (material number) in its key and by the InfoObjects OSALES (sales value) and OCURRENCY (currency) in its data fields.

```
REPORT ZQX_DATASTORE_EXAMPLE.
DATA:
  l_numrows LIKE bapi6116xx-numrows,
  l_s_data  LIKE bapi6116da,      "structure of the table l_t_data
  l_t_data  TYPE TABLE OF bapi6116da. "Table

DATA: BEGIN OF l_wa_data.
INCLUDE STRUCTURE /bic/aQ_DSTORE.
DATA: buff(1000).
DATA: END OF l_wa_data.
    l_wa_data-customer = '4711'.   "customer number 4711
    l_wa_data-material = '0815'.   "material number 0815
    l_wa_data-sales = 100.         "sales value 100
    l_wa_data-currency = 'USD'.    "US dollars

l_s_data-data = l_wa_data.
APPEND l_s_data TO l_t_data.       "append to internal tables

CALL FUNCTION 'RSDRI_ODSO_INSERT_RFC'
EXPORTING
  i_odsobject = 'Q_DSTORE'
IMPORTING
  e_numrows = l_lumrows            "appended records
TABLES
  i_t_data = l_t_data              "internal table with data
EXCEPTIONS
  data_target_not_ods = 1
  ods_type_not_transactional = 2
  active_table_name_not_found = 3
  record_key_already_exists = 4
  array_insert_failed = 5
  internal_error = 6
OTHERS = 7.

IF sy_subrc NE 0.
  WRITE:/ 'append or change failure'.
ELSE.
  WRITE:/ 'successfully appended records: '' l_numrows.
ENDIF.
```

The data model of each DataStore Object is defined using *key fields* and *data fields.* In both cases, the fields are InfoObjects (see figure 6–29).

Figure 6–29
Modeling of DataStore objects

6.3.1 Key Fields

The data in the DataStore objects are not primarily derived from the analysis requirements but from their relation to the operational data structures. It must be possible to properly process transaction modifications. A prerequisite is the ability to overwrite existing data (e.g., with a change in the order status, the previous status needs to be overwritten by the current status).

This is possible only if the fields that define a transaction (e.g., order number and order position) are defined so that all fields (e.g., order status) can relate to these fields.

To achieve this correlation, the fields that define a transaction are defined as key fields in the DataStore objects. Each data record in a DataStore object can thus be clearly identified through the combination of key fields. In the underlying transparent table, the key fields form the primary key for the table.

The definition of key fields of a DataStore Object requires deep knowledge of the existing structures in the source system. Don't assume or test key fields since errors in the definition can cause hardly traceable errors. You should only define the key fields of a DataStore Object when you are sure that you will not make a mistake.

With the definition of key fields, the following limitations have to be considered:

- Between 1 (minimum) and 16 (maximum) key fields have to be defined.
- The length of the key fields may not exceed 780 bytes in total.
- Key figures cannot be used as key fields.

6.3.2   Data Fields

Fields that are, from an operational point of view, dependent on the key fields (e.g., order status fields) are referred to as data fields in the DataStore objects. For transactional data, this includes all fields that are not part of the primary key (key fields), characteristics and key figures alike.

The use of data fields is subject to the following basic conditions:

- A maximum of 749 data fields can be defined.
- The maximum data record length of the DataStore table (including key fields) may not exceed 1918 bytes.

6.4   BasisCubes

BasisCubes form the basis of analysis-capable data models in BW. Data may be stored in different BW objects, but it is up to the BasisCubes to provide high-performance characteristics and key figures offering the full functional variety of BW for analysis purposes.

BasisCubes are basically built according to the snowflake schema, which was BW-specifically modified and enhanced to enable, for example, unbalanced hierarchies or the key date historiography of attributes. Thus, SAP refers to the data model of BasisCubes as *developed star schema* (enhanced star schema).

The enhancement of the regular star schema offers various options in data modeling; however, it increases the complexity of the data model at the same time so that modeling in BW should not be done without deeper knowledge of the data model.

In the following sections, the role of the *fact table,* the *master data ID,* and the *dimensions* of BasisCubes are explained. Then we'll explain the special form of *Real-Time InfoCubes.*

6.4.1   Fact Table

While the concept of the regular schema is only based on a central fact table, BW automatically defines *two* fact tables with the creation of a Basis-Cube:

- A normal fact table
- A compressed fact table

Both fact tables are identical in their structure; however, they have different tasks in the life cycle of analytical data.

The normal fact table is the first station for all data in a BasisCube. It is basically prepared for the analytical access to its data inventory and is thus functionally adequate to analytically process data inventory.

The normal fact table

Still, the normal fact table is designed to be an *intermediate station* only, which is to primarily enable the management[23] of data for a single loading (loading data is called *request* from now on). With each data record of the fact table, the so-called request ID with which it was written in the fact table is stored in a separate dimension. Thus, the data in the fact table is stored with a level of detail that is not necessarily required from a business perspective but is required from a technical perspective.

To write the data in the normal fact table in a high-performance way, the normal fact table does not dispose of a primary key in terms of the ABAP Dictionary.[24] If the data of a request is separated into packages, the data will—with the filling of the fact tables—not be aggregated across packages; therefore, the data of the BasisCubes will be detailed on the level of individual data packages.[25]

---

23. Part of this management task is to transfer new data to other data targets or the subsequent deletion of a request from the normal fact table.
24. The transaction SE11 shows a primary key; however, this key is not contained in the definition of the database table.
25. The detailing to individual data packages is not mapped in the data model of the normal fact table, but with the lack of a primary key, it is possible to store several records with identical key values in the fact table.

The compressed fact table

Depending on the data model of the BasisCube, the frequency of loadings, and the mixture of loaded data, the detailing of the normal fact table may have a serious effect on the data volume of the BasisCubes. Thus, an aggregation of data in data packages overall, together with the loss of the request ID, can reduce the data volume of the fact table by a multiple without having any negative effects from a business perspective (see figure 6–30).

Figure 6–30
Compression of the fact table

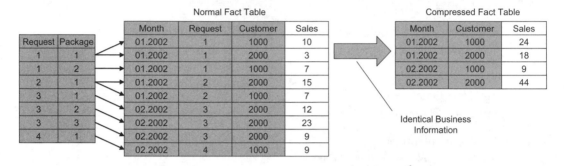

As counterpart to the normal fact table, each BasisCube has a compressed fact table that is less optimized to manage and realize loadings but rather optimized for analytical performance. This applies both to the storage structure[26] and the compression of the fact table with the loss of the request ID.

Interaction of fact tables

The use of the compressed fact table is optional. Without the explicit setting in BW, the compressed fact table will not be used. The data transfer from a normal fact table to a compressed fact table is made by the so-called compression.[27]

With the compression, BW moves data from a normal fact table into the compressed fact table (see figure 6–31).

From a data analysis view, it is transparent whether and how many requests are combined in the compressed fact table since the analytical engine considers both normal and compressed tables and automatically integrates the contents.

In large-scale architectures, if data from a BasisCube is transferred to another system, the request IDs that have been added since the last data transfer are required for the identification of new requests (delta process). In this case, only the requests that have already been delivered to the other system may be included in the compression.

---

26. Detailed explanations of the storage structure from a performance-tuning perspective are given in sections 7.3.1 (Range Partitioning) and 7.3.2 (Clustering).
27. SAP sometimes also refers to compression as condensation.

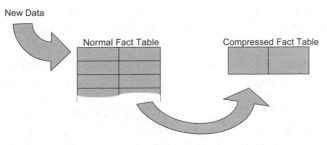

New Data

Normal Fact Table

Compressed Fact Table

Requests older than x days

Figure 6–31
Interaction of normal and compressed fact tables

The compression of a fact table can be made in InfoCube administration (see figure 6–32). Based on the request ID, you define which requests are to be compressed; i.e., the overall fact table or a part of the order requests can be compressed optionally.

Execution of a compression

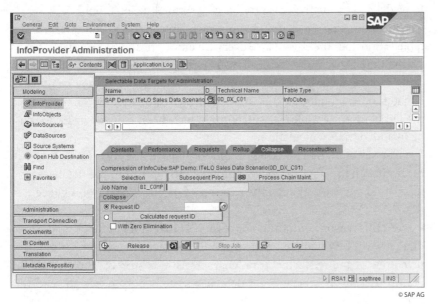

© SAP AG

Figure 6–32
Compression of BasisCubes

The compression process has an impact on running operations and considerably affects the data analysis. Thus, do not run a compression during analysis periods.

The compression of data through request IDs and packages often results in data records in the compressed fact table in which all key figures have the value zero. As long as there is no cube with content key figures or key

Elimination of zero values

figures with exception aggregation (i.e., only key figures with the aggregation behavior SUM), from a content perspective these data records can be deleted.

The deletion of zero values is automatically made after the compression if the check box With Zero Elimination is activated (see figure 6–32).

> The elimination of zero values may result in orphaned dimension entries, causing the desired performance advantages of the zero value elimination to not be completely achieved. Therefore, for cubes with zero value elimination, regularly perform dimension trimmings (see section 32.2).

The zero value elimination applies only to zero values created after activation of the zero value elimination check box. If zero value elimination is not activated in the design of a cube, zero values that already exist will have to be deleted explicitly. This process is described in section 9.2.3.

The compressed fact table for Inventory cubes

The compression of the normal fact table into the compressed fact table is only half the story, since every inventory has to be calculated based on the initial inventory taking. This is especially true for the compression of BasisCubes with inventory key figures. For example, if the inventory of a material for January 2004 is to be identified, all inventory changes since the initial inventory taking (which might have been realized in 1999) must be included in the calculation.

The selection of a booking period 01.2004 in a report would thus still mean that all previous periods would need to be read in the database, and this would particularly spoil the concept of database partitioning (see section 7.3.1).

For this reason, with the compression of Inventory cubes, the so-called markers will be calculated and stored in the fact table in which the final inventory of the respective time characteristic is stored. Thus, when the period 01.2004 is selected, the database system only needs to read this period (see figure 6–33).

For Inventory cubes, the compression of a fact table leads to another significant performance increase from the calculation of supporting points.

Updating markers in Inventory cubes

A particular feature of Inventory cubes is the option to prevent the supporting points from updating during compression (see section 6.4.1).

This is necessary if inventory changes were loaded into a BasisCube whose time reference is dated prior to the inventory initialization. In practice, this scenario is rather exceptional, so the option to prevent the markers update should be considered to be an exception.

Figure 6–33

Compression of the fact table for Inventory cubes[28]

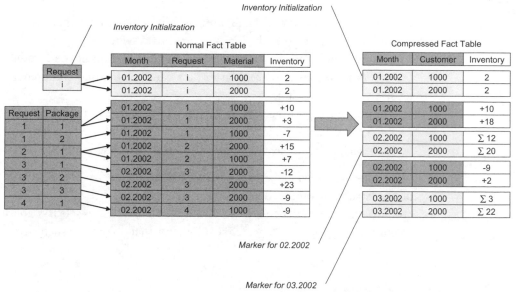

With the activation of metadata of a BasisCube, BW will automatically create both fact tables in the ABAP Dictionary. The naming conventions for these two tables are shown in the following table:

Naming convention

	Standard BasisCube	User-Defined BasisCube
Name of the BasisCube	0ttttttttt	{A-Z}ttttttttt
Fact Table	/BIO/F0ttttttttt	/BIC/F{A-Z}ttttttttt
Fact Table (compressed)	/BIO/E0ttttttttt	/BIC/E{A-Z}ttttttttt
Structure over All Characteristics/Key Figures	/BIO/V0tttttttttT	/BIC/V{A-Z}tttttttttT

6.4.2 SID Entries in Dimension Tables

The reference from master data to dimension tables is made by the SID of the respective InfoObject. In the dimension tables, only SIDs are stored, never the characteristic values (see section 6.1.1).

---

28. The design of data and markers shown here is simplified. In the technical realization, the markers will be combined in a separate storage area.

The use of SIDs is discussed widely since writing the direct master data keys in the dimension would be similarly effective and can be done easily. However, the use of SIDs has several advantages:

- The short 4-byte key of the SID may result in better data analysis performance compared to the long characteristic values.
- The referencing to the SID enables the encapsulation of the InfoObjects (and its master data). Master data can thus be used comprehensively across InfoCubes.
- The referencing to the SID of the InfoObject makes the functions of the master data, especially its texts, time-dependent information, and external hierarchies available with the use of the data model.

Enhancing the snowflake schema with SIDs has extensive consequences for the structure of the data model. Especially the use of navigation attributes, texts, time dependencies, and external hierarchies sets BW apart from most of the other data warehouse systems that do not use such structures as much.

6.4.3 Dimensions

The relation between a fact table and its dimension tables is made with the use of surrogate keys, the so-called DIM IDs (dimension identification). DIM IDs are system-generated, 4-byte long IDs that are created by BW when data is updated in a BasisCube.

Each BasisCube has a maximum of 16 dimensions. Thirteen of these dimensions can be defined individually for each BasisCube. Each dimension can take a maximum of 248 InfoObjects. This results in a maximum number of 13 x 248 = 3,224 freely definable InfoObjects per BasisCube (plus the attributes of each InfoObject).

Three of the dimensions are strictly defined for all BasisCubes: package, time, and unit.

Package dimension
The package dimension contains the *request ID*. This is a technical level of detail that describes the loading that transferred data into a Basis-Cube.

The detailing of data on a request ID level enables focused administration of single loadings (e.g., deletion of data from a BasisCube if found to be erroneous) as long as the data is still contained in the normal fact table.

The package dimension is also part of the compressed fact table, but it is only shown in a single initial record and has no further function.

The time dimension is used to add time characteristics in a BasisCube as far as they are the standard time dimensions such as 0CALMONTH or 0FISCPER provided by BW (see section 6.1.2). Proprietary time characteristics cannot be stored in this dimension.

Time dimension

Any key figure that describes a quantity or an amount needs to be defined as InfoObject with reference to a unit InfoObject. While the key figures are stored in the fact table, the unit InfoObjects are stored in the unit dimension (see figure 6–34).

Unit dimension

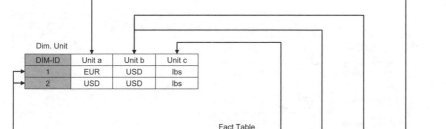

Figure 6–34
Use of the unit dimension (1)

In this way, each key figure is stored with an individually definable unit.[29]

Here, it is also possible that several key figures refer to the same unit InfoObject (in figure 6–34, these are the key figures 2 and 3). This should be applied if these key figures usually show identical units.

However, if all of a sudden such key figures show different units, the data can still be displayed correctly (see figure 6–35).

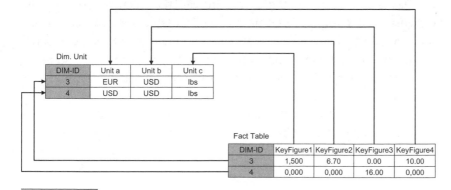

Figure 6–35
Use of the unit dimension (2)

---

29. As described earlier, the unit will *not* be stored in the dimension table. This is shown in a simplified way in figure 6–34. Instead, the SID for the respective unit will be stored in the dimension table.

In such a situation, it is disadvantageous that more data records than necessary are generated in the fact table (with the referencing from key figure 2 and key figure 3 to different units, this could be avoided). Thus, you should use several key figures to refer to the same unit only in exceptional cases in order to not unnecessarily increase the data volume of the Basis-Cube.

Naming convention   With the activation of metadata of a BasisCube, BW automatically creates all necessary tables for the dimensions in the ABAP Dictionary. The following table shows which these are.

	Standard BasisCube	**User-Defined BasisCube**
Name of the BasisCube	0tttttttt	{A-Z}tttttttt
Package Dimension	/BIO/D0ttttttttP	/BIC/D{A-Z}tttttttP
Time Dimension	/BIO/D0ttttttttT	/BIC/D{A-Z}tttttttT
Unit Dimension	/BIO/D0ttttttttU	/BIC/D{A-Z}tttttttU
1ˢᵗ Dimension	/BIO/D0ttttttttt1	/BIC/D{A-Z}tttttttt1
...	/BIO/D0ttttttt..	/BIC/D{A-Z}tttttt..
13ᵗʰ Dimension	/BIO/D0ttttttttD	/BIC/D{A-Z}tttttttD

6.4.4   Line Item Dimensions

A line item dimension is a special form of dimension table. Here, the fact table does not refer to the dimension table, which, via SID itself, refers to the master data table of an InfoObject. Instead, the SID that is found in the dimension table is directly taken into the fact table. As a consequence, a line item dimension can consist of only one single InfoObject (compared to a maximum 253 InfoObjects with normal dimensions).

Line item dimensions serve to improve performance and can always be used when the dimension consists of a single InfoObject.

A typical BasisCube with some "normal" dimensions and one line item dimension is thus defined as follows in the ABAP Dictionary:

Field	Data Element	Type	Check Table	Description
KEY_ZCUBEP	RSDIMID	INT4	/BIC/DZCUBEP	DIM ID
KEY_ZCUBET	RSDIMID	INT4	/BIC/DZCUBET	DIM ID
KEY_ZCUBEU	RSDIMID	INT4	/BIC/DZCUBEU	DIM ID
KEY_ZCUBE1	RSDIMID	INT4	/BIC/DZCUBE1	DIM ID
KEY_ZCUBE2	RSDIMID	INT4	/BIC/DZCUBE2	DIM ID
KEY_ZCUBE3	RSDIMID	INT4	/BIC/DZCUBE3	DIM ID
KEY_ZCUBE4	RSDIMID	INT4	/BIC/DZCUBE4	DIM ID
KEY_ZCUBE5	RSSID	INT4		SID (line item dimension)
KEY_ZCUBE6	RSDIMID	INT4	/BIC/DZCUBE6	DIM ID
/BIC/ZAMOUNT01	/BIC/oIZAMOUNT01	QUAN		amount key figure 1
/BIC/ZAMOUNT02	/BIC/oIZAMOUNT02	QUAN		amount key figure 2
/BIC/ZVALUE01	/BIC/oIZVALUE01	CURR		value key figure 1
/BIC/ZVALUE02	/BIC/oIZVALUE02	CURR		value key figure 2

In the SAP documentation, the use of line item dimensions is limited to cases where the InfoObject to be mapped has almost as many values as the fact table has in records. With the line item dimension, you can avoid performance problems from very large and continuously growing dimensions.

The line item dimension was developed initially to avoid such problems, but you don't need to limit their use. Line item dimensions are always advantageous for performance and they should always be used when the number of InfoObjects allows for the definition of one InfoObject per dimension.

6.4.5 Real-Time InfoCubes

Real-Time InfoCubes are a special form of BasisCubes that were initially used in the context of integrated planning in BW[30] (up to BW version 3.x, they were called transactional cubes).

The BPS functions have special requirements for the storing structure of the cubes used. With the planning and simulation functions of BPS, data

---

30. At that time, it was SEM BPS that was integrated in BW with release 3.5.

is not only read but also written. This is not mass data as found in the context of extraction or at staging, but single data records that are entered into the cube by several users and that may immediately be reread.

The procedures in BW 7 for timely analysis of data have similar requirements. which are written in a push method or from real-time-capable data sources into the cubes in very short time periods (see also chapter 22).

The functions of BW BPS, like push methods and the highly frequent data update, do not correspond with the initial concept of BasisCubes, so special enhancements were made that lead to the Real-Time InfoCube type.

Technical particularities   The technical challenge with a Real-Time InfoCube is dealing with several write accesses in parallel. With Oracle and DB2/UDB database systems, this requires different indexing of the fact tables (see section 7.2.1) and smaller extents. For all other database systems, the storage structure and the indexing of transactional cubes and standard BasisCubes are identical.

> The use of Real-Time InfoCubes is only required for the functions of integrated planning and real-time scenarios. Any BasisCube that should not have this function should not be created as a Real-Time InfoCube because it may be disadvantageous for data analysis performance.

To make a BasisCube transactional, you need to select the respective option when the cube is created (see figure 6–36).

If standard BasisCubes are subsequently to be turned into transactional cubes, this can be done with the program SAP_CONVERT_NORMAL_TRANS.

Integrated planning   If Real-Time InfoCubes are to be used for the functions of integrated planning, the load behavior of the cubes needs to be defined accordingly. The load behavior can be switched (and switched back) in running operations (see figure 6–37).

According to its load behavior, a Real-Time InfoCube can be loaded either from the staging engine processes or from the planning processor of integrated planning, but it cannot be loaded from both at the same time.

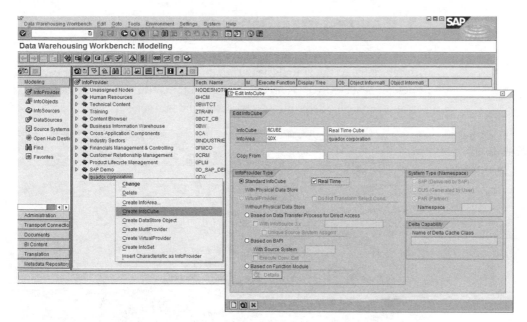

© SAP AG

Figure 6-36 *Creation of a transactional BasisCube*

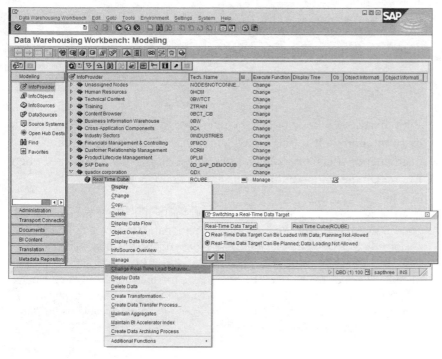

© SAP AG

Figure 6-37 *Switching the cube status in transactional cubes*

6.5   Source System Dependent Data

In some cases, it makes sense to store master data or transactional data with reference to the source system that provides it. For that purpose, the InfoObject 0SOURSYSTEM is predefined: it contains source system identification and can be loaded into the respective data target.

Figure 6–38
Source system dependent InfoObjects

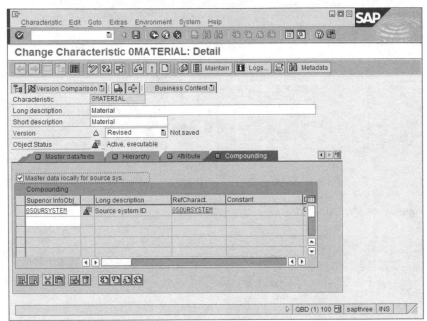

© SAP AG

Source system dependent InfoObjects

With master data InfoObjects, the reference to the source system is made by compounding it to the InfoObject 0SOURSYSTEM. Here, the InfoObject maintenance offers the setting *Master data locally for source systems,* where BW makes the compounding by itself (see figure 6–38).

The source system dependency of InfoObjects is not additional information but creates the total dependency of all master data to the source system ID. Prior to the definition of source system dependency, you should consider that the compounding of the InfoObjects 0MATERIAL to 0SOURSYSTEM will result in the fact that there will be no longer a material number 4711 but only the material numbers SYS1/4711, SYS2/4711, etc. They are physically totally independent material numbers, which may cause problems for data analyses (e.g., with ABC analyses).

7   Performance Tuning

In a data warehouse, the data volume can grow into sizes that may cause performance problems even for high-performance hardware. For this reason, SAP BW offers options to improve the data analysis performance.

In this chapter, we'll explain a selection of essential tuning measures that are directly related to the data model of *BasisCubes*. They are the basis for decisions in the data analysis and are thus at the center of optimization measures for read access.[31]

Performance tuning starts with the data model of a BasisCube that has been created without modeling errors. In too many cases, one tries to apply performance tuning measures to BasisCubes that have been created fundamentally wrong; the success of the tuning measures will often be a partial success only. Prior to each performance tuning attempt, be extremely careful not to make any modeling errors. Chapter 8 explains the most important basic rules of data modeling.

There are four approaches to optimization:

- Aggregation
- Indexing
- Partitioning and clustering
- Use of dedicated OLAP memory (BIA)

The technical basics of these approaches are very different, but in their implementation in BW, they correlate very much. Further, the implementation may focus very much on one of the two fact tables (normal/compressed), so for an understanding of the tuning approaches, the interaction of the two fact tables needs to be kept in mind (see section 6.4.1).

---

31. The optimization of write access to BW objects is explained in the context of extraction and staging in chapter 24.

Only the use of the BI accelerator as dedicated OLAP memory is different from the other tuning measures and in some way even competes with the these measures.

The approaches are described in the following sections together with the dependencies to be considered. In some cases, the tuning may require further analyses of the database or the basis system. In addition to the tuning measures described in this chapter, the part of the book on the Analytical Engine refers to tuning measures that aim at optimization of BW access to the database (see chapter 10 to 13).

7.1   Aggregates

Besides compression, there is another option in BW to reduce the data basis for read access: aggregates. An aggregate is redundant BasisCube data storage with low detailing and/or only a subset of BasisCube data.

> Aggregates are memory and administration intensive; however, they are very flexible and can be largely adjusted to the reporting requirements. With high data volumes, they are the most important tuning measure for data analysis!

An aggregate can always be used in reports when no further detailed information than available in the aggregate is required. The decision on whether a BasisCube or an aggregate is used for an analysis step will be made independently by the Analytical Engine; the decision will not be transparent for the user (see section 12.3).

Aggregates may be used for the optimization of BasisCubes only. This is one of the most important reasons why data analyses with large data volumes should always be based on BasisCubes and not on other data targets (e.g., DataStore objects). For each BasisCube, a discretionary number of aggregates can be created with the transaction RSDDV or the context menu of the BasisCube (see figure 7–1).

Aggregates can flexibly be created ex post and be aligned to reporting requirements. With a new creation, the aggregates are filled from the respective BasisCube. In running operations, the newly added data of a BasisCube will be transferred to the aggregates. This process is called **rollup.**

Figure 7–1
Creation of aggregates

The creation of many aggregates is suitable for reporting optimization; however, the creation and modification of aggregates in running operations require corresponding resources. To minimize resource needs in running operations, please consider the option to use so-called rollup hierarchies for the creation of aggregates (see section 24.6).

The reduction of data volumes in an aggregate may be achieved with the reduction of granularity or the accumulation of subsets, whereas in practice, both options are usually combined.

A reduction in granularity is achieved if, from the amount of Info-Objects that define the granularity of the BasisCube, only a subset is filled into an aggregate.

The following InfoObjects are to remain in the aggregate:

- Characteristics
- Time-constant navigation attributes

- Time-dependent navigation attributes
- Hierarchical nodes

However, all InfoObjects can be combined within an aggregate.

We'll explain how you can see what characteristics are required for the execution of a query (and when an aggregate is suitable for a query) in section 13.1, which also covers monitoring the Analytical Engine.

Aggregates for characteristics

Entering characteristics is the simplest form of aggregation. All characteristics that are defined in the BasisCube but not filled into an aggregate are aggregated in such a way that the detailing level of the aggregate is limited to characteristics that are filled into the aggregate (see figure 7–2). If there are any compound characteristics, the compounding will automatically be filled into the aggregate.

Figure 7–2

Characteristics aggregate

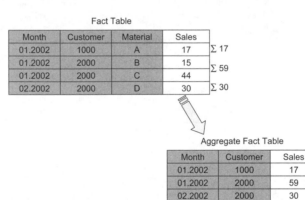

Basically, all key figures that are stored in the BasisCube will be filled into the aggregate. If there are key figures with exception aggregation, their reference characteristics will be filled into the aggregates of the cube.

The required entry of reference characteristics for the exception aggregation may in some circumstances have negative impact on the size of the aggregates (e.g., if for the key figure "average sales per customer", the customer number is always filled into the aggregate). For this reason, there is a so-called expert mode for the definition of aggregates (menu item *Extras→Expert Mode On*). With the expert mode, reference characteristics can be removed from the aggregates. These aggregates will be used by the Analytical Engine for a report only if the query does not contain any of the key figures that require this reference characteristic.

When a characteristic is filled into an aggregate, all of its time-constant navigation attributes are also available. In many cases, however, reporting will only require certain navigation attributes without the respective basic characteristic. Since the number of values of an attribute is usually less than the number of values of a characteristic (e.g., there are more customers than assigned countries), it can make sense to fill aggregates with the respective navigation attributes only.

Aggregates for time-constant navigation attributes

This form of aggregation can be modeled in the same way as the direct fill of characteristics.

As with time-constant navigation attributes, it can make sense to fill time-dependent attributes into an aggregate. However, this may be a problem since the data model of an aggregate is not suited to store the same data records for different values of time-dependent attributes (due to the different values of the respective key dates).

Aggregates for time-dependent navigation attributes

For this reason, from the filling of a time-dependent navigation attribute onwards, the complete aggregate is considered key date dependent. The key date is to be stored in the definition of the aggregate. This may be a fixed preset key date (see figure 7–3).

A time-dependently defined aggregate can be used for data analysis if the master data is requested for exactly this key date.

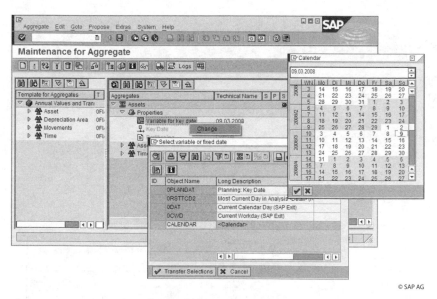

Figure 7–3

Aggregate for time-dependent navigation attributes

© SAP AG

Should the key date of an aggregate be designed dynamically, instead of a key date indication, an OLAP variable can be stored in the aggregate to set the key date. The value of this OLAP variable will be identified directly before the *filling* of the aggregate (and not when it is activated) and stored in the definition of the aggregate. This value is valid until a modification of all time-dependent aggregates has been made (see section 7.1.2).

> Time-dependent aggregates require a lot of administration because for each key date, an separate aggregate needs to be created (this is costly for you) or the existing aggregate must be modified (this is costly for the system). Time-dependent aggregates should be used only if they are absolutely required. In most cases, these requirements can be reconsidered in favor of normal aggregates.

Aggregates for hierarchy nodes

If external hierarchies are used for the data analysis, the complete external hierarchy of the respective InfoObject will be read from the BasisCube or the aggregate. For large external hierarchies with several thousand pages, this can be very time-consuming.

Therefore, this is not necessary if, for the analysis only, some hierarchy levels of the first display, but not all pages, are required. Thus, it makes sense to create aggregates with the respective hierarchy levels for these requirements. This can also be done with the modeling of aggregates (see figure 7–4).

Figure 7–4
Hierarchy aggregate

The creation of hierarchy aggregates makes sense only in combination with the read mode "read when you navigate or expand hierarchies" (see section 12.1.3). If the Analytical Engine does not use this read mode for a query, hierarchy aggregates cannot be used.

Apart from a reduction in granularity, the mapping of subsets is also an effective way to reduce the data volume of an aggregate. There, for one or several characteristics or navigation attributes of an aggregate, constant values (so-called fixed values) are stored that define the subset of the aggregate (see figure 7–5).

Mapping subsets

Figure 7–5
Fixed value aggregate

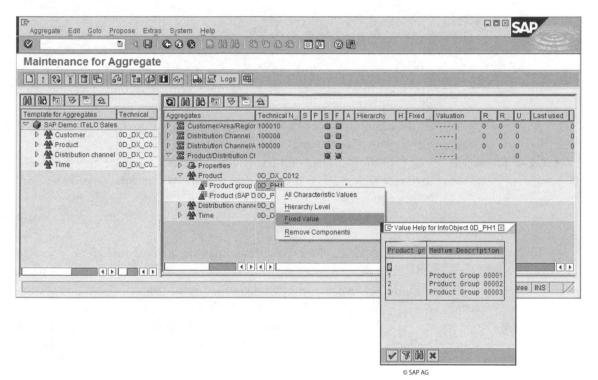

© SAP AG

Data records whose respective InfoObject does not contain these values are not filled into the respective aggregate. For each InfoObject, only one fixed value can be defined. The definition of several fixed values or intervals is not possible. If several InfoObjects are defined with a fixed value in one aggregate, they are treated as an AND conjunction when the data records are combined.

The modeling of fixed value aggregates especially makes sense if, for the data analysis, several characteristics are especially relevant and are thus selected more often (e.g., a certain company code or a certain customer classification).

The structure of the aggregates is analog to the data model of a Basis-Cube and has an individual fact table and individual dimension tables, which are stored in the ABAP Dictionary and in the database. The storage of characteristics is made with the use of the SID, same as with a Basis-Cube. Therefore, reports not only dispose of the characteristics of an aggregate but all navigation attributes of the characteristics.

The option in BW 3.5 to store aggregates in a multidimensional structure on the MS Analysis Server no longer exists in BW 7.

When you're creating aggregates, each aggregate gets its identification and the data model of the aggregate is defined. With activation of an aggregate, the technical name for the aggregate will automatically be created (similar to the technical name of a BasisCube) and the respective objects are created in the ABAP Dictionary.

Compression of aggregates

Like the fact table of a BasisCube, ROLAP aggregates also dispose of two fact tables: one fact table with and one without package dimension. With aggregates, the impact of compression is significantly higher than with BasisCubes. For this reason, aggregates are compressed by default after the rollup.

The compression of aggregates has the same consequences for the administration of a BasisCube as the compression of the BasisCube itself: compressed requests can no longer be deleted from the cube (see section 7.1).

Request-receiving aggregates

For this reason, it is possible to switch off the compression after the rollup so that the aggregates of a BasisCube are request receiving (see figure 7–6).

Please consider that request-receiving aggregates may considerably impact the effect of using aggregates. Only use request-receiving aggregates if it is absolutely necessary for administrative reasons and passable from a data volume perspective.

Line item aggregates
(flat aggregates)

For modeling dimensions in BasisCubes, so-called line item dimensions are available, where the fact table is directly filled into the SID of a characteristic. However, the use of line item dimensions is limited because for each line item dimension, only one InfoObject can be stored and the maximum number of freely defined dimensions per BasisCube is 13 (whether they are line items or normal dimensions).

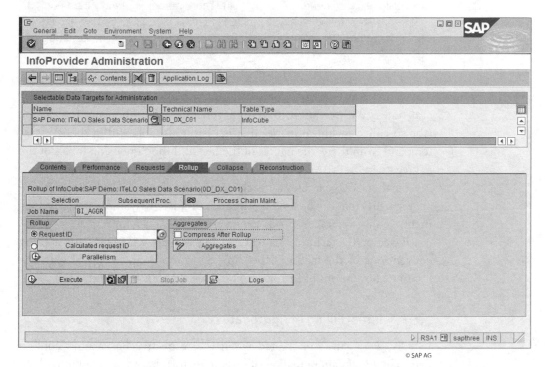

© SAP AG

The characteristics of a BasisCube that are filled into one of its aggregates are usually arranged by BW in dimensions analog to the BasisCube. All characteristics that are stored in the BasisCube of a dimension will also be stored in the aggregate in the respective dimension. If there is no characteristic of a cube dimension in an aggregate, this dimension will not be applied to the aggregate.

Figure 7–6
Rollup without compression of aggregates

If the number of characteristics in an aggregate is reduced to a maximum of 13, BW will not comply with the described process and will define all characteristics as a line item dimension.[32] Apart from the positive consequences this may have on performance of the data analysis, it enables BW to realize the rollup and the re-creation of these aggregates on the

32. Time and unit dimensions always remain normal dimensions.

database system only.[33] Thus, performance of the processes is significantly increased and the system load is reduced.

> Line item aggregates are, both from a data analysis and a staging point of view, significantly better performing and more resource friendly than normal aggregates. You should always try to fill a maximum of 13 characteristics in the aggregates to use the advantages of the thus-created line item aggregates.

Naming convention   The name of an aggregate can be chosen at random and even be used several times. With creation, BW itself generates a six-digit numeric name (the so-called technical name) that is distinguishable within the BW system, and from there, the names of the fact and the dimension tables of the aggregate in the ABAP Dictionary are derived.

Further, BW generates for each aggregate a systemwide distinguishable aggregate ID that can be used within the complete BW landscape (development, quality assurance, production system).

Based on the technical name of an aggregate (e.g., 101234), the naming conventions of the fact and the dimension tables are identical with the naming conventions of the BasisCubes (see sections 6.4.1 and 6.4.3).

7.1.1   Initial Filling of Aggregates

Usually, aggregates are created when the respective BasisCubes contain data. Thus, right after creation of an aggregate, it has to be filled initially to have the same dataset as the respective BasisCube and other aggregates of this cube. This is made in the aggregate maintenance under the menu item *Aggregate→Activate and fill* (see figure 7–7). If required, the necessary tables will be created in the ABAP Dictionary.

There are several limitations while an aggregate is being built:

- There can be no rollup of the aggregate (see section 7.1).
- (Systemwide) no change run is possible if the aggregate disposes of master data attributes.

Since the limitations described may exist for a period of several hours, it is advisable to use specific time slots to initially build aggregates.

---

33. This is not possible with aggregates for Inventory cubes. They are always built in the main storage.

In section 24.6, we'll explain how the filling of aggregates can be accelerated.

Figure 7–7
Activation and filling of
aggregates

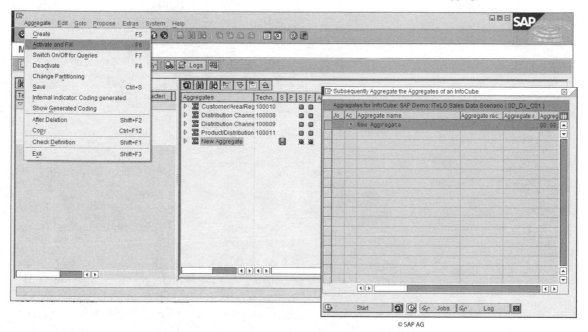

© SAP AG

If you define aggregates in the development system and transport them into the live system (see appendix B), do not fill the aggregate in the live system through aggregate maintenance as this would represent a new repair order. Instead, you can realize the initial filling of all new aggregates for a Basis-Cube using a process type in the process chain (see chapter 28).

7.1.2   Hierarchy and Attribute Changes

Aggregates can be built both for InfoObjects that are in the dimensions of an InfoCube and for the navigation attributes and hierarchies of these InfoObjects.

Whenever attributes and hierarchies of an InfoObject have changed, all aggregates using the attributes and hierarchies have to be modified to reflect these changes. Figure 7–8 shows a change of a customer attribute.

The aggregates can be adjusted in the so-called *hierarchy and attribute change run,* which is not part of the load process and thus has to be executed explicitly (menu item *Tools→Hierarchy/Attribute change* in the Data Warehousing Workbench).

Figure 7–8

Hierarchy and attribute change in aggregates

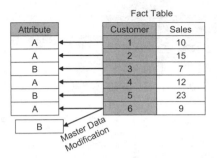

Depending on the modified master data and the aggregates to be adjusted, it is difficult to estimate the runtime of the change run. When using the ABAP program `RSDDS_CHANGE_RUN_MONITOR`, it is possible to identify the characteristics, hierarchies, and aggregates to be adjusted together with the runtime of the change run.

Master data changes will be effective only after a change run for the master data has been made. Until then, the data analysis is only possible for the old values of the hierarchies and navigation attributes.

The adjustment of aggregates with the change run may be time consuming. If not necessary, you should not define aggregates through navigation attributes or hierarchies but only with basic characteristics because these aggregates will not require a change run.

7.2   Indexing

With the realization of read access to database tables, in many cases the content of the complete table will not be read but only a specifically selected subset (e.g., all data records on a certain customer).

In these cases, the duration of the read process is less defined by the reading than by searching the respectively selected data records. If, for example, in 10,000 data records only 50 apply to a given selection, the search for these 50 records in the table takes significantly more time than the reading process itself.

If it was known prior to the reading process where in the database table the searched data records are located, the search could be dropped and the read access could be accelerated by a multiple.

Indexes pursue this approach. They are data structures that map the content of a database table in a specifically prepared form. Before the read access to the database table itself is undertaken, the database system using the index structure automatically identifies where in the table the searched data records are.

> When using indexing, please consider that with a change in table content, the content of index structures needs to be adjusted accordingly. Thus, the use of indexing is suitable not only to increase read access performance but also to increase the system load with write access at the same time.

There are two different index types that are suitable for different purposes: **B* tree indexes** and **bitmapped indexes.**

Since the early days of relational database systems, B* tree indexes have been used and they stood the test of time. Conceptually, B* tree indexes are based on binary search algorithms that are enabled by special index structures.

B* tree indexes

A B* tree index refers to one of several fields of a database table and displays the field values in a binary search tree whose nodes refer to the respective records in the database table (see figure 7–9).

For example, the figure shows that to search all data records with the customer number 7000 in the database table, the complete table will have to be searched; i.e., 12 data records would have to be read.

Using the B* tree index, however, from the start in the index root (5000), only three further records (8000, 6000, 7000) would have to be searched until all relevant data record positions in the database table are known.

The use of B* tree indexes is well suited to improve the performance of queries that make simple limitations to very selective table fields (e.g., selection of a certain customer).

Especially with data warehouse systems, queries are often complex and delimit the unselected fields (e.g., selection of products that are red or blue and were bought from customers who are located in the north).

Figure 7–9

B tree index*

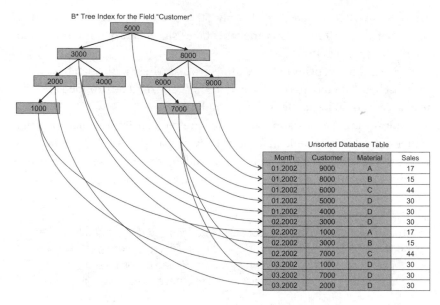

Bitmap indexes The described restrictions are not very selective, so from a performance view, it takes more effort to first read the large parts of the index and then read large parts of the table again than it does to search the complete table for the requested data records.[34]

To accelerate such unselected and complex queries in the database, Oracle and IBM provide their database management systems with bitmap indexes.

Bitmap indexes have no tree structure but can be displayed as a table with its separate data record for each value of the indexed field. Each data record of the indexed table reflects one field in the index table. The field content describes whether the respective field value (data record in the index) appears in the respective data record (field in the index) of the indexed table (see figure 7–10).

The example in the figure highlights that the use of bitmap indexes on fields with little values can be advantageous. This advantage is amplified when database queries contain a maximum of selections so that optimally, the relevant lines of the bitmap indexes can be linked to each other through logical operations (AND and OR).

---

34. The benchmark for the use of a B* tree index says that the selection of the respective field is to reduce the database volume to at least 15 percent.

SELECT * FROM fact table
WHERE
    color IN ("red", "blue") AND
    region = "North"

Line	Color	Region	Sales
1	red	North	17
2	blue	East	15
3	green	West	44
4	blue	South	30
5	blue	East	30
6	green	West	30
7	red	North	17
8	blue	East	15
9	red	East	44
10	red	South	30
11	green	West	30
12	blue	South	30

Figure 7–10

Bitmap indexes

Color	Line 1	Line 2	Line 3	Line 4	Line 5	Line 6	Line 7	Line 8	Line 9	Line 10	Line 11	Line 12
red	1	0	0	0	0	0	1	0	1	1	0	0
green	0	0	1	0	0	1	0	0	0	0	1	0
blue	0	1	0	1	1	0	0	1	0	0	0	1

Region	Line 1	Line 2	Line 3	Line 4	Line 5	Line 6	Line 7	Line 8	Line 9	Line 10	Line 11	Line 12
North	1	0	0	0	0	0	1	0	0	0	0	0
East	0	1	0	0	1	0	0	1	1	0	0	0
South	0	0	0	1	0	0	0	0	0	1	0	1
West	0	0	1	0	0	1	0	0	0	0	1	0

Furthermore, the binary structure of bitmap indexes is easily compressed by database systems and thus uses little storage compared to B* tree indexes.

The following sections describe the optimization options that BW uses with the different index types:

- BasisCubes
- DataStore Objects
- InfoObjects

Further, we'll explain the updating of statistics with database optimizers, which is necessary for the use of indexes.

7.2.1 Index Use with BasisCubes

With the modeling of BasisCubes, BW already creates diverse indexes in both fact tables and the dimension tables by default (see also figure 8–3 on page 175).

In a majority of instances, the indexes that are created are suited to post and read data in a high-performance way. Especially with large data volumes and with complex data models, modifications are required with the indexing of the fact tables.[35]

Figure 7–11

*Checking dimensions with
high cardinality*

The indexing of uncompressed and compressed fact tables is similar:[36] each dimension ID has a separate index. Whether this index is of type B* tree or bitmap has to be defined when the cube is created in the maintenance of the dimension by selecting ***High Cardinality*** (see figure 7–11).

If the dimension of a BasisCube disposes of a lot of data records (i.e., if it has high cardinality), a B* tree index is suitable to index this dimension. In this case, the dimension should be qualified as a dimension with high cardinality. At the same time, you should check whether the dimension is to be defined as a line item dimension too (see section 6.4.4).

Should the dimension not dispose of many data records, a bitmap index is better suited to index the dimension ID. This is the BW default value when a new cube is created.

---

35. Modification of indexing can also help to improve performance of badly modeled BasisCubes. This should only be done in special cases when the remodeling of the respective BasisCube is not possible.
36. The compressed fact table also disposes of a unique index over all dimension IDs. However, this only serves to optimize the compression process and has no effect on data analysis.

With database systems other than Oracle and DB2/UDB, the qualification of high cardinality is ignored. With these other database systems, indexes are only B* tree type, so each dimension will have this index type whether the index is suitable or not.

It is always defined by the relation to the fact table whether a dimension table holds "very many" data records. If a dimension table holds more than one-fifth (20 percent) of the data records compared to the fact table, one can speak of very many data records from a cardinality perspective.

With this calculation, please consider that a fact table grows over time while dimension tables will instead become a constant size. Thus, the calculation can be made only after some time periods have been stored in the cube. Sometimes, the indexing needs to be edited over the course of time. This makes cube modeling especially sophisticated.

In terms of indexing, transactional cubes are special. Transactional cubes give many users simultaneous read and also write access to the uncompressed fact table of the cube.

Indexing of transactional cubes

In the current database releases, bitmap indexes are not locked per record but only per page. Thus, simultaneous write access to the fact table would not be possible if there were any bitmap indexes.

For this reason, the dimensions of the uncompressed fact table of a transactional cube (where only simultaneous write access happens) have B* tree indexes only and they can be locked per record. With transactional cubes, the dimensions of the compressed fact tables are indexed as usual.

Thus, transactional cubes are less suitable for reporting than their standard counterparts since they cannot fully make use of the options of the database system (this is for Oracle and DB2/UDB). This becomes more noticeable when more data is in the uncompressed fact table. Thus, the regular rollup is very important, especially with transactional cubes.

All other database systems do not even offer a different form of indexing, so it is irrelevant whether a BasisCube is marked transactional or not.

7.2.2   Use of indexing on DataStore Objects

Other than BasisCubes, DataStore objects are primarily provided to support staging and are used for data analysis only in special instances. For this reason, DataStore objects have only a primary key[37] but no further indexes.

Figure 7–12

Indexing DataStore objects

In the case of DataStore objects, should data be selected for analysis purposes the respective key or data fields can be indexed. The definition of the indexes is part of the metadata of a DataStore object and is done in the object maintenance (see figure 7–12).

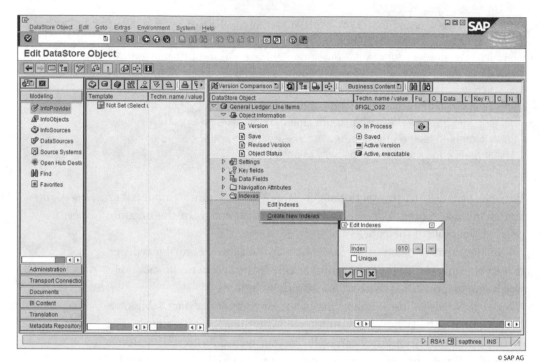

© SAP AG

7.2.3   Index Use on InfoObjects

While BasisCubes and their dimensions are completely indexed by BW, the master data IDs of the navigation attributes of an InfoObject (see section 6.2.2) are not indexed in order to not strain performance of master data load processes.

If a navigation attribute of an InfoObject is not only to be used for navigation in queries (drill down) but also to select data (e.g., selection of all customers with the same postal code), it may make sense to manually index the respective field in the navigation table of an InfoObject.

37. The primary key corresponds with a multiple index on the key fields of the Data-Store object. With write-optimized DataStore objects, in addition to the technical key (= primary key), an index will be given to the fields of the semantic key if this has been defined.

Indexes can be created using transaction SE11. First, you choose the respective table of the InfoObject (e.g., /BIO/XCUSTOMER for the master data table of the InfoObject OCUSTOMER). Then, you define and activate an index for the respective table field (e.g., S__POSTAL_CD for the navigation attribute OPOSTAL_CD). See figure 7–13.

B* tree indexes for InfoObjects

Figure 7–13

Indexing of navigation attributes using the customer postal code as an example

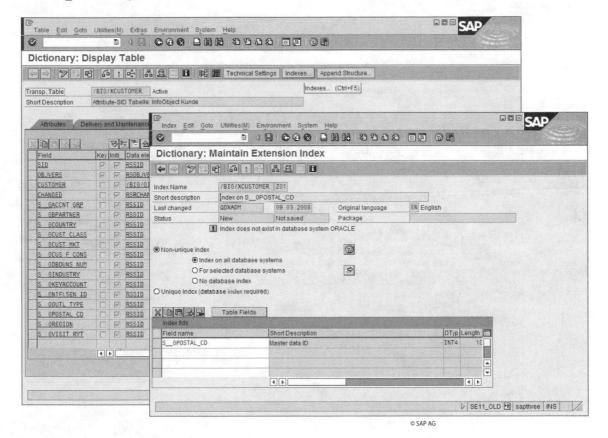

© SAP AG

An index created in such a way is always of B* tree type and thus only suited for selective attributes.

Specifically with the use of Oracle and DB2/USD database systems, it is possible to qualify navigation attributes with a bitmap index. Thus, attributes that are not very selective (e.g., the country of the customer) can be indexed.

Bitmap indexes for InfoObjects

To create a bitmap index, you first proceed as with a normal (B* tree) index. Prior to activation of the index, it will only be saved and the storage parameters will be edited respectively. For this purpose, from the index maintenance you can branch to the database utility, which offers an option to maintain storage parameters (see figure 7–14).

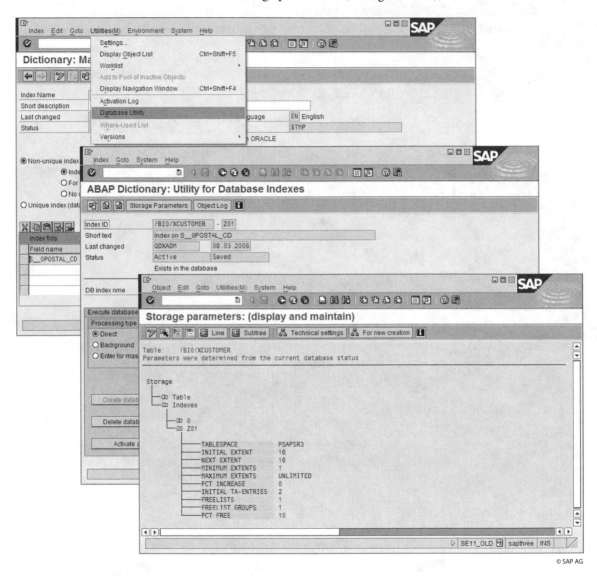

Figure 7–14

Set storage parameters for bitmap indexing (1)

Afterward, this index will be transformed into a bitmap index. For this purpose, the created index is chosen in transaction SE14 and the storage parameters will be edited so that the index will be created as a bitmap index with the next re-creation (see figure 7–15).

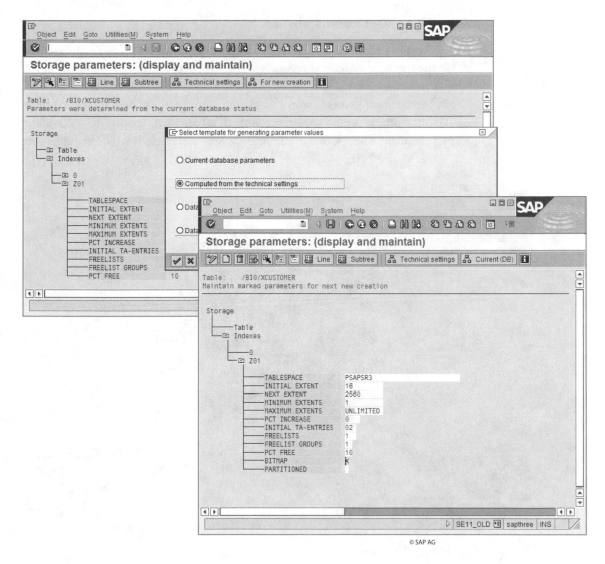

© SAP AG

Then, the index can be activated as usual and will be available as a bitmap
index.

> Bitmap indexes do not allow for locking of tables on the record level.
> Instead, tables that have bitmap indexes can only be locked completely.
> With the creation of bitmap indexes, you revoke the option to parallelize
> data packages during load processes (see section 24.1). Further, SAP will
> refuse support for errors that result from modified index structures.

Figure 7–15

Set storage parameters for bitmap indexing (2)

7.2.4 Optimizer Statistics

The use of indexes (both B* tree and bitmap indexes) is very difficult for the database system when queries are complex and more than one index is available.

The problem gets worse when data is not only to be read from a table but from several relationally linked tables—e.g., from the snowflake schema of a BasisCube where nearly every table field has its separate index (see figure 7–16).

Figure 7–16

B tree indexes in a star schema*

Month	SID
01.2002	1
02.2002	2
03.2002	3
indexed	*indexed*

SID	SID	SID	Sales
1	9	1	17
1	8	2	15
1	6	3	44
1	5	4	30
1	4	4	30
2	3	4	30
2	1	1	17
2	3	2	15
2	7	3	44
3	1	4	30
3	7	4	30
3	2	4	30

indexed   indexed   indexed

Customer	SID
9000	9
8000	8
6000	6
5000	5
4000	4
3000	3
1000	1
2000	2
7000	7

indexed   indexed

Material	SID
A	1
B	2
C	3
D	4

indexed   indexed

If a query ran on a star schema as shown in figure 7–16, where all sales to customer 2000, material D, and month 03/2002 were to be identified, first the customer number 2000 would be searched in the customer dimension to then identify the respective data records in the fact table. This result set would then be linked to the material and the time dimension. Since the customer number is very selective search criterion, only one data record would be read in the fact table from which the material and time dimension were to be read.

However, it would also be possible to first search for the month 03/2002 in the time dimension and to read the records of the fact table from there. In such a case, instead of one record, three data records would be found in the fact table that would have to be linked to the time and material dimension.

This simple example shows that the access sequence to relational databases is decisive with regard to performance. In practice, the snowflake models used in BW consist of up to a hundred relationally linked tables (fact, dimension, and master data tables), where not only the B* tree indexes but also bitmap indexes are used. Thus, the wrong access sequence can lead to a difference of 1,000 percent several times over in runtime for exactly the same query!

Keeping in mind that the access sequence is crucial for the perfor- *Rule-based optimizer* mance of a database, a so-called rule-based optimizer is used in relational database systems. With the concept of rule-based optimization, the queries (SQL commands) regulate the access sequence; i.e., the access sequence needs to be defined through the respective application in the SQL queries.

The rule-based optimization offers a simple way to influence the performance of database queries. At the same time, rule-based optimization requires deep knowledge regarding content of database tables.

With very complex structures as seen in the data models of Basis- *Cost-based optimizer* Cubes, such an optimization quickly reaches its limits—especially since there are usually no predefined queries in BW but an unforeseeable variety of queries are run on the cubes (selections, drill-downs, etc.).

For such circumstances, any relational database system nowadays works with the cost-based optimizer. It calculates by itself the optimal access sequence for queries to the database system.

Such a calculation requires the optimizer of the database system to have exact statistics in which the selectivity of indexes and the number of possible field values are stored.

Other than with index structures, the contents of the optimizer statistics will not be modified with a change in table content; instead, they have to be refreshed explicitly, especially after large data volumes have been written into a table.

For this task, each data warehouse system provides specific functions such as the tool BRCONNECT for Oracle database systems. In SAP BW (as in

SAP ERP systems), the database-specific tools are integrated into the DBA planning calendar (transaction DB13) from which the execution can be controlled.[38]

With transaction DB13 or the database-specific tools, the optimizer statistics of all tables of a database are usually refreshed. Especially in BW systems, this is not always desired; for runtime reasons, the optimizer statistics of BasisCubes are often refreshed but not the statistics of other tables.

Figure 7–17

Recalculation of optimizer statistics for all BasisCubes

For such reasons, there is the SAP_ANALYZE_ALL_INFOCUBES program, which refreshes only the optimizer statistics of BasisCubes. The basis for such calculation is the sample rate—i.e., the percentile share of data—and it can be added to the program as a parameter (see figure 7–17).

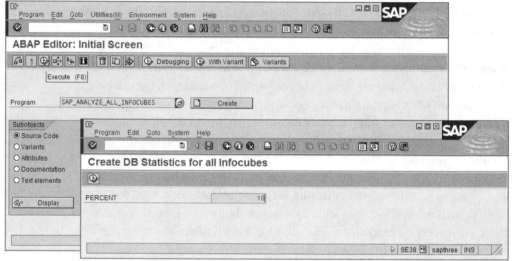

© SAP AG

A small sample rate saves time with the calculation of statistics but may have a negative effect on the quality of the statistics (and therefore on performance of database accesses).

With a normal distribution of data, 10 percent of the database should be enough to calculate database statistics. Should this normal distribution not be given—e.g., since 20 percent of the data volume is caused by one single customer (e.g., a CPD customer) and the remaining 80 percent by thousands of real customers—the percentile base for the calculation needs to be higher.

---

38. Some database systems rely on other BW-specific transactions.

If data is written in a few BasisCubes only, the program `SAP_ANALYZE_ALL_INFOCUBES` might take too long. For a targeted refresh of the database statistics for a single BasisCube, there is an option in the administration of the BasisCube to manually start the recalculation. Here, the sample rate can be defined as a percentile value too (see figure 7–18).

Figure 7–18

Recalculation of optimizer statistics for a single BasisCube

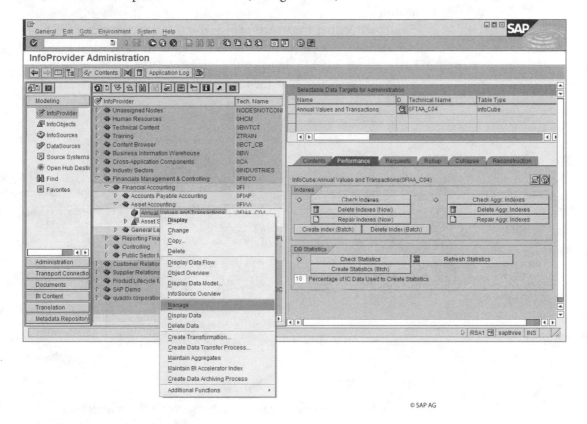

© SAP AG

Bad optimizer statistics are one of the main reasons for supposedly unexplainable performance problems in BW. For this reason, optimizer statistics should be refreshed on a regular basis.

Some database systems exclusively lock the database tables that are in use while statistics are refreshed and they cannot be accessed for read processes. Especially with large fact tables, this may result in downtime of several hours. In such cases, do not refresh the database statistics in running system operations but reserve special time periods. With Oracle database systems, updating the optimizer statistics will not result in locks to read access.

7.3   Partitioning and Clustering

Database tables often contain several million data records, so database operations of any nature are time-consuming for these tables. For such cases, the partitioning of a table is a very effective option to improve performance.

Figure 7–19

Partitioning of a fact table

With partitioning, the structure of a table in database systems will basically be defined to use a partitioning field to physically divide it into several database areas (tables, blocks, etc.). Figure 7–19 shows the structure of a partitioned fact table where the month is used as a basis for partitioning.

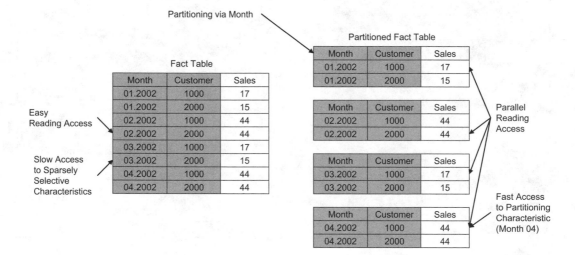

The partitioning of the tables has two advantages:

- Instead of having one read process that searches the complete fact table for the required information, several read processes can be executed *in parallel* in the individual partitions.
- When the read access to the partitioning characteristic is limited, a number of partitions may possibly be excluded from the read process, so the data base will be smaller and comprehensive data will be found and read significantly faster.

Technically, the partitioning can be implemented both on the database system level and on the BW metadata level. With partitioning on database system level, the database system effects the distribution of data to the respective partitions without any BW help. However, with partitioning on the application level, the application also needs to ensure that the data is written into and read from the right partitions.

> Each form of partitioning comes with a structural modification of the respective table, which can only be made as long as the table does not contain any data. Therefore, you should think about partitioning, especially with ODS objects and BasisCubes, before you even build the database.

In the following sections, we'll explain the usual forms of partitioning in BW and link them to the BW objects that can be partitioned in these ways:

- Range partitioning
- Clustering
- Model partitioning

7.3.1 Range Partitioning

Range partitioning is a database-specific form of partitioning that is supported in SAP BW 7 by the following database systems:

- Oracle
- MS SQL Server
- DB2/OS390DB2 for Z/OS
- DB2/400 (from V5R3M0 with DB Multi Systems)
- Informix

For the database systems DB2 for UNIX, Windows, and Linux, one can instead refer to database-specific clustering, which at least offers an equivalent form of partitioning (see section 7.3.2).

Users of the database systems MAX DB (formerly SAP DB or ADA-BAS D) miss out and cannot refer to any database-specific form of partitioning.

With range partitioning,[39] data records are distributed to the defined partitions based on the value of the required fields (partitioning field). Each partition can be compared to a database table in its physical structure, but the specified partitioning field will be defined for one value or one interval only.

---

39. The database systems listed might offer other specific forms of partitioning. SAP BW uses only range partitioning, which in a way represents the smallest common denominator of the named database systems.

What field will be used as a basis for range partitioning and what ranges will be defined depends on the respective database table. You have to differentiate between the following tables:

- The uncompressed fact table of BasisCubes and aggregates
- The compressed fact table of BasisCubes
- The compressed fact table of aggregates

Partitioning is defined (or to be defined) in different ways and will be explained for the named fact tables later. Apart from fact tables, BW supports range partitioning for only PSA tables. This is discussed with tuning of extraction and staging (see section 24.2).

Partitioning of the Uncompressed Fact Table of BasisCubes and Aggregates

The *partitioning of an uncompressed fact table* (see also section 6.4.1) will basically be made with the request ID, which is a mandatory component of each BasisCube and each aggregate; it identifies data that was entered into an uncompressed fact table during a loading/rollup.

SAP BW automatically creates and deletes partitions when new data is entered into a BasisCube or if the cube is compressed. This behavior cannot be modified of influenced.

Partitioning according to the request ID allows for easier management of requests that are still in the normal fact table. Therefore, the data of single requests can be deleted or moved systematically. Furthermore, it is (conditionally[40]) possible that several load processes write to a BasisCube in parallel since all read accesses come from several partitions and cannot interfere with each other.

Partitioning of the Compressed Fact Table of BasisCubes

The *partitioning of a compressed fact table* is not made according to the request ID. Instead, partitioning can alternatively be based on the time characteristic OFISCPER or OCALMONTH, which accordingly have to be part of the respective BasisCube. A partitioning based on other InfoObjects is not possible.

40. During the load processes, write accesses are made not only to the fact table but also to the dimension tables of a BasisCube. Since these cannot be partitioned in a similar way, two overlapping accesses to dimension tables may cause conflicts. The risk is relatively low but cannot be eliminated in practice.

For range partitioning of an uncompressed fact table, only the time characteristics `OFISCPER` and `OCALMONTH` are available. Therefore, when designing the data model, you need to make sure that for the relevant time characteristic of a BasisCube, only `OFISCPER` or `OCALMONTH` but no user-defined time characteristics are used.

You need to define in the BasisCube maintenance the characteristics on which partitioning will be based (see figure 7–20). If nothing is defined, the compressed fact table will *not* be partitioned!

Figure 7–20

Range partitioning of the fact table on the database level

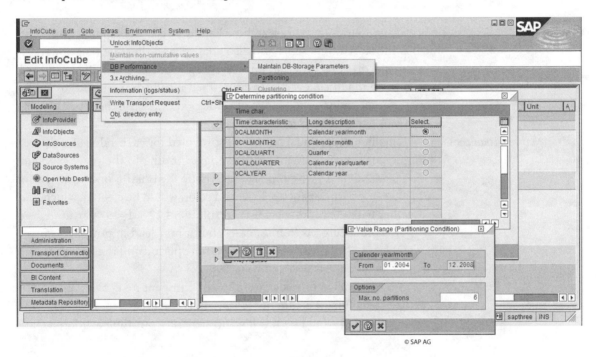

© SAP AG

Unlike the partitioning of the uncompressed fact table, the partitioning of the compressed fact table will not create a partition for a field value only when the respective data is entered into the cube. Instead, all required partitions will be created with the activation of the cube model, so the range of values of the partitioning characteristic needs to be determined at this point in time (and thus needs to be preset). For all characteristic values above the preset range, a specific partition will be provided. All characteristic values that are below the preset range will be entered into the partition with the lowest value.

Range of values for the partitioning criterion

Thus, there will be no errors if the range of values was not dimensioned big enough (even though this should be avoided for performance reasons).

> If the lower and upper limits of the partitioning are too narrow, the data that has not been mapped will be collected in the lowest and highest partition, which results in low-performing database accesses. A very broad design of partitioning will also result in performance losses as the administration effort of the database system increases with accesses to the partitioned fact table. Thus, when defining the range of values, you should always ensure that the design of the partitioning schema reflects the available data.

When old data is deleted or archived and new data is entered into a fact table, the stored time series will also change, and thus the range of values for the partitioning criterion must eventually become unsuitable and will need to be modified, even if it was defined ideally at the time. For subsequent modification of the range of values, you may use the repartitioning option as explained in section 32.1.

Number of partitions   Usually, an individual partition is provided for each value of the partitioning characteristic. With partitioning according to the range of values 01.2000–12.2007 for the time characteristic OCALMONTH, one partition for 01.2000, one partition for 02.2000, and so on would be created, which may (together with the lowest partition) result in 8 * 12 + 1 = 97 partitions.

This procedure fits in most cases, but it may lead to problems when a fact table is to be partitioned for a large time period and thus requires very many partitions.[41]

If a large range of values were to be "compensated" by relatively few data per partition, the administration effort for the database system with the partitioning would be too high to benefit from the partition advantages.

It also needs to be considered that the definition of a partitioning object requires a fixed share of storage space.[42]

---

41. In this case, it is tough to give a definition for "very many". Depending on the system, 50 partitions may be considered many. From approximately 100 partitions onward, a value is reached where one can speak of "many" partitions, and with 200 partitions, the term "very many" is justified at the very least.
42. In the case of an Oracle database, eight blocks are reserved per partitioning object. The size of a block is usually defined with 8 KB and stored in the database parameter DB_BLOCK_SIZE (indication in bytes). The value of the database parameter can be seen in the transaction ST04 → *Detailed analysis menu* → *Parameter changes* → *Active Parameters*.

A partitioning object is considered to be not only a partitioning of the fact table but also a partitioning of an index.[43] This may result in a very large number of partitioning objects, which is demonstrated, for example, with a BasisCube that has 16 dimensions completely defined and that contains 20 aggregates, where each has another 10 dimensions available.

A partitioning of the range of values 01.2000–12.2009 (= 121 partitions) would result for this cube in 121 partitions * ((1 fact table + 16 indexes in the fact table) + (1 aggregate table + 10 indexes in the aggregate tables) * 20 aggregates) = 121 * (17 + 10*20) = 26,257 partitioning objects. The 64 KB an Oracle database usually has per partitioning would lead to approx. 1.6 GB for the definition of the compressed fact table—and this is without even having entered one single data record into the cube!

Thus, it may make sense to limit the number of partitions by combining several values of the time characteristic in one partition. The respective presetting is made through the maximum number of partitions to be created (see figure 7–20).

If, for example, the range of values mentioned earlier from 01.2000–12.2009 was preset but reports are to show a quarterly and not a monthly view, then three months could be combined by presetting a maximum number of 31 partitions (30 partitions with three months each and an marginal partition for larger values).

Partitioning of the Compressed Fact Table of Aggregates

The partitioning of aggregates is the same as the partitioning of the Basis-Cube. Thus, the uncompressed and compressed fact tables of an aggregate are always partitioned in the same way as the fact table of the respective BasisCube.

For the compressed fact table, this procedure is not always advantageous, especially with smaller aggregates. The data volume of individual partitions may be so low from the compression and/or filtering that the effort to manage the partition may not be worth the benefits that could be produced from partitioning.

For this reason, there has been an option since the release of SAP BW 7 in the aggregate maintenance to specifically exclude individual aggregates from partitioning. The menu item *Change Partitioning* in the context

---

43. Indexes on the fields of a fact table are always partitioned the same way as the fact table of the indexed field; this applies to the uncompressed fact table as well as to the compressed fact table and to BasisCubes as well as to aggregates.

menu of aggregates changes the characteristic *partitioning* of the aggregate (see figure 7–21).

Figure 7–21

Exclusion of an aggregate from range partitioning

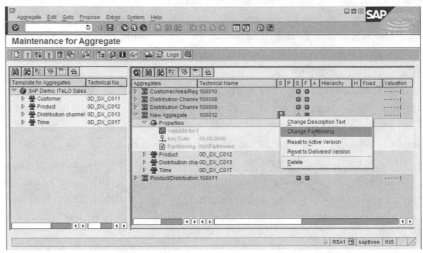

However, it's not possible to partition aggregates differently; i.e., the compressed fact table of an aggregate can be partitioned in the same way as the uncompressed fact table of the BasisCube or not at all.

7.3.2   Clustering

Especially with the database system DB2 UDB (UNIX, Windows, and Linux), clustering procedures are used instead of range partitioning. Basically, clustering is a physically comprehensive storage of data records with the same or similar field values within the partial objects of a database (for DB2 UDB, this is in so-called Extents, which may be referred to as cluster in this context).

From a variety of different clustering procedures, BW uses *index clustering* and *multidimensional clustering (MDC).*

Index clustering

With index clustering, the fields of an index (the clustering index) define the criteria according to which data records are to be combined within the clusters. This is not only about storage of data records with the same field values within a cluster. Rather, it's about a physically ordered storage of the clusters. Figure 7–22 refers to the structure of the B* tree index shown in figure 7–9 but considers it to be a clustering index, which results in a certain structure of the table.

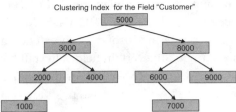

Clustering Index for the Field "Customer"

Figure 7–22
Table structure of index
clustering

Table Cluster

Customer	Month	Material	Sales
1000	02.2002	A	17
1000	03.2002	D	30
2000	03.2002	D	30
3000	02.2002	D	30
3000	02.2002	B	15
4000	01.2002	D	30
5000	01.2002	D	30
6000	01.2002	C	44
7000	02.2002	C	44
7000	03.2002	D	30
8000	01.2002	R	15
9000	01.2002	A	17

The index clustering enables significantly faster access to comprehensive data. Range scans especially benefit remarkably from the clustered structure of a table as far as data is selected according to fields in the clustering index. If the selection is made according to another field (e.g., month or material in the figure 7–22), the use of index clustering will not bring any advantage. If a clustering index comprises several fields, this is only advantageous if the selection is made from the first index fields onward.

Since the index clustering has an immediate effect on the physical storage of data, only one clustering index can be defined per table according to which the table is sorted. Therefore, index clustering only makes sense when accesses are usually made with defined selections.

There is another problem with index clustering when inserts or updates are made to the data in the table. If data areas are still unused in the defined clusters or if new clusters can be created, the sorted format will be kept. Should this not be possible, data might possibly only be written into clusters in such a way that data close to each other are in one cluster or that clusters with the same field value are "nearby". In the worst case, data may not be added to the sorted structure of the cluster and will have to be entered somewhere else in the database system. Thus, a recovery of the sorted clustering structure can only be achieved through a database reorganization.

Multidimensional clustering (MDC)

Since release 7, SAP BW also supports ***multidimensional clustering (MDC),*** which was first introduced with release 8 of DB2 UDB. Multidimensional clustering extends index clustering insofar as an extent (in this case called a block) is not only defined for a certain field value but for a combination of several field values and will only be used for the storage of data records with the designated field values. The selected fields are also called ***MDC dimensions.***

Additionally, multidimensional clustered tables get so-called ***block indexes*** that might replace existing secondary indexes to the MDC dimensions. These indexes no longer refer to individual data records of the table but only to blocks in which the same values of a field are combined. Block indexes are thus naturally smaller than normal secondary indexes and can be searched faster.

Each of the created block indexes describes the reference to the respective blocks for one MDC dimension; i.e., each field that is part of the MDC dimension will be provided with a block index. Additionally, a compound block index will be created for the fields of all MDC dimensions. Figure 7–23 shows multidimensional clustering with a table where the fields month and distribution channel are used as MDC dimensions.

Figure 7–23
Multidimensional clustering

Partitioned Table ***(MDC)***

Cluster	Month	Sales Channel	Customer	Sales
1	01.2002	01	1000	17
1	01.2002	01	2000	15

Cluster	Month	Sales Channel	Customer	Sales
2	01.2002	02	4000	18
2	01.2002	02	5000	9

Cluster	Month	Sales Channel	Customer	Sales
3	02.2002	01	1000	44
3	02.2002	01	2000	21

Cluster	Month	Sales Channel	Customer	Sales
4	02.2002	02	3000	23
4	02.2002	02	4000	12

Cluster	Month	Sales Channel	Customer	Sales
5	03.2002	01	1000	27
5	03.2002	01	2000	15

Cluster	Month	Sales Channel	Customer	Sales
6	03.2002	02	3000	11
6	03.2002	02	4000	17

Block Indexes

Month	Sales Channel	*Cluster*
01.2002	01	*1*
01.2002	02	2
02.2002	01	*3*
02.2002	02	*4*
03.2002	01	*5*
03.2002	02	*6*

Month	*Cluster*
01.2002	*1*
01.2002	2
02.2002	*3*
02.2002	*4*
03.2002	*5*
03.2002	6

Sales Channel	*Cluster*
01	*1*
01	*3*
01	*5*
02	2
02	*4*
02	*6*

The advantage of multidimensional clustering is that the acceleration of read access to a table is not limited to the selection of a single field (as with range partitioning and index clustering) but that each selection that limits one of the MDC dimensions may result in a respective performance gain.

However, the prerequisite for a real performance gain is the effective use of blocks, since for each value combination a complete block (= extent) is reserved even if the value combination exists only once.

If extents are too often reserved for a value combination that exists only once or so scarcely that the they will not be filled, the aspired performance gain will result in excessive storage usage since too many (half) empty blocks need to be read.

To achieve a performance gain with multidimensional clustering, the number of same value combinations in the selected MDC dimensions must be as high as possible. Thus, such fields are suitable as MDC dimensions that have low cardinality.

Which clustering procedure should be used at what time depends on the type of the database table. With BasisCubes, you have to differentiate between the following tables:

- The compressed fact table of BasisCubes and aggregates
- The uncompressed fact table of BasisCubes and aggregates

In the following sections, we'll explain how the clustering is or can be defined in both cases. Further, BW also supports the clustering of PSA tables and DataStore objects. This is explained with the performance tuning of extraction and staging (see chapter 24).

Clustering of the Compressed Fact Table

The compressed fact table of BasisCubes and aggregates is always built according to a clustering procedure. Up to release 3.x of SAP BW, this was always index clustering.

By default, the clustering index has comprised all dimension IDs of the fact table. At least the parts of the data analysis that accessed a range of time characteristics were accelerated (the time dimension is the first field of the clustering index). *Index clustering*

Index clustering is also used in release 7 of SAP BW for the compressed fact table by default. Here, regular database reorganizations are a prerequisite for a sustained high-performance use of the compressed fact tables.

Multidimensional clustering   Alternatively, the compressed fact table can be used for multidimensional clustering. However, this requires an explicit definition of the characteristics to be used as MDC dimensions that can only be realized manually and with knowledge of the data analysis to be accelerated. Thus, it cannot be provided as a default setting.

Thus, all key fields of the time dimension and all customer dimensions of an InfoCube are selectable as MDC dimensions, i.e., the dimension IDs or the master data IDs,[44] respectively (see also sections 6.4.3 and 6.4.4), and not the characteristics themselves. Exceptions are the time characteristics OCALMONTH and OFISCPER, which as such can form an MDC dimension. In this case, the master data ID of the used time characteristic[45] is directly added to the compressed fact table (such as with range partitioning).

> If multidimensional clustering is to be defined not only based on dimension tables but also on the basis of single characteristics, then these characteristics can be added as line items into the BasisCube. Usually, the use of line items is only a good option for characteristics with particularly many values; however, it may make sense for characteristics with few values. A typical example is user-defined time characteristics, which can thus be added directly to the fact table in a similar way as OCALMONTH and OFISCPER.

The definition of the MDC dimensions is made in the BasisCube maintenance as long as it does not contain any data (see figure 7–24). Should the multidimensional clustering be defined or modified for a data-containing BasisCube, reclustering can be used for this purpose (see section 9.3).

With the definition of MDC dimensions, a maximum of three dimensions can be named, including the time dimension/time characteristic. The time dimension or time characteristic does not necessarily have to be used as an MDC dimension, so three randomly customized dimensions can be used instead. The advantage is that multidimensional clustering also considers customized time characteristics whereas range partitioning only considers the time characteristics OCALMONTH and OFISCPER.

Basically, dimensions should be defined as MDC dimensions when the characteristics are often used in queries (i.e., some time characteristics should always play a role). However, it has to be considered that these

---

44. For line item dimensions.
45. In a BasisCube, only one of the two characteristics can be defined as an MDC dimension but not both.

dimension tables should not be very large. With high cardinality of the
dimension keys might come many blocks that cannot be used efficiently,
which may lead to a performance decline rather than an improvement.

Figure 7–24

Multidimensional clustering of BasisCubes

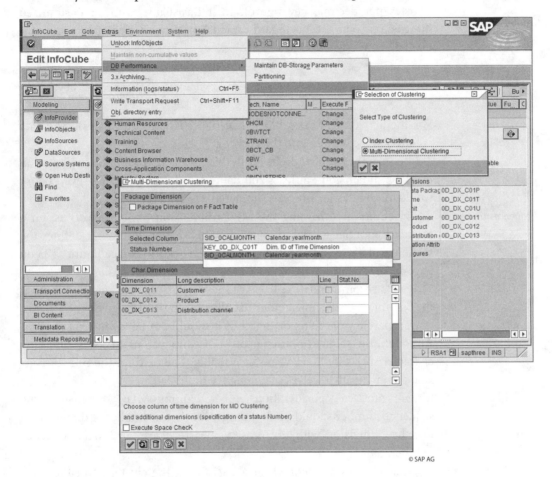

© SAP AG

To evaluate whether blocks are filled efficiently, it first has to be determined how many data records of the fact table can be stored in a block. On this basis, it can be estimated whether the database supplies enough data records to efficiently fill the blocks.

Calculation of block sizes

The size of a block conforms to the PAGESIZE and the EXTENTSIZE of the table space for the fact tables (data type DFACT). The standard value for the PAGESIZE is 16 KB, for the EXTENTSIZE 2 KB.[46] Thus, these standard values result in a storage area of 32 KB to be reserved per block.

46. In the releases prior to NetWeaver 2004s, it was still 16 KB.

The number of data records that can be stored in a block depends on the width of the data records. This is calculated from the number of dimensions (4 bytes per dimension) and the key figures contained in the cube (9 bytes per decimal key figure). In a BasisCube with 13 customized dimensions (plus the 3 standard dimensions) and 10 decimal key figures, the data record would thus require

$$(13 + 3)\,\text{dimensions} \times \frac{4\ \text{bytes}}{\text{dimension}} + 10\ \text{keyfigures} \times \frac{9\ \text{bytes}}{\text{keyfigure}} = 154\ \text{bytes}$$

For the above-mentioned block size of 32 KB (32,768 bytes), 212 data records can be written into the block.

To turn the number on its head, this means that for each combination of MDC dimensions, at least 200 data records should exist—even better would be a multiple of the denominated 212 data records.

Sequence numbers   In addition to naming the MDC dimensions, you need to assign a sequence number to each dimension. This sequence number defines the sequence of dimensions in the compound block index (see figure 7–23 on page 145).

SAP's recommendation to place these fields that are analyzed most at the beginning of the block index usually fails in practice given the absence of transparency of the reporting, thus it should not be taken too seriously. Although, the sequence number of MDC dimensions that describe time characteristics should be as low as possible. The field for the time dimension automatically receives the sequence number 1.

For practical considerations, for remaining MDC dimensions the sequence number should be declining with the cardinality of dimensions; i.e., the dimension with the most values receives the lowest sequence number.

Clustering of aggregates   If aggregates are defined for a BasisCube, the clustering of the Info-Cube will be assigned to them. If an aggregate for multidimensional clustering cannot map an MDC dimension of the InfoCube or if all Info-Objects of an MDC dimension are created as line item dimensions in the aggregate,[47] the clustering of the aggregate will be made in the remaining MDC dimensions. Should an aggregate not contain an MDC dimension of the InfoCube or only MDC dimensions, then index clustering will be used for this aggregate.

---

47. Such a deviant modeling of BasisCube and aggregates comes with the creation of line item aggregates.

Clustering of an Uncompressed Fact Table

By default, the uncompressed fact table of each BasisCube is provided with the clustering index for the time dimension. Thus, the performance of the reporting comes before cube administration—since otherwise, instead of the time dimension often used in data analysis, the package dimension should be the basis for the index clustering.[48]

If the compressed fact table is not clustered through an index but is multidimensional, the structure of the uncompressed fact table will comply with this definition. However, the package dimension will also be added as the first MDC dimension so that, in addition to the good performance during data analysis, a high-performance administration of the request in the BasisCube can be achieved.

Since the calculation of block sizes at the time of the modeling and the selection of MDC dimensions (see above) does usually not consider the additional inclusion of the package dimensions, the multidimensional clustering of the uncompressed fact table might result in an inefficient use of the blocks.

Calculation of block sizes

In fact, for the uncompressed fact table, an efficient use of blocks would be desirable too. When evaluating this disadvantage, however, it should be considered that the uncompressed fact table is only a better temporary location and that its data should be moved into a compressed fact table sooner or later regardless. Thus, the difficult modeling and the selection of MDC dimensions will not be unnecessarily complicated by considering the uncompressed fact table; this would increase the danger of a possible modification of the MDC dimensions on account of the compressed table.

7.3.3   Model Partitioning

With range partitioning and clustering, the database systems provide BW with powerful tools to manage large databases in BasisCubes and Data-Store objects.

However, range partitioning especially is not subject to a database system but may also be added or replaced through modeling on the application level when BW is run on a database system that does not offer any

---

48. In comparison, the Oracle implementation of BW partitions the uncompressed fact table according to the request ID and not according to time.

partitioning techniques[49] or when partitioning is to be made by using fields[50] other than the ones provided by default.

The unique character of model partitioning mostly comes from the fact that it is completely defined by the application—i.e., the customized data model—and thus needs special consideration during data modeling as well as staging.

> Partitioning on the application level not only increases performance, it also increases the complexity of the data model. In order to not make the administration of BW more complex than necessary, you should only use this form of partitioning if you are sure it's necessary.

A partitioning on the application level is made when explicit data targets (usually BasisCubes or DataStore objects) are defined for every desired partition. To gain a joint view on data of all partitions during the data analysis, the data has to be combined again with the use of a virtual InfoProvider (in this case, a MultiProvider). Figure 7–25 shows an example for partitioning according to three business units of a company.

Figure 7–25

Partitioning the fact table on the application level

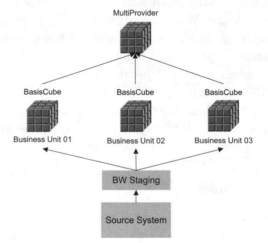

With the right configuration of the analytical engine (see chapter 11), the basic InfoProviders will be read in parallel processes when evaluating a MultiProvider. Detailed information on MultiProviders can be found in section 11.1.

---

49. In the current SAP BW release, this is only the case with the database system MAX DB (formerly SAP DB, which was formerly ADABAS D).
50. 0CALMONTH or 0FISCPER, respectively.

Further, the analytical engine can use a range of procedures to exclude single InfoProviders from the data analysis provided that it has been clarified that certain InfoProviders will not contribute any data to the report (e.g., with the selection of business unit 01 of the InfoProviders that were designed for storage of business unit 02).

For a specific case in which a BasisCube or a DataStore object stores one or several characteristics for only one single value, the analytical engine can (and should have been) configured in the design phase of the data model to exclude partitioned InfoProviders. This is made with the determination of so-called **_structure-specific properties_** in the metadata of a BasisCube or a DataStore object.

With BasisCubes, the structure-specific properties can be stored with the maintenance of the cube in the context menu of the respective Info-Object (see figure 7–26). As soon as a BasisCube contains any data, these settings can no longer be entered.

Structure-specific properties of BasisCubes

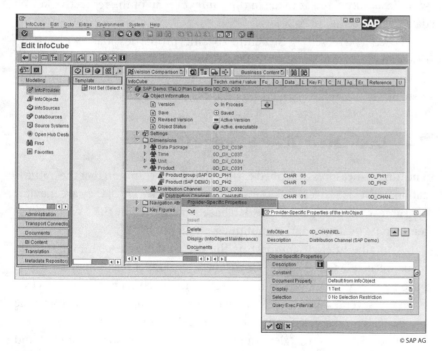

© SAP AG

Figure 7–26
Structure-specific properties of BasisCubes

Only static organizational characteristics that are subject to slight modifications (e.g., cost centers or business units) are suitable partitioning characteristics. With the use of continuous characteristics (e.g., time characteristics), a new BasisCube would have to be created for each value (or group of values). Thus, the partitioning of continuous time characteristics only makes sense for partitioning on the database level, where a larger number of partitions will not necessarily lead to higher (manual) administration effort.

> In consideration of the administration effort, you should not partition on more than approximately 5 BasisCubes. In exceptional cases, partitioning on up to 10 BasisCubes may make sense. However, a significantly higher maintenance effort is to be expected since each BasisCube needs to be managed and tuned separately.

Structure-specific properties of DataStore objects

Since DataStore objects do not focus on data analysis as much as BasisCubes do, the structure-specific properties are less relevant. Still, such settings can be made in the maintenance of the DataStore objects. Same as with BasisCubes, this is made in the context menu of the respective key or data fields (see figure 7–26).

Data distribution

When you're setting structure-specific properties, data will not be distributed with the transfer in BasisCubes and DataStore objects, so the distribution will have to be defined during staging. The definition of this distribution is explained in chapter 25.

7.4   Dedicated OLAP Storage (BIA)

The tuning measures described earlier all have in common that the optimization of the data structures is focused on SAP BW. Thus, they are inevitably subject to the options of the database system used by the BW basis system and its relational and monolithic paradigms.

A totally different approach is the use of database technologies that focus on data analysis and refer to massive parallel technologies for this purpose.[51] SAP competitors have been using such technologies successfully for several years. Further, there now are suppliers that offer the respective systems specifically for collaboration with SAP BW.

When SAP BW was developed, for pragmatic reasons relational and monolithic database technologies were chosen over massively parallel

---

51. The calculating units that work in parallel have their own self-contained and independently working CPUs and central memories.

storage technologies. With SAP ERP, SAP had a corresponding basis system at its disposal that also was to be used for SAP BW.

With the development of the search engine TREX, SAP also had a massively parallel storage technology, even though it was initially designed for storage and queries of unstructured data from documents. Especially designed to include structured data from SAP BW, TREX was enhanced with so-called BIA index types and is available to BW as ***Business Intelligence accelerator (BI accelerator).***

Massively parallel storage technology is used when the processing of data can be freely distributed to several calculating units because no dependencies exist between the different processing steps, thus the complete processing can be subdivided randomly.

Basics of parallel storage technologies

With reference to data warehousing, this is the case with reading the fact table of a star schema where data is basically added up. And since it does not make any difference whether the operation $1 + 2 + 3 + 4$ is made on one machine or the operations $1 + 2$ and $3 + 4$ are made on two separate machines and the result $3 + 7$ will only need to be added up in the end, a fact table can also be distributed to several calculating units. Figure 7–27 illustrates this theoretical approach.

Figure 7–27
Distributed data query

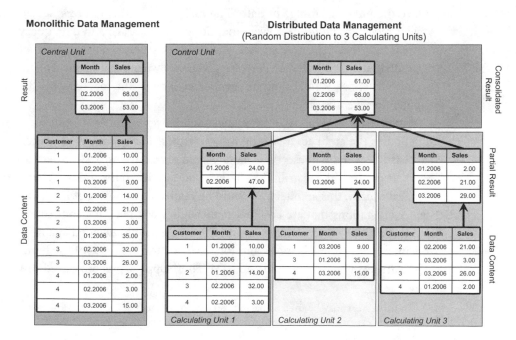

SELECT Month, SUM (Sales) FROM Cube GROUP BY Month

The distribution of data to several calculating units can be made in different ways: through content criteria (e.g., time characteristics), through hash algorithms, and even through chance-based procedures (as shown in the figure). After the explanations on partitioning (see section 7.3), the idea to distribute data to several storage areas is not a new one. The main difference is not only that data is organized differently within a storage unit but that it actually needs to be distributed to different calculating units.

In combination with the fact that the task at hand can be broken down into any number of partial tasks and that is has to be solved autonomously by the calculating units, the performance of the overall system can almost be scaled linearly by adding further calculating units.

The degree of the distribution of tasks to several calculating units depends on the chosen approach and the task itself. The focus of this approach can be centralistic, where only arithmetic problems are broken down and distributed; however, the approach may even include the distribution of physical storage and administration of the data. It always has to be considered that the approach used for a massively parallel query technique is subject to the use of the respective hardware and software architecture that supports the desired distribution of memory and read access.

Architecture of the BI accelerator
Here, SAP has decided to distribute both the calculation load and the storage of data (in the main memory) to the calculating units, but to centralize the physical storage of data. The main task in this interconnected system relies on the ***index servers*** that do the real storage and data query and execute the respective services (attribute services) for the query of each attribute. The index servers are the focus when scaling the system performance; i.e., with adding further index servers, the load can be distributed to several systems too.[52]

Apart from the index servers, the ***nameserver*** also has a significant function in the architecture of the BI accelerator. The nameserver (which consists of several nameservers that act as master/slave or backup server) basically controls the distribution of data and queries to the index servers.

Technically, this architecture could be realized by a series of independent workstations that are connected through a fast network connection and that share a common network drive. Here, SAP has decided against a free interconnection of servers and for the blade technologies of the hardware partners Hewlett Packard and IBM. They supply a preconfigured BIA

---

52. Index servers may be used as backup servers for other index servers. However, a detailed explanation of the system architecture is not warranted here.

with 64-bit Intel XEON-CPUs with SuSE Linux SLES 9. Currently, no other systems are supported.

> Even though the BI accelerator is based on the technology of the TREX search engine, it cannot be used as such. If TREX is to be run in addition to the BI accelerator, this has to be done on a separate entity. Should TREX be used on a 32-bit version, completely separate hardware will have to be used (which may make sense anyway) since the BIA only runs on 64-bit hardware.[23]

This so-called "BIA box" is a self-contained system not only in an architectural sense; it was (and is) developed independently from the SAP BW basis system. The BIA box interconnects several calculating units (blades) within a chassis with a central administration module that presents the blades to BW as a unit (the BIA server). Each of these blades has its individual CPUs and main memory but no disk memory.

Thus, the advantage of the BIA server is that, within a relatively compact design, a large number of CPUs and main memory can be integrated and that its mass (in GB and CPUs) can be scaled almost freely by adding new blades. The extension limits are only set by the respective hardware supplier. If applications are run on the BIA server, whose performance requirements mostly refer to CPU and main memory, then the performance of the BIA server can almost be scaled linearly to the "hardware mass".

The TREX technology meets this requirement; i.e., analysis processes are accelerated tremendously by caching of cube content in the main memory of the blades. This allows for faster access to the memory and also for parallelized access. This performance increase is only possible with a tremendous additional hardware cost for main memory as compared to disk memory.

Thus, the concept of the BIA will inevitably lose some of its effect if the main memory of the index server is not sufficient to contain all of the selected data. In this case, data will have to be removed from the main memory and read again from the file system, if required, which may result in performance losses. The main memory of the BIA should always be copiously equipped so that all BasisCubes to be accelerated by the BIA fit into its main memory. If this exceeds the technical and financial possibilities of the BW user, BIA should not be used at all.

---

53. The minimum equipment of a blade with 8 GB main memory exceeds the address room of 32 bits.

The use of the BI accelerator is mostly justified in BW systems that have to execute queries over particularly large databases in BasisCubes. Indeed, focused optimization using aggregates, indexes, etc. often leads to better results than the use of the BI accelerator; however, the specific advantage of the BI accelerator is that it ensures an average performance when the working method of the user is not known or not to be analyzed.

A particularly advantageous side effect is the fact that the change run is almost dropped (see section 7.4.3) and that the rollup of aggregates is limited to the modification of the BIA index. The BI accelerator can make the use of aggregates redundant and that is also advantageous for organizational reasons because it abolishes the often very time-intensive administration of aggregates.

However, the BI accelerator does not offer a free ride in terms of optimization of the BW system because the BIA is a mere analysis accelerator at the end of the information chain and it will be supplied with data only when the rest of SAP BW has processed the data. On top of that, the BI accelerator is a very "young" system. Downtime of the BI accelerator or the RFC connection between BW and the BI accelerator should not be ruled out; then, the BW database will be used as a fallback solution and should thus be prepared accordingly.

The following sections will explain these topics:

- BIA connection to SAP BW (section 7.4.1)
- Managing the BIA in BW (section 7.4.2)
- Structure of cube content (section 7.4.3)
- Organization of cube content (section 7.4.4)
- Creation and filling of BIA indexes (section 7.4.5)
- Hierarchy and attribute changes (section 7.4.6)

The settings and processes within the BI accelerator will be described from an SAP BW point of view; a detailed view on the BIA technology is beyond the scope of this book and is not included.

Apart from these topics, with the use of the BIA, implications on other areas of SAP BW need to be mentioned:

- OLAP caching and access sequences (see chapter 12)
- Rollup of BIA indexes (see section 24.7)
- Trimming of BIA indexes (see section 32.3)

The particular BIA details will be explained in the respective chapters.

7.4.1 BIA Connection to SAP BW

Communication between the BI Accelerator and BW is made via the SAP-specific RFC protocol (see also section 3.1.1). The settings of the RFC connection are made centrally in the administration of the BI accelerator. First, the connection information has to be stored in the RFC settings and then the RFC connection can be created (see figure 7–28).

Figure 7–28

BIA connection to a BW system

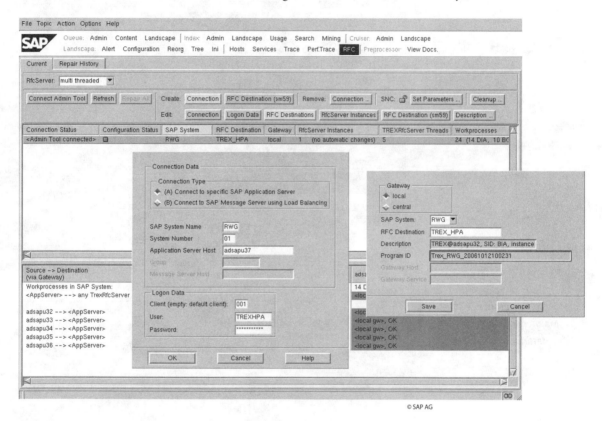

© SAP AG

With creation of an RFC connection in the BIA, all relevant information will be stored both in the BIA and in BW; i.e., the stored RFC destination from the connection data of the BIA will be created in BW (by default TREX_HPA). The RFC connection will be created as a registered server program and is stored in the BW transaction SM59 (see figure 7–29).

In addition to the connection settings made in the BIA, the RFC destination has to be entered into the field TREX_RFC_DEST of the maintenance view RSADMINA. For this purpose, the menu item *Settings→Global Settings* or the transaction RSCUSTA can be started (see figure 7–30).

Figure 7–29
RFC connection to the BIA in BW

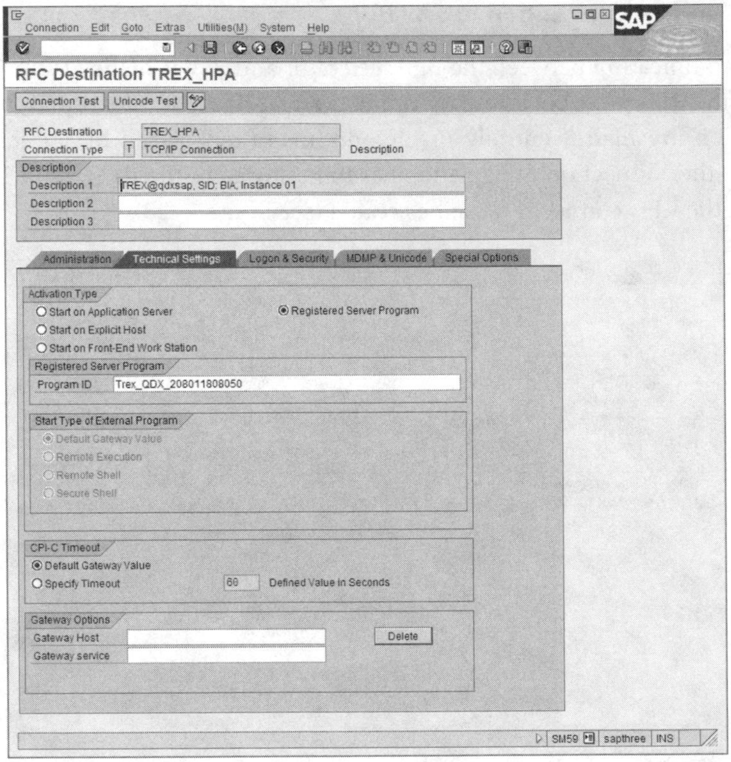

© SAP AG

Figure 7–30
Maintenance of the RFC destination to the BIA

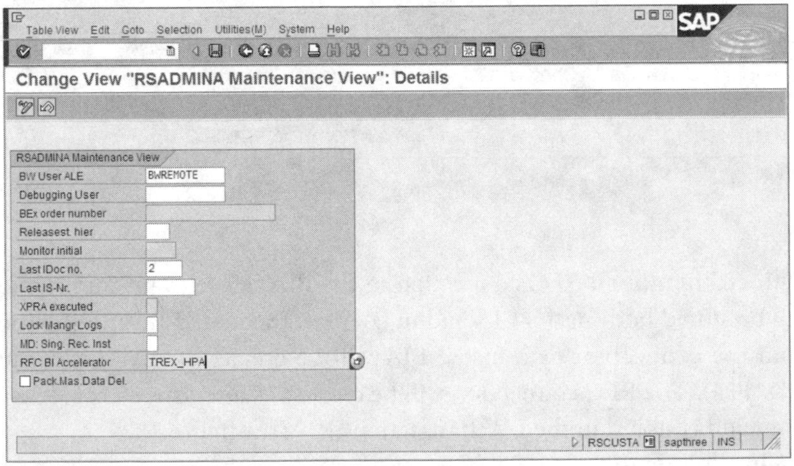

© SAP AG

Even though the RFC protocol in the area of SAP systems is an established, stable, and well-performing option for communicating, when this book went to press, the RFC connection between BW and the BI accelerator started to become a bottleneck or stood out for its instability.

If the BI accelerator cannot be reached, the data management in BW will be used as a fallback solution for 30 minutes until the BI accelerator can be accessed again for the first time. The danger of an unstable connection should be reason enough to keep the data models in BW "analysis-capable" in the near future, i.e., to provide them with the minimum amount of aggregates.

7.4.2   Managing the BIA in BW

The full stack of administration features for the BI accelerator is only available to the BIA itself. A small part of the configuration can be made in BW since the release of Service Patch 6. For these reasons, BW offers the transaction TREXADMIN, which offers a mapping of the most important administration features (see figure 7–31).

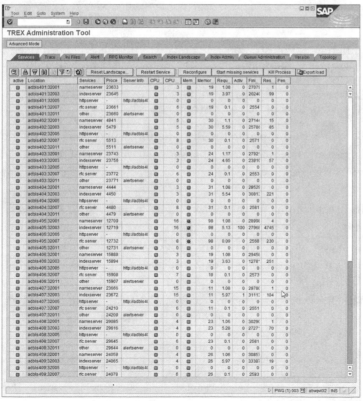

Figure 7–31

Managing the BIA in BW

Other features can be found in the transaction RSDDBIAMON2, which helps to restart the BIA host or the individual servers of the BIA (see figure 7–32).

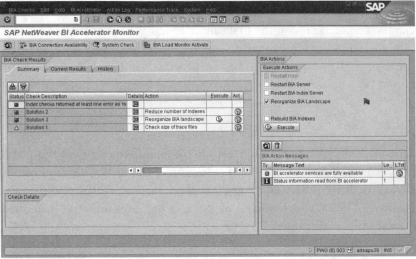

© SAP AG

The different administration functions will not be explained here. However, if required, they will be referred to in the following details on the BIA.

7.4.3   Structure of Cube Content

If a BasisCube is mapped in the BIA, the BIA will copy its structure. This means that all tables included in the snowflake schema of the BasisCube in BW will be copied into the BIA and will be read in the same way as tables in BW.[54]

In BIA terminology, the tables will be mapped in *BIA indexes,* but a BIA index has nothing to do with an index as used in relational databases (see also section 7.2); rather, a BIA index comprises metadata as well as data files, not only the links to data (indexes in the sense of relational database systems).

The BIA indexes related to one BasisCube will be combined by a logical index that contains the metadata of the snowflake schema.

---

54. Here, the BI accelerator can dissolve relational join connections between tables that are stored in the main memory of different index servers. The dissolution of such connections comes with a big network load; this is why the blades in a BIA box need to have very fast connections.

Related to the directory structure in the BIA,[55] the index structures are organized in such a way that in the directory /importfs/BIA/<*SID BIA*>/index[56]

- one corresponding subdirectory for BasisCubes exists in the content namespace (<SID BW>/BI0) and in the customer namespace (<SID BW>/BIC) where further subdirectories for the index files have been created, and

- one corresponding subdirectory per BasisCube exists where the logical index for the cube is stored. The subdirectory for the respective cube will follow the naming convention <SID BW>_<Cubename>. For example, the logical index for the BasisCube quadox of the BW system QX7 will be stored in the subdirectory qx7_quadox.

Figure 7–33 shows the directory structure of a BIA.

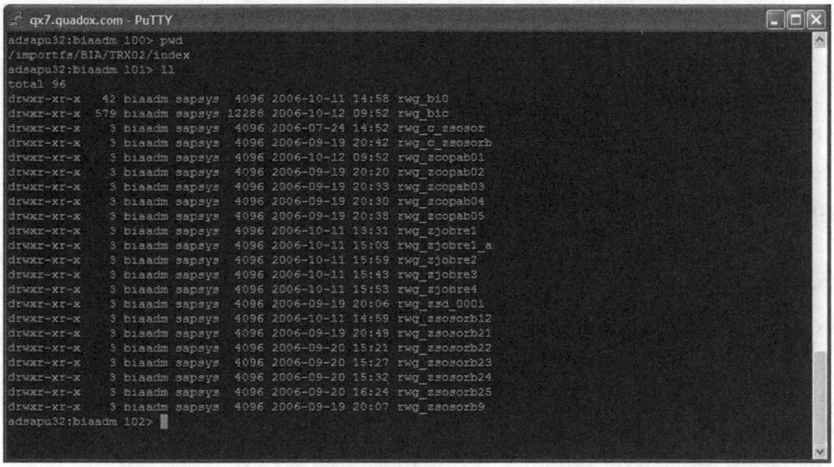

Figure 7–33
Index directory in the BIA

For each BasisCube mapped in the BIA, a logical index will be created that will be stored in the file named all-settings.ini in the directory for the logical index of the BasisCube.

Logical indexes

This logical index is a configuration file that contains metadata on the respective BasisCube. The metadata contains, in addition to some settings

---

55. The data structures within the BI accelerator will be treated here as if the data would only be stored in the file system. The particularities of caching in the main memory of the blades will be explained later.
56. <SID_BIA> stands for the system ID of the BI accelerator.

for the index, a description of all index files and the relations of the thus stored fact table, the dimension tables, and the master data tables.

Physical indexes

The storage of data is made in physical indexes (which are referenced in the logical index of a BasisCube). Each physical index maps the data of a table in BW, but the structure cannot be compared. Table columns are transposed in table lines and vice versa. Thus, the fields of a table map their data records while the data record number is kept as a table field.

A particular advantage of such storage is the fact that with one single access all content of a table field can be read, selected, and sorted. The reading of several thousand, or millions of, data records will not be necessary. This is relevant, since read accesses to the data of a BasisCube often involve field values of all data records in a table.

Memory consumption

Further, data is stored in a compressed form in the BI accelerator. To favor the use of compression procedures, data will only be stored as integer values. For this reason, the BI accelerator creates translation tables that can be compared to SID tables in BW and that describe references to the used integer values for all field values.

This enables a significant reduction in memory consumption of BIA indexes. The compression rate with regard to storage in the database system of BW depends on the database system used. Most notable are Oracle and MS SQL Server. While the database with Oracle is very efficient and experience shows that in the BIA, compression can only be made by factor 5; the compression rate with MS SQL Server can compress up to factor 30.

An estimate on the memory consumption of a BasisCube can be obtained from the program RSDDTREX_MEMORY_ESTIMATE (see figure 7–34).

The program provides, for each of the BIA-relevant tables of a Basis-Cube, the number of data records in BW in the right column and the estimated memory requirements in BIA in kilobytes in the left column.

On the file server of the BI accelerator, the reorganization of BIA indexes requires up to three times the data volume of an existing index. Please consider this number when calculating the memory space and intentionally dimension the memory larger than required for running operations.

When mapping fact, dimension, and master data tables in the BI accelerator, you should consider a variety of particular details.

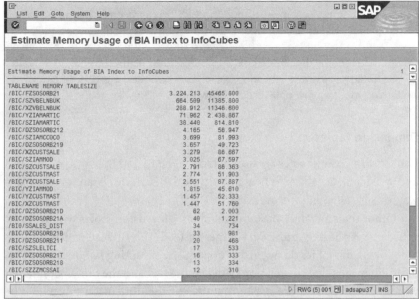

© SAP AG

Figure 7–34
Estimate on memory usage of the BIA index

Fact Tables in the BI Accelerator

The fact table of a BasisCube exists in BW in the form of an uncompressed fact table as well as in the form of a compressed fact table. The distribution of data to F and E fact table of a BasisCube is not duplicated in the BI accelerator since it does not make the same differentiation in fact tables for administration (F fact table) and performing data analysis (E fact table).

Instead, data from the F and the E fact table are kept in one single physical index. Here, no aggregation will take place; i.e., each data record of the BasisCube is available directly after the creation of the BI accelerator index and is contained here too. Data records from the E fact table are stored with an initial value for the request ID; data records from the F fact table will also be stored with the request ID in the BIA index.

Therefore, no compression is made in the BI accelerator while data is being stored. This also applies to the takeover of new requests during rollup; i.e., data records are always transferred to the BI accelerator as new data records but never as changes. The compression of the BasisCube does not have any effect on the BIA; data records that were originally taken over from the F fact table into the BIA will keep their request ID in the BIA after the compression of the BasisCube.

> Requests are never compressed in the BIA, as is the case with underlying BasisCubes. Especially for cubes with a lot of data modifications that are combined in BW during compression, the BI accelerator index may contain more data records than the underlying BasisCube. Thus, at regular intervals you should reorganize BIA indexes of BasisCubes where data changes often in order to avoid unfavorable growth of the BIA indexes.

Dimension Tables

Normal indexing

Usually, dimension tables are transferred to the BIA in the same way as fact and master data tables. When the physical BIA indexes are created this way, this is called *normal indexing*.

Flat indexing

Other than fact and master data tables, dimension tables will never be split up, even if they grow very large. Instead, the BI accelerator ensures that dimension tables do not grow too large by executing *flat indexing*. This basically means that the relation between the fact and the dimension tables will be dissolved and the master data ID of the dimension tables will be added directly to the fact table. The flat indexing in the BIA appears to model all characteristics as line item dimensions (see also section 6.4.4), but the maximum number of line item dimensions in the BIA is not limited to the usual 13 dimensions.

The BI accelerator engine decides whether the dimensions of a Basis-Cube are indexed normally or flat, depending on the proportions of dimension tables and fact table. If the number of data records in a dimension table exceeds 20 percent of the number of records in the respective fact table, the indexing of *all* dimension tables[57] will be flat.

Figure 7–35 shows the description of the fact table within the logical index for a normal indexing.

Figure 7–35
Structure of the fact table
using normal indexing

```
[attributes]
key_qdxcubep = INTEGER
key_qdxcubet = INTEGER
key_qdxcubeu = INTEGER
key_qdxcube1 = INTEGER
key_qdxcube2 = INTEGER
key_qdxcube3 = INTEGER
key_qdxcube4 = INTEGER
```

57. Only the package dimension will never be indexed flat in order to enable the deletion of single requests in the BIA too.

```
key_qdxcube5 = INTEGER
key_qdxcube6 = INTEGER
$bic$qdxkeyf01 = FIXED
$bic$qdxkeyf02 = FIXED
$bic$qdxkeyf03 = FIXED
$bic$qdxkeyf04 = FIXED
$bic$qdxkeyf05 = FIXED
$bic$qdxkeyf06 = FIXED
key_attributes =
key_qdxcubep,key_qdxcubet,key_qdxcubeu,key_qdxcube1,key_qdxcube2
,key_qdxcube3,key_qdxcube4,key_qdxcube5,key_qdxcube6
```

Figure 7–36 shows the same description of a fact table for flat indexing. Please consider that apart from the package dimension (key_qdxcubep), no other dimension ID is stored in the fact table. Instead, the master data IDs of the InfoObjects contained in the (original) dimensions are stored in the fact table (e.g., SID_Ounit for the characteristic unit that was originally stored in the dimension qdxcubeu).

```
[attributes]
key_qdxcubep = INTEGER
sid_Ounit = INTEGER
sid_Ocalday = INTEGER
sid_Obill_num = INTEGER
sid_Obill_item = INTEGER
sid_Opayer = INTEGER
sid_Osold_to = INTEGER
sid_Omaterial = INTEGER
sid_Omat_sales = INTEGER
sid_Osalesorg = INTEGER
sid_Odist_chan = INTEGER
sid_Oplant = INTEGER
sid_Osoursystem = INTEGER
$bic$qdxkeyf01 = FIXED
$bic$qdxkeyf02 = FIXED
$bic$qdxkeyf03 = FIXED
$bic$qdxkeyf04 = FIXED
$bic$qdxkeyf05 = FIXED
$bic$qdxkeyf06 = FIXED
key_attributes =
key_qdxcubep,sid_Ounit,sid_Ocalday,sid_Obill_num,sid_Obill_item,
sid_Opayer,sid_Osold_to,sid_Omaterial,sid_Omat_sales,
sid_Osalesorg,sid_Odist_chan,sid_Oplant
```

Figure 7–36
Structure of the fact table using flat indexing

The flat indexing of a fact table requires more memory consumption and thus results in worse performance during index creation and read access to the index. With the flat index, however, performance will still not exceed the approach of keeping the excessively large dimension table mapped. Therefore, with the use of the BI accelerator, the basic rules on modeling BasisCubes will absolutely have to be applied (see section 8.1).

Figure 7–37

BIA index with flat indexing

To recognize the flat indexing of dimension tables in the BI accelerator, one does not necessarily have to check the logical index of the BasisCubes. It is easy to recognize the type of indexing when checking the transaction

TREXADMIN in the *Index Hierarchy* tab (see figure 7–37). If the index hierarchy of an indexed cube (here, zjobre1) shows only the SID tables of InfoObjects rather than the usual dimension tables (here, szauthnam, szbakevpar, etc.), this is an indicator for flat indexing.

Master Data

The master data of an InfoObject in BW is shared in several tables (see also section 6.2.6). Only SID tables for time-constant and time-dependent navigation attributes are copied into the BIA; this is the X and the Y table of the master data. If the master date is a non-numeric characteristic, the SID table of the master data will also be copied.[58]

The attribute tables of the master data will not be copied; this is the P and Q table as well as the text tables. BW needs to enter these values and texts separately.

Master data is only stored once in the BIA—same as in BW. When a master date for a BasisCube is already indexed, no new indexing will be made for a further BasisCube that uses this InfoObject. Such indexes can be identified in the transaction TREXADMIN from the flag *shared* (see also figure 7–37).

7.4.4　Organization of Cube Content

The structure described earlier is an initial basis for the storage of data on the file server in the BI accelerator. As long as the storage is limited to the file server of the BIA, however, there are no architectural advantages compared to the storage in BW; since we also have a monolithic storage concept of the database. The advantages from the different data structure are not the sole, decisive factor for the use of the BI accelerator.

The performance advantage of the BIA only evolves when the physical indexes are cached in the main memory of the index server. Here, hard disk memory is replaced by extremely faster (and more expensive) main memory.

Storage in the main memory

The use of a file server for the BIA thus serves less for performance tuning than for the persistence of content where preparation may be very time intensive. For this reason, data is first stored on the file server of the

---

58. This simplifies transferring characteristic values to Integer values that are required to compress data in the BIA.

BI accelerator and loaded to the main memory of the index server only if required (i.e., when running a query).

With a restart of the BI accelerator, it becomes possible to create the cache content from the content on the file server without having to re-create the indexes from the data of the BW.

Split Indexes   Apart from the caching of index data, the distribution of index data to the individual blades of the BI accelerator box is also very relevant to the performance of queries on large databases. The basis for such distribution is already laid with the creation of the indexes on the file server of the BI accelerator. Up to now, indexing was always simplified so that a table in BW would always be mapped by exactly one physical index and thus by one index file on the file server.

In fact, the physical indexes of large fact and master data tables are split into several index files during the creation on the file server.[59] The split is made horizontally as well as vertically over the columns and rows of a table. These so-called index partitions will be distributed to the index servers of the BIA box and thus form the basis for parallelization.

From what size onward a split will be made depends on the configuration of the BI accelerator. By default, a table is split as soon as the product exceeds 100,000,000 bytes from the number of key figures and the number of data records. For example, a fact table with 40 key figures and 8,000,000 data records (320,000,000) would be split.

The number of partitions that are created in the case of a split from an index will be decided so that each index server receives as many partitions as it has CPUs. By default, the number of CPUs is two since standard blades currently have two CPUs. On a BIA box with six index servers, the table above would thus be split into 2 * 6 = 12 partitions. The settings for the number of partitions per host and the marginal value for the split can be found in the administration tool of the BI accelerator (transaction TREX-ADMIN) under the *Configuration* tab (see figure 7–38).

In the directory structure of the BIA, an index is stored in the directory /importfs/BIA/*<SID BIA>*/index/*<BI0>* or *<BIC>* in the subdirectory *<SID>_<BW-Object>*, where *<BW-Object>* stands for the technical name of the cube, the fact table, or the InfoObject. If the index of a fact table for a master data table is split, the individual partial indexes will get the suffixes ~1 to ~n. The partial indexes will be combined with the definition of

---

59. BIA indexes for dimension tables are not split. If a dimension table is very large, the dimension tables will instead be stored "flat", i.e., integrated into a fact table.

mappings within the logical index (e.g., see figure 7–39, where a fact table was split into eight partitions).

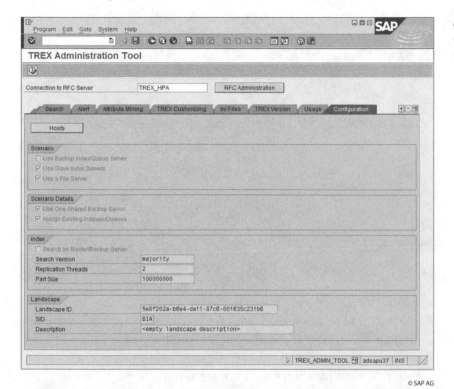

Figure 7–38
Configuration of the split in the BIA

© SAP AG

```
mappings = 1:rwg_bic:fqdxcube~01 10:rwg_bic:fqdxcube~10 2:
rwg_bic:fqdxcube~02 3:rwg_bic:fqdxcube~03 4:rwg_bic:
fqdxcube~04 5:rwg_bic:fqdxcube~05 6:rwg_bic:fqdxcube~06 7:
rwg_bic:fqdxcube~07 8:rwg_bic:fqdxcube~08
```

Figure 7–39
Description of split indexes in a logical index

For the distribution of index partitions to the index server of a BIA box, a range of different algorithms is available, ranging from a simple round robin procedure up to specialized procedures that can be defined in the system configuration of the BI accelerator. Such procedures could, for example, distribute partitions in such a way, that with the execution of joins between the partitions, the lowest possible network load occurs.

Distribution of index partitions

In the tab *Index Landscape* of the transaction TREXADMIN, the distribution of an index to the single blades is shown (see figure 7–40).

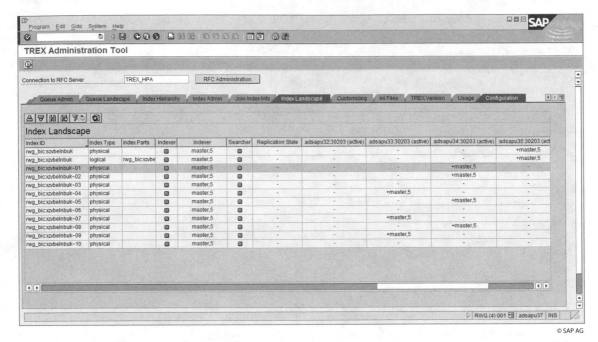

© SAP AG

Figure 7–40

Distribution of index blocks to blades

The distribution of data to the blades depends on the distribution of index data on the file server that was determined with the creation of the indexes. If new blades are added to the BI accelerator box, the index blocks on the file server of the BIA will remain unchanged until the new index has been created.

> Under certain circumstances, it makes sense to change the distribution of existing index blocks to the individual index servers. Information can be found in section 32.5.

7.4.5   Creation and Filling of BIA Indexes

Other than with aggregates, the content of BI accelerator indexes will not be defined explicitly. Rather, a complete BasisCube (or no part of it) will be provided for indexing in the BI accelerator. If a BasisCube is to be indexed via the BI accelerator, this can be done through the context menu of the BasisCube in the Data Warehousing Workbench (see figure 7–41).

Using the relevant wizard, the first step is creation of the index structures on the BIA and the second step is filling these structures. The filling can also be done by starting the program RSDDTREX_AGGREGATES_FILL, which is also started from the wizard.

Figure 7–41

Creation and filling of BIA indexes

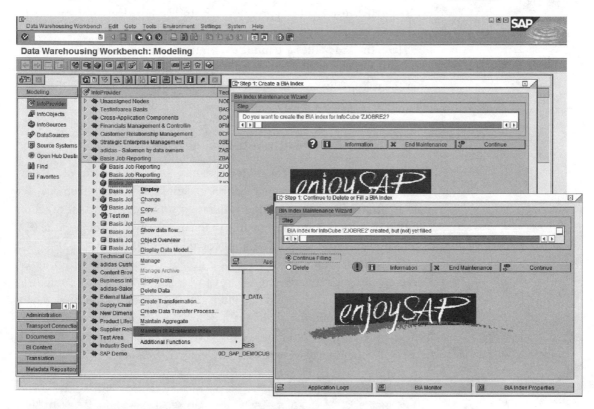

From the time BIA indexes are created and filled for a BasisCube, the data analysis will refer neither to the BasisCube nor to its aggregates, even if this might lead to better response times. The use of the BI accelerator can therefore not only increase but also decrease the performance! Thus, you should use the BI accelerator only after you have excluded the respective queries from the use of the BIA (see section 12.3).

The wizard to create (or delete) and fill BI accelerator indexes can always be started with the transaction RSDDV to manage indexes or to change index properties.

With the initial fill of BIA indexes, they are created on the file server of the BIA. Only when the first query is run will the data be transferred to the main memory of the BIA.

Rollup

If new data is entered into a BasisCube, similar to the rollup of aggregates, a takeover of the new data into the indexes of the BI accelerator needs to take place. This takeover is made though this rollup process, which is also used with aggregates; i.e., the rollup deals not only with aggregates but also with BIA indexes.

Here, the index files are modified on the file server of the BI accelerator and the cache in the main memory of the index server is invalidated; after the rollup, the modified indexes will need to be reloaded to the main memory of the index server.

7.4.6   Hierarchy and Attribute Changes

Like aggregates, BIA indexes are redundant storage for content of a BasisCube. However, while the aggregation of key figure values from master data attributes requires executing a hierarchy and change run (see section 7.1.2), this is not required for the BIA in the usual way since data in the BIA is not copied in compressed form but copied entirely.

The change run still needs to be executed when the BIA is used because master data tables are part of the redundantly stored content in BIA and they need to be updated after a modification of the master data attributes. Therefore, the change run as a process will remain, but it will behave differently with the use of the BIA insofar as modified content of the X and Y tables will have to be completely re-created.

The change run rules both the modification of aggregates and the management of the BI accelerator. Thus, you can replace aggregates with BIA indexes without modifying the defined process in running operations (see chapter 30).

8   Basic Rules of Data Modeling

The previous chapters explained the data models of BW and the related modeling options. Building on this, this chapter will serve as guideline for the translation of business requirements into the data model of InfoObjects and BasisCubes.

For this purpose, we'll look at the following topics from a modeling option point of view:

- Modeling BasisCubes
- Modeling InfoObjects
- Modeling hierarchies
- Modeling partner Roles
- Modeling key figures

The modeling of DataStore objects is crucial for staging and it will be explained in chapter 17.

8.1   Modeling BasisCubes

After the basic requirements from the data analysis have been determined in a BW project, the question will be which BasisCubes need to be defined. Basically, BasisCubes should focus on data of individual process parts since these will each form a structural unit in the data model.

For example, in distribution logistics, a BasisCube would map the data that comes with the order entry, the delivery, and the invoicing. These process parts contain individual information (e.g., delivery date, amount delivered) but also a variety of joint information (e.g., customer, material). To bring the data of all these process parts into context during data analysis, BasisCubes can be combined in MultiProviders and InfoSets, as explained with the virtual InfoProvider in chapter 11.

Fragmentation

A further distribution of process data to different BasisCubes should be made with the storage of key figures. Individual key figures are filled with data only sporadically, and the fact table would thus be fragmented. In such cases, it makes sense to build separate BasisCubes for single key figures and thus reduce the need for storage capacity (see figure 8–1).

Figure 8–1
Fragmentation of the fact table

Fragmentation of a Fact Table

Customer	Month	Sales	Receivables	Discount
4711	01.2002	1000.00		
4711	02.2002	500.00	125.00	
4711	03.2002		125.00	
4711	04.2002	1250.00		25.00
4711	05.2002	650.00		

Prevention of Fragmentation with several Cubes

Customer	Month	Umsatz
4711	01.2002	1000.00
4711	02.2002	500.00
4711	04.2002	1250.00
4711	05.2002	650.00

Customer	Month	Receivables
4711	02.2002	125.00
4711	03.2002	125.00

Customer	Month	Discount
4711	04.2002	25.00

You can consolidate data for the data analysis by adding individual Basis-Cubes to a MultiProvider (see chapter 11.1).

Granularity

The granularity of a BasisCube—i.e., the level of detail of the data—has a major impact on the data volume of a BasisCube and thus on performance. This applies to both the performance during data analysis and the performance during load processes.

The granularity is determined by the InfoObjects that are entered in a BasisCube as characteristics. From a granularity point of view, it is irrelevant how the InfoObjects are distributed to the single dimensions. The following example clarifies the impact of granularity of a BasisCube on its data volume.

A company with 1,000 customers is examined.

- Each customer places an average of five orders per month with this company.
- Each order contains an average of 10 positions with one material each.
- Each customer orders an average of 20 different materials.

Case 1: The data is stored on a monthly basis with information about the customer, the materials, and the order numbers in a BasisCube.
Memorizing this very detailed information means that

$$\frac{10\ \text{Materials}}{\text{Order}} \times \frac{5\ \text{Orders}}{\text{Month}} \times 1{,}000\ \text{Customers} = \frac{50{,}000\ \text{(Datarecords)}}{\text{Month}}$$

are written into the fact table.

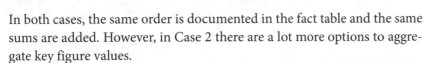

Case 2: The data is stored on a monthly basis with information on the client and the materials in a BasisCube.

The storage of this data means that every month only

$$\frac{20 \text{ Materials}}{\text{Customer} \times \text{Month}} \times 1,000 \text{ Customers} = \frac{20,000 \text{ (Datarecords)}}{\text{Month}}$$

are written into the fact table.

In both cases, the same order is documented in the fact table and the same sums are added. However, in Case 2 there are a lot more options to aggregate key figure values.

The smaller the number of data records in the fact table, the better the performance of the BW in managing the database.

Thus, with the modeling of BasisCubes, it should always be considered that the detail level of data is set as low as the business requirements allow. This rule becomes more important with increasing data volume.

While building BasisCubes is relatively easy, the distribution of the characteristics used in a BasisCube to the dimension of the cube is much more difficult.

Modeling dimensions

The information content of a BasisCube always stays the same, no matter how the individual characteristics are distributed to the dimensions (see figure 8–2). Thus, this is only about the physical data model.

The design of the dimensions has a direct and substantial impact on the performance, both when the cubes are filled with data and when the data is analyzed.

The reasons can be found in the concept of the star schema in general and in the implementation of the enhanced star schema by BW in particular. The basic conditions given with Web AS have to be considered in the same way as specific features of the given database system.

Due to the noticeable superiority of Oracle and DB2/UDB in the area of SAP BW and due to the fact that SAP BW intensively uses the features of these databases, the following explanations in this chapter will be limited to these two database systems. In addition, it is assumed that the database system can use bitmap indexes[60] (see also section 7.1).

---

60. Currently, no other database system has bitmap indexes but some try to re-create them in B* tree indexes and ultimately fail. The modeling rules for dimensions will not be dramatically changed, but the modeling goals will be re-created and will not really meet the requirements of other databases—same as for cube design overall.

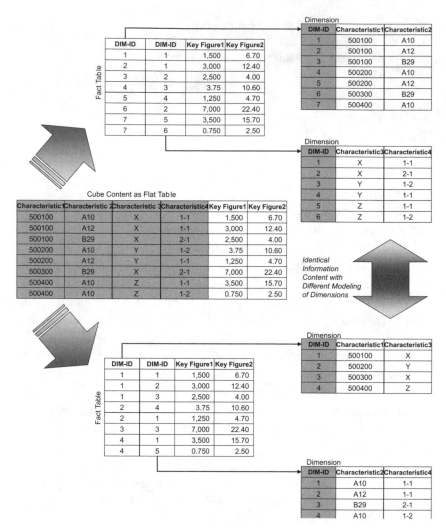

Figure 8–2

Same information content with different modeling of dimensions

For performance, the following data modeling correlations are crucial:

- Data analysis depends on the bitmap indexes of the DIM IDs of the fact table. To use them effectively, the DIM ID needs to show a *low cardinality* in the fact table. The number of values of the DIM ID should not exceed 10 per cent of the record number in the fact table.
- With selective access to the database, the data analysis depends on the fact that SID values of a selected characteristic can be found quickly in the dimension table. Since SIDs have B* tree indexes in the dimension tables, the SID within the dimension table needs to show a *high*

cardinality; i.e., the number of records in the dimension table should not exceed 10 times the number of characteristics of the SID.

- When you are filling a cube with data, for each SID combination in a dimension table, a corresponding data record will be searched and a new record might be created and a DIM ID generated. The bigger the dimension, the more often this check is made and the more time will be lost with the identification of new DIM IDs.

- When you are searching an existing SID combination in a dimension table, a B* tree index is used. It is defined for the first 16 SID fields[61] of the dimension. If more than 16 characteristics of a dimension are defined, the access via the index might take a very long time, especially when the first 16 SID fields are not the most selected.

Obviously, it is crucial to consider the indexing schema of the BasisCubes when designing the cube model. For better understanding, we show the enhanced star schema[62] of BW in figure 8–3 from an index perspective for the database systems Oracle and DB2/UDB.

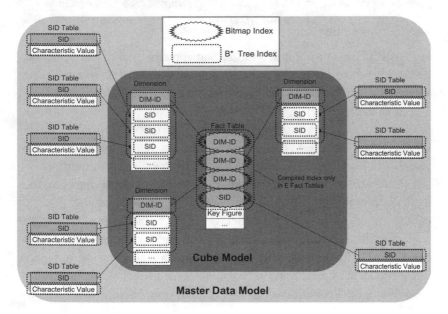

Figure 8–3
Indexing of the enhanced star schema with Oracle and DB2/UDB

---

61. A restriction from Web AS, in the ABAP Dictionary a maximum of 16 fields per key/index can be defined.
62. Only the compressed fact table that is relevant for data analysis will be considered. The indexes on the uncompressed fact table relevant for data loading are not of interest because these indexes can be deleted prior to a new data load anyway.

The objectives regarding the design of cube models can be summarized in one single goal: to keep the number of data records that are stored in a dimension as low as possible.

Specifically with the use of multidimensional clustering under DB2 UDB, the dimensions that are defined as MDC dimensions should be kept especially small (see chapter 7.3.2).

It is very important that not only single dimensions but all dimensions of a cube are designed as small as possible. The basic rule is the smaller the amount of data records of all dimension tables, the better the cube has been modeled.

The report SAP_INFOCUBE_DESIGNS offers a very simple option to get an overview on the quality of the modeling. The report shows the number of data records in the dimension tables and the F and E fact tables. Further, the size of each dimension table will be compared to the size of the compressed fact table and the so-called cube density[63] will be calculated, although in practice this has proven to be completely useless.

For BasisCubes with not much more than approximately 15 to 20 characteristics, a good cube model can be obtained when characteristics are not entered into a dimension if they have an n:m relation with each other (e.g., customer and material).

It is better to use a combination of characteristics that have a 1:n relation with each other (e.g., customer and postal code). To follow these basic rules, it is advantageous to fully use the 13 freely definable dimensions.

Unfortunately, large dimensions might not be avoidable, even with meticulous modeling. For example, if a comprehensive customer or product master, or even a record number, are included in the model, then the respective dimension tables will already become very large from this one characteristic. In this case, you might consider abandoning the respective dimension table by defining a line item dimension (see section 6.4.4). Since such a "deluxe dimension" can contain only one characteristic, the

---

63. The cube density is the quotient of the record count of the compressed fact table and the product of record counts of the dimension tables that are not empty. In theory, a cube model gets better with increasing cube density (maximum 100 percent). In practice, the cube density remains zero even with very good models, especially since line item dimensions are not considered as such.

remaining characteristics will have to be distributed to fewer dimensions, which may then make these dimensions bigger.

In any case, for very large dimension tables or line item dimensions, you must check whether the indexing of a DIM ID in the fact table with a bitmap index is suitable, or whether it should get a B* tree index since it is marked with high cardinality (see also section 7.2.1).

If more than approximately 15 to 20 characteristics that have a partially reciprocal relation to each other are to be part of a BasisCube, the complexity of the model, and thus the difficulty in modeling, will increase.

Modeling complex dimensions

In some cases, one can go so far as to claim ***that the development of an optimal cube design is impossible.*** At first, this statement might seem strange, but with a simple but allied example, the so-called "traveling salesman" problem, it will be made clearer.

With this problem, a number of n points (places) have to be connected in a single stroke (the travel route of the salesman). The shorter the stroke (that is, the travel route), the better the route because the same objective—that is, to reach each point—can be reached through a shorter and thus faster route. Figure 8–4 shows the traveling salesman problem based on a simple and a better route through five points.

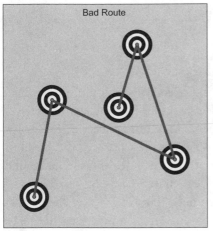 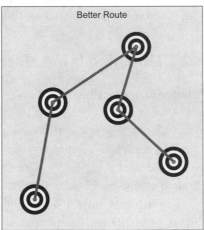

Figure 8–4

Traveling salesman problem

Mathematically speaking, both the traveling salesman problem and cube modeling are tasks for it can never be proven whether an approach to a solution was the best one or not. In theory, it is possible to review every possible model. Since the number of possibilities increases factorially with the number of characteristics, however, a simulation of all possible combinations cannot be economically realized with the processing power we have today.[64]

Thus, we have to accept that for the modeling of cube dimensions, as well as for the route planning of the traveling salesman, there is no procedure to identify the best possible design.

Especially for the traveling salesman problem, there is a range of algorithms that at least produce very good results. This was made clear during the U.S. presidential elections in 2002 where the optimal campaign route for the candidates could be identified only with specific algorithms.

For the modeling of cubes, such algorithms are not available. And the algorithms for the traveling salesman problem do not consider the general conditions of cube modeling. Further, with the existing algorithms, it is assumed that the quality of the routes will show in relatively little time (simple addition of distances). It takes a lot of effort, however, to identify the quality of a cube design because the size of dimension tables can be identified only with the simulation of comprehensive sample data.

Especially for complex models, the design of a BasisCube will inevitably prove to be an iterative and time-consuming process, and with some experience this will result in a good but never optimal model. Currently, quadox AG is the only provider executing such iteration processes where a tool-based procedure is used for this purpose.

8.2   Modeling InfoObjects

When you're modeling InfoObjects, the selection and use of master data attributes is important if the InfoObjects contain master data. In this section, we'll discuss frequently asked questions in this area.

The modeling of master data attributes depends on the business requirements that the historiography of the attributes and the navigation through attributes will have to meet (see section 5.1.2).

Current display   The requirement you'll most often need to meet involves the current display of attributes. In all cases where master data attributes are to be stored with the characteristics in their current form, they have to be stored as display or navigation attributes for the respective InfoObject. Thus,

---

64. While a travel route with five stops allows for only 120 combinations, there are 3,628,800 combinations with 10 stops and 2,432,902,008,176,640,000 combinations for 20 stops. The number of possible combinations with 50 stops is a 3 with 64 zeros. The modeling of cube dimensions is slightly more simple, but the available options (that may make sense) are similar.

during data analysis, BW can always refer to the current attribute values in the master data tables of the InfoObjects.

For a key date display of attributes, attributes for the respective InfoObject will also be defined, but here the option of a key date display is used (see figure 6–21 on page 81). *Key date display*

This option often reflects business requirements; however, the use of key-date-related master data attributes causes performance and administration problems. For this reason, especially for large master data tables, attributes should be stored key date related only when it cannot be avoided for business reasons.

The historic display cannot be realized with attributes. Instead, the attributes need to be added directly to the dimensions of the BasisCubes. There, they lose their reference to the respective characteristic where historiography is obtained. *Historic display*

From a performance perspective, this form of storage is the most favorable since the attributes are stored close to the fact table, which allows the database easier handling of these attributes in the reading processes.

The historic display represents a specific modeling of the respective BasisCube and can be used in addition to the current/key-date-related display.

A precondition for the use of attributes for navigation in queries or for the selection of data is the definition of the attributes as navigation attributes. Thus, these attributes will not only be stored as a value, but additionally as SID in the master data tables of the InfoObject (see also section 6.2.2). *Navigation attributes*

The result is that with load processes, special operations have to be made to identify or re-create the respective SID for the attribute values. To limit the additional delay in load processes, navigation attributes should be included only when necessary.

8.3 Modeling Hierarchies

In section 6.2.5, we explained the use of external hierarchies. The use of external hierarchies, however, is not the only option to map such structures in BW. In fact, there are three options:

- Use of external hierarchies
- Mapping hierarchies in master data attributes
- Mapping hierarchies in dimension attributes

Figure 8–5 shows the use of these three options in the data model.

Figure 8–5
Modeling hierarchies

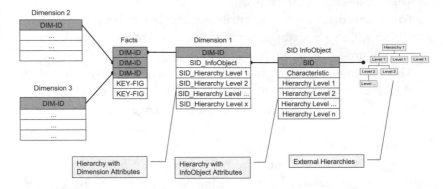

Each of these options has its specific pros and cons.

External hierarchies The advantage of external hierarchies is that they can be created and used in a very flexible way. Each InfoObject can own several external hierarchies at the same time, and they can be used independently for the data analysis (e.g., business-specific product hierarchies).

Further, the structure of hierarchies is flexible. Without further customizing the data model, you can define or modify the depth of the hierarchy or create an unbalanced hierarchy.[65]

During data analysis, hierarchies will also be displayed as such in the tools of the Business Explorer Analyzer (BEx Analyzer). The user is given a set sequence of hierarchy levels to facilitate navigation in the hierarchies.

The serious disadvantage of external hierarchies will become apparent in the review of the data model (see figure 8–5). As measured by the number of relations, external hierarchies are the furthest away from the fact tables. Thus, the use of external hierarchies will mostly come with a performance decrease; their use should be limited to small hierarchies, or should be strongly supported by the use of aggregates on the hierarchy level.

Hierarchies in attributes Each hierarchy consists of a number of hierarchy levels that map a certain characteristic. If measured by this characteristic, it is possible to store hierarchies in the form of attributes of an InfoObject.

For example, if for the InfoObject OMATERIAL the attributes product level 1, product level 2, and product level 3 are created, then this information is just as valuable as an external hierarchy with three respective hierarchy levels.

---

65. In unbalanced hierarchies, the different hierarchy branches show a different number of hierarchy levels.

Compared to external hierarchies, the performance gain is particularly advantageous with this form of modeling. However, there are also a number of disadvantages:

■ The number of hierarchy levels is set and identical (balanced) for each hierarchy branch.

■ Each modification to the hierarchy structure (hierarchy depth) needs to be realized with the modeling of the respective InfoObject. This requires considerably more effort than the use of external hierarchies. A versioning of the hierarchy is not available, nor are similar features of the external hierarchy.

■ Hierarchies in attributes will not be visually displayed as such in the tools of the Business Explorer Analyzer. The sequence of hierarchy levels is not preset for the user. Thus, the user needs to know that a certain combination of attributes represents a hierarchy.

Hierarchies in dimensions can be compared to hierarchies in attributes. While time-wise, hierarchies in attributes always come with the current version of the hierarchy, hierarchies in dimensions are used for the historic display of attributes (see section 5.1.2).

Hierarchies in dimensions

Given the closeness of the dimensions to the fact table, this form of storage is the most favorable from a performance point of view.

8.4 Modeling Partner Roles

Usually, partner roles are used in sales controlling (e.g., in the SD module of SAP ERP) to describe the roles of different customers that are engaged in an order. Usual partner roles are, for example, sold-to party, invoice recipient, and goods recipient For an order, these roles do not have to be assumed by the same customer and are thus to be entered individually.

From a business perspective, it can make sense to store order data with reference to all entered partner roles[66]. Here, the individual partner roles will have to be created as individual InfoObjects and stored separately, but it will not be necessary to load the respective master data for each Info-Object (this would mean that identical master data records are repeatedly loaded redundantly and stored in the master data tables).

---

66. For example, marketing measures are relevant for the dealings from the customer if he acts as sold-to party. For accounting, however, the dealings that he has to pay for as invoice recipient (regulator) are relevant.

In such cases it makes sense to work with referencing InfoObjects. An InfoObject will be created with master data (InfoObject customer) and all partner roles will reference it (InfoObjects, sold-to party, regulator, goods recipient).

Depending on the size of the master data tables and the frequency with which the partner roles differ, with the modeling of BasisCubes, the referencing InfoObjects can jointly be added to a dimension (see figure 8–6) or each InfoObject can be added to its individual dimension.

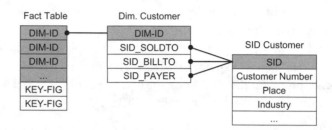

Figure 8–6

Modeling partner roles in small dimensions

Basically, it is recommended in larger dimensions (from approximately 10,000 data records) to store each partner role in a separate dimension in order to keep the individual dimensions as small as possible.

In addition, it makes sense not to add any further attributes to these dimensions and to define the dimensions as line item dimensions (see figure 8–7).

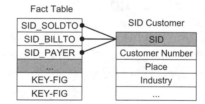

Figure 8–7

Modeling partner roles in large dimensions

8.5   Modeling Key Figures

Key figures are easy to model from a data model perspective since they can only be added to the fact table. You need to consider the arrangement of dimensions only for key figures with exception aggregation. In these cases, a reference characteristic has to be added to a dimension.

Still, even for key figures there are some basic rules that should be followed when modeling the individual key figures types:

- Key figures of characteristics type
- Grouped key figures
- Calculated key figures

8.5.1 Key Figures of Characteristics Type

In most cases, it can clearly be identified whether information is to be classified as key figure or characteristic. In some cases, however, the classification of the information is questionable.

For example, weight specifications can both be added as a key figure to the fact table and be processed through mathematical operations (usually addition). However, it may make sense to use weights as characteristics if a weight displays a grouping that can be the basis for an analysis (e.g., grouping of transportation cost according to the weight categories of products).

The following table offers some support for a decision about whether you should model information as a key figure or as a characteristic.

	Characteristic	Key Figure
Type of Information	Descriptive/categorizing information	Information that can be used for calculations (quantity or value)
Detailing	Information stored as a detailing level (e.g., for drill down)	Information that is aggregated to characteristics and can be displayed as a sum
Value	Agreed quantities of value or levels of information (e.g., weight class up to 1 lb, up to 10 lbs, up to 100 lbs)	Information that is indicated variably (e.g., 1.2 lbs, 34.0 lbs, 17.4 lbs)

8.5.2 Grouped Key Figures

During the evaluation of key figures that are relevant for analysis, the users often list key figures that are not pure key figures from a data model perspective but that are mixed up with a characteristic. In such cases, identifying key figures and characteristics in the information and modeling each as such is required.

The following table shows some examples.

Grouped Key Figure	Key Figure	Characteristic
Sales in previous year	Sales	Year
Turnover for business unit 01	Turnover	Business unit
Transportation period for materials up to 1 lb	Transportation period	Weight level

The respective value of the characteristics (previous year, business unit 01, weight category 1 kilogram) is relevant only for data analysis when a comparison to the previous year is defined.

8.5.3 Calculated Key Figures

In many cases, key figures provide information that only gains relevance with further calculations (usually with reference to characteristics or other key figures). There are three alternatives for the calculation of such key figures and the consideration of calculated key figures in the data model:

- Calculation of the key figure during analysis
- Use of exception aggregation
- Modeling the key figure in the BasisCube and calculation of the key figures when filling the BasisCube

The alternatives have very different pros and cons.

Calculation during analysis Key figures can be calculated spontaneously and flexibly at the time of the analysis through calculations in the respective analysis tool (e.g., in the BEx Analyzer).

Such calculations can be defined with little effort and without any deep BW knowledge. However, there are numerous disadvantages:

- The database for the calculation is limited to the query result that is passed on from the analytical engine to the evaluation tool. Thus, many calculations cannot be made due to an inadequate database.
- The calculation routines are not part of the Metadata Repository (possibly created by individual users) and are thus not transparent from a system administration perspective.
- The performance of the calculation is worse than with key figure modeling since the calculation will have to be redone with each navigational step.

The exception aggregation is a specific form of calculated key figure. With exception aggregation, the key figure will have to be part of the data model of a BasisCube, which results in some deviations from the normally calculated key figure:

Exception aggregation

- The calculation of the key figure is not made in the analysis tool but in the analytical engine. There, calculations can refer to a deeper level of detail than in the analysis tool.
- BW automatically ensures that the analytical engine received data with the respective level of detail. This even influences data modeling where reference characteristics of key figures will need to be added to a Basis-Cube.

An alternative to the calculation of key figures at the time of the data analysis (in the analysis tool or in the analytical engine) is to add certain key figures to the data model of BasisCubes and to precalculate them during the data transfer.

Modeling as key figure

Calculated key figures that are available on the data record level are usually cumulated in the data analysis with an addition. The consequence is that a precalculation of key figures will mathematically only be possible if the following is given:

Calculation(KeyFigure1) + Calculation(KeyFigure2)

= Calculation(KeyFigure1 + KeyFigure2)

For example, this is not the case when an average is calculated and when in the calculation

$$\frac{KeyFigure1}{Number1} + \frac{KeyFigure2}{Number2}$$

the reference values *Number1* and *Number2* are different (e.g., since the calculation is based on the number of all data records but the data analysis only selects part of the data). In such a case, the calculation can only be made using exception aggregation.

The advantage of this option is that key figures will need to be calculated only once with the filling of the BasisCubes (from a high-performance application server) and that they will be available for the analysis in a readily calculated form (in a not-so-well-performing PC). This makes sense if the calculation of the key figures is very complex and thus profits from the scope of the ABAP/4 language.

Another advantage comes with the fact that calculated key figures as well as the calculation procedures are stored in the BW metadata and are thus generally comprehensible.

Besides these advantages, there can also be a series of disadvantages. The entry of key figures in the fact table can strongly increase the data volume of an InfoCube. For this reason, calculated key figures should be modeled in the fact table only when it will not be a problem for the respective BasisCube from a data volume perspective.

Another advantage of calculated key figures in the fact table comes from the rigidity of the data model. Once key figures are modeled, they cannot be removed from a BasisCube and the entry of another calculated key figure requires modifying the data model.

Usually, calculated key figures are recommended for the fact table only if the following requirements are met:

- The calculation of the key figure is very complex or if the calculation is time-consuming.
- The formula for the calculation of the key figure is stable and will not be subject to change.
- The data volume of the respective BasisCube is not critical.

If these requirements are not fulfilled, then the key figures should be calculated only during the data analysis.

9 Data Modeling in the DWWB

Data modeling is performed in the Data Warehousing Workbench (see figure 2–2). Due to the number of objects that can be part of the modeling, all objects are structured in a hierarchic formation, the so-called InfoArea hierarchy.

This hierarchy is a structure of freely interchangeable, nested *InfoAreas* (e.g., financial accounting, human resources, and supply chain management) that together will make an InfoArea hierarchy. The structure of this hierarchy is preset by the BI content; however, it can be freely modified and expanded.

A specific InfoArea is the NODESNOTCONNECTED. Automatically, BW objects that are not assigned to any other InfoArea or that cannot be allocated to an InfoArea for technical reasons (e.g., if BW objects were acquired from the BI content without any existing corresponding Info-Areas) will be added to this InfoArea.

The Data Warehousing Workbench offers two different views on the objects of the InfoArea hierarchy: a view on all data targets (InfoCubes and DataStore objects) and a view on InfoObjects. The reason is that data targets and InfoObjects can be treated differently within a hierarchy.

For modeling in the Data Warehousing Workbench, data targets are arranged in the InfoProvider tree (see figure 9–1).

InfoProvider in the InfoArea hierarchy

Each data target needs to be assigned to exactly one InfoArea. It is not possible to place data targets right under the root of the hierarchy or to add them to the hierarchy more than once.

Like BW objects, InfoAreas are defined by a technical name and a description. Within the InfoArea hierarchy, data targets as well as Info-Areas can be moved by drag and drop.

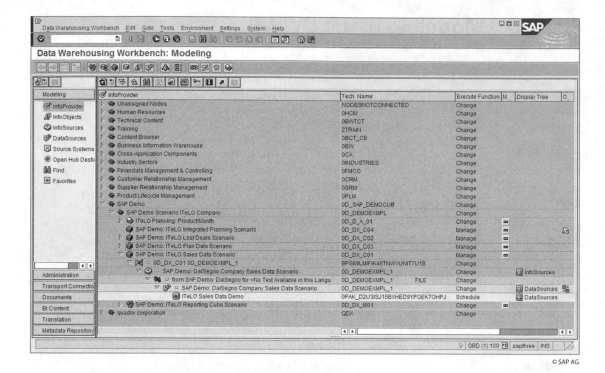

© SAP AG

Figure 9–1
InfoProvider tree

InfoObjects in the
InfoArea hierarchy

All data targets can be created under an InfoArea using the context menu, and each data target has a context menu available that allows for administration and maintenance.

While data targets with their unique data content can be assigned to exactly one node of the InfoArea hierarchy, this structure is very difficult for InfoObjects. For example, BasisCubes with data on order entry, delivery, invoicing, and complaints can be clearly allocated to the respective InfoAreas. However, all BasisCubes contain part of the same InfoObjects (e.g., customer number).

To repeatedly add InfoObjects to an InfoArea hierarchy, there are InfoObject catalogs. Similar to data targets, an InfoObject catalog needs to be assigned to exactly one node of the InfoArea hierarchy. However, each InfoObject catalog can contain a random number of InfoObjects, and each InfoObject can be part of a random number of InfoObject catalogs.

Using the InfoObject catalog, it is thus possible to assign an InfoObject to several InfoAreas. To achieve a clear organization of the InfoObjects, you need to differentiate when you create the InfoObject catalog whether the catalog is to acquire characteristics or key figures (see figure 9–2).

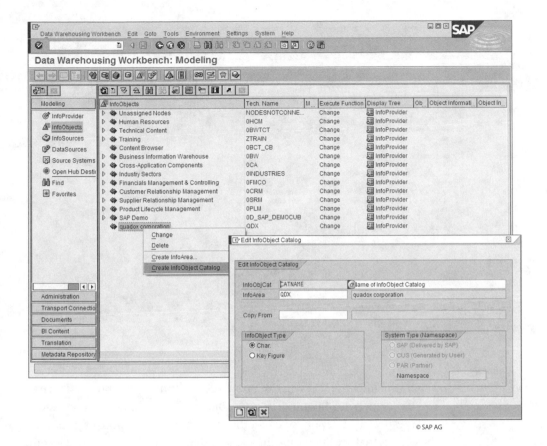

© SAP AG

Should an InfoObject not be contained in an InfoObject catalog, it will automatically be allocated to the catalog 0CHANOTASSIGNED (characteristics not assigned) or 0KYFNOTASSIGNED (key figures not assigned). If an Info-Object is allocated to an InfoObject catalog, it will automatically be removed from the catalog for unassigned InfoObjects.

Other than in the InfoProvider tree, the allocation of InfoObjects to the InfoObject catalog is *not* possible with drag and drop. Instead, the individual InfoObject catalogs will have to be maintained; i.e., single Info-Objects will have to be specifically added in the maintenance menu of the InfoObject catalogs (see figure 9–3).

The following sections explain how the modeling of InfoObjects, BasisCubes, and DataStore objects is done. The focus will not be on the modeling options in detail, which can be found in the BW online help, where there are additional details that are more current.

Figure 9–2
InfoObject tree

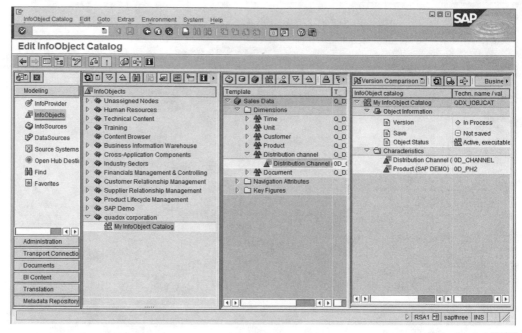

© SAP AG

Figure 9–3

*Maintenance of
InfoObject catalogs*

Rather, the intention is to give support on the limitations and particularities that come with the modeling of objects if they contain data already. This is especially relevant for changing InfoObjects, DataStore objects, and BasisCubes that are operating already and that cannot be remodeled "from scratch".

9.1 Modeling of InfoObjects

The easiest way to model an InfoObject is to create it in the context menu of the InfoObject catalog in which it is to be added.[67] Whether the InfoObject will be a characteristic of a key figure will be derived from the InfoObject catalog that has been designed for either key figures or for characteristics (see chapter 9).

With the creation of the InfoObject, you need to determine the technical name as well as the labeling. In the case of a referencing characteristic (see section 6.2.4), you need to indicate the reference InfoObject at this

---

67. The InfoObject can then be added to further InfoObject catalogs or removed from the original InfoObject catalog.

time, and you cannot change it afterward. Alternatively, an InfoObject can be used as template; its settings will be copied but can still be modified until activation[68] (see figure 9–4).

Figure 9–4
Creation of InfoObjects

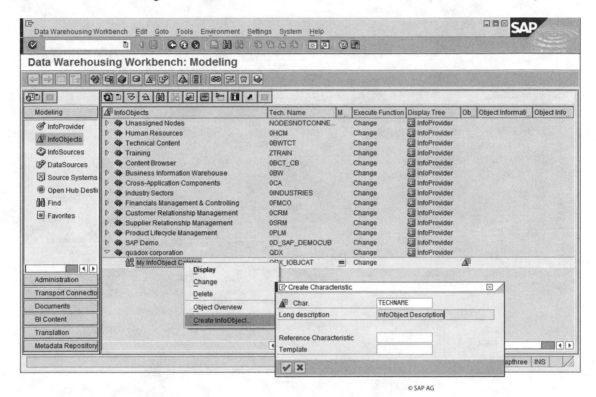

© SAP AG

If an InfoObject is not to be contained in an InfoObject catalog right away, you can also create it independently from an InfoObject catalog by using the menu item *Create→Objects→InfoObject* in the Data Warehousing Workbench or by using the transaction RSD1 (see figure 9–5).

With this direct editing of InfoObjects comes an option to compile and jointly edit several InfoObjects according to certain criteria (e.g., all InfoObjects of a data target). You can delete or activate large quantities of InfoObjects the same way.

Bulk processing

As long as an InfoObject is only modeled and activated, but not yet filled with master data or used in other objects, you can easily modify the settings. However, if an InfoObject is used in running operations, several modifications will no longer be possible.

Editing filled and used InfoObjects

68. The exception is the specification of a reference InfoObject.

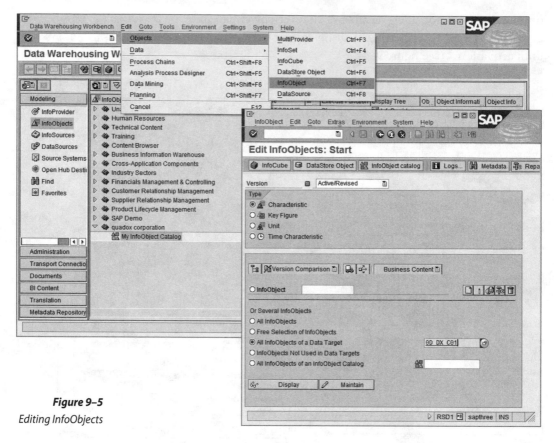

Figure 9–5
Editing InfoObjects

In the following table, you will find a summary of the modifications that can be made to InfoObjects where master data has been loaded. You must consider the different requirements of characteristics and key figure InfoObjects.

For key figure objects, it depends on whether they are already used in data targets (in BasisCubes or DataStore objects or as attribute in other InfoObjects).

Modeling of a Key Figure	Possible when used
Modify data type	✗
Change currency/quantity unit	✗
Modify standard aggregation	✗
Modify exception aggregation	✓

Modeling of a Key Figure	Possible when used
Change reference characteristic of the exception aggregation	✓
Modify flow values to inventory values and vice versa	✗
Modify inventory-changing InfoObjects	✗

To edit characteristics InfoObjects, it is crucial whether they already have master data entries or data records in their SID table.

Modeling of a Characteristic	Possible with Filled Data
Change data type	$(✗)^1$
Shorten key	✗
Lengthen key	$(✓)^2$
Enable lowercase letters	✓
Prohibit lowercase letters	✗
Activate attribute only	✗
Deactivate attribute only	✓
With master data tables	✓
Without master data tables	✓
With texts	✓
Without texts	✓
External hierarchies	✓
Without external hierarchies	✓
Activate language dependency	✓
Deactivate language dependency	$(✗)^3$
Change text length	✓
Activate time dependency	✓
Deactivate time dependency	✗
Display attributes	✓
Navigation attributes	✓

Modeling of a Characteristic	Possible with Filled Data
Expand compounding	✓
Reduce compounding	✗

1. It is possible to change the data type. However, the existing master data will then be deleted.
2. Only possible if the conversion routine ALPHA has not been stored. For compound InfoObjects, external hierarchies may become useless and might have to be reloaded.
3. The subsequent deactivation of the language dependency will still be possible if the text table of the InfoObject is previously emptied by the database system. The master data texts will then have to be completely reloaded after the modification.

Deletion of master data

Figure 9–6
Deletion of master data

If an InfoObject definition cannot be changed due to existing master data, it might help to delete the master data. To do so, you can use the context menu of the InfoObject in the Data Warehousing Workbench (see figure 9–6).

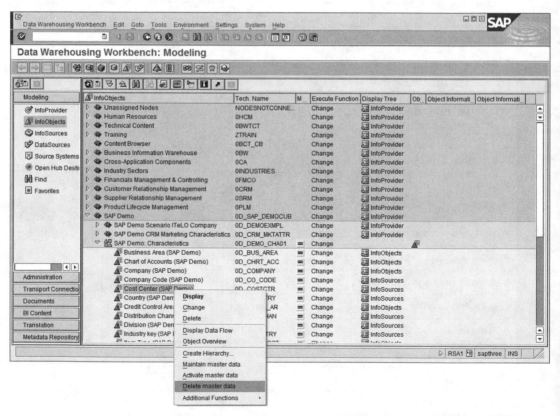

© SAP AG

At first, the deletion of master data is not serious since master data can usually be reloaded with little effort. However, it will be possible only if the respective SID values have not yet been referenced from the dimension tables of the BasisCubes.

For each master date to be deleted, BW checks whether it is used as such and it might then prevent the deletion so that only the deletion of the respective cubes would be an option.

In practice, it will be easier in such a case to replace the InfoObject in question with a new InfoObject and to remodel the replacement in the BasisCube. The remodeling of BasisCubes will be explained in section 9.2.

9.2 Modeling of BasisCubes

In the Data Warehousing Workbench, BasisCubes can be created in the context menu of the InfoArea to which the cube is to be a subordinate. You need to enter the technical name of the BasisCube as well as description. Alternatively, you can use a template; i.e., an existing BasisCube and its structure will be used as the basis for the definition of the cube (see figure 9–7).

Figure 9–7

Creation of a BasisCube in the Data Warehousing Workbench

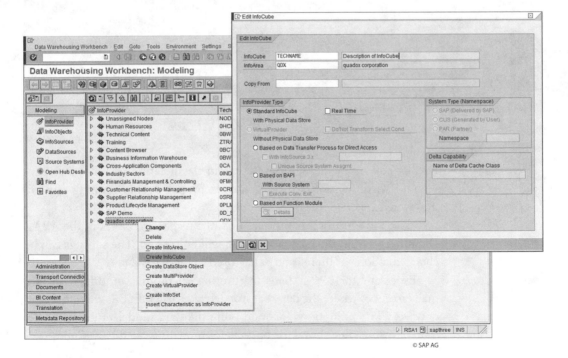

You set the dimensions of a BasisCube in the context menu of the dimensions in cube maintenance (see figure 9–8). The assignment of InfoObjects or key figures to the dimensions or to the fact table of the cube will be made by dragging and dropping from a template structure that has been chosen previously (InfoSource, DataStore objects, BasisCubes, etc.).

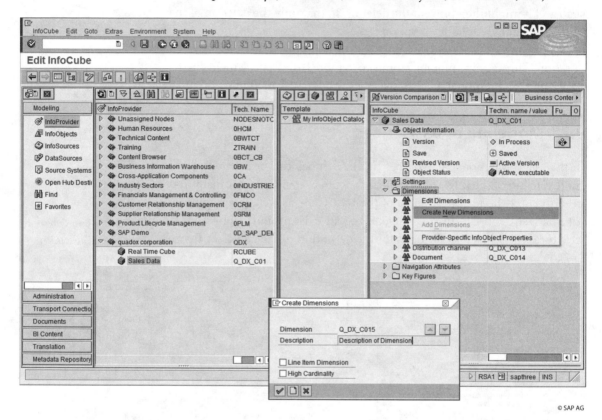

© SAP AG

Figure 9–8

Design of a cube model in the Data Warehousing Workbench

Further cube modeling settings (line item classification of dimension, cardinality of a dimension, structure-specific properties, partitioning, clustering) were explained in earlier chapters.

With the activation of a BasisCube, the respective tables in the ABAP Dictionary and in the database system will be created. The settings can be changed as long as there is no data stored in the BasisCubes.

Modification of filled cubes

Especially for BW systems in running operations, modifications are made to cubes where the data was not deleted earlier. In this case, there are only very limited options for modifying the data model of a BasisCube. The following table shows the options for modeling filled BasisCubes.

Modeling of a BasisCube	Possible with filled Cube
Enter characteristic with initial value	✓
Enter characteristic with defined value	x^1
Delete characteristic	x^2
Navigation attributes on/off	✓
Enter key figure with initial value	✓
Enter key figure with defined value	x^3
Delete key figure	x^4
Create dimensions	✓
Delete dimensions	✗
Change dimension allocation of a characteristic	✗
Change line item classification of a dimension	✗
Change cardinality of a dimension	✓
Modify structure-specific properties	✗
Partitioning	x^5
Clustering	x^6
Activate zero value elimination	✗
Inventory characteristics/time slice	✗

1.   Possible with limitations by remodeling dimension tables (see section 9.2.1).
2.   Possible with remodeling of dimension tables (see section 9.2.1).
3.   Possible with remodeling of the fact table (see chapter 9.2.2).
4.   Possible with remodeling of the fact table (see chapter 9.2.2).
5.   Modification possible during repartitioning system maintenance (see chapter 32.1).
6.   Modification possible with reclustering (see chapter 9.4).

If the data model of a BasisCube is be modified substantially—e.g., to modify the distribution of characteristics to individual dimensions for performance reasons—the only option will be to delete the cube content or to model a new cube.

You can make the following smaller modifications:

Remodeling of InfoProviders

■ Acquire characteristics with a defined value
■ Delete characteristics from a BasisCube

■ Replace existing characteristics with other characteristics
■ Acquire key figures with a defined value
■ Delete a key figure from a BasisCube

As an alternative to re-creating the cube to make these modifications, BW offers, from release 7, the option to *remodel InfoProviders*. The remodeling of a BasisCube can only be started from the context menu of the cube in the Data Warehousing Workbench (see figure 9–9).

Figure 9–9

Starting remodeling

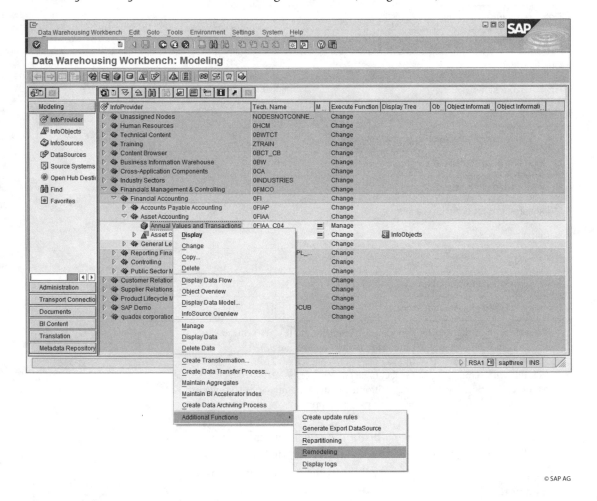

© SAP AG

Conceptually, remodeling is not only the modification of a BasisCube but the application of a range of modification instructions that specifically influence the content of selected dimension tables or the fact table of a BasisCube (with entry, deletion, or replacement of characteristics and key figures). These modification instructions are to be combined in a remodeling rule to be stored in the BW metadata and to be distributed to the individual BW systems through the transportation landscape.

> The execution of remodeling changes the metadata of a BasisCube. If the remodeling is not done in each system of a transportation landscape (see appendix C), there might be inconsistencies between the different systems in the definition of the BasisCubes and thus the BasisCube might no longer be transportable. When doing remodeling, please consider remodeling on all systems within a transportation landscape.

The individual change instructions that are part of a remodeling rule can be freely entered or deleted after the remodeling rule was named (see figure 9–10).

Figure 9–10
Definition of a
remodeling rule

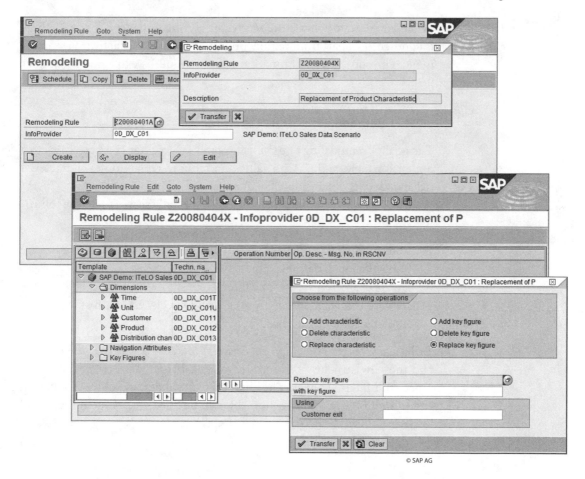

© SAP AG

The term *remodeling* is misleading because it is not the complete model of a BasisCube that can be changed conceptually; only individual dimension tables or the fact table can be manipulated when segregated from each other.

Which change instructions can be combined in a remodeling rule in detail and how these work is dealt with in the following ways:

■ Remodeling of dimension tables
■ Remodeling of the fact table

According to the SAP documentation, changing the settings for the range partitioning is part of remodeling. However, repartitioning is not performed to develop or change the data model but it is part of regularly recurring maintenance activities and is explained with model trimming in section 32.1.

Subsequent zero value elimination

When you need to activate the zero value elimination of a BasisCube, there is another tool apart from remodeling that meets with exactly this requirement. The subsequent elimination of zero values is explained in chapter 9.2.3.

9.2.1   Remodeling of Dimension Tables

The goal of remodeling of dimension tables is to enter characteristics to a dimension table, to fill it with values, and thus to replace other characteristics in *the same* dimension table, if required.

The remodeling of dimension tables especially serves to do the following:

■ Enter new characteristics to a filled cube where the characteristics are to be filled with defined values
■ Delete characteristics from a filled cube
■ Replace characteristics with other InfoObjects, e.g., with standardization of several BasisCubes

Technically, the remodeling procedure is made in a way that the existing and the new structure of the dimension table are transferred into each other with internal tables. The characteristics that have additionally been entered with the new dimension table can be filled with content that could be derived from the existing dimension table.

Of primary interest in this process is, therefore, probably the design of the rules according to which the newly entered characteristics can be filled. There, the consequences of a deletion or replacement of characteristics must be considered. How new characteristics are entered and how characteristics are deleted or replaced will be explained next.

Entering new Characteristics

Entering a new characteristic in a dimension table results in a structural expansion of the dimension table by the new characteristic or, to be more precise, by an SID that references the characteristic.

Such a structural expansion is possible with normal modeling too, even if a BasisCube already contains data. The particular significance of remodeling for entering new characteristics only comes with the fact that the new characteristic will be provided with the values that can be deduced from other characteristics of the *same* dimension.

Remodeling offers a range of simple ways to fill characteristics (see figure 9–10):

- **Constant:** The new characteristic will be filled with a given constant value.
- **Attribute:** The new characteristic will be filled with the value of the attribute that is deduced from another characteristic of the *same* dimension.
- **1:1 allocation:** The new characteristic will be filled with the value of another characteristic of the *same* dimension.

For more complex requirements that cannot be met with the allocation of constants, attributes, or other characteristic values, remodeling offers the possibility to identify values of the new characteristic via individual program coding.

Customer exit in the remodeling

The program coding is to be implemented as a class to the interface IF_RSCNV_EXIT. This is made in the transaction SE24, where first the class and also its properties[69] are defined (see figure 9–11).

If the class is created in this way, then the use of the interface IF_RSCNV_EXIT for the class needs to be defined from which the method IF_RSCNV_EXIT~EXIT of the class will be deduced (see figure 9–12).

---

69. Instantiation is always *public,* class type is always *usual ABAP class,* the class is always *Final.*

Figure 9–11
Definition of a class for remodeling

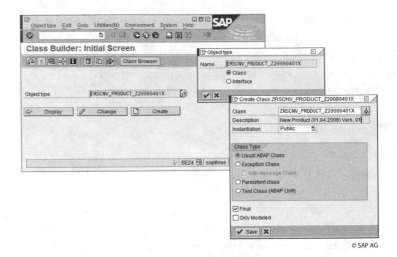

© SAP AG

Figure 9–12
Implementation of the method IF_RSCNV_EXIT~EXIT

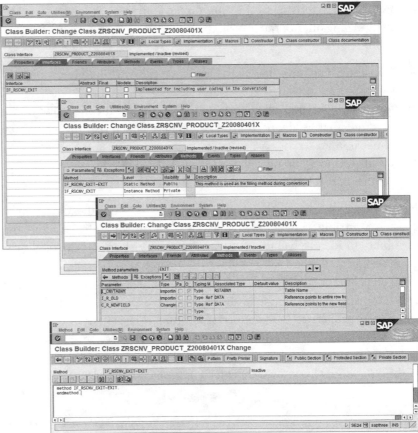

© SAP AG

The method `IF_RSCNV_EXIT~EXIT` is called for every data record of a remodeled dimension table and contains the following parameters according to the interface definition:

- **`I_CNVTABNM`**
Name of the dimension table[70] that is being processed during the remodeling. Since the implementation of the interface `IF_RSCNV_EXIT` can basically be executed for the remodeling of each BasisCube and each characteristic of each dimension, it makes sense to check in the coding whether the respective method is used for a suitable dimension. Otherwise, the remodeling would result in errors and aborts.

- **`I_R_OLD`**
Reference to the data record to be handled from the existing (old) dimension table. From this data record, the values of all characteristics for the respective data record of the dimension table can be deduced.

- **`C_R_NEWFIELD`**
Reference to the result of the calculation that describes the content of the new field.

The thus implemented class is available in the call input help of the customer exit to each remodeling rule (see figure 9–10).

The implementation of the method `IF_RSCNV_EXIT` does not automatically ensure that the method will only be used in remodeling rules that handle the respective dimension table(s). Basically, a totally different BasisCube or a characteristic of another dimension could be remodeled, which would result in errors and aborts. From the parameter `I_CNVTABNM` in the coding, you should check whether the method is selected to remodel a suitable dimension table.

The basic framework for the implementation of a class can be designed as follows:

```
METHOD if_rscnv_exit~exit.
  FIELD-SYMBOLS: <l_s_old> TYPE ANY,    "data record from old
                                        * dimension
                 <l_oldfld1> TYPE ANY,  "a field in old dimension
  <l_newfield> TYPE ANY.                "result of calculations
```

---

70. The name of the table in the ABAP Dictionary will be transferred; e.g., /BIC/DCUBE1 for the dimension 1 of the cube CUBE.

```
IF i_cnvtabnm = '/BIO/DOD_DX_CO11'.   "testing whether dimension 1
                                   * is remodeled by cube OD_DX_CO1.
* enter field symbols on reference tables/fields
  ASSIGN c_r_newfield->* TO <l_newfield>. "result of calculation
  ASSIGN i_r_old->* TO <l_s_old>.      "data record of old dimension
* enter field symbol <l_oldfld> on field SID_OCALDAY in old dim.
  ASSIGN COMPONENT 'SID_OCALDAY' OF STRUCTURE <l_s_old> TO
<l_oldfld1>.
* <l_oldfld1> contains an SID value.
* Deduce characteristics value from <l_oldfld1> and make further
* calculations. Then identify SID value for result and transfer to
* <l_newfield>.
ELSE.
* Create exception if wrong dimension table is remodeled.
  RAISE EXCEPTION TYPE CX_RSCNV_EXCEPTION.
ENDIF.
ENDMETHOD.
```

It absolutely needs to be considered that the field values of a dimension table will not be provided in the form of true characteristic values but in the form of SID values. Also, the value that is identified from the routine needs to represent an SID value.

A mandatory part of the program coding is thus the conversion of SID values of the old dimension table into the required characteristic values as well as the recalculation of the result into an SID value. For this purpose, the function modules RRSI_SID_VAL_SINGLE_CONVERT (conversion of the SID value of a characteristic into a characteristic value) and RRSI_VAL_SID_SINGLE_CONVERT (conversion of a characteristic value in an SID value of a characteristic) are available.

With the use of the function modules, at least the respective value to be converted as well as the InfoObject needs to be provided. The following example shows the conversion of the date 01/18/2007 of the InfoObject OCALDAY into its SID value and back into its characteristics value[71].

```
DATA: l_Ocalday_chavl type /BIO/OICALDAY,
      l_Ocalday_sid type RSSID.

l_Ocalday_chavl = '20070118'.

* Identify SID value for characteristics value
```

---

71. With the implementation of the user exit for the remodeling, the conversion order would be exactly the other way around.

```
CALL FUNCTION 'RRSI_VAL_SID_SINGLE_CONVERT'
EXPORTING
      i_iobjnm                  = 'OCALDAY'
      i_chavl                   = l_0calday_chavl
*     I_S_COB_PRO               =
*     I_CHECKFL                 = RS_C_FALSE
*     I_WRITEFL                 = RRSI_C_WRITEFL-NO
*     I_MASTERDATA_CREATE       = RS_C_TRUE
*     I_RNSID                   =
*     I_NEW_VALUES              = RS_C_FALSE
IMPORTING
      e_sid                     = l_0calday_sid
EXCEPTIONS
      no_sid                    = 1
      chavl_not_allowed         = 2
      chavl_not_figure          = 3
      chavl_not_plausible       = 4
      x_message                 = 5
      interval_not_found        = 6
      foreign_lock              = 7
      inherited_error           = 8
      OTHERS                    = 9
                    .
IF sy-subrc <> 0.
  RAISE EXCEPTION TYPE cx_rscnv_exception
  EXPORTING
  attr1 = ' RRSI_VAL_SID_SINGLE_CONVERT '
  attr2 = 'Error converting value to SID'
* attr3  = sy-subrc
       .
ENDIF.
* Identify SID value for characteristics value
CALL FUNCTION 'RRSI_SID_VAL_SINGLE_CONVERT'
EXPORTING
      i_iobjnm              = 'OCALDAY'
*     I_S_COB_PRO           =
      i_sid                 = l_0calday_sid
IMPORTING
      e_chavl               = l_0calday_chavl
*     E_S_NODESID           =
EXCEPTIONS
      no_value_for_sid      = 1
      x_message             = 2
      OTHERS                = 3
                  .
IF sy-subrc <> 0.
  RAISE EXCEPTION TYPE cx_rscnv_exception
```

```
        EXPORTING
        attr1  = ' RRSI_SID_VAL_SINGLE_CONVERT '
        attr2  = 'Error converting SID to value'
*       attr3  = sy-subrc
          .
      ENDIF.
```

Deletion of Characteristics

In addition to adding a new characteristic, it is possible to delete characteristics from a dimension table. This process is simply defined in remodeling, and at first, it results in only the respective characteristic being removed from the dimension table (see figure 9–13).

Figure 9–13

Deletion of a characteristic during remodeling

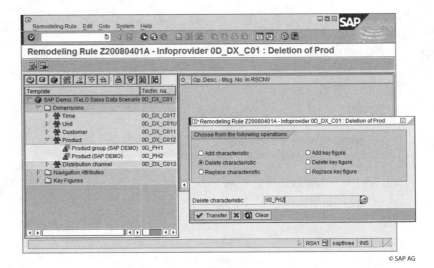

© SAP AG

Reduction of granularity

Contrary to the addition of new characteristics or the replacement of characteristics, it is possible that after the deletion of a characteristic, data records with an identical combination of SIDs exist in a dimension table. For example, if there were respective DIM-IDs in the dimension table prior to deletion of the characteristic that referred to the combination of product number 01 and product group A as well as to product number 02 and product group A, the two DIM-IDs in the dimension table would still exist after the deletion of the product number and they would refer to the same SID combination, in this case, product group A (see figure 9–14).

However, since the combination of all SIDs in a dimension table will always be described by a DIM-ID, the content of a dimension table will become inconsistent with the deletion of a characteristic if the deletion (as in the preceding example) will at the same time result in a reduction of granularity.

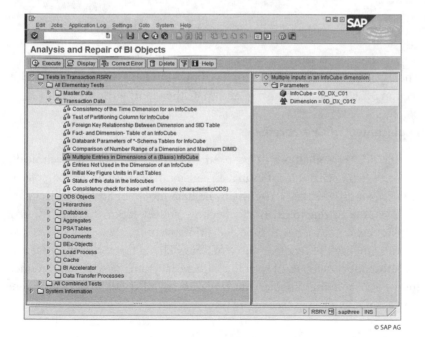

Dimension Table **before** Deletion of the Product

DIM-ID	Product	Product Group
1	01	A
2	02	A

DIM-ID	Product Group
1	A
2	A

Dimension Table **after** Deletion of the Product

Figure 9–14

Reduction of granularity in a dimension table with deletion of characteristics

This drawback will ultimately be detected when new data is entered into the BasisCube and the entering process will abort for exactly these inconsistencies.

To deal with inconsistencies that occur after a remodeling, BW offers a tool that looks for inconsistencies and corrects them. This tool is not started automatically after the remodeling. It should thus be started manually at the slightest suspicion of a possible reduction in granularity of a dimension table. This is the *search for multiple entries in dimensions of a (Basis) InfoCube* in the transaction RSRV (see figure 9–15).

Figure 9–15

Analysis of multiple entries to dimension tables

© SAP AG

After an analysis is executed, the detected inconsistencies (if any) will be shown as warnings in the error log and must be corrected via the *Correct Error* button.

Figure 9–16

Repair of duplicate entries in the dimension tables

Figure 9–16 shows the error protocol after the first analysis (18:10:19) and the subsequent error correction (18:10:56). The final analysis after the error correction (18:11:47) shows that no further duplicates can be found.

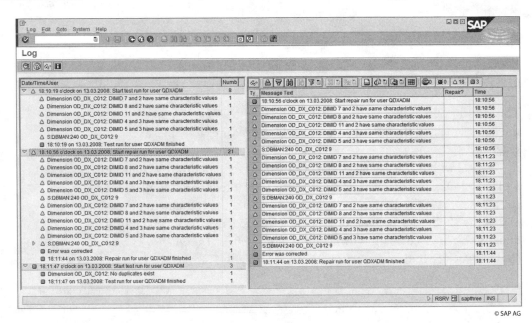

© SAP AG

The repair of duplicate entries in the dimension tables is also explained in section 32.2. Options on how to automate the repair will also be shown.

Replacement of Characteristics

In practice, remodeling will be used in particular cases to technically replace existing characteristics in a dimension table with other characteristics. This mostly makes sense when the data model of an InfoObject cannot be modified due to existing data content (see section 9.1) and where it is to be replaced by a newly modeled InfoObject.

To simplify the required entry of a new characteristic in this case and the subsequent deletion of the old characteristic during separate remodeling, the remodeling enables the replacement of a characteristic in one single remodeling step (see figure 9–17).

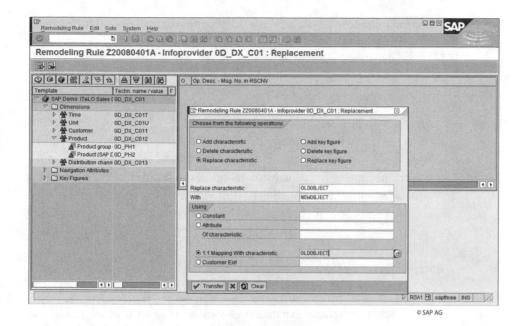

© SAP AG

All of the options that are available to enter a new characteristic are also available to fill this new characteristic. Thus, you won't need to fill the new characteristic with the same values as the old one.

Figure 9–17
Replacement of a characteristic with remodeling

The replacement of characteristics may lead to a reduction in granularity as described with the deletion of characteristics. Thus, you may be required to search for and delete duplicates in dimension tables.

A speciality with the replacement of characteristics is the option to replace a characteristic with itself (e.g., OCUSTOMER is replaced by OCUSTOMER). This at first glance senseless remodeling may be helpful if it was used to fill a characteristic differently than before.

Subsequent filling of characteristics

So, remodeling can be used to adjust historic data in a BasisCube if all the information that is corrected was available in the same dimension as the characteristic to be corrected.

9.2.2 Remodeling of the Fact Table

The remodeling of the fact table[72] is functionally mostly similar to the remodeling of the dimension tables and it serves to accomplish the following goals:

72. The following explanations always refer to both fact tables of a BasisCube, i.e., the uncompressed (F) fact table and the compressed (E) fact table.

■ To acquire new key figures in a filled cube where the key figures are to be filled with defined values

■ To delete key figures from a filled cube

■ To replace key figures with other InfoObjects, e.g., during standardization of several BasisCubes

Basically, with the remodeling of the fact table, an old structure will also be transferred into a new structure using internal tables. The remodeling has consequences for the key figure values of the fact table but not for the relational connection to the dimension tables or the number of data records.

Same as with the remodeling of dimension tables, some specific basic conditions and consequences have to be considered. We will explain them next.

Entry of New Key Figures

The entry of a new key figure causes a structural expansion of both fact tables. Such a structural expansion is also possible in normal modeling, even if a BasisCube contains data already. In this case, the key figure will be added with its initial value (zero) into the fact table.

The particular relevance of remodeling for the entry of new key figures comes from the option to provide the new key figure with specified values. However, to fill the key figure, only the definition of a constant value or the use of a self-coded user exit is provided (see figure 9–18).

Figure 9–18
Adding a key figure with
remodeling

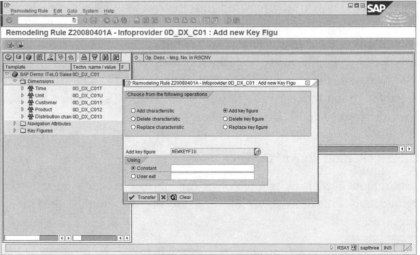

© SAP AG

Since the specification of a constant will in a majority of cases not meet the requirements, the use of the user exit (i.e., the implementation of a class to the interface IF_RSCNV_EXIT) is especially interesting.

Customer exit in the remodeling

The interface and the method to be implemented are the same as with remodeling of dimension tables (see section 9.2.1). However, crucial for the remodeling of the fact table is the fact that in the reference I_R_OLD, not only the key figures of the respective data record to be processed from the fact table can be found but also the dimension IDs of the data record in the fact table (or the SIDs in the case of line item dimensions).

On this basis, it is not only possible to refer to the key figures of the data record to be processed from the fact table to identify the key figure value but also to refer to the respective characteristic values and their attributes. This will be especially interesting when key figures that are attributed in the master data (e.g., weight of a product) are subsequently to be added as a key figure into the fact table.

To convert the SID values into characteristic values, you can use the function module RRSI_VAL_SID_SINGLE_CONVERT, as described in section 9.2.1.

Deletion of Key Figures

Same as with adding characteristics from dimension tables, it's possible to delete key figures from a fact table of a BasisCube. Only the key figure to be deleted needs to be indicated (see figure 9–19).

Figure 9–19

Deletion of a key figure with remodeling

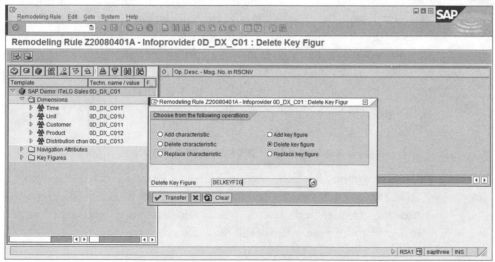

© SAP AG

Any given key figure of the BasisCube can be selected, but in the case of cubes with inventory key figures, the key figures that show inventory or the inventory changes cannot be selected.

The deletion of key figures plays a special role with BasisCubes where the compression of the F fact table is to be accompanied by an elimination of zero values (see section 6.4.1). It has to be considered that with the deletion of a key figure, data records with zero value may remain in the fact table (this is when the deleted key figure was the only key figure with this value).

These data records will *not* be deleted with the execution of the zero value elimination. They have to be deleted explicitly. In section 9.2.3, we'll explain how these zero values can be eliminated.

Replacement of Key Figures

In some particular cases, remodeling is used in practice to replace an existing key figure with another key figure. The most common reason is the need to use a key figure for the compilation of data in MultiProviders, either for its correlation with the key figure of another InfoProvider or because it has a different technical name. (see section 11.1.1). There are more reasons to replace key figures; however, they are too specific to be explained here.

To simplify the required entry of a new key figure and the subsequent deletion of the old key figure in a separate remodeling, there is an option to replace key figures in one single remodeling step (see figure 9–20).

By default, the value of the old key figure will be transferred to the new key figure. If another identification of the value of the new key figure was requested, it could only be made via a customer exit.

Same as with the deletion of key figures, data records with zero values can come up with the replacement and they will have to be removed with a separate zero value elimination.

9.2.3   Subsequent Zero Value Elimination

If the zero value elimination was not already activated with the design of a cube, the existing zero values will subsequently not be deleted during compression. The deletion of existing zero values needs to be executed rather explicitly to fully make use of the zero value elimination.

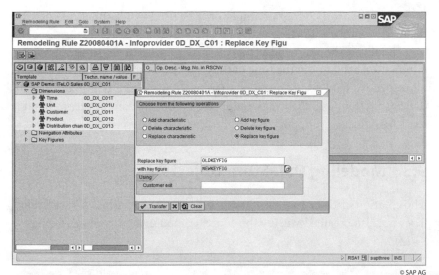

© SAP AG

Figure 9–20
Replacement of a key figure with remodeling

The program RSCDS_NULLELIM fulfills this purpose and deletes existing zero values from a BasisCube and its aggregates. The program can normally be started using the options shown in figure 9–21, but as an option, it can consider only the aggregates and not the fact table of the BasisCube (option NO_BASIS).

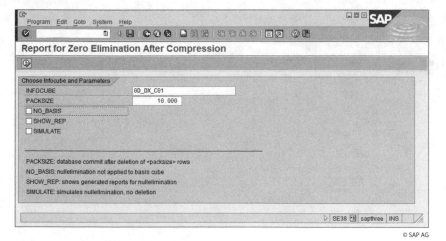

© SAP AG

Figure 9–21
Subsequent zero value elimination in the BasisCube

When using this program, you need to consider that for several reasons it will only be a mere workaround. The performance is poor and, depending on data volume and database systems, an excessive amount of archive logs is created so that the program might only be used in consultation with the database administration.

Thus, you should avoid using the program by having the zero value elimination activated at the time of the cube design. The "hard" deletion of all respective data records in a fact table using an SQL command on the database system usually brings better results, but we cannot recommend it since SAP does not support this procedure.[73]

9.3   Modeling DataStore Objects

Figure 9–22

Creation of a DataStore object in the Data Warehousing Workbench

The creation of DataStore objects is similar to the creation of BasisCubes. They are also created by using the context menu of an InfoArea (see figure 9–22).

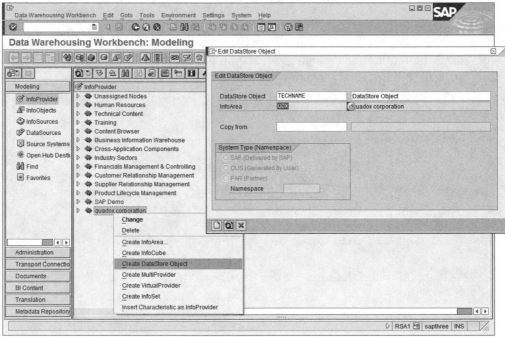

© SAP AG

At this point, however, you cannot indicate the type of DataStore object. This can only be stored in the properties of the DataStore object (see also figure 6–28 on page 93).

---

73.   The experiment-friendly reader will know how to interpret these lines.

The modeling of a DataStore object is much simpler than the modeling of a BasisCube insofar as you need to define only key and data fields and you don't need to configure settings to dimensions. A maximum of 16 characteristic InfoObjects can be used as key fields.

Similar to BasisCubes, there are limitations to modifying the data model of a DataStore object once the object has been filled with data. The following table shows the modeling options of filled DataStore Objects.

Modification of filled DataStore Objects

Modeling of a DataStore Object	Possible with Filled Object
Add key/data fields	✓
Delete key/data fields	✗
Move key/data fields	✗
Change DataStore type	✗

In practice, if the data model of a DataStore object was to be modified fundamentally, the content would have to be deleted or a new DataStore object would have to be modeled. Remodeling as with BasisCubes does not exist for DataStore objects yet.

9.4 Multidimensional Clustering

In section 7.3.2, we explained how to define multidimensional clustering for BasisCubes and DataStore objects. We mentioned that the selection of clustering characteristics of DataStore objects or the compilation of clustering dimensions of the BasisCube affects the performance gain from clustering. A bad selection of characteristics or dimensions may even result in poorer performance.

To modify the multidimensional clustering schema of BasisCubes and DataStore objects without prior deletion of data, you can use reclustering. It can be used in the following conditions:

- When the compilation of characteristics/dimensions creates blocks that are too small.
- When the characteristics/dimension builds the clustering schema in a wrong sequence.
- When a DataStore object or a BasisCube has not disposed of a multidimensional clustering schema.

Other than with range partitioning, no regular adjustments to the data structure have to be made with multidimensional clustering (see section 32.1) once an optimal design of the MDC fields and dimensions has been found. Until then, it might require a number of tests that only make sense with real data and are more easily realized with the option of remodeling than by a re-creation of the data targets.

Reclustering can be started from the context menu of the BasisCube or the DataStore object in the Data Warehousing Workbench, and it is identical to the configuration of the multidimensional clustering with an empty data target (see figure 9–23).

Figure 9–23

Reclustering of InfoProviders

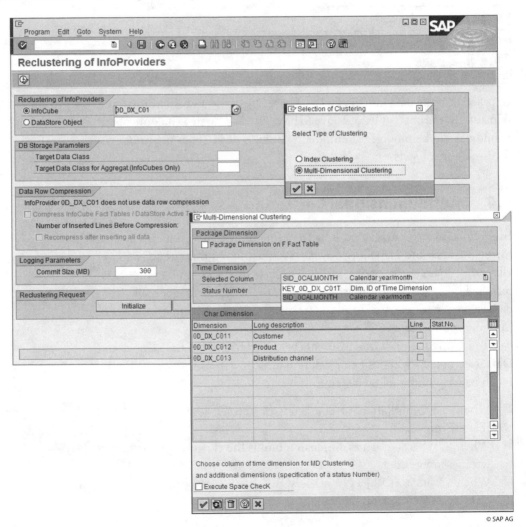

© SAP AG

Reclustering changes the metadata of an InfoProvider without enforcing compliance with a defined transportation route (see appendix C). Thus, inconsistencies in the definition of InfoProviders between the different systems in a transportation landscape can result and then InfoProviders can no longer be transported. When reclustering, consider reclustering in all systems within the transportation landscape.

With the execution of the reclustering, the E fact table[74] of the respective BasisCube or the table for active data of a DataStore object will be re-created in a so-called shadow table. The (initially empty) shadow table will be created and indexed similar to the existing tables but it will already be provided with the new clustering schema.

The data in the existing table will then be copied into the shadow table, which will represent a true copy of the existing table; the only difference being that it is provided with the required clustering schema.

On this basis, the existing tables will be exchanged for the shadow tables; i.e., the old fact table or the table for active data as well as the shadow table in the ABAP Dictionary remain identical, but the reference to the respective table in the database system will be modified. With this fast exchange, the data does not need to be copied back.

The shadow table that was created and filled during the reclustering will not be automatically deleted after repartitioning. The shadow table will only be deleted with a new repartitioning so that it can be used for the upcoming reclustering.

To free up memory space, you need to delete the shadow table manually in the ABAP Dictionary with the transaction SE11. You can identify the proper table in the monitor protocols.

Depending on the type and volume of reclustering, the shadow table that is created with reclustering may have significant data volume. The shadow table will not automatically be deleted by BW. However, it will lose its value when, after a successful reclustering, data is entered into the respective InfoProvider. Thus, after each reclustering, manually delete the shadow tables in the ABAP Dictionary.

---

74. Only the E-fact table comes with multidimensional clustering that has to be handled when reclustering.

III   Analytical Engine

All decision support systems (i.e., the analysis tools of the Business Explorer as well as third-party tools) refer to the data model of the data targets in the form of dimensions, characteristics, and key figures, and submit their queries to BW accordingly.

In BW, however, the data is stored only on a logical level in this way. For physical access, you refer to the different database tables of the enhanced star schema or the tables of DataStore Objects in the database system. Also, when you're accessing databases, you need to consider the status information on compression runs made, as well as the aggregates you can use to improve performance and many other factors.

Thus, the analytical engine stands between the decision support system (DSS) tools and the data management of BW, and it reformulates the queries it receives for the data targets in BW. The OLAP engine not only provides the DSS tools with BW data targets for reporting, it also defines its individual reporting objects. From a reporting view, the BW does not provide data targets but so-called **InfoProviders** as a basis for the data analysis.

Since the OLAP engine needs to consider status information from the staging engine (e.g., status of compression, usable aggregates), the analytical engine is very closely tied to data management and its basic design will be explained; even though it actually is a BI platform topic.

The following topics will be explained in detail in this chapter:

- Access to physically available data in InfoProviders
- Definition and access to virtual InfoProviders
- Use of the OLAP caching (including aggregates)
- Monitoring of the analytical engine

10 Access to Physical InfoProviders

Access to physically available data in BW (that is, data targets) is mostly accomplished by transforming the abstract data requirements of the OLAP engine that always refer to dimensions, characteristics, and key figures into physically available data structures.

Data models for reporting are the enhanced star schema of Basis-Cubes, the flat tables of DataStore Objects, and the master data tables of InfoObjects.

The result of the transformation can be the query of a simple table (for DataStore Objects), or the dissolution of relational correlations of the enhanced star schema (for BasisCubes), where attributes (possibly in consideration of a time dependency) and texts may be read as well and where inclusion tables of external hierarchies need to be dissolved.

Next we'll cover the following topics:

- Access to BasisCubes
- Access to DataStore Objects
- Access to InfoObjects

10.1 Access to BasisCubes

Cubes are created as the primary basis for data analysis and basically require no further treatment. The core task in the transformation of OLAP queries to BasisCubes lies in the dissolution of relational correlations between fact and dimension tables and even master data that is used in the query.

To ensure a consistent and nonvolatile view of the data, you must give particular consideration to the status of the staging engine. The forming of partial queries has particular significance to optimization of data analysis performance. How the status of the staging engine is to be considered and how partial queries are built will be explained in the following sections.

10.1.1 Status of the Staging Engine

In BW, data analysis is based on qualitatively assured and comprehensible data. To ensure this and to still meet the specific requirements for individual analysis of **consistency, completeness,** and **accuracy** of data, there are different access procedures:

- Dirty
- All
- Qualok
- Rollup

Dirty

With *dirty* access, all requests from a BasisCube will be read in the data analysis whether they are error free and completed or whether they have errors and are still being processed.

All

The *all* access method includes only error-free and completed requests in an analysis. Requests are considered error free when they are defined as error free in the data target administration. This can result from an automatic entry of an error-free technical request status but also from manual maintenance of the status request.

Qualok

The *qualok* access method expands the *all* access method with the condition that (error-free and completed) requests will go into the data analysis only if no requests are entered earlier that were not error free or completed.

The requests 95 to 99 shown in figure 10–1 are read by the *qualok* access method.[75] However, request 101 would only be read by the *all* access method.

Rollup

The *rollup* access method expands the *qualok* method by considering aggregates or Business Intelligence Accelerator (BIA) indexes. As long as the data target is a BasisCube with active aggregates of BIA indexes, requests will be considered by the *qualok* access type only when they are rolled up in the active and filled aggregates.[76]

For the BasisCube shown in figure 10–2, only the requests 95 to 98 were rolled up in aggregates and thus fulfill the criteria of the status *rollup*. The *qualok* access method, however, would also include request 99 into the analysis.

---

75. In the administration of InfoProviders, the SID of the request ID is shown. The allocation of SID to request ID can be identified in the table /BI0/SREQUID.
76. Not activated and unfilled agregates will not be considered.

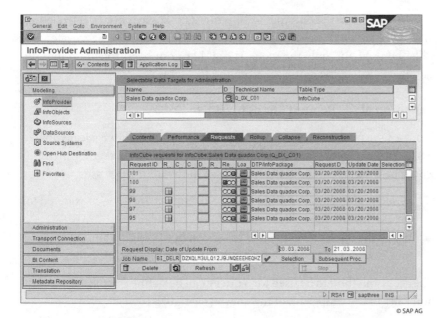

Figure 10–1
Requests with the status of qualok

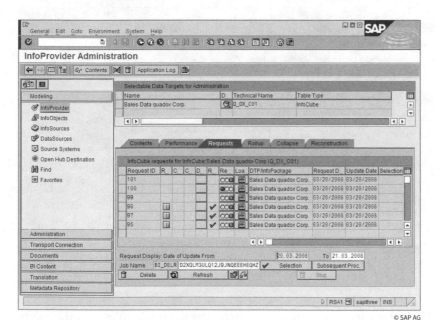

Figure 10–2
Requests with the status of rollup

By default, data analysis uses the *rollup* method. This is the only way to ensure that each query on a BasisCube always treats the existing data structures (i.e., aggregates or BIA indexes) optimally.

With the other access methods, requests that have not been rolled up into aggregates yet may need to be read. In this case, the aggregates will still[77] be used and only the requests that have not been rolled up into the aggregates will be read directly from the fact table.

Definition of the Request Status to Be Used

From a user perspective, the default access method *rollup* basically makes sense. However, there are special instances where other request methods would be desirable. This is especially true in the following cases:

- When requests that have not been rolled up yet are to be considered for the manual review of data quality
- When the most current data is to be shown too (e.g., planning requests that have not been completed), with the use of real-time cubes.

The access method to be used for a query can be defined using the transaction RSRT in the properties of the query (see figure 10–4).[78]

Figure 10–3

Definition of access methods in the query properties

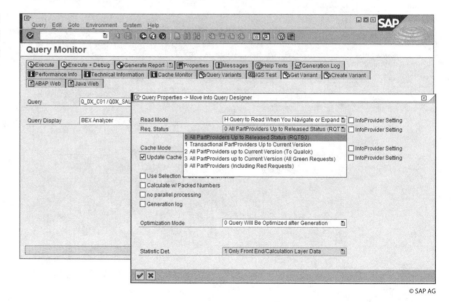

© SAP AG

The parameter value 1 plays a particular role. It basically uses the *rollup* access method; but, with real-time cubes it uses the *qualok* method, so that,

---

77. Different indications in various documentations are wrong.
78. 0 = rollup, 2 = qualok, 3 = all, 9 = dirty

specifically with real-time analyses and planning cubes, requests can be read that have been completed but not rolled up yet.

In addition to the ability to define the access method to be used in the properties of the query, there is an option to control the access method via the definition of the query.

This is basically possible by adding to a query the characteristic OREQUID, which is part of the package dimension of each BasisCube. Thus, the query will be changed to the *dirty* access method.

There is also the option to use the characteristic OREQUID in combination with predefined variables.[79]

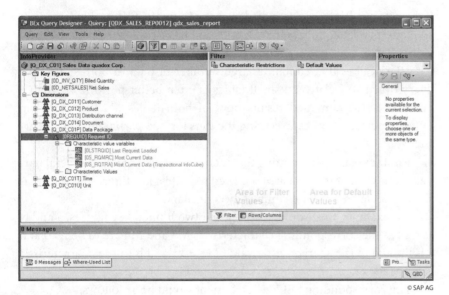

Figure 10–4
Definition of access methods in the query definition

Here, the variables OS_RQMRC (most current data) match the access method *qualok* and the variable OS_RQTRA matches the same method but is limited to real-time cubes.

Further, there is the variable OLSTRQID that describes the request IDs of the latest-entered request in a cube.

The access methods are to be defined in the current patch level 18 of SAP BW in the properties as well as in the definition of the query. With the next releases, it is to be expected that the current solution will be replaced by central maintenance of the access method in the query definition.

---

79. The variables are part of the BI content and need to be taken from it.

10.1.2   Partial Queries

The transformation of an OLAP query into a database query could basically result in a single SQL statement[80] that completely dissolves the relations of the enhanced star schema. However, the use of a single query does not always make sense from a performance perspective. Here there are especially two cases that need to be mentioned:

- BasisCubes whose data is distributed over both fact tables
- Limited key figures whose result pools are not congruent with each other

Partial queries on fact tables   If the data of a BasisCube is spread over the F and the E fact table (since not all requests were compressed yet), both fact tables will be considered individual BasisCubes and each will be read in its separate query. Especially with BasisCubes that contain a large number of data in both tables, the query over two (relatively) small tables is often better performing than a query over the compiled results pool of both tables. Further, BW can improve performance by executing the thus formed partial queries in parallel.[81]

Partial queries on limited key figures   Another reason for splitting the query on a data target into several partial queries is that the data area required to build a key figure and the actually read data area are not completely congruent.

For example, this would be the case if two limited key figures, a and b, as well as the corresponding characteristics M3 and M4 are to be read and a is limited to the characteristic value M1 = x1 and b to the characteristic value M2 = x2.

The corresponding SELECT statement would be as follows:

select M3, M4, a, b
from <cube and dimensions>
where (M1 = x1) or (M2 = x2)

The data area selected for a and b is unnecessarily large. Figure 10–5 shows the difference between the required data area and data area that's actually read using this example.

---

80. Master data attributes, text, and hierarchies will be read only in a second step.
81. The option to improve performance with parallelization uses BW for each type of partial query.

Characteristic M1	Characteristic M2	Characteristic M3	Characteristic M4	Key Figure a	Key Figure b
x1	b2	m12	m22	900	120
x1	c2	m11	m23	650	80
x1	c2	m13	m24	700	130
b1	x2	m14	m24	750	120
b1	x2	m14	m24	180	40
b1	x2	m13	m22	90	35

With a SELECT statement actually read amount of data

Characteristic M1	Characteristic M3	Characteristic M4	Key Figure a
x1	m12	m22	900
x1	m11	m23	650
x1	m13	m24	700

Characteristic M2	Characteristic M3	Characteristic M4	Key Figure b
x2	m14	m24	120
x2	m14	m24	40
x2	m13	m22	35

Required (queried) amount of data

Content will not be a problem if too much data is selected from the database since the analytical engine will again filter the data as specified in the definition of a query. However, the reading of unnecessarily large data quantities produces an unnecessarily high resource consumption, which results in poor performance. Further, with the OR clause for database systems, the SQL query generally requires more effort.

In such cases,[82] the analytical engine breaks a received query for the database system down into several partial queries and its results will later be put together again. For this example, this would be the following two partial queries:

Figure 10–5

Difference between the required and the selected data area

select M3, M4, a	*select M3, M4, b*
from <cube and dimensions>	*from <cube and dimensions>*
where (M1 = x1)	*where (M2 = x2)*

This functioning of the analytical engine can only be influenced with the definition of the OLAP queries.

---

82. Apart from the described combination, there are a number of other cases where the selected data volume is unnecessarily large. They are not dealt with in detail since here only the resulting functioning of the OLAP engine is relevant.

In particular, the creation of partial queries that refer to distinct limited key figures is relevant for tuning queries since these have to be dealt with in a special way with the definition of aggregates; they will come up again in this context in section 13.1.

10.2 Access to DataStore Objects

As per definition, data in InfoObjects and BasisCubes is suitable for reporting since, prior to it being entered in these data targets, its consistency in regards to content (e.g., correct date formats) and integrity (existence of SID values) is reviewed or created, if necessary. A detailed description of consistency and integrity tests can be found in chapter 23.

> DataStore Objects are not built according to a star schema and do not offer the option to build aggregates. Thus, you should absolutely avoid the use of DataStore Objects for data analysis if there are not compelling reasons to use them.

When data is being entered into DataStore Objects, no consistency test will be made, so characteristic values may be stored in a DataStore Object without existing master data (and master data IDs). These missing master data IDs will result in the fact that data in DataStore Objects might not meet the requirements of referential integrity and consistency. This would lead to problems if the data analysis was not only to refer to stored characteristics of the DataStore Object but also the navigation attributes of these characteristics. In this case, the necessary relations between the master data table and DataStore Object cannot be dissolved when master data records do not exist for the characteristic values to be entered. In the worst case, this might lead to different results, depending on the analyses.

Since release 7 of SAP BW, each DataStore Object is an InfoProvider at the same time and can be used for data analysis. The analysis capability, however, is limited to the use of InfoObjects in the key and data fields of the DataStore Objects. This definition is made in the maintenance of a DataStore Object (see figure 10–6).

The testing of existing master data IDs is integrated into the activation of new data for standard DataStore Objects (see section 17.1.2), so navigation attributes can be activated only with this type of DataStore Objects.

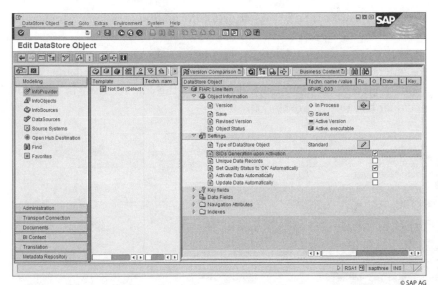

Figure 10–6
Generation of master data IDs for DataStore Objects

The validation regarding the existence of master data IDs in characteristic values can significantly decrease performance for the activation of new data. An alternative to the direct reporting of DataStore Objects is the use of InfoSets that can also access data of non-reporting-enabled DataStore Objects (see section 11.2).

In the case of DataStore Objects, the data analysis is always based on the table for active data. This table contains only error-free and completely loaded data, so that an explicit consideration of the staging engine status with the use of, for example, read pointers, will not be required.

Status of the staging engine

Unlike with access to BasisCubes, no partial queries will be created with access to DataStore Objects. Rather, the larger data volume on read accesses will be accepted in favor of a single query.

Partial queries

10.3 Access to InfoObjects

The master data attributes and texts of characteristic InfoObjects, as well as their external hierarchies, are usually only used for data analysis to categorize transactional data. In specific cases, it may make sense to provide master data of an individual InfoObject for the data analysis without establishing a relationship with transactional data. This is especially interesting when the identification of master data information (e.g., on customers or products) is an explicit task of the data analysis.

For this reason, InfoObjects with master data can be considered Info-Providers, just as BasisCubes and DataStore Objects, from a data analysis point of view. A precondition is the entry of the characteristic in the Info-Provider tree (see figure 10–7).

Figure 10–7

Inserting characteristics as InfoProviders

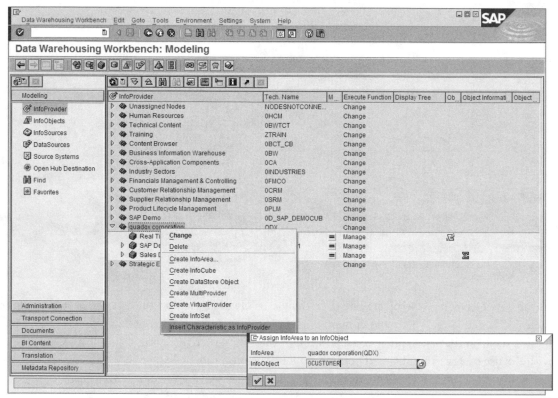

© SAP AG

Once a characteristics InfoObject is defined as an InfoProvider, it can be used as an InfoProvider and presents itself in the form of dimensions (one dimension for the characteristic and all its attributes) and key figures.

Since the navigation attributes of the InfoObject are available for the data analysis as characteristics, their attributes and external hierarchies are also available to the data analysis.

Handling of
master data versions

With access to the database, only the active master data will be read; i.e., master data of an InfoObject that will have to be activated in a change run (see also section 7.1.2) will not be considered for the data analysis. In this case, the analysis of InfoObjects is consistent with the use of Info-Objects in combination with BasisCubes or DataStore Objects.

For an InfoObject whose master data attributes or texts are time dependent, the indication of a respective key date on which the data is to be read is made in the same way as the analysis of master data with Basis-Cubes and DataStore Objects. This means that an OLAP query needs to indicate a key date on which the master data is to be read.

Handling time dependency

11 Virtual InfoProvider

Access to data targets with physically available data meets only part of the requirements demanded from an OLAP engine. During data analysis, it may be just as important to put several physical InfoProviders into context or even to get data from totally different sources.

For this purpose, BW offers different virtual InfoProviders—that is, metadata objects that are displayed as full InfoProviders but do not have individual data structures to store data. The data from a virtual Info-Provider is instead read from defined data sources at the time of the data analysis.

Depending on the goal to be achieved with the use of a virtual Info-Provider and the data sources to be referenced for the analysis, different types of virtual InfoProviders can be used:

- *MultiProviders* to consolidate data from other InfoProviders and to bring it into context
- *InfoSets* to relationally link data from BasisCubes, DataStore Objects, and InfoObjects
- *Service InfoCubes* to implement specific analysis requirements that can be met only with a user-defined program logic

The definition and functioning of MultiProviders, InfoSets, and Service InfoCubes will be explained in the following sections. *RemoteCubes* also belong to the group of virtual InfoProviders. RemoteCubes are used to analyze data in real time.

11.1 MultiProvider

MultiProviders have two functions within SAP BW: On the one hand, they bring data together from different InfoProviders (BasisCubes, InfoSets, InfoObjects, DataStore Objects). On the other hand, they form a logical layer over these selected InfoProviders and they thus abstract the reporting of physical databases.

MultiProviders as logical reporting layers

The function of the underlying InfoProviders will not be impacted by the creation of a MultiProvider. Thus, it will still be possible to extract data from the InfoProviders.

To form a logical layer over other InfoProviders, the use of MultiProviders makes sense even if only a single InfoProvider will be part of the MultiProvider because the underlying InfoProviders can be enhanced, modified, or even exchanged completely without any impact on the query definition of the MultiProvider. This option may be especially interesting for InfoProviders with physical data storage (BasisCubes, DataStore Objects, InfoObjects)—see figure 11–1).

Figure 11–1

Use of MultiProviders as logical reporting layers

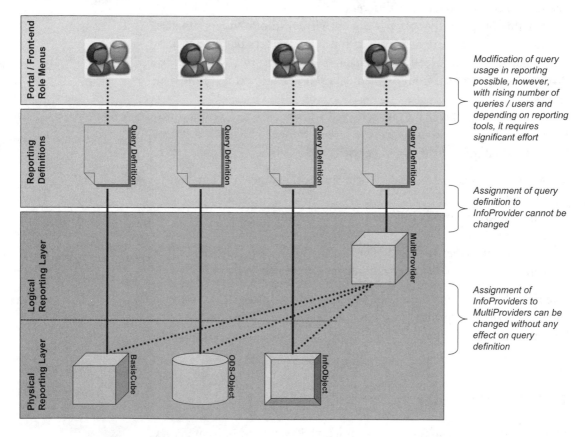

Thus, MultiProviders always have significant advantages in terms of flexibility for the further development of a BW system by disconnecting the definition of queries from the definition of the physical data model.

> Never develop queries based on BasisCubes, DataStore Objects, or
> InfoObjects. Instead, abstract the physical data management with the use of
> MultiProviders on which the queries are defined. This additional effort in
> terms of definition and maintenance of the MultiProvider quickly pays off in
> administrative advantages.

The actual task of MultiProviders, however, is not to provide a logical reporting layer, but rather to consolidate data from several InfoProviders, if required. This requirement can have different causes:

MultiProviders to consolidate InfoProviders

- There are several InfoProviders that represent self-contained areas from a management perspective. They have a joint subset (e.g., all InfoProviders have a customer number) but an otherwise heterogeneous data structure. The characteristics that form the intersection should be brought into context so that they can be consolidated for reporting.
- Data from different InfoProviders are to be brought into context and for technical reasons may not be stored in one InfoProvider (e.g., since structure-similar data is allocated to BasisCubes, virtual cubes, and DataStore Objects).
- Data is to be brought into context that was allocated to several InfoProviders for design reasons (e.g., planning and actual data).
- Data was allocated to different InfoProviders to improve performance and has to be consolidated for reporting (see also chapter 7).

Which InfoProviders are to be included in a MultiProvider will be indicated when the MultiProvider is created, but it can be changed at a later time. All InfoCubes (even RemoteCubes and Service InfoCubes but not other MultiProviders), DataStore Objects, InfoObjects, InfoSets, and aggregation levels of the integrated planning are available (see figure 11–2).

InfoProviders that are contained within a MultiProvider define the InfoObjects that a MultiProvider can provide for data analysis. Even though a MultiProvider is defined only in the metadata of BW, the definition is basically made in the same way as with BasisCubes; i.e., dimensions need to be defined and provided with InfoObjects, navigation attributes need to be defined, and so on.

However, this definition is completely independent from the design of the underlying InfoProvider. While a BasisCube is only to be modeled according to technical aspects (see section 8.1), InfoObjects in the

Figure 11–2

Creation of a MultiProvider

superordinate MultiProvider may be arranged in the dimensions according to business considerations.

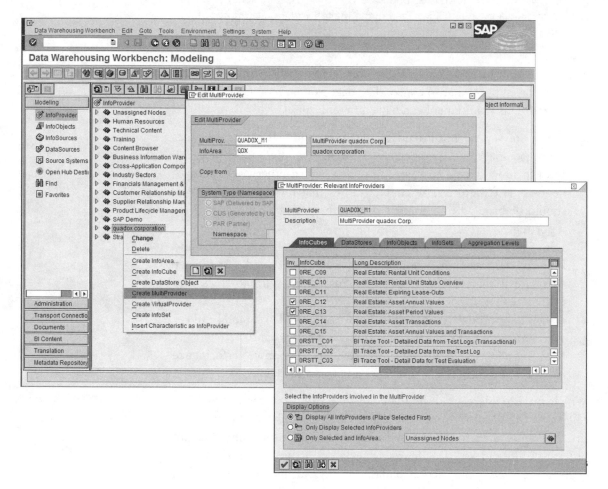

When you're configuring the consolidation of several InfoProviders into one MultiProvider, you need to consider several aspects:

- Rules to consolidate data
- Creation of subqueries to access MultiProviders (static and dynamic selection of the components of the MultiProvider for access)

The configuration of MultiProviders will be explained in detail in the following sections.

11.1.1 Consolidating Data

To consolidate several InfoProviders into one MultiProvider, BW uses the principle of a **UNION query;** i.e., all table fields (in this case InfoObjects in InfoProviders) with the same name will be mapped on each other. Key figure fields with identical names will be aggregated if they have identical characteristics keys (see figure 11–3).

Figure 11–3
Merging data in MultiProviders

MultiProvider (prior to aggregation by OLAP Engine)

Customer	Material	Month	Sales	Discount	Accounts Receivable
4711	ABC	01.2006	1,000.00	25.00	0
4711	ABC	02.2006	500.00	5.00	0
4711	DEF	04.2006	1,250.00	20.00	0
4711	ABC	05.2006	650.00	15.00	0
4711	ABC	01.2006	0	0	125.00
4711	ABC	02.2006	0	0	130.00
4711	#	04.2006	0	25.00	0

Σ

MultiProvider (after aggregation by OLAP Engine)

Customer	Material	Month	Sales	Discount	Accounts Receivable
4711	ABC	01.2006	1,000.00	25.00	125.00
4711	ABC	02.2006	500.00	5.00	130.00
4711	DEF	04.2006	1,250.00	20.00	0
4711	ABC	05.2006	650.00	15.00	0
4711	#	04.2006	0	25.00	0

InfoProviders

Customer	Material	Month	Sales	Discount
4711	ABC	01.2006	1,000.00	25.00
4711	ABC	02.2006	500.00	5.00
4711	DEF	04.2006	1,250.00	20.00
4711	ABC	05.2006	650.00	15.00

Customer	Material	Month			Accounts Receivable
4711	ABC	01.2006			125.00
4711	ABC	02.2006			130.00

Customer		Month	Discount
4711		04.2006	25.00

If an InfoProvider does not have an InfoObject that a MultiProvider refers to, then the respective InfoObject for this InfoProvider will be interpreted with the value # for characteristics and the value 0 for key figures.

> The most common erroneous belief about BW needs to be explicitly corrected at this point: During a query, MultiProviders do *not* run a joint query over the respective InfoProviders! The consolidation of the respective Info-Providers can instead be compared to a UNION query.

In a UNION query, only identical fields (here characteristic InfoObjects) would be mapped to each other. Especially with referencing objects (see section 6.2.4), it can be desirable to map different InfoObjects to each other

Consolidation of referencing characteristics

since they have the same master data and should thus be brought into context.

For example, an InfoObject 0MATERIAL from an InfoProvider and an InfoObject ZMATERIAL from another InfoProvider in the MultiProvider can be brought into context in the InfoObject 0MATERIAL (see figure 11–4).

Figure 11–4

Identification of the InfoObjects of a MultiProvider

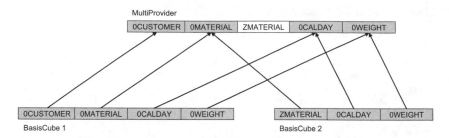

For such a special detail to be considered when mapping referencing characteristics, the characteristics need to be mapped in an ***identification*** when the MultiProvider is defined (see figure 11–5).

Figure 11–5

Identification with definition of MultiProviders

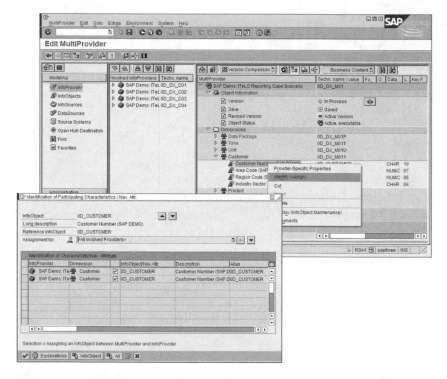

For the identification, BW attempts to map the same characteristics it would in a normal UNION query. In the case of referencing characteristics, the identification can be adapted. However, only characteristics that are basically the same can be mapped to each other; a completely unrestricted definition of the mapping is not possible.

Further, it is also possible to deactivate the identification even if it was technically possible. The MultiProvider will then be instructed to not read a characteristic from the respective InfoProvider but to supply the value # instead.

Selection of key figures

For key figures, there is no identification comparable to the characteristics. However, with a *selection,* you can define which key figures of an InfoProvider are to be provided to the MultiProvider (see figure 11–6).

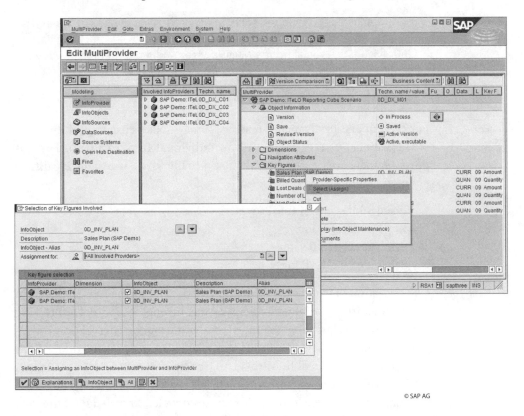

© SAP AG

If identical key figures (InfoObjects) of several InfoProviders are to be brought into context, they will be added to the MultiProvider. Key figures that are mapped in several InfoProviders by different InfoObjects will also result in different key figure objects in the MultiProvider. For example, if a

Figure 11–6

Selection of key figures with definition of MultiProviders

modeling error occurs and the key figure SALES is provided to the Multi-Provider once from the InfoObject ZSALES and once as SALES, the Multi-Provider will display both key figures independently from each other. To subsequently remove such modeling errors, key figure InfoObjects can be exchanged through remodeling (see section 9.2.2).

11.1.2 Creation of Subqueries

When a query is run that is based on a MultiProvider, this query is split into several subqueries, one for each underlying InfoProvider. Each of these subqueries can be compared to a query on the respective InfoProvider and can again be broken down into further partial queries.

In SAP terminology, the terms *subquery* and *partial query* are often not differentiated. For clarity, we will use the term *subquery* only for queries on InfoProviders that result from a MultiProvider and the term *partial query* to refer to the splitting of a query (which may be a subquery) into an InfoProvider.

Exclusion of InfoProviders   For content and performance reasons, it may make sense to prohibit individual subqueries (i.e., the query on individual InfoProviders). For this purpose, there are four options that are usually used for completely different motivations:

- Fixed addressing of InfoProviders
- Key figure selection
- Selection by fixed values
- Selection by OLAP hints

Fixed addressing of   The easiest way for individual InfoProviders to be specifically included in
InfoProviders   or excluded from a MultiProvider query is through the direct addressing (or the direct exclusion) of the InfoProvider during the query. For this purpose, the characteristic 0INFOPROV is available (in the package dimension) to help select individual InfoProviders (see figure 11–7).

The use of the characteristic 0INFOPROV is a flexible option to influence the analytical engine. However, it requires detailed knowledge of the data model and is to be selected specifically for particular requirements, such as error diagnostics.

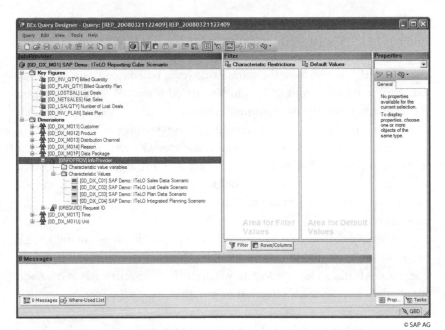

Figure 11–7
Fixed addressing of InfoProviders in MultiProvider queries

The fixed addressing of InfoProviders, however, is not a suitable basic tool to define queries since an adaptation of the data model also needs to come with a modification of all related queries.

Key figure selection represents another approach to selecting the Info-Providers to be read. Depending on the information requirements of a query, it will be decided which InfoProvider is to be included in a Multi-Provider query.

Key figure selection

This decision is influenced by the key figures selected in a query: If an InfoProvider does not supply any selected key figures, it will not be included in the MultiProvider query. If InfoProviders were not to be included in a MultiProvider query depending on the query or selection, it may make sense to define identical key figures (e.g., sales) in the form of two different InfoObjects that are distributed to two InfoProviders.

Another possibility to exclude InfoProviders depending on the key figures used in a MultiProvider query is via the key figure selection in the definition of the MultiProvider (see figure 11–6). If a key figure is not selected for a MultiProvider in this definition, the InfoProvider will appear to the MultiProvider to not contain this key figure and the key figure would not need to be read when asked for.

Selection by fixed values   The definition of fixed values for BasisCubes and DataStore Objects is suitable for performance optimization when the BasisCubes and DataStore Objects involved with a MultiProvider contain data where one or several characteristics always have the same value (e.g., when in a BasisCube only data for the business unit 0001 is to be carried forward). Such a situation was explained with the partitioning on the application level in section 7.3.

The analytical engine can consider these settings when running a query and exclude all BasisCubes and DataStore Objects where it is clear from the definition of a fixed value that they will not supply any data. Fixed values are to be installed with the definition of the respective data targets and the installation is limited to DataStore Objects and BasisCubes (see also figure 7–26).[83]

Selection by OLAP hints   An approach similar to the selection of fixed values is using OLAP hints, which are limited to accessing BasisCubes. Prior to running a sub-query, OLAP hints aim to identify whether the respective BasisCube will supply data for the given selection or whether its reading can be omitted right away.

Unlike with fixed values, it is not staticly defined which single values a BasisCube can deliver for certain characteristics. Instead, prior to running a subquery, it will be dynamically identified what values a BasisCube can supply for a certain characteristic and decided on this basis whether the cube is to be read or not.

The dynamic identification of characteristic values that a BasisCube can supply is based on the content of the dimension tables of a BasisCube. To identify what values a characteristic has in a cube, the dimension table that contains the characteristic will be searched for its characteristic values. Thus, the use of OLAP hints inevitably limits the characteristics in normal dimension tables. Characteristics in line-item dimensions cannot be used by OLAP hints.

The demand for small dimension tables (see section 8.1) is thus especially relevant for the use of OLAP hints. OLAP hints only bring performance advantages when the dimension tables can be quickly checked for the respective characteristic value. If a characteristic is to be analyzed in a large dimension table by OLAP hints, the search of the dimension table

---

83. The definition of fixed values must be made with the modeling of a data target and it will no longer be possible when data is contained in the data target.

prior to each evaluation will result in unjustifiably high effort and it will worsen rather than improve performance.[84]

> Dimension tables may contain characteristic values that can no longer be used in a BasisCube. This phenomenon mostly occurs after compression of the fact table with zero value elimination, after deletion of requests, and after selective deletion. So you should regularly trim the dimension tables of your BasisCubes to remove such entries. Details on dimension trimming can be found in section 32.2.

Given these disadvantages from the use of OLAP hints, the use of OLAP hints needs to be activated manually for each MultiProvider and characteristic by entering the MultiProvider and the characteristic in the table RRKMULTIPROVHINT. For this purpose, the Create Entries function in the transaction SE16 can be used (see figure 11–8).

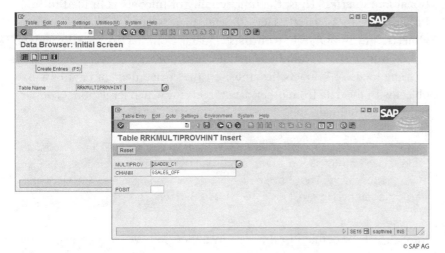

© SAP AG

Figure 11–8
Configuration of OLAP hints

The numerator defined the order in which tests are to be made. If a cube drops out after one value, the following values will not need to be tested. Thus, put characteristics with quick testing up front and move slower ones further in the back.

The problem with this system mostly results from the fact that a single unsuitably-modeled BasisCube within a MultiProvider will be enough to

---

84. Only the dimension tables of the BasisCubes but not the dimension tables of aggregates will be searched. The selection of suitable aggregates is made only after consideration of the OLAP hint so that the creation of aggregates does not have any advantages for OLAP hints.

make the use of OLAP hints for a characteristic disadvantageous. It would certainly have been better if OLAP hints were to be activated per Basis-Cube and dimension.

11.2 InfoSets

With release 7 of BW, InfoSets have significantly gained in functionality. Not only are they seen as a SQL-type appendix to the analytical engine, but the OLAP engine was enhanced by diverse, specific functions to further handle the result sets from InfoSets. In the broadest sense, InfoSets are thus an equivalent to MultiProviders. They are also used to consolidate data from several InfoProviders and to bring them into context.

Other than with a MultiProvider where similar data is consolidated in a sort of UNION query, InfoSets allow for data to be consolidated in relational *join queries.* Thus, the functionality of InfoSets is limited to Info-Providers with physical data storage; that is, BasisCubes, DataStore Objects, and InfoObjects with master data. Contrary to MultiProviders, virtual InfoProviders cannot be handled by InfoSets.

The focus of InfoSets lies, thus, on the enrichment of data of a BW object with the data from other data targets for which a relational connection is to be defined.

The term *InfoSet* was not selected wisely for BW. In SAP ERP, there is an InfoSet and an InfoSet query that are defined by the transactions SQ02 or SQ10, respectively. They have nothing to do with the InfoSet in SAP BW and are thus referred to as Classic InfoSets in BW context.

Creation of InfoSets InfoSets can be defined in the Data Warehousing Workbench or alternatively via transaction RSISET (see figure 11–9).

Contrary to the other virtual InfoProviders, the modeling of an InfoSet has no similarity to the modeling of a BasisCube. Rather, InfoSets are defined by the relational connection of the BW objects within the InfoSet. The individual BW objects are displayed in tables,[85] even if this

---

85. SAP BW offers two forms of display for the modeling of InfoSets: the display in a network plan and the tree display. All following explanations and figures refer only to the display in a network plan. The use of the tree display appears to us to be less intuitive. The display can be selected via the menu item *Settings→Display.* Depending on the patch level of the system, you may need to restart the InfoSet maintenance before the other form of display will be activated.

– as for BasisCubes – does not correspond with the physical model (see figure 11–10).

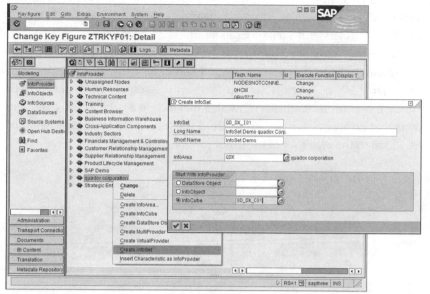

Figure 11–9
Creation of InfoSets

© SAP AG

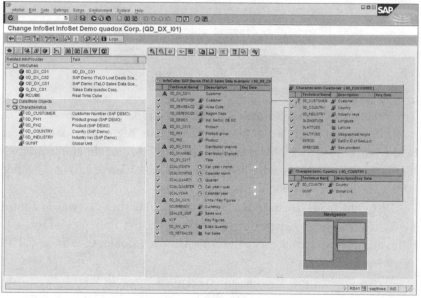

Figure 11–10
Definition of InfoSets

© SAP AG

To define the join condition between two tables within an InfoSet, you link the identical fields in both tables to each other. Thus, especially identical InfoObjects, or InfoObjects with the same basic characteristics, are suited. Technically, all InfoObjects that are identical in data type and field length can be connected with each other in a join connection.

Inner join   By default, any join condition is executed as an ***inner join*** (in the SAP documentation also referred to as *equal join*). Here, the data records from two related tables are consolidated to show the respective values in both tables of the connected fields. This also means that a data record from one table that does not have an equivalent in the respective other table will not be added to the result set of the inner join. (see figure 11–11).

Figure 11–11

Inner join (equal join)

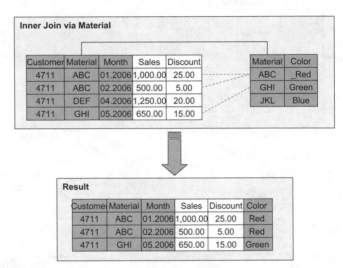

Multiplied key figure values   The modeling of an InfoSet requires special focus on the design of the relational connection. If this was omitted, erroneous key figure values might be the outcome. Two tables are always connected in a join connection so that each data record of a table is connected to each data record of the other table as far as a connection can be made.

Different from the example in figure 11–11, the material in figure 11–12 is not the full key of the material master but only part of the key. From an otherwise unchanged definition of the InfoSet, the result will be as shown in the figure.

When modeling a relation between two tables within an InfoSet, you must always ensure that no n:m relation is created. If there is only one table with a key figure, the InfoSet may describe a maximum of a 1:*n* relation where the key figure needs to be on the *n* side. If key figure values are extracted from both tables, the InfoSet may only describe a 1:1 relation.

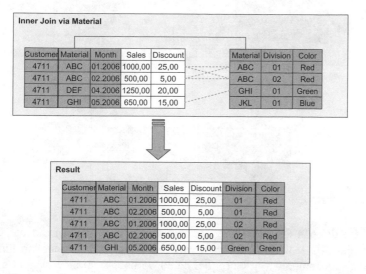

Figure 11–12
Multiplied key figure values in InfoSets

When modeling InfoSets, always ensure that the full key is mapped in the relationship of InfoObjects. You should avoid adding more than one Basis-Cube or one DataStore Object to an InfoSet; if this is not possible, you will have to be very aware of the relationship between the linked objects.

In some special cases, the records in a table are read by a join query even if there are no corresponding data records in the related table. For example, this makes sense if transitive attributes are to be read to an InfoProvider but it cannot be ensured that the master data of the attribute-carrying characteristics are available in the system.

Left outer join

For these purposes, a left outer join can be defined instead of an inner join. When a table is connected to another table via a left outer join, all data records from one table will be connected only to the respective data records from the other table (see figure 11–13).

Thus, the definition of a left outer join inevitably requires determining from which table all data records are to be read or from which table only the respective available data records or initial values are to be added. To explain this with the term *left outer,* it needs to be defined which table is to be placed at the "left" and which at the "right" side of the join.

Figure 11–13

Left outer join

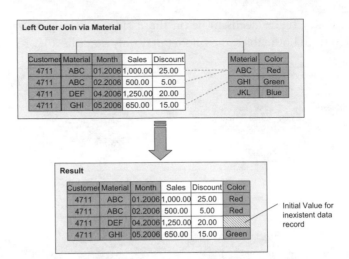

Before using a left outer join to define an InfoSet, you should consider whether it is really necessary or whether—possibly with meeting further basic requirements—an inner join could be used alternatively. Left outer joins result in significantly worse performance than inner joins and should thus be avoided.

BW supports the definition of left outer joins with the maintenance of InfoSets by showing the right operand in white (that is, the table for which the initial values are added if no corresponding data records are found from the join condition); otherwise, tables are usually shown in blue. In figure 11–14, the InfoSet from figure 11–10 has been modified so that the master data of the characteristic OD_COUNTRY is read with a left outer join so that nonexistent master data will not result in technical problems during the query.

Filter values in left outer tables

Particularly significant is the use of filter conditions on fields of the "right" table of a left outer join. Referring to the example in figure 11–13, such a filter condition would apply if the Color field was limited to the value Red.

Depending on whether the join is executed before or after the filter condition (in the WHERE clause) or whether the condition is part of the join (in the ON clause), there will be two different results as shown in figure 11–15.

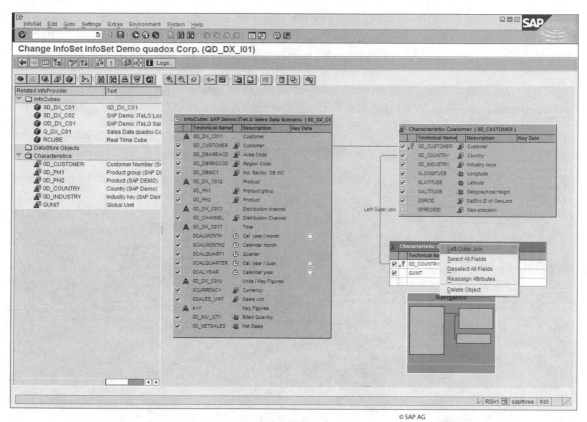

© SAP AG

Figure 11–14

Definition of the left outer join in InfoSets

Left Outer Join via Material

Filter Value: Color = red

Customer	Material	Month	Sales	Discount
4711	ABC	01.2006	1,000.00	25.00
4711	ABC	02.2006	500.00	5.00
4711	DEF	04.2006	1,250.00	20.00
4711	GHI	05.2006	650.00	15.00

Material	Color
ABC	red
GHI	green
JKL	blue

ON condition with JOIN

Where condition after JOIN
(Default Setting)

Result

Customer	Material	Month	Sales	Discount	Color
4711	ABC	01.2006	1,000.00	25.00	red
4711	ABC	02.2006	500.00	5.00	red
4711	DEF	04.2006	1,250.00	20.00	
4711	GHI	05.2006	650.00	15.00	

Result

Customer	Material	Month	Sales	Discount	Color
4711	ABC	01.2006	1,000.00	25.00	red
4711	ABC	02.2006	500.00	5.00	red

Figure 11–15

Filter values in left outer tables

By default, the filter condition of an InfoSet will be integrated into the WHERE condition of the SQL statement that will be executed after the join. If this behavior is to be changed so that the filter condition will be the ON clause of the SQL statement and will thus be run before the join, this can be determined by activating the option Left Outer: Add Filter Value to ON-Condition in the global properties of the InfoSet (see figure 11–16).

Figure 11–16

Global properties of InfoSets

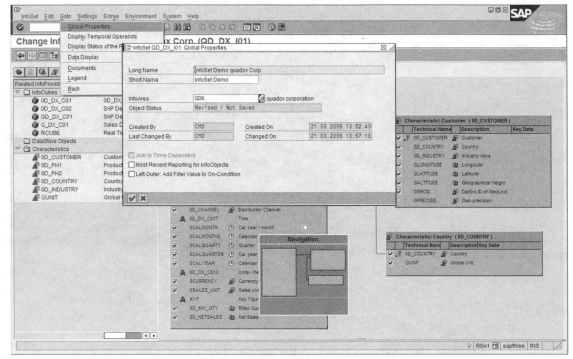

© SAP AG

This setting is valid for all left outer joins of the InfoSet and cannot be made specifically for individual joins within the InfoSet.

Limitations to the left outer join

When the left outer join is used, the right operand is bound to the following basic conditions:

- Right operands are not to be connected to other InfoProviders, so figuratively speaking, they will always form the end of a join connection.
- For performance reasons, BasisCubes are not available as right operands.

Physical access to data targets

Other than in previous releases of SAP BW, data access via InfoSets is not completely executed by the database system but can be handled by the analytical engine too. Thus, this results in a two-tier query in InfoSets: on the one hand from the database system that consolidates a basic population of data, on the other hand from the analytical engine that further limits or transforms data if required.

Here, the access to the individual BW objects is specifically regulated for InfoSets and does not correspond with the definitions that usually apply for access to physical InfoProviders (see chapter 10). In sections 11.2.1 to 11.2.3, we will explain how physical access to InfoObjects, Data-Store Objects, and BasisCubes is designed for InfoSets.

11.2.1 InfoObjects in InfoSets

Handling of InfoObjects is a significant reason for the use of InfoSets. If an InfoObject is used in an InfoSet, all attributes of the InfoObject will be available to the InfoSet, and with relational connections, they can flexibly be enriched by master data of other InfoObjects; that is the case whether they are navigation or display attributes (see sections 6.2.2 and 6.2.3) since only the P and Q tables of an InfoObject will be read.

So, master data attributes might be used transitively. This means not only the attributes of a characteristic but also the attributes of an attribute can be added to a query by defining the connection between the individual master data tables accordingly in the InfoSet.

Transitive attributes

For pure display attributes, there is no way to ensure that used attribute values actually exist in the master data of the respective characteristic. For example, the postal code 47111 can be stored in the master data table of the customer even though this postal code does not exist in the master data of the InfoObject postal code. An inner join to the master data table postal code might thus lead to an involuntarily reduced result set. To connect master data tables for display attributes, you should use a left outer join if possible.

Further, the way inactive master data is handled as well as time-dependent master data has to be considered. These topics will be explained in the following sections:

- **Most Recent Reporting,** which addresses the handling of inactive master data
- **Temporary join,** which addresses the time-dependency of master data

External hierarchies of InfoObjects (see section 6.2.5) are not available to InfoSets since they cannot be read relationally but only from an internal creation of inclusion tables.

Most Recent Reporting of Master Data

Master data that is not available in an active version needs to be activated with the change run (see section 7.1.2) before they can be considered in the "normal" reporting outside InfoSets.

However, when accessing the master data of InfoObjects, InfoSets can optionally also read attributes that are inactive, which is referred to as *Most Recent Reporting* in this context. Figure 11–17 shows the difference between regular reporting and Most Recent Reporting of master data using the example of the InfoObject OCUSTOMER that has a master data record for the customer 4711, which is available in an active and also in a new (still inactivated) form.

Figure 11–17

Most recent reporting of master data

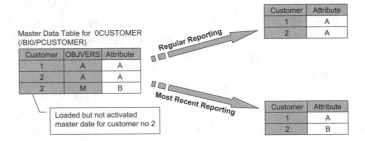

Whether the reporting of master data is to be made via an InfoSet in the form of normal reporting or in the form of Most Recent Reporting is determined in the InfoSet properties and will be valid for all InfoObjects within an InfoSet (see figure 11–16). A different handling of individual InfoObjects is not possible.

Temporary Join

With the temporary join, InfoSets offer a third option to access time-dependent master data tables where the time reference that is used is deduced from a time characteristic of the InfoSet.

This enables you to not only read a master data record from a time-dependent InfoObject (for a predefined key date) but also to identify a time reference per data record that will be used when time-dependent master data attributes are read.

The characteristics from which the time reference of a data record in the InfoSet is to be deduced are defined in the context menu of the InfoObjects in the InfoSet (see figure 11–18). InfoObjects that are marked in this way are also called *temporary operands.*

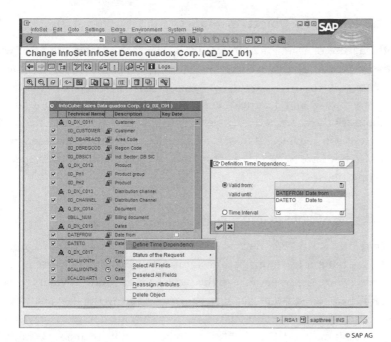

Figure 11–18
Definition of temporary operands

The temporary operands describe a period of validity that defines the time-dependency of the respective BW object to which the connection of time-dependent master data tables refers. The period of validity is deduced either from two key dates that describe beginning and termination of the validity or from a time interval.

The two key dates to describe a period of validity can be indicated in the form of time characteristics or characteristic InfoObjects of the date type. With time characteristics of the date type or the time characteristic OCALDAY, the exact key date described by the InfoObject is clear. When other time characteristics are indicated (e.g., OCALMONTH), it also has to be indicated what determines the exact point in time:

Key dates

- The first day
- The last day
- A certain day (e.g., the third day)

The beginning and the end of the period of validity can also be deduced directly from the time interval that is described by the time characteristics OCALWEEK, OCALMONTH, OCALQUARTER, OCALYEAR, OFISCPER, and OFISCYEAR. With the indication of the time characteristic OCALMONTH, for example, the first and the last day of the month will determine the period of validity.

Time interval

11.2.2 DataStore Objects in InfoSets

With the use of DataStore Objects in InfoSets, the DataStore table with active data will always be referred to independently from the type of DataStore Objects.

Here, all key and data fields are available for data analysis but not the attributes of the characteristic;, even if the DataStore Object is marked as being reporting enabled. If master data attributes are to be included in the analysis, they have to be added to the InfoSet by modeling of the respective join conditions.

11.2.3 BasisCubes in InfoSets

Since release 7 of SAP BW, data from BasisCubes[86] can be queried in Info-Sets. Last but not least, this option significantly enhances the use of Info-Sets and brings their relevance to the same level as MultiProviders.

All characteristics and key figures are available to the data analysis but not the attributes of the characteristics; even they are defined as navigation attributes. If master data attributes are to be added to an analysis, they will always have to be added to the InfoSet by modeling the respective join conditions.

For performance reasons, an InfoCube cannot be defined to be the right operand of a left outer join. During physical access to BasisCubes, the following processes occur:

■ Status handling of requests
■ Use of aggregates

Use of Aggregates

For a query on an InfoSet with an InfoCube, the run-time determines whether an aggregate can be used for the InfoCube. This is the case if all required InfoObjects of the InfoCube are available in an aggregate. The following InfoObjects are required:

---

86. SAP BW does not prohibit the addition of an arbitrary number of BasisCubes to an InfoSet. However, SAP AG supports a maximum of two BasisCubes within an Info-Set. Also, BasisCubes are limited by the performance capabilities of the database systems to run a query on a number of included tables. Further, the size of SQL statements is limited to a maximum of 64 KB (32 KB characters in Unicode systems). The more BasisCubes to be connected in an InfoSet, the faster the limit is reached.

- Key figures of the InfoCube that are selected in the query
- Basic characteristics of the InfoCube that are selected in the query
- Characteristics required for the join with other InfoProviders of the InfoSet

Another precondition for the use of an aggregate is that all data required by the InfoSet can be read with logical access. Within InfoSets with Info-Cubes, it is not possible to read part of the data for an InfoCube from an aggregate and to read another part of the data from another aggregate or the InfoCube itself.

> Within an InfoSet, it is not possible to use indexes of the BI accelerator. Especially when using the BI accelerator, you should try to avoid using InfoSets.

Status of the Staging Engine

As with "regular" access to the data of a BasisCube (i.e., outside InfoSets), the status of individual requests is checked when accessing an InfoSet (see section 10.1.1).

Other than with BasisCubes, however, the request status to be used cannot be defined in the respective query but in the InfoSet itself (see figure 11–19).

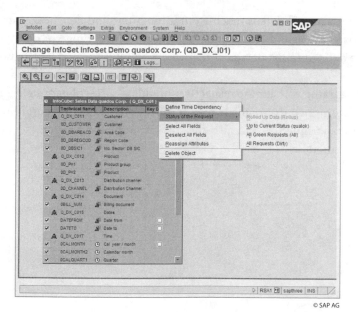

Figure 11–19

Handling of the request status in InfoSets

© SAP AG

11.3 Service InfoCubes

To implement specific analysis requirements that can only be fulfilled with self-defined program logic there are the Service InfoCubes. They enable the creation of an analysis independent from extraction and staging of the data for self-developed function modules.

> The name of the function module can be freely chosen, but this may lead to unmanageable developments within a very short period of time. Thus, when using Service InfoCubes, you should always choose a naming convention in which the name of the InfoCube refers to the respective function module.

Typical areas for the use of Service InfoCubes are complex financial calculations that cannot be made when queries include formulas and exception aggregation.

Even though a Service InfoCube is only defined in the metadata of BW, the definition is basically the same as with a BasisCube; i.e., dimensions need to be defined and provided with InfoObjects, navigation objects need to be determined, etc. During analyses, these cubes therefore present themselves in the same form as all other InfoCubes.

During the analysis, master data is usually read from the master data tables of the InfoObjects from which the data model of the respective cube is defined.

Transactional data is taken from a function module whose name can be chosen freely and whose interface comes with a range of options that can be defined in the details of the cube when it is created (see figure 11–20).

As a framework for the respective module, a series of parameters needs to be determined that regulate the modification of selection conditions for the function modules and also the import and export parameters of the function module.

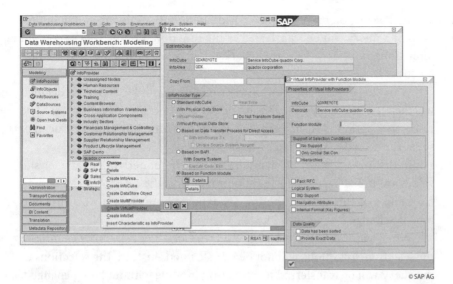

Figure 11–20
Creation of a service InfoCube

11.3.1 Transfer of Selection Conditions

With the execution of a query, the requested characteristics and key figures as well as the selection conditions[87] of the query are transferred to the function module. By default, all selection conditions are transferred. However, it can be determined in what way the selection conditions are to be modified (transformed).[88]

Support of selection londitions

> The transformation of selection conditions does not have any impact on the result of a query since the analytical engine will also process the selection after receipt of the result and it will independently filter possibly oversupplied data.

With you choose the option *No Limitations,* no selection conditions from the query will be transferred to the function module. When identifying the result, the function module will only have to orient itself at the selected characteristics and key figures.

No limitations

The selections made in the queries will only be processed from the analytical engine on the returned data.

---

87. Selection conditions are referred to as limitations in the details of the Service Info-Cube.
88. The limitation *simplify selections* had not been implemented when this book went to press and thus will not be described.

Only global limitations

With selection of the option *Global Limitations,* only the global limitations of a query will be transferred to the function module. These contain limitations in filter values, free characteristics, and drilled-down characteristics.

Hierarchies

With the implementation of the function module, it can be decided whether the selection of hierarchy nodes is to be supported or not. The respective option is to be activated when the function module does *not* support a selection of hierarchy nodes.

In this case, instead of hierarchy nodes, the underlying characteristic values are transferred to the function module as the selection. Depending on the use of this option, the import/export parameters of this function module change (see section 11.3.2).

No transformation of selection conditions

When you use the option *No Transformation of Selection Conditions,* the selection conditions will not be transformed. Instead, the selections of the query will be transferred to a function module without being changed.

With navigation attributes

The introduction stated that the function module does provide transactional data but that master data and texts are taken from the BW InfoObjects. Exceptions are the navigation attributes that can either be read from the master data of the InfoObjects or be provided by the function module.

If the option *With Navigation Attributes* is deactivated, the function module will not supply navigation attributes and the navigation attributes will be taken from the master data of the InfoObjects. Selection conditions on navigation attributes are in this case not transferred to the function module. If the option is activated, the function module will supply the navigation attributes as well.

11.3.2 Import/Export Parameter

The function module provides data for the reporting needs to be defined prior to creation of the cube and is to be provided with the following interface parameters:

```
IMPORTING
    i_infoprov      type rsinfoprov       "InfoProvider
    i_th_sfc        type rsdri_th_isfc    "required characteristics
    i_th_sfk        type rsdri_th_isfk    "required key figures
    i_t_range       type rsdri_t_range    "global limitations
    i_tx_rangetab   type rsdri_tx_rangetab "further limitations
    i_first_call    type rs_bool          "first call of the module
    i_packagesize   type i                "package size
    i_tsx_hier      type rsdri_tsx_hier   "hierarchy limitations
```

```
EXPORTING
  e_t_data          type standard table  "return table
  e_end_of_data     type rs_bool         "last data package
  e_t_msg           type rs_t_msg        "messages to front-end tool
```

With this defined interface, the following is assumed:

- Selections on hierarchy nodes are transferred to the function module in the form of nodes.
- Selections on characteristics are transferred to the function module in the form of characteristic values and not as SIDs.
- The function module is executed in the BW system and not (with the help of an RFC) in another system.

If limitations to hierarchy nodes are made in a query, the limitation will be transferred to the function module in the form of hierarchy nodes. For this purpose, a record with the field COMPOP = HI is generated in the table I_T_RANGE or I_TX_RANGETAB, respectively. The number that can be found in the LOW field of this record specified the record in the I_TSX_HIER table via the POSIT field, in which the respective hierarchy limitation can be found.

Cancellation of hierarchy limitations

If the function module cannot process such a selection, the analytical engine will transfer the limitation in characteristic values prior to the transfer. This is enabled by the option *Hierarchies*. The interface of the function module will thus need to be designed as follows:

```
IMPORTING
  i_infoprov        type rsinfoprov           "InfoProvider
  i_th_sfc          type rsdri_th_isfc        "required characteristics
  i_th_sfk          type rsdri_th_isfk        "required key figures
  i_t_range         type rsdri_t_range        "global limitations
  i_tx_rangetab     type rsdri_tx_rangetab    "further limitations
  i_first_call      type rs_bool              "first call of the module
  i_packagesize     type i                    "package size
EXPORTING
  e_t_data          type standard table       "return table
  e_end_of_data     type rs_bool              "last data package
  e_t_msg           type rs_t_msg             "messages to front-end tool
```

If the function module is designed so that the selection of hierarchy nodes is supported, it will inevitably have to support the limitation of characteristics by their SID values (instead of characteristic values) too.

This support is activated with the option *SID Support*. If this option is used, the analytical engine will do without the transfer of SIDs in

SID Support

characteristic values and vice versa, which will result in performance advantages. The support of SIDs by the function module also results in a modification of the interface of the function module:

```
IMPORTING
  i_infoprov      type rsinfoprov       "InfoProvider
  i_th_sfc        type rsdd_th_sfc      "required characteristics
  i_th_sfk        type rsdd_th_sfk      "required key figures
  i_tsx_seldr     type rsdd_tsx_seldr   "selection conditions (SID)
  i_first_call    type rs_bool          "first call of the module
  i_packagesize   type i                "package size
EXPORTING
  e_t_data        type standard table   "return table
  e_end_of_data   type rs_bool          "last data package
  e_t_msg         type rs_t_msg         "messages to front-end tool
```

Packing RFC The function module for the Service InfoCube can not only be called from the BW system but also from any other Business Application Programming Interface (BAPI) system (i.e., non-ERP systems).

For this purpose, a respective logical system needs to be defined in which the function module is called via RFC. Further, the parameter tables to call a module are packed in BAPI format, which results in a respective modification of the interface:

```
IMPORTING
  infocube           type rsinfoprov   "InfoProvider
EXPORTING
  return             type bapiret2     "return parameters (OK=0)
TABLES
  selection          type bapi6200sl   "selection conditions
  characteristics    type bapi6200fd   "required characteristics
  keyfigures         type bapi6200fd   "required key figures
  data               type bapi6100da   " generic data structure
EXCEPTIONS
  communication_failure
  system_failure
```

When the RFC call is used, only characteristic values but no SID values will be exchanged. The option *SID Support* cannot be used in connection with the RFC.

12 OLAP Caching and Access Sequences

To improve query performance, the analytical engine has a cache mechanism. Cache mechanisms are common and they basically aim to improve access to the database by buffering the data that's most often required. The performance improvement comes from the fact that the buffering is made in another (faster) *memory type*—e.g., the buffering of data in the main memory to avoid access to the slower disk drive.

Strictly speaking, the caching refers to a change from a slower to a faster, but *not persistent,* memory type. Content (and possibly also structure) of a cache is thus dynamically built and invalidated as soon as the underlying data is modified in the slower memory type.

With the OLAP cache, BW enhances the definition of a cache memory; apart from the interim buffering of often required data in faster memory types, the term also refers to interim storage of other *memory formats, memory places,* and *detailing levels* and in other *systems*. Therefore, even indexes of the BI accelerator and aggregates are linked to the OLAP cache concept, even though they are defined statically and their content is not only linked persistently but also in the staging process.

In this case, the OLAP cache is limited to InfoProviders that obtain their data from physically existing data targets—that is, not on Service InfoCubes, RemoteCubes, and InfoSets but also on BasisCubes, DataStore Objects, InfoObjects, and even MultiProviders if they obtain their data from BasisCubes, DataStore Objects, or InfoObjects.

The OLAP cache is made up of three cache levels that reside in different levels of the architecture:

Cache levels

- ■ Local cache
- ■ Global cache
- ■ Aggregate/BIA indexes

The cache levels and the targeted architecture models are shown in figure 12–1.

Figure 12–1
Cache levels of
the analytical engine

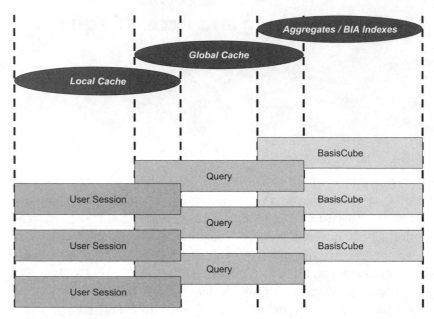

The functioning of the cache levels and interaction will be explained in detail in the following three sections.

12.1 Local Cache

The local cache can basically be referred to as original OLAP cache. Since release 3 of BW, its use would be obsolete for several reasons, but its established concepts are so fundamentally anchored in the analytical engine—and also in the other two cache levels—that it is always used.

The local cache aims at OLAP user navigation improvement by buffering the result sets of already undertaken navigation steps so that is it unnecessary to read again from the database when executing identical navigation steps.

The buffering is made with reference to the user session[89] of the respective user; it is bound to memory limits and cannot be used in another user session. Thus, if a certain view on the database is already buffered in the local cache of a user session, another user session for the same view will still have to access the database and cannot use the local cache of the first user session. This is where the *local* in *local cache* comes from.

---

89. A user session refers to all modes that a user is logged into.

The InfoObjects used in a query are used as benchmarks, and they will be differentiated between *filter characteristics, characteristics/key figures in rows, characteristics/key figures in columns,* and *free characteristics* (see figure 12–2).

Read mode

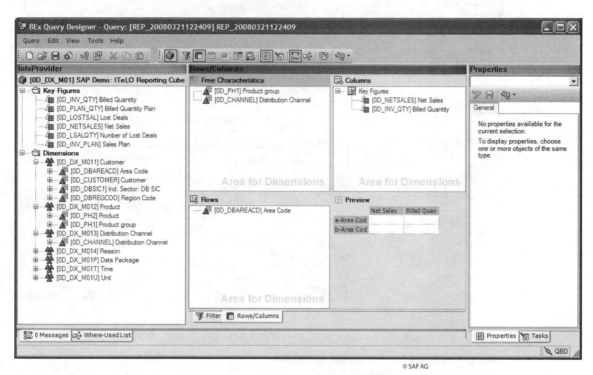

© SAP AG

Figure 12–2
InfoObjects in a query

While the InfoObjects *need* to be read from the database in filters, rows, and columns with the first execution of the query as a part of the result set, free characteristics will be used later only if the user decides to break data down to their free characteristics for further analysis.

The free characteristics can already be included in the query or, if required, when they will really be used. The cache will thus either be supplied with the data for all further navigations during the first navigation step, or it needs to be "refilled" with each navigation, after being read from the database.

For the respective configuration of the analytical engine, there are three options for each query:

- Read all data at once
- Read data during navigation
- Read when you navigate or expand hierarchies

The configuration is called *read mode* and can be defined with the transaction RSRT in the query settings (see figure 12–3).

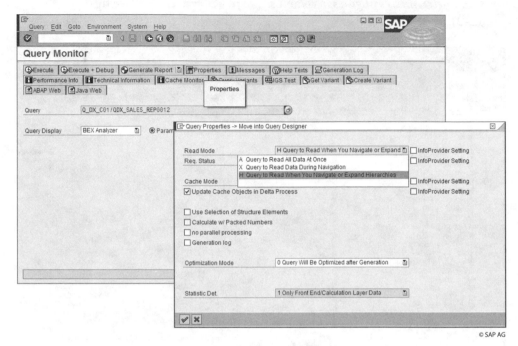

© SAP AG

Figure 12–3
Setting the read mode
of a query

By default, each new query will have the read mode "Read When You Navigate or Expand Hierarchies".

At first glance, it seems tempting to comprehensively supply the local cache with any required data to realize faster navigation within the result set. However, it needs to be considered that the initial read process can thus be significantly prolonged and that the result set might be so large that it will not fit into the local cache. Please also consider that the read mode plays a role for the use of aggregates and that aggregates may lose their impact with the selection of the wrong read mode.

The functioning and thus the respective advantages and disadvantages of the different read modes are explained in the following sections.

12.1.1 Read All Data at Once

When all data is read at once, with the first drill-down all defined Info-Objects in the query (also the free characteristics) will be loaded from the respective InfoProvider into the cache of the analytical engine. The cache comprises the data for all navigation steps that are possible for this query. During navigation, no further reading will be necessary but all navigation steps can be taken by aggregating the data in the analytical engine.

Thus, from the time the analytical engine has received all the data from the database, reading all data at once offers very good performance for the subsequent navigation steps of the query. However, there are two major disadvantages that very often make reading all data at once unsuitable:

- Keeping the data in the memory of the analytical engine is very advantageous for query performance; however, it might be cause for high memory requirements in the main memory of the application server. Depending on the number of users, the memory of the analytical engine can thus quickly become a bottleneck.
- Queries might be provided with a number of free characteristics to make the navigation in the query result as flexible as possible. Thus, in most cases, reading the data at once results in the fact that suitable aggregates can never be used. The fast navigation steps are out of all proportion to the initial loading of the OLAP cache.

For these two serious disadvantages, reading the data at once should only be used in individual cases and for particular queries. These may be queries with small result sets or queries where the consideration of free characteristics will result in only a slightly higher data volume in the cache since they almost have a 1:1 relation with the characteristics in the initial drill-down (e.g., the free characteristics postal code and industry when drilling down customer numbers).

12.1.2 Read Data during Navigation

When reading data during navigation, the analytical engine initially excludes the free characteristics from the read process. Only when a free characteristic is required from the navigation of the query result will the characteristics be considered in the read process.

Thus, there will be an individual read process for each navigation step where a new aggregate will be looked for each time. The cache of the analytical engine can be referred to only when an identical navigation step has been taken previously.

Reading data during navigation means slower navigation within a query result than with reading all data at once since a new reading process from the database is required for each navigation step. On the other hand, there is the advantage that reading the data during navigation is also suited for large numbers of free characteristics and aggregates might also be used. For large result sets, reading data during navigation should be preferred to reading all data at once.

12.1.3 Read When You Navigate or Expand Hierarchies

Reading when you navigate or expand hierarchies means that during navigation, you read the data that responds to the requirements of hierarchies.

If external hierarchies are used in queries, with reading the data during navigation, the complete hierarchy will be read even though the query definition might only require the expansion on a higher level or on a certain hierarchy node. The option Read When You Navigate or Expand Hierarchies considers the required hierarchy level or the expanded node, respectively, and reads only the relevant part of the hierarchy.

Especially with expansion on high hierarchy levels, the advantages of hierarchy aggregates will be used that can only be created up to a defined level themselves. Without this read mode, hierarchy aggregates are inefficient.

Reading when you navigate or expand hierarchies should always be used when you work with large hierarchies (from approximately 1,000 hierarchy nodes). For smaller hierarchies, the simple reading of data during navigation might be better suited since the complete hierarchy can quickly be read and the navigation within a hierarchy noticeably profits from the cache of the analytical engine.

12.2 Global Cache

With each navigation step, the data of the local cache will be searched first. If this test is negative, the data will be read from the next cache level, which is the global cache.

The global cache (also referred to as persistent cache or cross-transactional cache) came with BW release 3 as a supplement to the local cache and it remedied its biggest disadvantages.

The global cache is not limited to one user session. Thus, all user sessions of an application server can access the memory area used by the global cache. The executed analysis steps do not have to be identical with the content of the global cache (which is not the case with the local cache), but they can also display partial selections of the data in the cache (e.g., the selection of period 001.2005 if the interval of the periods from 001.2005 until 012.2005 is stored in the cache).[90]

The global cache can be stored in different ways, whereas the memory types intertwine, have specific functions, and thus practically represent further cache levels within the global cache. Basically, there is global main memory cache and the persistent cache.

12.2.1 Main Memory Cache

By default, the global cache of each query is located in the main memory of the respective application server. When you're using several application servers, each server uses its individual global cache that only users logged into it can access. The global cache levels of the individual application servers are managed separately and are not aligned with each other, so that they may represent similar but also completely different content.

This *cache mode* is referred to as *main memory cache without swapping* and is stored in the transaction RSRT in the settings of the respective query (see figure 12–4).

Main memory cache without swapping

For data storage, the main memory of the shared memory segment is used. The size of the shared memory segment is defined by the profile parameter `rsdb/esm/buffersize_kb` (size of the segment in KB) or `rsdb/esm/ max_objects` (maximum number of objects). Both are displayed in the program RSPARAM and maintained in the transaction RZ11.

What part of the shared memory segment is claimed by the global OLAP cache is defined in the cache parameters in the setting Local Size MB.[91] The cache parameters can be maintained with the transaction RSCUSTV14 (see figure 12–5).

---

90. Excluded form caching are queries with a replacement path variable (pre-query) and locally identical but still different selections (e.g., fixed vs. variable filters) where the common use of the OLAP cache is particularly impacted by the different analysis tools.
91. The term is confusing; however, the entry in Size Local MB has nothing to do with the local cache of the OLAP engine. The word local stems from the fact that the shared memory segment is limited to one application server and is thus not applicable to all application servers (globally).

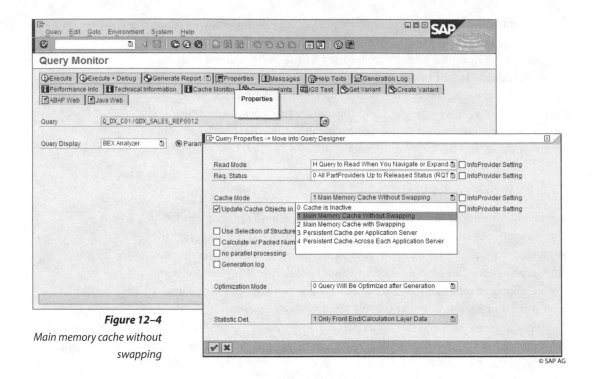

Figure 12–4

Main memory cache without swapping

If the addition of new cache content would exceed the upper limit of the cache size, the entries that have not been used recently will be eliminated. Large result sets that exceed approximately one-fifth of the shared memory segment are not stored in the global cache in order to avoid too much elimination.

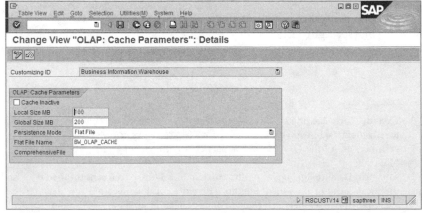

Figure 12–5

Cache parameters of the analytical engine

The use of the main memory cache mostly makes sense when a large number of users take similar navigation steps with manageable result sets, so that accordingly good hit rates can be achieved. If there is no agreement in the evaluation behavior of the users or if they even execute any ad hoc analyses, the cache should be deactivated since it will create overhead without creating any benefits.

Especially with a large number of queries, the reusability of query results in the cache and the elimination of "old" query results will compete for a relatively small main memory cache that cannot be freely expanded since most systems are short of main memory.

Main memory cache with swapping

For these cases, you should use the cache mode *main memory cache with swapping,* which can also be set in the transaction RSRT in the query properties (see figure 12–6)

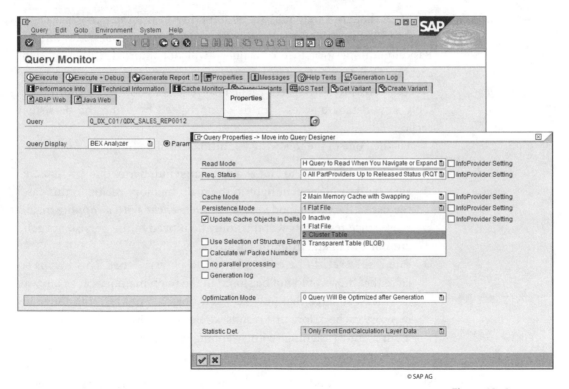

© SAP AG

Figure 12–6
Main memory cache with swapping

Here, the term *swapping* does not refer to the swapping of the operating system or such but rather to the removal of eliminated content to the next level of the global cache, which is the persistent cache, as explained in the next section.

12.2.2 Persistent Cache

In the case of persistent cache, the result sets will not be buffered in the shared memory of the respective application server but in database tables or files. The description of the cache level as "persistent" is technically incorrect as database tables or files basically can store data persistently. Still, the persistent cache—like the local cache and the global main memory cache—is invalidated with the modification of the underlying data targets and is thus not truly persistent.

Thus, the most obvious advantage of the persistent cache is its size since the used disk memory is substantially larger than the main memory. The maximum size of the persistent cache is defined with the transaction RSCUSTV14 in the entry of the cache parameter "Local Size MB" (see figure 12–5).

Application areas   Even though it may initially be tempting to use the persistent cache because of its size, the sensible use is limited by a range of basic conditions. Basically, the performance of a query will not improve with persistent caching if low I/O performance is the reason for the performance problem, because access to a persistent cache also requires good I/O performance. Only slow database access can be compensated by using the persistent cache.

Further, one of the following conditions must be fulfilled:

■ The buffering needs to aim at a very large number of queries that create a hard displacement fight in the main memory cache. In this case, the use of the cache mode ***main memory cache with swapping*** makes sense since result sets will thus only be moved to the persistent cache but not eliminated from the cache completely.

■ The results sets to be buffered need to be very large. This means so large that they would not be stored in the main memory cache anyway or at least so large that only very few objects would fit into the main memory cache before first results would be eliminated. In this case, no main memory caching (with swapping) should be realized at all; only buffering in the persistent cache should be made.

Should these preconditions not be met, the use of the persistent cache should be avoided so that the system will not be burdened with the respective administrative tasks.

With persistent caching, application-server-dependent and application-server-independent caching is differentiated. The cache mode to be used is defined with the transaction RSRT in the properties of the query.

Cache modes

The cache mode to be preferred mostly depends on user behavior and the organization of the application servers. If the application servers are used only for dynamic load balancing and if the users mostly run similar queries on all application servers, the cache mode ***persistent cache across all application servers*** is preferred.

If user allocation to the application servers is made according to organizational criteria, it is to be assumed that user behavior on the individual application servers will be different too. Individual queries will thus be made on only one of the application servers, so caching should be limited to this application server too. For such queries, the cache mode ***persistent cache per application server*** is used.

If the cache mode ***main memory cache with swapping*** is set, the swapping will refer to the persistent cache per application server; after all, the main memory cache already is mandatorily related to the respective application server, so a subsequent elimination of the cache across all application servers would not result in any advantages.

For the selection of the memory location for the persistent cache, there are different ***persistence modes*** available that can be selected for a persistent cache mode or for a main memory cache with swapping in the properties of the respective query with the transaction RSRT (see figure 12–6).

Persistence mode

On the one hand, the buffering of result sets in a cluster table or a transparent table with a BLOB field is available as persistence modes.

A completely different design approach is the use of the persistence mode ***flat file.*** Indeed, compared to database tables, the flat file format offers a relatively poor way to buffer result sets. In the special case of a very bad IO performance between the application server and the database server that is caused by a particular network topology, the buffering of result sets in a flat file provides an option to select a memory location for this network topology that is better suited than the database server.

For example, if the database server of a BW system was located in the United States and users in Europe were logged onto the BW system via this application server, the IO bandwidth between this individual application server and the database system would be rather low given the WAN connection. With the persistence mode flat file, result sets can be buffered in a flat file that is also stored on the server in Europe. Thus, at least accesses between application server and the persistent cache perform well;

the basically unsuited memory format of the flat file is compensated in this combination.

While memory locations for the persistence mode or cluster or transparent tables are definitely set, the memory locations for flat files need to be set manually. This is made in the cache parameter maintenance via the transaction RSCUSTV14 (see figure 12–5).

In the cache parameter maintenance, the entries Flat File Name and Across All Files are to be maintained with *logical file names*, where each entry refers to one flat file that includes result sets either specific to one application server or across all application servers.

For this purpose, BW provides the logical file names BW_OLAP_CACHE or BW_OLAP_CACHE_SPAN, respectively, that can be entered and modified in the parameter maintenance.[92] Should these two file names not be used, other logical file names can be entered; however, *no* physical data paths or names can be entered.

SAP arranged for the provided logical data names to be stored in the directory /usr/sap/<SID>/SYS/global/.[93] This directory can be replaced by enabled network directories too.

12.2.3 Cache Invalidation

As mentioned earlier, the term *cache* is used very liberally in this context. This results in the fact that the invalidation of the cache—which actually is a topic for each type of cache—only affects the type of the global cache. Only the global cache reasonably meets the understanding of a "true" cache: it is invalidated depending on the database[94] and it is filled dynamically depending on the data query.[95]

The validity of the global cache is invalidated as soon as data of the underlying InfoProvider has changed.[96] If the data analysis is only based on an InfoProvider, the invalidation is easy and does not require further explanation.

---

92. How logical data names work and how they are designed is described in a similar case (extraction of data from flat files) in section 15.1.4..
93. <SID> represents the three-digit ID of the BW system.
94. The local cache remains valid as long as the respective user session; aggregates and BIA indexes are not invalidated at all but updated only.
95. Aggregates and BIA indexes become statically persistent.
96. Additionally, the global cache will be basically invalidated when metadata, master data attributes, hierarchies, and exchange rates change.

The invalidation of the global cache is much different when the data analysis is based on a MultiProvider. Specifically, this form of cache invalidation will be explained in this section. The reason is that MultiProviders consolidate data from a number of data targets that can be provided with new data completely independently from each other.

This raises the question of whether the global cache for a query is to be completely invalidated if only the data of a data target is changed or whether only the data that concerns this one data target is to be invalidated. This apparently sensible form of invalidation is to be countered since in this case, data of the individual data targets needs to be separated in the cache and the global cache might thus require much more memory space. However, if the global cache can be invalidated even if only the data of a data target is changed, the data in the global cache can be better aggregated in favor of access speed and memory consumption.

In consideration of these arguments, BW offers, since release 7, different options for cache invalidation that have been subsumed under the term *SP Grouping*[97] (also referred to as delta caching) and that can be determined with transaction RSRT in the properties of the query (see figure 12–7).

Figure 12–7
Delta caching of a query

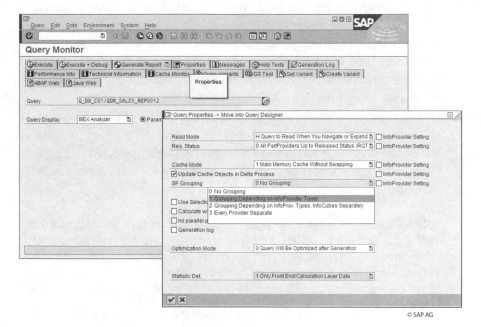

© SAP AG

97. The term is misleading. The type of partitioning that needs to be defined is not at all related to the partitioning of the data model (see section 7.3).

The following partitioning types can be selected:

- No Grouping
- Grouping Depending on InfoProvider Types
- Grouping Depending on InfoProvider Types, InfoCubes Separately
- Every Provider Separate

No grouping

By default, all queries are defined without grouping and the results are aggregated in the global cache. This partitioning type is suitable when the data of all data targets is changed in a common time frame and no real-time BasisCubes are involved in the MultiProvider.

Grouping depending on InfoProvider types

With Grouping Depending on InfoProvider Types, results are combined in the global cache referring to the InfoProvider types. Thus, the result sets of all BasisCubes, all DataStore Objects, and all real-time InfoCubes can be invalidated independently from each other. This type of partitioning is suitable when a MultiProvider combines "regular" InfoProviders with real-time InfoCubes or other InfoProviders and where the constant changes of data would never allow for a valid global cache.

Grouping depending on InfoProvider types, InfoCubes separately

A deviation from regular Grouping Depending on InfoProvider Types, there is another partitioning type that not only invalidates BasisCubes and real-time Cubes independently from each other but that generally invalidates all BasisCubes independently from each other. This partitioning type should be used when a MultiProvider has a large number of BasisCubes that are used for the period of time of the data analysis *and* independently from each other provided with fresh data.

Every provider separate

In the most extensive form of delta caching, all InfoProviders are invalidated separately from each other. This type of partitioning is suitable when not only the BasisCubes of a MultiProvider are updated during data analysis and independently from each other but also all other types of InfoProvider of a MultiProvider.

Data updates in the data targets of BW should basically be made outside analysis times. The possibilities of delta caching are not favorable to an overlap of analysis and load periods but only to lessen its negative impacts. Delta caching is particularly required if real-time InfoCubes are used. For the design of time periods for data analysis and data preparation, please see chapter 29.

12.3 BIA Indexes

If with access to analysis data, result sets are not found in either the local or the global cache, a physical read access of the InfoProviders in BW will be inevitable. If the content of the BasisCube is mapped in the BIA indexes, the BI accelerator and not the BasisCube will be read.

Access to the data of the BasisCube is thus not required with the use of the BI accelerator since it maps the complete content of a BasisCube. If not only the rolled-up (i.e., in BIA existing) requests were to be read but other access procedures were used also—e.g., *qualok, all* or *dirty* (see section 10.1.1—the data of the BasisCube would also need to be accessed.

The BI accelerator will not need to be used when a BasisCube is read as a component of an InfoSet. With the use of MultiProviders, however, the BI accelerator can be used without any restriction.

Thus, the BI accelerator competes with all procedures that aim at the tuning of the read access to BasisCubes (aggregates, compression, indexing, partitioning) since the data of a BasisCube is no longer read during data analysis when the BI accelerator is used.

> It seems that the use of the BI accelerator makes a large part of other tuning measures obsolete. Please consider, however, that the BI accelerator is a very new product that might suffer from some initial bugs. When the BI accelerator fails, the fallback solution will be to access the data in BW, so the established tuning measures should not be neglected completely.

Index preload

Since the BI accelerator, if used, has a central function in the data analysis, it should be ensured that it can work at full capacity. This is the case when the data of the BIA indexes are stored in the main memory of the index server.

However, this is not the case right after creation of the index; i.e., an index is first stored on the file server of the BI accelerator and only loaded into the main memory of the index server when required. Usually, this process only takes a few seconds, but as a precaution, this delay can be prevented with the first execution of a query on a BasisCube by loading the indexes of a BasisCube into the main memory of the index server.

This "preload" can be realized or scheduled with the transaction SE38 in the program `RSDDTREX_INDEX_LOAD_UNLOAD` (see figure 12–8).

Figure 12–8
Load data for a BIA index in
main memory

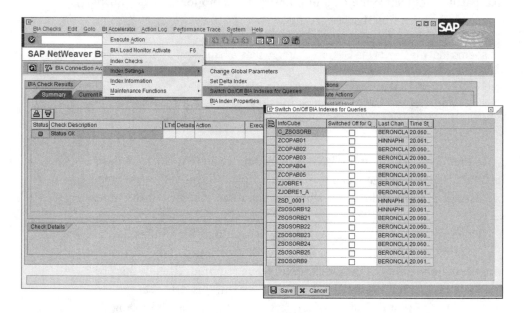

© SAP AG

Switch off BIA use   In the reverse case, it can make sense to temporarily switch off the use of
the BI accelerator for selected BasisCubes (especially for test purposes).
Switching the BIA use for a BasisCube on/off is possible with the menu
item *BI Accelerator→Index Settings→Switch On/Off BIA Indexes for
Queries* in the transaction RSDDBIAMON2 (see figure 12–9).

Figure 12–9
Switch on/off BIA indexes
for cubes

While it is only relevant for testing purposes to switch off the BIA use for a
complete BasisCube, the targeted switching off of the BIA use for an individual query may be continuously beneficial for BW in live operation. The
BI accelerator offers impressive access acceleration, but it does not come
up to the performance of especially small and well-built aggregates. Furthermore, if a query was so predictable that it will certainly use small

aggregates,[98] the use of the BI accelerator would result in a performance decrease.

To give such queries access to the aggregates while leaving the BI accelerator aside, in the transaction SE16 the field NOHPA in the table RSRREPDIR can be filled with the value X. The key to the table RSRREPDIR is the technical definition name of the query that can be identified through the technical information in the transaction RSRT (see figure 12–10).

Figure 12–10

Switch on/off BIA indexes for queries

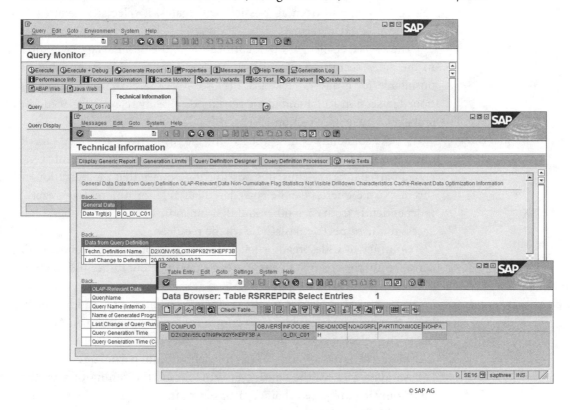

© SAP AG

12.4 Aggregates

If access to the BIA indexes is not possible, aggregates provide an excellent option to avoid physical read access to the data of a BasisCube as long as result sets are not found in either in the local cache or in the global cache.

---

98.   Above all, this requires a very restrictive use of free characteristics.

Since aggregates are precompressed data of a BasisCube or subsets of these data (see section 7.1) that were from the rollup completely involved in the BW staging process, they are not cache levels in the basic sense. However, since the analytical engine acts with aggregates as if there was another cache level, they are described in this context.

With each access to the data of a BasisCube, the analytical engine checks whether the same information content could be derived from other aggregates too, and from all possible aggregates, it selects the aggregate with the fewest data records.

The special challenge with identification of the optimal aggregates lies in the rules according to which an aggregate is considered suitable or unsuitable for a query. This closes the loop to the partial queries mentioned in section 10.1.1 and to the read mode already relevant for the local and global cache (see section 12.1).

Partial queries   So, the suitability of an aggregate for the respectively executed OLAP query is not measured from the query itself but from the subsequently generated partial queries. Thus, it is possible for a query that the execution of several partial queries can be considered suitable for different aggregates independently from each other and that for some of the partial queries an access to the respective BasisCube will be required.

Contrary to widespread belief, for the tuning of a query, you need to consider not the creation of *one* aggregate per cube but rather the creation of *one to n* aggregates per cube.

Read mode   Parts of partial queries are the characteristics/attributes and hierarchy levels that are imperatively required in the respective drill-down. According to the selected read mode, the free characteristics/attributes and further hierarchy levels are included in the definition of partial queries.

An aggregate will be considered suitable for the tuning of a partial query only if all required characteristics/attributes and hierarchy levels are included in its definition. The following is applicable:

- An attribute is also contained in the aggregate if its respective basic characteristic is contained in the aggregate. Thus, for example, the attribute OPOSTAL_CD (postal code) will not need to be added to an aggregate if the characteristic OCUSTOMER (customer) is already part of the aggregate since OPOSTAL_CD is an attribute of OCUSTOMER.
- A hierarchy is also contained in an aggregate when the respective characteristic is contained in the aggregate. Thus, the customer hierarchy

will not need to be added to the aggregate if the customer is already part of the aggregate.

■ A hierarchy level is also contained in an aggregate if a detailed level of the same hierarchy is part of the aggregate.

> The selection of the read mode (or the compilation of the free characteristics) is decisive for the use of aggregates. With an unsuitable read mode, in extreme cases either the potential of the local cache for a faster OLAP navigation will remain untapped or the existing aggregates remain unused, since they too often are considered unsuitable given the multitude of required information. Please consider that aggregates should at least compress the volume of the superordinate aggregates/cubes by a factor of 10. And this will not be possible when an aggregate is to map a multitude of characteristics.

For testing purposes, it may be relevant to circumvent certain aggregates for the evaluation of data without completely deactivating or deleting these aggregates since a rebuild can be very time consuming.

Switch aggregates on/off

For this purpose, individual aggregates can be switched on/off in the aggregate maintenance without having any impact on the data of the aggregate (see figure 12–11).

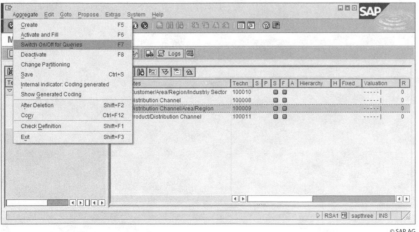

Figure 12–11
Switch aggregates on/off

A switched-off aggregate will no longer be used in a query systemwide, but it will still be considered in the rollup or the change run. Thus, without rebuild, switched off aggregates can be switched on instantly and used for data analysis.

13 Monitoring the Analytical Engine

You monitor the analytical engine to detect performance problems and to check individual queries in a focused way to identify optimization potential.

In the following sections, we'll describe working with the query monitor and the query runtime statistics, which are the core components of monitoring.

13.1 Query Monitor

The query monitor provides an option to review in detail the functioning of the analytical engine during the execution of a query. For this purpose, the query monitor can run a query and send messages on the upcoming process steps.

The query monitor is started with the transaction RSRT. There, the query to be reviewed can be selected and the analysis can be started via the *Execute + Debug* button (see figure 13–1).

The transaction RSRT can, with the help of the transaction RSSMQ, also be started with the ID of another user. This is especially helpful if problems with personalization or authorizations are to be detected.

The options offered by the query monitor to review a query are very comprehensive and at some points only relevant for SAP in support cases. At this point, we'll focus on how the query is split up and how these partial queries can be accelerated with the help of aggregates. For this purpose, you activate the Display Aggregate Found option, as shown in figure 13–1.

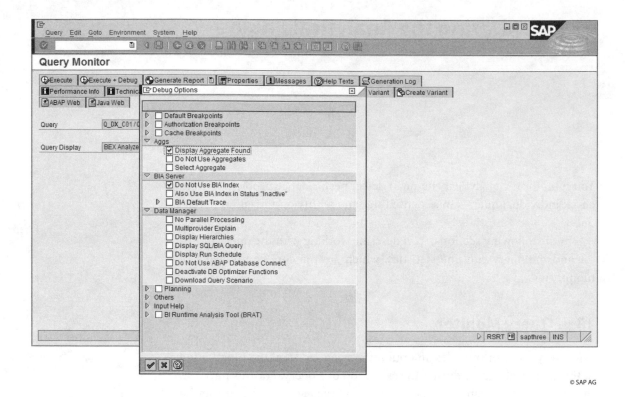

Figure 13–1
Debug options of the
query monitor

Here, for each partial query, the aggregate that is used will be displayed. If no suitable aggregate can be used, then the technical name of the respective BasisCube will be indicated. The characteristics required by a query can be found in the right column, and the characteristics offered by the respective aggregate can be found in the left column. With access to the BasisCube, not all characteristics of the BasisCube wil be shown in the left column.

Figure 13–2 shows the aggregate use in a query that is split into two partial queries. The first partial query cannot refer to an aggregate and thus reads directly from the respective BasisCube QUADOX_C2. The other partial query can be served from the aggregate 100009.

Based on such a review, an aggregate can be defined that contains the characteristics 0D_PH1 and QRESPCNTR, so the second partial query can also be accelerated. However, the existing aggregate 100013 and the characteristic 0D_PH1 could be enhanced just the same. Here, you need to consider the size of the aggregate, i.e., the compression achieved compared to the Basis-Cube.

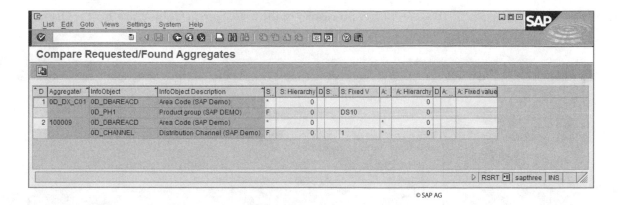

© SAP AG

Figure 13–2
Aggregates found for a query

This also applies to aggregates that are to be newly created. If it does not sufficiently compress the data of the BasisCube, it can be assumed that the aggregate will not lead to significant access acceleration and it should thus not be created.

13.2 Runtime Statistics of the Analytical Engine

At certain measuring points, the analytical engine is in a position to log the times and quantities of the execution. We will refer to these logs as runtime statistics.

For the interpretation of the runtime statistics, the front-end and calculation layer and the aggregation layer of the analytical engine have to be considered.

The front-end and calculation layer undertakes the execution of a query above the physical access to the data. This includes the interpretation of the OLAP command, the display of results, the generation of queries, the administration of the OLAP cache, conversions, and much more.

Front-end and calculation layer

Conspicuously long delays in this layer can point to problems with the front-end system, with the network, or in the definition of the query.

The runtime statistics of the aggregation layer map the timeframes that BW requires for the actual database accesses, for splitting partial queries, and for merging subqueries into a MultiProvider.

Aggregation layer

The review of these delays is the focus of the data model tuning in BW.

The simplest way to show runtime statistics for the execution of a query comes with the query monitor. You can see a display of statistics

Runtime statistics in the query monitor

that's similar to the display of the used aggregates by activating the Display Statistics Data option (see figure 13–3).

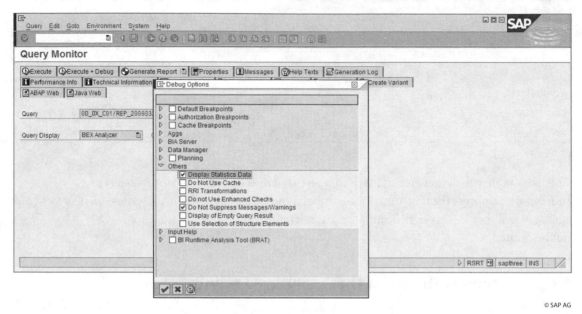

© SAP AG

Figure 13–3

Display of runtime statistics in the query monitor

The logged runtime statistics can be displayed as shown in figure 13–4. Here, the BasisProvider for each partial query is shown together with information on whether it had to be read or whether (in the case of Basis-Cubes) an aggregate could be accessed.

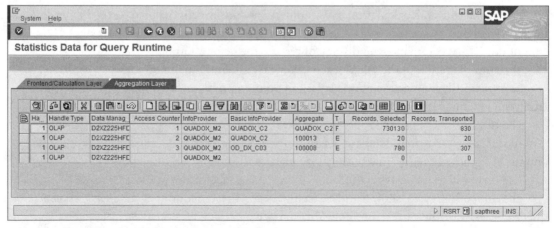

© SAP AG

Figure 13–4

Query runtime statistics in the query monitor

The example in figure 13–4 shows that the query was split into three partial queries.[99] The first partial query directly reads data from the BasisCube QUADOX_C2. From the 730,130 records that were read, only 830 will be transferred to the front-end and calculation layer; i.e., the read data records can again be massively compressed. This compression could also be made with an aggregate and that would significantly increase read delay.

For the second and third partial query, aggregates are used. In the case of the second partial query, the number of read data records is as high as the number of actually transferred records. In the case of the third partial query, the relation from read to transferred records is not optimal, but with a ration of 780:307, it is still so bad that the definition of a separate aggregate would be worthwhile. The definition of a separate aggregate should be considered from the factor 10:1 onward.

You may also use runtime statistics by logging these statistics independently from the query monitor. Runtime statistics can be used in this case to review the work of the analytical engine over a longer period of time and to actively search for tuning requirements.

Logging runtime statistics

The runtime statistics are not logged according to standard conventions. Rather, the analytical Engine needs to be told which queries, Info-Providers, workbooks, or web templates are to lead to the generation of log data. These indications are maintained in the transaction RSDDSTAT (see figure 13–5).

You need to define initially which individual objects to log. Alternatively, you can accept a default setting. You can accept the default setting for all object types in the menu item *Extras→Change Default*.

Further, you can define the level of detail for logging. You can use the default settings or select from the following levels of detail:

- 0 – Aggregated Data:
  In the data on the front-end and calculation layer, for each navigation, only an aggregated log entry will be generated. Logs from the aggregation layer are not filed.
- 1 – Front-end/Calculation Layer Data Only:
  The log entries from the front-end and calculation layer are filed in detail. The logs of the aggregation layer are filed only in an aggregated form.

---

99. The last entry describes the main process from which the partial queries are split.

- 2 – All:

  The logs from the front-end and calculation layer are filed in detail together with the logs of the aggregation layer. This logging corresponds with the display of runtime statistics in the query monitor.

- 9 – No Data:

  No logs are filed.

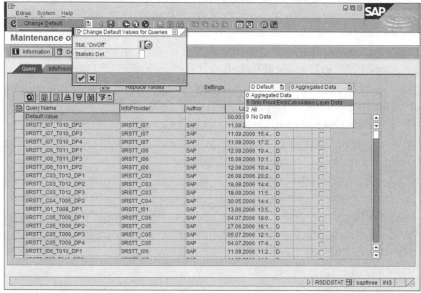

Figure 13–5
Control logging of
runtime statistics

© SAP AG

Especially for the review of MultiProvider queries, level 2 needs to be used to obtain information on access to the providers from the individual partial queries. When selecting the level of detail, you need to consider that the runtime statistics can generate large data volume. For example, if a web template is executed in four queries that each access a MultiProvider with five BasisCubes, and each access is split into four partial queries, this will result in 80 log records[100] only from the aggregation layer area.

With the settings for logging, there are overlaps in the settings for Info-Providers and for queries. For a query, different logging settings can be stored as compared to the underlying InfoProvider. Basically, the settings for an InfoProvider control the settings of the query. The only exception is when an InfoProvider is logged with default settings. In this case, the log

---

100. 4 queries x 5 InfoProviders x 4 partial queries

settings of the query will be used. If it is also set to default value, the default settings of the InfoProvider will be used.

The logging of web templates or work files only describe measuring values that are directly related to the object so that these settings can be made in any case and will not overlap with the settings of other object types.

The execution of a query is initiated by the front-end and calculation layer. At this point, the execution of a query will get a handle ID under which all partial queries of the query are executed. Typically, this handle ID is the basis for the analysis of logs. The handle ID is valid within a unique step ID (UID) that is executed for all data manager access within a navigation step.

Log analysis

To directly execute analysis on diverse tables that contain log entries, there are the views RSDDSTAT_OLAP and RSDDSTAT_DM, whose content can be shown with transaction SE16.

> The analysis of runtime statistics with the help of the views RSDDSTAT_OLAP and RSDDSTAT_DM is easily possible, but it is a little complicated. To enable an easy analysis, you can set the technical content that simplifies the analyses of runtime statistics in the Business Explorer (see appendix D.2.2).

The view RSDDSTAT_OLAP represents the logs of the front-end and calculation layer. In the following table, the fields in this view are briefly explained.

RSDDSTAT_OLAP

Field	Description
SESSIONUID	One-to-one identification of the user session
STEPUID	One-to-one identification of the user step
HANDLEID	Identification of a query runtime object to the STEPUID
HANDLETP	Type of query runtime object
EVENTID	Log step according to table RSDDSTATEVENTS
UNAME	User name
STEPTP	Type of step (BI Front-end Tools, broadcasting, OLAP BAPI, etc.) according to table RSDDSTATSTEPTP
STEPCNT	Counter of the navigation step with query execution
UTIME	Time of day from field STARTTIME

Field	Description
CALDAY	Calendar day from field STARTTIME
RUNTIME	Duration of a step in seconds
INFOPROV	InfoProvider
OBJNAME	Name of the runtime object (e.g., query, web template)
OBJPROP	Encryption of the object properties: First place: read mode (see also section 12.1). >>A<< = query to read all data at once >>X<< = query to read during navigation "H<< = query to read when you navigate or expand hierarchies Second place: data update (see also section 10.1.1). 0 = rollup 1 = qualok for real-time cubes, otherwise rollup 2 = qualok 3 = all 9 = dirty Third place: delta caching on/off (see also section 12.2.3). "X<< = on " << = off Forth place: partition mode (see also section 12.2.3). 0 = no provider partitioning 1 = partitioning in groups 2 = partitioning in groups, BasisCubes separated 3 = each provider separate Fifth place: cache mode (see also section 12.2.2). 0 = cache is inactive 1 = main memory cache without swapping 2 = main memory cache with swapping 3 = persistent cache per application server 4 = persistent cache across all application servers Sixth place: persistence mode (see also section 12.2.2) 0 = inactive 1 = flat file 2 = cluster table 3 = transparent table
STATLEVEL	Level of detail for runtime statistics (0, 1, 2)
EVTIME	(Net) runtime
EVCOUNT	Counter (not required for all execution steps)
EVENTIDCNT	Number of calls of this execution step
STARTTIME	Start time of the step in the format yyyymmddhhmmss, mmmuuun

The view RSDDSTAT_DM contains the logs of the aggregation layer. The fields of this view are also explained in the following table.

RSDDSTAT_DM

Field	Description
STEPUID	UID of the user step
HANDLEID	ID of a query runtime object
HANDLETP	Type of the runtime object
DMUID	UID for the data manager access
UTIME	Time of day from field STARTTIME
CALDAY	Calendar day from field STARTTIME
UNAME	User name
OBJNAME	Name of the runtime object (e.g., query, web template).
INFOPROV	InfoProvider
PARTPROV	Partial provider of the MultiProvider (if a MultiProvider is contained in the field INFOPROV)
AGGREGATE	Technical name of the aggregate or the BIA index (if applicable)
ACCESSTP	Type of read access (component or delta)
TABLTP	Type of fact table (F or E) if access to InfoCube or aggregate is made
TIMEDMPREP	Data access preparation time
TIMEDMPOST	Data post-processing time
TIMEREAD	Time to read the data
TIMESID	Time to calculate/define new SIDs
TIMENAVATTR	Time to update master data
TIMEHIERARCHY	Time for hierarchy handling
DBSEL	Number of records read from a database
DBTRANS	Number of records transferred to front-end and calculation layer
WP_ID	ID of the work process in which the (possibly parallel) data read access was realized
PROCESSCNT	Count of data accesses during execution step

Field	Description
SLOT	Slot for parallelization
STARTTIME	Start time of the step in the format yyyymmddhhmmss,mmmuuun

As an alternative to the analysis of runtime statistics based on the views RSDDSTAT_OLAP and RSDDSTAT_DM, the technical content also offers a predefined extraction of the respective database tables and a transfer in predefined InfoCubes as well as the respective queries to analyze the relevant data. An explanation of the technical content can be found in appendix D.2.2.

IV Extraction & Staging

In this part on extraction and staging, we will explain how the data flow can be defined from the source systems up to the data targets (BasisCubes, DataStore Objects, InfoObjects). The data flow can usually be displayed in a cascaded arrangement where data passes several logical layers in which it is transformed, homogenized, validated, and error-corrected. Due to the cascaded arrangement of the layer, this process has been named staging (see figure IV–1). The controlling processes involved in the staging are combined under the term *staging engine*.

Users of versions up to 3.5 of the BW will find significant changes in this area. On the design level, they are reflected in the fact that extraction and processing of data are strictly separated from each other and thus completely different forms of delta processing are enabled. On a technical level, the new concepts are manifested in the fact that different forms of processing need no longer be defined (transfer rules, update rules). Now, the data flow is to be defined with a common technology, the transformation.

Reference architecture

Since the design of the data flow is no longer defined by the architecture of the staging engine with BW release 7, and since it can be designed (and disfigured) rather freely, this chapter emphasizes giving the description of the staging a reasonable structure.

Basically, we would like to not describe staging and data models according to individual requirements but to define an architecture at the beginning of the development that either determines staging and data modeling systemwide or at least develops a limited set of design options.[101] This helps when looking for errors, it serves system documentation, and it especially facilitates the enhancement of the staging to meet new requirements.

At first, it is more time-consuming to define such an architecture than to start with the implementation right away and to neglect the long-term benefits of an architecture (as short-term demands of business requirements often claim). To find the trade-off between long-term planning and the fulfillment of short-term goals is thus one of the most important tasks of the extraction and staging design.

The basic recommendation for BW design is the displayed reference architecture in figure IV–1. This architecture describes the layers we prefer and serves as reference architecture for all architecture elements explained in the next sections

---

101. BW cannot determine any conventions for the definition of the staging. Thus, the definition of a reference architecture needs to be made on an organizational level.

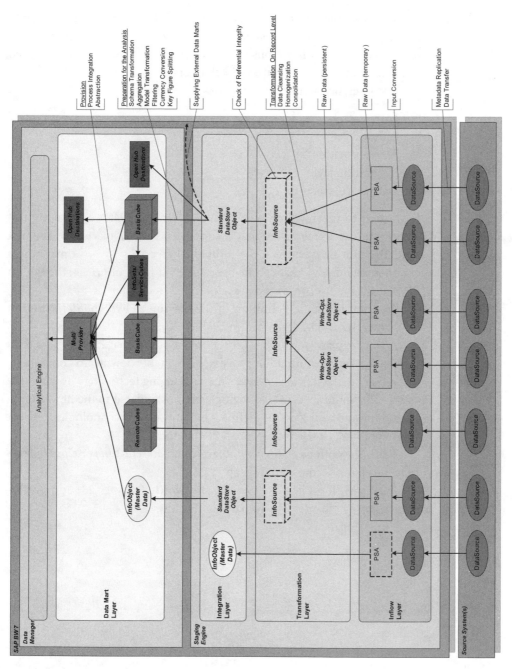

Figure IV–1 Reference architecture

The reader is asked to critically review each solution approach according to the respective circumstances and to customize it to the specific requirements. Typical customizations to the reference architecture are described in the chapter on BW design and in chapters 25 to 27.

The reference architecture includes the following layers:

- Extraction layer
- Inflow layer
- Transformation layer
- Integration layer
- Data mart layer

Compared to previous releases, SAP BW 7 rather follows the design of enterprise data warehousing that is supported by data marts. For the first time, the data flow between the individual layers in BW 7 is made by a common technology that can be used for each form of processing within BW. This is the *transformation,* as described in chapter 19.

To bring the static definition of the staging to live, the *definition of load processes* will be explained in chapter 20.

All the explanations focus on the new options that BW 7 offers with the concept of transformation processes. To enable downward compatibility among others, BW also masters the old staging technology down to the release 3.x. Some areas of the staging were not updated to the new staging procedure and will thus be defined using the old technologies. **Direct staging** of BW 3.x will be explained in chapter 21.

Then, the options on how to integrate data in *real-time* or *close to real-time* into BW are considered (chapter 22).

Finally, we'll explain the topics *data quality* (chapter 23) and *performance tuning* (chapter 24) from a staging view.

14 Extraction Layer

Before SAP BW can access data from source systems, the source systems have to be enabled to transfer data to SAP BW. In the most simple cases, the credentials to sign into the source system are stored in BW but it may also be the case that source systems need to be customized to actively transfer data to BW.

The structure and content of data that is transferred to BW have to be known to BW. The metadata of the extraction layer needs to be available for each data source, and for BW, it will be either explicitly made known or implicitly used. In section 14.1, the metadata of the extraction layer will be explained first.

Based on this background knowledge on metadata of the extraction layer, the specific preparation of the different source systems (SAP ERP, SAP BW, files, web services, UD connect, third-party ETL tools) will be described in sections 14.2 through 14.8.

14.1 Metadata of the Extraction Layer

The basis for the extraction is the metadata that describes the data to be extracted from the source systems.

In the case of SAP ERP, SAP BW, and third-party ETL tools, BW gets the metadata from the source systems. File systems and relational database systems, however, do not supply this information, so metadata related to them needs to be manually defined in the inflow layer.

The transfer of metadata from the source systems and the manual maintenance is described with the inflow layer (see section 15.1). In the following sections, we'll explain the metadata of the extraction layer and the meaning of this information. The metadata is as follows:

- Available data sources and structure of data
- The application component hierarchy
- Supported delta procedures of the data sources

14.1.1 Data Sources and Data Structure

The data sources and data structures in the extraction layer are contained within what is called a *DataSource*. A DataSource is a business-management unit of master and transactional data (e.g., customer master data, sales order documents) that can be extracted from a source system. The metadata of the source system contains all DataSources available to BW from this source system.

There are four DataSource types:

- Transactional data DataSources
- Master data DataSources for attributes
- Master data DataSources for texts
- Master data DataSources for external hierarchies

From a source system point of view, every DataSource comes with information and programs that describe how the extraction is to be made. These are specific for each data source type and each DataSource within the source system, so we can describe only the technical basics but not the background of the extraction as regards content.

From a BW point of view, each DataSource is a flat structure that is compiled from a range of data fields and that describes a business-management unit (customer master attributes, order entries, etc.).

14.1.2 Application Component Hierarchy

Each source system can provide a number of DataSources. When you're using the BI contents (see appendix D), there may be some hundred DataSources. So that they can be displayed in a manageable way, the DataSources are organized in an application component hierarchy.

Like DataSources, the application component hierarchy is part of the metadata of each source system and is either provided by the source system (SAP ERP, SAP BW, third-party ETL tools)[102] or needs to be maintained manually.

---

102. This means that each of these systems can dispose of its own application component hierarchy, which is independent from other application component hierarchies.

Figure 14–1 shows the application component hierarchy as well as the DataSources of a file system contained in it.

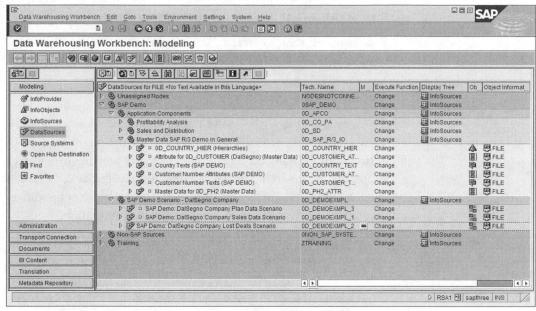

© SAP AG

Figure 14–1
Application component hierarchy with DataSources

14.1.3 Supported Delta Procedures

There are two different forms of extraction when data are extracted from source systems:

- Complete extraction of all data (full upload)
- Extraction in a delta procedure (delta upload)

For the ***complete extraction*** of all data of a DataSource (e.g., all customer orders), all data that is available in a data source is extracted. If there is already data in BW, it might have to be deleted prior to a new full upload.[103] This procedure is the easiest to implement, but especially for large data volume, it can be too runtime intense to lead to success in a reasonable time frame.

For this reason, it makes sense for master data and for transactional data to only extract information that has been newly created, modified, or deleted since the last extraction ***(delta extraction).***

---

103. In BW, the deletion of old data is a specific function that needs to be run explicitly.

Depending on the respective data sources, there are different options to display delta information in DataSources. Some DataSources might not even be in a position to supply delta information. To describe the respectively used delta mode, two pieces of information are relevant:

- The delta mode of each extracted data record
- The used delta mode in a DataSource (delta procedure)

Delta Mode of the Data Records

Each data record that describes delta information can do so differently. Thus, each data record needs to contain some information on the type of delta so that it can be handled accordingly during processing in the staging. To enter this information, there is the InfoObject 0RECORDMODE that can be supplied by the DataSources. The following table comprises the different delta modes that can be used to describe a delta information.

Name	0RECORDMODE	Description
New Image	'N'	The record describes the state after the creation of a new record.
After Image	' '	The record describes the state after the modification of a record. Depending on the DataSource's capabilities, an after image might also mean the creation of a new record.
		If the data of a DataSource does not contain the InfoObject 0RECORDMODE, an after image is automatically assumed.
Before Image	'X'	The record describes the state before a modification. All summable attributes have an inverted sign. Before images are always supplied in combination with other delta mode.
Additive Image	'A'	For summable attributes, the record describes the changes. For non-summable attributes, it describes the state after the change or after the creation.
Deletion	'D'	The record only transfers the key and thus marks that the record was deleted.
Reverse Image	'R'	The record is identical to a before image. Technically, there is a difference in the processing of such records in standard DataStore Objects (see section 17.1.2): if a record with the same key is found in the DataStore Object, it will be deleted even though the attributes might not be identical.

Delta Procedures of DataSources

Depending on the delta mode to be used in a DataSource, the DataSource describes in its metadata a certain delta procedure. Thus, BW can decide with the modeling of the staging whether a DataSource is suitable for the planned processing. Like the structures of the DataSource, the delta procedure of the DataSource is also supplied with the metadata of the extraction layer (SAP ERP, SAP BW, third-party ETL tools) or it needs to be stored manually in the inflow layer. The following table shows the individual delta procedures.[104]

Delta	Description	Full Upload Only	New Image	After Image	Before Image	Additive Image	Deletion	Reverse Image
	(=FULL) Full Upload. Delta can be identified via the standard DataStore Object.	✓						
A	Master data delta (always After Image).			✓				
ABR	Complete delta with deletion mark over delta queue (cube-capable).		✓	✓	✓			✓
ABR1	Like ABR, but serialization only on request.		✓	✓	✓			✓
ADD	Additive extraction via extractor (e.g., LIS infostructures).					✓		
ADDD	Like ADD, but via delta queue (cube-capable).					✓		
AIE	After Images via extractor.			✓				
AIED	After Image with deletion mark via extractor.			✓			✓	
AIM	After Images via delta queue.			✓				
AIMD	After Image with deletion mark via delta queue.			✓			✓	
CUBE	InfoCube extraction.					✓		
FIL0	Delta with After Images.			✓				
FIL1	Delta with Delta Images.					✓		
NEWD	Only new records (inserts) via delta queue (DataStore capable).		✓					

---

104. The currently existing delta procedures can be found in the table RODELTAM.

Delta	Description	Full Upload Only	New Image	After Image	Before Image	Additive Image	Deletion	Reverse Image
NEWE	New records only (inserts) via extractor (DataStore capable).		✓					
ODS	Extraction from DataStore Object.		✓	✓	✓			✓

Furthermore, there are the delta procedures D, E and X. These are old delta procedures that were developed for the extractors of BW release 1.2. These procedures are still supported for compatibility reasons; however, they are no longer used in newer extractors.

Identification of delta procedure
In some cases, it is helpful to identify the delta procedures of a Data-Source from the metadata. The delta procedure is always stored in the ABAP Dictionary table RSOLTPSOURCE (field DELTA) and can be identified using the transaction SE16.

14.2 Extraction from SAP ERP

The basis for the extraction from SAP ERP systems are the extractors that need to be installed as plug-ins in the respective SAP ERP systems. They provide the technical basis for the provision of metadata as well as the processing of data requirements and the execution of the extraction.

A prerequisite for the communication with the BW system is the creation of a CPIC background user (profile S_BI-WX_RFC) as well as the implementation of the required RFC destination in the source system. In the case of SAP ERP systems from release 3.0E onward, the implementation is made during the automatic source systems coupling by BW. With SAP R/3 systems in release 3.0D, the implementation has to be made manually as part of the basic administration.

For each DataSource, the extraction of data is made specifically for the respective data source (see figure 14–2).

The provision of DataSources and the application component hierarchy as well as the module-specific extraction are defined in the BI content that needs to be activated after the installation of the extractors (plug-ins). The activation of the BI content is described in appendix C.1.6.

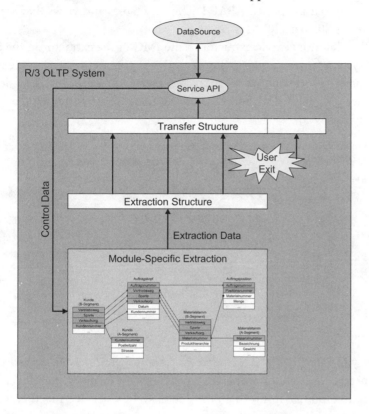

Figure 14–2
Data flow in the source system during extraction from SAP ERP systems

If the extraction is not based on the DataSources of the BI content (e.g., since self-developed ABAP Dictionary tables are to be extracted), generic DataSources can be defined.

Furthermore, enhancements to the DataSources of the BI content or the generic DataSources can be made when the data content of the Data-Sources basically meets requirements but needs to be customized.

In the following sections, we'll explain these topics:

- Defining generic DataSources
- Enhancement of DataSources

14.2.1 Defining Generic DataSources

When you define generic DataSources, you have the option to extract data from any ABAP Dictionary table, view, or even a function module. Thus, such data can be extracted from SAP ERP systems where the extraction was not predefined in the DataSources of the BI content. In practice, these are mostly self-developed ABAP Dictionary tables and views that are not part of the standard ERP systems.

You define a generic extractor in the IMG of the extractor in the SAP ERP system (transaction SBIW) or directly via transaction RS02. To ensure the correct processing of the extracted data in BW, you need to define whether the generic DataSource is transactional data, master data, or texts (see figure 14–3).

Figure 14–3

Maintenance of generic DataSources

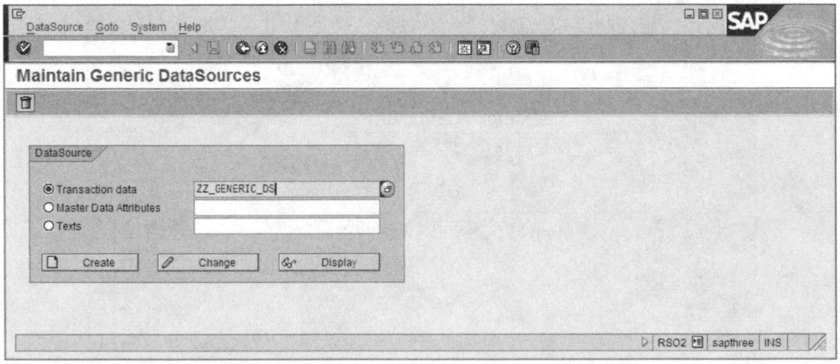

© SAP AG

After you categorize a DataSource as transactional, master, or text data, you need to indicate a transparent table,[105] a view on a transparent table or a function module from which the data is to be extracted together with a descriptive text regarding the DataSource.

The extraction of data for external hierarchies is not possible with the use of generic DataSources. For the extraction of hierarchies, you instead use flat files. A separate program needs to be developed that writes the hierarchic data in a suitable flat file. The design of such flat files is described in section 14.5.

Additionally, you need to determine an application component to which the generic DataSource is to be assigned. This assignment has no meaning to the functioning of the DataSource; it serves only to help clearly organize all DataSources in the application component hierarchy (see figure 14–4).

---

105. The extraction of data from pool and cluster tables is not possible in SAP R/3.

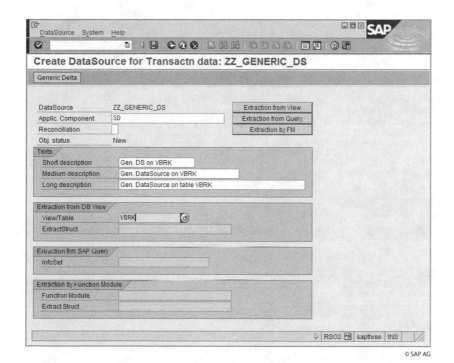

Figure 14–4
Creation of a generic DataSource in SAP ERP

In the following sections, we'll describe the *extraction from views/tables* and the *extraction from function modules.* Further, we'll explain how the extraction can be made via generic DataSources using *delta procedures.*

Extraction from Tables and Views

For extractions using generic DataSources, either a transparent table or a view can be assigned. All table fields of the table/view are available for the extraction.

When you generate a DataSource (see figure 14–5), you can define the fields BW is actually to be offered in the DataSource structure and which of these fields can be used during extraction for the selection of data (see section 15.4.1).

In the SAP ERP environment, a client is a legally and organizationally independent system participant (e.g., one of several companies that share an SAP ERP system). For each logon[106] to an SAP ERP system, exactly one client will be logged on.

Cross-client extraction

---

106. This applies to all forms of logon, i.e. for dialog users and also for CPIC users or such that are used for the logon of other systems to an R/3 system.

Figure 14–5

*Definition of the structure and
selection fields of generic
DataSources*

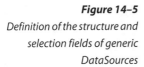

DataSource   Edit   Goto   Utilities(M)   System   Help

DataSource: Customer version Edit

Header Data
DataSource   ZZ_GENERIC_DS   Package $TMP
Description   Generic DataSource

Extraction
ExtractStruct.   Z0XQBD0006
Direct Access   1
Delta Update   ☐   DataSource for Reconciliation   ☐

Field Name	Short text	Selection	Hide field	Inversion	Field only
COMP_CODE	Company code	☑	☐	☐	☐
ASSET_MAIN	Main Asset Number	☑	☐	☐	☐
ASSET	Asset Sub-number	☐	☐	☐	☐
ASSET_AFAB	Depreciation Area Real or Derived	☐	☐	☐	☐
FISCYEAR	Fiscal year	☐	☐	☐	☐
FISCPER3	Posting period	☐	☐	☐	☐
FISCPER	Fiscal year / period	☑	☐	☐	☐
FISCVARNT	Fiscal year variant	☑	☐	☐	☐
SEQ_NUMBER	Sequence number of asset line items in fi	☐	☐	☐	☐
TRANSTYPE	Asset Transaction Type	☐	☐	☐	☐
RECORDMODE	BW Delta Process: Record Mode	☐	☑	☐	☐
CURRENCY	Currency key	☐	☐	☐	☐
ACQ_VAL_TR	Acquisition value for transactions	☐	☐	☐	☐
INV_SUP_TR	Investment support of the transaction	☐	☐	☐	☐
ORD_DEP_TR	Ordinary depreciation on transactions	☐	☐	☐	☐
SPC_DEP_TR	Special depreciation on transactions	☐	☐	☐	☐
UPL_DEP_TR	Unplanned depreciation for the transactior	☐	☐	☐	☐

RSO2   sapthree   INS

Application and customization data of an SAP ERP system is usually stored
related to the client so that a logged-in system/user can use only the application and customization data of the respective client.

Technically, the separation of application and customization data is
made via an additional field in the primary key of the data-containing table
that contains the client number. This is always a field with the name MANDT
and the data element has the same name. Each access to a table with the
field MANDT is automatically limited by SAP ERP according to the login.

In addition, the connection of an SAP ERP system to a BW system
always refers to a certain client; technically, to the logical system that
defines this client (see section 15.1.1).

Therefore, during the extraction from ERP systems, the data of the
respective client is selected for DataSources of the BI content as well as for
generic DataSources. This needs to be kept in mind especially because the

field MANDT will not appear with the definition of DataSources and load processes and will simply be suppressed by the system.

> Especially with the use of views, you should consider that the extraction can only be client related when the field MANDT is also part of the view. If the field MANDT is not part of the view, the underlying table will in each case be read cross-client, which will usually result in key violation in BW since the field MANDT is no longer part of the key in BW.

When texts are modeled for InfoObjects in BW, they are often defined as being language dependent (see also section 6.2.1), partly because this is the default setting for new InfoObjects and partly because it sounds so nice to offer language-dependent texts.

Language-dependent extraction of texts

In this context, for the creation of generic DataSources for texts you should consider whether BW expects texts to be language dependent.

If this is the case, DataSources will need to provide a respective field (preferably the field SPRAS with the data element of the same name) that indicates the language of the respective text.

If the design of the data model, the extraction, and the staging are made without particular alignment, this is in practice often the point in time when a customization of one of the areas is made based on the conditions in the source system.

Extraction from Function Modules

Under certain circumstances, the data to be extracted from an SAP ERP system is not available as a transparent table and cannot be compiled in a view.

Before developing a program to fill a transparent table (as was common with former extractor versions), the extraction can directly access a function module that needs to be developed by the user.

The indication of a function module always needs to be made in combination with an *extract structure* that defines the structure of the Data-Source. Such an extract structure can be created in the ABAP Dictionary using the transaction SE11.

The function module will be called repeatedly:

■ The **first call** is to initiate the function module as well as to possibly review the input parameter. Primarily, the selection criteria (see section 15.4.1) and the maximum package size of the extraction (see section 24.1.1) for the further calls to the function module are to be buffered in the initial call.

■ All **further calls** serve to read and transfer data. With the first call and typically prior to the read access itself, an OPEN CURSOR is to be made in the required tables. For all later calls, the read access (FETCH) will be sufficient. If no further calls are required because the data was read, this will have to be communicated to the Service API by starting the exception NO_MORE_DATA.

The interface of the function module is strictly defined and needs to show the following structure:

	Parameter Name	Typing	Reference Type	Optional	Value Transfer	Description
Import Parameters	I_REQUNR	TYPE	SRSC_S_IF_SIMPLE-REQUNR	✗	✓	Request ID in BW system
	I_DSOURCE	TYPE	SRSC_S_IF_SIMPLE-DSOURCE	✓	✓	Name of the DataSource
	I_MAXSIZE	TYPE	SRSC_S_IF_SIMPLE-INITFLAG	✓	✓	Expected data package size
	I_INITFLAG	TYPE	SRSC_S_IF_SIMPLE-INITFLAG	✓	✓	Flag initialization
	I_READONLY	TYPE	SRSC_S_IF_SIMPLE-READONLY	✓	✓	(No meaning)
	I_REMOTE_CALL	TYPE	SBIWA_FLAG	✓	✓	Flag remote call
Tables	I_T_SELECT	TYPE	SRSC_s_IF_SIMPLE-T_SELECT	✓		Selection criteria
	I_T_FIELDS	TYPE	SRSC_S_IF_SIMPLE-T_FIELDS	✓		Fields to be extracted from the extract structure
	E_T_DATA	LIKE	<Extract Structure>	✓		Transfer structure according to definition of Data-Source
Exceptions	NO_MORE_DATA					Signals that all data was read and FB will not to be called any more
	ERROR_PASSED_TO_MESS_HANDLER					Extraction erroneous

The presetting of a data package size in the parameter I_MAXSIZE represents a desired size that the calling BW systems expect. This size should be kept, if possible; however, it is not mandatory. In some cases (e.g., with complex selections from several tables), it is almost impossible to keep the package size. Even the DataSources of BI content supplied by SAP do not always keep the indicated package sizes.

The following coding example is for a function module that can be used in a generic extractor. The task of this module is to extract from the table ZTABELLE using the fields SFIELD1 and SFIELD2 as selection criteria.

```
FUNCTION Z_BW_EXTRACT_ZTABLE.
*"----------------------------------------------------------------
""Local Interface:
*"      IMPORTING
*"            VALUE(I_REQUNR) TYPE  SRSC_S_IF_SIMPLE-REQUNR
*"            VALUE(I_DSOURCE) TYPE  SRSC_S_IF_SIMPLE-DSOURCE
*"                            OPTIONAL
*"            VALUE(I_MAXSIZE) TYPE  SRSC_S_IF_SIMPLE-MAXSIZE
*"                            OPTIONAL
*"            VALUE(I_INITFLAG) TYPE  SRSC_S_IF_SIMPLE-INITFLAG
*"                            OPTIONAL
*"            VALUE(I_READ_ONLY) TYPE  SRSC_S_IF_SIMPLE-READONLY
*"                            OPTIONAL
*"          VALUE(I_REMOTE_CALL) TYPE  SBIWA_FLAG
*"                          DEFAULT SBIWA_C_FLAG_OFF
*"      TABLES
*"            I_T_SELECT TYPE  SRSC_S_IF_SIMPLE-T_SELECT OPTIONAL
*"            I_T_FIELDS TYPE  SRSC_S_IF_SIMPLE-T_FIELDS OPTIONAL
*"             E_T_DATA STRUCTURE  ZTABELLE OPTIONAL
*"      EXCEPTIONS
*"            NO_MORE_DATA
*"            ERROR_PASSED_TO_MESS_HANDLER
*"----------------------------------------------------------------

TABLES:
ZTABELLE.  "This table is to be extracted by FB
DATA:
   L_S_SELECT TYPE SRSC_S_SELECT. "Supporting structure to
*                                  include selection criteria

STATICS:
   S_S_IF TYPE SRSC_S_IF_SIMPLE,  "Initialization Parameters
   S_COUNTER_DATAPAKID LIKE SY-TABIX,  "Data Record Count
   S_CURSOR TYPE CURSOR.              "Cursor
```

```
RANGES:
   L_R_SFIELD1  FOR ZTABELLE-SFIELD1, "Range for selection fields
   L_R_SFIELD2  FOR ZTABELLE-SFIELD2. "SFIELD1 and SFIELD2

* Call for Initialization
IF I_INITFLAG = SBIWA_C_FLAG_ON.

* Initialization Call: Buffering Initialization Parameters

* Option check of the input parameters can be made here
* Buffer initialization parameters for further calls
   S_S_IF-REQUNR  = I_REQUNR.   "Request ID of Extraction
   S_S_IF-DSOURCE = I_DSOURCE.   "Name of DataSource
   S_S_IF-MAXSIZE = I_MAXSIZE.   "Maximum Data Package Size
   APPEND LINESOF I_T_FIELDS
       TO S_S_IF-T_FIELDS.

* Call for data transfer
   APPEND LINESOF I_T_SELECT
       TO S_S_IF-T_SELECT.
ELSE.

* Read call: OPEN CURSOR + FETCH with first call
* for further calls FETCH only
   IF S_COUNTER_DATAPAKID = 0."OPEN CURSOR with first call

      LOOPAT S_S_IF-T_SELECT  "Selecting the
         INTO L_S_SELECT  "selection criteria
         WHERE FIELDNM = 'SFIELD1'.  "for field SFIELD1

         MOVE-CORRESPONDING L_S_SELECT TO L_R_SFIELD1.
         APPEND L_R_SFIELD1.
      ENDLOOP.

      LOOPAT S_S_IF-T_SELECT  "Selecting the
         INTO L_S_SELECT  "selection criteria
         WHERE FIELDNM = 'SFIELD2'.  "for field SFIELD2

         MOVE-CORRESPONDING L_S_SELECT TO L_R_SFIELD2.
         APPEND L_R_SFIELD2.
      ENDLOOP.

      OPEN CURSOR WITH HOLD S_CURSOR FOR
      SELECT (S_S_IF-T_FIELDS)
         FROM ZTABELLE
         WHERESFIELD1  IN L_R_SFIELD1
         ANDSFIELD2   IN L_R_SFIELD2.

   ENDIF.
      FETCH NEXT CURSOR S_CURSOR  "Fetch for all read calls
         APPENDING CORRESPONDING FIELDS
         OF TABLE E_T_DATA
         PACKAGE SIZE S_S_IF-MAXSIZE.
```

```
IF SY-SUBRC <> 0.
CLOSE CURSOR S_CURSOR.
RAISE NO_MORE_DATA.
ENDIF.
S_COUNTER_DATAPAKID = S_COUNTER_DATAPAKID + 1.
ENDIF.
ENDFUNCTION.
```

If there are errors in the execution of a function module, they can be handed over to the Service API with the call of the macro LOG_WRITE. The error also needs to be signaled to the Service API by starting the exception ERROR_PASSED_TO_MESS_HANDLER.

The respective ABAP coding can be designed as follows:

```
LOG_WRITE'E'      "Message type E (error)
     'Zxy'        "Message class (acc to transaction SE91)
     '001'        "Message number within the class
     I_DSOURCE    "Content 1 (here name of DataSource)
     ' '.         "Content 2 (here no values)
RAISE ERROR_PASSED_TO_MESS_HANDLER.
```

Generic Delta

Especially if the data volume supplied by a generic extractor leads to performance problems, the use of the delta procedure is inevitable (see section 14.1.3).

The use of the delta procedures will be supported by generic extractors *Delta-defined field* if changed or newly created data records can be delimited from the data records already extracted with an attribute. For this purpose, the value of such an attribute needs to increase monotonically with the changed/newly created data record.

Such a monotonically increasing attribute could be, for example, one of the following:

- A time stamp as a DEC15 field in the format YYYYMMDDhhmmss
- A calendar day as a DATS8 field in the format YYYYMMDD
- A numeric pointer

With the definition of the delta procedure, you should indicate a respective field in the DataSource and define whether it is a time stamp, a calendar day, or a numeric pointer (see figure 14–6).

Figure 14–6
Creation of a generic
DataSource with the delta
procedure

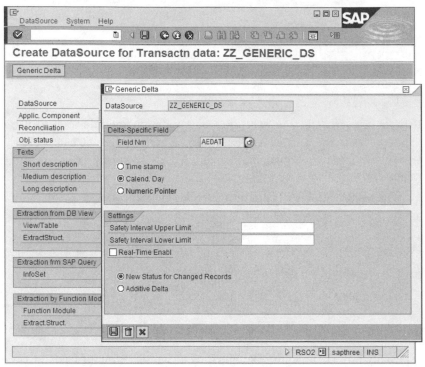

© SAP AG

The sales document number of the sales orders (tables VBAK and VBAP) would not be a suitable example for a delta pointer since this number is a consecutive numeric pointer and sales orders can change over time; the sales order will thus not monotonically increase with the changes.

The sales order of the invoice receipts, however, would be well suited since it is a monotonically increasing numeric pointer (invoices do not change subsequently).[107]

> With the definition of a generic delta, it is necessary to know the content of the data to be extracted. If a delta procedure is created on a numeric pointer/calendar day/time stamp that does not increase monotonically, this will lead to major errors (that are usually sneaky since they are well hidden).

Use of two
delta-defined fields   In many cases, a change date will be combined with the creation data in SAP ERP systems when the field with the creation data is first filled with

---

107. In the area of orders and invoices, you should consider that, despite the given examples, the content DataSources of the logistic extraction should be applied anyway.

the creation of the data record and the change date is first filled with the first change. Thus, the creation date is suitable only as a delta-defined field to identify newly created data records (but no changes) while the change date as a delta-defined field can only be used to detect changes (but not creation).

To define a delta extraction with the use of two fields combined this way, you can define two generic DataSources that each supply part of the delta (creation/changes). You need to consider that individual data records that can be created and also be changed prior to extraction can be supplied by both DataSources.

With the extraction from generic DataSources, the extractor in SAP ERP systems internally reviews the content of the transferred data, and in the administration of the delta queue, it remembers the highest value transferred to BW.

Delta administration for numeric pointers

The next extraction involves all data records in which the content of the delta pointer is above the value that was stored in the delta queue with the last extraction. After the extraction, the next higher value is stored in the delta queue, etc. (see figure 14–7).

Figure 14–7

Generic delta extraction on the basis of numeric pointers

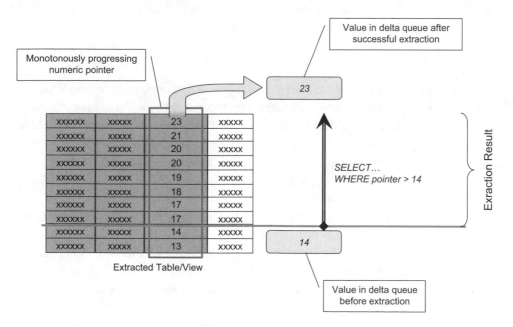

This is all automatically done by the interaction of extractor and SAP BW and does not need to be considered any further during the modeling of extraction and staging.

Delta administration of time stamps and calendar days

For the use of time stamps and calendar days, the delta mechanism known from numeric pointers will be expanded. So, not only is the highest extracted value of the last extraction used as the *lower limit* for the next extraction, the current date/time stamp is used as *upper limit.*

For example, the generic delta extraction on the calendar day of 01/18/2005 would not supply any data records if the calendar day is after 01/18/2005 (an exception is the use of security intervals, as explained next).

Figure 14–8

Generic delta extraction on the basis of time stamp/calendar day

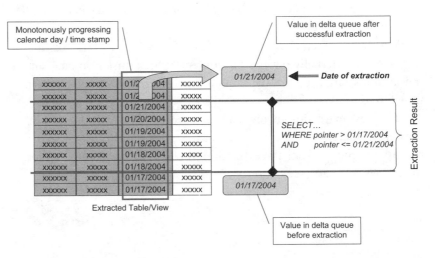

Security interval

Delta administration is an acceptable tool that ensures for numeric pointers that only all new or changed data records are considered for extraction.

Especially if during extraction new data records are generated, there might be serious errors in the delta administration of calendar days/time stamps. For example, if data was extracted on 01/18/2008 at 23:45 hrs, the transfer of all data records that were created on 01/18/2005 after 23:45 hrs would not be secured.

This reason for errors could theoretically be limited by setting the extraction time exactly to 23:59:59 hrs if possible (not to 00:00:00 since the upper limit would then be the following day!). However, this is not practical from a technical or business point of view.

To counter this problem, two *security intervals* can be defined (see figure 14–6):

- **Security Interval Upper Limit:** The determination of an upper limit is not to read the data source up to the current time/date but to deliberately select a smaller upper limit. Setting an upper limit prevents errors that occur from extracting and generating data records simultaneously (as far as the security interval at least covers the duration of the extraction). At the same time, setting an upper limit leads to the fact that the most current data will never be extracted.

- **Security Interval Lower Limit:** The determination of a lower limit also refers to data records in the extraction that are below the last highest extracted calendar day/time stamp. The underlying principle is to extract data records multiple times rather than to not extract them at all. The extracted data volume is thus bigger than necessary but the most current data can also be included in the extraction. The use of security intervals for the lower limit always needs to be linked to a DataStore Object in BW (to be discussed additionally later in this section).

Both security intervals can be used individually or in combination with each other. The combination of lower and upper limits, however, makes sense only in specific cases since a larger data volume than necessary will be created and the most current data will still not be extracted.

Depending on whether the delta administration is made using the calendar day or using a time stamp, a unit in the security interval means either one day or one second.

The delta administration with security intervals is outlined in figure 14–9.

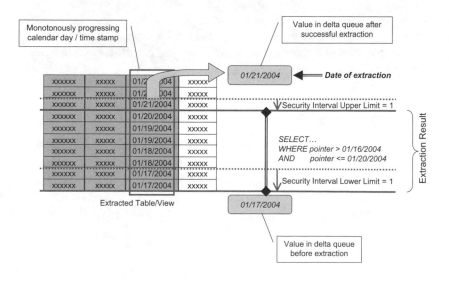

Figure 14–9

Generic delta extraction with security intervals

Delta mode of
generic delta DataSources

As regards delta administration and security intervals, the use of generic delta procedures is mostly understood as a user development with specific properties. Unlike the DataSources of the BI content, the SAP ERP extractor cannot itself provide information on the generic data records' delta mode type (see section 14.1.3.1).

With the definition of a generic delta procedure, whether an extractor displays its data to BW as **additive images** or as **after images** needs to be determined. Other delta modes are not available for the definition.

The right selection of the delta mode plays a decisive role for the processing of data in the integration layer and the data mart layer (see chapters 17 and 18). Only additive images can be directly updated in a BasisCube while after images need to be updated in a DataStore Object to be transformed into an additive image there.

You need to consider that the provision of data records as additive images will be realistic only in the delta administration with a numeric pointer. For the calendar day/time stamp, an additive image will still be possible if the security interval is used as upper limit.

With the use of a security interval for the lower limit, the determination of the after image will be out of the question.

Only mark a generic delta procedure as additive when you have fully understood the properties of the delta procedure and the mode and the additive nature of the DataSource is ensured. The effort to create DataStore Objects that are required to process after images in BW (new condition for changed records) is manageable and should be preferred for design considerations, anyway, i.e., also for additive images. Because a data source only creates new data records but does not change any, you can easily mark a delta procedure as an after image even with an additive image. In practice, cases where this does not apply are rather rare, so you are at least on the safe side with the after image.

14.2.2   Enhancing DataSources

In some cases, the information from existing DataSources will not exactly meet all requirements. For this reason, the extractors offer an option to enhance DataSources per field. It can be filled with individual ABAP routines.

The enhancement of DataSources is made in three steps:

- Enhancing the DataSource structure
- Filling the enhanced data fields
- Editing the application component hierarchy

The starting point for the planned enhancing is always the introductory guideline to BW extractors that can be found in the respective source system in the transaction SBIW (see figure 14–10).

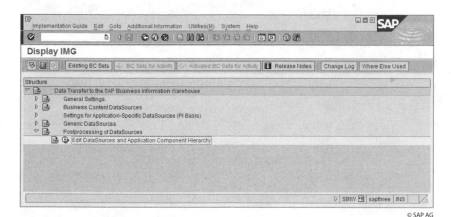

Figure 14–10
Editing DataSources

© SAP AG

The basis for the enhancement of the DataSource structure is the data flow of the extraction from SAP ERP systems, as shown in figure 14–2. Accordingly, the data from the module-specific extraction is first compiled for each DataSource in a flat structure—the *extract structure*. The extract structure is preset by either the BI content or the generic DataSources and it *cannot* be changed.

After the extracted data is adjusted to the format of the extract structure, it is transformed into the format of another structure—the transfer structure. The transfer structure determines the design of the respective DataSource, and at first, the design will be identical to the extract structure. Unlike the extract structure, the transfer structure can be enhanced with additional fields if required (this also enhances the structure of the DataSource).

You can enhance the transfer structure by editing the DataSource via the *Enhance Extraction Structure* button (see figure 14–11).

With the enhancement, an append to the transfer structure will be created in which the new fields are defined by field names and the respective data elements. The enhancement is possible for each DataSource that extracts flow and master data. However, only fields in the structure of the

Enhancing the DataSource structure

Figure 14–11
Editing the DataSource
structure

append can be maintained. Changing or deleting existing fields in the DataSource is not possible.[108] DataSources for the extraction of texts cannot be changed.

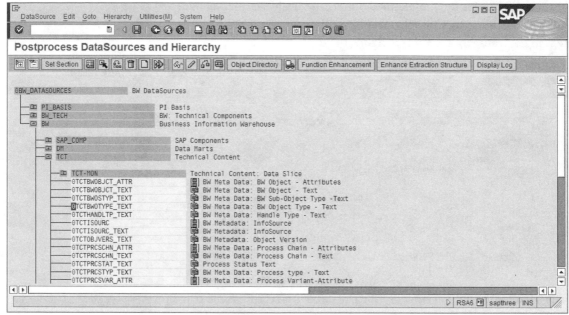

© SAP AG

When you use DataSources to extract hierarchies, an enhancement is not possible since these DataSources basically keep a preset structure and the hierarchy structure can be enhanced only by manipulating the data content.

Filling enhanced data   After you enhance a DataSource, the additional fields are contained in the DataSource but they are not supplied with content during extraction. To supply additional fields with data, the extractors provide user exits in which the fields can be filled.

> You should not enhance DataSources for the calculation of values that could also be calculated in the BW staging. If all required data is supplied by one DataSource and no specific functions of the source system are required for the calculation, it will be easier and more traceable to calculate data in BW than in the user exits of the extractors.

---

108. Besides, fields can be hidden from BW (see figure 14-5) or content can be changed during extraction.

The coding of user exits can be reached via the *Function Enhancement* button when you edit the DataSources (see figure 14–11). Depending on the data type, one of the following user exits is used:[109]

- Enhancing transactional data:
  EXIT_SAPLRSAP_001
- Enhancing master data attributes:
  EXIT_SAPLRSAP_002
- Enhancing master data texts:
  EXIT_SAPLRSAP_003
- Enhancing external hierarchies:
  EXIT_SAPLRSAP_004

To use these user exits, you need to create a new project and activate it using the transaction CMOD, to which the SAP enhancement RSAP0001 is added.

Data is packaged during extraction. Thus, the user exit may not dispose of all the supplied data from data delivery. The package sizes refer to the technical conditions (package sizes), not to content rules. The definition of package sizes is further explained in section 24.1.1.

Enhancing DataSources is usually finished with enhancing the structure and the programming of the respective user exits. If requested, the existing application component hierarchy can be edited as part of the enhancement.

Editing the application component hierarchy

The application component hierarchy can be edited in the source system using the transaction RSA6 or in the introductory guidelines of the extractors (transaction SBIW, *Edit DataSources→Edit Application Component Hierarchy*, see figure 14–12).

When you edit the application component hierarchy, you can change the hierarchy by rearranging, deleting, or re-creating hierarchy nodes and existing DataSources can be rearranged within a hierarchy.

---

109. This list includes the underlying function modules that are to be considered when using transaction SE37.

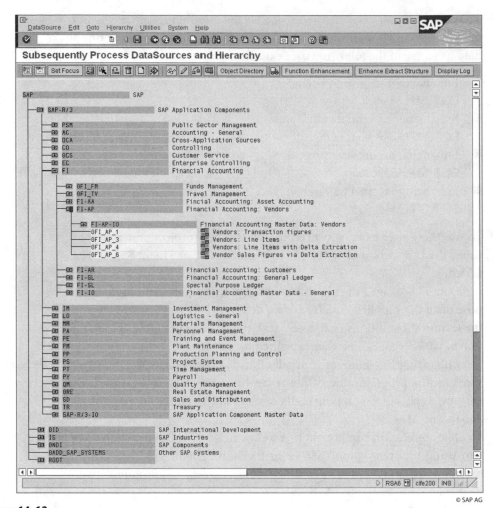

© SAP AG

Figure 14–12

Editing the application component hierarchy in SAP ERP

14.3 Extracting from BW Systems

Especially in large-scale architectures, a BW system is not only the data recipient, it also needs to be able to provide data for other systems. For this purpose, BW makes use of export DataSources in addition to the generic DataSources used in ERP systems (see section 14.2.1).

Export DataSources are generated for data targets in BW and they make DataSources available for extraction. The DataSources can be used for extraction by other BW systems to which the supplying BW system is connected as source system.

Up to release 3.x, it was common to also use export DataSources for transferring data within the BW system. BW used itself as source system (the so-called Myself source system). For the system-internal transfer of data, from now on you should use the new technology for transformation and data transfer processing (see chapters 19 and 20) that no longer need to rely on export DataSources.

Export DataSources can be created for the following data targets:

- BasisCubes
- DataStore Objects
- InfoObjects with master data/hierarchies

For this purpose, it is sufficient to select in the context menu of the respective data target in the Data Warehousing Workbench the menu item *Generate Export DataSource* (see figure 14–13).

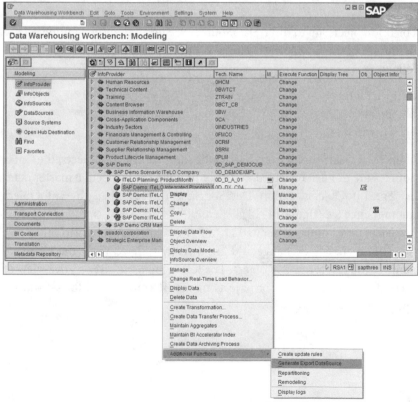

Figure 14–13

Creation of export DataSources for transactional data

© SAP AG

Export DataSources for cubes and DataStore Objects

For BasisCubes and DataStore Objects, BW thus supplies a DataSource for transactional data. This DataSource can supply data in one complete delivery or in a delta procedure to another system (the delta procedure is CUBE or ODS).

Components of the DataSource are all characteristics and key figures of the cube or the DataStore Object, but not the attributes of the characteristics! If required, these need to be manually added by expanding the extract structure and by programming the user exit for extraction (see section 14.2.2).

For BasisCubes, the delta is formed from the request ID that identifies load processes in a BasisCube. For DataStore Objects, the change log is used to provide delta information. The change log is further explained in the description of the integration layer (see section 17.1.2).

> If several systems are to be supplied by the export DataSource, the delta procedure can only be used by one system.

Export DataSources for InfoObjects

For InfoObjects, up to three DataSources are generated (depending on the definition of the InfoObject). There will be one DataSource for each of the following:

- Attributes
- Texts
- Hierarchies

Unlike the DataSources from BasisCubes and DataStore Objects, the DataSources are not delta enabled and only provide the respective master data.

For InfoObjects, export DataSources are created in the InfoObject maintenance (see figure 14–14).

Naming convention

The names of the generated DataSources are transferred to other systems via metadata exchange and are directly derived from the technical name of the respective BW object. The following table gives an overview of these dependencies both for objects of the BI content and for self-developed BW objects.

BW Object	Name of the BW Object	Name of the DataSource
Cube/Data-Store Object	0ttttttttt / ttttttttt	80ttttttttt / 8ttttttttt
InfoObject (attributes)	0ttttttttt / ttttttttt	80ttttttttM / 8ttttttttM
InfoObject (texts)	0ttttttttt / ttttttttt	80ttttttttT / 8ttttttttT
InfoObject (hierarchies)	0ttttttttt / ttttttttt	80ttttttttH / 8ttttttttH
PSA table	0ttttttttt_XX / ttttttttt_XX	70ttttttttt_XX / 7ttttttttt_XX

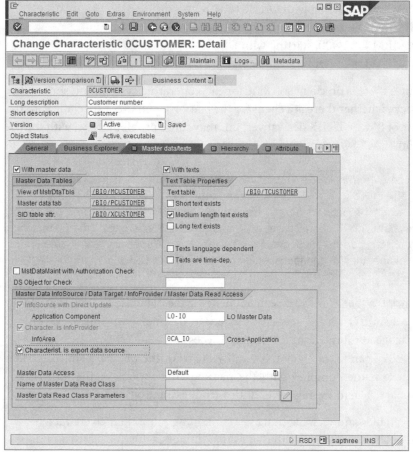

Figure 14–14
Creation of export
DataSources for master data

© SAP AG

14.4 Extracting from Database Systems

To make data sources outside the SAP ERP and the SAP BW world accessible to BW, there is the option to directly connect relational database systems to BW. SAP BW refers to the respective interface as DB connect.

Supported database systems   To extract data, SAP BW logs onto the respective database systems like a regular client and reads the required data. SAP BW can work only with client software of the following databases:

- SAP DB, starting with SAP DB 7.2.5 Build 3
- All IDS releases of Informix, series 7 and 9, that are maintained by IBM/Informix
- Microsoft SQL Server 7.0 and MS SQL Server 2000
- Oracle, starting with Oracle 8.1.7.3
- IBM DB2/390, starting with DB2/390 V6
- IBM DB2/400, starting with DB2/400 V4R5
- IBM DB2 UDB, starting with DB2 UDB V7.1

Since there is no client software for each operating system, you should first check whether there is a client for the platform you use. Especially with the use of BW on UNIX derivatives, this may cause problems (e.g., with the client for MS SQL Server).

There are numerous alternatives to using the DB connect, such as the use of flat files (see section 14.5.1) or extracting using the JDBC driver (see section 14.7). However, please consider that the connection to a database system via DB connect is easily made (from a BW perspective) and that the transfer performance beats any alternative. Especially with large data volume, the DB connect should be used if the preconditions are fulfilled.

Database user   Since BW behaves like a regular client for the database system, you should create a user for the respective database schema. With this user, you can manage authorizations for database access.

Restrictions   BW can extract any table and view from the database source system whose name complies with the naming conventions of the ABAP Dictionary. The following are excluded from extraction:

- Tables and views with names containing more than 26 characters
- Tables and views with names that do not exclusively consist of uppercase letters, figures, or the underscore character (_).

- Tables and views with field names that exceed 16 characters
- Tables and views with field names that do not exclusively consist of uppercase letters, figures, or the underscore character (_).
- Tables and views with reserved field names (e.g., count)

Further, BW has a basic problem with using date formats since BW itself does not create any date fields in the database (date fields of BW are always of NUMC type).

To solve the problems regarding naming conventions and date formats, it is recommended that you use views that can be created on the tables to be extracted and change table and field names and possibly even make format adjustments. Thus, BW does not directly extract from a table but from the respective view.

BW can determine selections for the extraction of data. Here, BW assumes that the database system works with the code page >>cp850<< and the sort sequence "bin". If this is not the case, errors with pattern search (e.g., >>LIKE 1B*<<) or area search (e.g., >>BETWEEN 1B00 and 1BZZ<< or >> >1B00<<) can occur.

Sort sequence and code page

In these cases, you should ensure that the selection of data is made using the first 127 ASCII values but no special characters.

A selection of DEC type fields is not possible at all.

If the database system works with multibyte code pages—i.e., character records with more than 256 characters (e.g., Kanju, Chinese, etc.)—characters may be distorted.

Texts are provided language dependent in the language in which the database user has logged onto BW.

Texts

Hierarchy data cannot be supplied via a DB connect.

Hierarchies

14.5 Extracting from Files

When you extract data from files, you have a universal and very flexible option to import external data into BW without defining the data source explicitly as an own source system in BW.

The file interface especially makes sense when it's not worthwhile to make a connection from the respective source system to BW because, for example, only one single DataSource is to be extracted from the source system or if a connection from the source system is technically not possible.

You can typically extract master and transactional data from the following sources:

- MS Excel sheets
- External systems (e.g., SAP R/2, SAP R/3 prior to release 3.0D, Baan, JDE, etc.)
- SAP ERP systems in the case of self-defined hierarchies

This type of extraction requires that the source systems that have to provide data in a file format play an active role. How such a file is created is up to each source system.

> The file interface existed from the earliest BW releases, and it can be functionally replaced by another interface, especially since the new interfaces can often directly extract from the data sources where the source systems do not need to play an active role. You need to consider in this case that the performance of file interfaces is very convincing with large data volume and is exceeded only by DB connect. Prior to the use of UD connect, the SOAP connection, or a complex third-party ETL tool, the use of the file interface should be reviewed quite favorably.

The following sections explain the requirements for the available data so that they can be processed in BW. We'll explain requirements for the file format and the data structure for transactional data, attributes, texts, and hierarchies.

14.5.1   File Format

When reading from file systems, BW can process only *flat files*. These are files with a firmly structured design that is identical for each row of the file. Files with other structures (e.g., hierarchical structures) cannot be read into BW.

> BW can skip a preset number of rows in the beginning of the flat file. This allows for storage of information such as field names in the beginning of the flat file.

A particular difficulty with flat files is to type and format individual fields so that they are correctly processed in BW.

Typing   Regarding typing, there is now an option in BW 7 to read data in the internal format of BW via a flat file. The content of the flat file is stored **binarily;** e.g., a value INT4 is not stored as the number displayed but as a 4-byte value (as required for storing). This form of data input leads to high-performance processing since no further conversions are necessary in BW.[110] However, if errors occur during the processing, they are hard to trace if they are content errors from the data input.

In this regard, it is easier to use data content in ***ASCII format,*** which was mandatorily used up to the releases 3.x of BW. For processing in BW, this data only needs to be converted via a generic adapter into the internal BW format and this slightly decreases performance. *Formatting*

With the use of the ASCII format, there are two options to describe the fields within a file:

- Fixed data record length (ASCII with CR separator)
- Comma Separated Variables (CSV)

Further, both file types are expanded in a conversion to map numeric values.

For file types with fixed data record length, not only the length of the data records but also the length of each individual field will be preset (in BW, this definition is made in the inflow layer). *Fixed data record length*

Each data record in the flat file needs to end with the carriage return (CR) separator. If the CR separator is recognized before the defined data record ending, it will be assumed that the data records end earlier.

Due to the simple structure of this file type, extraction is easy and implementation is stable and very well performing.

The definition of the transfer structure in BW, however, can be time consuming and prone to error, so extraction from flat files in CSV format is easier to implement.

> For files with fixed data record length, all fields absolutely need to have the defined length. If this length is not reached (e.g., with a shorter customer number), padding the fields with blank spaces (for alphanumeric fields) or zeros (for numeric fields) needs to be done.

For CSV format also, the fields created in the flat file as well as their sequence need to be determined and defined in the BW inflow layer. The CSV format, however, does not rely on keeping a fixed length of the individual fields or data records. *Data format (CSV files)*

---

110. With the definition of DataSources in the inflow layer, the file data is loaded by generating adapters.

Instead, the end of a field is marked by a *data separator*. The data separator is a preset character (a semicolon by default) that marks the end of the fields.

In some specific cases where the data separator itself is part of the field content, this can be marked by an *escape sign* (an apostrophe by default). Thus, field entries can be provided with data separators that BW will not treat as data separators per se.

The following table contains some examples for the use of the escape sign.

Field Content to Be Described	Display in CSV Format
abcdef	abcdef
abc;def	abc";def
abc""def	abc""def
abc;def "	abc";def ""

In the example in the table, the semicolon is used as a data separator and the apostrophe as an escape sign. This definition corresponds with the standard BW settings, but it is not binding and can be freely determined during load processes in BW.

Number format   The display of numeric values also needs to be made in ASCII format. A particular problem is the use of thousands separators[111] and decimal points.[112]

To accommodate different types of display, the characters can be chosen freely. In BW, they will only be interpreted according to their definition during the load process.

By default, BW interprets a comma to be a thousands separator and a point to be a decimal point and thus it follow the standard U.S. notations.

14.5.2 Data Structure

Depending on the data to be described in a flat file, the flat file needs to follow a certain structure or provide a minimum amount of fields. The data structure for extraction shows the following components:

---

111. Thousands separators are often used to display big number in a readable way (e.g., 3,000,000 for three million).
112. Decimal points are used to separate positions.

- Transactional data
- Attributes
- Texts
- Hierarchies

Extracting Transactional Data

There are no further restrictions for the design of flat files for flow data. The number and sequence of the fields can be defined freely as long as a flat structure with fixed data record length or the CSV format is given.

Regarding content, the flat file can either deliver all data completely or deliver it in a delta procedure. There are two possible delta procedures:

Delta extraction

- Only after images are provided (in BW defined as FIL0).
- Only additive images are provided (in BW defined as FIL1).

If no delta procedure is to be used, the provided data will also be described by the delta procedure FIL0, which is the standard used for flat files in BW.

Extracting Attributes

The design of a flat file for master data attribute delivery depends on the compounding and the attributes of the InfoObject to be filled as well as the time dependency of its attributes.

The following table describes the design of a flat file to provide *time-independent* attributes for the InfoObject ZCHAR that is *not* compounded to another InfoObject.

Field Name	Description
ZCHAR	Character key
ATTR1	Time-independent attribute 1
ATTRx	Time-independent attribute x

In the case that the InfoObject ZCHAR is compounded to the InfoObject ZCOMPOUND and has a *time-dependent* attribute, the following fields need to be part of the structure of the flat file.

An InfoObject can have time-constant and also time-dependent attributes and thus, depending on the provided attributes, a different flat file structure might be required. It results in the fact that two flat files will have to be created to supply an InfoObject: one for time-constant attributes and one for time-dependent attributes.

Field Name	Description
ZCOMPOUND	Key of the compounded characteristics (if characteristic available)
ZCHAR	Characteristics key
DATETO	Valid until – date (only for time-dependent master data); CHAR 8
DATEFROM	Valid from – date (only for time-dependent master data); CHAR 8
ATTR1	Time-dependent attribute 1
ATTRx	Time-dependent attribute x

Extracting Texts

To provide BW with master data texts, you need to meet file structure requirements similar to the requirements for attributes.

The following table describes the required fields of a flat file for the provision of the InfoObject ZCHAR that shows language and time-dependent texts of short, medium, and long length and that is compounded to the InfoObject ZCOMPOUND.

Field Name	Description
LANGU	Language key (E for English; D for German); CHAR 1
ZCOMPOUND	Key of the compounded characteristic (if characteristic available)
ZCHAR	Characteristics key
DATETO	Valid until – date (for time-dependent master data only); CHAR 8
DATEFROM	Valid from – date (for time-dependent master data only); CHAR 8
TXTSH	Short text; CHAR 20
TXTMD	Medium text; CHAR 40
TXTLG	Long text; CHAR 60

In practice, master data texts will be designed in a simpler way so that the fields LANGU (language-dependency), ZCOMPOUND (compounding), and DATETO/DATEFROM (time-dependency) and defined text lengths can be omitted.

External Hierarchies

The structure of a flat file to display a hierarchy is more complex than with attributes and texts. The following table describes the structure that needs to be followed for such flat files. Unlike with attributes and texts, the sequence of fields is relevant in this case.

Field Name	Description
NODEID	Internal ID (with leading zeros) that clearly describes a hierarchy node. The NODEID 0000001 exists exactly once in each hierarchy and describes the hierarchy root. The NODEIDs of all other nodes can be selected freely (usually numbered sequentially).
INFOOBJECT	If a hierarchy node is described by a characteristics node, the field needs to contain the technical name of the characteristic (e.g., 0MATERIAL). If the hierarchy node is to describe a text node, the InfoObject 0HIERNODE needs to be entered into the field (this marks the node as text node).
NODENAME	For a characteristics node, the key value of the InfoObject needs to be contained. For text nodes, this field contains the respective (discretionary) text.
LINK	If the hierarchy node is a link node (that is, a node of two parent nodes), this needs to be marked by an X in this field. With the use of link nodes, two records that contain the same NODEID are supplied in the flat file. The first record describes the "normal" node and leaves the field LINK blank. The second record describes the link node and contains an X in the LINK field. For normal nodes, this fields needs to be left blank.
PARENTID	In the field PARENTID, the NODEID of the superordinate node (parent node) needs to be entered. In the case of the hierarchy root, this is 00000000. In the flat file, the hierarchies always need to be described decreasingly; that is, the PARENTID needs to have a smaller NODEID than the described NODEID. Thus, BW can check whether there is a PARENTID when loading.
CHILDID[1]	For sorted hierarchies, there is a defined first subordinate node for each node. In this field, the NODEID of the first subnode needs to be entered. If there is no subnode, the CHILDID needs to have the value 0000000. If there is no sorted hierarchy, the field must not be contained in the file structure.

Field Name	Description
NEXTID[2]	For sorted hierarchies, there is a defined next node for each node.
	In this field, the NODEID of the next node needs to be entered. If there is no other node in the same hierarchy level, the NEXTID needs to have the value NEXTID.
	If there is no sorted hierarchy, the field must not be contained in the file structure.
DATETO/ DATEFROM[3]	In the case of time-dependent hierarchy structures, the fields DATETO and DATEFROM need to contain a validity period.
	If the hierarchy structure is not time dependent, these fields must not be contained in the file structure.
LEAFTO/ LEAFFROM[4]	For hierarchies with intervals, the fields LEAFTO and LEAFFROM need to provide the upper and lower limit of the interval (same as the field NODENAME).
	If there is no hierarchy with intervals, these fields must not be contained in the file structure.
LANGU	If a text node is described by the node, this fields needs to describe the language of the texts in the following fields.
	If texts are to be provided in several languages, several records need to be provided for the respective hierarchy node in the file and they describe the different languages.
TXTSH/TXTMD/ TXTLG	If a text node is described by the node, the short, medium, and long text of the hierarchy node is to be defined.

1. This field is mandatory for sorted hierarchies only.
2. This field is mandatory for sorted hierarchies only.
3. These fields are only required for time-dependent hierarchy structures.
4. These fields are only required for hierarchies with intervals.

In the following, an example for the description of a hierarchy with a flat file is given. A sales structure to the InfoObject ZREGION with the hierarchy nodes *North, East, South,* and *West* in hierarchy level 1 is to be described.

The hierarchy nodes *North, East,* and *West* are characteristics nodes that can be posted to. The hierarchy node *South* is a text node that has two subordinate nodes. These nodes are the characteristics nodes *South1* and *South2* that can be posted to.

The hierarchy to be described is not time dependent and not sorted and does not allow for any hierarchy intervals. Figure 14–15 shows the hierarchy together with the master data of the InfoObject.

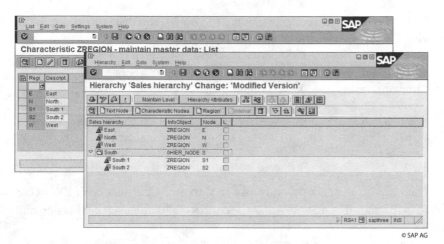

Figure 14–15
External hierarchies from flat files

© SAP AG

The following table shows the structure and content of the connected file. The characteristics keys for the regions are N, E, S1, S2, and W

NodeID	InfoObject	Node Name	Link	Parent ID	Language	TXTSH
00000001	OHIER_NODE	ROOT			D	Sales
00000002	ZREGION	N		00000001		
00000003	ZREGION	E		00000001		
00000004	OHIER_NODE	S		00000001	D	South
00000005	ZREGION	S1		00000004		
00000006	ZREGION	S2		00000004		
00000007	ZREGION	W		00000001		

14.6 Extracting via Web Services

To extract XML documents, an HTTP service based on Web AS ABAP has been available since BW release 3.0. This is the SOAP service[113] that helps to transfer data in XML format into BW.

In this section, we'll explain the basic conditions for XML documents to be extracted. It should quickly become obvious that this is less a universal

---

113. SOAP (Simple Object Access Protocol) is an HTTP-based object protocol that enables the exchange of XML documents.

XML interface than a concept tailored to SAP XI, and that is, in our opinion, vital for a reasonable use of the SOAP interface.

> In the area of metadata definition, XML is an excellent data format. To exchange mass data, XML is rather unsuited given its large overhead, and thus the SOAP service is provided only for the exchange of small data volume. If you're using the SOAP service at all, you should use it only for very small amounts of data; preferably, alternative data sources (e.g., flat files) should be used.

Each XML document that is transferred to the SOAP service of BW needs to be packaged as a SOAP message consisting of an envelope, header, and body.

Envelope
The envelope is the first element of the XML document; it's the element by which it is identified as a SOAP message and it envelops all other parts of the message.

Header
Optionally, XML documents can be provided with an additional header that contains additional information on the XML document. By default, BW does not consider this header any further.

Body
The core of the XML document is the body that describes the master and transactional data provided by the XML document. An extraction of hierarchy data is not possible with XML documents.

The structure of the data in the body needs to exactly match the structure that is expected in BW—comparable to flat files where the structure is also defined by BW.

Within the body, the individual data records are describes as *items* that are each compounded by the HTML tags <item> and </item>. Within such an item, the fields of the respective data record need to be transferred in a flat structure (and in exactly the sequence BW expects). A modified sequence or even a hierarchic structure is not permitted even though the XML taxonomy would allow for it.

Push mechanism
Other than with the remaining source system types, XML documents are not extracted by BW but are actively transferred from the source system to the BW SOAP service; this is referred to as a *push mechanism*.

Since the SOAP service of BW receives data from all kinds of DataSources, it needs to be defined within the SOAP message how the data is to be processed in BW after the SOAP service has received the message.

For this reason, the body of the SOAP document needs to start with the indication of a *function module*; its calling writes the data in the provided delta queue of BW. The function module is generated with the definition of the transfer structure for the XML source and is thus only explained in section 15.2.1. Also, you need to indicate the name of the *DataSource* that has been provided in BW to receive the XML data.

Thus, the content of an XML document relies more heavily on the implementation of BW than the creators of the XML model had thought.

As an example, figure 14–16 shows a SOAP message where a data structure consisting of the fields SALESORG, POSTAL_CD, SALES_OFF, SALES_DIST, and SALES_GRP is delivered to the DataSource 6AQSALES_STRUC in BW. The called function module is named /BIC/QI6AQSALES_STRUC_RFC.

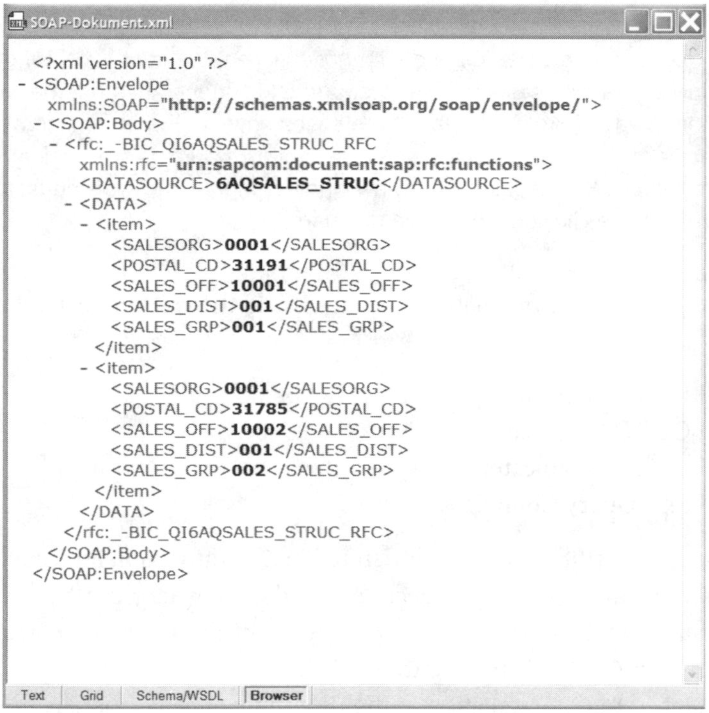


```
<?xml version="1.0" ?>
- <SOAP:Envelope
    xmlns:SOAP="http://schemas.xmlsoap.org/soap/envelope/">
  - <SOAP:Body>
    - <rfc:_-BIC_QI6AQSALES_STRUC_RFC
        xmlns:rfc="urn:sapcom:document:sap:rfc:functions">
        <DATASOURCE>6AQSALES_STRUC</DATASOURCE>
      - <DATA>
        - <item>
            <SALESORG>0001</SALESORG>
            <POSTAL_CD>31191</POSTAL_CD>
            <SALES_OFF>10001</SALES_OFF>
            <SALES_DIST>001</SALES_DIST>
            <SALES_GRP>001</SALES_GRP>
          </item>
        - <item>
            <SALESORG>0001</SALESORG>
            <POSTAL_CD>31785</POSTAL_CD>
            <SALES_OFF>10002</SALES_OFF>
            <SALES_DIST>001</SALES_DIST>
            <SALES_GRP>002</SALES_GRP>
          </item>
        </DATA>
      </rfc:_-BIC_QI6AQSALES_STRUC_RFC>
    </SOAP:Body>
  </SOAP:Envelope>
```

Figure 14–16
SOAP document

14.7 Extracting from JDBC, XML/A, and ODBO Sources

The J2EE connector architecture (see section 3.1.3) technically enables you to develop any data source in the form of connectors or resource adapters for the J2EE engine and to supply the thus available data via SAP JCo to the BW system (Web AS ABAP).

The technical possibilities are interesting for the development of specific applications, but it would certainly require too much effort for each SAP user to redevelop the access to common relational and hierarchic interfaces such as JDBC, XML/A, and ODBO.

BI Java Connector

For this reason, SAP provides for these interfaces predefined Java connectors and resource adapters: the *BI Java Connectors* that give the applications of the J2EE engine access to the interfaces.

Universal Data connect

To also give Web AS ABAP (i.e., BW) access to the BI Java Connectors, the Web AS Java has a *UD connect* that shows the BI Java Connectors of BW abstracted from logs and specifics as a unified UD connect data source. The communication is made via SAP JCo.

The UD connect creates redundant functionalities; the connection of some relational database systems, flat files, and SAP queries has been enabled by other means from the earlier BW releases onward. For architectural reasons, the UD connect is slower than and not as stable as the original specific solutions. You should thus review whether there might be a better alternative than the UD connect for the planned data source.

Configuration of BI Java Connectors

The BI Java Connectors that BW can access via the UD connect are as follows:

- BI JDBC Connector
- BI ODBO Connector
- BI XML/A Connector
- BI SAP Query Connector

Access to a specific data source is defined in the connection information of a BI Java Connector. The connections for the connector can be found in the visual administrator of the J2EE engine in the tab *Cluster→Services →Connector Container* (see figure 14–17).

Right from the installation of the BI Java Connector, there is only one connection template per connector. For every single connection, the respective template of the connector to be used needs to be copied and configured via the *Clone* button. The prefix SDK_ has to be used in the name of the cloned connection since only connections with this prefix will be recognized by the UD connect as BI Java Connectors.

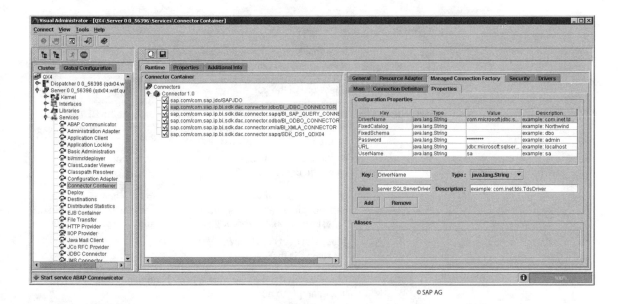

© SAP AG

The configuration of the connection parameters for the respective connection is stored in the tab *Managed Connection Factory→Properties,* as shown in figure 14–17. The parameters are stored as key values (this is the parameter to be configured) and with a respective value. We'll explain how JDBC, ODBO, XML/A, and SAP query connectors are each to be configured in the following sections.

Figure 14–17

Configuration of BI connectors

14.7.1 Installing a BI JDBC Connector

The BI JDBC Connector provides the connection to relational data sources for which a corresponding JDBC driver has been installed in the J2EE Engine (in the tab *Cluster→Services→JDBC Connector*). JDBC is not limited to one platform, so drivers are available for the most operating system platforms and database systems.[114]

The adoption and acceptance of JDBC is so widespread that there are even drivers for data sources that are not relational—e.g., MS Excel and text files.

The following table describes the interface parameters to be configured for JDBC data sources.

---

114. An overview on the currently available JDBC drivers can be found at http://servlet. java.sun.com/products/jdbc/drivers.

Feature	Description
USERNAME	User that has on the respective database systems at least read rights to the UD connect data source to be extracted.
PASSWORD	Password of the user.
LANGUAGE	Double-digit language abbreviation (e.g., EN) that the BI Java Connector is to use for the connection; e.g., if error messages are to be provided. This feature does not impact the JDBC connection. The indication of this parameter is optional; without an indication, EN will be used.
URL	URL of the server where the database can be reached and the name of the database, as shown in this example for the database SalesEurope on the server qdx04.wdf.quadox.corp: jdbc:microsoft:sqlserver://qdx04.wdf.quadox.corp; database=SalesEurope
DRIVERNAME	Class name of the driver for the JDBC connection, as shown in this example to access MS SQL Server: com.microsoft.jdbc.sqlserver.SQLServerDriver
FIXED_CATALOG	Indication of the database catalog for which metadata access is to be limited. Metadata access will be relevant if in the installation of the data flow you're asked for a selection of the available database tables. The indication of this parameter is optional; without indication, no limits are set.
FIXED_SCHEMA	Indication of the database schema to which the metadata access is to be limited. This parameter is to be used analog to FIXED_CATALOG.

14.7.2 Installing a BI ODBO Connector

The BI ODBO Connector provides a connection to multidimensional ODBO data sources. This connection is based on the Windows platform-specific COM log, so this connector can only be used on J2EE servers in combination with a Windows platform.

Examples of ODBO data sources are the MS Analysis Service in MS SQL Server, the MS PivotTable Service, and even other data warehouse systems such as SAS or SAP BW itself if they are also operating on a Windows platform.

The following table describes the interface parameters to be configured for ODBO data sources.

Feature	Description
USERNAME	User who has on the respective ODBO source system at least read rights for the UD connect data source to be extracted.
PASSWORD	Password of the user.
LANGUAGE	Double-letter language abbreviation (e.g., EN) that both the data source and the BI Java Connector are to use for the connection. The default language is EN.

CONNECTION_STRING	Character sequence with connection information to access the ODBO provider. The design of the string is subject to the respective ODBO provider and typically contains information on the memory location, the server, and the description of the ODBO provider.
	
	 Examples:
	
	 Access to the OLAP cubes of the SQL Server MSSQUADOX:
	
	 `Provider=MSOLAP;Data Source=MSSQUADOX`
	
	 Access to OLAP cubes of a local MS Analysis Service installation:
	
	 `Provider=MSOLAP;`
	`Location=\"c:\\public\\SalesEurope.cub\"`[1]
	
	 Access to OLAP cubes[2] of the BW system QX4, client 100:
	
	 `Provider=MDrmSAP;`
	`Data Source=QX4;`
	`SFC_CLIENT=100;`
	`SFC_LANGUAGE=DE`

1. The signs " and \ are considered special signs and they are to be started with the sign \.
2. In BW, the queries enabled for ODBO are considered OLAP cubes.

14.7.3 Installing a BI XML/A Connector

The BI XML/A connector provides the connection to multidimensional XML/A data sources. Other than with multidimensional ODBO data sources, data is exchanged platform independently in XML format via the SOAP log.

In a number of cases, multidimensional data sources can provide their data both via ODBO and via XML/A. While ODBO usually offers better performance, XML/A is platform independent.

The following table describes the interface parameters to be configured for XML/A data sources.

Feature	Description
USERNAME	User who for the XML/A source system has at least read rights to the UD connect data source to be extracted.
PASSWORD	Password of the user.
LANGUAGE	Double-letter language abbreviation (e.g., EN), that the BI Java Connector is to use for this connection; e.g., if error messages are to be provided. This feature does not impact the XML/A connection. The indication of this parameter is optional; without an indication, EN is used.
URL	URL to reach the service, e.g., `http://qdx04.wdf.quadox.corp:8100/sap/bw/xml/soap/xmla` for the XML/A service of the BW system `qdx04.wdf.quadox.corp`[1] on port 8100 or `http://qdx04.wdf.quadox.corp:6100/isapi/msxisapi.dll` for the XML/A service of a MS SQL server with the same name on port 6100
DATASOURCE	Name of the XML/A data source
STATEFULNESS	Indication of whether the connection to the XML/A service is to be made stateful or stateless (values true/false); that is, whether the session is to be kept or whether it can be terminated after each data transfer. The indication of the parameter is optional; by default, the connection will be stateless.

1. The URL prefix of a BW system can be identified by calling the function module RSBB_URL_PREFIX_GET in the transaction SE37. Here, the parameters are to be entered as follows: I_HANDLER = CL_RSR_MDX_SOAP_HANDLER; I_PROTOCOL = HTTP; I_MESSAGESERVER = X. The URL path will always be /sap/bw/xml/soap/xmla.

14.7.4 Installing a BI SAP Query Connector

The BI SAP query connector provides the connection to SAP queries on a Web AS ABAP. The Web AS ABAP can be either an SAP ERP system on the basis of Web AS 6.40 or even the BW system itself.

Prior to the use of the BI SAP query connector, the use of a generic data source (see section 14.2.1) for the respective source system should be considered in any case. This can also extract data from an SAP query and usually provides a faster and more stable solution.

The following table describes the interface parameters to be configured for SAP query data sources.

Feature	Description
USERNAME	User who has at least read rights on the respective SAP source system to the UD connect data source to be extracted.
PASSWORD	Password of the user.
R3NAME	System ID of the SAP system, e.g., QX4.
APPLICATIONSERVER	Application server of the SAP systems, e.g., `qdx04.wdf.quadox.corp`
CLIENT	Client in which the login has to be made, e.g., 100.
SYSTEMNUMBER	System number of the server entity, e.g., 00.
LANGUAGE	Double-letter language abbreviation (e.g., DE) that is to be used by the data source as well as by the BI Java Connector.
QUERYAREA	Definition of an area to which metadata access is to be limited. The metadata access is relevant if for the installation of the data flow a selection from the available SAP queries is to be mapped in the SAP system. As a parameter value, either an initial entry for the (client-dependent) standard work area or an X for the (cross-client) global work area can be defined.
SERVERGROUP	Indication of the logon group when load balancing is used.
MESSAGESERVER	Host name of the message server for the logon group, e.g., `msgserver1.quadox.com`. The indication of the message server is required only with the use of a logon group.
SNCMODE	Flagging on whether SNC (secure network communication) is to be used. The indication of the parameter is optional; without an indication, no SNC will be used.
SNCLEVEL	Indication of the SNC level if SNC is used. Parameters can be as follows: 1: Authentication 2: Integrity 3: Encryption
SNCPARTNER	SNC name of the service user on the application server if SNC is used.

Feature	Description
RFCTRACE	Indicates whether database calls, the calls of lock management, and the remote calls of reports and transactions from the SAP system are to be recorded in a trace file. (parameter value 1) or not (parameter value 0).
	The indication of the parameter is optional; without an indication, no trace file will be recorded.

14.8 Extraction with Third-Party ETL Tools

Another option to support the extraction is the use of third-party tools. With the next layer, the inflow layer (see chapter 15), we will describe how these tools are installed in SAP BW. Each tool functions differently during extraction, so you should review the documentation of the respective supplier.

15 Inflow Layer

The inflow layer is the interface between the extraction layer and further processing of data in SAP BW. The inflow layer describes the metadata for the source systems on the one hand and for the DataSources within the source systems on the other hand.

Further, the inflow layer controls extraction from the source systems and stores the extracted data in the persistent staging area (PSA), from which processing can draw for further layers. Thus, in terms of processing, the inflow layer separates further processing of data in the following layers from the extraction.

We'll cover the following topics in this chapter:

- Metadata of source systems
- Metadata of DataSources
- Persistent staging area (PSA)
- Definition of extraction processes

15.1 Metadata of Source Systems

In BW, the data flow is defined based on the source systems connected to BW and their metadata. You must first create the source systems in BW. This is done in the Data Warehousing Workbench in the modeling of source systems (see figure 15–1).

There are several source system types, each with its own specific characteristics. In the following sections, we'll explain the settings for each source system type.

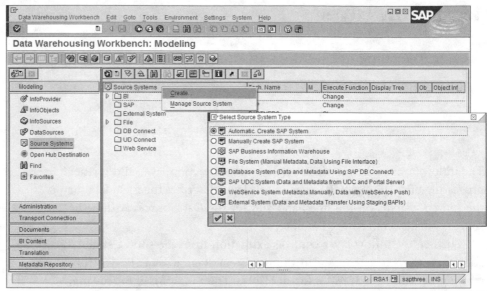

Figure 15–1

Creation of source system connections

> The creation of source systems is like a repository modification that cannot be transported and needs to be made in the respective BW system directly (even in live operations). For this reason, to create source systems you need to allow for system modifications (see appendix C.1.6).

The chapter ends with the definition of source system IDs, whose maintenance is often forgotten in practice. It only comes up when problems occur. When creating new source systems, do not forget the maintenance of their source system IDs!

15.1.1 Creating SAP ERP Source System Connections

The creation of an SAP ERP source system is very much supported by BW, so it is largely created automatically.

> The creation of an SAP ERP system is conceptually incorrect. It is not an ERP system but a *logical system* that is connected to SAP BW. This is defined by a *client* of the SAP system. If several clients are created on an SAP system, they can all be connected to BW. Each of these clients represents an individual logical system, and thus, BW treats it as individual source system.

There are two ways to create SAP ERP source systems:

- Automatic creation
- Manual creation

For automatic creation, BW needs to be provided with only the host name, the system ID, and the system number of the source system.

The host name, system ID, and system number can be found in the transaction SM51 in the source system. The listed systems are created according to the scheme server_<SAPSID>_<systemno>. For example, the entry QR000009_BW3_00 would describe the host name QR000009 with the system ID BW3 and the system number 00.

Further, you need to select a user ID for the background user under which SAP BW communicates with the source system (see figure 15–2).

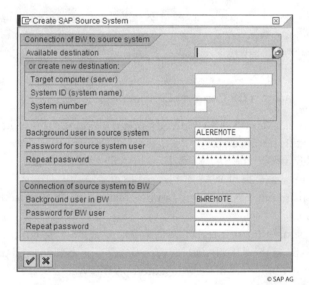

Figure 15–2

Automatic creation of SAP ERP source systems

© SAP AG

The background user in the source system is suggested by BW. The default value can be defined in the transaction RSCUSTV3. To supply data to BW, all SAP ERP systems use a standard user in BW that can be defined in transaction RSBWREMOTE.

In the second step, BW requires a source system login as system administrator (for authorization purposes) and automatically creates a background user and RFC destination for the communication with BW. Further, the RFC destination for the respective source system is created in BW. If it exists already (for example, since RFC destinations are always created as part of the system installation), the existing RFC destination can be indicated instead of the host name.

For a manual creation (only from SAP R/3 3.0D), the required RFC destinations need to be maintained in parallel both in BW and in the source system.

15.1.2   Creating a BW System Connection

BW systems represent a separate source system type, but they behave in the same way as SAP ERP systems when it comes to creation. The procedure and all settings correspond with the approach for the creation of SAP ERP source systems (automatic creation).

Each BW system is also connected to itself—this is the so-called Myself source system. This source system is created by default and does not need to be created manually.

15.1.3   Creating a DB Connect Connection

When started, Web AS ABAP already opens a connection to its database server. For this purpose, respective database clients as well as the respective database library for the SAP kernel are installed on the Web AS.

Since release 6.20 of WAS, it is capable of a MultiConnect; i.e., further connections to database systems can be created in addition to the default connection.

In the simplest case, the database to be connected via DB connect is of the same type as the default database, so the database client and the respective database library are already installed on the Web AS. If not, you need to install them.

When you create the DB connect in the source system tree of the Data Warehousing Workbench, you first indicate a logical system name to be used for the database connection and a descriptive text. Then, you need to indicate the connection information (see figure 15–3).

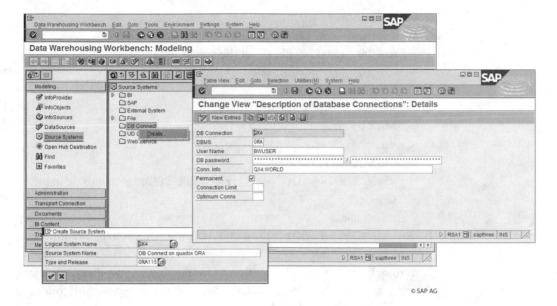

© SAP AG

The connect information contains the following:

■ An indication on the database management system *(DBMS)* of the data source.

■ The *user name* of the database user who opens the connection to the database.

■ The *password* of the database user. The password needs to be indicated twice and will be stored encrypted.

■ *Connection information* on how to open the database connection. Syntax and semantics of the connection information are database specific and usually contain the database host and the name:

  • **DB2 UmDB:**[115]

    DB6_DB_NAME=<database name>

  • **DB2/390:**[116]

    PORT=<Port>;

    SAPSYSTEMNAME=<sapsystemname>;

    SSID=<ssid>;

    SAPSYSTEM=<sapsystem>;

    SAPDBHOST=<sapdbhost>;

    ICLILIBRARY=/usr/sap/D6D/SYS/exe/run/ibmiclic.o

Figure 15–3

Description of database connections for DB connect

---

115. On the DB connect to DB2 UDB, see also OSS notes 523622 and 200164.
116. On the DB connect to DB2/390, see also OSS notes 523552 and 160484.

- **DB2/400:**[117]
  AS4_HOST=<host name of the database server>;
  AS4_DB_LIBRARY=<library of the server job>
  AS4_CON_TYPE=<connection type OPTICONNECT or SOCKETS>
- **Informix:**[118]
  <database name>@<database server>
- **MAX DB:**
  <database server>-<database name>
- **MS SQL Server:**[119]
  MSSQL_SERVER=<database server> MSSQL_DBNAME=<database name>
- **Oracle:**[120]
  <TNS alias>

■ An indication on whether the database connection is to be ***permanent.***
A permanent connection is reviewed with every source-system-related
transaction whether a connection to the database is given and whether
the transaction can be executed or not. For nonpermanent connections, this review will not be made and a possible transaction abort will
be accepted.

In any case, the definition of the DB connect will remain.

15.1.4 Creating Flat File Connections

The connection to file systems will be defined in the source system tree as
with all other source system types. However, no further settings have to be
stored in the file system, so the creation of this source system type is only a
formality.

The relevant settings for the extraction of flat files are made with the
definition of the DataSources (see section 15.2). Therefore, it is irrelevant
from a technical point of view whether a file system will be created for all
file DataSources or whether an individual source system will be created for
each file DataSource.

For clarity, the use of a single file system is certainly preferred. It may
make sense to create several file systems only if the identification of the
respective source system is to be contained within the transferred data so

---

117. On the DB connect to DB2/400, see also OSS notes 523381 and 146624 (to AS/400)
     or 445872 (to iSeries).
118. On the DB connect to Informix, see also OSS notes 520496 and 181989.
119. On the DB connect to MS SQL Server, see also OSS notes 512739 and 178949.
120. On the DB connect to Oracle, see also OSS notes 518241 and 339092.

that the file systems reflect this display of the source system. The identification of the source system is made in the source system IDs, which are explained in section 15.1.8.

15.1.5 Creating Web Service System Connections

The creation of web service source systems is identical to the creation of file source systems. It's a formality since the relevant metadata will be defined only with the definition of the DataSources.

The SOAP service of the web application server is used to receive SOAP documents. At any rate, it will be there after the installation and does not need to be configured anymore. However, the SOAP service needs to be active. This can be controlled and defined in the transaction SICF (see figure 15–4).

Figure 15–4

Activation of the SOAP service

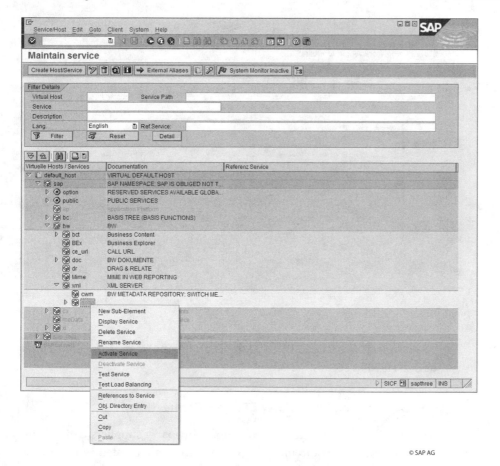

Via the SOAP service, source systems can actively transfer data to BW. Unlike with all the other source system types, there will be no extraction according to the pull principle. The use of the SOAP service is one option to supply BW with data close to real time; however, given the large overhead, this procedure is suitable only for processing very small amounts of data.

15.1.6   Creating a Universal Data Connect Connection

Figure 15–5
Creation of an SAP UD CONNECT source system connection

To extract data via the Universal Data connect of the J2EE Engine, you need to indicate the RFC connection to the J2EE Engine as well as the connector to be used. Thus, the definition of a UD connect source system connection always refers to a connector of the J2EE Engine (see figure 15–5).

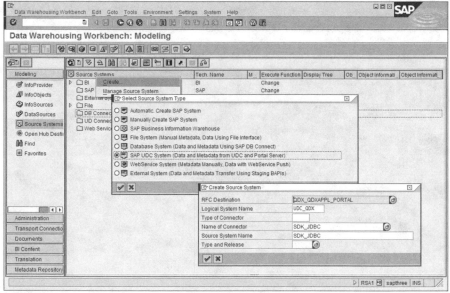

© SAP AG

The connection between BW and the J2EE Engine needs to be configured as described in section 3.1.3.

15.1.7   Creating Third-Party ETL Tool Connections

The creation of an extraction tool from third-party suppliers depends on the different tool requirements. When the tools are created in the inflow layer, only the how the extraction tool starts is defined. It corresponds with the RFC server program call to a BW application server and a host (indicating the target machine) of the respective user's client workstation (see figure 15–6). Here, the call is initiated by BW.

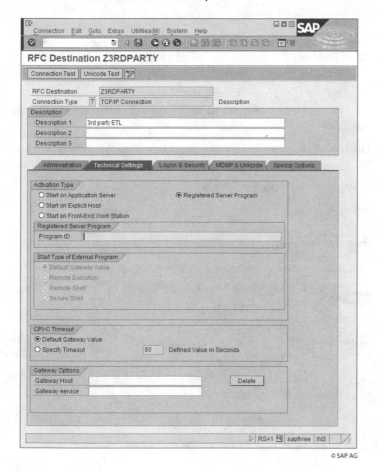

Figure 15–6
Connecting third-party ETL tools

The detailed settings that are required for the creation of an extraction tool depend on the tool specifications and can be found in the documentation provided by the supplier.

15.1.8 Source System IDs

In some cases it makes sense to further process or store data with regard to the source system from which data were extracted. This is the case for the following types of data:

■ *Master data* that is to be stored with reference to the supplying source system and is thus compounded to the source system ID.

■ *Transactional data* that is to be stored with information on the source system for data validation purposes or for the drill-through functionality in the reporting.

Since the names of the source systems change in a transport landscape,[121] you should not use the names of the respective source systems for the definition of the data flow. Instead, the source systems of all BW systems need to have identical IDs. Here, development, testing, and production environments of the source system are to be described with the same ID in each BW system.

The maintenance of source system IDs is made in the Data Warehousing Workbench via the menu item *Tools→Assignment of Source System to Source System ID* (see figure 15–7).

Figure 15–7

Maintenance of source system IDs

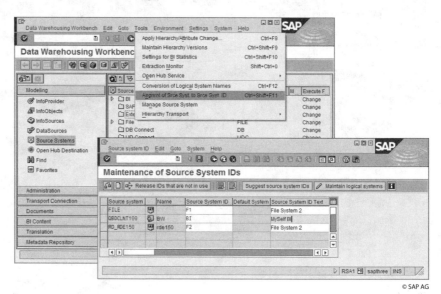

© SAP AG

The assignments are stored in the master data of the InfoObject 0SOURSYSTEM. During data transfer, the assignment of the source system to the source system ID defines the value that is written for the InfoObject 0SOURSYSTEM. Thus, all source-system-dependent data structures need to contain the InfoObject 0SOURSYSTEM.

---

121. Usually, different source systems are created in the development system and in the test or production system.

To enable a consistent assignment of source system IDs to source system names across all systems, you can also define IDs for source systems that might not have been created in the respective BW system.

> The IDs can consist of only two letters. In more comprehensive architectures, it will thus be difficult to give the IDs descriptive names. Especially for globally dispersed source systems, it may be useful to make a geographical assignment with the first sign of the ID.

The use of the defined source system IDs during staging is part of the transformation layer and is described in section 6.5.

Source System IDs in Data Mart Architectures

For the transfer of data from BW to another system, the receiving system must not work with source system IDs because the original source system ID would then be replaced by the source system ID of the supplying BW system. Instead, the original source system IDs need to be transferred to the target BW, and there they may not be replaced by the source system IDs of the supplying BW system. Figure 15–8 shows this connection using a part of a hub-and-spoke architecture (see chapter 27).

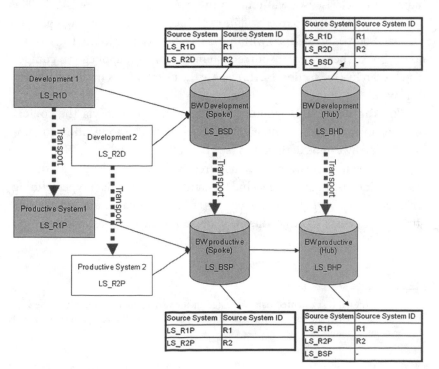

Figure 15–8

Transfer of source system IDs in large-scale architectures

15.2 Metadata of DataSources

After the creation of source systems in BW, you will know which systems are provided for extraction and how BW can communicate with these systems.

Further, you need to define for each data source within a source system how the data to be extracted is structured, what delta procedures the data sources are capable of, and so on. The definitions of this metadata of a data source within a source system are combined in a ***DataSource.***

There are two different objects behind the definition of a DataSource in BW: one for the new DataSources of BW 7 and one for the 3.x Data-Sources of former BW releases.

The new DataSources of BW 7 provide a real-time data acquisition option (see section 22.1.2) to directly access master data (see section 22.2.1) and to remotely activate the DataSources (see appendix D.1). In addition to the staging with transformation and data transfer processes (see chapters 19 and 20), the 3.x DataSources also support the direct staging of master data (see chapter 21), which is no longer supported by the new DataSources in BW 7.

The definition of old and new DataSources is very different. If not indicated otherwise, we will refer to the new DataSources of BW 7. The definition of 3.x DataSources will be explained within direct staging.

DataSources are defined within the DataSource tree in the Data Warehousing Workbench. Each source system has an own application component hierarchy (see section 14.1.2) where the DataSources in the system are displayed.

You can define a DataSource for the source system via the context menu of an application component to be selected. The application component hierarchy can be defined too (see figure 15–9).

When you're creating a DataSource, you need to enter a source-system-wide distinguishable technical name as well as a data type defining whether the data is to be processed as transactional data or as master data attributes or texts (so that they will be stored in the master data of an InfoObject).[122]

---

122. Hierarchies and segmented data are listed in the drop-down menu, but in the current BW release, they are only available for replicated DataSources and they cannot be created manually.

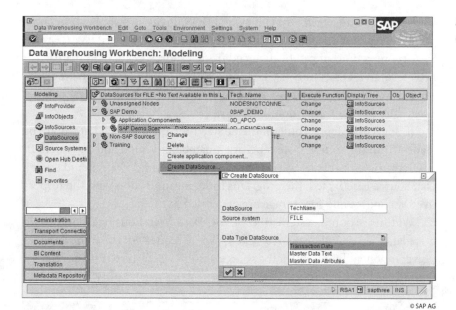

Figure 15–9
Creating a DataSource

In the general DataSource settings that are to be made next, you first need to enter only a name for the DataSource (figure 15–10).

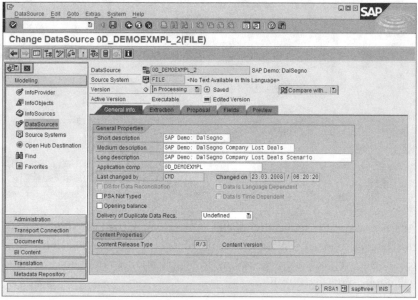

Figure 15–10
DataSource definition for file DataSources: general information

Depending on the source system type, DataSources and application component hierarchies need to be completely defined within SAP BW (flat file, SOAP connection) or can be deduced from a source system template (SAP ERP, SAP BW, DB connect, UD connect, third-party ETL tools); i.e., the source system already uses metadata that can be modified in defined places but that cannot be defined freely.

Metadata replication for SAP and third-party source systems

If source systems contain metadata, the metadata will need to be loaded from the source system before it can be modified and activated. In BW terminology, this is called **metadata replication.** When metadata of a DataSource is activated, the programs for communication with the respective DataSource and for storage are generated in the inflow layer.

Within a source system tree of the Data Warehousing Workbench, metadata for a complete source system can be requested. Here, the application component hierarchy of the source system will also be transferred (see figure 15–11).

Figure 15–11
Metadata replication in source systems containing metadata

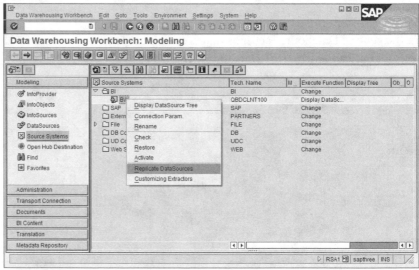

© SAP AG

Alternatively to the replication of all DataSources, in the DataSource tree of the Data Warehousing Workbench, metadata of a DataSource can be replicated selectively. Changes regarding the application component hierarchy will not be transferred to BW.

If the replicated DataSource is a new DataSource for BW 7, it can be decided during the replication whether the DataSource is to be created as such in BW or as a 3.x DataSource[123] (see figure 15–12).

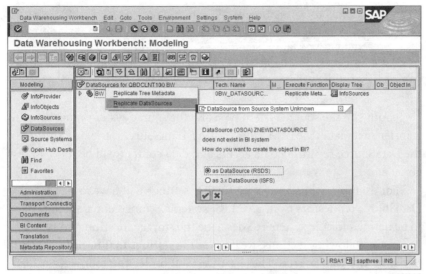

Figure 15–12
Selection of DataSource version

© SAP AG

The selection of the DataSource version is not final since with the transaction RSDS, one DataSource version can be migrated into the other version (see figure 15–13).

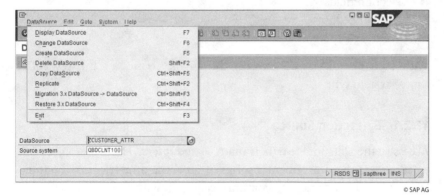

Figure 15–13
Migration of DataSources

© SAP AG

---

123. In this case, a new DataSource can also be used for the direct staging of master data.

If a DataSource cannot handle the new functionalities of BW 7, it will automatically be created as a 3.x DataSource. In any case, the new staging can be applied via transformation and data transfer processes.

> For the replication of DataSources in the test or production system of a transport environment (see appendix C), it does not matter what version was selected for the DataSource. With the transport, the DataSource version will be overwritten by the version from the development system anyway.

Depending on the source system type and the source system capabilities to transfer metadata to BW via the existing DataSources, the description of the DataSource regarding data access and data content will be more or less complete.

For example, while almost no further settings will have to be made for DataSource replicators from SAP ERP systems, a range of parameters need to be defined for file systems to describe the storage location and type.

Metadata on DataSources   In the following sections, we'll cover the settings that need to be made to define the DataSource. These settings fall under the following categories:

- Extraction source
- Data structure
- Input conversion
- Selection fields
- Delta procedures
- Inventory key figures

With each category, we'll explain the characteristics of the respective source system type.

15.2.1 Extraction Source

Adapter   Access to the DataSource data is made via *adapters.* These are object-oriented classes that implement a series of predefined interfaces. The interfaces enable the adapters to communicate both with the inflow layer and with the interfaces to the respective source systems.

A significant change came for adapters with SAP BW release 7 with the scalability of the underlying framework; i.e., with the implementation of the respective interfaces, individual adapters can be developed to access

DataSources. For this purpose, the developed methods need to be declared using the SM34 in the accumulated view RSDSACCESS (see figure 15–14).

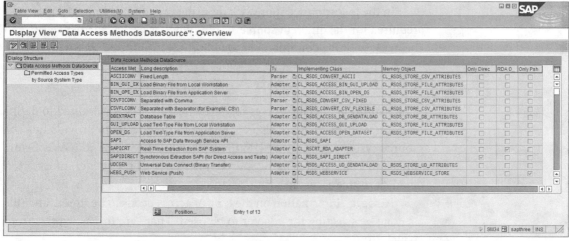

© SAP AG

What adapter is to be used in a certain case is usually deduced from the respective source system type—for example, there is an adapter that's exactly suited to connect a database via DB connect. However, especially with SAP and file systems, with definition of a DataSource, an adapter needs to be chosen from a selection of several adapters.

Figure 15–14

Definition of adapters and parsers

Depending on the adapter, the use of a data format parser will follow the extraction. It deals with conversion of extracted data in the typed structure that is defined by the DataSource (see section 15.2.2).

Data format parser

Whether the use of a data format parser is required depends on whether the adapter supplies the data in the structure defined by the Data-Source[124] (in this case, no parser is required) or whether it only supplies data as a table of strings[125] (in this case, the use of a parser is required to convert the table of strings into the defined structure of the DataSource).

If the use of a parser is required with the use of an adapter, you must configure the respective settings regarding the format to be changed. In the current version, the setting is limited to indicating whether the source data consists of strings with fixed length or data separated by separators.

124. In this case, SAP also uses the term generating adapters.
125. In this case, SAP also uses the term generic adapters.

If no indication is to be made for a parser, the data source will be shown in BW as *already binary* (see example DataSources for the DB connect, figure 15–17).

In the following sections, we'll describe the adapter and parser settings required for the different source system types as well as further settings to be made with the definition of a DataSource.

Data Sources for SAP Source Systems

The definition of DataSources for SAP source systems is limited to defining DataSources that are also contained in the metadata provided by the source systems in the extraction layer. Each DataSource in BW is firmly linked to a data source in the source system so that no further information on data source access needs to be stored.

Adapters However, information on the type of access needs to be stored, and this is done by selecting the adapter to be used. There are three adapters from which to choose:

- ▪ SAPI to access SAP source systems via the Service API that controls "normal" extraction from SAP source systems.
- ▪ SAPICRT to access real-time-enabled DataSources in SAP systems (see chapter 22).
- ▪ SAPIDIRECT for synchronal extraction from SAP source systems. It is used for direct access to DataSources (see section 22.2.1) as well as for debugging (see section 31.4.3).

Typing The adapters SAPI and SAPICRT require the use of a data format parser to convert the data structure with fixed-length fields in the typed structure of the DataSource.

Number format In addition to configuring the settings for adapters and parsers, you must indicate the number formats (decimal points, thousands separators) you plan to use in the DataSources for SAP source systems. You can either do this at runtime from the master record of the respective user that starts the loading or predefine them in the DataSource (see figure 15–15). We don't recommended that you set the user master record as a configuration source for the number format since this may make the system behave unpredictably because the result of an extraction can be different depending on the respective user.

For each InfoPackage, BW offers default values for thousands separators and decimal points. These default values can be changed using the transaction RSCUSTV1.

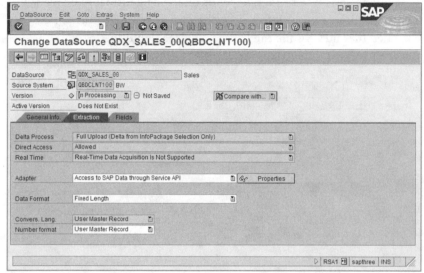

© SAP AG

Figure 15–15
DataSource for SAP source systems

Data Sources for File Systems

A core component for the definition of file data sources is the indication of the file to be read and the file type.

Both indications are combined in the adapter to be used. These are the options:

Adapters

- To load *binary files,* there are the adapters BIN_GUI_EX (load from workstation) and BIN_OPE_EX (load from application server[126]).
- To load *text-type files,* there are the adapters GUI_UPLOAD (load from workstation) and OPEN_DS (load from application server[127]).

With the use of the adapters BIN_GUI_EX and GUI_UPLOAD for the extraction of files from a local path of the workstation, the load process needs to be run in sync with the respective client workstation, and (e.g., in standard operations) it cannot be planned in the background.

126. From the application server or from a file server that accesses the application server.
127. From the application server or from a file server that accesses the application server.

Typing The adapters for loading text-type files (GUI_UPLOAD and OPEN_DS) require the use of a data format parser: the parser ASCIICONV to convert files with fixed-length fields and the parser CSVFLCONV to convert files with fields that are separated with separators.

Which parser is to be used depends on the data format to be read, and it is also indicated in the settings for the data source. The formats ASCII-separated file and CSV file can be selected (see figure 15–16).

Figure 15–16
DataSource for file systems

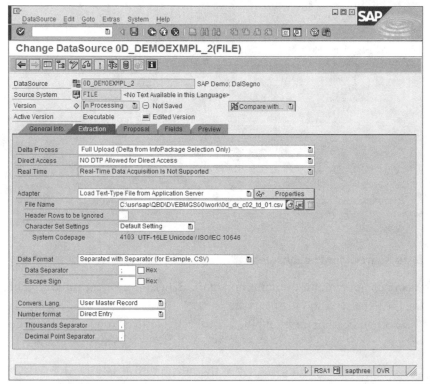

© SAP AG

For CSV files, the data separator and the escape sign also need to be indicated (see section 14.5.1).

For a file in CSV format, the data separator and the escape sign need to be defined. The default values for the data separator and the escape sign can be changed using the transaction RSCUSTV1.

In any case, the core setting for the data source is the definition of the file name—in the form of a physically existing file, in the form of a logical file name (see section 15.1.3), or as the result of an ABAP routine.

File name

Especially in initially improvised systems, the definition of a physically existing file offers quick results. For live operations, the use of a clearly determined file name results in two significant disadvantages:

- If BW is used in a transport landscape in which the respective BW systems are to access different file servers, the file names will be invalid after the transport of the InfoPackages.
- If files are loaded in regular intervals, in many cases dynamic file names are used (e.g., with an encrypted full date). This does not apply for predefined file names.

To avoid these disadvantages, there is the option to work with logical file names. With the definition of logical file names, system-specific variables as well as parameters generated during runtime can be used. The definition of logical file names is explained in detail in appendix B.

In addition to defining physical or logical file names, you can define a file name using a self-developed ABAP routine. As parameters for the routine, only the parameters P_FILENAME with the name of the file and P_SUBRC with the error code of the routine are to be returned (0 = error-free, 4 = erroneous).

```
program filename_routine.
* Global code
*$*$ begin of global - insert your declaration only below this line
* TABLES: ...
* DATA:   ...
*$*$ end of global - insert your declaration only before this line
*   ----------------------------------------------------------*-*
form compute_flat_file_filename
  changing p_filename type RSFILENM
           p_subrc like sy-subrc.
*$*$ begin of routine - insert your code only below this line    *-*
         p_filename =
*....
         p_subrc = 0.
*$*$ end of routine - insert your code only before this line    *-*
endform.
```

Character set settings

Especially for Unicode systems, additional settings can be stored regarding the character set used for binary files. This is necessary in order to correctly interpret the binary display of signs.

Number format

As with SAP source systems, you need to set the number formats you will use in the data source (decimal point, thousands separators).

Data Sources for DB Connect Source Systems

With a DB connect, the database source system supplies with the database catalog all tables, views, and field details that the database offers BW for extraction.

If the naming convention hasn't been followed (see section 14.4), not all tables and views might technically be suitable for extraction. Further, usually only selected tables/views are relevant for extraction.

For this reason, after installation of the DB connect, the tables and views that are to be reflected in the definition of DataSources need to be defined first. When you define the data source, you need to indicate the table/view on which you will base a DataSource (see figure 15–17).

Figure 15–17
DataSource for DB connect

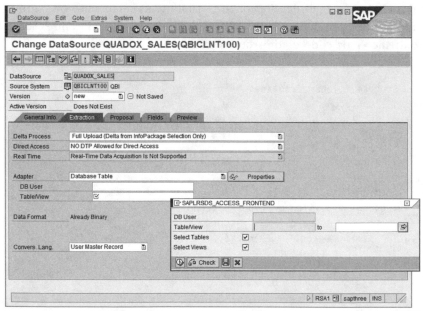

In any case, the adapter DBEXTRACT is used to access the database systems. *Adapters*
There are no other adapters available. The supplied data is always typed so
that no further settings regarding the data format need to be made.

Data Sources for Web Services

As for flat files, the extraction layer does not supply any metadata on web
services. Thus, the DataSource needs to be defined manually in the inflow
layer. The data source for a web service is a function module that is SOAP
runtime enabled and that needs to be indicated in the body of SOAP-com-
pliant XML documents (see section 14.6).

Usually, this function module is generated with the creation of a SOAP
DataSource. The name of the function module is derived from the technical name of the DataSource, and the prefix /BIO/CQ as well as a numeric
suffix are added (see figure 15–18).

Alternatively, an own web service can be stored—i.e., a function mod-
ule that has been enabled for the SOAP runtime. The name of the module   ***Figure 15–18***
is always to be stored in the field Fixed Service Name.   *DataSource for web services*

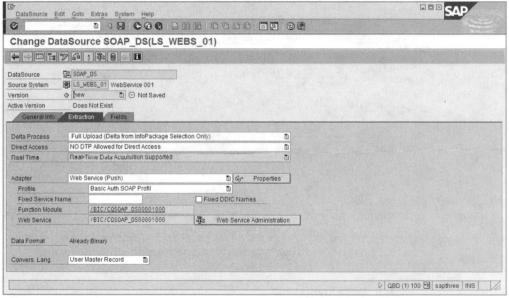

© SAP AG

The adapter used for web services is the WEBS_PUSH adapter. The supplied   *Adapters*
data is always typed so that no further settings regarding the file format
need to be made.

Given the characteristics of the push procedure, the extraction via SOAP runtime is not described in the same way as the other source system types. The use of SOAP runtime will be explained with real-time and push technology.

Data Sources for UD connect

With the definition of the source system connection, the J2EE Engine and the connector to be used are already set (see section 15.1.6). Thus, only the naming of the source object within the UD connect remains to be defined for the data source—that is, the name of the database table for JDBC connectors or the name of an OLAP cube for the ODBO connector (see figure 15–19).

Figure 15–19
DataSource for UD connect

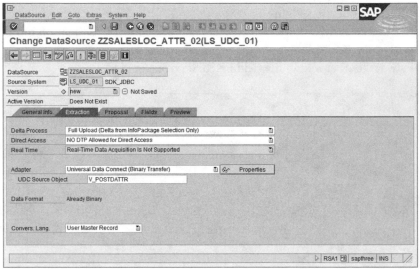

© SAP AG

Adapters   No matter what type of connector was used, the adapter UDCGEN is always used for the extraction via UD connect. The supplied data is always typed so that no further settings need to be made regarding the file format.

15.2.2   Data Structure

For the extraction of data from source systems, the inflow layer needs to describe the structure of the extracted data. We'll refer to this structure as the *transfer structure*.

For SAP and third-party source systems, this structure is transferred to BW via the metadata of the systems, and it available when the DataSource is defined and can't be changed.

DataSources for Universal Data connect

The UD connect comes with metadata in the form of source object elements, which are the fields (for JDBC and SAP query) or characteristics/key figures (for ODBO and XML/A) that the respective BI Java connector offers for extraction.

Transfer structure for source systems without metadata

For all other source systems, the transfer structure needs to be defined manually with the definition of the DataSource. Each field of the DataSource needs to be manually defined together with the data type and length (see figure 15–20).

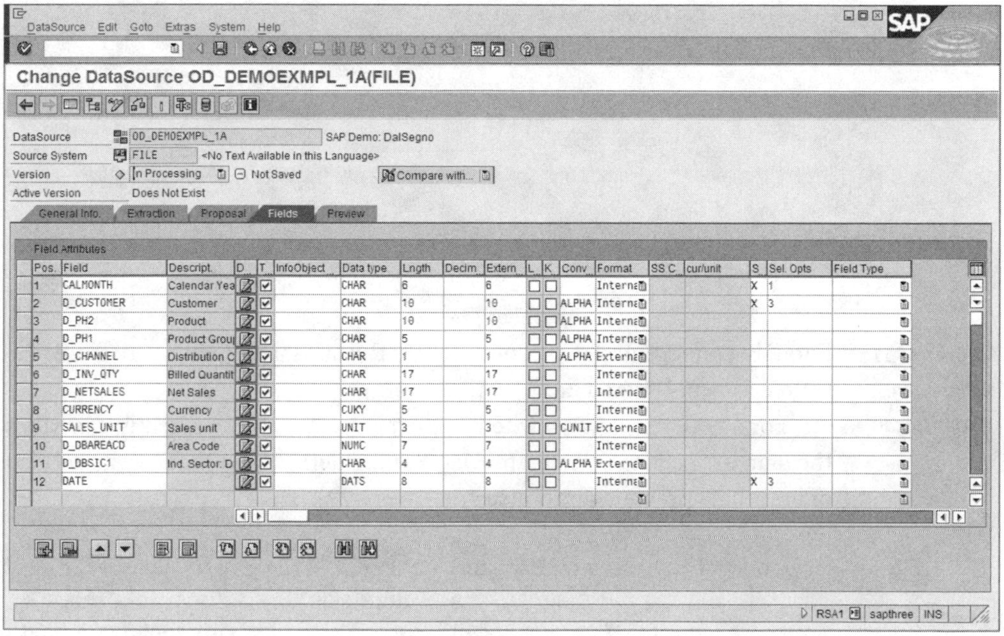

© SAP AG

As a recommended alternative to manually entering all field names, types, and lengths, you can derive the fields of the transfer structure from InfoObjects that are defined as templates.

Figure 15–20
Data structure for file systems: Fields tab

For DataSources for file systems, DB connect, and UD connect you can use default values to configure the transfer structure. For file DataSources, the default value is generated from a preset number of sample records for which the parser to be used (CSV or ASCII) needs to be indicated (see figure 15–21).

Proposal for data structure for file systems, DB connect, and UD connect

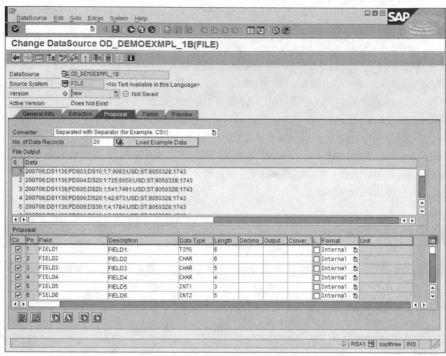

© SAP AG

Figure 15–21
Data structure for file systems:
Proposal tab

For DB connect and UD connect, this proposal is generated from the source systems' metadata.

For a better review on whether the preset structure correctly describes the data of the data source, the DataSource definition for file systems also offers a data preview option (see figure 15–22).

The default values for the structure of file data sources are suitable for the number and the minimum lengths of the fields. Even if the data preview provides plausible results at first glance, you should ensure that the default values correspond with the actual data fields and types.

Application Structure

To process the data of a DataSource, you must provide not only the description of the file structure in the data source (i.e., the transfer structure) but also the description of a data structure for further data processing within SAP BW.[128]

---

128. Especially to store data in the persistent staging area (see section 15.3).

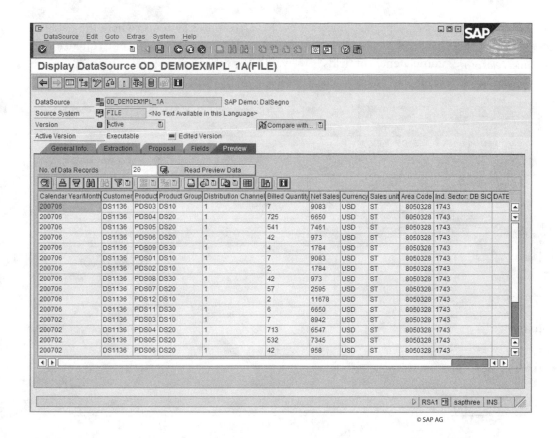

Figure 15–22

Data structure for file systems: Review tab

In view of the simple tasks of the inflow layer, this structure (referred to as the application structure) will in most cases be identical to the transfer structure, and in the following layers, totally different structures will be used.

In some cases, variations between transfer and application structure may make sense if not all fields of the transfer structure will be taken over into the application structure. This especially makes sense if by omitting single fields during extraction of data, SAP BW can create a pre-aggregation to reduce the data volume during extraction.[129]

The fields that are to be taken over from the transfer structure into the application structure are defined in the field structure of the DataSource in the Transfer column (see figure 15–23).

The definition of fields that are to be taken over into the application structure can basically be made for all source system types; however, this

---

129. This is an option for DataSources from SAP systems and for web services.

Figure 15–23

*Selection of transfer fields of a
DataSource*

option especially makes sense for SAP source systems (where the field list itself cannot be changed) and for file systems (where the sequence and completeness of fields is relevant). For other source system types, the same result can be obtained by omitting fields from the field list.

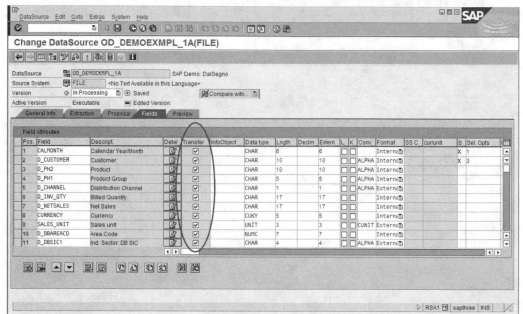

15.2.3 Input Conversion

If InfoObject values are stored in the database system, the format used for storing needs to meet the requirements of the conversion routine that is provided for the respective InfoObject (see section 6.1.1).

Basically, BW does not check fields' values for their compliance with conversion routines; i.e., if BW contains noncompliant values, they are processed and physically entered into the BW data targets. An exception are InfoObjects with the conversion routines ALPHA, NUMCV, and GJAHR; there are checks at specific points on whether they have the correct internal format (see section 23.2).

In previous SAP BW releases, this procedure often led to problems, especially if erroneous data was already partially processed (and already physically stored) and was found erroneous and rejected only very late in the staging process.

In release 7, BW offers a comprehensive solution to check field values for compliance with a conversion routine (and to convert the values) with input conversion,[130] which is configured with the definition of the data structure of a DataSource (see figure 15–24).

Figure 15–24

Settings for input conversion

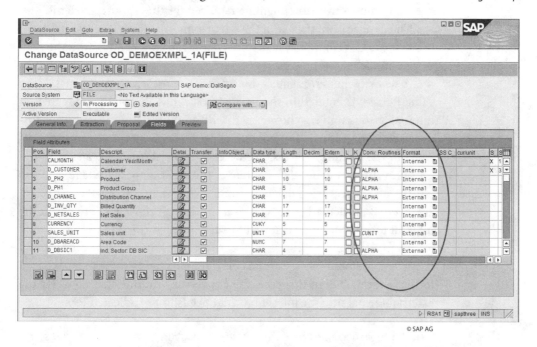

© SAP AG

The input conversion is already made when the data is handed over to the BW transfer structure[131] and it thus offers maximum security from non-compliant field values.

You define whether an input conversion is made in the Format column in the definition of the DataSource structure.

If each value is stored internally, BW assumes without any further review that it is compliant with the internal format expected by the conversion routine.[132] Thus, the values are directly entered into the data targets without prior input conversion.

Not running an input conversion

Especially for the data takeover from SAP ERP and SAP BW, one should be able to assume that the data is already provided in the internal

---

130. The input conversion existed from SAP BW release 3 onward; however, with releases 3.x, it only supported InfoObjects with the conversion routines ALPHA, GJAHR, and NUMCV.
131. That is *prior* to storage of raw data in the PSA (see section 15.3).
132. In this context, it is also referred to as "trusted" internal format.

format. In fact, SAP ERP and SAP BW both use conversion routines—and for identical information, these should be identical conversion routines.

However, it is wrong to consider this assumption to be a general default condition. Especially if generic DataSources and user exits are used, an input conversion might be required for these source systems.

Review format   The danger from the use of the trusted internal format is that field values that are not compliant with conversion routines can get into the data targets and lead to problems.

A security measure against this error is the review of the format. If the value Review is entered in the Format column, BW still assumes that an internal value is given—however, it will double-check this value. If unexpectedly the value is not compliant with the conversion routine indicated in the column conversion, the extraction aborts with an error and thus prevents erroneous data content at the earliest possible stage.

Conversion execution   If DataSources from diverse systems other than SAP ERP or SAP BW are given, it particularly needs to be assumed that the values are not in the internal format but in an external format and a conversion to the internal format needs to be made.

It can be stored in the Format column that a field's value in an external format is available. In this case, the conversion routine that converts the external format into the internal format needs to be indicated too.

> The compliance check as well as the execution of the input conversion result in runtime for the extraction. Thus, do not automatically activate input conversion for each field; only do so if required.

15.2.4 Selection Fields

To limit the data volume of the extraction, it may make sense to specifically select data for extraction. The fields that are available to a DataSource for extraction depend on the definition of the DataSource in BW as well as in the source system.

For a selection, BW itself only assumes that the selected fields in the application structure are defined as field types CHAR, NUMC, DATE, TIME, and INT4.

SAP ERP   For DataSources of the BI content or for generic DataSources, the
SAP BW   fields available for selection are defined by the metadata in the source sys-
Third-party   tem and cannot be changed in BW. In the extraction layer, the selection fields for generic DataSources can be defined with the definition of the

structure and selection fields (see section 14.2). For DataSources of the BI content, these selection fields cannot be changed.

For all other source systems, the selectable fields need to be manually defined in the metadata of the DataSource. For this purpose, the Selection and Sel. Opts (selection options) columns are available in the maintenance of the DataSource structure (see figure 15–25).

DB connect

Flat File

UD connect

SOAP connection

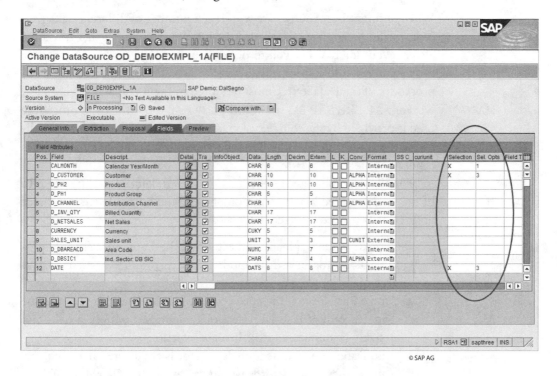

© SAP AG

If a field is marked as a selection field in the Selection column,[133] the following selection options will be available:

Figure 15–25

Selection options for file DataSources

- ▦ 0 (selection options undefined): The selection options are not limited (advisable for selections from ABAP routines, see section 15.4.1).
- ▦ 1 (selection EQ permitted): Only single values can be selected.
- ▦ 2 (selection BW permitted): Only intervals can be selected.
- ▦ 3 (selection EQ, BT permitted): Only single values and intervals can be selected.
- ▦ 7 (selection EQ, BT, CP permitted): Only single values, intervals, and patterns can be selected (e.g., >>10*<<).

133. X = selection possible; M = selection required.

Reminder: This is not about the selection itself but only about the definition of fields that are to be available for a possible selection. The selection itself will only be made in the InfoPackage (see section 15.4.1).

15.2.5   Delta Procedure

When different DataSources are working, a number of different delta procedures can be applied (see section 14.1.3) and the knowledge thereof is also relevant for BW. For you to decide whether data from a DataSource can be entered into a specific data target[134] and how to proceed, the delta procedure of the DataSource must be stored in the metadata.

SAP ERP
SAP BW
Third-party

For SAP ERP, SAP BW and third-party ETL tools, the delta procedure used is provided by the source system and gets to the BW system by replicating the DataSources. Thus, a manual definition of the delta procedures is not required.

File
DB connect
UD connect
SOAP connection

For all other source system types, the applied delta procedure needs to be manually entered in the definition of the DataSource. There is a choice of three delta procedures (see section 14.1.3):

- ■ FULL (delta via full upload): Indicates that the DataSource cannot provide data records in a delta mode. Data records from such a DataSource can be entered as follows:
  a) Into a BasisCube if the cube content is deleted earlier. This can be avoided only if through selections during extraction, a delta can reliably be duplicated (e.g., by date selection).
  b) Into DataStore Objects if no data records are deleted from the data source; these data records would remain in the DataStore Objects unless the content of the DataStore Objects are deleted prior to their entry.
  c) Into the master data of an InfoObject (other than with DataStore Objects, master data is not deleted in BW anyway).
- ■ FILO (delta with after images): DataSource only supplies modified records in form of the new state (after image). Data records from such a DataSource can be entered as follows:
  a) Into DataStore Objects.
  b) Into the master data of an InfoObject.

---

134. As an example, after images can only be rewritten into data targets that support an overwrite of old values by new values—this prevents rewrites in BasisCubes.

■ FIL1 (delta with delta images): The DataSource only provides modified records in form of additive deltas. Data records from such a Data-Source can be entered as follows:
a) Into DataStore Objects.
b) Into BasisCubes.

The indication of the delta procedures used is given in the extraction settings of the respective DataSource (see section 15.2).

15.2.6 Inventory Key Figures

With the extraction and processing of inventory key figures in normal operations (see section 6.1.3), only the reference key figures from which the inventory key figures are determined are updated. The inventory key figures themselves are updated only once with the initialization of the beginning inventory, if there is an initialization at all.

For this reason, the extraction of inventory key figures needs to be made from two DataSources: one DataSource to extract the beginning inventory to initialize the inventory key figure and another DataSource to extract the inventory changes in the form of regular cumulative values.

> Please consider that beginning inventories are not to be transferred to DataStore Objects, but always directly to BasisCubes. In this context, DataStore Objects are only suited to store inventory changes.

Thus, it needs to be explicitly defined in the DataSource whether it is a DataSource to initialize inventory or whether it is a DataSource with inventory changes (i.e., a conventional DataSource).

For DataSources from SAP ERP, SAP BW, and third-party ETL tools, it is already stored in the metadata of these systems whether the respective DataSource is to supply beginning inventories or inventory changes. This setting cannot be changed as it describes the fundamental job of the Data-Source. *SAP ERP* *SAP BW* *Third-party*

DataSources from file systems, the DB connect, or the UD connect need to be manually marked as suppliers of beginning inventories. This is done by activating the Opening Balance option in the general settings of the DataSource (see section 15.2). *Flat file* *DB connect* *UD connect*

For the extraction via web services, no option to extract beginning inventories is provided. *Web services*

15.3 Persistent Staging Area (PSA)

The persistent staging area (PSA) is a collection of database tables in which the data supplied from the extraction layer are stored directly[135] upon arrival in BW and from which they are available to other layers for processing.

The PSA exists since the first SAP releases, and in terms of structure, it has not changed significantly since then. However, SAP has redefined the conceptual significance of the PSA with each new SAP release.

> In the administration information as well as the PSA documentation, the term *ODS* often comes up. Up to release 2.0A, the PSA was called ODS. This changed with release 2.0B when the term *ODS* was introduced for what is now referred to as DataStore Object. You should be aware that the term *ODS* might still appear even though *PSA* is meant.

The definition that SAP has given with release 7 is the most convincing from a functional point of view, and it should finally get a chance to survive future release changes on SAP BW. The price that PSA paid was that it lost almost all of its performance tuning function.

Decoupling of extraction and transformation

In BW release 7, the PSA is mostly to be characterized as the ***processing stack*** for the requests extracted from the source systems; it decouples the extraction from the transformation. Thus, from the point of view of the other layers, the PSA represents an independent data source that provides data in a delta procedure.

The delta of the data to be newly provided is derived from all new, error-free requests. Thus, the PSA is no longer an optionally used data container where error-free as well as erroneous requests can be created and managed freely.

Rather, the PSA is an administratively maintainable and obligatory memory source of all requests that are to be processed in further layers; the transfer of all error-free requests is pursued with such consequence that even old requests can overwrite the data of new requests if an erroneous request receives the status error-free at a later point in time (i.e., after newer requests were already processed).

---

135. It is impossible to manipulate data prior to its being stored in the BW PSA. The only exception is the input conversion that is made before the storing in the PSA (see section 15.2.3).

Completely different than in the releases up to 3.5, BW does not make any tests here to ensure the completeness or the sequence of the entries. Thus, the PSA needs to be managed especially in view of further entries of the requests; erroneous requests are to be dealt with immediately or be replaced by error-free requests (and deleted) in order to not create any problems with the entry sequence.

If you already have experienced BW prior to release 7, you might find the lack of diverse tests during the data entry from the PSA very strange. You should experiment with the new system behavior to take it in. Regardless of your evaluation of whether it makes sense or it's nonsense, the consideration of the new system behavior is absolutely required to manage the system.

The management of DataSource requests is made in the context menu of the DataSource in the Data Warehousing Workbench (see figure 15–26).

Figure 15–26

Managing the PSA

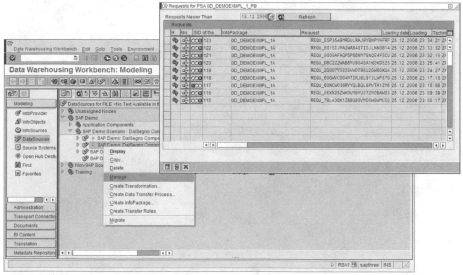

© SAP AG

The new function of the PSA as processing stack makes a significant difference to the BW releases up to 3.x: The PSA must be kept "clean" in terms of quality; i.e., it needs to be "cleansed" from double requests. Erroneous requests should also be deleted to prevent later status changes. Please remember to change the definitions for the management of the system accordingly.

Structure of the PSA   To store extracted data, BW generates at least one database table for each DataSource in the PSA. The structure of this table corresponds with the application structure of the DataSource (see section 15.2.2) as well as the fields REQUEST, DATAPAKID, and RECORD, which provide information on the respective loading. Figure 15–27 shows the structure of a PSA table in the ABAP Dictionary.

Figure 15–27
Structure of a PSA table in the ABAP Dictionary

Thus, there is no aggregation during the storing of data in the PSA; raw data of the source systems is stored with the same level of granularity as provided by the source systems.

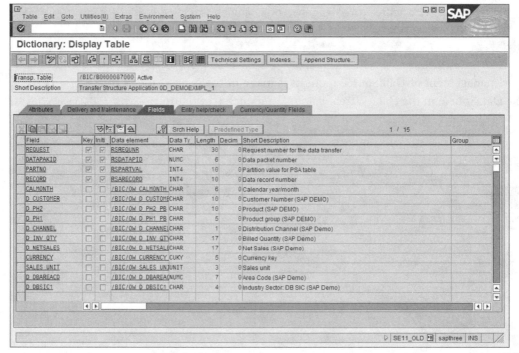

© SAP AG

The PSA content is not automatically deleted after processing. Since data in the PSA is stored on a very granular level, the PSA may soon require a large portion of the overall system capacity. Thus, it is highly recommended that you only persist the data temporarily[136] and delete it after it and its processing has been found to be error free.

136. In the BW architecture since release 1.2B, the PSA has experienced several changes to its scope and its name, so the term can be regarded as only an artifact of an older system.

If the requirements for extraction are changed, you may be required to modify the DataSource structure, and this usually results in a modification of the application structure and thus the PSA table.

Versioning of the PSA structure

To avoid changing the structure of existing data in the PSA, BW only changes PSA tables with field expansions. However, for other changes, the existing PSA tables are not modified; instead, new PSA tables are created with a new version number (the old table remains unchanged).

Each of the thus-versioned PSA tables internally receives a validity period so that it can be determined when working with PSA content which PSA table is valid for the respective period. Therefore, even after a change in the transfer structure, both old and new requests can be accessed in the PSA.

> The programs to process the data in the following layers are *not* versioned by BW in this way. Thus, you need to ensure that after a change in the application structure, further processing can be made using the old as well as the new structure (if required).

The name of a PSA table in the ABAP Dictionary depends on the name of the DataSource, the source system, and the version of the transfer structure. Based on this dependency, the system generates the names;[137] they are in the namespace /BIC/B0000xxxxxx.

PSA tables

To manage PSA tables, BW uses the transparent table RSTSODS. In this table, the name of the transparent table of a DataSource is stored in the field ODSNAME_TECH. The respective data record can be found in the content of the field USEROBJ,[138] which contains the technical name of the Data-Source as well as the respective source system.

The PSA structure is derived from the application structure that is defined with the DataSource. This structure maps field types that are *expected* but not field types that are actually supplied.

Typing of PSA segments

When the fields of the application structure are not of the type CHAR, problems can arise if a source system does not provide the requested field type (e.g., a string for a date field).

---

137. The ABAP Dictionary table is automatically created and activated with the activation of the transfer structure.
138. This only applies to new DataSources of BW release 7. Administrative entries for DataSources of the release 3.x are found via the key field ODSNAME. Its content is derived from the name of the respective DataSource and a two-digit suffix for the source system and it is stored in the table RSTS for DataSource and source system.

Problems should be solved by entering a suitable conversion routine for the respective fields in the DataSource so that through input conversion, the field value is stored in the PSA with the correct typing.

If there is no conversion routine to reliably convert a field value into the required format or if it cannot be ensured that a source system provides field values in the expected format, problems from the entry of raw data into the PSA can be prevented by storing the PSA untyped. The option can be found in the general settings of the DataSource maintenance (see figure 15–10).

When a PSA table is filed untyped, all fields of the PSA table are defined as characteristics fields. Thus, at least all data records can always be written up to the PSA. However, this does not replace the handling of the respective data records—if all else fails, this is done by manually correcting PSA content. However, sooner or later dubious field values in the raw data need to be dealt with adequately.

15.4 Definition of Extraction Processes

With the configuration of the extraction and the inflow layer, all requirements are fulfilled to extract raw data from the source systems and to store it in the PSA. Except with former SAP BW releases, defining a further data flow is no longer required. The extraction process instead represents an independent part of the staging process that concludes with storing the extracted data in the PSA.

The use of the PSA is mandatory with the use of the new staging process in SAP BW 7. Unlike with releases up to 3.x, with release 7, InfoPackages control only the handover of data to the PSA but not the further processing in the following layers.

InfoPackages   The definition of extraction processes is thus stored in *InfoPackages*. InfoPackages are created for each DataSource of a source system, and they describe the control parameters for the data flow up to the PSA.

Each InfoPackage for the extraction of data from source systems is described by a freely chosen (and ambiguous) name. The unambiguous technical identification of the InfoPackage is automatically generated by the system.

For the setup of standard operations and monitoring, it has proven helpful to add the technical name of the DataSource to the name of the InfoPackage.

It is possible to define several InfoPackages for each DataSource. Which package is used when can be determined when the system ist started manually or in the subsequent definition of standard operations.

If an extraction process is started from an InfoPackage, it receives a systemwide unambiguous ID directly with the data request: the *request ID*. This *request* comprises all monitor logs that are related to this process and generated during the extraction process. It is further referred to the processing logs in other layers.

InfoPackages are created in the DataSource tree of the Data Warehousing Workbench for the respective DataSource (see figure 15–28).

Figure 15–28
Creation of InfoPackages

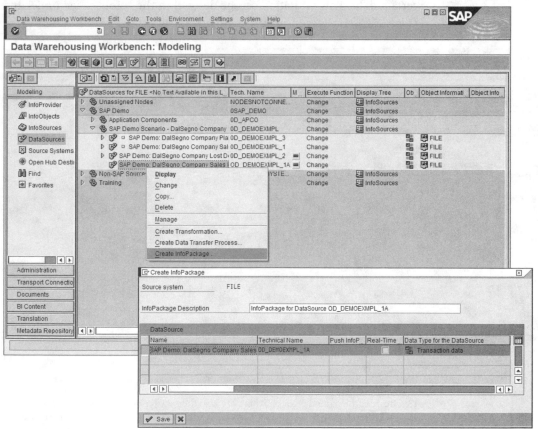

© SAP AG

The settings made in the InfoPackages partially depend on the source system and data type. There is a range of registers[139] available in the settings of the InfoPackage maintenance:

- Data selection
- Extraction
- Processing
- Update
- Schedule

The different settings will be explained in the following sections.

15.4.1 Data Selection

Figure 15–29
InfoPackage:
Data Selection tab

In many cases, it is desirable to limit the extraction from a DataSource to certain data. This limitation can be defined in the InfoPackage under the *Data Selection* tab (see figure 15–29).

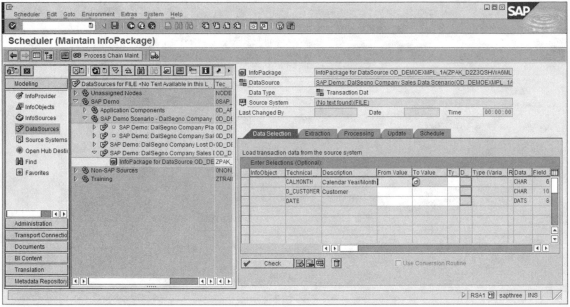

© SAP AG

---

139. Besides the named registers, there are also the register *data targets*. They are specifically for staging processes with BW 3.5 DataSources. For the new staging processes in BW release 7, the register *data targets* are less relevant and will not be explained any further in this context.

The fields that a DataSource offers for selection depend on the definition of the respective DataSource (see section 15.2.3).

The simplest form of selection is the definition of fixed values. To obtain a dynamic selection, there is a range of selection types available that can be selected with the definition of an InfoPackage:

- Date selection (type 0 to 4)
- Free timely limitation (type 5)
- Selection through ABAP routine (type 6)
- Selection through OLAP variable (type 7)

After entering the respective selection type and confirming with Enter, you can make further type-specific settings.

The definition of an empty selection—i.e., the selection of a field value with initial content—is not possible when a fixed value has been predefined. However, you can define the empty value by selecting an ABAP routine (type 6).

Selecting the Date

The date can only be selected for fields of the DATS type. There are five types that stand for an automatically set date. The following table shows the types 0 to 4.

Type	Name	Description
0	Yesterday	12:00 a.m. until 23:59 p.m. of the previous day
1	Last Week	Monday to Sunday of the previous week
2	Last Month	First to last day of the previous month
3	Last Quarter	First to last day of the previous quarter
4	Last Year	January 1 to December 31 of the previous year

Selecting the date is especially helpful in cases where the dates are to be loaded periodically and the selection is to refer to different periods based on the date of the load request.

Depending on the nature of the data source, a delta mechanism can be realized with the selection of the date if the DataSource itself is not delta enabled (e.g., generic DataSources or flat files).

Free Time Delimitation

The free delimitation of time allows for dynamic selection of characteristics fields similar to that for date fields.

For this purpose, the delimitation of time offers an option to indicate an interval from which, depending on the number of loads, further steps are taken (see figure 15–30).

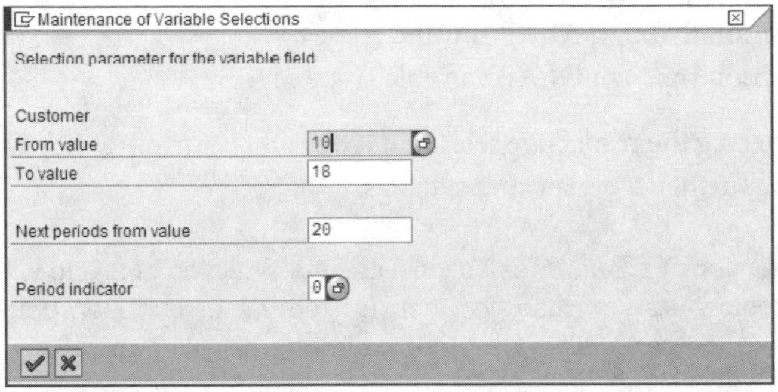

© SAP AG

Figure 15–30
InfoPackage: free time delimitation

The free delimitation is shown in the following example:

From value	10
To value	18
Next periods from value	20
Period indicator	0

Here, with the first load the values 10 to 18 are selected. With the second load, the values 20 to 28 are selected, with the third 30 to 38, and so on.

Should these values be date fields despite their data type, then the period type 1 (year/similar period) should be selected instead of the period type 0. Thus, it is possible in a dynamic selection to use months and years as calculating units.

Selection through ABAP Routine

There may be cases where the option of constant selections and date selections do not sufficiently delimit data. For this purpose, there is the selection type 6, where an ABAP routine is to identify the content of the selection field. The routine is executed after all other selections and thus it has access to the content of all selection fields.

With the start, a separate program will be generated for each InfoPackage to which the code of the ABAP routine will be integrated. The structure of the ABAP routines is linked to a predefined schema consisting of the following items:

- A global data declaration part
- A parameter part
- A code part

The global declaration part is given for all selection routines of an Info-Package. Here, data can be declared that is to be valid for all selection routines of the respective InfoPackage. On the one hand, this relates to the pure declaration; on the other, it relates to content that can be reused in other routines.

Global declaration part

```
program conversion_routine.
*    Type pools used by conversion program
type-pools: rsarc, rsarr, rssm.
tables: rssdlrange.
*    Global code used by conversion rules
*$*$ begin of global – insert your declaration only below this line –
* TABLES: ...
* DATA:    ...
*$*$ end of global – insert your declaration only before this line –
```

The parameters of the form routine have the following relevance and effect:

Parameter part of the form routine

- L_T_RANGE
  In the internal table L_T_RANGE, the existing selections are transferred. At the same time, this internal table serves to return the selections evaluated in the ABAP routine.
- P_INFOPACKAGE
  This parameter contains the technical name of the InfoPackage for extraction.
- P_FIELDNAME
  This parameter contains the field name of the selected field.
- P_SUBRC
  With the return parameter P_SUBRC, the routine needs to indicate whether a selection was successful (P_SUBRC = 0) or not (P_SUBRC ≠ 0).

```
* --------------------------------------------------------------
*   InfoObject     =
*   Fieldname      = CALMONTH
*   data type      = CHAR
*   length         = 000006
*   convexit       =
* --------------------------------------------------------------
form compute_CALMONTH
  tablesl_t_rangestructure rssdlrange
  using p_infopackagetype rslogdpid
       p_fieldnametype rsfnm
  changingp_subrclike sy-subrc.
*   Insert source code to current selection field
```

Code of the selection routine All ABAP functions are available in the code part of the selection routine, so the decision on the selection can be made according to complex rules.

```
*$*$ begin of routine – insert your code only below this line    -
data: l_idx like sy-tabix.
read table l_t_range with key
     fieldname = P_FIELDNAME.
* P_FIELDNAME is in this case the string "CALMONTH"
l_idx = sy-tabix.
* Example to fill OCALMONTH with the selection of 12.2006…
l_t_range-low = '200612'.
l_t_range-sign = 'I'.
l_t_range-option = 'EQ'.
modify l_t_range index l_idx.
* …or the period 01.2000 – 12.2000
l_t_range-low = '200001'.
l_t_range-sign = 'I'.
l_t_range-option = 'BT'.
l_t_range-high = '200012'.
append l_t_range.
* End of Example
modify l_t_range index l_idx.

p_subrc = 0.
*$*$ end of routine – insert your code only before this line     -
endform.
```

With the creation of the routine, coding is already provided to access the field content of the field to be selected as well as to modify the selected content of this field (e.g., the field CALMONTH).

Selection routines only provide options to dynamically fill selection fields. Selection routines cannot run a filter over the already transferred data records. The selection criteria are evaluated before the extraction requirements are sent to the source systems, and they are transferred together with the data request.

Selection through OLAP Variable

A special selection type is the selection through a variable that was defined for the selection of characteristics values in queries (type 7).

OLAP variables generally serve the purpose to make the data analysis more flexible and to define individual parameters for each analysis action (e.g., selection of a certain customer number). Such variable content can be either deduced from the user input during analysis (manual input, replacement path, authorization) or calculated from a user exit[140] (or SAP exit for supplied variables).

OLAP variables with user exits might show values that are also relevant for the data selection. To avoid having to develop identical ABAP coding for the OLAP variables as well as for the data selection, the results of the value evaluation from the OLAP variable with user exits can be directly integrated into the selection of InfoPackages (see figure 15–31).

15.4.2 Extraction

The settings in the *InfoPackage Extraction* tab are similar to the settings for the extraction source that have already been made with the definition of the DataSources. The selected settings are copied into the InfoPackages on the DataSource; however, they can be overwritten with other values. The only exceptions are settings on the delta procedure and the adapter used.

Figure 15–32 shows an InfoPackage for the DataSource defined in figure 15–16.

---

140. The identification of the OLAP variable is made in the function module `EXIT_SAPLRRS0_001`.

Figure 15–31
InfoPackage: selection
through OLAP variables

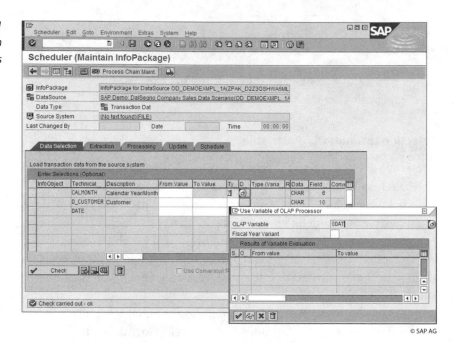

© SAP AG

Figure 15–32
InfoPackage: settings for
extraction

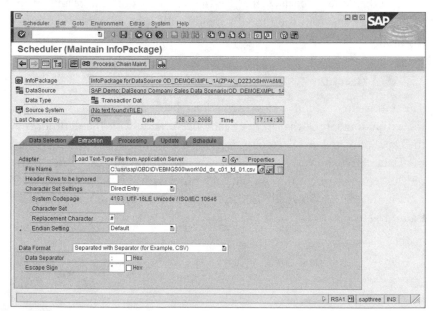

© SAP AG

15.4.3   Processing

The settings regarding processing are mostly relevant for the direct staging with BW 3.5 DataSources. Here, you indicate how the timely sequence of processes between PSA and the following layers is to be managed (see chapter 21).

For the new staging in BW release 7, the question of a coordination of processes in the single layers does not come up any longer since entries are made only in the PSA and in no other layers. Thus, the settings on processing are limited to the entries in the PSA or, more precisely, the parallelization of data entry. The parallelization of entries is a performance-relevant topic and will be explained in section 24.1.

15.4.4   Update

The settings in the update parameters define whether data is to be extracted as a full upload or whether a delta procedure is to be used, if possible (see figure 15–33).

Figure 15–33

InfoPackage: Update

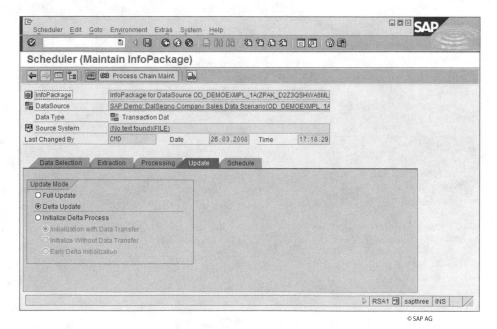

© SAP AG

While the full upload can be done anytime, the use of a delta procedure requires an initialization. During the initialization, all data is extracted from the DataSource and (depending on the extractor) a respective pointer will be placed from which new and changed data records are identified during a delta procedure.

For the structure of standard operations, it has been proven helpful with the use of delta procedures to not switch between initialization and delta update in one InfoPackage but to create one InfoPackage for the initialization and a separate one for the delta update.

When the delta procedure for a DataSource has been initialized, a load status is logged for each delta load process. For error-free load processes, the pointer in the extractor will be adjusted accordingly. For erroneous load processes, the pointer will stay in place, and with the next load process, the same delta needs to be reloaded.

Figure 15–34

InfoPackage: deleting a delta initialization

If the initialization needs to be repeated (e.g., since a delta load process could not be repeated), the old initialization will have to be deleted first (see figure 15–34).

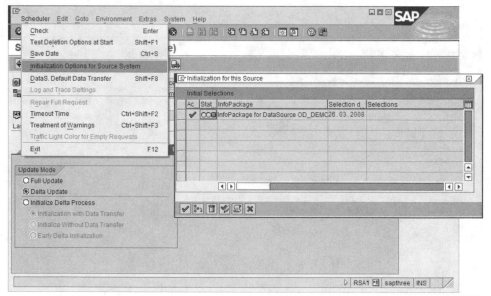

15.4.5 **Scheduling**

With the scheduling of an InfoPackage, the starting conditions for the load process are determined, and a job is scheduled and enabled via the *Start* button according to the starting conditions (see figure 15–35).

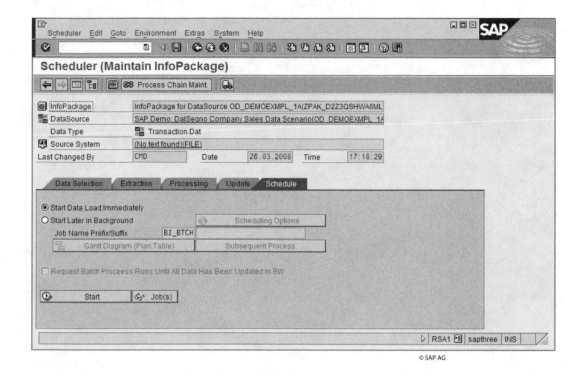

© SAP AG

More specific explanations on scheduling options and postprocessing can be found with the description of event controlling for the BW basis system (see section 28.1).

Figure 15–35
InfoPackage: scheduling

16 Transformation Layer

Data that BW receives from a source system is available in the form used by the source system. This may have consequences for semantics, structure, and display of the data:

- **Semantics:** Business objects are described differently in the source systems, as in these examples:
  - Identical customers are described with different customer numbers in the source system.
  - Identical customer numbers describe different customers in the respective systems.
  - Supplied key figures do not have identical meaning (e.g., sales with/without VAT/GST, item or pallet quantities).
  - Different systems provide different key figures (e.g., a system provides only sales revenue, another only sales volume).
- **Structure:** Information is structured differently and might need to be deduced (e.g., combination of several information components encrypted in one field).
- **Validity:** Data might be erroneous and must be identified as such (and possibly separated). Examples for erroneous data are manifold:
  - Lowercase letters are used incorrectly.
  - Data is not supplied in compliance with conversion routines or cannot be converted (e.g., the erroneous date 02/31/2006).
  - The referential integrity of the data is not kept.

Especially in heterogeneous and established system landscapes, the extracted data is to be interpreted very differently and is, in its raw form, of little use for the data analysis. Before data from source systems can be evaluated, it needs to be qualitatively enhanced or prepared by being transformed into a structural and semantic standard format.[141]

---

141. The transformation of data is also referred to as homogenization.

The functions running this homogenization are all concentrated in a preferred[142] architecture in the transformation layer. With this architectural requirement, errors can quickly be analyzed and corrected. Compared to BW architectures where the transformation is located in different places according to the staging process, the standardized architecture is much easier to manage and enhance.

In practice, the evaluation on what data modifications are to be made as part of the transformation layer and what processes are to be executed at a later stage (i.e., in the data mart layer) is often very difficult, and it usually gets even more difficult the clearer (!) the analytical requirements are the system must fulfill. The need for a corresponding separation only becomes obvious with complex architectures from which the need for a transformation layer is deduced.

As such, it is the task of the transformation layer to undertake all general processing steps that are required from all analytical applications as well. These include not only the previously mentioned structural and semantic homogenizations of data but also the filtering and correcting of errors (data cleansing/data scrubbing) and the data quality testing.

The target structure of the transformation is defined according to the architecture by DataStore Objects of the integration layer (see chapter 17) or within the transformation layer by InfoSources.

Besides the general preparation of data, a specific data preparation might be required for single analytical applications. However, this is not in the scope of the transformation layer and will be executed in the data mart layer with the application-specific preparation of data (see chapter 18).

From the deliberate shift of the application-specific processing to areas closer to the application and the concentration of application-independent preparation in the transformation layer comes the initial statement that the more complex the system, the easier it is to define the tasks of the transformation layer. Especially in complex systems, it can be evaluated right away which requirements come from all analytical applications and which requirements come specifically from one single application.

In the following sections, we'll discuss BW objects that (can) assume a function for the transformation layer. These are **InfoSources** (section 16.1) and **write-optimized DataStore Objects** (section 16.2).

---

142. Always consider that the described architecture is not a mandatory for SAP BW but what we consider to be the most sensible variant for a range of requirements.

The actual rules that describe how data content should be enhanced in the transformation layer—i.e., the *transformation*—are not available in the transformation layer. Instead, this is a central component of the staging engine and will be described separately in chapter 19.

16.1 InfoSources

As mentioned initially, the data preparation in the transformation layer requires the definition of a target structure into which data is to be transferred. In the reference architecture, such a target structure is preferably defined with standard DataStore Objects in the integration layer, but there are also reasons to define the target structure in the form of an InfoSource.

In BW releases prior to release 7, InfoSources were the central element to control the staging process and they were required for the definition of any data flow. *InfoSource* was included in BW 7 as a term but not as a technology. Now, it is only a target structure for staging, and it is only an optional component.

Since an InfoSource does not have its own data storage, it does not provide any value for the staging at first glance. However, InfoSources are used in the preferred reference architecture if the result from the transformation is not transferred to a DataStore Object in the integration layer. Otherwise, they form the target structure of the transformation; if they do not exist, the InfoSources will assume this function and transfer the data themselves to the next layer.

InfoSources are to be created in the InfoSource tree of the Data Warehousing Workbench. An object template needs to be provided, and it should be as close as possible to the desired target structure (which is typically a target structure in the next layer). However, the structure of the InfoSource can be modified freely (see figure 16–1).

Creation of InfoSources

The definition of fields of an InfoSource is made based only on InfoObjects whose technical characteristics thus also influence the definition of the InfoSource (see figure 16–2). However, in the ABAP Dictionary a structure for each communication structure will be created and it is based on the data elements of the InfoObjects.

Figure 16–1

Creation of InfoSources

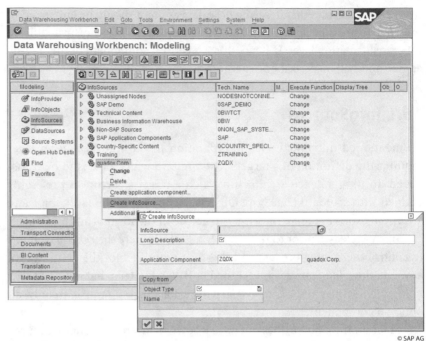

Figure 16–2

InfoSource as target structure in staging process

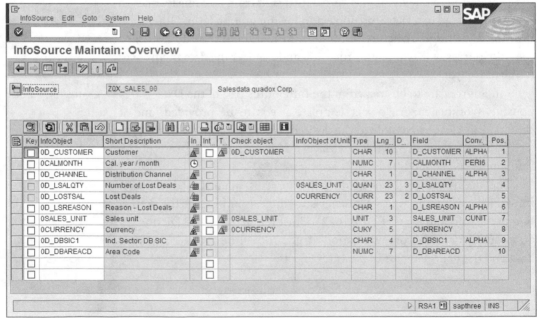

In addition to the description of a target structure for the homogenization, an InfoSource can assume a range of further functions in the staging that justify its use:

- Test of the referential integrity of field content
- Aggregation of data
- Conversion of currencies and units

Here, the specific advantage lies in the fact that these functions are all executed in one single place. Thus, the use of InfoSources is especially suited to map the branching of the staging process in general transformation (source structures to InfoSource) and for data-target-specific preparation (InfoSource to target structures).

This advantage of an InfoSource becomes especially visible when data with an n:m relationship is transferred between source and target structure; in these cases, the use of an InfoSource is well suited to reduce the number of transformations to be defined between data sources and data targets (see figure 16–3).

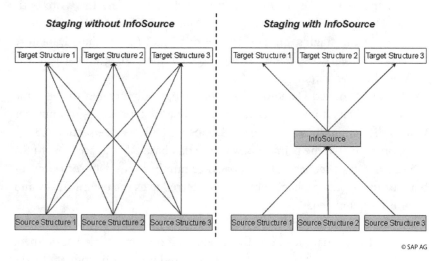

© SAP AG

Figure 16–3

Standardization of staging with InfoSources

The fact that a shared InfoSource can be used to process several transformations does not have any effect on load process execution. The load processes can be defined per transformation and can be executed independently (and in parallel too).

16.2 Persisting of Raw Data

With the persistent staging area, BW already offers an option to persistently store extracted data. Above all, the goal is to validate and manage recently loaded data and the handling of errors during staging. Thus, the PSA is especially relevant as a memory media for requests that have not been finally processed yet or that have not been released by the quality assurance.

However, the PSA is less suited to persist raw data permanently in order to build single data targets from the raw data ex post facto; apart from an increased management effort (selection of available requests since there might be double or erroneous requests), it is helpful to prepare raw data fundamentally—even if this only consists of filtering data records with zero values in key figures.

SAP itself supports the argument that the PSA is not provided to permanently persist data since it does not offer any option in release 7 to archive data in the PSA[143] (see chapter 33).

For the permanent storing of extracted data, there are the write-optimized DataStore Objects. These are DataStore Objects that are fully involved in the staging process on the one hand (other than DataStore Objects for direct access) and that store data in the same granularity as the PSA on the other hand.

Write-optimized DataStore Objects are basically created in the same way regular DataStore Objects are created, but the type write-optimized is to be indicated in the settings of the DataStore Objects (see section 6.3).

Consequently, the primary key of the database table as well as of PSA tables consists of request ID, data package number, and data record number within the data package. This key is referred to as the technical key and it cannot be changed.

In addition, a semantic key can be defined. Its fields are provided with a UNIQUE secondary index by the database. If no semantic key is defined, all fields of the DataStore Object can be entered into the list of data fields; the secondary index will then be dropped.

If a semantic key is defined, the uniqueness of the data records regarding the semantic key will be checked when the DataStore Object is filled. When data records that already exist from a semantic key perspective are

---

143. This function was announced earlier, but with release 7 it is no longer under discussion.

to be written into a DataStore Object, it will lead to an error during the entry.

If this behavior is not desired, the option Do Not Check Uniqueness of Data can be activated in the settings of the DataStore Object (see figure 16–4). In this case, the semantic key is no more and no less than a regular secondary index.

Figure 16–4

Semantic key of write-optimized DataStore Objects

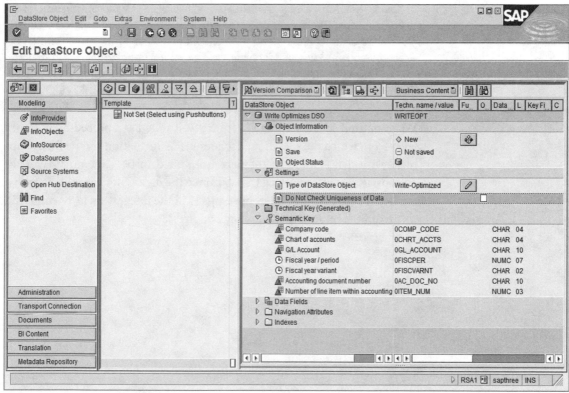

© SAP AG

The uniqueness of all data records in a write-optimized DataStore Object is ensured by the composition of the technical key anyway; i.e., data records are never overwritten with newer data (even if they have the same semantic key).

Thus, all data is stored in the granularity and sequence at which they were transferred to BW. Each single modification of a field from one extraction to the other will be exactly recorded so that write-optimized DataStore Objects form a sufficient data basis to transfer data changes to the data analysis.

In practice, this requirement is (unfortunately) relatively rare, but it can be found in particular cases. Due to the huge data volume that comes from such a detailed storing of data, write-optimized DataStore Objects should only be used in special cases.

Write-optimized DataStore Objects are fully integrated into the staging and can basically be provided with completely transformed data. However, you should always be aware that this is not the task of write-optimized DataStore Objects. The processing steps prior to entry in write-optimized DataStore Objects should instead be limited to the filtering of redundant data records and very simple, technical, and structural transformations that have almost no error potential. The actual preparation of data in the transformation layer should be made only after the write-optimized DataStore Object.

Write-optimized DataStore Objects are well suited as a preceding memory layer from which the specific subsequent transformation can be freely supplied with data. However, they are not suited to be a memory layer for enterprise data warehousing (EDW) since the data is not available in transformed form. Only the DataStore Objects in the integration layer can fulfill this requirement (see the following chapters).

17   Integration Layer

The integration layer is sort of an "extended arm" of the transformation layer and is defined by storing enhanced transactional data and master data.

In the underlying reference architecture, the integration layer only receives data from InfoSources because the objective is to create a standard design that is independent from the source system. However, this is not a mandatory part of transformation in BW 7; i.e., data can be transferred from the transformation layer to the data mart layer without this "detour".

There are different reasons, depending on different design options, that transactional data and master data are stored in the integration layer.

17.1 Transactional Data in the Integration Layer

For transactional data, three goals are pursued with the use of the integration layer that can be weighted very differently depending on the system architecture:

- Persistence
- Delta generation
- Data integration

The technical means to reach these goals are standard DataStore Objects that form the core of the integration layer. In the following sections, we'll explain how the use of *standard DataStore Objects* responds to these tasks. The following sections also describe the functioning of standard DataStore Objects.

When cumulative data is supplied, the use of DataStore Objects is a problem since different business cases might be supplied in several data records but with the same characteristics combinations and thus no unique key can be found. If the use of DataStore Objects is not possible, you should still aim for a standard architecture where the target structures of the homogenization are clearly defined. In these cases, such a target structure can best be defined by an InfoSource in the transformation layer (see also section 16.1)

17.1.1 Persistence

The persistence of transformation results offers an option to transfer transformed data at a random point in time (independent from the time of transformation) to the next layer—e.g., to rebuild[144] modified BasisCubes, to initially fill new BasisCubes, or to provide data for other purposes.

The structure of the DataStore Objects in the integration layer is derived directly from the structure defined by the transformation layer; i.e., if an InfoSource is used, the DataStore Objects have the same structure as the respective InfoSource from which they are filled. Like the transformation layer, the integration layer has the task to provide data in a generally valid form and to leave the application-specific data preparation to the data mart layer.

To fulfill their task and be a universal data supplier, data is stored in the DataStore Objects of the integration layer in the same granularity as in the source systems. Each individual data record can be unambiguously identified by the classification criteria (e.g., sales order and receipt position) that are key fields in the DataStore Object (see also section 6.3.1).

Standard DataStore Objects

The DataStore Objects of the integration layer thus need to be of "standard" type (see section 6.3) that on the one hand enables the filling during the staging process (contrary to DataStore Objects for direct write) and on the other hand is organized according to business-relevant classification criteria (e.g., sales order and receipt position) compared to write-optimized DataStore Objects that have a technical key.

---

144. Usually BasisCubes are modeled in such a way that they meet reporting requirements. Experience shows that after a certain time in live operations, requirements are redefined and cannot be met with the existing data model of a BasisCube. Usually, the only solution is to rebuild the BasisCube, which often cannot be done with data from the source systems (e.g., since it was archived already).

Standard DataStore Objects offer the option to overwrite fields' values in data fields if the same key values are available. Thus, duplicate supplies can be identified from the key values and old values can be overwritten by new ones. The primary goal of the storing on receipt level is thus to create a mapping of the operative systems in the integration layer.

Depending on whether there is a chance that the transformation of data could be erroneous or the requirements for the transformation could subsequently change, DataStore Objects should not only contain the results from the transformation but also the raw data from which they were derived.

In terms of enterprise data warehousing as propagated by SAP for some time, DataStore Objects form the memory layer referred to as the data warehouse layer, which is used to supply any data mart. Whether DataStore Objects form the data warehouse layer of an enterprise data warehouse or whether they are only the persistent form of transformation is technically irrelevant and basically depends on the evaluation and use of DataStore Objects.

Enterprise Data Warehousing (EDW)

There might certainly be opposing opinions and approaches at this point. However, the design of a BW architecture follows our personal opinions and experiences; we refuse write-optimized DataStore Objects as a basis for the EDW layer since they offer no convincing options for correction of errors or data integration. For noncumulative data, the use of write-optimized DataStore Objects is the only possibility to store such data in an EDW.

17.1.2 Delta Generation

The organization of data in standard DataStore Objects according to content keys enables you to not only provide data fields with changed values prior to data transfer but also to recognize and log the changes.

In the generated "log", the changes are stored in the generally adopted delta procedure ODS.[145] With help from DataStore Objects from extracted data of various delta procedures, it is thus possible to generate standard delta information (see figure 17–1) that can be processed by any discretionary data target in BW. This is helpful since, for example, BasisCubes

---

145. Operational Data Store (ODS) objects were the forerunners of standard DataStore Objects. The name change from ODS objects to DataStore Objects has not been adopted for the technical keys of the delta procedure, so the delta procedure ODS still exists.

cannot process all used delta procedures and thus rely on a suitable delta procedure (e.g., the delta procedure ODS).

Figure 17–1

Delta generation of standard DataStore Objects

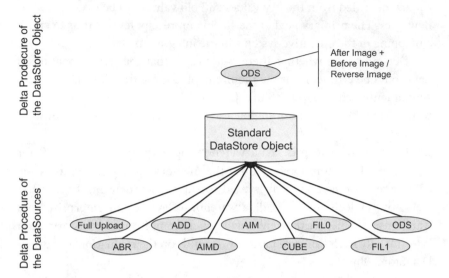

Thus, even from the data of a full upload, delta information can be generated.

> With the help of standard DataStore Objects, even the data from a full upload can be transformed into delta information. In this case, the delta information describes all changes and newly generated data records. Deleted data records (that were not supplied with the full upload) will not be represented in the delta information.

The delta mode of a respective data record that is updated in a DataStore Object and that is to be transformed into the delta procedure ODS is handed over from the InfoObject ORECORDMODE to the DataStore Object. If the InfoObject is not supplied by the data source during the transformation, BW always assumes an after image. The content of the InfoObject ORECORDMODE can be manipulated during transformation. Further information will be provided in section 19.4.2.

It is possible to overwrite data fields only if the used delta mode of the update DataSource enables the generation of before and after images. If this is not the case, data fields cannot be overwritten, even with DataStore Objects. DataSources with the delta procedures D, E, and X (old extraction from LIS infostructures of the LO module in SAP ERP) can be processed by DataStore Objects only if a suitable delta mode is assigned to the InfoObject ORECORDMODE in the transfer rules.

To identify delta information, you need to compare new data and existing data. Since the sequence in which data records are written into a DataStore Object[146] is crucial for the result of the delta generation, the comparison is not made right after the data is entered into a DataStore Object; this is because the correct sequence of data cannot be ensured at the time of the entry given the parallelization of entries (see section 24.1) or the parallel entry of several requests.

Activation queue

For this reason, new data is first entered into a separate table and only in the second step (and in the right sequence) compared with the actual data of the DataStore Object. The actual data of a standard DataStore Object is called **active data** in BW terminology; the table into which data is entered before the comparison is referred to as the **activation queue.** The comparison process is called **activation.**

The activation queue is a transparent table, and its structure is similar to the DataStore Object. In addition, the activation queue has a request ID, data package number, and data record number that were transferred from the extraction. It is thus possible to write several requests and data packages into an activation queue at the same time and to still keep the correct sequence of data records during activation.

While in write-optimized DataStore Objects and DataStore Object for direct write, new data can be found in the active data immediately after the data entry, the data of the activation queue needs to be transferred through explicit activation in the DataStore Object. Any use of new data (for data analysis or data transfer to the next layer) thus depends on the activation of the DataStore Object.

The delta information identified during activation is recorded in the *change log* (see figure 17–2).

Change log

The change log is a table of the PSA that is automatically created for each standard DataStore Object. Further, for each standard DataStore Object, an export DataSource will be created that serves as data source for the transfer of data from the change log to other data targets.

---

146. For the result of the comparison, it crucial whether, for example, the order status is first overwritten by an A and then by a B or vice versa.

Figure 17–2

*Generation of the change log
with activation of new data in
standard DataStore Objects*

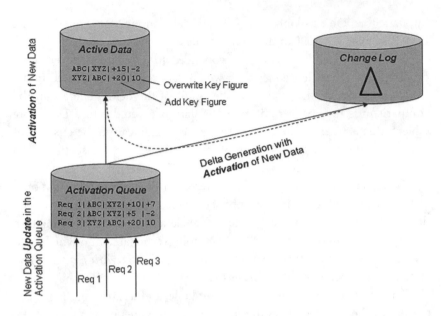

The delta information calculated with the activation of new data has its own data requirements from a PSA point of view. These are not identical to the activated requests of the activation queue, but they are newly identified by the system.

To define the transfer of data from the change log to the next data target, you need to define only a transformation into the data target where the DataStore Object is indicated as data source.

Naming convention

In addition to the naming conventions that are described with the data model of the DataStore Object (see section 6.3), the following table contains naming conventions for the staging with DataStore Objects.

	Standard DataStore Object (BI Content)	Standard DataStore Object (Self-Defined)
DataStore Object	0ttttttt	{A-Z}ttttt
Active Data	/BIO/Attttt00	/BIC/A{A-Z}ttttt00
Activation Queue	/BIO/Attttt10	/BIC/A{A-Z}ttttt10
DataSource of the Change Log	8tttttttt	8{A-Z}ttttt

17.1.3 Data Integration

It was described in the previous chapters how the options of a DataStore Object to overwrite data fields with changed values can be used to identify delta information.

The same technical functionality can have a completely new meaning for DataStore Objects if data records are composed from parts of different data sources. The only precondition is that all data sources can supply the complete key of the DataStore Object.

The application cases for this form of data integration are as different as the processes in the different source systems. While it may be important for a company to merge planned and actual delivery dates from two different data sources in one joint data record, this requirement might be irrelevant for another company.

Figure 17–3 shows how data can be integrated into a DataStore Object and what results the same process would produce with a BasisCube as data target without any option to overwrite data fields.

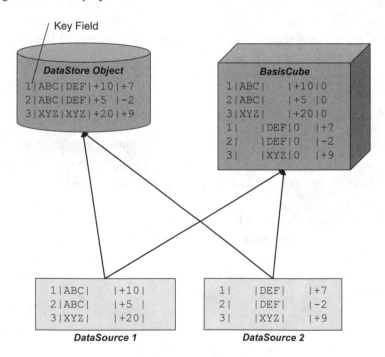

Figure 17–3

Data integration with standard DataStore Objects

For simplification purposes, the activation queue and change log are not shown in the figure but they are used as usual. With the creation of change

logs, delta information can be transferred to the next data targets so that
BasisCubes with the same integrated data can be supplied too. Thus, there
may be a significant difference whether a BasisCube is filled from the
DataSources directly or whether it is filled from the preceding standard
DataStore Objects.

> If the data fields that are transferred from the individual DataSources to a
> DataStore Object have common subsets, then the last request will always
> overwrite the data fields of the preceding requests (unless the data field is
> not taken over into the DataSource). This may be an error source, but it may
> also be a practical option to manipulate erroneous content in data fields in a
> targeted way.

17.2 Master Data in the Integration Layer

Other than transactional data, master data often exists in the integration
layer in the requested form so that a transfer to the subsequent layer is not
required. The reason is that there can only be one view on master data
cross-system,[147] and given their uniqueness, they only need to be stored
once in the system.

As a consequence, master data can be stored in the integration layer
without having to be transferred to following layers as with transactional
data.

So, the storing is not done in DataStore Objects but directly in the master data containing InfoObjects. These InfoObjects use similar mechanisms for persisting and data integration as are found with DataStore
Objects. Only the option to identify delta information is not available for
InfoObjects.

Direct update   Up to release 2.x of SAP BW, the unambiguity and uniqueness of master data was assumed with such consequence that there was no other
option systematically but to transfer the data of a master data DataSource
into exactly one InfoObject. The reason was the concept of direct update of
master data attributes, texts, and hierarchies.

Direct update is also used in the current version of SAP BW, even if it
is no longer "state of the art" given the new transformation in BW 7.

---

147. E.g., the postal code or address of a customer does not change with the respective
     application that uses the master data.

However, it can be defined easier and it is still required to load hierarchy data.[148] The direct update is further explained in chapter 21.

However, if InfoObjects of the integration layer are not to be filled with the outdated direct update but via the transformation of BW 7, it is first necessary to add the master data of the respective InfoObject into the data mart layer (see section 18.2).

DataStore Objects for master data

In this case, it makes sense to fill the master data in the data mart layer from the DataStore Objects in order to create a standard staging architecture, as is done for transactional data on the BW architecture level.

Especially for InfoObjects with large master data tables, the use of standard DataStore Objects may be advantageous since it comes with the option the generate delta information. If master data is distributed to several InfoObjects in the data mart layer, the volume of the distribution will be reduced significantly.

> With the use of DataStore Objects for master data, never activate the creation of SIDs with the activation of new data (see section 10.2). With the activation of new data, the creation of SIDs would generate initial master data records that would only be filled with the transfer of delta information from the DataStore Object and would generate a massive number of data records in the M versions. This would consequently lead to unnecessary problems in the change run.

---

148. Up to Support Package 18, the transformation cannot process data for external hierarchies, yet.

18 Data Mart Layer

The architecture of the layers described in the previous chapters always aimed at preparing and providing data in a general rather than an application-specific form. The transformation layer forms a structural layer that can be persistent in the integration layer in order to provide data in an integrated way, whether or not a source system is available. In the sense of enterprise data warehousing, the layer could be described as a data warehouse layer.

Up to and including the integration layer, data is available in a general, application-independent form. In the simplest case, this structure will meet the requirements of the analytical application. In this case, InfoObjects can be used unchanged. For performance reasons, transactional data should be transferred into the star schema of BasisCubes; however, no changes to the content are required.

In numerous cases, the requirements from the analytical application(s) differ so strongly from the data structure in the transformation or the integration layer that they first need to be prepared semantically in order to be used. The preparation can be designed in a way that it can be used by several applications; however, it may also happen that each analytical application requires its own preparation.

The concept of the data mart layer makes sense because it provides a dedicated memory of prepared data in a layer within BW.[149] Thus, the homogenization of the preceding layers is followed by an individualization.

In BW terminology, data marts stem from the view of complex data warehouse systems or are considered to be a specialty of enterprise data warehousing. However, the application-specific display of data that is the intention behind data marts remains the same for each mapping of data in

---

149. Data marts can be outside of SAP BW. We are describing data marts in the context of large-scale architectures.

the InfoProviders, whether the mapping matches the structure of the transformation layer or whether it comes with complex preparation or overcoming system boundaries.

Thus, we decided to basically refer to the layer that forms the basis for analytical applications as the data mart layer. A design was chosen in which a small BW system can be scaled up to an enterprise data warehouse without fundamental change to the architecture. Further information on the use of the data mart layer in so-called large-scale architectures (that also include the EDW) can be found in chapter 27.

In the following sections, we'll explain the scope of the data mart layer in relation to *transactional data* and *master data* as well as the transfer of data to file systems and database tables using *open hub destinations.*

18.1 Transactional Data in the Data Mart Layer

In regard to transactional data, BasisCubes are the central component of the data mart layer. They represent the objects designed as the basis for the data analysis, and thus they ideally meet the application-specific reporting requirements.

The transfer of data to the data mart layer can serve a range of purposes that are related to both structural and semantic changes of data:

- Schema transformation
- Aggregation
- Filtering
- Process integration
- Abstraction
- Model transformation
- Currency conversions

The meaning of these tasks will be explained in the following sections The tasks that really need to be executed with the transfer of data to the data mart layer (or whether data can be taken over unchanged from the integration layer) partially depend on the requirements of the respective application.

Keep in mind that not all requirements have to be met by one cube. Rather, identical data can be prepared several times in different cubes, depending on application requirements.

18.1.1 Schema Transformation

The schema transformation is the central reason to provide transactional data in the data mart layer (i.e., in BasisCubes) and never to build the data analysis on the data structures of the integration layer (i.e., basically on DataStore Objects), because the schema transformation describes the transfer of data from the flat structures of the transformation and integration layers into the enhanced star schema of BasisCubes.

The motivation for the schema transformation is always the optimization of read performance during data access. This is enabled by the data model of BasisCubes itself and also by specific tuning measures[150] (e.g., partitioning, indexing, aggregate).

This optimization is the reason the data mart layer should be used even when no other tasks come with the transfer of data into the data mart layer.

18.1.2 Aggregation

On integration layer level, it is inevitable that data will be stored on a granular level. For the data analysis, however, this granularity is often not required so data records can be aggregated with the transfer into the data mart layer. Such an aggregation is another advantage of the schema transformation.

18.1.3 Filtering

Besides aggregation, the filtering of data records may result in another reduction of the data volume. Not all analytical applications require all data provided by the transformation/integration layer.

In some cases, some data may not even be desired. Thus, with the transfer of data to BasisCubes of the data mart layer, data records can be filtered according to individual rules.

In simple cases, the filtering can be made using the data transfer processes that transfer data into the BasisCubes (see section 20.2). In complex cases, the start or end routine of the transformation can assume the filtering of data records (see sections 19.2 and 19.5).

---

150. Details on the tuning of BasisCubes can be found in chapter 7.

18.1.4 Process Integration

The analysis of data in the data mart layer does not need to be limited to the data of a data structure in the transformation layer or the data of a DataStore Object in the integration layer. Rather, data from different process parts can be brought into context in an analysis.

The integration of different processes is usually made on the analytical engine level with virtual InfoProviders, specifically with MultiProviders or InfoSets (see chapter 11). The physical integration of different process data into a BasisCube (by filling the BasisCube from different data sources) is not usually recommended; in terms of content, the result is identical to the data merge in a MultiProvider, but the consolidation of several data sources in one BasisCube is more difficult to manage.[151]

Further, the quality of the data model may suffer if data that does not have identical structures is consolidated in this way—fact and dimension tables of the cube will thus turn into "Swiss cheese" with an unnecessarily high number of entries of which single fields are not filled.

18.1.5 Abstraction

Abstraction is a consequence of the use of MultiProviders as well as a reason to create them; with the use of MultiProviders, a logical layer is placed between BasisCubes and the data analysis and decouples the data analysis (in the form of queries) from the data model.

Thus, data analyses can be defined based on a MultiProvider for which the analytical engine will identify only the relevant BasisCubes at the time of the analysis. Since the structure of the MultiProvider can be changed freely, even the BasisCubes underlying the MultiProvider can be exchanged without the acknowledgement of the data analysis.

To increase the flexibility of the data model, the data analysis should thus never be defined based on BasisCubes but only based on MultiProviders. This implies the recommendation to define MultiProviders even if they integrate a single BasisCube only (i.e., even if they do not represent any direct functional value-add).

---

151. Especially for rollup and compression, dependencies between the individual data sources need to be considered. A request can only be rolled up/compressed if all requests loaded earlier are error free. Thus, this might result in the situation that a request from data source A cannot be rolled up/compressed since another request from data source B is not error free.

18.1.6 Model Transformation

Whether the mapping of key figures is to be made in a key figure or an account model can usually be deduced from the data structures (see section 5.3). Usually, data is already provided by the source system in the respective format; it is transferred accordingly by the transformation and integration layer and can also be stored in the data mart layer.

However, if a form of storing that is different from the source system is required, the conversion of the key figure and the account model and vice versa can be made with the transfer of data into the BasisCubes of the data mart layer.

Such a conversion of models is usually made when data from processes is to be integrated into the data mart layer where each is stored in a matching but not the same model. Here, the conversion of models serves to achieve standardization.

Besides this pure transformation of a model between key figure and account model, there are several other reasons to convert data records in key figures and vice versa. One example is a typical sales controlling scenario: Salesman 0001 has sold 15 units of a product to a customer. Salesman 0002 has not been involved in the deal; however, the sale was made in his sales area. In such cases, the sales volumes are to be split in a 2/3 to 1/3 relation.

The resulting request often requires generating two data records that each contain only one sales key figure from one single data record (indicating both salesmen in two fields with one sales amount). This example will be used in section 19.3 to discuss the technical realization during transformation.

18.1.7 Currency Conversion

Up to the integration layer, value fields are carried over in the currency in which they were supplied from the data sources. Usually, this is the local currency and/or sales order currency.

The currency can be transferred to the data mart layer without change, and it can be converted into other currencies at the time of the data analysis, if required.

However, if value fields are to be provided for the data analysis in converted form, the conversion should be made at the time of data transfer into the data mart layer. If required, not only a simple conversion will be made but even complex forms of conversion with reference to the data's time reference.

18.2 Master Data in the Data Mart Layer

Other than transactional data, BW provides for master data to use the data stored in the integration layer when transactional data is analyzed; the master data tables of the respective InfoObjects map the memory structures of the integration layer.

The design is based on the assumption that master data is never to be used in a way that's specific to an application but that it is always easily applicable (see section 17.2).

Figure 18–1
Definition of InfoObjects as InfoProviders

This idea was dropped with release 3 of SAP BW, and master data can now be handled in the same way as transactional data. To have this option, it is absolutely necessary to first enter the respective InfoObjects as data targets in the InfoProvider tree (see figure 18–1).

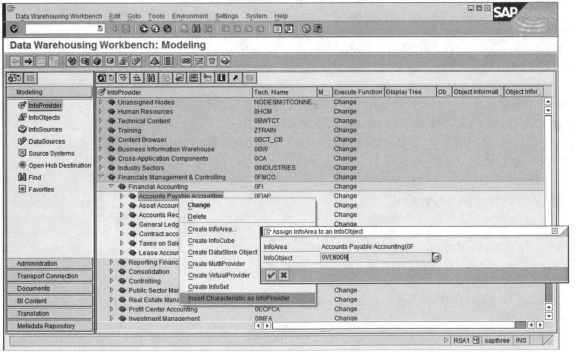

© SAP AG

As soon as an InfoObject has been entered to the InfoProvider tree as a data target, it can be used as a data target for a transformation.[152] In this case, it will be handled during the staging in the same way as a data target for transactional data.

> Please consider that with a change of master data—with direct or flexible staging—all changed master data will first be stored in an M version and it will become active data only with the execution of a change run (see section 7.1.2).

When InfoObjects are entered to the InfoProvider tree, you can build analyses directly on them without having to use BasisCubes or DataStore Objects. This is especially useful for reporting of master data.

18.3 Open Hub Destinations in the Data Mart Layer

In the previous chapters, data warehousing with SAP BW 7 was considered only under the precondition that data is processed to be prepared for data analysis by the BW InfoProviders. Systems other than SAP BW were in this regard considered to be only decision support tools or data suppliers for extraction.

Especially in complex system landscapes, in reality this might be different. SAP BW might be only one of several data warehouse systems, and it might assume certain tasks regarding data preparation; however, it may transfer this data over to other systems where it might be further prepared or at least used for analysis.

To transfer data to other systems, you can define open hub destinations in BW. These can provide data either in file format or as a database table. From there, the third-party systems need to handle the data acquisition.

Each data or database table that is to be provided with data can be defined as an open hub destination. For this purpose, the Data Warehousing Workbench provides a separate tree for the definition of open hub destinations (see figure 18–2).

---

152. At the same time, the InfoObject will be enabled for reporting. For reporting from the master data of InfoObjects, see section 10.3.

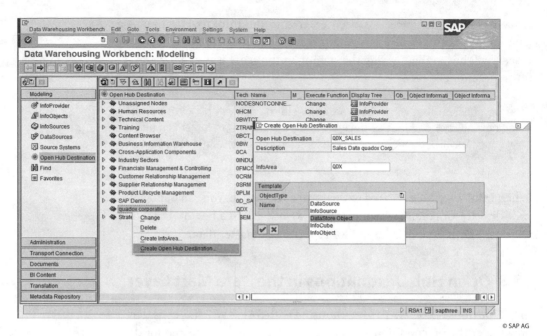

© SAP AG

Figure 18–2

Creation of open hub destinations

Field list of an open hub destination

The provision of an open hub destination is completely integrated into the staging; i.e., data preparation for the target structure can be controlled via the transformation and data transfer process (see chapters 19 and 20). With its tight integration into the BW staging processes, the idea of the open hub destination even replaces the InfoSpokes of the open hub services used until release 3.

With the creation of an open hub destination, you need to indicate a template object from which the proposal for a field list of the open hub destination is deduced. However, it is possible to individually modify the list of fields to be provided for an open hub destination. Here, it makes sense to deduce the fields from InfoObject requirements; the fields of a field list can also be created and typed without any reference to InfoObjects (see figure 18–3).

Further, you need to indicate with the definition of the open hub destination how the data is to be transferred to the target system. There are several transfer options:

- ▨ Via a CSV file on an network drive
- ▨ Via a CSV file on the application server
- ▨ Via a database table
- ▨ Via a third-party tool

The use of network drives as targets for the data to be generated with an open hub destination is the easiest form of open hub destination from a configuration point of view; the definition is limited to indicating a directory that SAP BW can access. Further, you need to indicate the separator to separate the field values in the generated files (see figure 18–4).

Transfer to CSV files on network drives

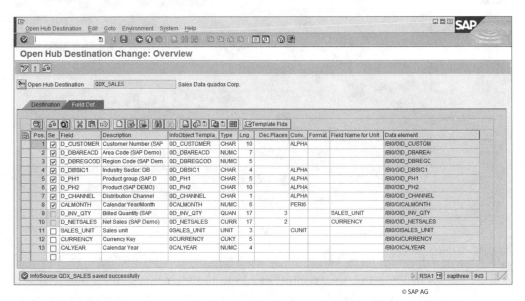

© SAP AG

Figure 18–3

Field list of an open hub destination

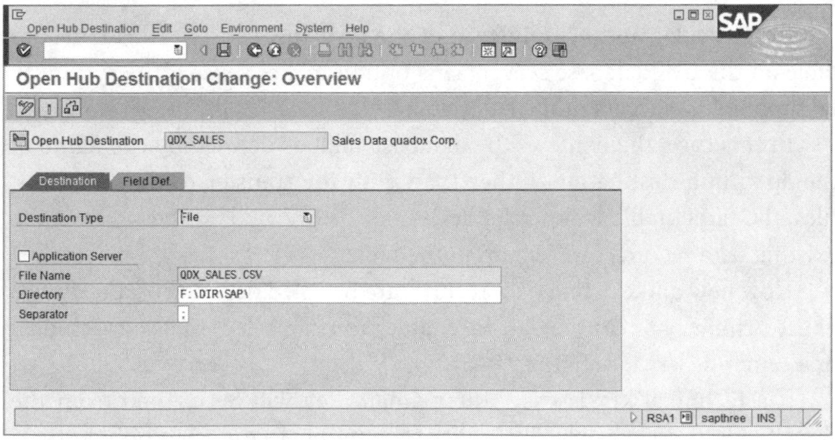

Figure 18–4

Transfer to files on network drives

The file name is automatically derived from the name of the open hub destination and cannot be changed. For structure, only CSV files are permitted.

Transfer to CSV files on the
application server

As an alternative to the use of network drives, you can also create CSV files in the WORK directory of an SAP BW application server. Here, the file name is derived from the name of the open hub destination, and it cannot be changed either (see figure 18–5).

Figure 18–5
Transfer to files on the
application server

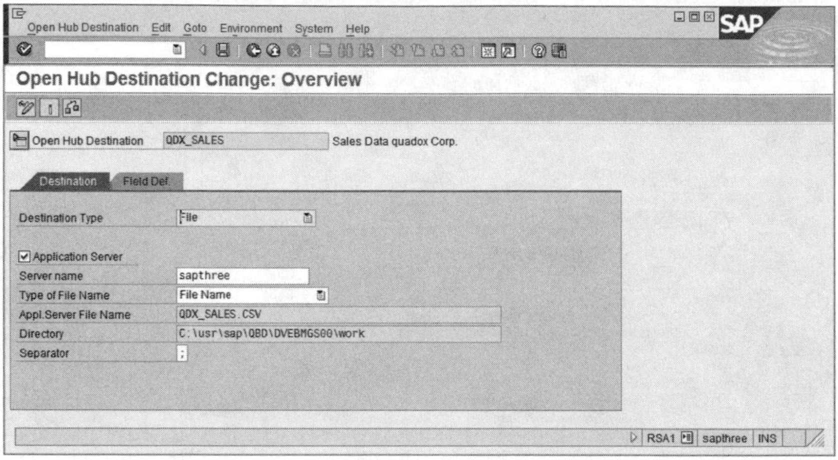

© SAP AG

However, there is an option to use a logical file name instead of the derived file name and, for example, to add to the file name a suffix that changes daily. A detailed description on the use of logical file names is given in appendix B.

Transfer to database tables

In particular instances, instead of the CSV file, you can fill a database table on the BW database server. This option makes sense if the system to be supplied has access to the BW database.

In this case, the name of the database table is defined by the name of the open hub destination. Other than with the transfer to data via CSV files, the target table will not be deleted prior to data transfer. Rather, the existing data records can remain in the table.

How new and existing data records are handled depends on the choice of the primary key for the database table. You can select to use a technical or a semantic key (see figure 18–6).

If a technical key is used, the primary key will be formed from the three fields; these are: OHREQUID (ID of the supply to the open hub destination), DATAPAKID (data package), and RECORD (data records within the data package). Each data record is unambiguous beyond the supply of the open hub destination, so new data is always added to existing data in the table.

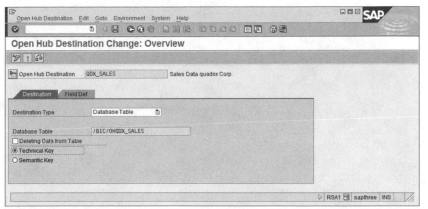

Figure 18–6
Transfer to database tables

With the use of a semantic key, the fields that form the key are to be selected from the fields list of the open hub destination with the Semantic Key option (see figure 18–3).

The fields of this semantic key form the primary key of the table. If data records are to be written into the table for which key data records already exist, then the existing data records will be overwritten with the new ones.

Often, you not only need to create a CSV file or fill a database table, you need to integrate the system to be supplied into the delivery process. For this purpose, there is an option to control the supply of the system via RFC calls.

Transfer to third-party tools

This requires that the system to be supplied can handle the RFC log that is used by BW open hub destinations and that it is certified accordingly. The system to be supplied is to be indicated with its RFC connection or with its server program, respectively (see figure 18–7).

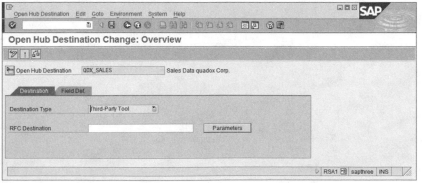

Figure 18–7
Transfer to third-party tools

19 Definition of Transformations

In BW 7, transformation is the central technology through which the processing of data in all layers is defined. Thus, transformation replaces the transfer and update rules in the BW releases up to 3.x by a standard technology.

The task of transformation is to describe a rule set to transfer data from a source structure into a target structure. A target structure consolidates the data of identical processes with the same granularity so that, for example, all data sources that provide data on customer orders on a position level can be transferred into a joint data structure.

Data from different processes or of different granularity (e.g., sales order documents and delivery data or document headers and document positions) are each transferred into individual data structures. Basically, the use of a joint data structure for data from different processes does not make any sense, even if the data is to be consolidated at a later stage.[153]

The source and target structures of the transformation are combined differently depending on the characteristics of the architecture and the layer. The following table shows the objects that can be used in BW as a source or target structure.

Source and target structure of the transformation

BW Object	Data Source	Data Target
DataSource	✓	✗
InfoSet	✓	✗
InfoSource	✓	✓
DataStore Object	✓	✓
BasisCube	✓	✓
InfoObject	✓	✓
Open hub destination	✗	✓

153. The analytical engine provides better options with its InfoSet and MultiProvider.

Figure 19–1

Creation of a transformation

A transformation can be created in the context menu of the BW object that is to be used as data source for the transformation (see figure 19–1 for a transformation with a DataSource).

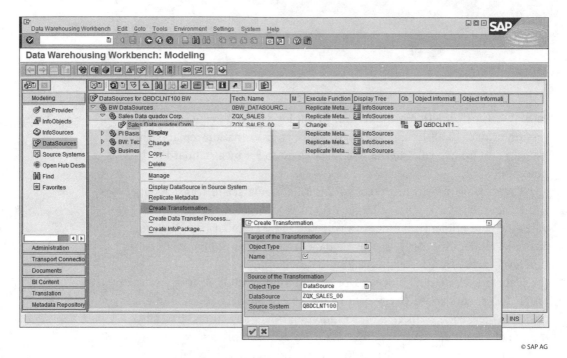

© SAP AG

A transformation is modeled graphically. It is most important to first deduce the field values of the target structure from the fields of the source structure (see figure 19–2).

You need to keep in mind that a transformation is not focused on handling individual data records. The definition of a rule set instead refers to the handling of **data packages,** i.e., the consolidation of several data records that are to be created with the data acquisition from the respective data source.[154]

During a transformation, the data records of a data package go through one of two rule sets: the **transformation** or the **expert routine.** The rule set of the transformation consists of several levels that assume different tasks. This chapter focuses on the transformation rule set.

The expert routine should be used only in exceptional circumstances, and it is described in section 19.6.

---

154. Details on the creation of data packages can be found in section 24.1.4.

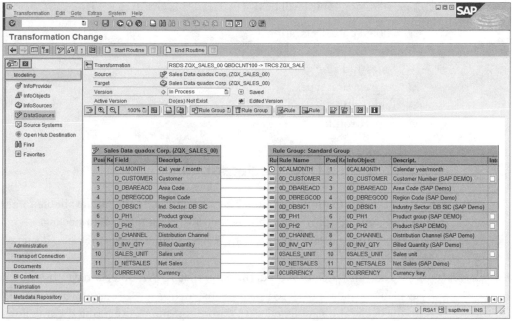

© SAP AG

A closer look reveals that the transformation rule set is much more complex and able to meet the comprehensive data preparation requirements. Figure 19–3 shows the components of the transformation rule set.

Figure 19–2

Transformation maintenance

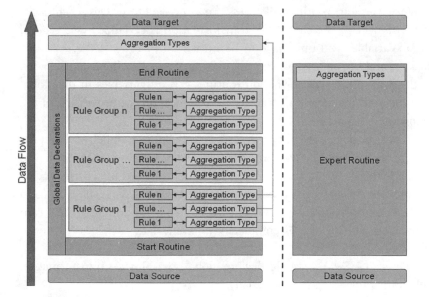

Figure 19–3

Transformation rule set

The following topics will be discussed in this chapter:

- Global data declarations
- Start routine
- Rules and rule groups
- Aggregation types
- End routine
- Expert routine

19.1 Global Data Declarations

Each transformation uses global data declarations that are available to all ABAP routines during the processing of the complete data package—i.e., the start routine, end routine, and ABAP routines access the same declarations.

Package-related data   The full range of type definitions that ABAP objects have to offer is available. If data is declared via DATA instructions, its life span will be linked to the declaration context, i.e., the process instance executing the transformation for a data package.

Cross-package data   It is different for global data declarations that are defined by CLASS-DATA. Static variables to which all objects of the class within a process instance have access are declared.

If all data packages of a request are processed in the same process instance, the start routine will access the same data to process each package. This will be the case if the transformation is serialized (see section 20.3). Variables will only have to be initialized to process the first data package and can be used by the start routine of all following data packages. In this way, other transformation routines can fill variables in the global data too, and they can thus transfer information on the processing of the following data packages.

If data packages are not processed serially but in parallel, several process instances might be used for data package processing when it can also not be foreseen which data package is to be processed by which process instance. In this case, the declaration of variables via CLASS-DATA leads to the fact that the respective variables can be filled at random with data from previous or subsequent or completely different data packages (or not at all).

Thus, CLASS-DATA should declare global variables for transformation only if the processing is done serially.

19.2 Start Routine

At the beginning of the processing of each data package, the staging engine tries to run the start routine. It is the task of the start routine to *filter data records* that are to be excluded from processing within a transformation and that are not to be included in the result of the transformation and to *initialize global data declarations.* Any other changes to the content of the data packages to be processed are rather unusual but technically possible, such as, for example, correcting fields' values as well as adding new data records.

The definition of a start routine is not mandatory, so its execution might be neglected. If a start routine is to be created, this can be done in the transformation maintenance via the menu item *Edit→Start Routine Create* (see figure 19–4).

Figure 19–4

Start routine in transformation

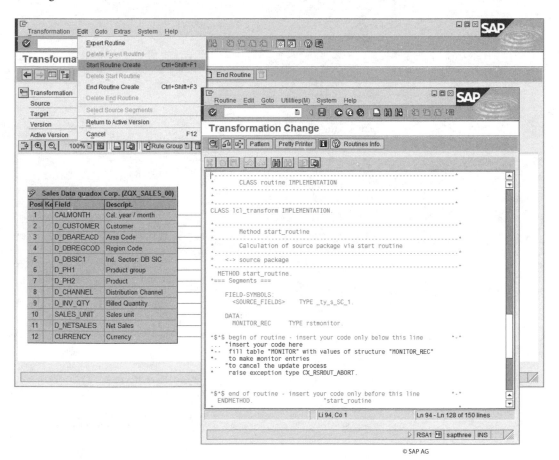

© SAP AG

The structure of the start routine is predefined in BW and consists of three components:

- Definition area of the class
- Signature of the method
- Implementation area of the class

Definition area of the class In the definition area, the TYPES to describe the data package that is to be handled in the start routine are stored. The TYPES are deduced from the source structure of the transformation.

The definition of TYPES is followed by the global data declarations that were explained in the previous chapter and that can be stored between *$*$ begin of global ... and *$*$ end of global ....

```
CLASS routine DEFINITION.
  PUBLIC SECTION.

    TYPES:
      BEGIN OF _ty_s_SC_1,
* Field: /BIC/MM1. "sample declaration of the characteristic MM
      /BIC/MM1          TYPE C LENGTH 4,  "in the source structure
* Declaration of other fields in the source structure.
*        Field: RECORD record number.
        RECORD             TYPE RSARECORD,
      END   OF _ty_s_SC_1.
    TYPES:
      _ty_t_SC_1         TYPE STANDARD TABLE OF _ty_s_SC_1
                         WITH NON-UNIQUE DEFAULT KEY.
  PRIVATE SECTION.

    TYPE-POOLS: rsd, rstr.

*$*$ begin of global – insert your declaration only below this line
..."insert your code here
*$*$ end of global – insert your declaration only before this line
```

Signature of the method The following parameters that are passed on to the start routine are defined by the signature of the method:

```
METHODS
  start_routine
    IMPORTING
      request                type rsrequest
      datapackid             type rsdatapid
    EXPORTING
      monitor                type rstr_ty_t_monitors
```

```
       CHANGING
         SOURCE_PACKAGE              type _ty_t_SC_1
       RAISING
         cx_rsrout_abort.
```

The parameters of the method have the following meanings and effects:

- **Importing parameters** REQUEST **and** DATAPAKID
  These parameters transfer the request ID and the number of the data packages currently to be processed.
- **Exporting parameter** MONITOR
  With the use of the internal table MONITOR, self-defined messages can be transferred to the monitoring of the transformation. The transfer of error messages to the monitoring is the same in the start routine as in the ABAP routines that are explained in section 19.3.4.
- **Changing parameter** SOURCE_PACKAGE
  In the internal table SOURCE_PACKAGE, the data package to be processed is provided. In the start routine, SOURCE_PACKAGE can be not only read but also modified. In addition to the fields of the source structure, the internal table SOURCE_PACKAGE also has the field RECORD that indicates the number of the data record in the package.

Further, there is the option to abort the processing of the current data package by starting the exception CX_RSROUT_ABORT. This form of "parameter transfer" is helpful if the errors occurring during processing are so serious that the processing of the complete request does not make any sense and is to be aborted.

The implementation area of the class adopts the program code that is to be entered between *$*$ begin of routine... and $*$* end of routine.... Within the routine, all elements of the programming language ABAP Objects are available.

Implementation area of the class

> ABAP Objects does not support all language elements of the structured ABAP. Do not use includes to connect subprograms; use only function modules and subroutine pools. Do not declare variables with the command STATICS but with CLASS-DATA, and do not define internal tables with headers but create an explicit work area with the supplement LINE OF.

In the following example, all data records that have the field QCUSTOMER filled with an initial value are deleted in the start routine.

```
*----------------------------------------------------------------*
*        Method start_routine
*----------------------------------------------------------------*
*        Calculation of source package via start routine
*----------------------------------------------------------------*
*    <-> source package
*----------------------------------------------------------------*
  METHOD start_routine.
*=== Segments ===

    FIELD-SYMBOLS:
      <SOURCE_FIELDS>     TYPE _ty_s_SC_1.

    DATA:
      MONITOR_REC       TYPE rstmonitor.

*$*$ begin of routine — insert your code only below this line *-*
*--  fill table "MONITOR" with values of structure "MONITOR_REC"
*-   to make monitor entries
...  "to cancel the update process
*     raise exception type CX_RSROUT_ABORT.
    DELETE SOURCE_PACKAGE where QCUSTOMER is INITIAL.
*$*$ end of routine — insert your code only before this line  *-*
  ENDMETHOD.                        "start_routine
```

19.3 Rules and Rule Groups

Rules and rule groups form the **value-related** definition of the transformation as well as the **operation-related** definition.

Rule groups The operation-related definition of the transformation rule set deals with the processing framework for creating data records in the target structure from data records in the source structure. This implies the possibility that a data record in the source structure can create not only one but several data records in the target structure.

From the start routine to the end routine of a transformation, each data record of a source structure runs through the data preparation not only once but possibly several times. Each definition of such a preparation is called a rule group. By default, there is only the **standard rule group** at first; however, it can be supplemented with further rule groups. In this case, a data record in the source structure creates one data record in the target structure, and another data record in the target structure will be created for each additional rule group.

The distribution or merging of data records from the source structure mostly caters to the application-specific preparation of data in the data mart layer. With the preparation of data in the transformation layer, data records are to be transferred from the source structure into the target structure one by one and the transformation is only made on a field level. Only the deletion of data records in the start or end routine is a common operation for transformations in the transformation layer.

Figure 19–5 shows an example where the generation of two target records from one source record is used for splitting sales revenue.[155]

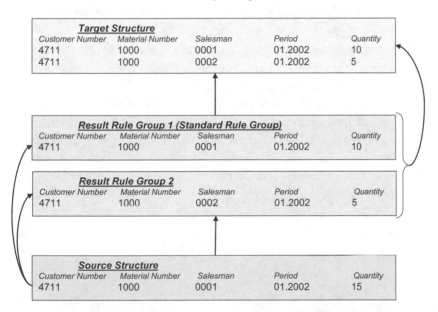

Figure 19–5

Data flow with rule groups

The use of rule groups to multiply a data record of the source structure is suitable only if the number of data records in the target structure is set. If this number has to be dynamically identified during the transformation, multiplication can only be achieved in the start/end routine or in the expert routine. An option that corresponds with the return table in the updating routines as known in releases up to 3.x has not been provided up to the current patch level 18 of BW 7.

---

155. The example shows a typical scenario from sales controlling: Salesman 0001 has sold 15 units of a product to a customer. Salesman 0002 was not involved in this deal, however, he would basically be responsible for this sales area. In such cases, the sales quantities are to be distributed in the 2:3 and 1:3 relation.

The result of all rule groups is consolidated in the target structure of the transformation and entered into the target objects afterward (BasisCubes, DataStore Objects, InfoObjects).

The number of data records in the target structure does not necessarily have to be multiplied by the number of rule groups. Rather, data records with identical key values are filtered; i.e., if other rule groups provide identical keys, these will be filtered.

Within a transformation, key fields can be recognized by the key symbol in the target structure (see figure 19–2). The criteria according to which they are built depend on the respective target objects that define the target structure of the transformation. This topic is explained in detail section 19.4.

Rules

The ***value-related*** definition of the transformation forms the central component of the rule set. It defines the identification of field values for the target structure of the transformation.

The graphic display of rule groups shows from which entry parameters (i.e., fields of the source structure) the value of a field in the target structure is deduced (see figure 19–2). For example, if the addition of two key figure values in the source structure is to form a key figure in the target structure, the arrows from both key figures of the source structure will point to the key figure in the target structure.

Rule types

There are different rule types to identify the field values (see figure 19–6):

- Constant
- Direct Assignment
- Formula
- No Transformation
- Read Master Data
- Routine

Additionally, all rule types will execute conversion exits if these have been defined.

Especially with the transformation of key figures, the handling of units and currencies is relevant. Rule types, conversion exits, and the handling of units and currencies will be explained in the following sections.

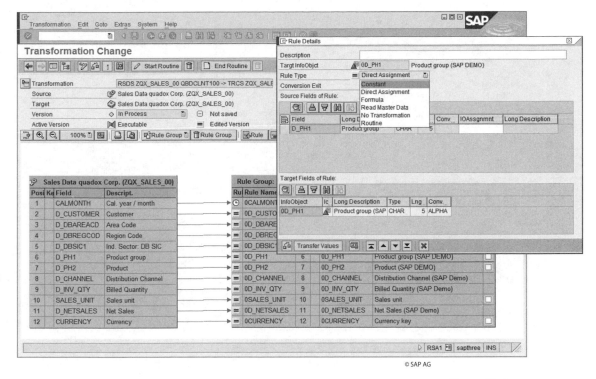

© SAP AG

Figure 19–6
Rule types

19.3.1 Assignment of Constants

It may make sense to assign a constant value if a DataSource does not supply information but either of the following conditions apply:

- The information needs to be supplied due to compound InfoObjects.
- A constant value seems to be the right for a DataSource or should be used subject to the DataSource.

With the definition of a transformation, only the constant value needs to be stored in order to provide all data records this value.

19.3.2 Direct Assignment

Mapping is a simple form of identifying information. It is assumed that a field of the source structure will match the field of the target structure without being changed. In this case, the respective field value can simply be transferred (see figure 19–7).

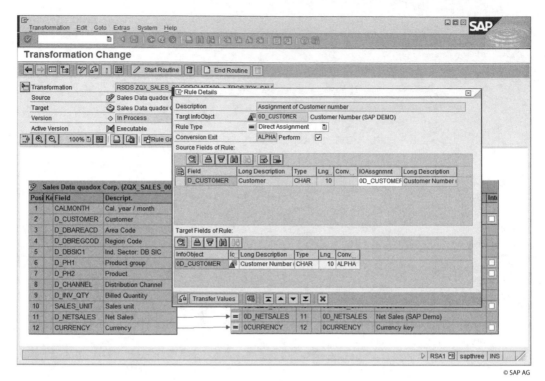

© SAP AG

Figure 19–7

Direct assignment in the transformation

Time characteristics

To create a transformation, BW first tries to make a proposal for corresponding fields. This proposal is not binding and can be changed.

The handling of time characteristics during the transformation takes a special role. As with any other InfoObject, time characteristics can be provided with values. However, you also have the option to automatically convert time characteristics.

This enables you to derive time characteristics from other time characteristics if they are exactly the same. The conversion (e.g., day date into month) is automatically made in BW;[156] i.e., a mapping of the calendar day to the calendar month can be defined without storing further information on how this mapping is to be handled.

Figure 19–8 shows how the time characteristics provided by BW can automatically be derived from each other.

The figure shows how calendar week and calendar month can be derived from the calendar day; however, the calendar month cannot be derived from the calendar week.

156. Under the condition that it is a time characteristic predefined by BW.

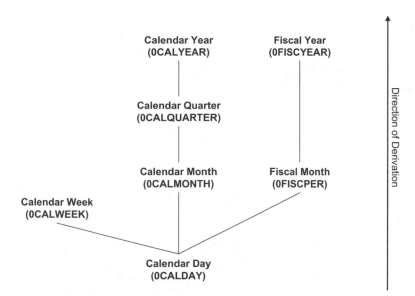

Figure 19–8
Automatic derivation of time
characteristics

The use of automatic time conversion offered in BW is not mandatory and can be replaced by self-developed routines. In the most cases, the automatic time conversion, however, will satisfy your needs.

19.3.3 Master Data Attribute of an InfoObject

With master data changes, master data attributes for InfoObjects are always displayed in the data analysis with their current values (see section 5.1.2). If master data attributes are to be archived in the data model, the respective attributes of the InfoObjects need to be written directly into the data targets (in the dimensions of BasisCubes or the key fields of DataStore Objects).

To identify the attribute value of an InfoObject with the transformation, BW offers an option to automatically read these values with the indication of the InfoObject (see figure 19–9).

With the use of this data source, all InfoObjects are available that have the same InfoObject as an attribute whose value is to be identified in the target structure.

As a condition to read master data, the master data attribute needs to be identical in the target structure to the InfoObject to be transformed. If there is no correspondence, the identification of master data attributes can only be made using ABAP routines.

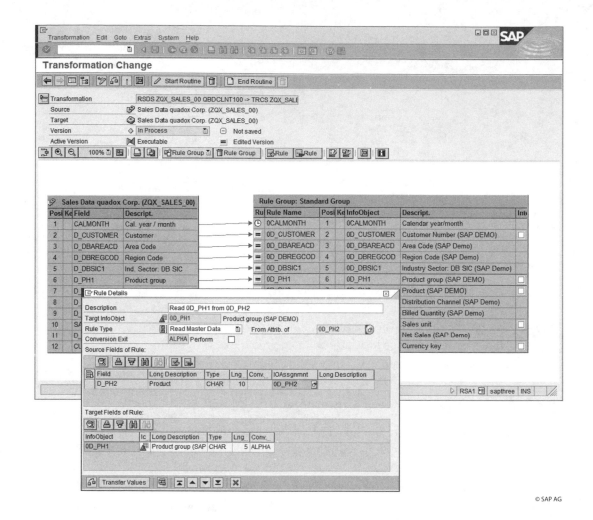

© SAP AG

Figure 19–9

Read master data attributes
in the transformation

19.3.4 Routines

In some cases, the assignment of constants or the direct assignment of field values is not enough to run the transformation as desired. In order to define complex transformations, the rule type *routine* provides an option to program the transformation using the program language ABAP Objects.

Routines are local ABAP classes with a predefined structure consisting of a definition area, the signature of the method, and its implementation.

Definition area of the class

In the definition area, the TYPES for the entry and exit parameters of the method are stored. The TYPES are deduced from the predefined fields that are set as source fields for the routine (see figure 19–10).

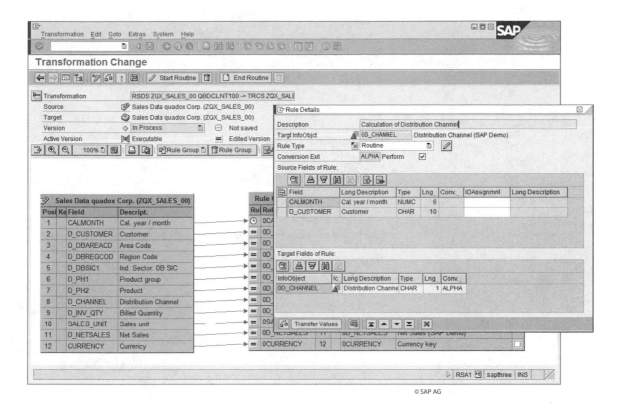

© SAP AG

The entry parameters can be found in the definition of the TYPES _ty_s_ SC_1 and the exit parameters in the definition of the TYPES _ty_s_TG_1.

The definition of the TYPES is followed by the global data declarations. The following shows the definition area of a routine; the definition area describes the fields CALYEAR and D_CUSTOMER as entry parameters and the field D_CHANNEL as exit parameters.

Figure 19–10

Setting entry parameters for routines

```
*------------------------------------------------------------*
*       CLASS routine DEFINITION
*------------------------------------------------------------*
*
*------------------------------------------------------------*
CLASS lcl_transform DEFINITION.
  PUBLIC SECTION.

    TYPES:
      BEGIN OF _R_4,
*       InfoObject: 0CALYEAR.
        CALYEAR            TYPE /BI0/OICALYEAR,
```

```
*         InfoObject: OD_CUSTOMER.
          D_CUSTOMER                TYPE /BIO/OID_CUSTOMER,
        END   OF _R_4.
      TYPES:
        BEGIN OF _ty_s_TG_1,
*         InfoObject: OD_CHANNEL Sales Channel (SAP daemonstration).
          D_CHANNEL                 TYPE /BIO/OID_CHANNEL,
        END   OF _ty_s_TG_1.
    PRIVATE SECTION.
      TYPE-POOLS: rsd, rstr.

*$*$ begin of global - insert your declaration only below this line
... "insert your code here
*$*$ end of global - insert your declaration only before this line
```

Signature of the method   With the signature of the method, the following parameters are defined.

```
METHODS
  compute_OD_CHANNEL
    IMPORTING
      request                       type rsrequest
      datapackid                    type rsdatapid
      SOURCE_FIELDS                 type _ty_s_SC_1
    EXPORTING
      RESULT                        type _ty_s_TG_1-D_CHANNEL
      monitor                       type rstr_ty_t_monitor
    RAISING
      cx_rsrout_abort
      cx_rsrout_skip_record
      cx_rsrout_skip_val.
```

The parameters of the method have the following meanings and effects:

- **Importing parameters REQUEST and DATAPAKID**
  These parameters transfer the request ID and the number of the data package that is to be processed currently.
- **Importing parameter SOURCE_FIELDS**
  In the structure SOURCE_FIELDS, the data record to be handled is provided for the transfer structure.
- **Exporting parameter MONITOR**
  Using the internal table MONITOR, self-defined messages can be passed on to the monitoring of the transformation.
- **Exporting parameter RESULT**
  The variable RESULT serves to return the result from the transformation.

Further, the exceptions CX_RSROUT_SKIP_RECORD, CX_RSROUT_SKIP_VAL, and CX_RSROUT_ABORT for the return of messages are available:

- RAISE EXCEPTION TYPE CX_RSROUT_SKIP_RECORD aborts the processing of the current data record in all rule groups (!) and continues processing the next data record. The triggering of an exception is *not* considered to be an error per se; it is only another option to filter data records. This exception is only considered to be an error in combination with an error message in the exporting parameter MONITOR.
- RAISE EXCEPTION TYPE CX_RSROUT_SKIP_VAL will set the initial value for the target field of the transformation if it is a characteristic. If it is a key figure, this exception will be changed into the exception CX_RSROUT_SKIP_RECORD.
- RAISE EXCEPTION TYPE CX_RSROUT_ABORT aborts the processing of the current data package and marks the package with the status erroneous. Thus, the complete load process is considered erroneous.

The implementation area of the class takes in the program code that is to be entered between *$*$ begin of routine... and $*$* end of routine.... Within the routine, all elements of the program language ABAP Objects are available. At the time of the generation, this method is nested into the local class of the transformation program.

Implementation area of the class

```
*-------------------------------------------------------------------*
*       CLASS routine IMPLEMENTATION
*-------------------------------------------------------------------*
*
*-------------------------------------------------------------------*
CLASS lcl_transform IMPLEMENTATION.

  METHOD compute_OD_CHANNEL.

*   IMPORTING
*     request      type rsrequest
*     datapackid   type rsdatapid
*     SOURCE_FIELDS-D_CHANNEL TYPE C LENGTH 000001
*   EXPORTING
*     RESULT type _ty_s_TG_1-D_CHANNEL

    DATA:
      MONITOR_REC    TYPE rsmonitor.

*$*$ begin of routine – insert your code only below this line    *-*
... "insert your code here
*-- fill table "MONITOR" with values of structure "MONITOR_REC"
*-  to make monitor entries
```

```
...  "to cancel the update process
*     raise exception type CX_RSROUT_ABORT.
...  "to skip a record
*     raise exception type CX_RSROUT_SKIP_RECORD.
...  "to clear target fields
*     raise exception type CX_RSROUT_SKIP_VAL.

      RESULT = '00'.

*$*$ end of routine – insert your code only before this line     *-*
      ENDMETHOD.                    "compute_OD_CHANNEL
   ENDCLASS.                        "routine IMPLEMENTATION
```

The goal of the implementation is to identify a value for the export parameter RESULT (and possibly the export parameter CURRENCY or UNIT).

If data is to be exchanged via global data declarations between the routines of individual InfoObjects, the sequence for the execution of routines is relevant. The sequence of calls corresponds with the sequence of fields in the target structure and it cannot be modified without modification to the target structure.

Transfer of monitor messages

In a transformation, BW usually looks after the transfer of informative error messages to the monitoring. With the use of ABAP routines, however, errors, warnings, or other information need to be forwarded to the monitoring by the ABAP routine.

For this purpose, the export parameter MONITOR can be used. The following program example shows the transfer of error messages to the monitoring.

```
*------------------------------------------------------------------*
   METHOD compute_OCUSTOMER.
     DATA:
       MONITOR_REC    TYPE rsmonitor.
*$*$ begin of routine – insert your code only below this line     *-*
if l_error = true
   monitor_rec-msgid = 'ZQUADOX'. "Message ID
   monitor_rec-msgty = 'E'.  "E=Error, W=Warning, I=Information
   monitor_rec-msgno = '001'.     "Message Number
   monitor_rec-msgv1 = 'There has been an error'.
   monitor_rec-msgv2 = 'More error text'.
   monitor_rec-msgv3 = 'Even more error text'.
   monitor_rec-msgv3 = 'No more error text possible'.
   "monitor_rec-DETLEVEL = . "Detailing level in application log
   "monitor_rec-RECNO = . "Data record number in source structure
   "monitor_rec-SKIPPED = . "rec. was filtered & will not be booked
      RAISE EXCEPTION TYPE CX_RSROUT_ABORT.
   else.
```

```
      RESULT = .  "return value of routine
    endif.
*$*$ end of routine – insert your code only before this line    *-*
    ENDMETHOD.                      "compute_OCUSTOMER
*-----------------------------------------------------------------*
```

19.3.5 Formulas

Formulas have the same goal as routines: They identify a value depending on different fields of the source structure. For this purpose, formulas offer simple calculation designs and conditions (see figure 19–11).

Figure 19–11

Formulas in the transformation

© SAP AG

All fields of the source structure are available as a basis for the formula calculation. Formulas are defined more easily than ABAP routines and they provide an option to make comprehensive calculations without ABAP knowledge. However, complex rules (e.g., with access to transparent tables) can only be created using ABAP routines.

> If errors occur during the calculation of formulas (e.g., division by zero), no error code will be sent to the monitoring but initial values for the calculated fields will be returned. Thus, when designing formulas, you should consider possible errors.

19.3.6 Conversion Exit

With the use of input conversion (see section 15.2.3), the inflow layer should supply only characteristics values. However, if it cannot be ensured during transformation that characteristics values are available and compliant with their conversion exit (e.g., since they are identified by ABAP routines or formulas), an input conversion can be made after the execution of the rule type (see figure 19–12 using the example of the InfoObject 0D_CUSTOMER that is provided with the conversion exit ALPHA).

The option to perform an input conversion with the transformation is the "last resort" if data has already made it into BW that is not compliant with its conversion exit. However, you should try to run the input conversion in the inflow layer and not at a later stage with the transformation. Especially in regards to performance, input conversion should not be executed if it's not actually required.

Figure 19–12

Conversion exit in the transformation

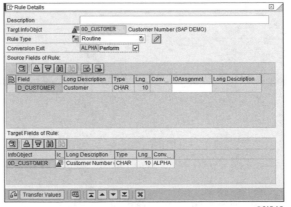

© SAP AG

19.3.7 Handling of Units

With the definition of a transformation, the objects that describe the quantity and currency units of the used key figures need to be added to the target structure. The exceptions are key figures with a fixed unit (see section 6.1.3).

With the transformation, the filling of InfoObjects that describe the quantity units and currencies of key figures is not defined explicitly, but it is firmly linked to the identification of the respective key figure. So for each key figure, you can set the field of the source structure from which the unit is to be taken (see figure 19–13).

© SAP AG

Figure 19–13

Unit calculation in the transformation

As an alternative to the takeover of units from the source structure, a conversion of quantity and currency units is possible. Here, the respective conversion types[157] are to be indicated.

> Please consider that the conversion of currencies and units in the transformation can result in a loss of information (the information on the original unit/currency will be lost). Thus, make the conversion only on the way to the data mart layer but not before it's stored in the integration layer. If required, the conversion of currencies and units can be made at the time of the data analysis.

---

157. Conversion types are explained in the appendix (see appendix A).

Handling of units in routines Specifically for the identification of key figure values through routines, apart from the known rule type *routine* there is also the rule type *routine with unit*.

For routines with units, it is the routine's task to identify not only the value of the key figure but also the value of the unit. For this purpose, the signature of the method uses two additional export parameters: CURRENCY to return currencies and UNIT to return quantity units.

The identification of the requested units is up to the programming of the routine. For the conversion of currencies, the function modules RSW_CURRRENCY_TRANSLATION or CONVERT_TO_LOCAL_CURRENCY are available, among others.

19.4 Aggregation Types

Apart from the creation of data records and field values for the target objects, it is no less important how data records of the target structure are to be treated when they are already in the target objects, especially if they are in the target objects together with other values.

The question of whether a data record already exists or not is linked to the field combination of the key fields (they were already relevant for the filtering of duplicate records by rule groups; see section 19.3).

How to treat fields that do not belong to the key fields is regulated by the aggregation types that are stored with the definition of the transformation rule. The options are the summation,[158] the update, or keeping old values[159] (see figure 19–14).

Since the possibilities to execute different operations are limited by the target objects in different ways, the definition of the aggregation types will be explained in relation to the target objects of a transformation.

---

158. Only for key figure InfoObjects. Depending on the selected standard aggregation, maximum/minimum values may be defined as an alternative to summation (see also section 6.1.3).

159. If you keep initials, this is not an aggregation type but shown as the rule type *no transformation*.

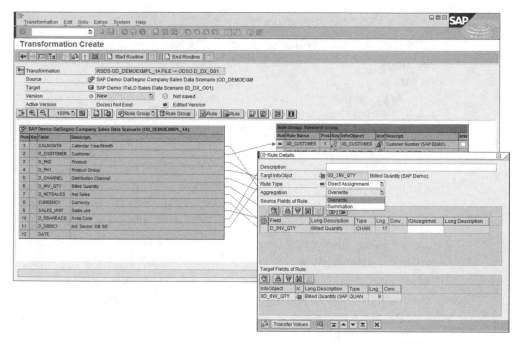

© SAP AG

Figure 19–14
Aggregation types

19.4.1 Aggregation Types for BasisCubes

For BasisCubes, the aggregation types are kept very simple. The key to the target structure is defined by the combination of all characteristics.[160] However, as per definition, only key figures can be added.

Technically, existing data records are not changed in the fact table of a BasisCube. Only new data records are written into the fact table which is similar (during data analysis) to a summation. Data records are only technically combined in the fact table of a BasisCube during the compression (see section 6.4.1).

> With the addition of the request ID, the transformation of BasisCubes cannot update existing key figure values. For this reason, DataSources that provide pure after images (i.e., after images without before images) or deletions cannot be processed. Thus, as delta types for BasisCubes, only the types ABR, ABR1, ADD, and FIL1—as well as for compatibility reasons with BW release 1.2 the types D, E, and X—are permitted.

If a key figure is not transformed, the key figure will have the result value 0.

---

160. Technically, the key is formed by the dimension IDs that are created from a combination of characteristics within a dimension. This corresponds with the key that consists of all characteristics.

19.4.2 Aggregation Types for DataStore Objects

DataStore Objects for direct update (see section 6.3) are not provided to be filled through staging, and thus, they are basically dropped in this regard.

Write-optimized DataStore Objects use a technical key with which—similar to BasisCubes—only new data records are transferred. Thus, the same aggregation types as used for BasisCubes are applicable.

Only with *Standard DataStore Objects* are the existing data records physically overwritten with new objects, so apart from the summation of key figures in the data fields, overwriting of data fields can be considered.

Because the data fields are updated, it's possible to update receipt-related structures (e.g., status fields), and they can be used both for alpha-numeric data fields and numeric fields. Numeric fields are usually over-written if data in BW is stored at the same detailing level as in the source systems (e.g., order quantities on the level of order number and position number).

The tasks that overwriting data fields in standard DataStore Objects fulfill were explained in section 17.1. Figure 19–15 shows the consequences of overwriting data fields for DataStore Objects and BasisCubes.

Figure 19–15

Overwriting data fields in DataStore Objects

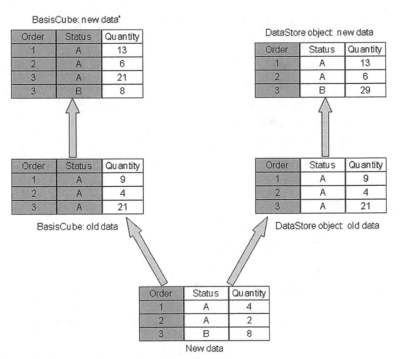

*For simplification, the request ID and the data packages are not displayed.

In this figure, an order number as key field and a status as well as a quantity are defined. The status is to be overwritten, and the quantity is to be added in the same way as with BasisCubes. In the BasisCube, the status can only be defined as characteristic and thus forms part of the key since it is not a numeric InfoObject.

By default, characteristics InfoObjects in the data fields are overwritten by standard DataStore Objects. Alternatively, the aggregation type *no transformation* can be selected. In this case, the content of the respective data field remains unchanged.

Depending on the data source, for key figure InfoObjects not only the overwrite but also a summation might make sense. This depends on the delta mode of the respective data source (see section 14.1.3). With the definition of a transformation, BW offers only aggregation types that may make sense in connection with the delta mode of the respective data source.

Figure 19–16

Overruling the delta mode in the transformation

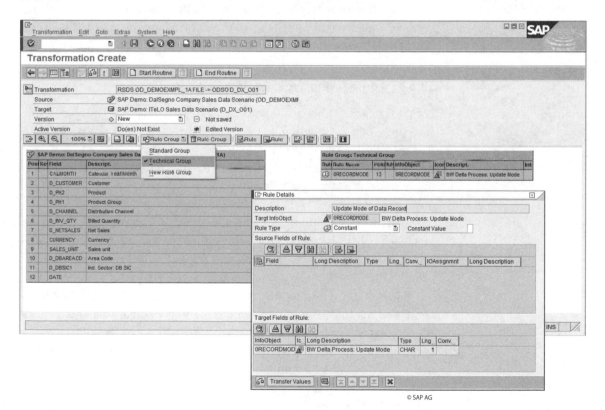

© SAP AG

The delta procedure on the respective data records is processed with the transformation in standard DataStore Objects in a separate rule group; this is the technical rule group. There, it is stored in the InfoObject ORECORDMODE. It is possible to overrule the delta procedure provided by the data source (see figure 19–16). If this option is used, then all aggregation types are available in the key figures of the standard rule groups. The delta procedure can be overruled, not only in the technical rule group but also in the start, end, and expert routines. Here, the InfoObject ORECORDMODE is contained in the target structure of the transformation.

19.4.3   Aggregation Types for InfoObjects

The aggregation behavior of InfoObjects corresponds mostly with the aggregation behavior of standard DataStore Objects, but it is slightly simpler since summation and the formation of minimum/maximum values is not possible.

There is only an option to overwrite attributes of an InfoObject or to define no transformation at all. If no transformation is defined, the existing attribute values remain unchanged, the same as for the data fields of the DataStore Objects.

19.4.4   Aggregation Types for InfoSources

For the transformation in InfoSources, aggregation types do not play a role since InfoSources only define a data structure and there are no existing data records that could be overwritten.

A possible use of an InfoSource is to transfer transformed data records to the respective target objects without any aggregation whatsoever. Here, duplicate data records will not be filtered.

Apart from the option to pass data records through with unchanged granularity, there is the option to use InfoSources to aggregate data. The aggregation is made when key fields are defined for the InfoSource (see figure 19–17).

Suitable key fields for the aggregation are all characteristics Info-Objects of the InfoSource. All key figures will be added. If characteristics InfoObjects are not aggregated as key fields, they will be filled during aggregation with the respective field value of a freely chosen data record that is part of the aggregation. Instead of not defining a characteristics InfoObject as a key field, it is better to remove the respective InfoObject from the InfoSource.

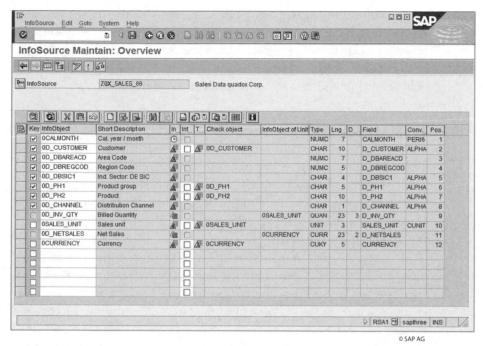

© SAP AG

Figure 19–17
Key fields in InfoSources

The aggregation of data during staging is (only) relevant if the subsequent transformations are to work on the levels of this aggregation. However, an aggregation to compress storage (e.g., in an BasisCube) is not required since the entry of data in data targets already implies an aggregation.

19.4.5 Aggregation Types for Open Hub Destinations

For open hub destinations, the aggregation behavior depends on whether the open hub destination has a technical or a semantic key (see section 18.3).

For open hub destinations with a technical key, the transformed data records are forwarded to the target structure without aggregation. Here, it needs to be considered that the data records of different rule groups receive the same technical key values that are filtered during aggregation. Any rule group apart from the standard rule group will thus remain unaffected since the results will be filtered.

Aggregation behavior with technical key

For open hub destinations with a semantic key, the data records for the target structure are aggregated via the key fields. All key figures are added. If characteristics InfoObjects are not defined as key fields, they will be

Aggregation behavior with semantic key

overwritten during aggregation with field values of the subsequent data records that result in the same key combination. If the subsequent data records are distributed to several data packages that are processed in parallel, it is freely chosen which data record is to be handled last and which field value is thus identified as the result of the aggregation type.

19.5 End Routine

The end routine is the counterpart of the start routine, but it differs slightly. The end routine is also very well suited to filter data records from transformed data records. Unlike with the start routine, the transformed fields' content is available as criteria for deletion while the start routine can access the data from only the source structure.

Further, the end routine is better suited to change the content of the data packages since it, contrary to the start routine, does not use the source structure but instead uses the target structure of the transformation as result structure. Thus, the content of the target structure can be changed directly.

Like the start routine, the end routine is not necessarily part of the transformation. If an end routine is to be created, this can be done in the transformation maintenance using the menu item *Edit→End Routine Create* (see figure 19–4).

The definition area of the class, the signature of the method, and the implementation area of the class are (apart from the result structure) identical to those elements in the start routine.

19.6 Expert Routine

If the concept of the transformation does not meet the transformation requirements, the expert routine can be used.

The expert routine completely replaces the use of start/end routines, aggregation types, rule groups, etc. and combines the rule set of the transformation in one single routine, the expert routine, instead. If an expert routine is created, it replaces the definition of the transformation (see figure 19–18).

Signature of the method   The specialty of the expert routine is that in the signature of the method, both the source structure (SOURCE_PACKAGE) and the target structure (RESULT_PACKAGE) are transferred to the transformation as parameters.

```
METHODS
  expert_routine
    IMPORTING
      request                type rsrequest
      datapackid             type rsdatapid
      SOURCE_PACKAGE         type _ty_t_SC_1
      log                type ref to cl_rsbm_log_cursor_step
    EXPORTING
      RESULT_PACKAGE         type _ty_t_TG_1.
```

Thus, the expert routine is especially suitable in cases where the performance of generated ABAP coding has absolute priority over a transparent definition of the transformation; this is because the expert routine neglects the complete overhead that automatically results from the rule set of the transformation.

At this point, we contradict the officially given reason for the use of the expert routine, which is to increase functional freedom for the definition of the transformation. In terms of content, the transformation can meet any requirement, same as the expert routine. Especially for the transformation in DataStore Objects, the expert routine is no substitute for the transformation since key figures are only handled with the aggregation behavior *overwrite*. A summation of key figure values is not possible when the expert routine is used.

Figure 19–18

Creation of an expert routine

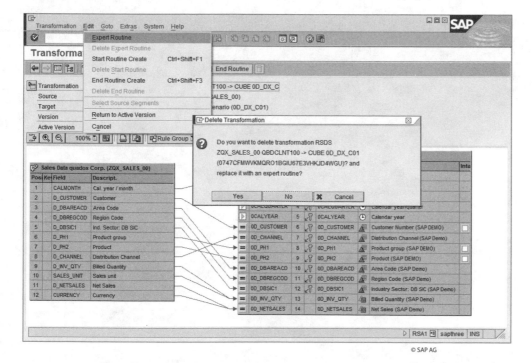

© SAP AG

20 Definition of Load Processes

The definition of transformations reflects only the content aspect of the data flow definition. The execution of a transformation is defined separately by *data transfer processes*.

The definition of a data transfer process is stored in the Data Warehousing Workbench with either the target or the source object of a transformation where the transformation is thus to be indicated (see figure 20–1).

Figure 20–1
Creation of a data transfer process

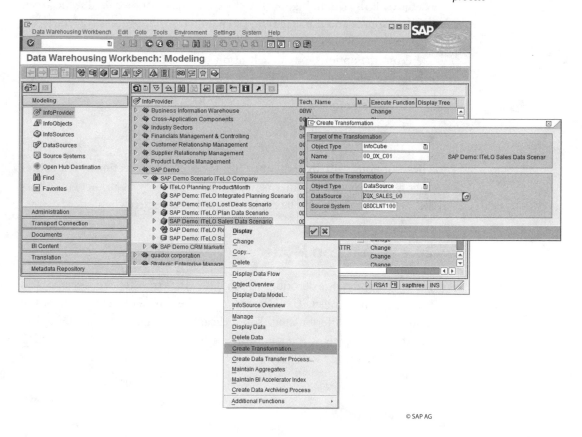

© SAP AG

A data transfer process always relates to exactly one transformation whereby data source and data target are implicitly defined. An exception is transformation where an *InfoSource* is involved. In these cases, in a data transfer process, the transformation that the InfoSource has as a target structure as well as the transformation that the InfoSource has as a data source are executed. A data transfer process always describes the data flow between two objects with physical data management.

> Up to BW release 3.x, there has been an option to indicate several data targets with the definition of a loading process. This option no longer exists for data transfer processes in BW 7. If data is to be transferred to several data targets, then for each data target, an individual data transfer process must be defined and executed.

With the start of a data transfer process, a request is created that reads the respective data from the source object and transfers it to the target object. A request is thus unambiguously defined for exactly one data flow between the data source and the data target. If a data transfer process is restarted, a new data flow will be executed under a new request.

From the options for the definition of a data transfer process, the following are relevant:

- Extraction mode
- Filter
- Serialization

These options will be explained in the following sections. The other options are relevant in other aspects (usually quality assurance, monitoring, and tuning) and will be explained in the respective chapters.

20.1 Extraction Mode

The extraction mode describes which data a data transfer process is to read from the source object. The "extraction" of the source object in delta or full mode has to be differentiated. You indicate the mode to be used for a data transfer process right after you create the data transfer process, and it cannot be changed (see figure 20–2).

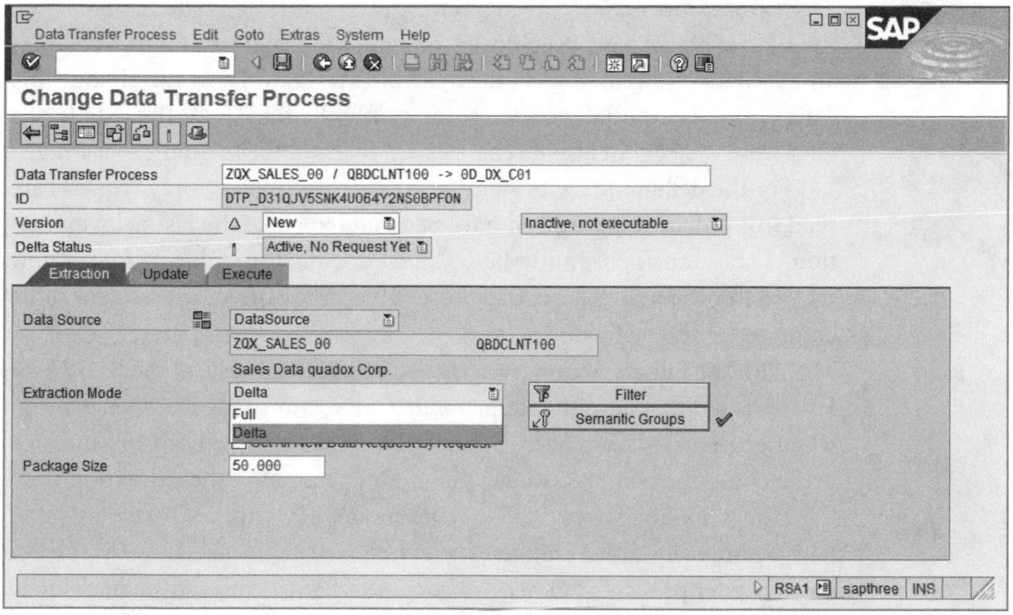

© SAP AG

Figure 20–2

Selection of the extraction mode for a data transfer process

For the extraction in delta mode, you need to consider that the administration of deltas is made per transformation. Thus, it is possible to fill a data target from the change log of a standard DataStore Object daily and to fill another data target only once per week.[161]

The data that is read is specific to the respective source object.

DataSource

For **DataSources,** with a full upload all error-free requests of the PSA to the respective DataSource are extracted. Keep in mind that the DataSource does not necessarily need to contain all requests that have been extracted from the DataSource. Rather, older requests may have been deleted by the information lifecycle management (see section 33.3).

If a DataSource is extracted in delta mode, all error-free requests in the PSA are read that have been added since the most recent delta extraction from the data transfer process. Here, the sequence of requests in the PSA is *not* relevant; if an old request in the PSA receives the status error-free much later, then it will be extracted in the delta even if more recent requests were extracted in the delta.

---

161. In comparison, in BW releases up to 3.x, the delta management was defined by the source object and was expressed in one single status that described the supply of all data targets. So, data targets could be supplied from the change log of a DataStore Objects either once daily or weekly.

DataStore Object If ***DataStore Objects*** are extracted in full mode, the data is taken from the table of active data. Specifically for standard DataStore Objects, there is an alternative to receive data during full extraction from the change log. This option is especially relevant if not only the display of the data in the DataStore Object but also its changes are relevant for further processing.

For the delta mode with standard DataStore Objects, only requests are read from the change log that have been added since the last delta extraction. The same applies to write-optimized DataStore Objects for all new requests in the active data. DataStore Objects for direct access cannot be extracted in the delta mode.

BasisCube With the full extraction from ***BasisCubes,*** all requests of the BasisCube are extracted that have the status *rollup* (see section 10.1.1). It is irrelevant whether requests have been compressed already since both the uncompressed and the compressed fact tables are included in the extraction.

If a BasisCube is extracted in delta mode, BW reads only requests that have been newly added with the status *rollup* since the execution of the last data transfer process. You need to consider that the relevant requests may not be compressed earlier since the identification of delta information is only made based on the request IDs in the uncompressed fact table.

InfoObject ***InfoObjects*** can only be extracted in full mode, and then they access the active master data records (i.e., records with the master data version A).

InfoSet ***InfoSets*** can also be extracted in full mode only, and they access the databases they defined. Here, the settings regarding most recent reporting and the status to be read are considered, which may result in the fact that master data records from InfoObjects or requests from BasisCubes are extracted that would not be read with a direct extraction of these data sources.

20.2 Filter

Whether data is extracted from a source object in delta or in full mode, it can be filtered when it is read. This makes sense if the data target of a transformation is provided for only a part of the data from the data source and filtering data records during reading brings better performance than filtering during the transformation (in this case, larger quantities of data would need to be read).

Any field of the data source can be used as filter criteria. The values to be filtered can be defined as fixed or they can be taken from an OLAP variable or a routine (see figure 20–3).

Figure 20–3
Selection of filter values for data transfer processes

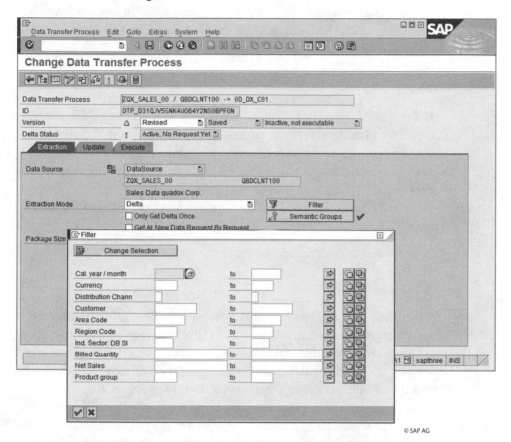

© SAP AG

The filter value will already be placed when the data is read from the respective database tables so that unrequested data will not even be read.

20.2.1   OLAP Variable

If the selection of data is to be designed dynamically, then filter values can be taken from the OLAP variables. OLAP variables actually serve the purpose of making data analyses more flexible. However, if the content of OLAP variables is identified via a user exit[162] or an SAP exit, the underlying

---

162. The determination of OLAP variables is made in the function module
    `EXIT_SAPLRRS0_001`.

program coding often offers a logic that is also desirable for the identification of filter values for data transfer processes (in most cases, this refers to date selections to identify the current year, the previous month, etc.).

To avoid having to repeatedly develop the coding of an OLAP variable with a user exit or SAP exit, you can use OLAP variables as selection criteria for the filter of a data transfer process.

20.2.2 Routine

If the options from the OLAP variables are not sufficient to dynamically create the filtering, then filter values can be identified with self-developed ABAP routines. Routines are executed at runtime after all other selections have been made, and thus they have access to the content of all other selection fields.

The design of the ABAP routines follows a defined schema, consisting of the following components:

- Global data declarations part
- Parameter part
- Code part

Other than with routines in the transformation, the routines to filter field values are not programmed in an ABAP object but in the procedural ABAP; if requested, this makes it easier to move coding sections that were initially stored in the data selection in InfoPackages (see section 15.4.1) into the coding sections of the filters for data transfer processes.

Global data declarations part

The global data declarations part exists for all filter routines of a data transfer process. Here, data can be declared that is to be valid in all filter routines of the respective data transfer process. On the one hand, this applies to the pure declaration, and on the other to the content that can be reused in other routines.

```
program conversion_routine.
* Type pools used by conversion program
type-pools: rsarc, rsarr, rssm.
tables: rssdlrange.
* Global code used by conversion rules
*$*$ begin of global – insert your declaration only below this line -
* TABLES: ...
* DATA:   ...
*$*$ end of global – insert your declaration only before this line -
```

The parameters of the form routine have the following meanings and effects:

Parameter part of the form routine

- L_T_RANGE
  The existing selections are transferred in the internal table L_T_RANGE. At the same time, this internal table serves to return the selections calculated in the ABAP routine.
- P_SUBRC
  With the return parameter P_SUBRC, the routine needs to mark whether a selection could be successfully created (P_SUBRC = 0) or not (P_SUBRC ≠ 0).

```
*  ------------------------------------------------------------------
*   InfoObject     =
*   Fieldname      = CALMONTH
*   data type      = CHAR
*   length         = 000006
*   convexit       =
*  ------------------------------------------------------------------
form compute_CALMONTH
  tablesl_t_rangestructure rssdlrange
  changing p_subrclike sy-subrc.
*   Insert source code to current selection field
```

In the code part of the selection routine, all ABAP functions are available so that the selection decision can be made according to complex rules.

Code of the selection routine

With the creation of the routine already, coding is provided to access the content of the field to be selected as well as for the modification of the selection content of this field (in following example, this is the field CALMONTH).

```
*$*$ begin of routine — insert your code only below this line    -
data: l_idx like sy-tabix.
read table l_t_range with key
     fieldname ='CALMONTH'.
l_idx = sy-tabix.
* Example to fill OCALMONTH with the selection of 12.2006…
l_t_range-IOBJNM = 'OCALMONTH'.
l_t_range-FIELDNAME = 'CALMONTH'.
l_t_range-sign = 'I'.
l_t_range-option = 'EQ'.
l_t_range-low = '200612'.
if l_idx <> 0.
modify l_t_range index l_idx.
```

```
else.
  append l_t_range.
endif.
* …or the period 01.2000 – 12.2000
l_t_range-low = '200001'.
l_t_range-sign = 'I'.
l_t_range-option = 'BT'.
l_t_range-high = '200012'.
append l_t_range.
* End of Example
p_subrc = 0.
*$*$ end of routine – insert your code only before this line    -
endform.
```

20.3 Processing Mode

To improve performance during the transformation, BW tries to basically parallelize the processing of data packages. How this works from a technical perspective is shown in section 24.1.2.

However, the parallelization of the processing is not relevant only from a performance perspective. Rather, you need to keep in mind that for content reasons, not every transformation can be freely parallelized and that it might have to be serialized. This involves transformations where the self-defined ABAP coding relies on receiving global data declarations data package by data package and that global data declarations execute via CLASS-DATA (see section 19.1).

If the data packages of a request are not to be processed in parallel but serially, the processing mode *serially in the dialog process* is available to the data transfer process (see figure 20–4).

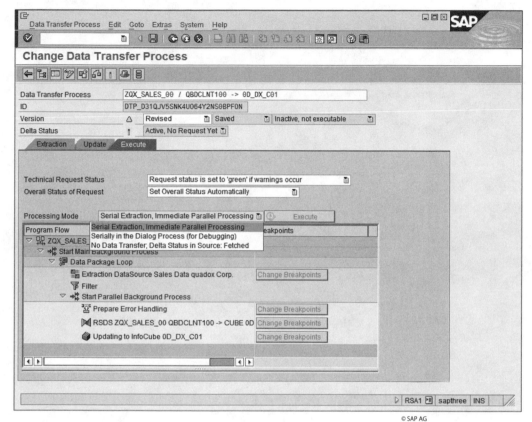

Figure 20–4 *Definition of the processing mode for data transfer processes*

Decision Support Systems

Data Warehouse

E

Da

Extraction Layer

21 Direct Staging

The previous explanations on staging have dealt only with the technologies of transformation and data transfer processes that are new in BW 7. We haven't included a detailed discussion of the staging used in BW releases up to 3.x because, at least in the area of transactional data, all functionalities of the old staging technology can be replaced by transformation and data transfer processes.

In the area of staging for master data, there are two reasons to continue to use the old staging technology from BW 3.x and earlier; on one hand, it is much easier to define, and in most cases, it meets all requirements. On the other hand, only direct staging currently provides an option to load external hierarchies, so the old staging technology cannot be omitted.

This chapter focuses on the staging of master data and this does not refer to the so-called flexible update (this can be directly replaced with transformation) but only the direct update.

The term *direct update* is used because the extraction and inflow layers exist in the form described in the reference architecture; however, data moves from the inflow layer directly into the master data of the InfoObjects that also define the target structures into which the data is to be transformed.

At the center of direct update are **InfoSources** that can only be condi- *InfoSource*
tionally compared to the InfoSources of BW 7 (see section 16.1) since they assume many more staging functions in BW 7.

With direct staging, the target structures of all homogenized and consolidated data that is related to an InfoObject are all *mandatorily* combined in one InfoSource. In this case, the target structures are called **communication structures,** and they are directly derived from the structure of texts, attributes, and hierarchies of the InfoObject. Thus, the InfoSource for the direct staging of master data of an InfoObject comprises, depending on the definition of the InfoObject, separate communication structures for attributes, texts, and hierarchies.

Figure 21–1

Creation of InfoSources for direct staging

The communication structures cannot be modified unless the definition of the respective InfoObject is changed. The creation of an InfoSource for the direct staging of master data is made in the InfoSource tree in the Data Warehousing Workbench (see figure 21–1).

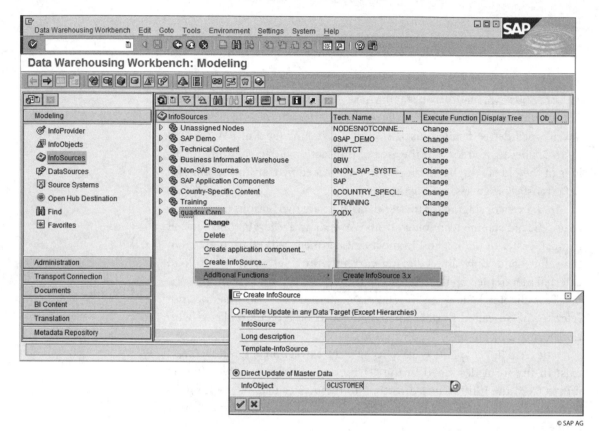

© SAP AG

A characteristic of direct staging is that the InfoSource not only describes the target structures, it also combines the ***transfer rules*** that make the connection between DataSources and communication structures. Further, the ***definition of metadata in the inflow layer*** and the ***definition of extraction processes*** directly depend on the InfoSource.

In this chapter, we'll discuss the following topics as they relate to the direct staging of master data:

- Definition of metadata in the inflow layer
- Definition of transfer rules
- Definition of extraction processes

21.1 Definition of Metadata

As with staging in BW 7, DataSources need to be defined in the BW inflow layer for staging in BW 3.x. Metadata of these DataSources is provided as usual (depending on the source system type) by the extraction layer of the source systems (SAP ERP, SAP BW, DB connect, third-party ETL tools), or it needs to be updated manually (flat file, UD connect, SOAP connection).

However, how the DataSources are defined is fundamentally different from the definitions in the new staging in BW 7. In the following sections, we'll explain how a 3.x DataSource in the inflow layer of BW is defined for the different source system types:

- Creation of a 3.x DataSource
- Selection fields
- Hierarchy properties

21.1.1 Creation of a 3.x DataSource

The definition of a 3.x DataSource is based on the replicated metadata of a source system (as far as it supplies metadata). The starting point for the definition is the data structure of the DataSource, which needs to be linked to the InfoSource of an InfoObject before the DataSource can be activated in the inflow layer.

The link can be made in the context menu of the administrator workbench for the communication structure to be filled. For this purpose, first the source system and then the DataSource need to be selected (see figure 21–2).

Each communication structure can be supplied from a freely chosen number of DataSources. This makes it possible to provide master data from several different DataSources (e.g., filling customer master data from a DataSource for general customer attributes, a DataSource for A-B-C classifications, and a DataSource for credit rating).

The assignment of a DataSource to an InfoSource directly branches into the maintenance of transfer rules; when they are activated, the DataSource is created too. A detailed description of transfer rules can be found in section 21.2.

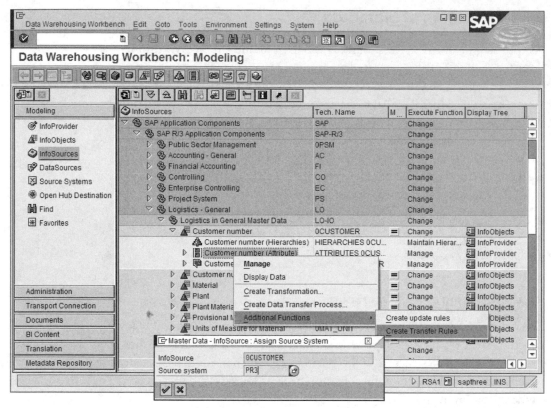

Figure 21–2
Connect DataSources with
an InfoSource

Each 3.x DataSource can be linked to only one InfoSource. Thus, one Data-Source can provide only one InfoObject with master data. To distribute master data to several InfoObjects, you should use the new staging with transformation and transfer processes.

How the data structure of a DataSource is defined depends on the source system type and will be explained in the following sections.

DataSources for SAP and Third-Party Source Systems

With the initial assignment of a replicated DataSource to an InfoSource, the field structure of the DataSource will automatically be used as a template for the DataSource structure in the inflow layer. Figure 21–3 shows the definition of the DataSource structure (also referred to as transfer structure).

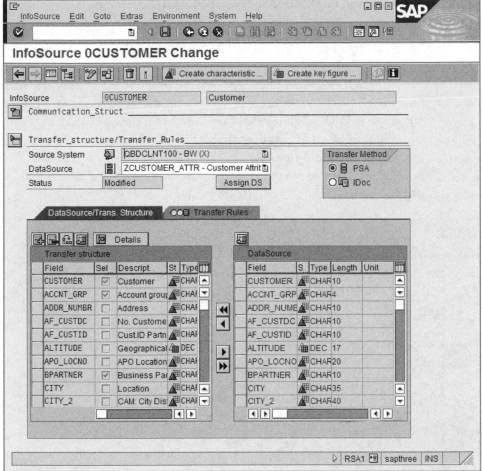

© SAP AG

Figure 21–3

Creation of transfer structures with DataSource template

Usually, the template structure can be adopted without modification; however, it is also possible to omit fields from the template. This is especially relevant if a DataSource has too many fields that won't show in the BW data flow but cannot be deleted from the DataSource in the source system for whatever reasons.

If the DataSource changes in the source system, the DataSource replicates and the transfer structure in BW will remain the same at first. Only with a new replication of metadata will the DataSource replicate be modified. The transfer structure in BW needs to be manually modified to meet the new requirement before new fields of the DataSource can be used in the data flow.

DataSources for DB Connect Source Systems

With the DB connect, the database source system provides with the database catalog all tables, views, and field details that the database offers BW for extraction.

Through violation of naming conventions (see section 14.4), possibly not all tables and views are technically available for extraction. Further, usually only selected tables/views are relevant for the extraction.

For this reason, after the creation of the DB connect, you need to determine the tables and views for which a DataSource is to be defined. The available tables and views can be read from the database catalog via the context menu of the source system (see figure 15–17).

Figure 21–4

Selection of DataSources for
DB connect

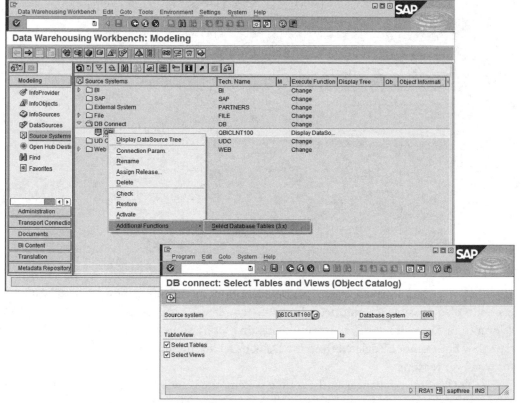

© SAP AG

Thus, for selected tables/views, DataSources can be generated where the fields to be adopted as well as the DataSource type can be defined (transactional data, master data attributes, or master data texts—see figure 21–5).

Texts are provided language dependent in the language that the BW database user uses to log onto the database. Hierarchy data cannot be supplied from a DB connect.

Figure 21–5
Generation of DataSources
for DB connect

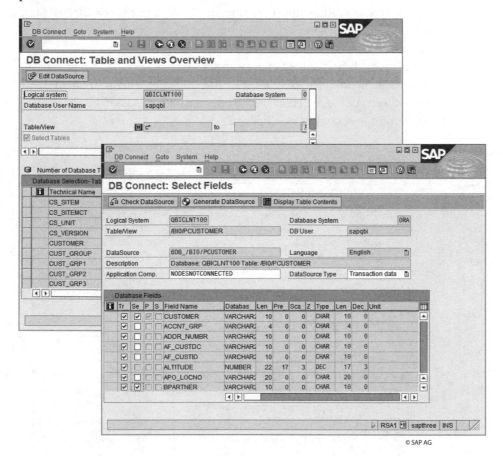

© SAP AG

The generation of the DataSources is made in BW and not in the database source system; i.e., the definition of a DataSource is not replicated from the source system but directly stored in the metadata of the inflow layer.

After the generation of the DataSources, the DataSources can be linked like "regular" DataSources from SAP source systems via transfer rules to an InfoSource and a transfer structure can be defined.

DataSources for Flat File Source Systems

For flat file source systems, the extraction layer does not provide any metadata. Thus, the transfer structure cannot be derived from a replicated

DataSource but needs to be maintained manually, and it defines the Data-Source.

If an InfoSource is thus provided with a flat file source system in the DataSource allocation, then the respective DataSource is not selected (as is the case with SAP source systems) but the respective transfer structure is defined.

Here, each field of the flat file is described with a respective field of the transfer structure. The definition of the transfer structure is made with InfoObjects; i.e., each field of the transfer structure needs to be represented by an InfoObject in BW (see figure 21–6).

Figure 21–6

Creation of transfer structures without a template

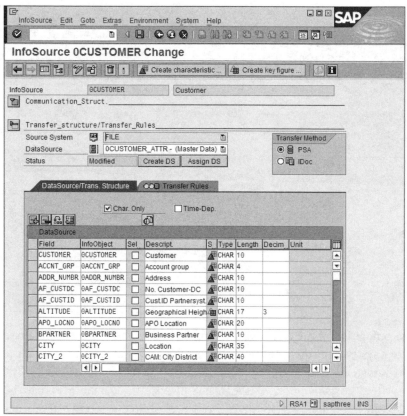

© SAP AG

As a template for the transfer structure, you should select the structure of the InfoSource to which the flat file source system is connected. Depending on the structure of the file to be extracted, this structure can or must be modified to meet the requirements.

With the activation of the transfer rules, the transfer structure in the ABAP Dictionary is created and the DataSource is stored in the metadata of BW.

DataSources for Universal Data Connect

The UD connect comes with metadata in the form of source object elements—i.e., the fields (for JDBC and SAP query) or characteristics/key figures (for ODBO and XML/A) that the respective BI Java Connector offers for extraction.

From which of these fields the respective DataSource is to be composed is defined with the creation of the DataSource. The DataSource is created in the maintenance dialog of the assigned InfoSource (see figure 21–7).

Figure 21–7
Create DataSource with UD connect

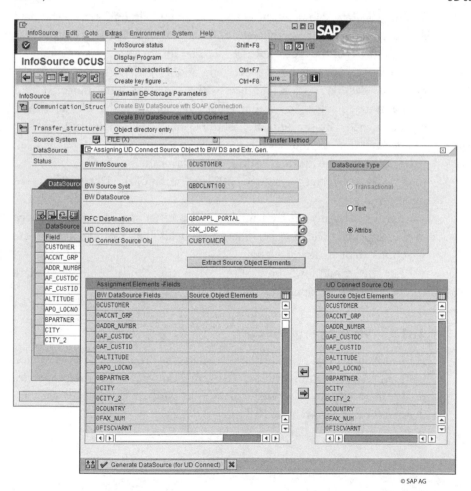

© SAP AG

To define the DataSource with the UD connect, the connection following information for the UD connect source object needs to be stored:

- The RFC destination of the J2EE servers
- The UD connect that contains the connection information to the respective data source (see sections 14.7.1 through 14.7.4)
- The source object within the UD connect, i.e., the name of the database table (for JDBC) or the name of an OLAP cube (for ODBO)

After the indication of the connection information, the source object elements of the UD connect can be displayed and transferred into the structure of the DataSource.

21.1.2 Selection Fields

To limit the data volume of the extraction, there is an option to select data for extraction if the respective selection field in the definition of the transfer structure is of the type CHAR, NUMC, DATE, TIME, or INT4.

SAP ERP
SAP BW
Third-party
For DataSources of business content and for generic DataSources, the available selection fields are defined by the metadata in the source system and cannot be changed in BW. For generic DataSources, the selection fields can be defined with the definition of the DataSource (see figure 14–5).

DB connect
Flat file
For DB connect and flat file source systems, the selectable fields need to be defined in the metadata of the inflow layer.

For DB connect, this is done with generation of the DataSources (see figure 21–5).

For flat files, this setting is made in the transfer structure maintenance of the respective DataSource. There, the fields that are relevant for the selection can be marked (see figure 21–8).

UD connect
SOAP connection
For the extraction from a SOAP connection and the universal data connect, there is no option to select fields.

21.1.3 Hierarchy Properties

For DataSources that provide hierarchy data, the properties of the supplied hierarchy data need to be stored. Thus, BW can verify that the properties of the hierarchy to be loaded correspond with the properties that are defined for this hierarchy in BW.

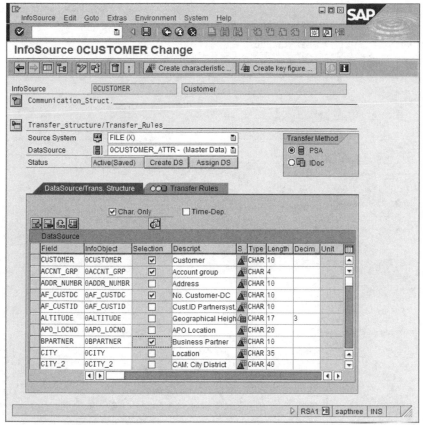

Figure 21–8
Definition of selection fields for flat files

The hierarchy properties are as follows:

- Hierarchy sorting
- Time-dependency of the hierarchy structure
- Use of hierarchy intervals

For SAP ERP and BW source systems, hierarchy DataSources provide with the metadata replication all required information to describe the properties of the extracted hierarchies. This is the same for third-party ETL tools as far as they are able to provide hierarchy data in the format that BW requires.

SAP ERP

SAP BW

Third-party

For flat files, the hierarchy properties as well as the DataSources and transfer structures need to be maintained manually. This is done with the definition of the transfer structure (see figure 21–9).

Flat file

Figure 21–9

*Definition of hierarchy
properties (flat file)*

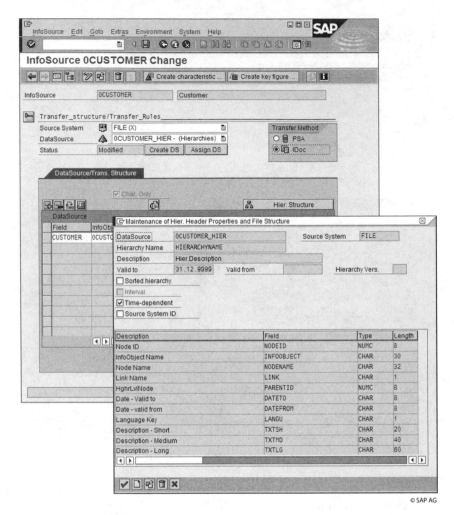

© SAP AG

The maintenance of the hierarchy properties has an impact on the transfer structure and thus on the required file structure (see section 14.5.2.4).

DB connect   All other source systems are unable to provide hierarchy data, and BW
UD connect   allows for other source systems to extract only transactional data, master
SOAP connection   data attributes, and texts.

21.2 Definition of Transfer Rules

The tasks of the transformation in BW 7 are distributed for staging in BW 3.x through a combination of transfer rules and update rules. Transfer rules control the data flow from DataSource to InfoSource while update rules control the data flow from InfoSource to data target. For direct staging, update rules are not used, so we won't explain them any further. Instead, the preparation of data needs to be defined completely by transfer rules for direct staging.

The maintenance of transfer rules is started in the InfoSource tree of the Data Warehousing Workbench in the context menu of the respectively linked DataSource (see figure 21–10).

Figure 21–10

Maintenance of transfer rules for a DataSource

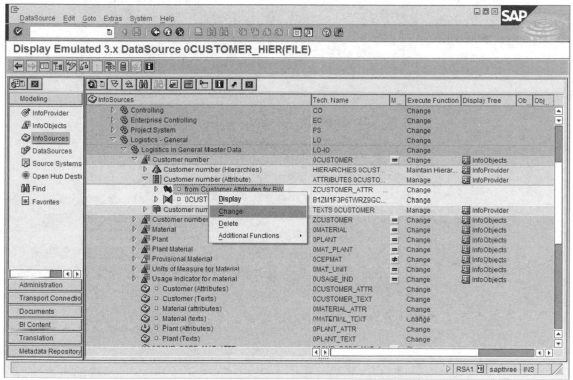

© SAP AG

Transfer rules can identify field values of a communication structure (i.e., the fields' values in the master data tables of the InfoObject) in the form of *direct assignment, assignment of constants,* or *ABAP routines* or with *formulas.* As with transformation, a *start routine* will be executed with the execution of transfer rules (however, an end routine does not exist).

Specialities are the definition of the *input conversion* and the handling of *source system dependent data.*

21.2.1   Start Routine

Before the transfer rules are processed, the staging engine tries to update each data package to execute the start routine of the transfer rules. The start routine can be defined individually for each DataSource of an Info-Source, but it is not necessary to use it (see figure 19–4). If a request consists of several data packages, then the start routine will accordingly be started several times.

Figure 21–11
Start routine in the transfer rules

© SAP AG

The start routine is programmed in ABAP/4, and it can be used to initialize global variables and internal tables that are required by the transfer rules of the data package.

The actual transformation of data should always be left to the transfer rules and not be made in the start routine. However, it makes sense to use the start routine to delete data records that are not relevant for the staging. Thus, the staging will be easier and the performance improved.

The structure of the start routine is firmly defined by BW and consists of three components:

- Global data declarations part
- Parameter part of the start routine
- Code of the start routine

The global declarations part initially consists of the declaration of the DataSource structure in the ABAP structure TRANSFER_STRUCTURE. This is required to access the data of the data package to be handled.

Global data declarations part

Further, in the global data declarations part, separate variables and tables can be stored that can be initialized and accessed by all subsequent transfer rules.

```
PROGRAM CONVERSION_ROUTINE.

* Type pools used by conversion program
TYPE-POOLS: RS, RSARC, RSARR, SBIWA, RSSM.

* Declaration of transfer structure (selected fields only)
TYPES: BEGIN OF TRANSFER_STRUCTURE ,
*    Record number to be filled in case of adding row(s)
*    to enable 'error handling'
     record       TYPE rsarecord,
*    InfoObject OCUSTOMER: CHAR - 000010
     CUSTOMER(000010) TYPE C,
*    InfoObject OACCNT_GRP: CHAR - 000004
     ACCNT_GRP(000004) TYPE C,
*    InfoObject OADDR_NUMBR: CHAR - 000010
     ADDR_NUMBR(000010) TYPE C,
*    InfoObject OAF_CUSTDC: CHAR - 000010
     AF_CUSTDC(000010) TYPE C,
*    InfoObject OAF_CUSTID: CHAR - 000010
     AF_CUSTID(000010) TYPE C,
END OF TRANSFER_STRUCTURE .

* Declaration of Datapackage
TYPES: TAB_TRANSTRU type table of TRANSFER_STRUCTURE.
```

```
* Global code used by conversion rules
*$*$ begin of global – insert your declaration only below this line
*-*
* TABLES: ...
* DATA:   ...
*$*$ end of global – insert your declaration only before this line
*-*
```

Parameter part of the start routine

The parameter part of the start routine transfers the routine information on the data package that is to be transformed with the transfer rules.

```
FORM STARTROUTINE
   USING    G_S_MINFO TYPE RSSM_S_MINFO
   CHANGING DATAPAK type TAB_TRANSTRU
            G_T_ERRORLOG TYPE rssm_t_errorlog_int
            ABORT LIKE SY-SUBRC. "set ABORT <> 0 to cancel datapackage

* (Code of the start routine)

ENDFORM.
```

The parameters have the following meaning:

- **G_S_MINFO**
  In this structure, information on the respective load process is stored. These include information on *request, data package number, InfoSource name, InfoSource type,* and much more. An overview of all fields can be found in the ABAP Dictionary structure RSMINFOHEAD.

- **DATAPAK**
  In the internal table DATAPAK, the data package to be handled is provided. Not only can DATAPAK be read in the start routine, it can be modified too.

- **G_T_ERRORLOG**
  With the use of the parameter G_T_ERRORLOG, messages can be transferred to the monitoring, e.g., if processing errors occur. The transfer of error messages to the monitoring in the start routine is analogous to the ABAP routines that are explained in section 19.3.4.

- **ABORT**
  ABORT <> 0 stands for a serious processing error. The processing of the request will be completely aborted.

Code of the start routine

The code part of the start routine records the program code and initializes global variables, changes the data package, and possibly provides the variable ABORT with an error status.

The parameter G_S_MINFO-LOGSYS contains the logical system name of the source system that may be different within one transport landscape for development, test, and production system. This is a problem if routines are to execute different functions depending on the respective source system. To make routines work the same for all BW systems of a transport landscape, you should first identify within the routine the source system ID for the logical system from the table /BIO/SSOURSYSTEM and design the processing depending on the source system ID. The installation of the source system ID is explained in section 15.1.8.

In the following example, all data records are deleted in the start routine where the field ZATTRIB is filled with an initial value.

```
*$*$ begin of routine – insert your code only below this line    *-*
* DATA: l_s_datapak_line type TRANSFER_STRUCTURE,
*         l_s_errorlog TYPE rssm_s_errorlog_int.

  delete DATAPAK where ZATTRIB is INITIAL. "Deletion of all
                     * data records without entry of customer number

* abort <> 0 means skip whole data package !!!
  ABORT = 0.
*$*$ end of routine – insert your code only before this line    *-*
```

21.2.2 Direct Assignment

Direct assignments represent a simple form to identify field values. It is assumed that fields of the filled communication structure correspond with a field of the DataSource. The respective fields can in this case be assigned to each other (see figure 19–7).

With the creation of a transfer rule, BW first tries to make a proposal for matching fields. This proposal is not binding and can be changed. Also, assignments can be made that are not proposed by SAP BW.

Consider with the creation of transfer rules that after the mapping, global transfer routines might need to be executed or constant InfoObjects might be given, so assigned values might change at a later stage even with simple mapping (see sections 21.2.3 and 21.2.4).

Figure 21–12

Mapping in the transfer rules

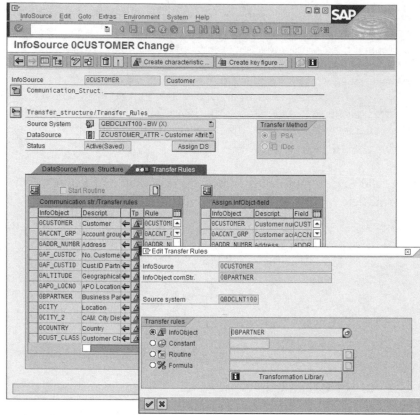

© SAP AG

21.2.3   Assignment of Constants

It may make sense to use the assignment of a constant value instead if a DataSource does not supply the information but one of the following is true:

- The information absolutely needs to be provided if there are compound InfoObjects.
- A constant value seems to be right for a DataSource or is to be used subject to the DataSource.

For the assignment of constants, there are two options:

- The assignment of constants in the transfer rules
- The assignment of constants in the InfoObject

The assignment of constants in the transfer rules always makes sense if the same constant is not assigned to all DataSources but individually defined for certain DataSources.[163]

Figure 21–13 shows the assignment of constants.

Constants in the transfer rules

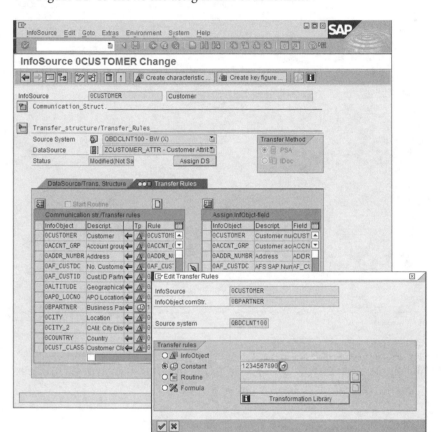

Figure 21–13
Constants in the transfer rules

If InfoObjects always have the same constant assigned, it makes sense to not make the assignment several times (for each DataSource) but to store the constant with the InfoObject.

For this purpose, the assignment of constant is provided in the InfoObject maintenance (see figure 21–14).

Constant InfoObjects

---

163. For other DataSources, in this case formulas or simple mapping can be used if the transfer structure provides the respective information.

Figure 21–14
Constant InfoObjects

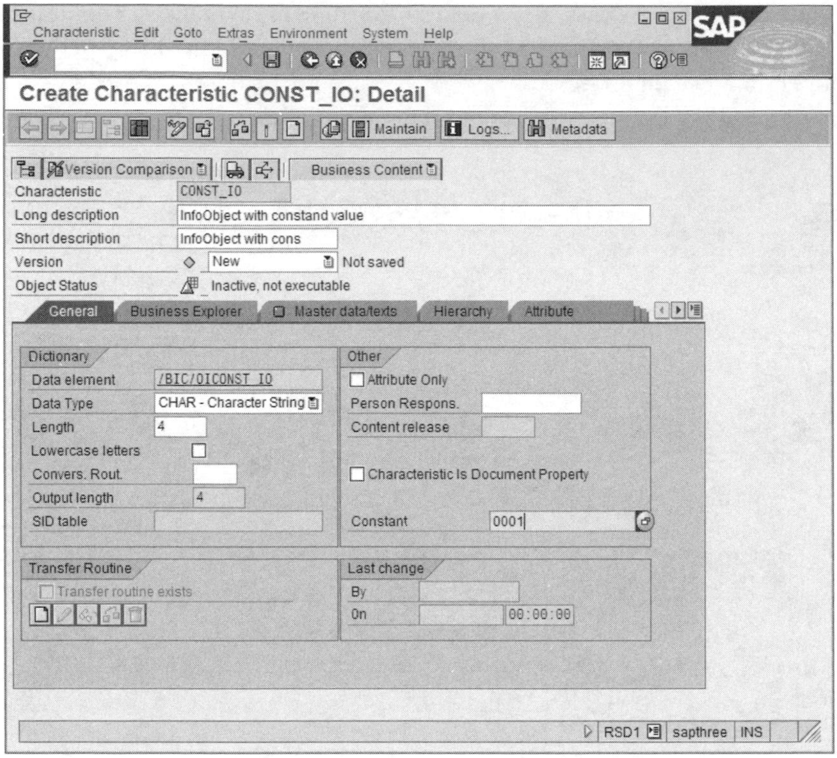

© SAP AG

Special handling is required for the assignment of the constants <SPACE> (for alphanumeric data types) and 0 (for numeric data types). In these cases, the constant is to be marked by #.

21.2.4   ABAP Routines

In some cases, the mapping of InfoObjects or the assignment of constants is not enough to prepare DataSources from different data sources in a homogeneous way. Given the ABAP functions, there are vast options to describe individual assignments with ABAP routines.

ABAP routines can be stored as either local transfer rules or global transfer rules.

Local Transfer Routine

For local transfer routines, an ABAP routine is stored as a transfer rule with the InfoSource (see figure 21–15). This makes sense if for different

DataSources, different ABAP routines are to be stored or if the calculation of an InfoObject is based on more than one field of the DataSource.

Local ABAP routines are form routines that are integrated into the program that is generated from the transfer rules. In these form routines, all functions of the ABAP programming are available.

Figure 21–15

Local transfer routines

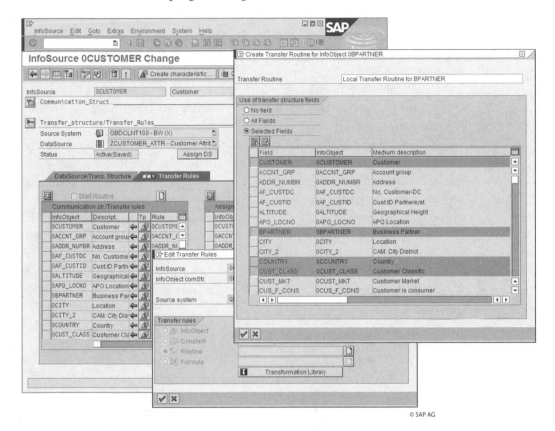

© SAP AG

Local transfer routines have several components that provide the schema of the routine:

- Global data declarations part
- Parameter part of the form routine
- Code of the form routine

Further, the transfer of messages to the monitoring is relevant.

The global data declarations part exists for all transfer rules of a Data-Source. Here, data can be declared that is to be applied to all local transfer rules for the respective DataSource.

Global data declarations part

```
program conversion_routine.
*$*$ begin of global – insert your declaration only below this line
* TABLES: ...
* DATA:    ...
*$*$ end of global – insert your declaration only before this line
*
```

This affects the pure declaration as well as the data content. With the use of global data declarations, interim results can be used in other routines, or the results of the first call can be reused with another call of the same routine.

If data is to be exchanged between routines of individual InfoObjects via the global data declarations, it is necessary to execute the routines in the correct sequence.

For example, the InfoObjects account plan and company code are identified with routines. With the identification of the account plan, content that needs to be available for the routine that identifies the company code is stored in the global variables. It is absolutely necessary for this procedure to first execute the routine for the identification of the account plan. The sequence of calls of the single transfer rules corresponds with the sequence of fields in the InfoObject.

Parameter part of the form routine The parameter part describes the parameters that are to be transferred to the transfer rule as well as the parameters that the routine needs to return.

```
form compute_<InfoObject>
       using
           record_nolike sy-tabix
           tran_structuretype transfer_structure
           g_s_minfotype rssm_s_minfo
       changing
           result    type /BIO/OICOMP_CODE
           g_t_errorlogtype rssm_t_errorlog_int
           returncodelike sy-subrc
           abort     like sy-subrc.
* (Code of the form routine)
ENDFORM.
```

The parameters of the form routine have the following meanings and effects:

■ **RECORD_NO**
In the variables RECORD_NO, the number of the data record to be handled is provided to the transfer structure. Since the data deliveries from

the source system are packaged if they exceed a certain minimum size, the record number refers to the package just handled and not to the complete number of all extracted data records.

■ **TRAN_STRUCTURE**
In the structure TRAN_STRUCTURE, the data record to be handled is provided to the transfer structure.

■ **G_S_MINFO**
In this structure, information on the respective load process is stored. This contains information on request, data package number, Info-Source name, InfoSource type, and much more. An overview of all fields can be found in the ABAP Dictionary structure RSMINFOHEAD.

■ **RESULT**
The variable RESULT serves to return the results of the transfer rule.

■ **G_T_ERRORLOG**
With the use of the parameter G_T_ERRORLOG, messages can be transferred to the monitor, e.g., if errors occur during processing.

■ **RETURNCODE**
With the variable RETURNCODE, errors can be signaled to the conversion program. RETURNCODE <> 0 signals an error; i.e., the processing of the remaining data records will be continued. If the PSA is used for the load process, the respective data record will be marked erroneous in the PSA request.

■ **ABORT**
ABORT <> 0 stands for a serious processing error. The processing of the request is completely aborted.

The code part of the form routine records the program code of the transfer rule and returns the result of the routine via the variable RESULT. Besides the variable RESULT, the RETURNCODE and ABORT also need to be provided with values.

Code of the form routine

```
*
*$*$ begin of routine - insert your code only below this line    *-*
   result = TRAN_STRUCTURE-AMOUNT.    "Assign InfoObject 0AMOUNT
                                      * from transfer structure
* returncode <> 0 means skip this record
   returncode = 0
* abort <> 0 means skip whole data package !
   abort = 0.
*$*$ end of routine - insert your code only before this line     *-*
*
```

If the assignment options provided by BW (mapping, assignment of constants, formulas) are used, BW sends error messages to the monitoring, if required. Errors, warnings, and other information need to be transferred to the monitoring via the ABAP routine.

For this purpose, the parameter G_T_ERRORLOG can be used. The following program example shows the transfer of error messages to the monitoring.

```
form compute_month
    using  record_nolike sy-tabix
           tran_structurelike z1x001x
           g_s_minfotype rssm_s_minfo
    changingresultlike /bic/vcube-calmonth
           g_t_errorlogtype rssm_t_errorlog_int
           returncodelike sy-subrc
           abort     like sy-subrc.
*
*$*$ begin of routine – insert your code only below this line     *-*
DATA: X_ERRORLOG like RSSM_S_ERRORLOG_INT.
(…)
  if error = true.
   X_ERRORLOG-RECORD = RECORD_NO.
   X_ERRORLOG-MSGTY = 'E'. "E=Error, W=Warning, I=Information
   X_ERRORLOG-MSGID = 'ZQUADOX'.
   X_ERRORLOG-MSGNO = '001'.
   X_ERRORLOG-msgv1 = 'An error has occurred'.
   APPEND X_ERRORLOG to G_T_ERRORLOG.
   returncode = 4.
   abort = 0.
  else.
   returncode = 0.
   abort = 0.
   result.
  endif.
*$*$ end of routine – insert your code only before this line *-*
*
ENDFORM.
```

Global Transfer Routine

For each InfoObject, a transfer routine can be stored that is always executed *right after* the transfer rules of the communication structure,[164]

---

164. From the part of the local transfer rules, there is no option to prevent the following explanations on global transfer routines.

whether the transfer rules are described by mapping, constants, ABAP routines, or formulas. The use of global transfer routines makes sense if an InfoObject is always to be transformed with the same ABAP routine *and* the calculation is made based on only a single field of the DataSource (since only one value can be transferred to the routine).

Global transfer rules are very well suited to execute checks or conversions—e.g., from lowercase into uppercase letters.

The transfer routines for an InfoObject are created in the InfoObject maintenance (see figure 21–16).

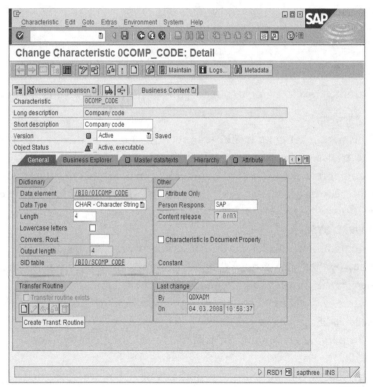

Figure 21–16
Creation of global transfer routines

© SAP AG

Like local transfer routines, global transfer routines are based on a fixed, defined program framework consisting of a data declarations part, a parameter part, and code.

```
PROGRAM CONVERSION_ROUTINE.
* Type pools used by conversion program
TYPE-POOLS: RSD, RSARC, RSARR.
TYPES: DE_OCOMP_CODE(000004) TYPE C.
* Conversion rule for InfoObject OCUSTOMER
*      Data type      = CHAR
*      ABAP type      = C
*      ABAP length    = 000004
FORM CONVERT_OCOMP_CODE
   USING     RECORD_NO LIKE SY-TABIX
             SOURCE_SYSTEM TYPE RSA_LOGSYS
             IOBJ_NAME TYPE RSIOBJNM
   CHANGING RESULT TYPE DE_OCOMP_CODE " InfoObject value
             RETURNCODE LIKE SY-SUBRC.
*$*$ begin of routine – insert your code only below this line   *-*
   RESULT = '0001'.
   RETURNCODE = 0.
*$*$ end of routine – insert your code only before this line   *-*
ENDFORM.
```

The parameters of the global transfer routine have the following meanings:

- **RECORD_NO**

  This parameter contains the data record number of this data record of the transfer structure that is just being processed. The data record number refers to the record number within the respective data package of a request (load process) and not the overall number of all data records.

- **SOURCE_SYSTEM**

  The parameter SOURCE_SYSTEM describes the logical system name supplied by the DataSource. With the use of this parameter, it is possible to design the transfer rules depending on the source systems (e.g., if the source systems supply different sign codes).

- **IOBJ_NAME**

  This parameter contains the technical name of the InfoObject.

- **RESULT**

  This parameter contains the actual value that was assigned to the InfoObject by mapping or assignment of constants or local transfer routines in the transfer rules. The result of this calculation in the global transfer routine also needs to be stored in this parameter. If no assignment is made, the current value will be kept.

■ **RETURNCODE**

If errors occur during the calculation, the transformation layer can be notified using the parameter RETURNCODE. Each value <> 0 marks an error and leads to an abort of the processing of the overall package in which the data record was provided. The data package is displayed erroneously in the monitoring and can be reprocessed. The return of a detailed monitor log is not possible.

21.2.5 Formulas

Formulas have the same goal as local ABAP routines: they are meant to calculate a value depending on different fields of the transfer structure. For this purpose, formulas offer simple calculation designs and conditions that are identical to the formulas in the transformation (see section 19.3.5).

All fields of a transfer structure are available as a basis for the calculation of a formula. Formulas are easier to define than ABAP routines, and they offer the option to make comprehensive calculations even without any ABAP knowledge. Complex rules (e.g., with access to transparent tables), however, can only be realized with ABAP routines.

> If errors occur during the calculation of formulas (e.g., division by zero), no according error codes are returned to the monitoring but only initial values for the calculated field. When designing formulas, you should consider that errors may occur.

21.2.6 Input Conversion

With the new staging with transformation and data transfer processes, the execution of an input conversion is also relevant (see section 15.2.3). However, it only focuses on the conversion exits ALPHA, GJAHR, and NUMCV, i.e., the conversion exits that are checked when data is entered.

If DataSources are extracted from third-party source systems, DB connect source systems, flat files, UD connect, or web services, the input conversion is basically executed for all relevant fields of the DataSource (and different from any other transfer rule before the data is stored in the PSA).

3rd party DB connect

Flat file, UD connect, web service

Especially with the data transfer from SAP ERP and SAP BW, BW assumes that the data is already in the correct internal format and the effort of an input conversion is spared.

SAP ERP, SAP BW

However, the assumption that all InfoObjects that are defined with the conversion exits ALPHA, GJAHR, and NUMCV would also be provided by the source system in the respective format is often wrong. Especially if generic DataSources and user exits are used, an input conversion might be required for these source systems. This is noticeable if BW does not report compliant values during the load processes.

To still execute an input conversion for these InfoObjects, a respective optional field can be activated in the transfer rules (see figure 15–24).

Figure 21–17

Settings for input conversion

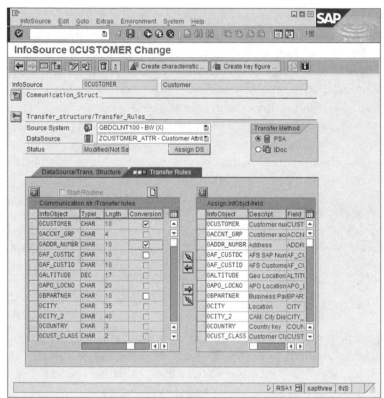

© SAP AG

21.2.7 Source-System-Dependent Data

In some cases, it makes sense to store master data related to a source system (see section 15.1.8). For this purpose, the InfoObject 0SOURSYSTEM is predefined; it is recognized during the definition of the transfer rules as a special case and is automatically assigned with the ID of the source systems (see figure 21–18).

Figure 21–18
Source-system-dependent
communication structure

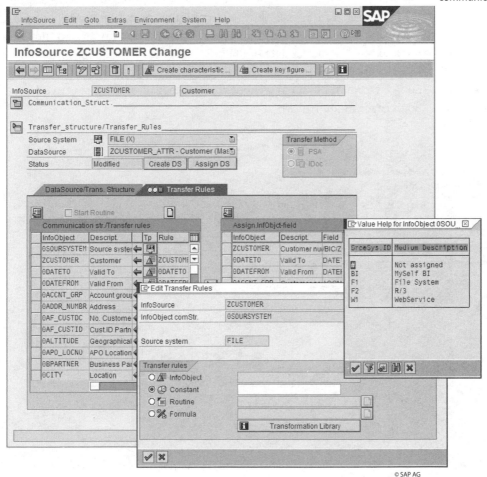

© SAP AG

The InfoObject 0SOURSYSTEM can be added as an attribute of the InfoObject to be filled. However, the InfoObject can also be compound to 0SOURSYSTEM. For this case, the InfoObject maintenance provides an automatic mechanism with which the source system dependency can be made via a check box (see figure 6–38).

InfoObjects with direct staging

Only master data attributes can be stored related to a source system. For external hierarchies and texts, this is not possible.

21.3 Definition of Extraction Procedures

Particular to direct staging, the execution of extraction and load processes is not separated from each other but combined in a joint controlling element. These are the known InfoPackages that write not only into the PSA but also into the master data of the InfoObject.

Figure 21–19

Creation of InfoPackages

The creation of InfoPackages for the direct staging is made in the Info-Source tree of the Data Warehousing Workbench of the respective Data-Source (see figure 15–28).

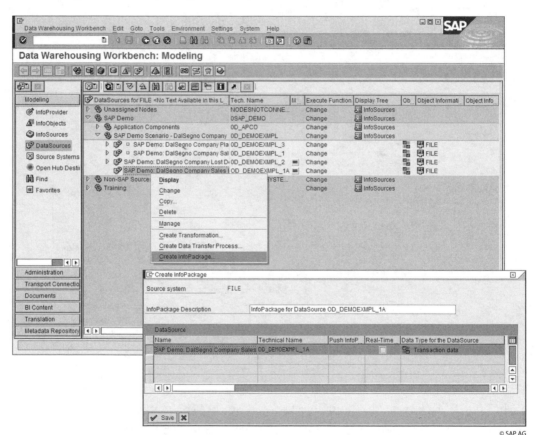

© SAP AG

The settings that are made in the InfoPackages for direct staging are similar to the settings for InfoPackages for the new staging of release 7. There are exceptions for the tabs *External Data* and *Processing*. For the extraction of *external hierarchies*, there is also the *Hierarchy Selection* tab. The different settings are explained in the following sections.

21.3.1 External Data

For the extraction of data from SAP ERP systems, the following data sources as well as display rules are known from specific agreements for all SAP systems:

- Thousands separators
- Sign for the decimal point
- Currency conversion
- Number of headers

For external data from flat files or third-party ETL tools, both the data sources and the display need to be defined. This is done differently than in the new staging in BW 7; it's not done in the definition of the DataSources but under the *External Data* tab with the definition of InfoPackages (see figure 21–20).

> BW offers for each InfoPackage a choice for thousands separators and decimal point. The proposed values can be modified using the transaction RSCUSTV1.

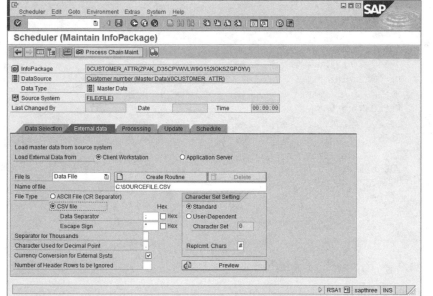

Figure 21–20
InfoPackage: external data

© SAP AG

The settings for the *memory location* and *file type* are identical to the respective settings that are made during the staging in BW 7 in the Data-Source. Particular to the direct staging in BW 3.x, the definitions can alternatively be derived from a control file that can also be preset in the Info-Package.

Control File

Usually, control files are used if the settings in the external data of Info-Packages with a lot of external data or many different settings seem to cause too much effort or seem to be error prone.

Control files are ASCII files and thus needs to be designed as follows:

```
* Name of the flat file to be loaded
FILENAME = c:\temp\qwertz.abc
* Typy of the file to be loaded (binary, CSV or ASCII)
FILETYPE = BIN or CSV or TXT
* Memory location of the flat file (application server or client
* workstation)
LOCATION = A oder C
* Data separator
FS = ;
* Escape sign
ESCAPE = \
* Thousands separator
1000SEPARATOR = .
* Sign for the decimal point
DECIMALPOINT = ,
* Number of records in file
RECCOUNT = 985
* Length of a record in flat file
RECSIZE = 53
* Number of records in an IDOC package
PACKETSIZE = 1000
* Selection date
SELDATE = 19989893
* Selection time
SELTIME = 112305
```

21.3.2 Hierarchy Selection

The loading of hierarchies comes with a range of characteristics that do not exist in any other load processes and relate to the following:

- Selection of the hierarchy to be loaded
- Update method of the hierarchy
- Saving the hierarchy
- Activation of the hierarchy

Selection of the Hierarchy to Be Loaded

An InfoPackage relates to exactly one DataSource in a source system. Thus, the data source for InfoPackages with transactional data, master data attributes, and texts is clearly defined. However, several hierarchies can be offered for extraction by one DataSource.

For this reason, as part of the InfoPackage definition for hierarchies, the hierarchy to be loaded needs to be selected after the list of all available hierarchies has been requested via the *Available Hierarchies from OLTP* button (see figure 21–21).

Figure 21–21

InfoPackage: hierarchy selection

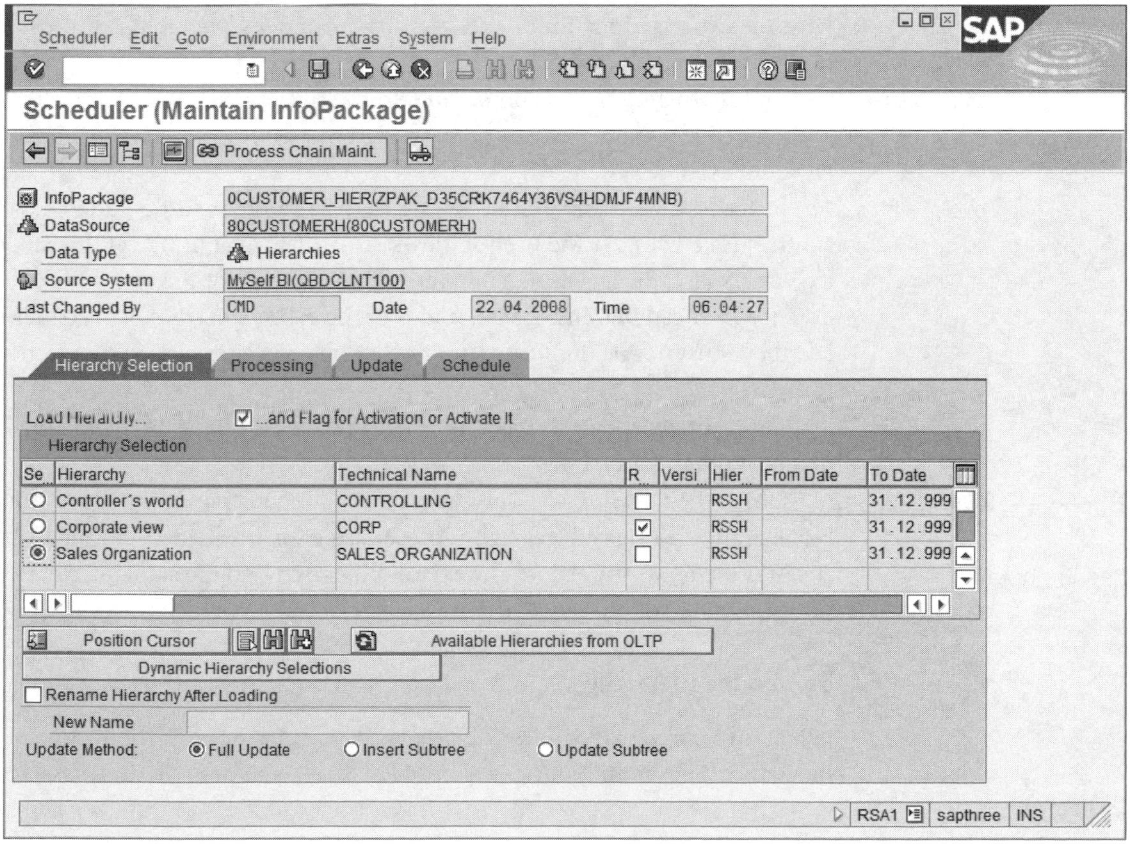

© SAP AG

The list of all available hierarchies might be comprehensive and thus unclear. For this reason, for the hierarchies relevant to the load processes, you can choose the check box in the Relevant for BW column.

The thus marked hierarchies are subsequently listed immediately with the hierarchy selection. Then, the *Available Hierarchies from OLTP* button only needs to be used for a listing of all further (unmarked) hierarchies. However, the relevant hierarchies are only marked for reasons of usability.

Update Method of the Hierarchy

A hierarchy can either be loaded completely from a hierarchy in the source system or composed of several hierarchy parts.

Full update
If a hierarchy is completely mapped from a hierarchy in a source system, the existing hierarchy will be overwritten with the ***full update*** or created with the initial load of a new hierarchy.

In this case, the hierarchy only identifies itself with its technical name, which is expanded for time- and version-dependent hierarchies by "date until" or a version number.

Subtree update
The ***subtree update*** is comparable to the full update; however, in BW the respective hierarchy will not be completely overwritten with the hierarchy of the source system.

Instead, the hierarchy node of the new hierarchy will be added as a subtree directly under the root of the existing hierarchy in BW. If the subtree exists already, it will be completely overwritten by the new subtree. You need to keep in mind that all nodes of the subtree need to be distinct; i.e., they must not be duplicated at another place in the existing hierarchy in BW.

The subtree update is capable of composing a hierarchy from fragments of other hierarchies.

Subtree insert
Other than during the subtree update, the ***subtree insert*** does not replace an existing subtree with the subtree to be loaded. Instead, it repastes the new subtree into the existing hierarchy, so the same hierarchy node might be found several times in a hierarchy.

Storing the Hierarchy

When a hierarchy is loaded in BW, it will be stored under the technical name that it has in the source system. However, this does not always make sense (e.g., since a hierarchy from a source system must not overwrite the hierarchy from another source system).

Especially when a hierarchy is composed of subtree updates and inserts, the hierarchies to be loaded will only in the rarest cases all have the same technical name.

For this reason, in the loading process hierarchies are stored in temporary hierarchy tables and not in the M version of the hierarchy master data as with master data attributes (see section 7.1.2).

Before hierarchy data is transferred from the temporary hierarchy tables, a hierarchy can be renamed to enable subtree updates and inserts from different hierarchies of the source systems into the same hierarchy in BW.

The technical name that a hierarchy is given can be predefined with the hierarchy selection in the InfoPackage.

The migration of hierarchy data into the temporary hierarchy tables is directly executed with the execution of the InfoPackage, and possibly the technical name of the hierarchy will be changed at the same time.

> If an InfoPackage is executed to load hierarchy data in a process chain (see chapter 28), the hierarchy is not stored (and possibly renamed) as part of the InfoPackage. Instead, the additional process type *save hierarchy* needs to be executed after the load process.

Activation of the Hierarchy

No matter whether a hierarchy is part of aggregates or not, after the loading, the hierarchy data is basically all stored in the M version of the hierarchy master data. This is necessary to ensure the consistent state of a hierarchy in BW even with the execution of subtree updates and inserts.

To accommodate this peculiarity the hierarchy selection in the InfoPackage offers an option to directly activate the loaded hierarchy right after the load process; i.e., to migrate the data of the M version into the A version of the hierarchy master data (see figure 21–21).

This option makes sense if a hierarchy is loaded as a full update. For subtree updates/inserts, a hierarchy should only be activated with last InfoPackage or manually in the hierarchy maintenance of the DWWB (see figure 21–22).

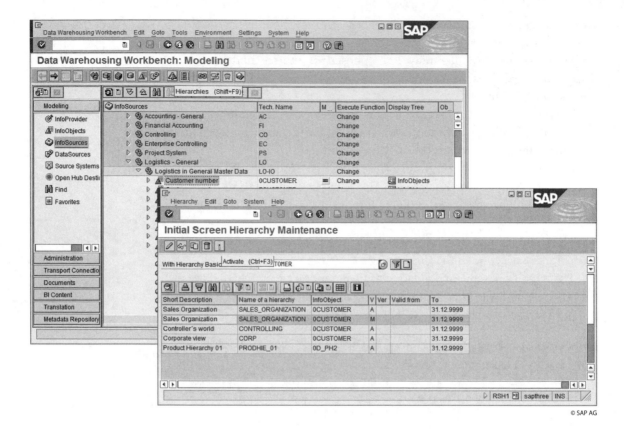

© SAP AG

Figure 21–22
Manual activation of new hierarchy data

If a hierarchy is in aggregates, the activation of the hierarchy will not replace the change run. In this case, the hierarchy is only *marked* for activation and will be included in the next change run.

21.3.3 Processing

The settings regarding processing consist of definitions for consistency checks as well as entering options for data (see figure 24–4).

Consistency check of characteristics values

The settings on consistency checks are embedded into a comprehensive concept that aims at data quality assurance and is explained in detail in the context of all related functions in section 23.2.

Posting options

The settings on data posting define the cooperation of the inflow layer (in the form of the PSA) with the integration layer (in the form of data targets).

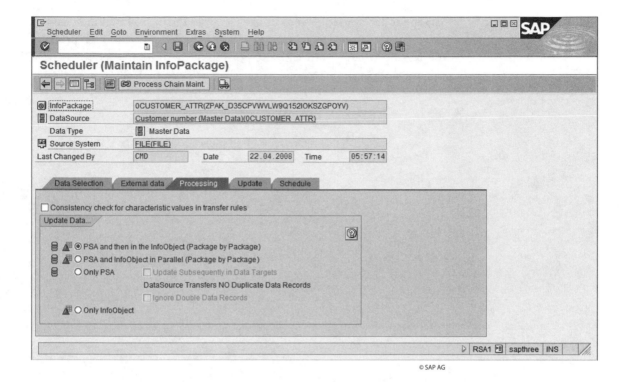

© SAP AG

With these settings, you can determine whether the PSA is to be used as memory space and how the time sequence of the processing steps from the PSA into the data targets is to be designed (InfoCubes, ODS objects, InfoObjects).

Figure 21–23
InfoPackage: settings for
processing using direct

The time sequence of the processing steps is a central topic for the performance tuning of load processes. For this reason, BW tries, by default, to improve performance by parallelizing processing steps. The parallelization is explained in detail in section 24.1. You can set BW to not use parallelization through the option Only PSA or the combination of this option with the subsequent option Update Subsequently in Data Targets.

The processing option Only PSA enables you to first store all extracted data in the PSA without transferring it to the master data tables of the InfoObjects. This allows for a comprehensive validation of the extracted data before it is further processed (manually).

Only PSA

If the processing option Only PSA is enhanced with the check box Update Subsequently in DataTargets, then after all data packages of a request are posted into the PSA, the posting of a request into the Info-Object is started.

Only PSA and update
subsequently in data targets

The use of this variant brings utmost security during extraction since the extraction from the source systems will be executed fast with high priority. If errors occur afterward with the posting of the InfoObjects, the data is still available in the PSA and can possibly be systematically reposted (per package).

22 Real-Time Staging

In the shadow of the strategic decision making that BW technologies have focused on, real-time reporting that mostly aims at supporting tactical decisions has developed. From a technical point of view, tactical decisions are characterized by the fact that they do not refer to a long-time series of historic data but to a relatively small but updated database.

Technically, there are two different procedures for executing a data analysis using the most current data records:

- *Real-time data acquisition* that extracts data with a high frequency from the source systems and migrates it to BW
- *Direct access* to the source systems, where data is not physically migrated into BW but read rights for the data analysis are directly transferred to the respective DataSource.

When InfoProviders that are used for real-time data analysis are combined with other InfoProviders in a MultiProvider, the real-time staging is directly linked to the respective settings for the delta caching. The explanations in section 12.2.3 are thus supplementary to the explanations in this chapter.

22.1 Real-Time Data Acquisition

The concept of the real-time data acquisition (RDA) is a novelty in BW 7 and is at first very easily described: extracted data runs through the extraction and transformation processes as it does during regular data transfers, but it does it more often, possibly even every minute.

This seems to make a new technical concept unnecessary since the transfer is not in true real-time and a high data transfer frequency should have been achieved from the planning of extraction and staging processes. The real-time data acquisition thus seems to be more a question of time frames in live operations (see chapter 29) than a technical question. However, a data transfer every minute will actually fail for a number of reasons.

On the part of the extraction layer, it needs to be said that DataSources are not really prepared to immediately supply small data quantities. They are instead made to provide large data quantities. If during an initialization phase, several minutes are needed to collect data, this is hardly relevant for regular staging if several million data records are transferred subsequently.

The staging engine in BW would quickly reach its limits with the execution of a load process every minute. For regular extraction and load processes, comprehensive log entries are generated to ensure that monitoring is as detailed as possible. This is not a problem if load processes are executed daily or even more infrequently. However, if a load process is executed every minute, the daily newly generated logs for 1,440 requests in extraction and transformation would blow up the management tables of BW in such a way that the effort to manage the log entries would dramatically decrease performance of the staging.

There are a couple of preconditions to execute the real-time data acquisition: the concept of request generation or logging in BW needs to be changed and DataSources in source systems need to be able to react as quickly as possible to new data requirements. This requires that DataSources for real-time data acquisition are delta enabled. The transfer of data in a minute cycle would not be possible with full upload even if only a reasonable data volume needs to be migrated. However, if the data source is very small, the use of direct access is better suited than the real-time data acquisition (see section 22.2).

How staging behaves in the extraction layer of the source systems and in the staging of BW is explained in the following sections Additionally, we'll explain how to control the real-time data acquisition, which centers on the so-called daemon processes.

22.1.1 RDA in the Extraction Layer

The technical possibilities of the real-time data acquisition do not cover the full range of source systems that can be considered with "regular" staging. The core of the RDA is the SAP source systems (ERP and BW). Other source system types can be linked to the concept of RDA only if they act as a web service and transfer data via SOAP messages to BW.

For SAP source systems, the DataSources that are to be connected to   *SAP source systems*
BW via RDA need to be explicitly marked as real-time enabled. Whether
this is the case can be read from the settings of the data source (see also
figure 15–15 using the example of a DataSource that is a not real-time
enabled).

> Real-time-enabled DataSources could only be defined since the release of
> the BI service API of SAP NetWeaver 2004s. For an SAP release 4.6C with
> the plug-in 2004.1, this option has been available since service pack 10.

For DataSources from the BI content, SAP has invariably defined whether
a DataSource is real-time enabled or not. The decision mostly depends on
whether the applications in the source system can supply the delta queue in
real-time so that during extraction no waiting times occur from data collection.

For generic DataSources, you can define yourself whether the Data-
Source is able to handle accesses in real time. For delta-enabled Data-
Sources, an option is available in the DataSource maintenance (see figure
14–6).

The decision on whether a generic DataSource should be marked as
real-time enabled mostly depends on how generic deltas are created. Two
conditions should be met:

- The delta-defining field should enable high-performance access to
  new/modified data; i.e., it should be indexed by a B* tree index. The
  delta-defining field must be selective; it must be effected via a maximum number of different values (the number of different values
  should be at least one-tenth of the number of data records in the
  extracted table).
- The identification of relevant data records from the delta creation
  should contain only data records that have truly been newly created or
  modified since the last extraction (possibly the extraction that was executed one minute earlier). The use of a security interval can become a
  problem when RDA is used since thousands of records can be
  neglected if data records are extracted daily or even less frequently but
  not if the extraction is to be executed in every minute.

SOAP messages do not find their way into BW through an extraction pro-   *Web services*
cess; they are written into the PSA of the SOAP DataSource through the
SOAP service. Thus, BW does not need to execute an extraction but can
directly access PSA data that is further processed in a delta procedure.

22.1.2   RDA in BW Staging

The concept of real-time data acquisition does not comprise all areas of staging in BW. It is limited to the inflow and integration layers, whose objects must be used in a predefined architecture in which data is extracted from the PSA in delta mode and written into DataStore Objects. For web service source systems, data is already available in the PSA, while for SAP source systems, the extraction from the PSA also needs to be considered in the RDA design.

There are always three requests involved in the RDA: the PSA request that contains the raw data of the source system, the DTP request that describes the transformation into the DataStore Object, and the change log request that contains the activated data of the DataStore Object.

However, these three requests are not generated in the same way as with regular staging. Instead, the requests are created synchronically and closed if they contain a defined number of data records. Thus, the requests do not contain the data from the extraction of load process but a firmly defined number of data records that can be distributed to a multitude of extraction and load processes.

To keep the participating requests synchronous, extraction, the data transfer process, and activation of new data in the DataStore Object cannot be executed as usual—that is, independently from each other. Control is instead handed over completely to a **daemon.** Thus, RDA is not only a technology but also a particular form of automation in standard operations.

The precondition for the execution of extraction and staging by a daemon is the corresponding definition of the staging. For web services, this definition comprises only the data transfer process between PSA and DataStore Object since the data is written into the PSA from the source system in a push procedure and thus is transferred to the PSA in real time by default.

DataSource for RDA

For SAP source systems, the controlling of the extraction needs to be explicitly defined for RDA. First, this comprises a corresponding qualification of the DataSource for the use of RDA. This is because the option to use RDA as defined in the metadata of the DataSource is only one *optional* form of usage. Only with the selection of a corresponding adapter will the execution be effected in real time (see figure 22–1).

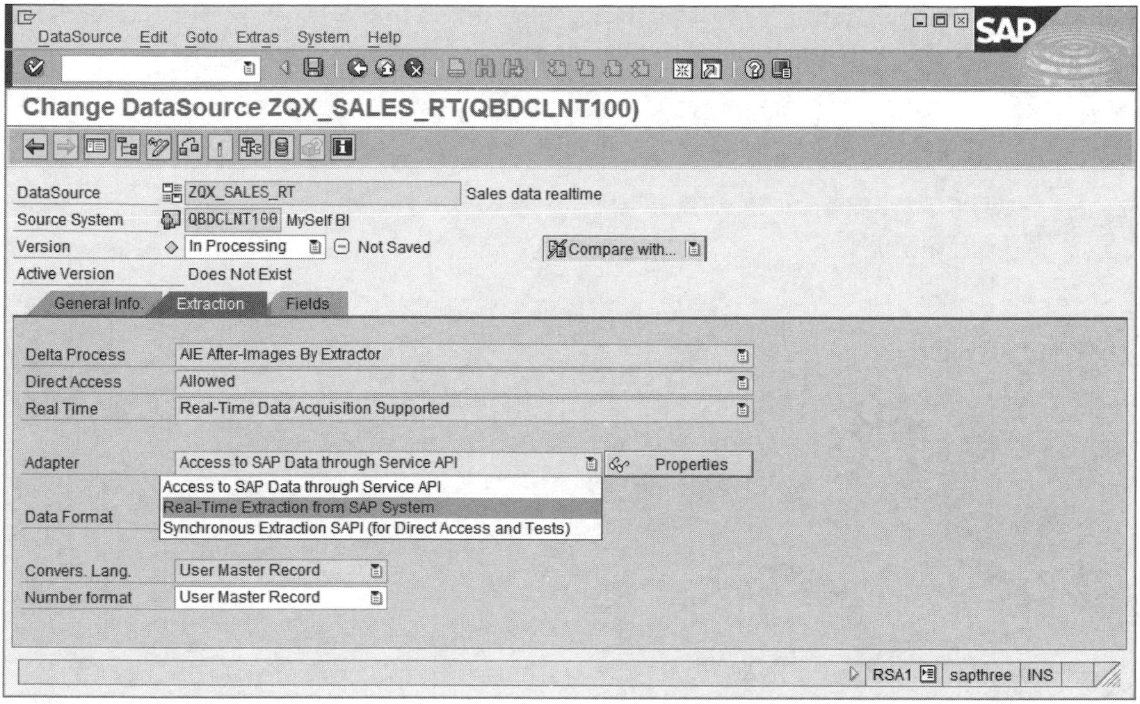

Figure at top of page:

Change DataSource ZQX_SALES_RT(QBDCLNT100)

DataSource Edit Goto Extras System Help

DataSource	ZQX_SALES_RT	Sales data realtime
Source System	QBDCLNT100 MySelf BI	
Version	In Processing / Not Saved	Compare with...
Active Version	Does Not Exist	

General Info. | Extraction | Fields

Delta Process	AIE After-Images By Extractor
Direct Access	Allowed
Real Time	Real-Time Data Acquisition Supported

| Adapter | Access to SAP Data through Service API | Properties |

Access to SAP Data through Service API
Real-Time Extraction from SAP System
Synchronous Extraction SAPI (for Direct Access and Tests)

| Data Format | |

| Convers. Lang. | User Master Record |
| Number format | User Master Record |

RSA1 | sapthree | INS

© SAP AG

Figure 22-1
*Create DataSource for
real-time data acquisition*

In any case, DataSources for real-time data acquisition are based on delta information that supplies the respective DataSources. If a DataSource is extracted via RDA, no regular delta extraction is possible in parallel. This does not interfere with extraction of data in full upload.

InfoPackages for RDA

To control the extraction, an InfoPackage is to be created that is explicitly defined to support RDA (see figure 22–2).

> InfoPackages for real-time data acquisition can be defined with SAP source systems only if the delta procedure was initialized and a data transfer process was created. Information on the details of initialization of the delta procedure for real-time data acquisition can be found in section 21.3.

For a DataSource for real-time data acquisition, only one InfoPackage for real-time data acquisition can be defined. However, the InfoPackage must also be provided if data is transferred to BW via web services (even if the data is directly written into the PSA and not really extracted).

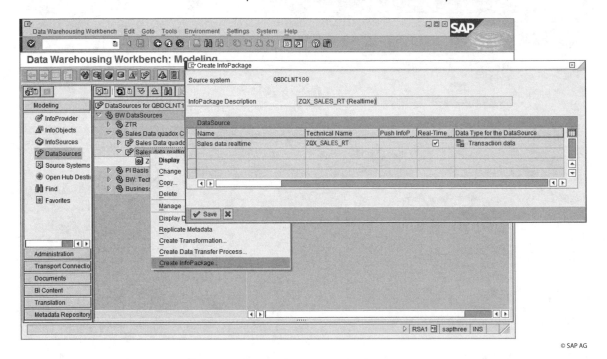

© SAP AG

Figure 22–2
Create InfoPackage for real-time data acquisition

The creation of InfoPackages for RDA and the respective qualification are necessary to control the special request management. You can preset that all requests (PSA, DTP, change log) are closed if the PSA request reaches the limit of 100,000 data records and if it is open for more than one day. The request is distributed to 10 data packages of 10,000 data records each. The request size can be modified in the processing settings of the Info-Package for RDA (see figure 22–3).

The size of the data packages within the requests should be left unchanged. However, if there are compelling reasons, the size can be changed if the change is made by the debugging user. Which user is referred to as debugging user is defined in the management settings (see figure 22–4).

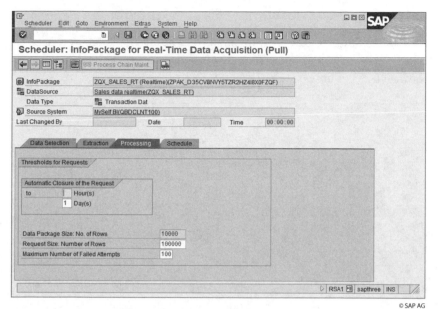

Figure 22–3

Processing options of InfoPackages for real-time data acquisition

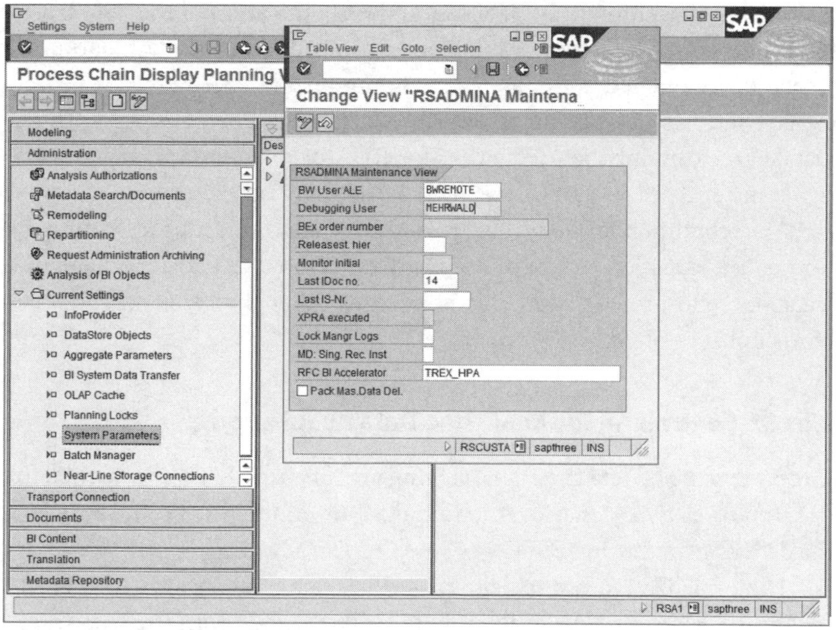

© SAP AG

Figure 22–4

Definition of the debugging user

© SAP AG

Data Transfer Process for RDA

As a precondition for the creation of an InfoPackage for RDA, you need to select the type *DTP for Real-Time Data Acquisition* with the definition of the data transfer process (see figure 22–5).

Figure 22–5
Create DTP for real-time
acquisition

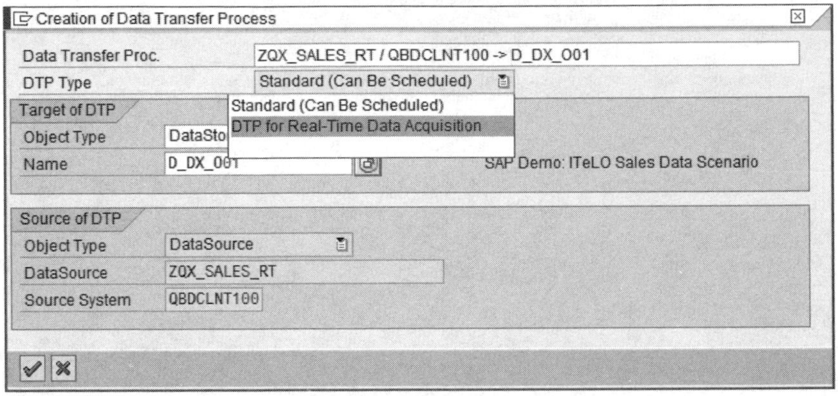

© SAP AG

As with the definition of InfoPackages, the qualification of the data transfer process mostly serves the purpose of modifying request handling. Requests are opened and closed depending on the PSA requests; i.e., no explicit settings need to be made. Here, it needs to be considered that a DataSource can only be used either for RDA or for standard staging. The two transfer types cannot be executed at the same time.

A precondition for being able to define a data transfer process for real-time data acquisition is to have one DataStore Object as data target and one DataSource to provide source data. Designs other than this one are currently not supported by RDA.

22.1.3 Controlling the Real-Time Data Acquisition

The processing of data through a staging architecture that was designed for RDA involves two scenarios: the initialization of the delta procedure and the data transfer during RDA.

Delta initialization   The initialization of the delta procedure is necessary at first to create the InfoPackage for RDA. If the initialization is made with the data transfer, the initialization request cannot be handled by the defined data transfer process since it can only be started via the daemon that controls and monitors the RDA.

Subsequently, the handling of the initialization request of the data transfer process needs to be switched to default behavior. In the definition of the data transfer process, the *Change to Standard DTP* button is available (see figure 22–6). If the initialization request was processed and posted into the DataStore Object, the type of the data transfer process needs to be switched back and can subsequently only be started via the respective daemon.

Figure 22–6
Switching DTP types

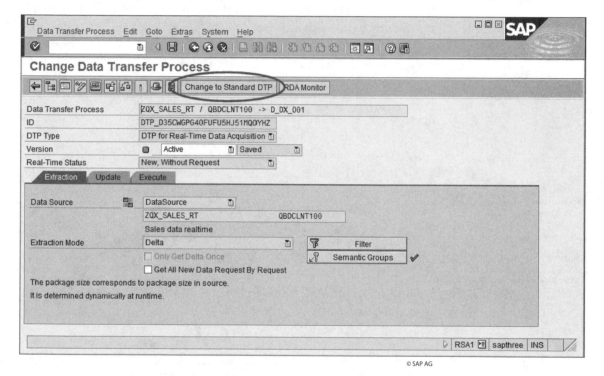

© SAP AG

If a delta initialization was processed and the respective request was activated in the DataStore Object, controlling InfoPackages, data transfer processes, and activation of new data in the DataStore Object can be transferred to a daemon that controls and monitors the staging for the real-time data acquisition.

Daemon for RDA

A daemon is a continuously running a background job that switches into sleep mode between the single extraction processes. However, to improve main memory usage, it regularly ends the job and reschedules itself again.

One or several InfoPackages and data transfer processes can be assigned to each daemon, and it executes them in the predefined cycles. With the first execution, the daemon opens a request in the PSA where the data of the following extraction processes are stored. At this time, the DTP request and change log are not opened, yet.

If through extraction, data is first posted into the opened PSA request, the synchronic DTP and change log requests are opened to immediately transform extracted data after it is posted in the PSA and to post it into the DataStore Object. With a standard DataStore Object, the data is immediately written into the active data and into the change log. The activation queue is not used for real-time data acquisition.

If the PSA request reaches its limits in terms of size or age, the PSA request as well as the DTP and change log request will be closed. With the next execution of the daemon, the PSA request will immediately be reopened and the execution restarted.

Definition of a daemon

A daemon for the real-time data acquisition is created in the transaction RSRDA. There, you can create a daemon to which subsequently the previously defined InfoPackage (in form of the DataSource) and the data transfer process need to be assigned (see figure 22–7).

Figure 22–7

IP assignment for RDA to DTP

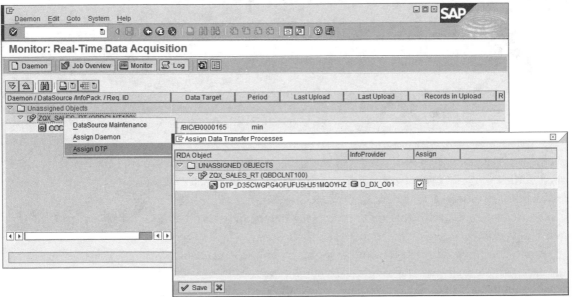

© SAP AG

With the creation of the daemon already completed, the cycle of the background job needs to be defined. The daemon is started from its context menu.

22.2 Direct Access

Another way to map current data is through the direct access to data in the source systems. This renounces the basic concept of data warehousing by leaving the analysis to the source systems instead of transferring, preparing, and storing the BW data in structures that are optimized for data analysis. Direct access is thus suitable only for data sources with especially small data volume and for a small number of accesses.

Direct access is relevant both for transactional data and for master data, and it is mapped by *virtual providers* that are defined like regular BasisCubes and regular InfoObjects but exist only in the metadata of the BW system. There are two different types of virtual providers:

- Virtual providers with staging connect
- Virtual providers with BAPI (for transactional data only)

We'll explain the two types of virtual providers in the following sections.

22.2.1 Virtual Provider with Staging Connect

Virtual providers with staging connect offer an option to access the data of a source system through the DataSources of the source system and to use the known transformation procedure for the supply. Virtual providers are defined for transactional data as they are for master data.

Virtual providers for transactional data are modeled as InfoCubes, but you need to select the type that only stores the definition in the metadata (see figure 22–8).

Transactional data

If a virtual provider is created for transactional data, it accesses the DataSource in the source system for the characteristics and key figure. However, it always reads master data of the characteristics from the existing master data tables in BW.

Should the access to master data also be transferred to a DataSource, then it needs to be defined in the respective InfoObject as remote access and the InfoObject needs to be declared as InfoProvider (see figure 22–9).

Master data

Figure 22–8

Creation of virtual providers with staging connect (transactional data)

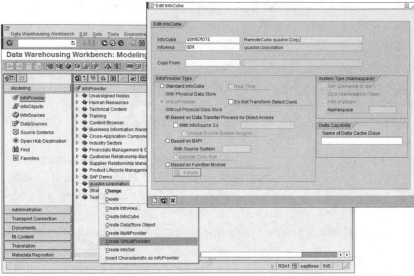

© SAP AG

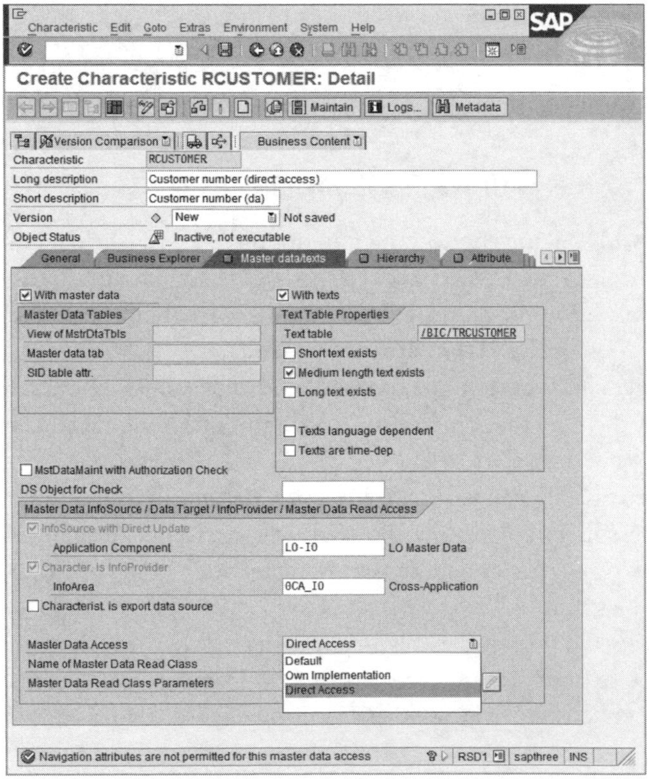

Figure 22–9

Creation of virtual providers with staging connect (master data)

© SAP AG

If one considers that the navigation attributes in the master data tables of InfoObjects are usually stored twice for performance reasons (attribute value and SID), it becomes quickly obvious that remote access to master data can have very negative effects on the data analysis performance. For this reason, attributes in such InfoObjects can be defined as only display but not as navigation attributes.

Each virtual provider can access a random number of DataSources. The precondition is the ability of the respective DataSource to provide data to the BW via direct access. Only SAP source systems offer DataSources that are to be read, in this case, with the adapter SAPIDIRECT. The Data-Source is defined accordingly in BW (see figure 22–10).

Figure 22–10

Definition of DataSources for direct access

```
┌──────────────────────────────────────────────────────────────────────────┐
│ DataSource  Edit  Goto  Extras  System  Help                    □ □ ☒  SAP│
│ ⊘              ▌ ◁ ▐ | ⟲ ⟰ ⊗ | ⬜ ⯗ ⯗ | ⯑ ⯑ ⯑ ⯑ | ⬚ ⬚ | ⊘ ⬚              │
│ Change DataSource ZQX_SALES_RT(QBDCLNT100)                                  │
│ ⬅ ➡ ⬜ ⬚ ⬚ ⬚ ▐ ⬚ ⬚ ⬚ ⬚ ▌                                                 │
│                                                                            │
│ DataSource     ▦ ZQX_SALES_RT              Sales data realtime             │
│ Source System  ⬚ QBDCLNT100 MySelf BI                                      │
│ Version        ◇ In Processing ▤ ⊕ Saved        ⧎ Compare with... ▤        │
│ Active Version      Executable    ═ Edited Version                         │
│    General Info.  ╱Extraction╲  Fields                                     │
│                                                                            │
│ Delta Process    AIE After-Images By Extractor                     ▤       │
│ Direct Access    Allowed                                           ▤       │
│ Real Time        Real-Time Data Acquisition Supported              ▤       │
│                                                                            │
│ Adapter          Real-Time Extraction from SAP System        ▤  ⚙ Properties│
│                  ┌──────────────────────────────────────────────┐         │
│                  │ Real-Time Extraction from SAP System          │         │
│ Data Format      │ Access to SAP Data through Service API        │         │
│                  │ Synchronous Extraction SAPI (for Direct Access and Tests)│        │
│                  └──────────────────────────────────────────────┘         │
│ Convers. Lang.   User Master Record     ▤                                  │
│ Number format    User Master Record     ▤                                  │
│                                                                            │
│                                              ▷ RSA1 ▣ sapthree  INS        │
└──────────────────────────────────────────────────────────────────────────┘
```
© SAP AG

Not all DataSources are able to use the SAPIDIRECT adapter. Keep in mind that especially DataSources for delta procedures might not be enabled to supply data to virtual providers.

The connect between a DataSource and a virtual provider is defined as with regular staging by a transformation and a data transfer process.

If exceptions are produced during the execution of transfer rules (e.g., conversion error with the use of erroneous data type assignments), this does not lead to aborts or error messages in the case of queries on virtual providers. Rather, the respective data records are filtered without comment. For this reason, with the transformation of virtual providers, the particular focus should be on assigning the correct type.

How many DataSources supply data to a virtual provider depends on the defined transformations and data transfer processes. With the definition of the data transfer processes, you should select the option *Do Not Extract from PSA but Access Data Source* and the adapter for synchronic extraction (see figure 22–11).

Figure 22–11

Create data transfer process for direct access

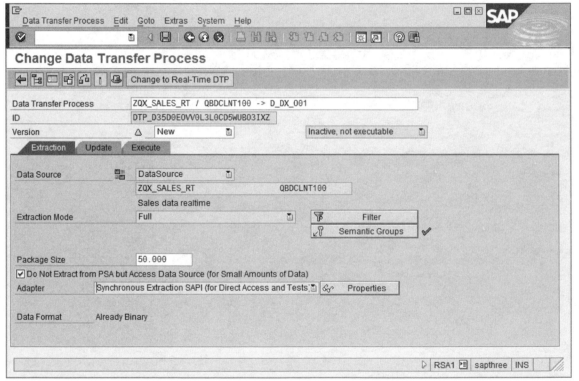

© SAP AG

The data sources that are actually to be read with direct access need to be redefined explicitly. This is done in the context menu of the respective target structure (master data attributes or texts or cube) and is activated via the *Activate Direct Access* menu item (see figure 22–12).

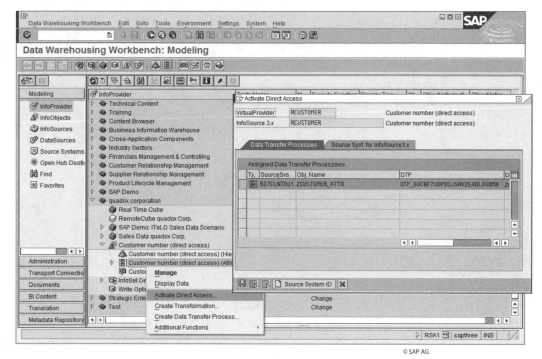

© SAP AG

Figure 22–12
Activate direct access

22.2.2 Virtual Provider with BAPI

Using virtual providers with BAPI,[165] the systems from third-party suppliers can be used to retrieve data from these systems. The principle is similar to the virtual provider with staging connect, but the obtained data is not even processed in a transformation. It needs to be already supplied in the form required for the analysis.

The data requirement is not directed to the DataSources of the source system but requires a specifically prepared third-party source system that provides a corresponding BAPI to exchange data.

The creation of the virtual provider with BAPI is similar to the creation of a virtual provider with staging connect, where the type Based on a BAPI is selected and the RFC destination to the respective third-party source system is indicated (see also figure 22–8).

Virtual providers with BAPI are used in special cases if data is to be obtained from a market data supplier (e.g., AC Nielsen or Dun & Bradstreet).

165. Up to release 3.x of BW, BAPI was referred to as general RemoteCube.

23 Data Quality

There is the danger with all processing steps in extraction and staging that erroneous data will be supplied to SAP BW or that it will be prepared erroneously in BW. This applies to master data as well as to transactional data.

To make sure erroneous data doesn't make its way to the user, BW offers numerous options within the staging process to avoid or recognize different errors, both content and technical errors.

The basis (or rather the result) of each form of quality assurance is a status management view that displays the quality status of a request. Depending on the status, requests that depend on the start of subsequent processes in standard operations can be evaluated or requests for the data analysis can be released.

Each extraction and data transfer process is equipped with its own *overall status,* which describes the processing status as well as the status of the respective request in the target structure. The differentiation of request status and the data target status as it was used up to release 3.x is no longer required for staging in BW 7 since the data target and request have a 1:1 relation.[166]

Which part of the staging is described by the quality status of the request depends on the request type. Requests of the PSA describe the status of an extraction, while a request in the data transfer process describes the status of this process.

It can directly be deduced from the status of a request whether the request can be further processed; i.e., whether a request in a DataStore Object can be activated, rolled up into aggregates, or released for a data analysis. If the review of the data quality *prior* to a processing of new requests is crucial, this might not always be desired, even if the status of the

---

166. In staging up to release 3.x, the request of a load process could be written into several data targets so that each of these processes could be terminated with a different status.

Figure 23–1
Setting of the overall
status of a request

request is to be considered error free from a technical and content perspective. Whether an overall status of a request is to be set automatically or manually is determined in the definition of the respective data transfer process in the option *Overall Status of Request* (see figure 23–1).

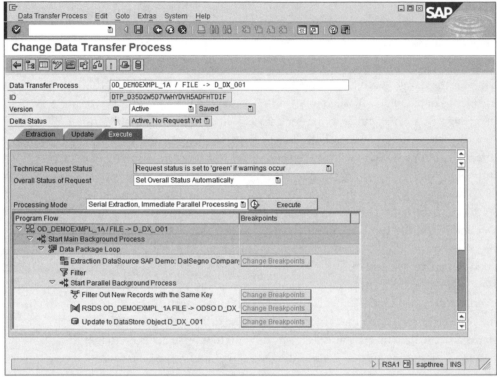

If the status is not set automatically, it needs to be set manually in the management of the respective data target. A corresponding traffic light (see section 31.2) can be used as button to change the quality status in a data target. However, if in standard operations further processes are to follow the execution of the load processes (as in most cases), then the overall request status needs to be marked as error free right after the processing; i.e., it needs to be set automatically.

The data check for content is complex and usually takes much time. This hampers the timely provision of information. You should carefully consider whether you can assume this task before deciding to manually maintain the data-target-related request status.

The handling of warnings requires special treatment. Warnings occur if the content of a request is found to be neither erroneous nor error free; they can result from self-developed error treatment in the transformation but also be supplied by BW or the extractor in the source system.

Treatment of warnings

If a warning occurs, the technical evaluation is unclear and the request is considered as "undecided". However, especially for the design of standard operations, it is necessary to either abort further processing of the request (i.e., to interpret the warning as an error) or to continue processing (i.e., to interpret the warning as only information).

The status a request is to receive when warnings occur ***during the extraction*** is determined in the definition of the InfoPackage (see figure 23–2).

Figure 23–2
Treatment of warnings during extraction

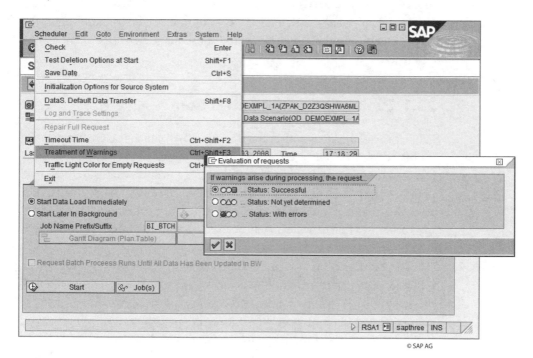

© SAP AG

The status a request is to receive when warnings occur ***during data transfer processes*** needs to be defined in the definition of the data transfer process in the option *Technical Request Status* (see figure 23–1).

The error checking that leads to the overall status of a request varies greatly and is distributed to different stages in the staging process. These are as follows:

Error checking

■ Evaluation of the extraction
■ Consistency tests
■ Testing of master data integrity
■ Testing of referential integrity

Besides, with self-developed **routines** within the *transformation,* error situations can be signaled. How this works can be found in section 19.3.4 on page 434. Such an error treatment can also be used for own rule sets to signal possible data quality problems.

The error checking is mandatory in BW, but it can also be designed to meet individual requirements. In the following sections, we'll explain the function of the individual tests and describe how the tests can be modified to meet individual needs.

Error treatment   The chapter ends with a description of how the error handling in the staging can be configured and how the subsequent error treatment can be defined.

23.1 Evaluation of the Extraction

While processing steps within the staging in BW can at least technically be evaluated as error free or erroneous, the evaluation of extraction processes is more complex. Often, the extraction is *not* a process that is defined by a program start and a program end in the classical sense. The difficulty with an evaluation of extraction processes is rather the evaluation of the distributed processes that can alternately be executed in the source systems and in BW.

End of extraction process   The extraction process in the source system is started asynchronously to the request process in SAP BW; i.e., it only sends asynchronous feedback messages to BW, so aborts of this process are not recognized per se. There are two very different ways to recognize aborts of the extraction processes in the source systems, these are: **wait time** and **polling**.

Wait time   The wait time is a vehicle that was especially significant in the releases prior to BW 3.x, but it is still in use. The wait time is defined within BW as a systemwide threshold at which a PSA request will be considered erroneous when exceeded. The time period is measured from the data request to the source system until the *termination* of the posting in the PSA.

The wait time is defined in seconds and can be defined using the transaction RSCUSTV2 (see figure 23–3).

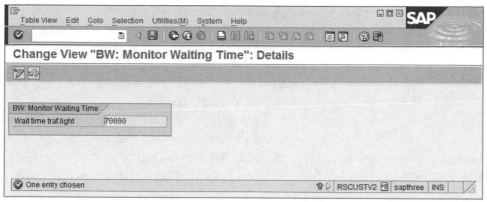

© SAP AG

Especially if very large requests are written into the PSA (e.g., with transfer of legacy data), large runtimes occur that depend on a waiting time that would be inappropriately long for regular load processes. On the other hand, there are waiting times that end so quickly that the systemwide-defined waiting time would be too long.

For these reasons, the systemwide waiting times can be explicitly defined for individual InfoPackages (see figure 23–4).

Figure 23–3

Definition of the monitor waiting time

Figure 23–4

Definition of the monitor waiting time per InfoPackage

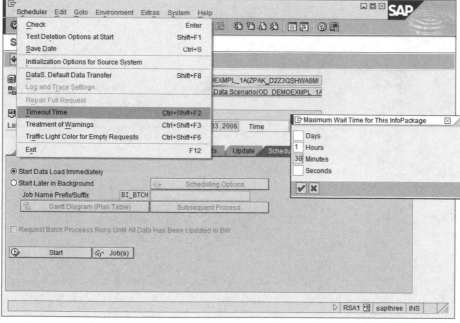

© SAP AG

The evaluation of a request based on the waiting time does not result in a processing abort. If a request is to be processed error free, even though it has already been evaluated as technically erroneous because of a waiting time that was calculated too small, the processing will still be continued. However, the overall status of the request will in this case be erroneous and need to be corrected manually (see section 31.4.1).

Polling

The evaluation of a load process based on its runtime is an imprecise and error-prone procedure to determine the status. Erroneous load processes that are aborted in the source system might be detected as being erroneous too late and error-free requests might be considered erroneous only because they have a runtime that is too long.

Figure 23–5

Activation of the polling procedure in process chains

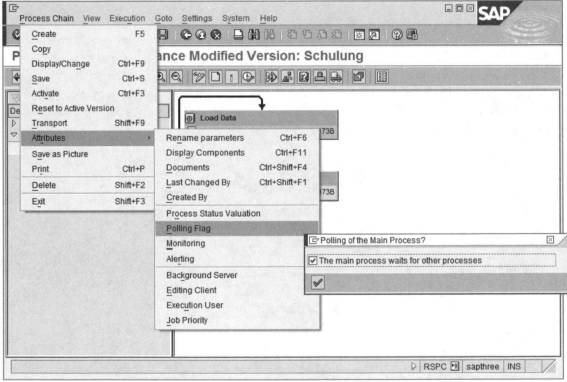

In addition to the waiting time, with the use of process chains,[167] a so-called polling procedure can be used that offers a significantly more reliable evaluation of the extraction. With the use of the polling procedure,

---

167. Process chains will be discussed in detail in chapter 28. Here, the reference to polling is made only to point to an alternative to the waiting time.

the requesting batch process in BW continues to run, and it periodically checks the status of the remotely started process every two minutes so that the load process can be evaluated on a current basis and correctly.

To activate the polling procedure, you need to place the polling flag in the definition of the respective process chain (see figure 23–5).

The resource requirements for the main process that executes the polling is minimal from a performance perspective, but an additional batch process is to be provided for this main process. Especially with parallelization of several load processes, several additional batch processes will thus need to be provided in the system administration.

If the polling procedure is used to run load processes, then the waiting time is irrelevant and can thus be calculated more generously.

Another peculiarity with the evaluation of extraction processes is the handling of data deliveries that are error free from a technical perspective but that indicate a possible error by not supplying any data.

Evaluation of empty data delivery

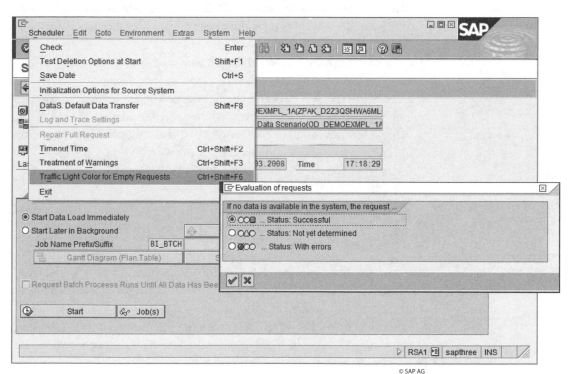

© SAP AG

Especially with the use of the delta procedure, an empty data delivery may be correct (e.g., because no new data was generated since the last load process); however, it may also indicate an error that needs to be investigated.

Figure 23–6
Evaluation of empty data supplies

How BW evaluates an empty data delivery is defined in the definition of the respective InfoPackage[168] (see figure 23–6).

23.2 Consistency Check

During extraction and staging, characteristics and attributes values can be created that may in context be considered invalid or implausible; i.e., they are considered *inconsistent*. Characteristics and attributes values need to meet the following requirements to be considered consistent:

- **Plausibility of date and time fields:** The data type of the InfoObject defines the respective date or time field. For example, the InfoObject OCALMONTH needs to be in the form JJJJMM, where JJJJ needs to be higher than 1000 and MM between 01 and 12.
- **Correct evaluation of the conversion routines** ALPHA, GJAHR, **and** NUMCV: Characteristics values with these conversion exits need to comply with the conventions for the internal display of the conversion routines.
- **Use of letter values in NUMC type fields:** Only number values can be assigned to InfoObjects of the NUMC type.
- **Use of lowercase letters and special signs:** The use of lowercase letters and special signs is permitted only for display attributes but not for characteristics values or navigation attributes unless they are explicitly permitted (see also section 6.1.1).

The consistency check is actively supported by BW and is considered in two places:

- Mandatory consistency checks with posting into data targets
- Optional consistency checks

Mandatory consistency check with posting into data targets

Directly after the posting of data into data targets (i.e., after a transformation is executed), a consistency check will be made. This consistency check is mandatory and cannot be avoided.

If errors are found during the consistency check, the update of the processed data package will be aborted. All other data packages within the respective request are further processed.

---

168. As for the treatment of warnings, the status for direct staging (see also chapter 21) is defined as a systemwide setting in the transaction RSMONCOLOR.

Special cases are standard DataStore Objects. If the generation of master data IDs is activated (see figure 10–6), then the consistency check will be made with the activation of new data in the activation queue. For DataStore Objects that do not generate any master data IDs with their activation, the consistency check is not applied.

Especially when dropping the consistency check with the filling of standard DataStore Objects, inconsistent values can "survive" part of the staging process and will only cause problems at a later time.

Even though it may seem problematic at first glance to not always run a consistency check on values prior to posting in DataStore Objects, it may make sense. Inconsistent values can still be filtered at a later time or they might be the basis for further calculations. In these cases, the consistency check might not necessarily make sense and can even be disruptive because DataStore Objects are, above all, staging objects that do not have any relation to the data analysis yet.

In numerous cases, it makes sense to not wait until BW runs the consistency check but to enforce it as early as possible.

Optional consistency check in the inflow layer

For example, if inconsistent values are written into a standard DataStore Object that does not identify any master data IDs with its activation, BW will find an error when the DataStore Object is posted into a BasisCube. However, it was obvious at the time of the posting of the characteristics values into the DataStore Object that the values would result in errors at a later stage.

For such cases, BW offers an option to individually identify for each field of a DataSource whether an additional consistency check is to be executed prior to the posting of data into the PSA. This enables a very early consistency check before a single data record from the PSA is further processed.

With the explanations regarding input conversion in section 15.2.3, we pointed out that with the definition of the DataSource structure you can run a format check to see whether field values are compliant to their conversion exit (see figure 15–24). This check not only refers to the conversion exit but also to the preconditions of the consistency check. A format check may also make sense for fields for which no conversion exits are stored because format consistency and plausibility are checked too.

The permission to use lowercase letters is defined separately but not for the SAP source systems because, in this case, using lowercase letters is defined in the properties of the fields in the source systems (see figure 23–7).

With a large number of characteristics, the additional consistency check in the inflow layer can affect performance in the extraction. Thus, only activate the optional consistency check for necessary fields.

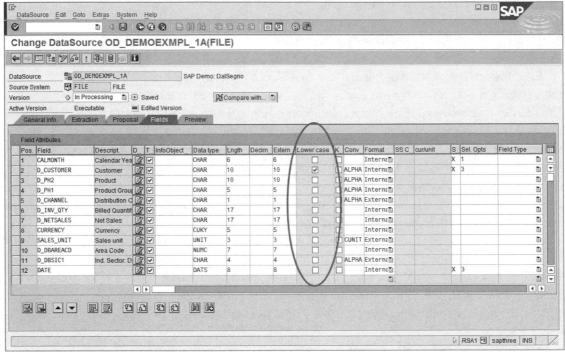

© SAP AG

Figure 23–7
Consistency check in the
inflow layer

The mandatory consistency check of the characteristics values with the posting in BasisCubes, or with the activation of DataStore Objects with SID identification, is always executed.

23.3 Master Data Integrity

When data targets are filled with new data, characteristics values are not entered by their true values into the data targets but rather by their master data IDs (SIDs). The concept of the SIDs was explained in section 6.1.1.

The following is true of SIDs of characteristics values:

■ They are stored when transactional data is loaded into the dimension tables.

- They are checked for their existence or generated when new data is activated in standard DataStore Objects that create master data IDs (see section10.2).
- They are stored when master data is loaded into the master data tables of a characteristics if they are navigation attributes (see section 6.2.2).

If, for example, when the InfoObject OCUSTOMER is filled in a data record, the navigation attribute OINDUSTRY = 0102 is entered into the master data, then the SID for OINDUSTRY = 0102 is identified from the table /BIO/ SINDUSTRY, and this value is entered into the field S_OINDUSTRY of the respective data record in the table /BIO/XCUSTOMER.

The behavior of BW is interesting if the InfoObject OINDUSTRY has master data but this master data does not contain the characteristics value that is to be entered. Consequently, no SID can be identified. The same applies to transactional data if a characteristics value is to be entered into a Basis-Cube for which there is no master data even though the InfoObject has master data.

For this case, there are two posting options (update modes):

- The data record will still be entered. Thereby, a new master data record is generated for the respective characteristic with initial values and the SID of this new record is used.
- The data record is excluded from the entry and is considered erroneous.

The update mode can be preset in the definition of the respective data transfer process (see figure 23–8).

Update mode for transactional data

It is thus possible to control the review of the master data integrity in a dedicated way for each staging process. At the same time, the update mode applies to all characteristics of the respective data transfer process; i.e., everything or nothing at all is reviewed.

> For BasisCubes and InfoObjects, the review of the master data integrity is made at the time of the entry. For standard DataStore Objects, the review is made only when new data is activated; i.e., at the time of the entry, errors cannot be detected yet.

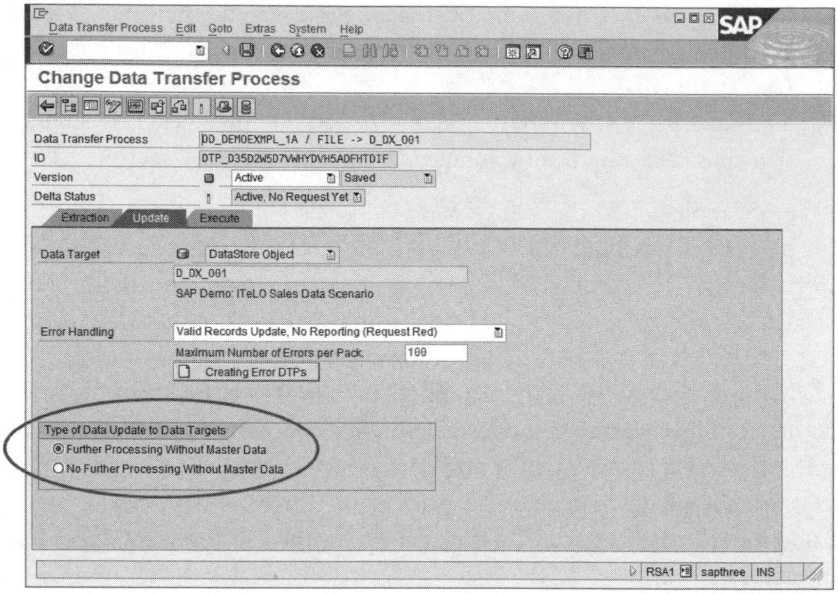

Figure 23–8

Check on attribute SIDs during update

Update mode for direct staging

With direct staging of master data (see chapter 21) as well as with the manual maintenance of master data in BW, the update mode is taken from a systemwide setting. This setting can be defined using transaction RSCUSTV9 (see figure 23–9).

The correct selection of the update mode depends on the respective requirements and the general conditions. Even with nonexisting attribute SIDs, the entry significantly reduces maintenance efforts for the load processes. However, especially in the initial phase of standard operations, it may result in wrong master data and longer runtimes since, in addition to the loaded master data, SIDs for the attributes need to be generated.

The check on existing attribute SIDs ensures data quality, but it may come with increased maintenance effort. The right sequence of the load processes is especially important for this update mode: Before transactional data can be loaded, all master data needs to be loaded. Before the master data of an InfoObject is loaded, first the master data of all respective navigation attributes is loaded.

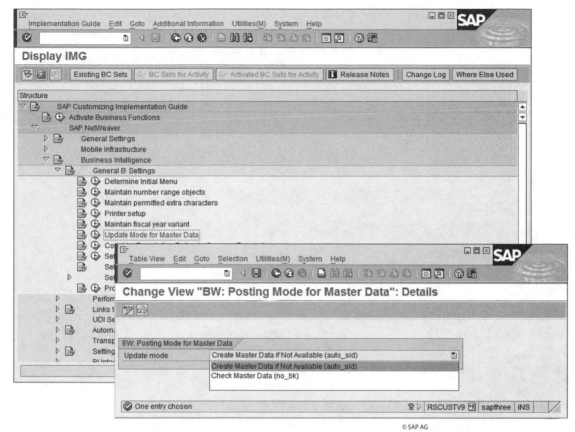

© SAP AG

Figure 23–9
Update mode for master data

23.4 Referential Integrity

The previously described settings on the update mode that controls the check on master data integrity are, in most cases, not distinct enough or they come with other disadvantages:

- With the execution of a data transfer process, the selected update mode applies to *all* InfoObjects of the target structure.
- For standard DataStore Objects where master data IDs are generated, the master data integrity is checked only when new data is activated.
- For DataStore Objects where no master data IDs are generated, the master data integrity is not reviewed at all.
- When master data attributes that are defined as display attributes but not as navigation attributes are loaded, the master data integrity is not reviewed at all.

Due to these disadvantages, the concept of the master data integrity seems to be so impractical that it is hardly ever used. Only the referential integrity helps to execute a distinct review of the integrity.

Referential integrity check against master data

Whether the referential integrity of characteristics values is to be checked is basically determined in the definition of the respective transformation. For this purpose, there is an optional field that activates the referential check against the master data of the respective InfoObject (see figure 23–10).

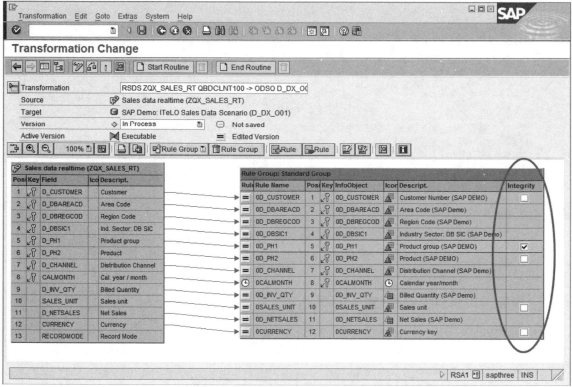

© SAP AG

Figure 23–10
Referential integrity check against master data

From a content perspective, the check of the referential integrity against master data is similar to the known integrity check; i.e., BW also reviews whether a characteristics value has an existing SID.

However, since the referential check against master data is more flexible you can decide which InfoObjects to check. For example, as shown in figure 23–10, the integrity would be checked for the InfoObject 0D_PH1 but not for the other InfoObjects.

As an alternative to activating the integrity check in the transformation, the integrity check can also be activated in the definition of an InfoSource (see figure 23–11). If an InfoSource is used for staging, the procedure is especially advantageous if the InfoSource was filled from several data sources, and the integrity check will automatically be applied to all transformations. Thus, the check does not need to be activated in the definition of each single transformation.

Figure 23–11

Definition of the referential integrity check in InfoSources

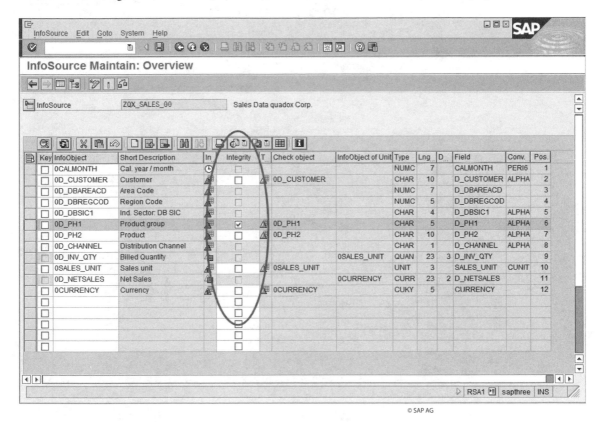

© SAP AG

In specific cases, it may make sense to refer the referential integrity check to another test table rather than to the loaded master data of an InfoObject. In practice, this makes sense if the following is true:

Referential integrity check against Datastore Objects

- There is a list of valid entries but no master data is provided for it in the source system (the test table is larger than master data of the InfoObject).
- From the amount of loaded master data, only part of the characteristics values is valid (the test table is smaller than the master data of the InfoObject).

A DataStore Object can be used as test table. It needs to be stored in the metadata of the InfoObject to be checked (see figure 23–12). The Info-Object to be checked needs to be contained in the key part of the DataStore Object.

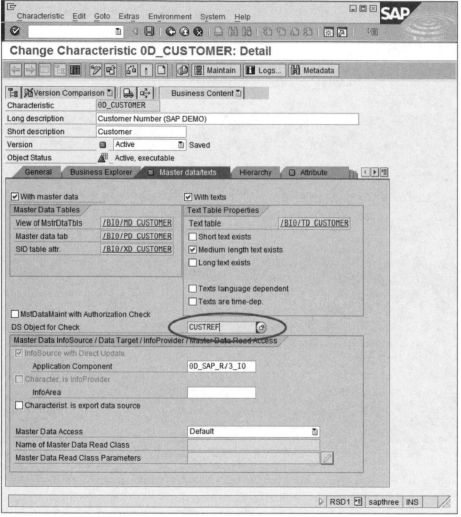

© SAP AG

<span></span>

Figure 23–12
Referential integrity check
against DataStore Objects

For thus defined InfoObjects, the referential integrity check is made against the DataStore Object but no longer against the master data of the InfoObject. As an example, figure 23–12 shows a definition of the Info-Object 0D_CUSTOMER with which the DataStore Object CUSTREF is checked.

> If DataStore Objects are to take on an overload of actually existing characteristics values, then master data IDs must not be generated during activation because the overload of values can only be stored in the DataStore Object where SID values do not need to be given at the same time.

23.5 Error Handling

The previous chapters described how errors in the data flow can be detected. For this purpose, you can apply a range of consistency and integrity checks as well as self-developed ABAP routines. Besides the detection of errors, the handling of errors is especially interesting. There are different options that can be selected in the definition of the data transfer process (see figure 23–13).

The different options are described in the following sections.

Figure 23–13

Error handling during update

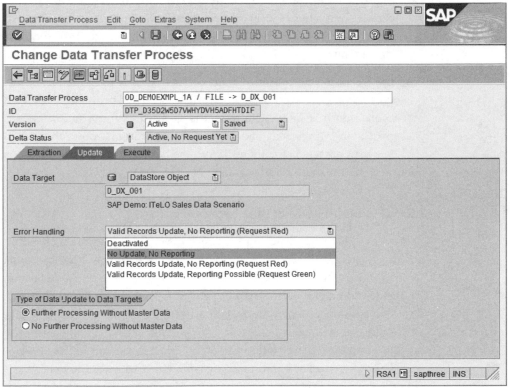

© SAP AG

23.5.1   System Behavior without Error Handling

In the simplest case, error handling is deactivated.[169] If an error is detected, the processing of the respective data package is aborted and the respective data records are marked erroneous in the PSA. If there are further erroneous data records in the respective data package, they will not be checked again and might possibly even be detected in further loading attempts. All other data packages of a load process are processed further.

One option for handling errors is to correct the data records marked erroneous in the PSA; they can then be rewritten into the respective data target. This system behavior assumes the following:

- For each erroneous data package, there is an option to manually intervene and to correct the data in the PSA.
- The data correction in the PSA can be made in an acceptable time frame for operations.
- The BW administrator has time and energy to receive with a data package only a message on the first erroneous data record for each load process and to detect only the next error with execution of the next load attempt.

In practice, these preconditions are often not met and a request with several million data records might wait for further processing until an erroneous sign in a single data record is clarified with the source system administrator (who usually takes a four-week vacation around this time). When a load process is finally restarted, the next erroneous data record is detected and the drama starts again.

23.5.2   Continuation of the Check

BW makes the completeness of the check easier since it aborts the posting of a data package after an error is detected and the error check can continue. For this purpose, you can select the option *No Update, No Reporting* in the definition of the data transfer process (see also figure 23–13).

The advantage lies in the fact that not only the first erroneous data record but all erroneous data records of a data package are logged in the first load attempt of the monitoring and marked erroneous in the PSA.

This form of error handling comes into effect when in the field *Maximum Number of Errors per Package,* a number larger than zero is entered.

---

169. This was the default behavior up to BW release 3.x.

The number defines from what point in time a continuation of the check is no longer of any interest since it might be a systematic error that no longer allows for a manual treatment of erroneous records.

23.5.3 Continuation of the Posting

A logical consequence of continuing the check when errors occur is the option to continue the posting of error-free data records but to exclude erroneous data records from posting and to separate them in the *error stack,* which can be handled manually and completely separated from the running load process.

If an error is detected by an ABAP routine (see section 19.3.4) and the MONITOR table is filled, then the respective data record will not be written into the error stack per se but it will still be entered into the target structure. If the erroneous data record is to be separated in the error stack, the exception CX_RSROUT_SKIP_RECORD also needs to be started. For start routines, the number of the erroneous data record also needs to be transferred to the monitoring in the RECORD field.

For the handling of error-free data records of a request, there are two possible forms of error handling (see also figure 23–13):

- **Valid Records Update, No Reporting:** The request is posted but is still considered erroneous. Further processing in the staging can be made only after the quality status of the request has manually been categorized as error free.
- **Valid Records Update, Reporting Possible:** The request is posted and considered error free by the monitoring. The processing of data can be continued right after the load process.

This form of posting offers more flexibility insofar as erroneous data records do not "obstruct" the data flow of error-free data and that it can be handled and posted at a later time.

However, to separate only erroneous data records would not lead to the desired result because, especially with the entry of data in standard Data-Store Objects, the sequence in which data records are entered plays an important role since older field values in data fields can be overwritten by new ones.

For example, if data of a document was separated in an error stack because one field shows invalid content, the separated data record could not be reentered at random. After all, it may happen that in the meantime, the same data record is again written into the DataStore Object (this time with the correct field content and several other changes). If the returned data record is handled first and manually reentered into the DataStore Object, it would overwrite the new information that was meanwhile received with the old field values.

Semantic groups

The use of the error stack absolutely implies an option that after the separation of a data record, subsequent data records can be separated that generate the same key values in the target structure and would thus generate problems in keeping the correct sequence. The criteria according to which error-free data records are considered is defined in semantic groups in the respective data transfer process (see figure 23–14).

Figure 23–14

Definition of semantic groups in data transfer processes

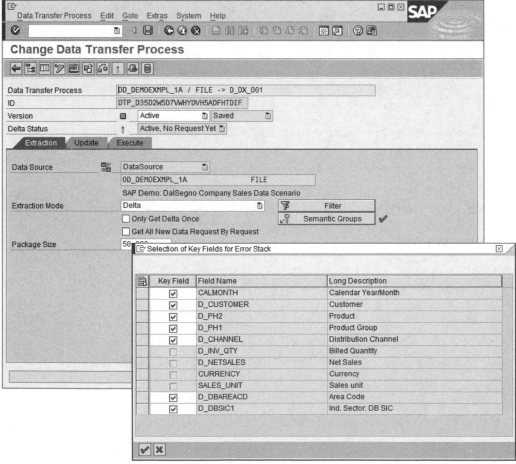

© SAP AG

If a data record makes it into the processing that has the same semantic key as another data record that is still in the error stack, then this data record will also be written into the error stack.

In an optimal case, the semantic key is derived from the key fields of the target structure (usually a DataStore Object). It is ensured that only error-free data records that show the same key as erroneous records are separated. A wrong sequence in the entry of erroneous and error-free data records is thus impossible.

However, the selection of fields that can be defined as key fields for the error stack is not derived from the target structure of the transformation but from the source structure, i.e., usually from the DataSource. If this has different fields, another key needs to be formed that can also prevent an incorrect processing sequence.

The definition of semantic groups not only ensures that the processing sequence for erroneous data records is kept correctly over several load processes (requests), it also ensures that subsequent data records are written into the error stack with the same semantic key, even from within a request if an erroneous data record precedes them—that is, even if the entry of data packages could be parallelized in the request.

Sorted reading from the PSA

This is possible for BW because the PSA data is not processed in the same way as it came into the PSA. The data is rather sorted according to a semantic key.

> By default, errors are entered into the error stack and are thus written sorted from the PSA. At first glance, this procedure is attractive from a content perspective, but it unnecessarily uses resources if there are usually no errors and this form of error handling could thus be omitted. Thus, you should always question the use of error handling in order to possibly avoid sorted reading from the PSA.

The error stack in which erroneous data records and subsequent records are written is technically another PSA table that is linked to the target structure with the same transformation as the original target structure (= DataSource). Thus, no further transformation needs to be defined; only a respective data transfer process needs to be created that explicitly reads the error stack of a DataSource. The creation of this so-called error DTP is made in the definition of the original data transfer process[170] (see figure 23–15).

Error DTP

---

170. Impossible with data transfer processes for direct access.

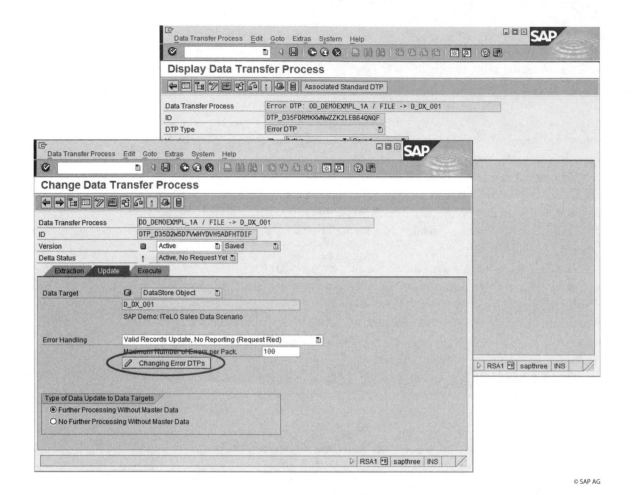

Figure 23–15
Creation of an error DTP

From then onward, the error DTP is found in the data transfer processes and can be used to jump into the error stack as far as data records in the error stack can be corrected.

24 Performance Tuning

In part, performance tuning was already discussed with data modeling (see chapter 7). The goal of performance tuning is to optimize reading and also writing access to data through the respective modeling of BasisCubes.

This chapter describes performance tuning of staging-related processes. BW 7 offers a fundamental tuning mechanism through the parallelization of partial steps within a process. For example, the rollup of aggregates of a BasisCube can be separated into several parallel steps that rollup in an aggregate.

Parallelization

The parallelization of independent partial steps within a process especially aims at tuning an individual process and depends on sufficient available system resources. If several processes are being executed already (e.g., several rollup processes on different BasisCubes), this is already one form of parallelization that requires accordingly comprehensive resources. For further parallelization of each single process, there might not be enough resources available, so the overall performance of all processes might even be decreased rather than increased through parallelization. Thus, do not consider parallelization to be a wonder drug but rather an option that needs to be used in a targeted and well-considered manner.

Options for parallelization were already known in BW release 3.x, but not all areas of the staging were covered and parallelization was subject to numerous restrictions. A particular downside to the "old" parallelization was that the execution of parallel processes was usually made via dialog processes that were controlled through a central batch process. Thus, the parallelization was subject to the usual restrictions of dialog processes and often aborted due to the restriction regarding the maximum runtime of work processes, among others.

With release 7, BW offers with a central batch management the option to control the parallelization in a standardized and integrated way; here, the parallelization is made through batch processes so that even processes with a long runtime will not cause any problems. The degree of parallelization can be separately defined for each process type in the batch manager, which can be reached through the management of the Data Warehousing Workbench or via transaction RSBATCH (see figure 24–1).

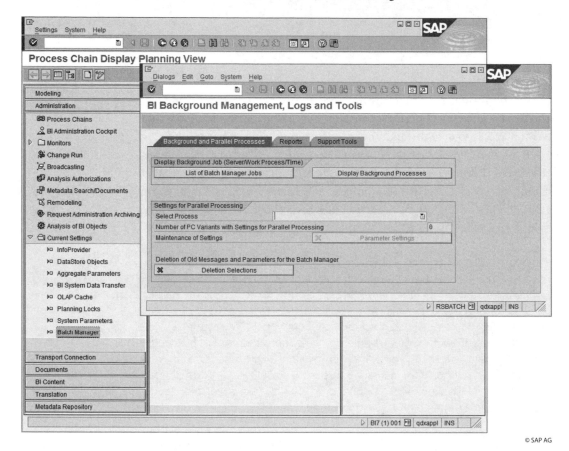

© SAP AG

The settings on parallelization relate to the execution of processes that are started manually (usually in the Data Warehousing Workbench). If process variants for process chains were created with the design of the standard operations (see chapter 28), then the degree of parallelization for the process can be defined in a dedicated way for each single process variable.[171]

The parallelization of the staging deserves particular consideration (i.e., the parallelization in the extractor and in the staging). With the parallelization of these processes, you need to keep in mind general conditions

171. This setting can also be made in the maintenance of the process variables.

beyond the configuration of the batch manager. Section 24.1 deals with the *parallelization of extraction and staging* in more detail.

Beyond parallelization, there are a number of options to improve the performance of staging-related processes. In the following sections we'll explain a range of selected tuning measures that refer to different levels of staging:

Further tuning options

- Input processing in the PSA
- Index management
- Compression of BasisCubes
- Activation of new data in DataStore Objects
- Aggregate management

Apart from specific measures that focus on the tuning of individual staging areas, it needs to be generally considered that log entries are made for all processing steps and for all requests in the tables RSMON* and RS*DONE. These tables grow rapidly with each new request, so after some time during operations, the management of request logs alone will take up considerable effort in terms of the staging. Thus, it makes sense to regularly archive and delete the logs in these tables. Details can be found in section 33.4.

24.1 Parallelization of Extraction and Staging

Given a minimum size, each request is composed of several data packages. These correspond with the "partial deliveries" in which a source system distributes the data of a complete load process. If the data records within a data package are considered a unit, they can be processed (from a technical perspective) in parallel to the data records of other data packages.

Since individual data packages can be processed, at least up to the PSA, completely isolated from each other, the *extraction from the source systems* offers ideal conditions for parallelization, so the performance improvement can be proportional to the degree of parallelization.

With the *execution of load processes* from the PSA into the data targets, similar parallelization options are offered, but depending on the transformation definition, the individual data packages cannot be processed if they are isolated from each other.[172] Technically, the parallelization needs to be defined differently too.

---

172. In the transformation, the use of global variables that are declared by CLASS-DATA does not allow for a parallelization (see section 19.1).

In this chapter, we'll cover the following topics:

- Parallelization in the extractor (section 24.1.1)
- Parallelization in the transformation (section 24.1.2)
- Parallelization through direct staging (section 24.1.3)

The basis for parallelization is the breakdown of a request into **data packages** that are processed in parallel. The formation of data packages is explained in section 24.1.4.

In section 24.1.5, we'll focus on the preconditions for a parallel posting of data.

Staging via **real-time data acquisition** takes on a special role when it comes to parallelization. Here, the concept of the parallelization of data packages does not apply since there are usually not so many data records in the synchronously executed processing units that they would need to be distributed to several data packages. The options for parallelization with real-time data acquisition are explained in section 24.1.6.

24.1.1   Parallelization in the Extractor

With the extraction of data in the source system, the respective data is not read entirely. Rather, whenever a certain number of records are read, the records are transferred to SAP BW after the termination of the read process as data packages within a load process.

Instead of waiting after the delivery of each package until SAP BW has completely processed it, the extractor can continue to read data and can send the next data packages to SAP BW even if it has not finished processing the previous package yet. The data packages are processed in parallel in BW.

In order to not burden BW too much with many data packages that are to be processed in parallel, you need to define an upper limit for parallel processes and the source systems need to comply with this when transferring new data packages. If the upper limit is reached,[173] the source system will hold the extraction until BW signals that one of the open processing activities is terminated.

---

173. Parallelization is based on the precondition that the extraction of data in a source system is faster than the posting in BW. Practice has shown that this precondition is usually met.

Figure 24–2 shows the parallelization in the extractor interacting with the BW staging engine. The figure refers to an upper limit of three parallel processes and assumes that the processing of a package is terminated with the posting in the PSA (more information on the respective options can be found in section 24.1.2).

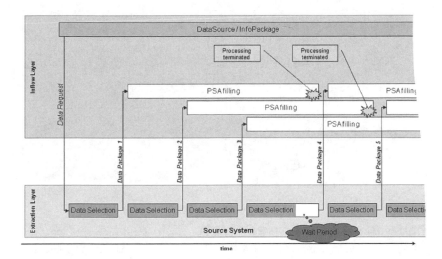

Figure 24–2

Parallelization in the extractor

The degree of parallelization—i.e., the maximum number of processes to post data into the PSA—is defined in the *extraction layer of the respective source system* and not in the BW system.[174]

Degree of parallelization

For SAP ERP and BW systems,[175] you define the number of parallel processes the extractor is to generate in SAP BW when you're customizing the (transaction SBIW) in the respective source system (see figure 24–3).

SAP ERP

SAP BW

The control parameters are maintained separately for each client in the source system (i.e., for each logical system). The logical system for which parameters are maintained is defined in the table key in the Src. System (source system) field. If no parameters are maintained for a logical system, a maximum of two to three processes will be assumed by default.

From all parameters, only the entry in the Max. Proc. field is relevant for the degree of parallelization. Here you enter the maximum number of processes the extractor may start in parallel.

---

174. For the extraction from third-party ETL tools, you should refer to the documentation of the respective supplier.

175. As far as data is transferred in a data mart scenario from one BW system to another.

Figure 24–3
Control parameters for data transfer from SAP source systems

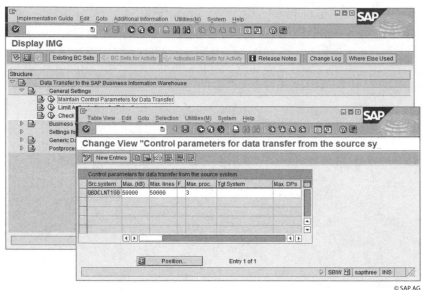

© SAP AG

The control parameters for data transfer that are stored in the BW system only apply if BW acts as a source system for other BW systems. Also, these settings apply if BW extracts from the Myself system, i.e.. from itself (e.g., with the further processing of data from DataStore Objects).

Flat file With the definition of the metadata, settings for flat files need to be made manually in the inflow layer—except with SAP ERP systems that dispose of metadata themselves. The settings on parallelization are similar; they do not need to be stored in the flat file source system but in BW.

You need to consider that the parallelization can be controlled via either the BW 7 batch manager or the old system of the previous BW releases (not applicable for 3.x DataSources). With the new form of controlling, the degree of parallelization can be defined directly in the batch manager (process type LOAD_NEWDS) or in the maintenance of the InfoPackage (see figure 24–4).

If the number of parallel processes is set to the value 1, it does *not* deactivate parallelization. Instead, the batch manager is in this case avoided and the extraction is made synchronously (with the option *Synchronous PSA Load*). An "old" DataSource for direct staging is always loaded synchronously; the batch manager will not be used.

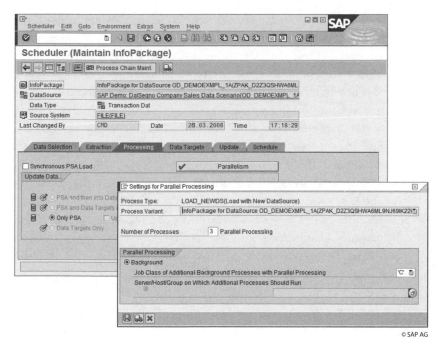

Figure 24–4
InfoPackage: settings for processing

With synchronous loading, BW goes back to the old controlling that was still used for parallelization with the extraction of flat files in release 3.x. The parallelization of flat files cannot be controlled explicitly. Instead, the control parameters are applied that are defined for the extraction from the BW system (see figure 24–3). The control parameters must be stored in the BW system and not with the flat file system.

DB connect
UD connect
Web services

The synchronous filling of the PSA is also applicable with DB connect, UD connect, and web services. For these DataSources, the Myself system settings apply for the degree of parallelization, but there is no alternative to using the batch manager.

Differentiability of parallelization

The control parameter setting for data transfer in an SAP source system applies for a complete logical source system (client). For the extraction layer, this means that the setting is applicable independently from the extracted DataSource and the type of extraction (full/delta).

This means that for the inflow layer, the settings apply to all BW systems that extract data from a source system. If several BW systems with different capabilities extract data from the same SAP ERP system, the settings will have to be oriented toward the weakest system.

Especially the control parameters in the BW system are applicable both for the transfer of data to other BW systems and for the extraction from flat files (synchronous extraction), DB connect, UD connect, and web services; thus, they partially refer to their own system and partially to other systems.

There is not much difference in the control parameters and this is further increased because the control parameters are applicable per request (load process). If. for example, a maximum of 4 parallel processes are permitted and 5 load processes are executed in parallel, this can generate up to 20 processes in SAP BW.

Thus, the limitation of parallel processes in the control parameters is only conditionally suited to limit the load for the BW system. The control parameters rather need to always be considered in combination with the actually executed load processes.

Since extraction processes in standard operations of SAP BW are usually parallelized, the interaction of parallel processes/load processes in BW is an extremely complex system. Therefore, the ideal setting cannot be foreseen but needs to be found out step-by-step during standard operations.[176]

24.1.2   Parallelization in the Transformation

Since BW release 7 offers for the first time with transformation and data transfer processes a central option to control the processing between the individual layers, this is also the first time the parallelization is controlled centrally.

Thus, it is irrelevant for the configuration from what data sources a transformation receives its data and into which data target the data is written. For example, the parallelization in the extraction layer does not have any impact on the parallelization of the transformation process in BW since the data source (in this case, the PSA) is extracted separately.

The degree at which a data transfer process is parallelized is defined in the batch manager settings (see figure 24–1). The respective process type is DTP_LOAD. Alternatively to configuring the general settings for the parallelization of data transfer processes, the degree of parallelization can be defined for a single data transfer process. This variable is selected for the use of DTP in process chains (see figure 24–5).

---

176. The testing of new settings can only be conditionally isolated (i.e., on test systems). Truly clear results can usually be found only in the real environment of the production system.

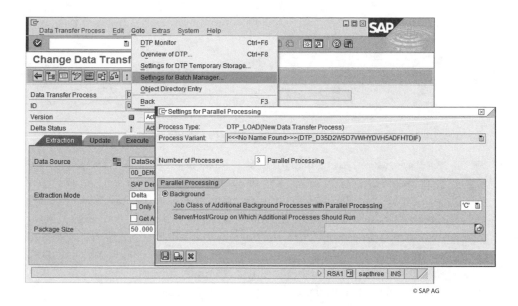

© SAP AG

The extraction from the data source is always made serially; however, the processing of the packages is made in parallel. The processing of a data package is considered terminated when it has gone through the transformation and is entered in the respective target structure (see figure 24–6).

Figure 24–5

Parallelization in data transfer processes

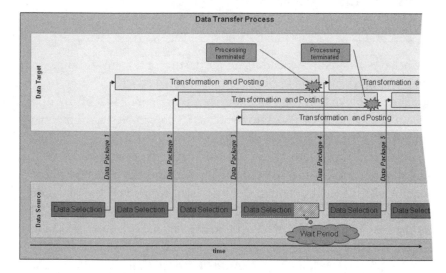

Figure 24–6

Parallelization of the transformation

You should keep in mind that not every transformation can be parallelized freely and the processing needs to be serialized instead. This is especially necessary if, in the transformation, global variables with CLASS-DATA are declared to exchange static variable content between several data packages (see section 19.1)

> The parallelization of write accesses in BasisCubes is subject to conditions for Oracle database systems. Please make sure you read section 24.1.5.

24.1.3 Parallelization through Direct Staging

Unlike with the transformation, the extraction and the subsequent processing are closely linked in BW when it comes to direct staging, and they cannot be considered isolated from each other. The package sizes that are created by the extractor during the data transfer to the PSA are also a factor for further processing. Also, the degree of parallelization that is applied to writing into the PSA is significant and it cannot be changed in BW. Still, BW influences performance tuning by defining how the interaction of PSA and data targets is designed.

The respective settings are part of the definitions for the processing of an InfoPackage (see section 21.3.3) and they are referred to as posting options. The following ***posting options*** are available:

- Only PSA (and Update Subsequently in Data Targets)
- PSA and Then into Data Targets (by Package)
- Only Data Target
- PSA and Data Targets in Parallel (by Package)

BW behaves differently depending on the posting option. In addition, each posting option can create its own unique problems.

Only PSA (and Update Subsequently in Data Targets)

The posting option *Only PSA* was shown in figure 24–2. Further processing of data from the PSA into the data targets can be started manually from the PSA or from the load monitor.

However, further processing into the data targets should usually be started automatically instead of manually. For this purpose, the posting option *Only PSA* can be combined with the subsequent update in the data targets. In this case, the posting of data in the PSA is executed in parallel but the subsequent update of all extracted data packages into the data targets is made in a serialized process (see figure 24–7).

The posting option *Only PSA (and Update Subsequently in Data Targets)* is especially suitable for system environments that focus on very fast extraction and where the subsequent posting of data into data targets is secondary.

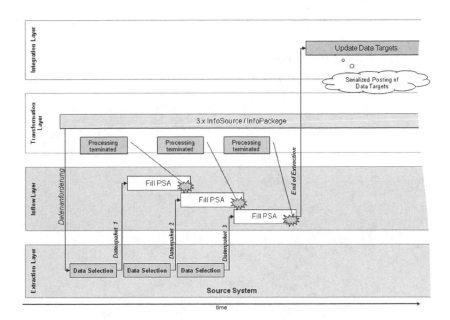

Figure 24–7
Parallelization with direct staging: Only PSA (and Update Subsequently in Data Targets)

At the same time, this posting option aims at burdening BW itself in the least possible way by serializing the processing. Thus, this posting option is particularly suitable *for BW systems with weak hardware* or volatile utilization.

This resource-friendly handling of the BW system results in an extremely disadvantageous overall runtime for the extraction and staging since the runtime-intense staging process is not parallelized. For systems with powerful hardware, the use of the posting option *PSA and Data Targets in Parallel (by Package),* which also guarantees a fast extraction from the source systems, should thus be considered.

The posting option *PSA and Then into Data Targets (by Package)* aims at improving the total runtime of extraction and staging by parallelizing the posting package by package.

PSA and Then into Data Targets (by Package)

For this purpose, directly after the posting of a package in the PSA, the execution of the transfer rules and the posting of the data package into the data targets is started. Technically, another dialog process is started that first rereads the package from the PSA and then processes it. The processing of a data package is considered terminated only when the processing activity, including posting, is terminated.

Compared to the posting option *Only PSA (and Update Subsequently in Data Targets),* the overall runtime of extraction and staging is significantly increased. However, the limit on the degree of parallelization can result in wait periods in the source system, so the extraction process may take longer (see figure 24–8).

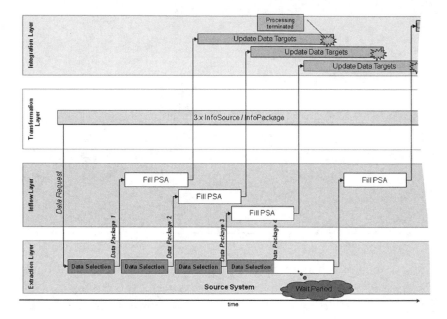

The posting option *PSA and Then into Data Targets (by Package)* is suitable if the overall runtime of extraction and staging is the focus and the time periods on the source system allow for wait periods.

In this case, the burden on the BW system is higher with the parallelized processing activities than with the posting option *Only PSA (and Update Subsequently in Data Targets),* but overall it is still limited by the degree of parallelization.

Only Data Target   The posting option *Only Data Targets* simplifies the load process by omitting the PSA. With this option, all data packages are transferred to the integration layer directly after the extraction without being stored in the PSA (see figure 24–9). The processing of a data package is considered terminated with the posting of the package into the data target.

The omission of the PSA can reduce the BW system load. However, it is mostly felt in the area of storage requirements. From a runtime perspective, the posting of data in the PSA plays only a subordinate role.

The disadvantage of this posting option is that there is no assurance of the quality of the data in the PSA. If errors occur, the data will have to be extracted again, which may cause problems, especially with the use of delta procedures.

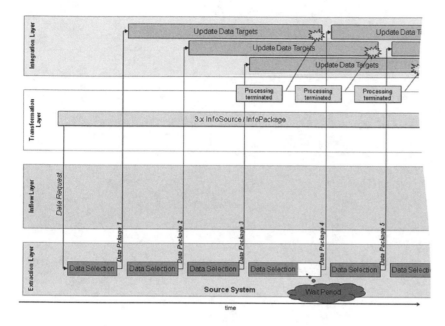

Figure 24–9

Parallelization with direct staging: Data Targets Only

The posting option *Only Data Targets* is thus particularly suited for internal workflows in the BW system (e.g., subsequent posting of data from DataStore Objects) and should not be used for the extraction from source systems.

The posting option *PSA and Data Targets in Parallel (by Package)* aims at optimizing the extraction period and at the same time optimizing the total runtime of extraction and staging.

PSA and Data Targets in Parallel (by Package)

As with the posting option *PSA and Then into Data Targets (by Package)*, the posting of data packages in the PSA is followed by the subsequent processing of the data packages. However, the processing of the data package is already considered terminated with its posting into the PSA.

The limitation on the degree of parallelization thus refers only to the posting of data packages in the PSA, while the parallelization of the subsequent processing is limited only by the number of free dialog processes (see figure 24–10).

The parallel posting into the PSA and into the data targets can result in a significant time saving for the staging; however, BW is further burdened. Since the posting into the PSA and the processing of data packages might compete with free dialog processes in extreme cases, the time schedule of the individual processes can be hard to trace.

Figure 24–10

Parallelization with direct staging: PSA and Data Targets in Parallel (by Package)

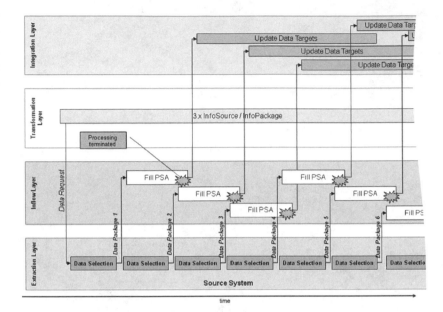

As with the posting option *Only PSA,* this posting option is suitable for the extraction from company-wide and time-critical source systems. However, for large data volume, ***powerful hardware*** needs to be used to cope with the parallelization of the processing activities.

24.1.4 Packaging

Depending on the size, requests are broken down into several data packages with the extraction from the source systems, from the PSA, or from the change log. These data packages form the unit in which data is parallelized during processing.

Since the data package is processed completely in the main memory, the size of the data package has a direct effect on the main memory requirement of the overall system (and the system load). The smaller the data package, the smaller the main memory requirement (and vice versa).

Additionally, smaller package sizes enable parallel processing of several packages even for small data deliveries. Such data deliveries might otherwise consist of one single package and would not be parallelized at all.

On the other hand, the percentage of internal management effort compared to the overall processing period for a data package significantly increases the smaller the data package. Also, the compression of data with the posting in BasisCubes is very low with small data packages.[177] Considering the processing period, the management effort, and the compression of data, the processing performance of a data package increases as the package size gets bigger (given that there is sufficient main memory).

The optimal size of a data package can thus not generally be defined for a system; it is the trade-off between parallelization and management effort that needs to be identified individually for each processing activity.

When the package sizes are defined, extraction and data transfer processes need to be considered individually. For data transfer processes, the package sizes are basically defined with the definition of a data transfer process no matter which data source they are to be read from (see figure 24–11).

Package sizes for data transfer processes

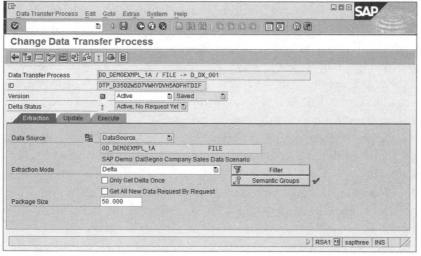

Figure 24–11
Package sizes for data transfer processes

Thus, with the execution of data transfer processes, the package sizes of requests in the PSA and in the change log are irrelevant since with the extraction from the PSA, other package sizes are formed.

---

177. When data is transferred to BasisCubes, only the data within the data package is compressed. When writing into the cube, no further compression takes place. Another compression can only take place by compressing the BasisCube.

Package sizes with direct staging

It is different with direct staging where extraction and subsequent processing in BW are closely linked. Here, the package sizes that are formed by the extraction layer in the PSA are also used for further processing in BW. Depending on the source system type from which data is extracted, the settings need to be defined in different places.

These source-system-related settings are to be considered maximum sizes that will serve as general protection from packages that are too large. Optionally, the package sizes can be decreased specifically for each single DataSource.

SAP BW

The source-system-specific definition of the package size for SAP ERP and SAP BW source systems is made in the control parameters for the data transfer that also defines the parallelization degree (see figure 24–3).

The definition of the *package size* aims on the one hand at not further burdening the source system with large data packages during extraction and on the other hand at not burdening the subsequent processing in BW with too many *data records* per package.[178] Package size and record number are not completely independent from each other, but combinations are possible where a very large number of data records is contained in relatively small packages (low record width) or where very few data records generate very large packages (high record width).

For this reason, with the control parameters for data transfer during extraction from SAP ERP systems, the maximum size is indicated both in kilobytes and in data records. The value that results in the strongest limitation for the extraction is relevant (i.e., the smallest value for the respective DataSource). By default, 100,000 records or 10,000 KB per data package are applied.

As with the setting on the parallelization degree, the definition of the package size applies to all supplied BW systems of an SAP ERP or SAP BW system as well as for the Myself system of a BW system.

Flat file

Unlike with SAP ERP systems, the storage strain in SAP BW is only secondary. The focus is instead on the number of data records that define the runtime of the subsequent processing. Thus, for the extraction of flat files, the transaction RSCUSTV6 enables customizing to indicate the maximum permitted size of data packages in the form of a record number (see figure 24–12).

---

178. From a performance perspective, it is crucial for the further processing of data how many data records are updated. In comparison, the creation of new data records is so important that the data volume behind a package can be neglected.

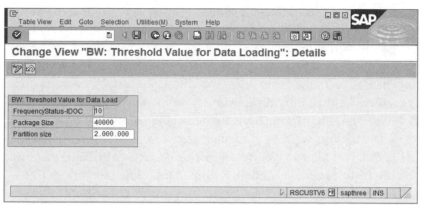

Figure 24–12
Control parameter for data transfer from flat files

As for the settings on the degree of parallelization, the settings on the package size refer to each individual extraction procedure. The main memory requirements of extractions executed in parallel thus require in BW a multiple of the defined package size.

The same applies to UD connect and DataSources of the SOAP connection. For these DataSources, the respective settings in the transaction RSCUSTV6 define the package size.

UD connect
SOAP connection

Specifically for the DB connect, since BW 7, the transaction to define package sizes is RSCUSTV18.

DB connect

The source-system-related maximum size of data packages provides a general protection from data packages that are too large, and as such it should be as generous as possible. The specific tuning should be made only with the selection of the package size for specific DataSources.

DataSource-specific package size

Even though the DataSource-specific package size applies to all Info-Packages of a DataSource, the respective settings are made in the InfoPackage maintenance for any freely chosen InfoPackage (see figure 24–13).

It can make sense to reduce a source-system-related maximum size by reducing a DataSource's specific package size:

- In a specific load process during transformation, a large number of data records can be generated with rule groups from a single data record (see section 19.3). Thus, huge packages can be created during transformation that are to be avoided by packages that are set particularly small in the extraction.

■   If a load process generally supplies relatively few data records to BW, the processing in BW might not be parallelized since all extracted data packages fit into one single package. Smaller data packages enable optimization of such load processes by parallelization. For this reason, especially with the use of delta procedures, the package sizes should be set smaller than with full uploads.

■   Depending on the complexity of the staging process, the processing of a data package can take particularly long. Depending on the parallelization procedure in BW, the processing is executed in dialog processes and their maximum runtime is limited by a time-out period. If there are problems for specific DataSources with the time-out, then the DataSource-specific package size can be decreased.[179]

Figure 24-13

Define DataSource-specific package sizes

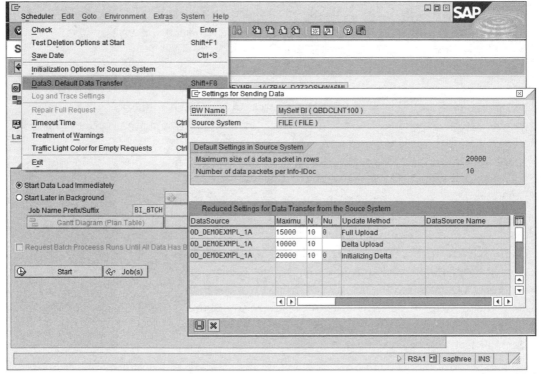

© SAP AG

---

179. If time-out problems occur more often and for several DataSources, this should be taken as an indication that the source-system-specific package size was defined too large.

24.1.5 Preconditions for the Parallelization

For each form of parallelization, the structure in the database system needs to be designed to enable parallel write access for the processing activities. Usually, this can be done only through the selection of the primary key or the partitioning; the only exception is the parallelization of data transfer processes that write into BasisCubes under an Oracle database.

The fact tables of BasisCubes do not use a clear primary key, so several data records with the same key can easily be pasted. Also, the indexes on the fact table can be modified without problems with parallel write accesses from the database system.

Only for Oracle database systems, a bitmapped index on the fact table is created in addition to the usual B* tree indexes.[180] With an update, this cannot be locked per line but only per partition, so parallel write accesses to the fact table can result in lock conflicts and program aborts.

Lock conflicts with bitmapped indexes

By the way, this applies only to regular BasisCubes. For transactional cubes, several write accesses in parallel need to be made in a BasisCube so that these cubes are created without the bitmapped index.

For regular BasisCubes, the lock conflict problem can be circumvented by deleting and re-creating the indexes immediately before the execution of the load processes (see section 30.1.7).

The deletion of indexes results in a drastic decrease in response times for the data analysis. This is one of the reasons the loading of new data and the data analysis should not overlap in time. In practice, load processes are often designed so that all load processes that are finished by the start of the analysis automatically delete and rebuild the indexes while all (extraordinary) load processes during the analysis periods process their data packages serially.

24.1.6 Parallelization in RDA Scenarios

With the use of real-time data acquisition, the concept of the parallelization of data packages does not usually apply because the complete request with numerous data packages isn't processed, only data records that are read from a DataSource within the short extraction intervals.

The number of these synchronously processed data records is usually not so high that several data packages could be filled. Often only part of a

---

180. DB2 UDB databases use bitmapped indexes too. However, these are not created persistently but dynamically and thus they do not cause any lock conflicts.

data package needs to be processed, and in any case, it will not be enough for a successful parallelization with the standard means of BW.

If a parallelization of processing is to be enforced despite the lack of options in BW, this can be enabled by creating and parallelizing processing units along content criteria. Technically, a single data transfer process for real-time data acquisition will no longer extract the delta information from the PSA; it will extract several data transfer processes that define their respective "work package" through filters (see section 20.2).

These single, so-called split deltas need to be disjunctive, but together they have to map all data records that are to be processed. Thus, for each data transfer process, smaller data quantities can be processed with high performance. The same DataStore Object or several DataStore Objects can be filled over all data transfer processes.

> To avoid lock conflicts and problems with adherence to the correct sequence of the posting, the filter conditions do not only need to be disjunctive regarding the PSA fields but also regarding the key fields of the DataStore Objects into which the data is posted.

In the definition of the daemon for the real-time data acquisition, all data transfer processes to which data was assigned need to be added for the parallelization of the transformation.

24.2 Inbound Processing in the PSA

The PSA are flat table structures that are defined per DataSource in the ABAP Dictionary. With reading from and writing into these simple table structures, the limit to performance is basically defined by the data volume that is stored in the PSA table.

A performance increase in the area of the PSA can be achieved by keeping the size of PSA tables relatively small (for deletion of requests from the PSA, see section 33.3). Depending on the database system, the flat table structures of the PSA cope with several million data records without experiencing a noticeable performance decrease.

Partitioning of the PSA

If very large data quantities are written into a PSA table (several million data records per day), without an adequate deletion of old requests being enabled, partitioning of the PSA tables can produce relief.

For the database system *DB2/UDB,* this partitioning means index clustering via the request ID of the PSA table. The default settings are used for the index clustering, so there are no options for further tuning.

For the database systems *Oracle* and *DB2/400,* the partitioning method is range partitioning. With the use of DB2/400, the partitioning first needs to be activated through the RSADMIN parameter DB4_PSA_PARTITIONING = 'X'.[181] For Oracle databases, range partitioning is automatically used.

Here, the partition sizes are controlled by BW by changing the value of the partitioning field (PARTNO) according to a number of data records to be predefined. The setting for how many data records are predefined before a new partition for the PSA table is created is made using the transaction RSCUSTV6 (see figure 24–14).

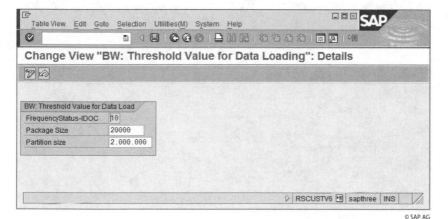

Figure 24–14
Partitioning of PSA tables

© SAP AG

The setting on the partition size for PSA tables applies systemwide to all PSA tables. The limitation of this setting to individual PSA tables is not possible. If no partition size is indicated, the default value 1,000,000 is applied.

24.3 Index Management

Numerous indexes are stored in the fact tables of BasisCubes and their aggregates. These indexes are a precondition for a high-performance execution of the data analysis on BasisCubes.

---

181. Further information can be found under the reference 815186 in the SAP Service Marketplace.

However, for write access, these indexes need to be modified by the database system, which can result in substantial performance losses. To accelerate write access in BasisCubes, it is possible to delete indexes of the respective cube and re-create them after the write access is terminated.

There are two different options to delete indexes: deleting them in the cube management and deleting them in the process chain.

Index deletion in the cube management
The indexes of a BasisCube can be deleted in the cube management under the *Performance* tab (see figure 24–15).

Figure 24–15

Deletion of indexes for BasisCubes

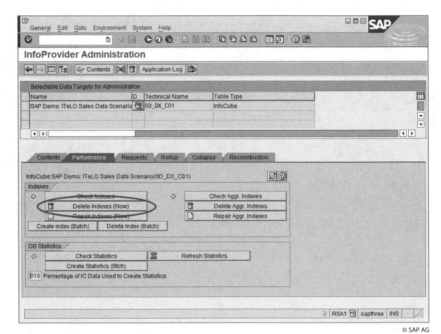

© SAP AG

When you delete indexes in the cube management, all indexes of a Basis-Cube as well as its aggregates are deleted with the exception of the primary key of the compressed fact table.

Deleting indexes prior to posting new data makes sense only if the subsequently necessary rebuild of the indexes does not take more time than is gained with the deletion itself. This is usually the case if one of the following conditions are true:

- BasisCubes are initially filled with a large amount of legacy data (e.g., with initialization of the delta procedure).
- A delta upload that writes more than 10 to 15 percent of new data into the uncompressed fact table takes place.

This option for deleting indexes is a relic from old BW releases, and given its sweeping effect, it is used in only a few cases without substantial disadvantages. However, there are no particular advantages that result from the radical deletion of all indexes since all processes that would benefit from this (rollup, compression) handle the deletion of relevant indexes in their own way.

A significantly better-suited procedure to delete indexes comes from process chains, which are explained in detail with the description of standard operations. The deletion of indexes is explicitly explained in section 30.1.7.

Index deletion in process chains

With process chains, the deletion of indexes comprises only the indexes of the uncompressed fact table of a cube. These indexes should—given regular compression—be empty or very small, and thus there should be no problem with the subsequent rebuild of indexes.

In the following sections, when we refer to index deletion, it is assumed that indexes are deleted through process chains, not through the cube management.

24.4 Compression of BasisCubes

Compression is a single process that cannot be parallelized and that moves the data of a BasisCube on a record level from its F fact table to the E fact table.

Because the E fact table is updated on a record-by-record basis, the compression can be slower than, for example, the posting of the same data in the BasisCube. Each data record is reviewed to determine whether an insert or an update of an existing record is necessary.

In the very specific case that all records that are to be posted in a Basis-Cube are disjunctive, the compression of the update on a record level can be basically omitted and a significantly better-performing array insert can be executed instead.

There usually are disjunctive data records if data records are entered into a BasisCube on the transaction data detailing level (e.g., record number, record position). Basically, the precondition is *never* met with Basis-Cubes with noncumulative values.

To configure BW to assume that disjunctive data records are included with compression of a BasisCube and to use a fast array insert, in the transaction SE16 in the table RSDCUBE, put an X in the COMP_DISJ field (see figure 24–16).

INFOCUBE	BWAPPL	ACTIV	PROTECFL	INFOAREA	NCUMTIM	BCTCOMP	CUBETYPE	COMP_DISJ	CUBESUBTY	SVRESTR	SVRESTRNO	SVRESTRGLOB	SVRESTRSEL	SVSUPP
0D_DX_C02	BW	X		0D_DEMOEXMPL			B							X
0D_DX_C03	BW	X		0D_DEMOEXMPL			B							X
0D_DX_C04	BW	X		0D_DEMOEXMPL			B							X
0D_DX_M01	BW	X		0D_DEMOEXMPL			M							
0D_FI_C01	BW	X		0D_FIAP			B	X						
0D_FI_C02		X		0D_FIAR			B							
0D_IB_01	BW	X		0D_IB			B							
0D_IB_02	BW	X		0D_IB	0CALMONTH		B							
0D_PP_C01	BW	X		0D_PP			B							
0D_PL_C01	BW	X		0D_MMPUR			B							
0D_SC_C03		X		0D_SD_GEN			B							

Data Browser: Table RSDCUBE Select Entries   86

© SAP AG

Figure 24–16
Compression of disjunctive records using the example of the cube 0D_FI_C01

If the data records of a BasisCube are thus marked as disjunctive, BW will omit all (time-consuming) checks when executing the compression. If there are no disjunctive data records despite the assumption, this will lead to a compression abort from the database system.

> If there are disjunctive data records in a cube, the compression will not be a compression (in its true meaning) but only a data shift from the F fact table into the E fact table. This makes sense when Oracle and DB2/UDB database systems are in use because their E fact tables come with suitable partitioning and bitmapped indexes. For any other database systems, the compression of disjunctive data records is a complete waste of time.

24.5 Activation of New Data in DataStore Objects

Given the simple table structure of the tables of DataStore Objects[182] (active data, activation queue) write accesses are well performing and cannot be optimized any further.

For standard DataStore Objects, with the start of the activation queue, further resources are used. To optimize the activation, which might be very time consuming, there is a range of options:

---

182. The change log is a table in the PSA.

- Simplification of delta determination
- Limitation of the main memory requirement during activation
- Avoiding SID determination
- Abandoning optimizer statistics
- Clustering of DataStore Objects

The tuning options will be explained in the following sections. Keep in mind also that, with the partitioning of the PSA, in section 24.2 we described another influencing factor on the performance of the activation since the change log that is written with the activation of new data in a DataStore Object is in fact a PSA table.

24.5.1 Simplification of Delta Determination

With the activation of new data in a standard DataStore Object, BW compares each single record of the activation queue with the active data of the DataStore Object.

Usually, this comparison and the resulting generation of delta information in the change log is inevitable from a content perspective. It needs to be assumed that when data records are posted into a DataStore Object that these data records already exists with identical key fields in the active data of the DataStore Object. In exceptional cases, however, DataStore Objects are provided only with data records where the keys do not exist in the active data of the DataStore Object (i.e., there are disjunctive data records as described in section 24.4).

In this case, the comparison of each single data record with the active data of the DataStore Object takes too much time (since it is redundant); after all, the data of the activation queue is only added to the active data, without a single existing data record being changed.

To improve the performance in this case, BW can omit the comparison on single record level and execute a single record insert or an array insert instead. For this purpose, the option *Unique Data Records* is provided in the properties of the DataStore Object (see figure 24–17). Depending on the database system and the DataStore Object, the required time frame for the activation of new data in DataStore Objects can be improved by 10 to 30 percent.

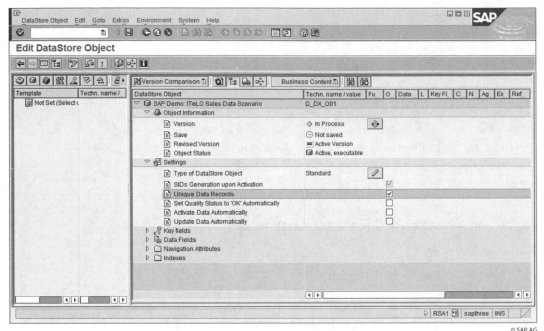

Figure 24–17 *Provision of DataStore Objects with unique data records*

Unfortunately, the option regarding the unique data records is defined as a property of the respective DataStore Object and thus applies to all load processes of the DataStore Object. The individual setting of this option for single InfoPackages is not possible. You should thus carefully consider whether the option can really apply to all load processes of the DataStore Object.

The decision whether a DataStore Object is provided only once with each key needs to be made individually and case by case. You need to ensure that, with the extraction, a DataStore Object defined as such is really only provided with unique data records. If this determination is violated, the activation of new data in DataStore Objects will be aborted. In the worst case, the property needs to be deactivated, and luckily this can even be done when the DataStore Object is filled with data.

24.5.2   Limitation of the Main Memory Requirement

With the activation of new data in a standard DataStore Object, BW tries to manage the data of the activation queue in the main memory and to thus accelerate the comparison of active data with the new data. This is only possible if the activation queue is accordingly small (less than 1 million data records). If this is not the case, the activation will be made in several steps, which results in a significantly worse activation performance.

To keep the data of the activation queue small, new data in DataStore Objects should be activated as often as possible. Possibly, the activation in standard operations should take place several times between single load processes if the data of several requests would generate too much data volume.

24.5.3 Avoiding SID Determination

For the data analysis, you need to ensure that there are respective SID values for the stored characteristics values. For this reason, with the posting of data in BasisCubes and DataStore Objects, corresponding tests on the SID tables of the InfoObjects need to be made to possibly abort the process activities or to generate master data with default settings.

This testing and master data activation activity takes up a noticeable part of the processing time for the activation of new data. Since, in many cases, DataStore Objects are only used as objects for the staging and not for the analysis, this test is by default not made with DataStore Objects.

To make DataStore Objects available to the analysis, a determination needs to be made in the DataStore Object's settings (see figure 10–6). However, this setting should be used only if DataStore Objects have a clear role during data analysis and navigation attributes of the characteristics are part of the data analysis.

If data of a DataStore Object or characteristics values are analyzed only in exceptional cases and if their navigation attributes are not part of the analysis, then the determination of SIDs should absolutely be avoided.

24.5.4 Abandoning Optimizer Statistics

To realize the staging function, accesses to a DataStore Object can very easily be characterized by the fact that reading is always done via the primary key of the involved database tables (with activation) or that a full scan of the tables is made (with extraction from active data).

For these operations, the available primary keys are sufficient. However, in numerous cases, it makes sense to optimize other accesses to a

DataStore Object—e.g., the targeted reading of data records via self-defined indexes (see section 7.2.2).

By default, BW assumes that a DataStore Object is used for the data analysis and that accesses are to be made via indexes. As a consequence, BW assumes that the optimizer statistics (see section 7.2.4) must be current, and after each activation of new data, it updates the optimizer statistics of the tables for new and active data of the DataStore Object.

This activity is hardly relevant for small DataStore Objects, but with large DataStore Objects (especially if they have secondary indexes), this can take up a significant portion of the activation time. If in fact a DataStore Object is used only for the staging, this update of the database statistics could be abandoned.

The update of the optimizer statistics can be suppressed using the program RSSM_SUPPRESS_STATISTICS (see figure 24–18).

Figure 24–18

Suppression of optimizer statistics with DataStore Objects

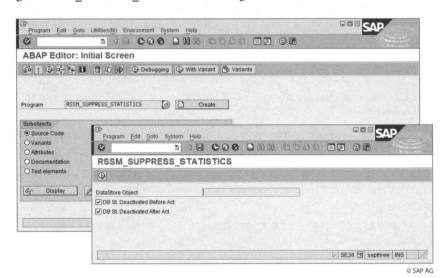

© SAP AG

With this program, an entry in the field ANALYZE_SID of the table RSODS-SETTINGS is filled. It gives a quick overview of which DataStore Objects optimizer statistics are updated and which are not.[183]

---

183. The value 0 indicates that optimizer statistics are updated. The value −1 marks the suppression of the update.

24.5.5 Clustering of DataStore Objects

Especially for the database system DB2/UDB,[184] SAP BW offers an option to cluster DataStore Objects (see section 7.3.2). Here, the activation queue and the change log as well as the PSA are provided with an index cluster on the request ID. Write-optimized DataStore Objects are also clustered in this way because they principally map the PSA structure. This form of clustering is preset and cannot be changed, and thus there is no option to influence performance.

However, the clustering of tables for active data of standard DataStore Objects and DataStore Objects for direct writing is different. By default, these are not clustered but can be provided with a user-defined multi-dimensional clustering (MDC) (see figure 24–19). Data analysis and other read accesses as well as the activation of new data can benefit from this option.

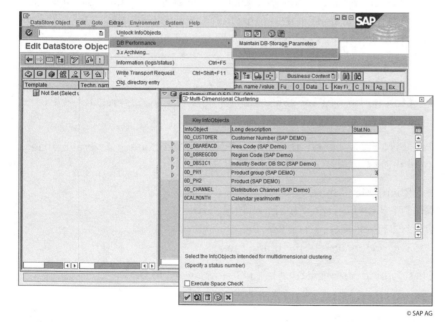

Figure 24–19

Multidimensional clustering of DataStore Objects

© SAP AG

If DataStore Objects are also to be used for data analysis or other accesses to active data, then the MDC dimensions (that are only defined by key

---

184. It was announced with the development of BW 7 range partitioning of DataStore Objects would be implemented for Oracle database systems. This feature was not implemented.

fields of the DataStore Object) are formed from only those fields that specify the access. Here, you need to consider that these are not very selective fields (see section 7.3.2). Possibly, the indexing of fields with a B* tree index might be better suited than multidimensional clustering since indexing via B* tree index is especially suited for selective fields and can also be used for data fields (see section 7.2.2).

If multidimensional clustering is used "only" to improve performance with the activation of new data, it will be enough to only add to the MDC dimensions a good selection of key fields that will result in good block sizes given their selectivity.

24.6 Management of Aggregates

Given their compressed and redundant databases, aggregates are suited to improve performance of the data analysis. However, during staging, aggregates need to be managed, and this binds system resources. The management processes are as follows:

- Initial creation of new aggregates
- Rollup of existing aggregates
- Modification of master data attributes in the aggregates with the change run

There is a range of options for the optimization of one or several management processes.

- Rollup hierarchies
- The delta procedure of the change run
- The block size for rebuild
- The pre-analysis of the filling process

These options are explained in the following sections.

24.6.1 Rollup Hierarchy

With the creation of aggregates, all required data is read from the fact table of the respective BasisCube. Depending on the size of the BasisCube, reading the fact table can be very time consuming. Reading the fact table is not really required, because there might already be other aggregates that could be used as a database.

For this reason, with the ***rollup,*** the ***initial filling of new aggregates,*** and the ***change run,*** BW first tries to find aggregates that already exist and from which the aggregate to be handled could be derived.

To efficiently use the option to derive aggregates from each other, BW *automatically* creates dependencies to the aggregates for each BasisCube and determines the optimal sequence in which aggregates are derived from each other.

The thus determined rollup hierarchy cannot be influenced manually and can be displayed via the menu item *Goto→Aggregate Tree* (see figure 24–20).

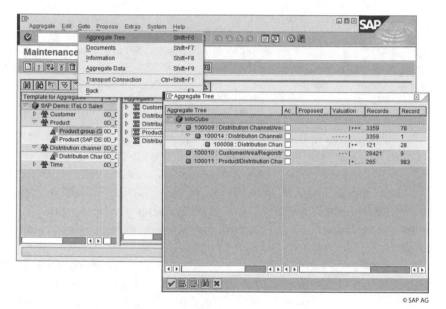

Figure 24–20

Display of the rollup hierarchy of aggregates

This form of optimization that BW makes automatically can be substantially supported if it is considered with the creation of the aggregates that a rollup hierarchy can possibly be determined. Then, aggregates can always be derived from other aggregates if their characteristics form a subset of an existing attribute. A subset is also given if attributes can be derived from a basic characteristic.

In some cases, it may even make sense to create large aggregates on purpose so that they could serve as basis aggregates for the creation of subordinate aggregates. However, even these aggregates should be smaller than the BasisCube itself by at least the factor 10.

24.6.2   Delta Procedure of the Change Run

In the early releases of BW, the execution of a change run resulted in the complete rebuild of all affected aggregates. This procedure was adequate for cases where a majority of hierarchies/attributes were modified. However, in cases where only a small part of the master data was changed, the complete rebuild was very disadvantageous from a performance perspective.

For this reason, a delta procedure has been specifically implemented for the *change run.* With this procedure, the changed master data is handled sequentially and the old content[185] is posted negatively and the new content is posted positively into the respective aggregates.

> The delta procedure is suitable for all summable key figures as well as for noncumulative key figures. If a BasisCube contains key figures with the aggregation MAXIMUM or MINIMUM, then the aggregates are always recreated entirely.

This procedure multiplies the effort per data record compared to an entire rebuild. However, if only part of the master data is affected by the change, the overall run time of the change run is significantly improved.

The threshold value from which an entire rebuild is more favorable than the delta procedure depends on a multitude of parameters that BW cannot evaluate itself. For this reason, the threshold value needs to be set manually.

For this purpose, there is the transaction RSCUSTV8, which helps to make a determination in percentages (see figure 24–21). If the share of changed master data exceeds the indicated limit, the delta procedure will be dropped and an entire rebuild of the aggregates will be made. If the threshold value is set to 0, then the rebuild will always be executed.

To find the ideal threshold value, SAP recommends testing the performance with different values. However, this may be very time consuming and difficult. Experience has shown that a suitable value is a delta limit of approximately 15 to 20 percent and this can be used as a starting point for the optimization.

---

185. Until the change run is finished, both the old and the new master data are stored in separate versions.

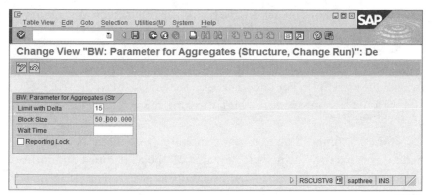

Figure 24–21
Change run in the delta procedure

24.6.3 Block Size for the Rebuild

With the *initial fill of a new aggregate,* the respective data is either read from the BasisCube or (if enabled by the rollup hierarchy) from a superordinate aggregate. Then it is written into the F table of the aggregate and compressed in the E table.

For large data volume, the composition of all data for an aggregate can require several hundred megabytes or even several gigabytes of main memory, which brings many systems to the limits of their resources.

For this reason, the data from BasisCubes (or the superordinate aggregates) are read, sorted, and aggregated per block and entered into the aggregate so that the building of an aggregate can be distributed into several smaller processes where each binds fewer resources.

> Aggregates of inventory cubes cannot be built per block, so the initial build may require an excessive amount of main memory. Please consider that the initial creation of aggregates on inventory cubes may require excessive resources and thus select low-traffic load periods in which to build these aggregates.

By default, the block size is 100,000,000 data records; however, it should be modified according to the individual requirements of the respective system. The setting on block size is made system-wide in the transaction RSCUSTV8 (see figure 24–21).

For systems that are low in resources, it may make sense to determine a relatively small block size in the first phase of live operation since experience shows that in this phase, several aggregates are newly built in parallel.

Block sizes for database
systems with partitioning

In a later phase of live operation, the block size can be increased since the rebuild of aggregates will only rarely take place.

Especially for database systems that support partitioning, BW tries to build the reading blocks according to the respective partitioning characteristics of the BasisCube. For uncompressed fact tables, this is the request ID, and with the compressed fact tables, the time characteristic OCALMONTH or OFISCPER.

From the composition of blocks configured with the respective partitioning characteristic, tedious table scans can be abandoned and instead one or several partition tables can be read completely. The performance improvements that can be achieved may reduce processing times by several factors!

If the block size for such database systems is set too small to hold the data of the complete partition, BW needs to abandon the composition of blocks based on the partitioning characteristic and compose the blocks differently. A considerable potential performance improvement would be wasted.

Thus, on partitioned database systems, the block size should be set so large that the data of a complete partition fits into it. This corresponds with the number of records per load processed (= request) or the number of records per time unit (depending on which number is bigger).

Information on the so-called block characteristic on which the building of blocks is based on can be found in the pre-analysis of the fill process (see section 24.6.4).

24.6.4   Pre-analysis of the Fill Process

In practice, there are often situations in which the ***initial filling of new aggregates*** is followed by unexpectedly poor performance without the definition of the aggregate being responsible itself.

In the most cases, an unsuitably selected block size (and thus an unsuitably selected block characteristic; see section 24.6.3) or poor database statistics (see section 7.2.4) cause the poor performance.

Support of the review on performance problems comes from the pre-analysis of the fill process that can be called from the aggregate maintenance (see figure 24–22).

The most important function of the pre-analysis is the display of the SQL statement[186] used for the fill. If this is linked to the display of the

---

186. With a filling per block, only the SQL statement for the first block is shown.

execution plan, it can be evaluated whether the database optimizer has identified the ideal access method based on its statistics.

Further, if the block size is under suspicion to have caused an unfavorable block characteristics, then for testing purposes another block size can be determined for use in the pre-analysis. Thus, you can test which block size enables the most favorable block characteristic or selection of blocks according to the partitioning characteristic.

Figure 24–22
Pre-analysis of the aggregate fill

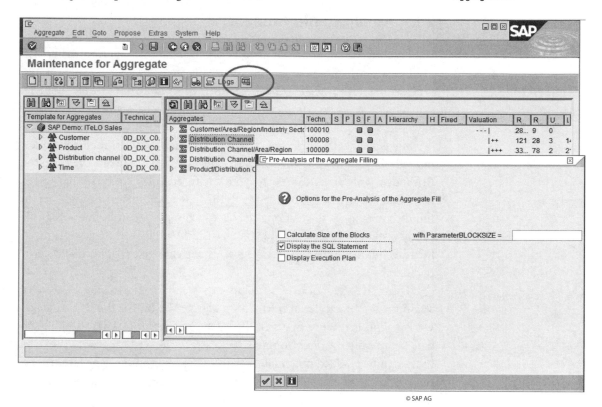

© SAP AG

 Unfortunately, the block size can only be determined system-wide. Thus, please be aware that optimizing the aggregate fill by changing the block size will have consequences for the fill process of aggregates in all other Basis-Cubes at the same time.

Since the blocks are always composed using the same block characteristic, the blocks are usually sized differently and they never exactly meet the indicated block size. To calculate the size of the individual block exactly, the option Calculate Size of the Blocks is available.

Through the calculation of the block size actually achieved, it can be evaluated whether the selected block size is basically unsuitable or whether, for example, it causes an unfavorable combination in single cases only. The calculation of block sizes may take a long time depending on the size of the fact table of the superordinate aggregate or the BasisCube respectively.

24.7 Rollup to BIA Indexes

With the execution of the rollup, not only the relational aggregates but also the indexes are modified in the BIA. This involves the indexes for the dimension tables as well as the index for the fact table of the cube. Dimension tables are always completely rebuilt in the BI accelerator, which is usually done very quickly since dimension tables are relatively small.[187]

Since the fact tables are much larger compared to the dimension tables, instead of a rebuild only the respective new request are taken over into the BIA index. This procedure corresponds with the rollup of relational aggregates that are also only provided with the new request. You should keep in mind that changes to relational tables of aggregates can be made significantly faster and easier than to changes to BIA indexes that are optimized for read but not for write access, given their changed structure and compression.

Thus, the execution of a rollup can result in a significant resource strain for the BI accelerator, which gets larger the bigger the BIA index. A workaround is the use of a so-called delta index. This contains either no data yet or only the data from few requests, so the write access to the delta index can be realized much faster than to the main index. The strain is on the read performance since the data from the main and the delta index needs to be combined at read time.

To keep the delta index of a fact table small, it needs to be regularly consolidated with the main index in standard operations (see section 32.3). The strain on the system resources is thus not removed but only deferred or concentrated.

---

187. No indexed dimension table contains more than 20 percent of data records in the fact table. If there is a bigger dimension table in BW, then the dimension table will be indexed flat; i.e., it will not be indexed but will be integrated into the index of the fact table instead (see section 7.4.3).

Delta indexes can be created in the transaction RSDDBIAMON2 via the menu item *BI Accelerator→Index Settings→Set Delta Index* (see figure 24–23). In the same menu, the delta index for a BIA main index can be switched off. In this case, the BIA will consolidate the delta index with the main index during the next indexing so that a cancellation of the delta index can result in significantly higher run times for the subsequent rollup.

Figure 24–23

Activation of the delta Index for BIA indexes

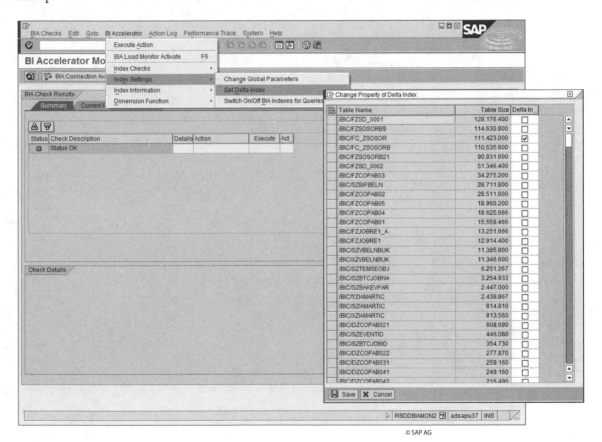

© SAP AG

The use of the delta index is suitable for the fact tables of all BasisCubes where data is regularly changed. Decision support comes from the basic test *BI Accelerator→Suggest Delta Index for Indexes* in the transaction RSRV. This test finds a delta index reasonable if in the last 10 days new values were written into the index more than 10 times.

If a delta index was switched on for a main index in the BIA, it will be used from the next delta indexing onward.

V   BW Design

In the section on extraction and staging, we showed you a reference staging architecture explained in detail (see figure Figure IV–1). This reference architecture is suited to meet a large part of all requirements of a BW system.

In certain cases, you may need to modify this reference architecture, in terms of both the extraction and staging as well as the data model. The reasons may lie in a certain form of extraction (e.g., real time), in an inhomogeneity of process data, or in particularly extensive requirements regarding availability, data capacity, and scope of work.

The following chapters describe possible modifications to the reference architecture that can be used to respond to the preceding requirements:

- Partitioned InfoProviders
- Partitioned staging
- Large-scale architectures
- Real-time architectures

This list is not complete. Rather, these are architectures that have stood the test of time in practice from our perspective. Depending on the specific project requirements, these architectures need to be modified further.

25 Partitioned InfoProviders

The distribution of data to several BasisCubes—i.e., the partitioning of one BasisCube into several BasisCubes—may make sense for different reasons: In section 7.3.3, we explained how data access can thus be accelerated. The inhomogeneity of the data structure within a process may also give reason to split the data of a process into several BasisCubes (see section 8.1).

The distribution always aims at physically separating data but to present it on the logical level (i.e., during data analysis) as one unit. In BW, this means distributing data to single BasisCubes with the transfer from transformation/integration layer to the data mart layer and to reconsolidate them for the data analysis with a MultiProvider (see figure 25–1).

Technically, data is distributed to the different BasisCubes by filtering the data records that are unnecessary for the BasisCube. In simple cases, the filtering can be done via the data transfer processes that transfer data into BasisCubes (see section 20.2). In complex cases, the start or end routine of the transformation can assume the filtering of data records (see sections 19.2 and 19.5).

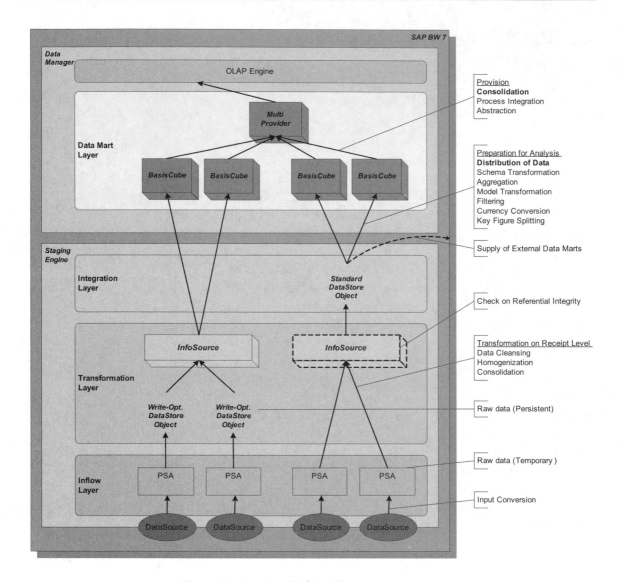

Figure 25–1 Partitioned InfoProviders

26 Partitioned Staging

The integration of data from several data sources into one DataStore Object provides an option to integrate subsets that use only a joint key (see section 17.1.3).

If the data sources provide only distinct (i.e., one-to-one) values, then the integration aspect is less relevant. If structural differences in the data sources are added, the memory capacity of the DataStore Object will be used inefficiently for the data of each data source; fields of the DataStore Object that are not provided by a data source stay empty.

In this case, the staging process can be partitioned completely along the DataSources. For this purpose, for each data source individual DataStore Objects are defined whose data is integrated only in the data mart layer (see figure 26–1).

The structure of the thus partitioned DataStore Objects is typically very similar, but it is not identical.

A distribution mechanism as described in the previous chapter (partitioned InfoProviders) is no longer required with partitioned staging; this is because the definition of the data flow from the data source to the DataStore Object is already limited to the data from the data source.

Partitioned staging can be combined with the architectural option of the partitioned InfoProviders so that, for each data source, not only an individual DataStore Object but also an individual BasisCubes in the data mart layer are defined. In this case, the advantages from the architecture and the additional management effort and subsequent development of the system are balanced.

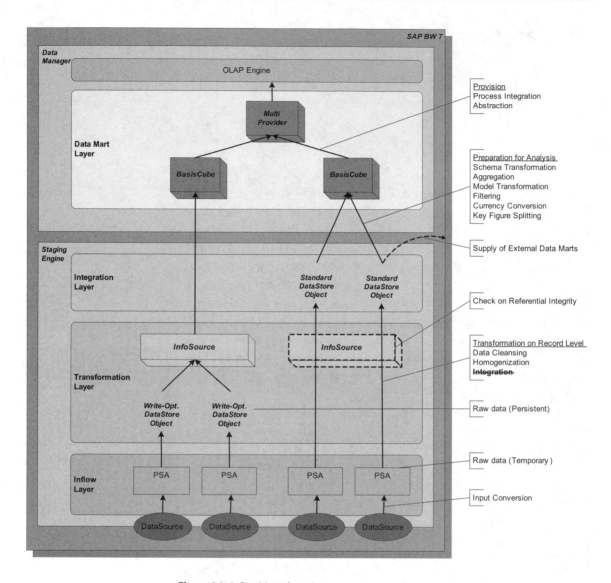

Figure 26–1 Partitioned staging

27 Large-Scale Architecture

The term *large-scale* describes data warehouse systems that need to meet particularly comprehensive requirements in certain areas, such as these, for example:

- Coverage of many function areas/modules/proprietary developments
- Job coordination for several project groups
- Management of large data volume or comprehensive load processes
- Global distribution of users
- Global distribution of source systems, different availability of source systems

These requirements need to be explicitly considered when the architecture is designed, and they may result in very different technical and organizational results.

The handling of many and complex tasks is rudimentarily considered for the design of the data mart layer in the reference architecture by allowing analytical applications to build specific InfoProviders (especially Basis-Cubes) in this layer. This not only technically meets the needs of large-scale architectures. It is also a tribute to the organizational and technical complexity that needs to be managed with the design and implementation of such applications: Each application can decide autonomously on further processing of the centrally provided data and is not in danger of being exhausted in endless merges with other applications.

Data Marts in large-scale architectures

With all the freedom that the analytical applications enjoy, you need to consider that the transformation and integration layers are centrally positioned in a data warehouse and that they have sovereign tasks regarding the provision of data. To use consistent and explainable data along all analytical applications, it is absolutely necessary to accept the sovereign task of the transformation/integration layers and to use their data as a basis. Data marts that have a unique, agreed data basis are sometimes called *architected data marts* or *dependent data marts*.

With the implementation of an analytical application, often it is quickly decided to also directly build a central database for the process data to be mapped. However, this procedure is as ambitious as it is wrong! At the beginning of such a project, you should consider whether there is such a data basis already. And should this not be based on an SAP BW but on another data warehouse system, it is no reason not to accept and use it as the central data basis.

Hub-and-spoke architecture

In addition to technical and organizational complexity, particular requirements regarding data volume or availability can be a characteristic of large-scale architectures. These are (figuratively) not only to be solved by quality but especially by quantity. To be clear, this means distributing the BW system physically and logically to several data warehouse systems[188] and still—this is about class—not giving up on the demand to create a very centric overall system.

The solution for such a task is to use hub-and-spoke architectures that distribute data to different physical systems (partially redundant) but consider all systems and databases as part of a standardized data warehouse architecture. As with the data marts, the databases of the single subsystems are *architected* too!

The term *hub-and-spoke architecture* is derived from its centralistic structure where a hub (central data slice) receives data from or gives data to the surrounding spokes (operative source systems or data marts).

For hub-and-spoke architectures where the spokes consist only of BW systems, export DataSources are used for the data transfer. The transfer of data to external systems is enabled by open hubs. Please also read section 14.3.

Depending on the technical or organizational requirements, there are two basic types of hub-and-spoke architecture: the *replicating* architecture, covered in section 27.1, and the *aggregating* architecture, covered in section 27.2. The options described in these sections can be used without modification or they can be combined, depending on the requirements. As a particular form of such a combination, the virtual hub-and-spoke architecture will be explained in section 27.3.

---

188. This do not necessarily need to be SAP BW systems, even though this type of large-scale architecture is in our focus.

The design of a large-scale architecture with several BW systems impacts the transport landscape. Please see appendix C.1.4.

27.1 Replicating Architecture

Replicating architectures aim to remove resource shortages during the data analysis that may occur because of the following conditions:

- The data analysis of the system is especially strained by large data volume or many users.
- Due to connectivity problems (e.g., regional spreading of users), no central analysis platform can be used.
- Data analysis and staging cannot be separated time-wise and they noticeably interfere with each other.
- The data analysis is to be supported by specific tools (e.g., SEM, CRM, or APO) that each require a dedicated BW system.

For these reasons, the data is integrated into a central BW system (the hub) and prepared and distributed to the surrounding BW systems (the spokes). figure 27–1 clarifies this architecture.

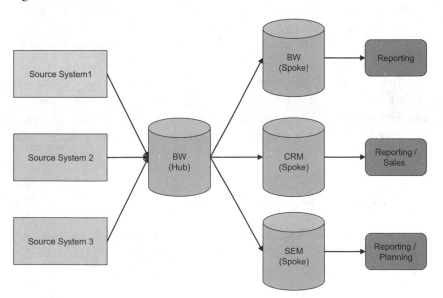

Figure 27–1
Replicating architecture

The hub basically corresponds with the reference architecture up to the integration layer, while the spokes are the data mart layer that was "only" transferred to other BW systems. The use of the integration layer in the hub is necessary since the spokes draw their data from the hub independently of each other (pull principle), and thus the data needs to be persistent in the hub.

Contrary to the reference architecture, however, the spokes do not only serve the purpose to prepare the data of the hub in an application-specific manner; if the same application is distributed to several spokes, these spokes can prepare data identically. In practice, this scenario is found when the spokes are used for load balancing.

There is also the option to specifically build spokes for each single application. In this case, for each spoke parts of the database are transferred individually, and if required, they are further aggregated or prepared in the spoke.

Since spokes in a replicating architecture are only provided with already prepared data and there is already a persistence layer in the hub, the spokes themselves do not need the persistence layer and do not need to deal with the transformation of data again.

Extraction from the hub   Technically, the hub is the (only) source system of all spokes. A direct connection from the real source systems is only made to the hub.

The transactional data of the integration layer is always extracted from the hub and transferred to the spokes in BasisCubes (possibly after prior preparation for specific applications). Given the performance-critical relevance for the data analysis, the persisting of the data in the physical models of the BasisCubes is inevitable.

However, with less performance-critical master data, there is a choice on whether extraction processes are to be defined and controlled or whether the master data is drawn in a direct access from the hub (see section 22.2.1). This decision mostly depends on the size of the master data tables and the availability of the hub.

27.2 Aggregating Architecture

Contrary to the replicating architecture, the data preparation is considered to be resource intensive with the aggregating architecture. This may be the case because of the following:

- The data-supplying source systems are geographically separated (connectivity problem).
- The data volumes from the supplying source systems are too large to be processed by BW.
- Data analysis and staging cannot be separated time-wise and they noticeably interfere with each other.

For these reason, in an aggregating architecture the data from several BW systems (spokes) is collected and prepared and then further transferred to a central BW system (the so-called hub; see figure 27–2).

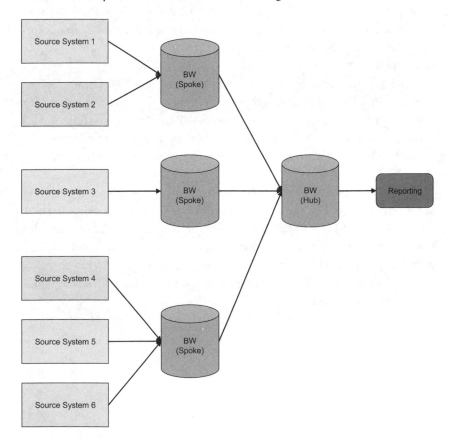

Figure 27–2

Aggregating architecture

In this case, the spokes basically correspond with the reference architecture up to the integration layer, while the hub is the data mart layer. The system is similar to the replicating architecture; it is only that the tasks of hub and spoke are swapped.

If such architectures emerge due to geographical distribution of the source systems, it is especially customary to also run data analyses on the spokes and to only provide aggregated data to the hub (since regional reporting requires more detailed information than global reporting).

In this case, spokes do not use only an integration layer but also an individually designed data mart layer.

27.3 Virtual Hub-and-Spoke Architecture

Besides the already described options to distribute data to several BW systems, there is also the option to "virtually" distribute the data; i.e., not to store it in hub/spokes but to exchange data between the systems at the time of the data analysis.

The technical basis for this architecture forms the SAP RemoteCubes. These are InfoCube definitions that are defined in the metadata repository but that are not created in the database. Remote objects (cubes and InfoObjects) do not store any data, but for each request they access the respective source system in which the respective data is stored (see also chapter 22).

With the use of remote objects, both a replicating and an aggregating architecture can be built to reduce the organizational complexity of a system. You should keep in mind that each data request results in transfer times in the network that only occur once with the data distribution in a genuine hub-and-spoke architecture. The use of virtual architectures is thus limited to areas where the timeliness of data is especially relevant and where the data volume is low.

VI BW in Live Operation

The previous chapters provided the necessary background to completely design and implement a BW system from an architectural perspective. We explained the data model, the definition of the data flow, and also the data access from the analytical engine.

We outlined the manual execution of load and management processes (e.g., loading master data and transactional data, change run, rollup, etc.).

Now that the static view on the BW system is completed, the processes need to be harmonized, automated, and controlled; i.e., they need to be migrated to operative standard operations.

The technical basis for the automation forms the *process chains,* and their control mechanisms are explained in chapter 28.

The basis for the design and the setup of standard operations are *time slots* on the one hand (see chapter 29) and the detailed *organization and sequence* of all processes on the other hand (see chapter 30). While time slots define at what points in time processes are to be executed, in the organization and sequence phase, the processes to be executed are sorted and a dependency is created. In chapter 30, we also describe how the execution of processes is to be defined through controlling of the process chain.

> Please do not underestimate the need to carefully design the standard operations of your BW system. Implementing an incompletely designed standard operation too quickly often results in excessive manual tasks related to the maintenance of BW systems and in extreme cases leads to performance problems if load and analysis processes are executed without any coordination and in parallel and therefore create resource shortages.

The explanations of the regularly executed processes in standard operations end with chapter 31, where we explain the *monitoring* of standard operations and the analysis of errors that occurred during the monitoring.

In addition to the regular executions and the monitoring of processes, the operation of SAP BW requires some maintenance activities to keep the system continuously stable and performing well. These are explained in chapter 32 with *model trimming* and in chapter 33 with the *information lifecycle management.*

28 Process Chains

Up to release 3.x of BW, three different technical designs were used to auto-mate processes in BW: event chains, automatisms, and process chains. The designs differ regarding their mapped flexibility and complexity and they compete to a certain degree.

With SAP BW release 7, the existing automation functionalities are supported for backward compatibility, but new processes can only be inte-grated in process chains (especially in the area of staging). In the following sections, event chains that represented the ruling form of automation in BW release 2 are only outlined as basic technology onto which process chains are based. Automatisms[189] are no longer used for transformation and data transfer processes in BW 7, and they are not dealt with in this book.

Process chains aim to support process sequences if the definition is particularly complex and the parallelization and status-dependent branch-ing needs to be considered. Further, process chains offer central control-ling and central monitoring of all process steps defined in them.

In a process chain, the dependencies of all process steps within a time slot of standard operations are bundled. For reasons of clarity and admin-istration, it is possible to subdivide a process chain into several subchains (see section 28.3.1).

The process chain maintenance can be reached via the Data Ware-housing Workbench or via transaction RSPC, and it offers three different views on process chains (see figure 28–1):

Views on a process chain

- ▪ **Planning view:** Overview on all existing process chains and on the definition of process chains. In the plan view, process chains are cre-ated and maintained.

---

189. With an automatism, the activation of new data in a DataStore Object could be started automatically after new data is posted to a DataStore Object.

■ **Checking view:** Results from the syntactical and semantic testing of a process chain that was defined in the plan view. With the change to the check view, the testing of the respective process chain is executed.

■ **Log view:** The log on the execution of a process chain selected in the plan view (more detailed explanations on monitoring of process chains can be found in section 31.3).

Figure 28–1

Process chain maintenance

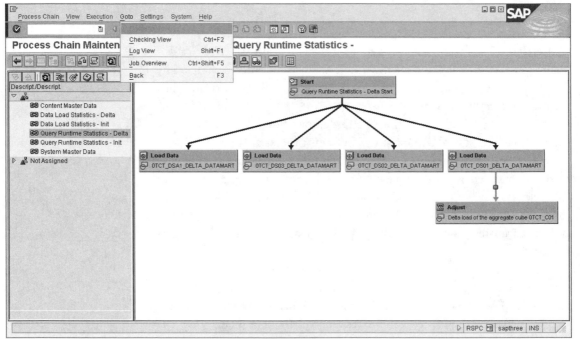

© SAP AG

The dependency of processes is graphically displayed in the modeling of a process chain. Here, you determine the execution sequence and dependency of two processes using drag and drop, and you define whether the displayed sequence is applicable to the error-free or erroneous execution of the preceding process (see figure 28–2).

Process types

The task a process has within a process chain is defined by the respective *process type*. All available types are divided into the following categories (see figure 28–3):

■ General services
■ Load process and post-processing
■ Data target administration
■ Reporting agent
■ Other BW processes
■ Other

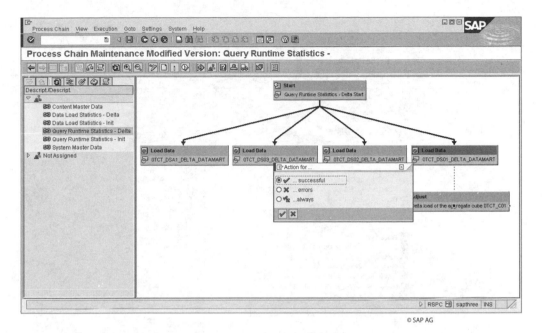

© SAP AG

Each process type needs to be used in combination with a variable that defines the parameterization of the respective process step—e.g., which InfoPackage is to be executed for a load process or which cube needs to be compressed up to which request.

> If processes are entered into a process chain, BW automatically adds further processes for numerous process types that could make sense in the context of the new process (e.g., execution of the change run after the loading of master data). This approach is sometimes very disturbing and it can be switched off in the process chain maintenance via the menu item *Settings→Default Chains*.

Variables to a process type are not related to a process chain or a process step but can be used by (a freely chosen number of) other process chains.[190] It is thus possible to change the functioning of several process chains by maintaining a single variable.

Figure 28–2

Status-dependent process sequences in process chains

Process type variables

---

190. The exception are process chain starters (see section 28.3).

Figure 28–3

Process types in
process chains

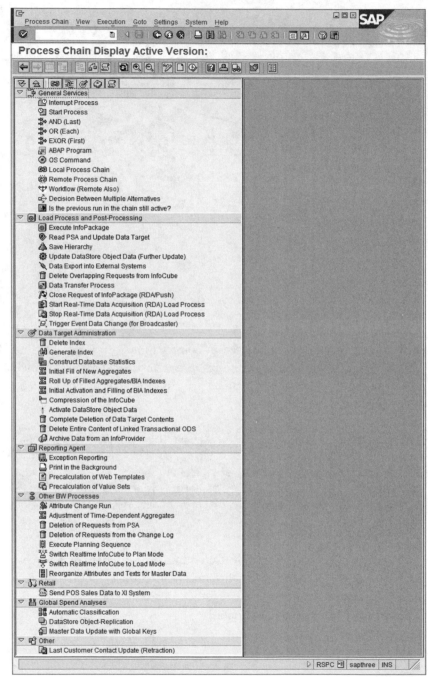

Depending on the process type, the parameterization of a process step can be clearly defined by the variable (e.g., indication of a BasisCube), or it can refer to other process steps within the same process chain. With this relative addressing, a data transfer process can be used, for example, to parameterize a rollup. In this case, the requests of the specific BasisCube that is filled during the data transfer process are rolled up.

Fixed and relative parameterization

Figure 28–4 shows the relative addressability of process types. The figure shows only addressing that can be utilized with the new staging with transformation and the data transfer process. The process types that can use a data transfer process for addressing offer the option to address objects from an InfoPackage. However, these are InfoPackages for the "old" staging up to release 3.x of BW, which is not considered in the figure.

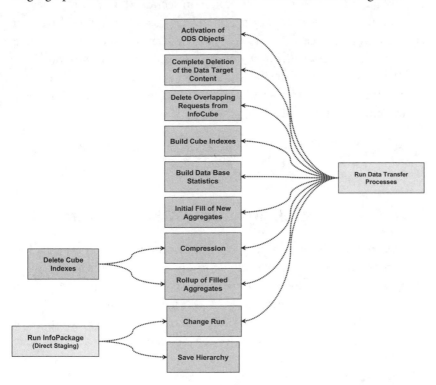

Figure 28–4
Relative addressability of process types

With the relative addressability of InfoPackages, the parameterization usually refers to **data targets** that are posted by the InfoPackage. In exceptional cases, the relative addressing of InfoPackages, however, can refer to the **request** that was last loaded by the InfoPackage:

- With the activation of new data in DataStore Objects, only requests that were loaded by the addressing InfoPackages are activated. If several requests are to be activated, all respective InfoPackages are executed in the addressing.
- With the compression of a BasisCube, it is compressed up to the request that was last loaded by the addressing InfoPackages.
- With the rollup of filled aggregates, it is rolled up to the request that was last loaded by the addressing InfoPackage.

Initially, the definition of a process chain describes, on only the metadata level, what processes are to be executed and in what dependency to each other. Technically, the control concept is based on the *event controlling of the BW basis system,* which we'll explain in section 28.1.

The *controlling concept of process chains* uses the technical basis of event controlling as explained in section 28.2. Here, the specific controlling mechanisms for *parallelization* and *serialization* are addressed too.

With a summary on the particular options to *start process chains* and their integration in cross-system processes, the description of process chains ends with section 28.3.

The different process types that fill a process chain with life (from a content perspective) are explained with organization and workflow in chapter 30.

28.1 Event Controlling of the BW Basis System

The controlling of events in the BW basis system is based on the scheduling of batch jobs that are managed by the job scheduler of the basis system. Using *events,* you set the start time to be dependent on previous jobs so that jobs can be linked to each other in a certain workflow.

Each job that is to cause subsequent activities can generate an event when it is finished. This is a signal for the job scheduler that a certain state in the system has been reached. The job scheduler then looks for released jobs that wait for this event and it starts them.

With their termination, the jobs can in turn start further events and so on. Figure 28–5 shows this dependency.

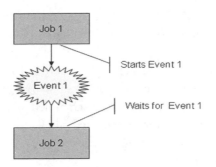

Figure 28–5
Simple process chain

The figure shows how the dependency between two jobs can be realized in the system. Since the controlling concept of process chains uses this form of dependency but hides it behind the framework of graphical modeling, the less-interested reader may skip the following paragraphs and continue with section 28.2.

The first step to controlling events is to define the events that link the single jobs in the system. The event maintenance can be reached via transaction SM62 (see figure 28–6).

Definition of events

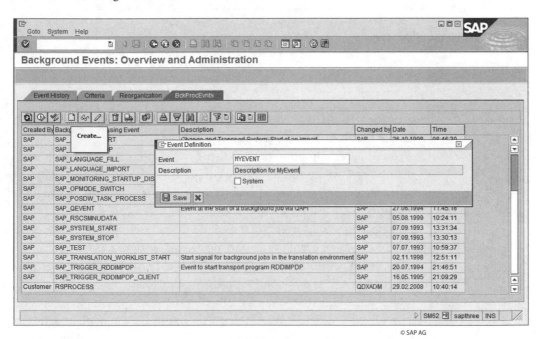

© SAP AG

Figure 28–6
Definition of events

Events can be created as system events or as user events. However, this is only a categorization; it has no functional consequences. Since system events are defined by SAP and might come with different functions in a release change, only user events should be defined for the design of standard operations.

Event parameters Basically, the use of events is enough to define dependencies between jobs. Additionally, there is an option to combine events with event parameters that are transfer parameters for the scheduled job.

Depending on how an event is activated and which selection is defined for a subsequent job, the starting conditions are very different. This is shown in the following table.

Activated Event/Parameter	Job Scheduled In	Job Started
Event: E Parameter:	Event: E Parameter: P	No
Event: E Parameter: P	Event: E Parameter: P	Yes
Event: E Parameter: X	Event: E Parameter: P	No
Event: E Parameter:	Event: E Parameter:	Yes
Event: E Parameter: X	Event: E Parameter:	Yes

Scheduling of jobs For jobs to be started after an event occurs, you need to define in the job schedule the event/parameter a job is to start.

You can add a program to a job using transaction SM36, in which a job is defined and where the respective program can be added to the job as another step. Here, you can also determine a variant to run the program (see figure 28–7).

To define the start event for a defined job, a starting condition can be defined to mark an event as the starting event (see figure 28–8).

You select periodic execution if the job is to be started with *every* incidence of the event and not only with the first incidence.

The start of the first job in a defined event chain will in most cases be set for a fixed time (periodically too). Alternatively, it may make sense to also let the first job of an event chain start after an event. This can be activated manually using the transaction SM64.

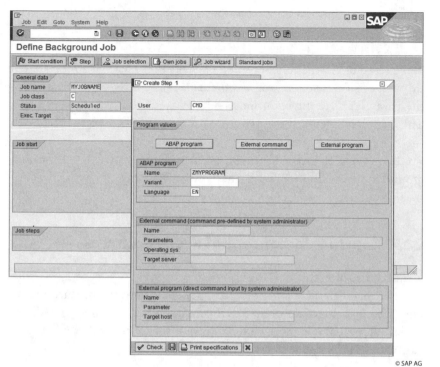

Figure 28–7
Job scheduling for programs

© SAP AG

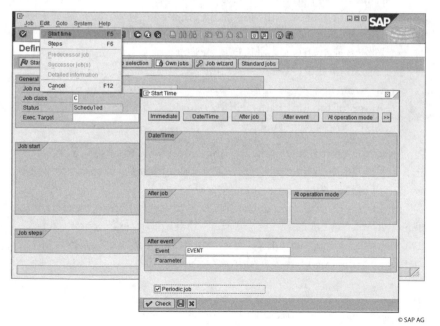

Figure 28–8
Job scheduling according to events

© SAP AG

Subsequent events   When you're scheduling jobs for the basis system, you can define start events, but no subsequent events that are to be activated after the execution of a job can be stored.

As a solution, the function module RSSM_EVENT_RAISE can be started through a self-developed program that activates the requested event with the parameter. The function module RSSM_EVENT_RAISE is RFC enabled. Thus, an event can also be activated from another system to start a job there (e.g., a load process).

However, with SAP standard programs, a framework can only be built around the standard program in the same way as with the workflow controlling of the process chains (see section 28.2).

28.2 Controlling Concept of Process Chains

With the use of events, job workflows are controlled decentralized. With the job scheduler, there is a central component to activate the start of a job after the incidence of the event, but the definition of each single job determines what event it is started after and what subsequent event it will activate with its termination. This comes with a number of disadvantages:

- The *chaining of jobs* by events takes a lot of effort, and it is error prone, especially if changes to the job chain are made.
- The *integration capability* of job chains is limited to programs that are enabled to activate self-qualified[191] events for subsequent processes.
- If a program aborts before it could activate a subsequent event (e.g., from erroneous programming or a system-caused dump), then the execution of the job chains will be paused and a manual intervention in the workflow is inevitable.

Process chain controlling addresses these problems to ensure a consistent and stable controlling of processes. The *chaining of process steps* will be explained in the following section.

In numerous cases, the definition of a process chain represents more than a simple sequence of process steps that are to be executed consecutively. Process chain definitions also come with different process strings that are to be executed *alternatively* (depending on the status-based

---

191. The activation of events is qualified if, depending on the status of the execution (error free/erroneous), different events can be activated.

branching) or *in parallel* (to improve the overall runtime) in the workflow of the process chain.

The chaining of process steps and the handling of alternative or parallel execution strings is discussed in the following sections. We will then describe how *programs are integrated* into process chain controlling.

28.2.1 Concatenation of Process Steps

Each process step in a process chain corresponds with a released job in the BW basis system whose start conditions are by definition dependent upon an event. Other than with event chains, these jobs that are part of a process chain do not need to be scheduled manually.

Instead, the scheduling of all jobs involved in a process chain is done when the *Activate and Schedule* button is activated in the process chain maintenance. Here, it is possible to prioritize jobs (see figure 28–9).

Figure 28–9

Scheduling of jobs with process chains

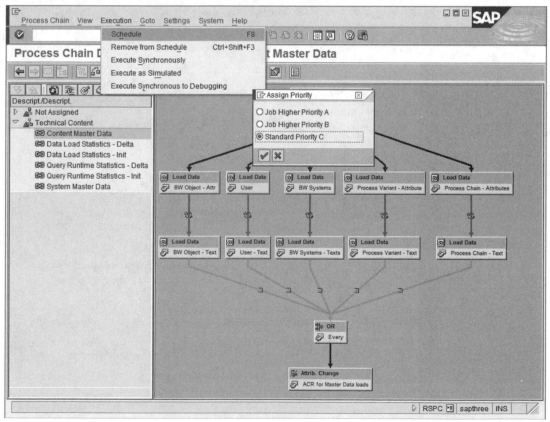

© SAP AG

By default, the jobs are scheduled under the ID of the background user that is also stored for extraction and staging in the transaction RSBWREMOTE (see section 15.1.1). However, via the menu item *Process Chain→Attributes→ Execution User,* another user ID can be defined.

> At first, the use of a separate user ID facilitates the monitoring of the otherwise anonymous processes in BW. On the other hand, the use of another user ID comes with numerous problems if, for example, a user is locked because of the wrong password entry and thus all jobs of this user can no longer be executed. Further, the execution of the process chain is also linked to authorizations from the execution user. Thus, you should only use a user other than the default user in exceptional cases and for testing purposes.

Definition of events

To get a dependency of process steps using the event controlling of the BW basis system, all dependencies are realized through event parameters for the user event RSPROCESS. Each process step activates the event RSPROCESS and combines it with a generated, unambiguous event parameter that can be found via double-clicking on the process connection (see figure 28–10).

Figure 28–10
Event dependency
of process steps

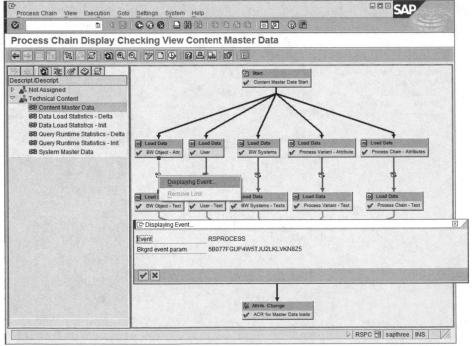

© SAP AG

You can thus make sure that the work with process chains doesn't result in the definition of an unmanageable number of events.

With the definition of process steps, you can define either a ***simple dependency*** or a ***status-based dependency.***

With the simple dependency, the event RSPROCESS is always activated through a process step with the same event parameter whether the process step was executed error free or erroneously.

Simple dependency between process steps

The type of event parameter for a process step results from the definition of the dependency for the first subsequent process in the process chain maintenance (see figure 28–2).

If more than one subsequent process is defined for a process step, the simple dependency applies to all the following processes since each process step only activates exactly one event with its termination, which all subsequent processes need to use as entry event.

As an alternative to the simple dependency, a process step can activate the event RSPROCESS with two alternative event parameters—depending on whether the process step was executed error free or erroneously.

Status-based dependency between process steps

With the status-based dependency, similar to the simple dependency, the definition of the first following process determines that all further processes are to be scheduled on the basis of status.

If the simple dependency is to be combined with the status-based dependency, a simple dependency can be obtained by linking a following process to both possible entry events (error free/erroneous; see figure 28–11).

If a process step is linked to both entry events, the functionally is like that of a simple dependency. However, technically this is realized by scheduling the following process on the error-free as well as on the erroneous entry event, i.e., twice.

So, the definition of such a dependency comes with a warning from the process chain maintenance and ***should be avoided.*** A better alternative to the combination of simple and status-based dependencies is the use of the EXOR process that is also used to collect alternative execution strings (see section 28.2.2).

Another option to dynamically design the workflow of a process chain is the use of decision processes. Through decision processes, a definable number of different events can be activated so that the workflow of a process chain can be designed variably.

Dependency from external parameters

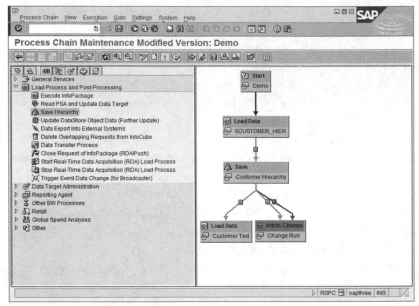

© SAP AG

Which event is activated by a decision process is basically independent from the status of the process chain and only refers to external parameters that are primarily taken from the system variables and that can be evaluated with a simple formula. The formula always needs to be designed so that it returns a boolean result value (see figure 28–12).

Decision processes are suitable if a process chain is to be executed depending on the day of the week (rollup of BIA indexes from Monday to Sunday, rebuild of the indexes on Sunday, etc.) or on the time of day (change run not after 6 a.m. for example).

28.2.2 Collection of Alternative Execution Strings

In numerous cases, status-based branchings in the process chain are defined and later recombined to form a string.

For example, suppose a change run is to start based on status if a load process for master data was executed error free. However, the subsequent load process for transactional data is to be executed no matter what; i.e., it is to follow the change run as well as the erroneous termination of the load process for master data.

In such a case, it is tempting to organize the collection in a process chain, as shown in figure 28–13.

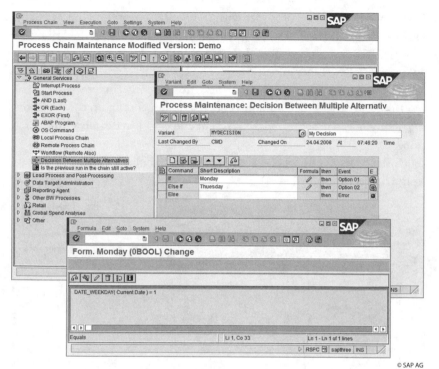

Figure 28–12
Definition of decision processes

© SAP AG

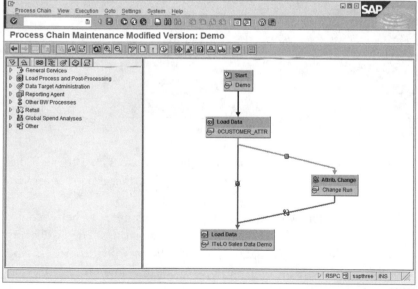

Figure 28–13
Incorrect collection of alternative execution strings

© SAP AG

Basically, the desired goal is met with the definition of the process chain. However, technically BW will implement this by scheduling the following process after the entry event of the one execution string as well as after the entry event of the other execution string; i.e., it will be scheduled twice.

The definition of such a dependency subsequently comes with a warning from the process chain maintenance, and depending on the monitoring, it might lead to some disarrangement and errors in the job administration.

Instead, an EXOR process should be used to collect alternative execution strings (see figure 28–14).

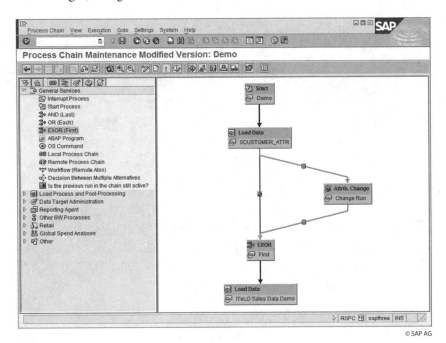

Figure 28–14

Correct collection of alternative execution strings

The EXOR process starts its own subsequent processes after the termination of the *first* process. The termination of all further processes remains without impact.

The process following an EXOR process thus needs to be scheduled only once, even if it follows alternative execution strings. The EXOR process is now scheduled several times, but specifically with this process type, it is clear that several jobs belong to one and the same process step in a process chain.

28.2.3 Collection of Parallel Execution Strings

From performance aspects, it can make sense to parallelize processes in standard operations (see chapter 30).

Process chains – internal collection

Within a process chain, the parallelization is made when several processes are defined that have the same status dependency to the first process (e.g., linking several load processes to the start process).

If these parallel execution strings within a process chain are again to be serialized, an AND process can be used. The process following an AND collection process is started only after *all* preceding processes (whether error free or erroneous) are terminated.

Figure 28–15 shows the serialization of execution strings using the AND process for the parallelization of master data load processes and the subsequent serialization for the change run.

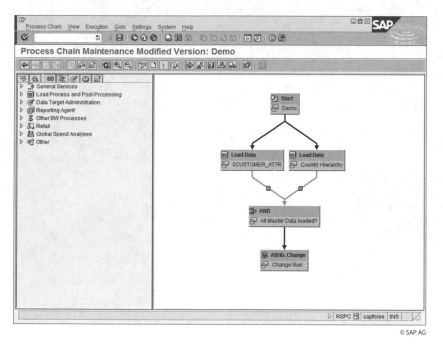

© SAP AG

Figure 28–15
Process chains:
internal collection of
parallel execution strings

In some cases, execution strings are parallelized outside the process chains and are to be serialized again prior to or during the execution of the process chain. This may be the case, for example, if several source systems independently activate events in BW that all together are to trigger the execution of a process chain. Such a situation occurs with initiated time slots (see section 29.1.2).

Process chains – external collection

The collection processes of process chain controlling refer only to events that are activated within the same process chain; they do not react to events that are activated outside the process chain. For this purpose, there are *interrupt processes*. They interrupt the execution of a process chain until a defined event is activated in BW (see figure 28–16).

Figure 28–16

Interrupt processes for process chains

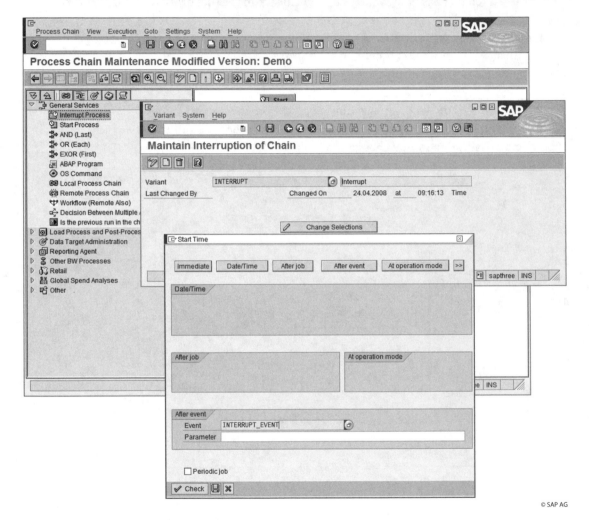

© SAP AG

It is thus possible to make a process chain wait for the activation of several internal events that either lead to the process chain starting or continuing at a given stage.

Technically, a job for the interrupt process is scheduled during the execution of a process chain. The job waits for the defined event and starts the continuation of the process chain with activation of this event. Thus, the interruption of a process chain does not require any resources since the chain is not active during the wait period but actually put on hold.

Since the job of the interrupt process only waits for its event as long as the process chain is interrupted, the activation of such an event is important for the process chain only while it is interrupted and waits for the respective event.[192] If the events of interrupt processes are activated before or after the interruption of a process chain, this will not have any effect on current or subsequent executions of the process chain.

Thus, if a process chain is to wait for several events before executing, then it needs to be already running. The start condition in the start process of the chain itself may not be part of the events that the process chain is waiting for; a continuous repetition of the process chain is better—e.g., by having the process chain reactivating itself continuously.

28.2.4 Integration of Programs

Each program for the execution of a process step (load processes, rollup, compression, etc.) is only an indirect part of the respective job in the process chain. A direct part of the job is the program RSPROCESS, which starts the actual program to be executed.

Consistency in execution

The advantage is that the RSPROCESS program can check the execution of the respective process step regarding its consistency before the actual program is called. The execution of a process step is consistent if the preceding process that was defined in the process chain was executed. This prevents a process step from being manually activated with the activation of the event RSPROCESS with a respective event parameter.

Central monitoring

Further, the RSPROCESS program can generate log entries with its start and its termination so that a central monitoring of the execution of all process steps within a process chain is possible (for monitoring process chains, see section 31.3).

Encapsulation of local calls

Besides the secured consistency of process chain controlling and central monitoring, a fundamental advantage of the RSPROCESS program lies in the encapsulation of the programs to be called. The RSPROCESS program needs to be able to activate the process chain definition events accordingly. However, the called program does not need to care about the definition of the respective process chain or the definition of the subsequent

---

192. The job of the interrupt process is done after the activation of the respective job.

jobs. It needs to neither activate events nor adhere to particular conventions with its termination. It only needs to be scheduled regularly (i.e., it must not abort with a short dump) and leave the rest completely to the RSPROCESS program.

Figure 28–17

ABAP program variants in process chains

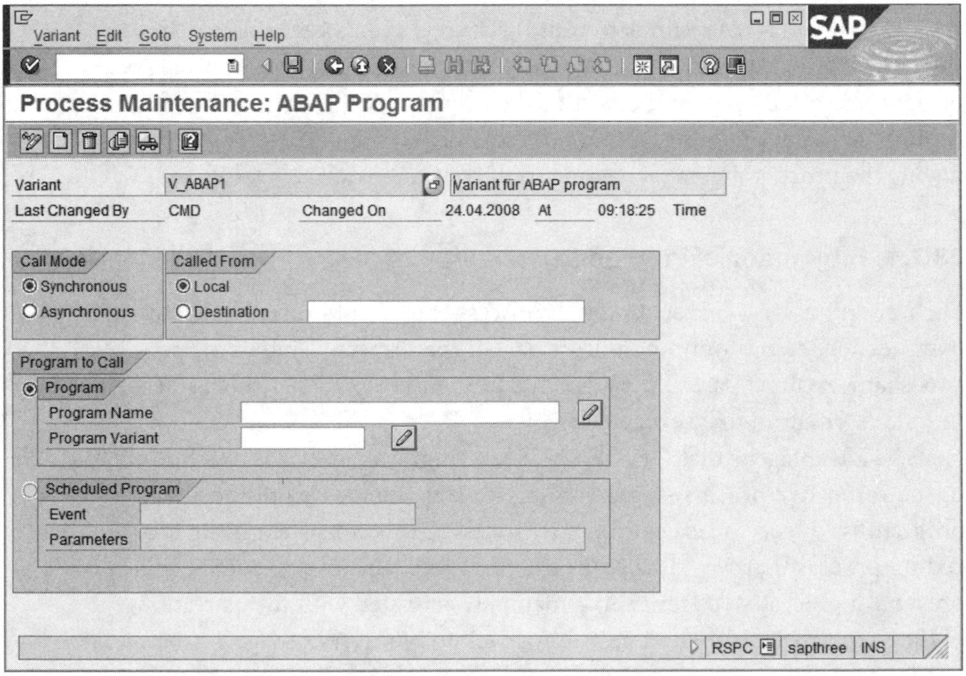

This enables a freely chosen integration of ABAP programs into the definition of a process chain. Only the process type *ABAP program* is available, and in its variant only the name of the ABAP program and the program variant[193] are stored (see figure 28–17).

© SAP AG

As long as the respective ABAP program is to be executed locally (i.e., on the same BW system as the process chain), the program can be called synchronously with process chain controlling. This means that the process chain controlling waits for the termination of the ABAP program and then starts the subsequent processes.

Should the ABAP program abort, the controlling will be notified with an error code and it can react to this error accordingly.

193. The program variant defines the entry parameters of the ABAP program and it can be maintained with the program. It is not to be confused with the process variant that stores process-related information for the process chain.

Further, process chains provide an option to integrate ABAP programs into the standard operations of other SAP systems.[194] For this purpose, the ABAP programs need to be scheduled as background jobs in the target system and they need to wait for an event that is activated from the process chain via RFC to the target system (see section 28.1 on the scheduling of jobs for events).

Remote ABAP programs

In this case, instead of the ABAP program, the target system and the respective event that activate the start of an approved job need to be indicated. The start of the remote program is thus made asynchronously; the controlling of the process chain is not able to recognize the termination. The termination of the distributed process instead needs to be indicated by the process itself so that a true encapsulation is thus not given.

To call the following processes of a remote program, the process chain controlling needs to be informed by the remote system of the termination of the program. For this purpose, the remote program needs to call (via RFC) the function module RSPC_ABAP_FINISH and indicate the process variant in the original BW system. The process chain controlling thus recognizes the error-free termination of a remote program and can then start the following processes.

Encapsulation of distributed processes

With individually-called ***extraction processes, remote process chains,*** and ***remote workflows,*** this feedback is already integrated into the called programs so that no further provisions need to be made. However, if random ABAP programs are started asynchronously, you need to take care yourself that the respective ABAP program[195] gives feedback.

28.3 Starting Process Chains

For several reasons, the start of a process chain fundamentally differs from regular job scheduling.

First, the start of a process chain is defined with its modeling via the process chain starter (in the following called start process). Each process chain needs to have exactly one[196] start process, which is the first job of the chain and can be followed by a freely chosen number of processes. The

Process chain starter

---

194. SAP ERP and BW systems.
195. Or the following steps in the started job.
196. It is possible to make a process chain wait for several events and thus to use several start conditions for a process chain. More information can be found in section 28.2.3.

start process defines the scheduling options for the start of the complete chain (see figure 28–18).

Figure 28–18

Scheduling the start process

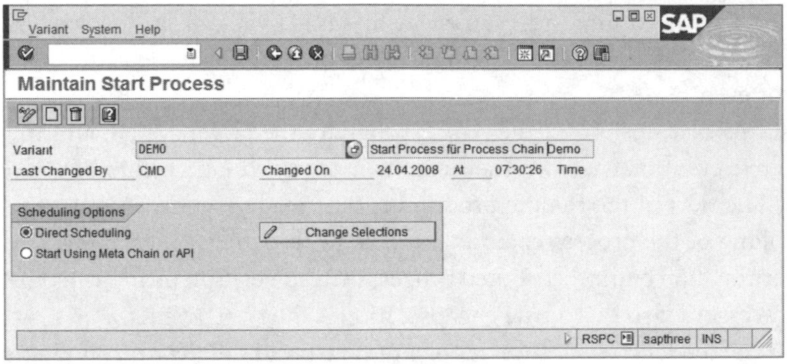

© SAP AG

In all other areas of the BW basis system, the definition of jobs is an exclusive functionality of the job scheduler and thus not part of the metadata of BW or the ABAP Dictionary. It is only with process chains that the job definition is part of their metadata.

This detailed examination is especially relevant for the use of the transport method (see appendix B). While the definition and scheduling of jobs is usually made separately for each system of a transport landscape and cannot be transported, the scheduling options for a process chain are transported.

Additionally, the start process and all jobs related to a process chain are immediately scheduled and linked during the transport procedure so that the complete process chain is in use immediately according to the start process. A change of the scheduling is not provided in the target system; i.e., it needs to be executed by changing the start process and the subsequent transport.

Particularly with the definition of process chains, it is especially relevant to already consider the role of the process chain when the standard operations are organized. Which scheduling options are suitable for which purpose depends on whether a process chain is to be started locally or from a remote system. The following sections address these two cases.

28.3.1 Starting Local Process Chains

As described in section 28.2.1, the scheduling of jobs related to a chain is made via the *Activate and Schedule* button (see figure 28–9).

There are two alternatives on how to start the first process step of a process chain, the start process:

■ Direct scheduling as a job
■ Via a metachain/API

Direct Scheduling of Local Process Chains

The start process of a process chain can be scheduled like regular jobs, i.e., at certain points in time or on user events (see figure 28–18).

If a process chain is to always be started at the same time and in periodic intervals (daily, weekly, monthly, etc.), the direct scheduling of the start process is favored.

Start at certain points in time

Here, the time for the first start of the process chain needs to be stored in the scheduling options, and subsequently, the periodic execution needs to be defined.

As an alternative, the immediate start of the process chain can be defined in the scheduling options too. However, this makes sense only for testing purposes since a productively used process chain would thus immediately be scheduled and activated in the production system after the transport of the chain.

If the starting time of a process chain cannot be generalized so it can start at certain points in time, the periodic scheduling of the start process is available.

Start upon system events

In this case, the chain is always started when the event is activated, which can be configured manually using the transaction SM64 or with calling the function module RSSM_EVENT_RAISE (see section 28.1).

System events like, for example, the entry of a certain operation mode or the termination of other jobs can also be used as scheduling options for the start of a process chain.

Start via Metachain/API

With the start of a process chain via a metachain or the respective API, neither the start process nor the other process steps of a process chain are scheduled as jobs. Instead, the scheduling of the process steps is only done with the calling of the start process as a metachain/API.

The start process of a process chain can be called by another process chain. In this context, the calling process chain is referred to as a

Start via metachain

metachain while the *called process chain* is referred to as the local process chain or *subchain.*

Figure 28–19

Call of a local subchain

For the definition of such a call, the process type *Local Process Chain* is available. It can be defined as an individual process step for a process chain (see figure 28–19).

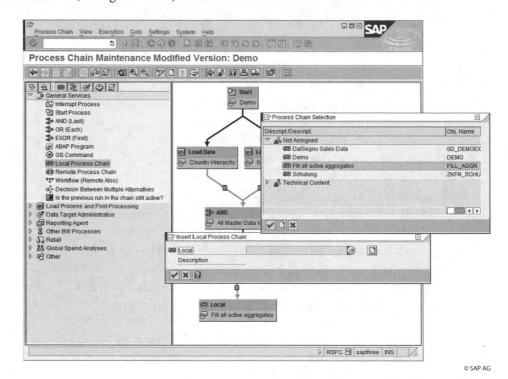

© SAP AG

The labeling of a process chain as metachain or subchain is always done in relation to another process chain. Each metachain can also be a subchain of another metachain and vice versa. In practice, a hierarchical organization of metachain and subchains has been established, as shown in figure 28–20.

Figure 28–20

Organizing metachains and subchains

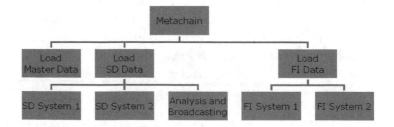

The subcategorization of process chains in a metachain and several sub-chains should be made so that all parts of a process chain that form a closed complex in itself and whose start can thus also make sense outside the process chain should it be outsourced to a subchain.

After a subchain is called, the metachain awaits a completion confirmation as well as an error status. Based on the error status, the concatenation of the subsequent processes in a metachain can basically be defined as status dependent. You need to consider that the error status of a subchain results from all process steps contained therein; i.e., a subchain is considered erroneous if at least one of its process steps is erroneous.

Error status of local process chains

If within the subchain an erroneous process step is handled through respective branching, it often does not make sense to evaluate the subchain as erroneous anyway. If erroneous processes are instead to be considered error free when they have a respective subsequent process that starts error free according to the status, this can be defined in the menu item *Process Chain→Attributes→Process Status Valuation* (see figure 28–21).

Figure 28–21

Status valuation of local process chains

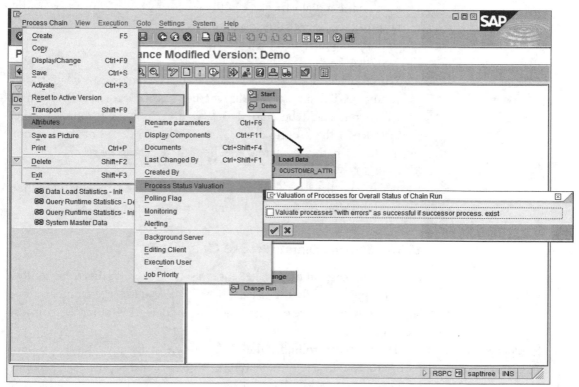

© SAP AG

Start via API call   The call of a subchain within a metachain is technically made by calling the function module `RSPC_API_CHAIN_START`. This can also be used outside a metachain to start a process chain.

The start of a process chain via API can make sense when you're starting a chain from a self-developed program. Even if a subchain is to be executed outside its metachain, the use of the API may make sense.

The import and export parameters of the function module `RSPC_API_CHAIN_START` have the following meaning:

- `I_CHAIN`
  Technical name of the process chain.
- `I_T_VARIABLES`
  Parameters that are transferred to the process chain as variables. To date, there are no process types that work with variables.
- `I_SYNCHRONOUS`
  With transfer of the parameter X, the process chain is started synchronously; i.e., the first process after the start process is synchronously executed in a dialog process of the executing user. With the synchronous call, process chains can be started where the start process would actually require a direct scheduling.
- `I_SIMULATE`
  With transfer of the parameter X, the start of the process chain is only simulated. The simulation tells whether a process chain actively exists, whether it could be started (i.e., it does not go through another instance of the process chain), and (for an RFC call of the function module) whether the target system of the RFC can be reached.
- `E_LOGID`
  Log ID of the process chain run that is returned from the function module. More on the log ID can be found in section 31.3.

28.3.2 Starting Remote Process Chains

In numerous cases, it may make sense to start process chains from another system. This is usually the case if several BW systems exchange data in a large-scale architecture or if time slots are initiated by source systems (see section 29.1.2).

Start by activation of events   The event controlling of the BW basis system already offers a very simple option to start a job from a remote system. For this purpose, the job to be started (for process chains this would be the start process) needs to be scheduled periodically for an event.

Same as with local chains whose start follows an event, the function module RSSM_EVENT_RAISE can also be used for remote process chains. Since it is RFC enabled, the call can be made system-wide.

The following code example shows how the event ZTEST can be activated via remote call in the system QBW (logical system name LS_QBW_100) in order to, for example, start a process chain that reacts to this event.

```
REPORT Z_EVENT_RAISE.
CALL FUNCTION 'RSSM_EVENT_RAISE'
DESTINATION                      'LS_QBW_100'
EXPORTING
EVENTID                   = 'ZTEST'
*    EVENTPARM                 = ' '
*    TARGET_INSTANCE           = ' '
*    EXCEPTIONS
*    BAD_EVENTID               = 1
*    EVENTID_DOES_NOT_EXIST    = 2
*    EVENTID_MISSING           = 3
*    RAISE_FAILED              = 4
*    OTHERS                    = 5
            .
IF SY-SUBRC <> 0.
*    MESSAGE ID SY-MSGID TYPE SY-MSGTY NUMBER SY-MSGNO
*    WITH SY-MSGV1 SY-MSGV2 SY-MSGV3 SY-MSGV4.
ENDIF.
```

The call of a remote process chain from a local process chain is simpler. *Start via metachain* Same as with the integration of local subchains, the call to a remote subchain is defined as an individual process step in a process chain.

For this purpose, you can use the process type *Remote Process Chain,* which needs to be given the technical name of the process chain to be called as well as the logical name on which the process chain is defined and to be executed (see figure 28–22).

The call to a remote subchain is made asynchronously, so you need to not only indicate the system needs on which the remote process chain is to be called, but also the calling BW system since, after the termination of the remote process chain, it receives a completion confirmation with error status to which the calling metachain can react.

From a technical perspective, the start of a remote process chain is *Start via API call* configured similarly to the start of a local process chain, which is through function module RSPC_API_CHAIN_START.

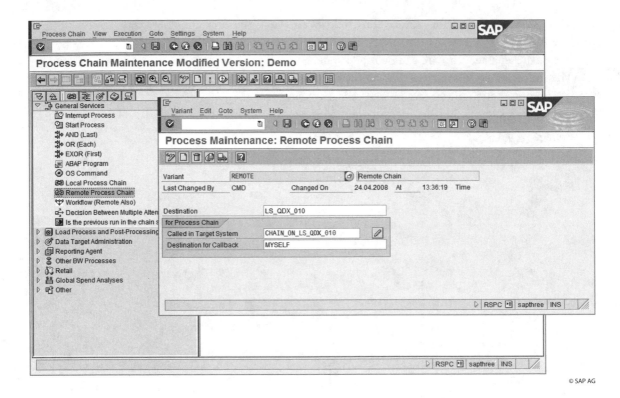

© SAP AG

Figure 28–22

Call to a remote subchain

Since this function module is RFC enabled, it can be called not only from the local process chain of a BW system but also from a remote SAP ERP system.

29   Time Slots

When designing standard operations, you need to consider that they basically differ from the analysis operations. While the analysis operation requires a number of dialog processes, often accesses the same data in read mode, and does not place any exclusive locks on data, the processes in standard operations mostly run in the background (batch), they change the database, and they interfere with other processes by placing lock entries.

For this reason, the execution of standard operations and analysis operations should be coordinated timewise, especially to isolate processes in standard operations that would massively limit a running analysis operation that is running in parallel.[197]

In the simplest case, the design of standard operations assumes that there are two fixed time slots that define the time period (usually nighttime) for load and administration processes and the time period (usually daytime) for analysis activities. Optimally, the load and the administration processes start with the change of the business mode[198] from DAY to NIGHT and they provide current data on time the next morning. Further, all users work in a shared time zone and they are interested in using BW only between 8 a.m. and 6 p.m.

However, the optimal case is only an idealistic vision that is rarely found in reality. The time slot for load and administration processes instead needs to be defined in alignment with the source system and it

---

197. This is especially the case with the change run, rollup, and compression runs that cause temporary inconsistencies and locks as well as load processes if they are combined with a deletion of indexes. Displacement of data in the cache of the database and the buffers for the application server result in further conflict potential between standard and analysis operations.
198. From a system perspective, the operation mode primarily determines the number of batch and dialog processes in the BW system. The change of the operation mode comes with the activation of the event SAP_OPMODE_SWITCH and the event parameter DAY or NIGHT (for reactions to events, see section 28.1).

often collides in large interconnected systems with the daily analysis operations.

> In this chapter, we describe solutions that can be used with BW systems in large, complex, and hardly predictable interconnected systems. Should you be in the lucky position to extract data from source systems that provide data on time and where the data is (at least halfway) reliable, you may skip this chapter. The approaches we describe are sometimes strenuous and should not be attempted without compelling reasons.

The combination of system-specific general conditions and requirements for data preparation results in an inexhaustible variety of possible solutions for the design of time slots.

In the following sections, different problems and their specific solution approaches will be explained:

- Fixed time slots
- Initiated time slots
- Source-system-specific time slots

The solution approaches can be combined to meet individual basic conditions of a BW system.

29.1 Fixed Time Slots

For the extraction, SAP BW works according to the "pull principle" and collects data without waiting for a source system.

From a technical perspective, a source system is ready at any given time to supply data to BW. For example, the extraction of sales order documents in the delta procedure can be made at any given time—only sales order documents that were available at the start of the extraction will be extracted. Thus, independently from the source system, a point in time could be defined when SAP BW is to run load processes.

However, if the same sales order documents are not entered manually and over the whole day but, for example, supplied to the order entry via batch input[199] in one piece from another system, it does not make sense for the BW system to execute the load process two hours earlier.

---

199. Batch input is a technology from SAP R/3 to execute an automated transaction entry based on external controlling information (e.g., files).

In these cases, the extraction time needs to be aligned to the conditions of the respective source system. In practice, the points in time for an extraction need to be defined not only per source system but also per process (e.g., order entry, delivery, invoicing, creation of the receipt, etc.).

> If the determination of supply times comprises several source systems and processes, you should create corresponding time plans and have agreements with everybody involved (i.e., the source system responsible). In practice, if this is missed, corresponding agreements will be undermined or forgotten over time.

29.2 Initiated Time Slots

As far as the time of the data supply for a data source can be defined, the extraction can be made at fixed times as described in the previous section However, this is not possible if the time of the supply is unknown.

In such a case, it makes more sense to initiate the extraction through the source system. For each DataSource, you need to determine how its readiness to supply can be identified (e.g., termination of the invoice run) and how at the time of the readiness an appropriate message can be given to BW.

> The initiation of an extraction through a source system often requires modifications in the source system operations that cannot be made in BW. At this point, you should always include source system administrators.

Basically, with the initiation of the extraction through a source system, the question comes up regarding what is to happen if the readiness to supply is signaled "too late"—e.g., if the supply is signaled at 7 a.m. instead of at 5 a.m. even though it is clear that extraction and staging will still be running when the analysis operations start at 7:30 a.m.

There are the following options:

- The extraction is executed no matter what; i.e., the BW system reacts to an identical supply signal at any time.
- The extraction is not executed; i.e., the BW system no longer reacts to a supply signal after a fixed time.
- The extraction is pushed up; i.e., from a defined time onwards, the BW system no longer waits for the supply signal but prematurely starts the extraction itself.

Which one of these alternatives to use is mostly based on the organizational requirements from the system. Technically, the conditions for the initiated start of process chains are met with conditions regarding the chaining of process steps (see section 28.2.1).

29.3 Source-System-Specific Time Slots

In the previous discussion of time slots, it was assumed that there is a clearly defined time when the extraction from a DataSource is to start. However, transactional data especially is often extracted from several source systems, for example, since globally, several SAP ERP systems are used for decentralized order entry, but the data is consolidated centrally in BW.

If the extracted data is to be consolidated in the staging in one place, this partially results in a serialization that leads to long downtimes. Usually, the activation of new data in DataStore Objects, the rollup of aggregates, and the compression of BasisCubes can be executed only when all data transfer processes are completed.

However, with the different DataSources, the time of the completion will vary substantially if the supplied data volumes differ. This becomes more evident, for example, with an extraction at 10 p.m. Central European Time and there is still a high system load on the U.S. systems so that the extraction needs to start at least four hours later there.

It may happen in such cases that the data from several source systems has been updated for a long time but that it is still not available to the user since the activation of new data in DataStore Objects, rollup, and compression still wait for one single source system.

The solution to the problem is not to design the time sequence of the single processes. Instead, the goal of the design of the data model and the staging needs to be an execution that is parallelized without dependencies on each other. An example for such architecture was given in chapter 26. There, we have data targets and staging workflows for each DataSource that can be executed and managed independently from each other.

The final consolidation of all data should only be made with the use of a MultiProvider, but given its virtual design, the MultiProvider does not represent a serialization of the data flow (see figure 26–1).

The design of dedicated data targets (DataStore Objects, BasisCubes) for each DataSource basically makes sense with several source systems even if the consolidation of the data flow would not be a problem from a time perspective. Here, the advantage lies in the fact that the data from single source systems can be managed individually (deleted, rebuild, reorganized, etc.).

30 Organization and Sequence

As soon as the design of the time slot for standard operations is completed, the question of the components of standard operations comes up. A large number of processes are involved in completely designed standard operations that are to be executed in a sometimes very complex dependency.

Usually, the processes within a time slot for administration and load processes are executed in a statically defined sequence. The following description assumes an ideal sequence schema of processes that offers a comprehensive integration of all process types into the standard operations.

Figure 30–1 shows the sequence schema of processes in standard operations. Here, the use of the reference architecture as described in the chapters on extraction and staging is assumed.

In addition to the listed processes, each standard operation requires a range of supporting processes through which the physical structures in the database system can continuously perform well. These processes are dealt with model trimming in chapter 32.

Supporting processes

In many cases, the time slots for load processes are calculated very small so that the highest possible transfer rate needs to be achieved. Besides corresponding tuning measures (see also chapter 24), this can also be achieved with a high level of parallelization. For this reason, with the description of processes, we'll also explain the options of parallelization.

If despite all tuning measures no time slot for the staging can be found that is outside analysis times, then the staging processes and the data analysis inevitably need to overlap.

Standard operations with overlapping staging cycles

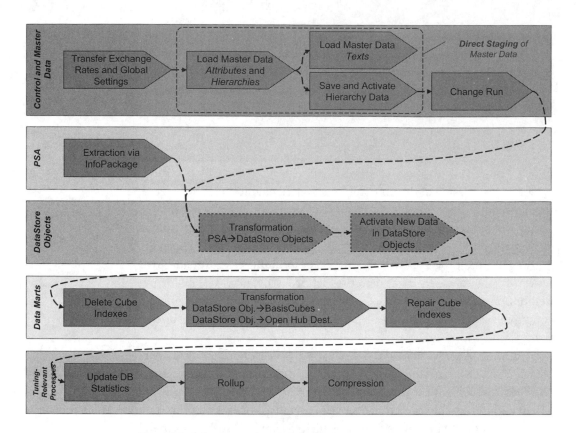

Figure 30–1 *Sequence schema of processes*

If staging processes and data analysis overlap, then performance short-comings are inevitable, but at least lock situations can be avoided. Appendix E.1 describes which processes can be executed in parallel and which lock each other.

In this case, the processes of the standard operations can be separated into different overlapping cycles where especially processes that have little impact on the performance of the data analysis can overlap with the analysis operations.[200] However, processes that come with considerable impairment of the data analysis are executed in an independent cycle that strictly adheres to the time slots defined for the analysis operations.

With the separation of the cycles, the extraction into the PSA, the transformation in DataStore Objects, and the activation of the DataStore

---

200. In an extreme case, these processes can run around the clock.

Objects are usually combined into one cycle that can run around the clock, if required. The loading of control and master data, the governing of data marts and the tuning-relevant processes, however, are separated in cycles that need to adhere to the predefined time slots.[201]

In the following sections, the single processes are explained in the sequence in which they should be arranged in standard operations. The loading of master data attributes, hierarchies, and texts is combined under the term *master data*. With the description of each process, we also explain how the respective process types are to be defined from the perspective of process chain controlling.

The description of process chains thus refers to the explained organization of processes and is limited to the required process types. However, a complete description of all available process types is not the goal, here, especially since some process types can only be found in the old staging up to BW release 3.x.

30.1 Transfer of Exchange Rates and Global Settings

If currency conversions are made with data integration, BW always needs to dispose of the current exchange rate information and global settings (see section 19.3.7).

The requirements on current exchange rate information and global settings are very individual for each system. For example, measurements might not be changed in some companies for 10 years. However, the need for current information is never to be excluded, and since the effort for the supply of current information is very low, the transfer of current exchange rates and global settings should be part of each standard operation.

Basically, the transfer of current exchange rates and global settings should be made prior to all other processes in standard operations so that all processes can access current information. The parallelization of this data transfer is irrelevant given the short runtimes.

With process chain controlling, the transfer of exchange rates and global settings needs to be made by calling ABAP programs since there is no respective process type for this task.

---

201. This is to separate the rollup of aggregates, the compression of the fact table, the execution of the change run, the deletion of indexes, and the entry of new data in BasisCubes from the analysis operations.

The following programs are to be called:

- RSIMPCURFILE to transfer exchange rates from a file
- RSIMPCURR to transfer exchange rates from an SAP ERP source system
- RSIMPCUST to transfer global settings from an SAP ERP source system

These are the same programs that are executed with the manual transfer of exchange rates and global settings in the Data Warehousing Workbench.

Prior to the initial scheduling of these programs, you need to add a branch to the manual transfer of exchange rates (see appendix A) and the selection made needs to be stored as a variant (see figure 30–2 using the example of the program RSIMPCURRFILE).

Figure 30–2

Set variant to transfer exchange rates

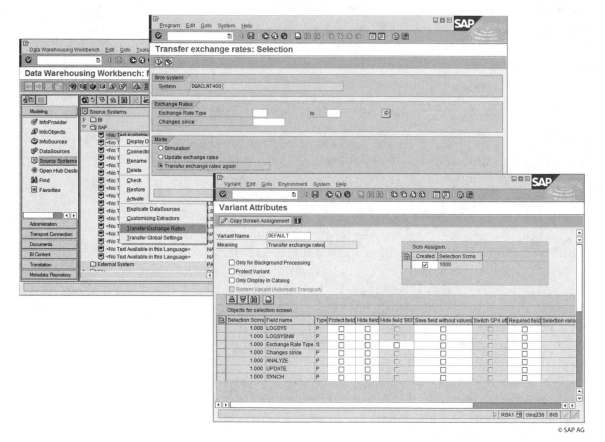

© SAP AG

The thus-stored variant can be used when the program is scheduled and it determines the source system for exchange rates.

Since some global settings can only be transferred completely (e.g., currency translation ratios), for the interconnection of several source systems, there needs to be a clear definition of the global settings. You should always select a source system that you consider to be the leading system for global settings.

30.2 Loading Master Data

For master data, the loading sequence cannot be freely defined but comes with a range of limitations.

On the one hand, dependencies among InfoObjects need to be considered. Each InfoObject can be the attribute of another InfoObject or be used as a characteristics node in external hierarchies. Figure 30–3 shows these dependencies using the example of client- and sales-relevant master data.

Figure 30–3

Dependencies of InfoObjects

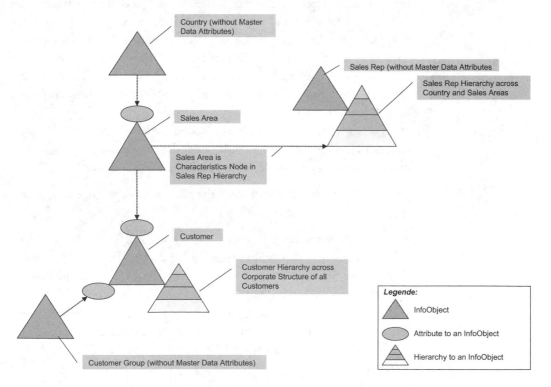

The consideration of dependencies is absolutely necessary if, for data quality assurance purposes, the integrity of the master data attributes is checked during the loading (see section 23.3).

Referential integrity

The referential integrity check assumes that navigation attributes for an InfoObject are loaded only if all master data was loaded for the supplied attribute values. The sales area North would thus be accepted as an attribute value in the customer base only if the InfoObject sales area already contained a master data record for the sales area North.

If the integrity is not reviewed, the evaluation of the dependencies among InfoObjects is still recommended for performance reasons since for nonexisting attribute values, default values need to be created in the attribute InfoObjects[202] and this may be very time consuming.

So, possibly for integrity reasons but certainly for performance reasons, the sequence of the load processes for master data should be oriented toward the following general conditions:

- Master data attributes for an InfoObject (see section 6.2.2) may be loaded only if the master data attributes of all navigation attributes were loaded already. If the navigation InfoObjects do not have any master data, they do not need to be loaded previously.
- External hierarchies (see section 6.2.5) may be loaded only if the master data of the respective InfoObject and also the master data of possibly available characteristics nodes were loaded. If the InfoObject of the characteristics nodes does not have any master data, it does not need to be loaded previously either.
- Texts (see section 6.2.1) are always loaded (together) at the end since this can be done without further dependencies and also parallel to other processes (e.g., parallel to the subsequent change run).

Considering these general conditions, the sequencing for the example in figure 30–3 could be made as follows:

- At first, only the master data attributes (country) for the InfoObject *sales area* are loaded. All other InfoObjects do not contain any master data or have the sales area as a navigation attribute (client). The external hierarchies cannot be loaded either since they have the sales area as a characteristics node (sales hierarchy) or the master data to the respective InfoObject is not loaded yet (client hierarchy).
- In the next step, the *sales rep hierarchy* as well as the *client base attributes* (client group) are loaded in parallel. The loading of the

202. This only applies to navigation attributes. Pure display attributes are not impacted by this disadvantage.

client hierarchy is not possible in this step since the client master data needs to be loaded first.

- The last step is the loading of the *client hierarchy.*
- All *master data texts* can then be loaded in parallel (also parallel to the subsequent change run).

This example shows that even with a very simple combination, comprehensive dependencies need to be considered. The structuring of dependencies even makes sense for the design of standard operations if it could be left out for performance and integrity checks.

With the process chain controlling, for the loading of master data, the process type *execute InfoPackage* is available; it also looks after the entries into the master data tables of the InfoObjects (if direct staging is given). With the execution of the InfoPackage, all parameters are used that were set with the definition of the InfoPackage (see section 15.2.3).

Particularly with the loading of hierarchies, you needs to consider that the saving, renaming, and activating of hierarchy data might have to be done in separate processes. This is especially the case when a hierarchy is combined from several subtrees so that the saving and activating can only be done after the loading of all subtrees (see section 21.3.2).

Save and activate hierarchy

When external hierarchies are loaded, the saving of the hierarchy explicitly needs to follow the loading of hierarchy data. Here, you can use the process type *save hierarchy,* which can only be used in combination with the previously executed InfoPackage for the loading of the hierarchy data (see figure 30–4).

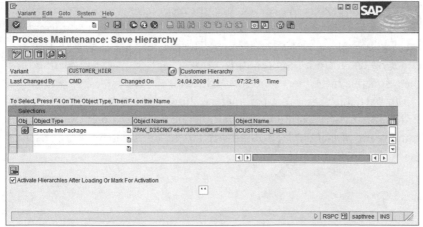

Figure 30–4

Process type: save hierarchy

© SAP AG

This InfoPackage to load hierarchy data also serves to parameterize the process type *save hierarchy*. As parameters, the loaded hierarchy and possibly the technical name are used. The hierarchy needs to be renamed prior to saving.

If a hierarchy is not activated or marked for activation through a process chain, the activation/marking can be done manually in the hierarchy maintenance or with the program RRHI_HIERARCHY_ACTIVATE.

30.3 Change Run

After the loading, master data attributes and external hierarchies are only immediately actively available if they are neither used in aggregates nor used in the indexes of the BI accelerator—that is almost never the case with large BW systems that require tuning.

In this case, master data first needs to be activated in the change run before it is available for the data analysis (see section 7.1.2). This process needs to be executed after the loading of master data attributes or after the activation of external hierarchies.

Due to possible lock situations, the change run must not be executed in parallel to loading master data attributes or external hierarchies. However, it may be executed if master data is loaded since master data does not need to be activated.

The staging of transactional data should not be executed parallel to the change run either if the staging depends on master data content (e.g., with the storing of master data attributes).

In the process chain maintenance, the respective process type *attribute change run* comprises a multitude of different parameterization forms that can also be combined with each other. The master data to be activated can either be taken from the preceding InfoPackage or be clearly defined for the respective InfoObjects and hierarchies (see figure 30–5).

In particular cases, the parameterization in the form of InfoPackages and hierarchies is justified, especially if the change run is not a central component of standard operations but is to be isolated for a subset of master data when it is executed.

The definition of InfoPackages, InfoObjects, and hierarchies in the change run only appears to isolate different change run variants from each other. The execution of the change run is limited to the preset parameters, but systemwide, only one instance of the change run can be executed. Thus, you should always coordinate the execution times of the change run systemwide for all applications on a BW system.

Process Maintenance: Attribute Change Run

Variant	CR1		Change Run
Last Changed By	CMD	Changed On 24.04.2008 At 07:32:41 Time	

To Select, Press F4 On the Object Type, Then F4 on the Name

Selections

Obj	Object Type	Object Name	Object Name	
	Execute InfoPackage	ZPAK_D35CRK7464Y36VS4HDMJF4MNB	0CUSTOMER_HIER	
	Data Transfer Process			
	Hierarchy			
	InfoObject			
	Execute InfoPackage			
	Report Varaints			

✕ Parallel Processing

☐ Deactivate BIA if Error During Change Run
☐ Fill Deactivated Aggregates After Change Run
Error Tolerance in Change Run as Percentage

RSPC sapthree INS

© SAP AG

Mostly, the change run is a central component of the standard operations that is to activate all new master data. For this purpose, the explicit consideration of each InfoObject and each hierarchy in the process type variant of the change run is very complex and accordingly error prone.

A simple option to execute a mass activation of new master data with the change run is provided with the report variant. Here, in the transaction SE38, an ABAP variant is stored with the report RSDDS_AGGREGATES_ MAINTAIN (this is the change run), which subsequently is available as a report variant for the change run (see figure 30–6).

The advantage of the report variant is mostly that InfoObjects and hierarchies can also be determined with the * sign so that all InfoObjects/hierarchies in the change run are considered.

Figure 30–5

Process type: attribute change run

Parameterization through report variants

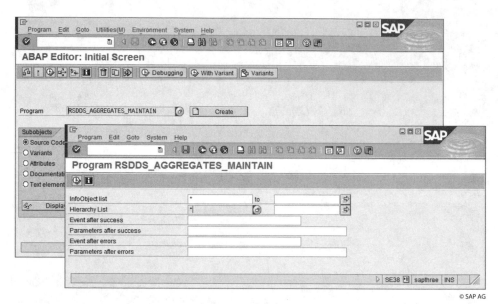

© SAP AG

Figure 30–6
Process type: attribute
change run (report variant
maintenance)

30.4 Extraction into the PSA

The extraction of transactional data into the PSA can be done at any given time—i.e., also parallel to the loading of master data. It is important that the new staging is being used with transformation and data transfer processes since they write InfoPackages for extraction only into the PSA and do not start any further postings into the data targets.

In the process chain controlling, the extraction is made with the process type *execute InfoPackage,* which receives the InfoPackage to be executed as a parameter. Thus, all required parameters for extraction are defined.

Specifically with file DataSources, the parameters set in the DataSource for the selection of data and the external data parameters can be overruled (see section 15.2). However, there is no impact on the settings on the data targets that are only a relic from the staging up to BW release 3.x.

30.5 Transformation: PSA into DataStore Objects

The transfer of transactional data from the PSA into the DataStore Objects requires that the extraction was made into the PSA and that all exchange rates, global settings, and master data are available in the system.

The loading of transactional data into DataStore Objects can be parallelized freely. It can even be written into the same DataStore Object from several processes at the same time. Here, the parallelization is only limited by the BW resources and the source system.

For the entry of PSA data into the data targets, the process type *data transfer process* needs to be added into the process chain after the InfoPackage.

30.6 Activation of DataStore Objects

To transfer the data from a standard DataStore Object from the activation queue into the active data and to make it available as a change log, the new data needs to be activated (see section 17.1.2).

Standard DataStore Objects

Since the activation of new data in DataStore Objects only considers requests that are completely posted, the activation should be executed only after all load processes for a DataStore Object are terminated.

For write-optimized DataStore Objects, the activation of new data is not applicable since with these objects, data is written directly into the change log and delta information is not identified.

Write-optimized DataStore Objects

In the process chain controlling, the process type *activate DataStore Object data* is available. It needs to receive either the DataStore Objects to be activated or the data transfer processes as parameters.

Only one single activation process per DataStore Object can be executed at a time. To improve the performance of the overall system, several different DataStore Objects can be activated at the same time. However, for this purpose, several process steps need to be added to a process chain. The entry of several DataStore Objects in a process type variant only results in a serialized activation of all indicated DataStore Objects.

> Please consider that the relative addressing from a data transfer process does not refer to the data target posted in the data transfer process but to the most recently loaded request by the data transfer process.

By default, with the activation of new data in DataStore Objects, all requests to be activated are integrated into a joint request in the change log of the DataStore Object. This integration (condensing) of all requests to be activated in a joint request in the change log comes with performance advantages involving the activation period as well as the further processing in the subsequent data targets.

Integration of requests in the change log

For the particular case that all requests from a DataStore Object are to be deleted after they were previously activated, BW needs to make a sort of recalculation to the state prior to activation where the data of the change log is used as a basis for the recalculation. If, with the activation, several requests were condensed to one joint request in the change log, all of these requests can only be deleted together, which is often not desired from an administrative perspective.

The activation of new data in DataStore Objects can be redesigned in such a way that for each request, an individual request is generated in the change log, which later enables the deletion of this one request.[203] For reasons of traceability and error finding, it may make sense not to condense requests with the activation.

The activation behavior can be influenced through the parameter *Do Not Condense Requests into One Request When Activation Takes Place* of the process type variant (see figure 30–7).

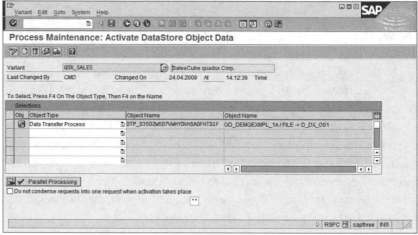

30.7 Deletion of Cube Indexes

With the posting of data in a BasisCube, the database structure needs to adapt the index structures of the change tables to each new and modified

---

203. Only if the respective request is the last to be activated. If, subsequently, further requests were activated, then at first these need to be deleted too, so requests are not freely deletable from the ODS objects.

data record. This (noticeable) effort is not applicable if the indexes of the fact table are deleted prior to the posting (the indexes of all other tables are still required).

The subsequently required complete rebuild of indexes can be much faster than running all other required single updates. Whether it really results in a performance advantage depends on the relation of new/changed records to the existing data records of the fact table.

Trade-off between index customization and index design

If only one record is added to a fact table with several million data records, the collapse of the indexes will not be worthwhile since the rebuild will take significantly more time than the customization of the index structures for a data record. If a million data records are written into an almost empty fact table, then the rebuild of the index structures is much more efficient than the customization of each single data record. The decision on whether indexes are to be deleted prior to the loading always results from a trade-off between new and existing data volume.

The use of cube compression plays a significant role; in BW, the deletion of indexes is limited to the indexes of the uncompressed fact table (F fact table).[204] If, with the cube compression, data is regularly moved from the uncompressed into the compressed fact table, then the uncompressed fact table is relatively small even if the BasisCube contains much data. If a cube is compressed regularly, the deletion of indexes will be worth it even before the posting of smaller data volumes.

Index deletion and compression

The deletion of indexes is only mandatory for Oracle database systems if the posting of data packages in the BasisCubes is parallelized (see section 24.1.5).

Index deletion with Oracle and DB2/UDB

The deletion of indexes results in the fact that reports are practically made impossible due to performance reasons until the indexes are rebuilt. If analysis activities from the user cannot be ruled out at this time of the standard operation, then the parallel posting of data packages should be dropped so that indexes do not need to be deleted.

In any case, indexes should not be deleted unnecessarily early. Optimally, they should only be deleted prior to the posting of new data.[205]

---

204. This only applies to the deletion of indexes with process chains. With the deletion of indexes from the cube administration, all indexes of a BasisCube and its aggregates are deleted (see section 24.3).
205. Some SAP documentation states that the deletion of indexes should be executed as the first process in standard operations. This is unnecessarily early since it already impacts the analysis operations at an early stage where indexes might still exist.

To delete indexes with the process chain controlling, the process type *delete index* is available, and as a parameter, the BasisCube whose indexes are to be deleted needs to be transferred (see figure 30–8).

Figure 30–8
Process type: delete index

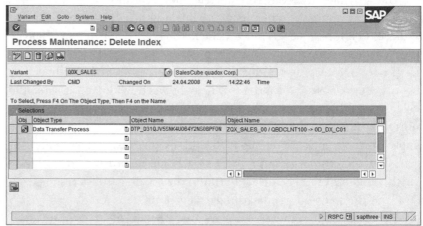

© SAP AG

Here, the deletion of indexes refers to the indexes of the uncompressed fact table of a BasisCube but not to the indexes of the compressed fact table.

If the compression of the respective BasisCube is executed regularly, the rebuilding of the indexes after the posting of new data will not result in an unusual system load since the majority of data is in the compressed fact table whose indexes will remain. However, if compression is not executed regularly, the posting performance advantage from the deletion of indexes is balanced with the additional runtime that comes from the rebuilding of the indexes.

30.8 Transformation: DataStore Objects in Data Marts

After the deletion of cube indexes, data is posted into the data targets of the data mart layer—depending on whether DataStore Objects are used for staging from the change log of the DataStore Objects or from the PSA.

The data targets of the data mart layer are mostly BasisCubes that are used for the data analysis but also open hub destinations to supply other systems.

If the data mart layer is filled from the change log of DataStore Objects, then the delta creation of the DataStore Objects ensures that only new records or changes are transferred to the data mart layer.

Posting from the change log

The data transfer is made via data transfer processes that extract data in a delta procedure. This is the simplest option to supply the data mart layer since the data mart layer receives all data fully prepared.

However, if the data mart layer is directly filled with DataStore Objects from the PSA, then the delta ability of the respective DataSources in the extraction layer will become especially relevant; while with the posting of new data in DataStore Objects, existing data can be overwritten with new data, this is not possible with BasisCubes. Here, only new requests can be written into the fact table without changing the existing requests.

Posting from the PSA...

This procedure is correct if the loaded data is delta information. However, if a DataSource is not able to use a delta procedure, then the posting of full information would result in the fact that new data is added to the existing data and values and quantities are accounted for several times.[206]

To prevent this, existing data needs to be deleted from the respective BasisCube before/after new data is loaded. Here, the difference between **complete** deletion and **selective** deletion needs to be explained.

...with BasisCubes

The **complete deletion** of the total BasisCube makes sense if, after a new request is loaded, only this request is to be contained in the BasisCube. The deletion needs to be made before data of the new request is entered into the data target.

The deletion of data target content can be defined in the process chain controlling through the process type *complete deletion of data target contents,* which can be parameterized with the respective data target or the data transfer process (see figure 30–9).

Sometimes, with the loading of a request, not the complete content of a BasisCube but only certain requests are to be **selectively** deleted after the posting of new data.

This may be the case if data from several sources systems is updated in a BasisCube and each of the source systems provides a full upload. In this case, with a new load process only old requests that come from the same source system may be deleted from the BasisCube.

This functionality is available in process chains with the process type *delete overlapping requests from InfoCube.* The selection of the requests to

---

206. This might be correct; e.g., if the time of loading is a call date that is part of the data analysis.

be deleted is made immediately after the start of the data transfer process with the settings made in the process variant. However, the deletion itself will take place only when the new request is completely updated (see figure 30–10).

Figure 30–9
Process type: complete deletion of data target contents

© SAP AG

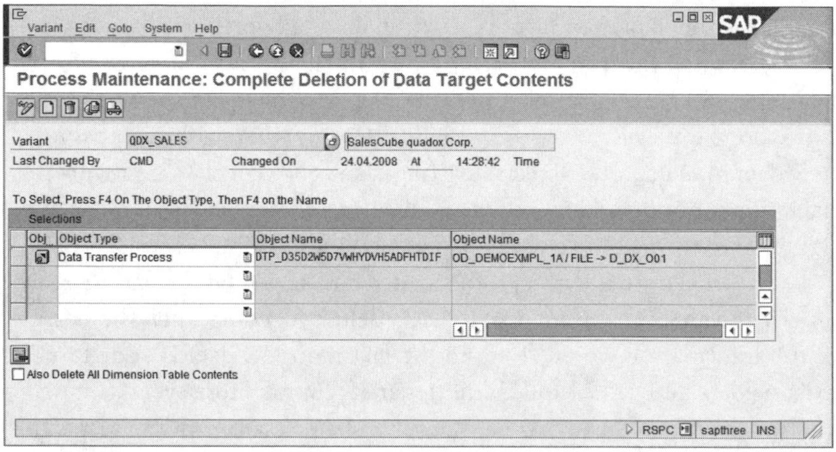

Figure 30–10
Process type: delete overlapping requests from InfoCubes

© SAP AG

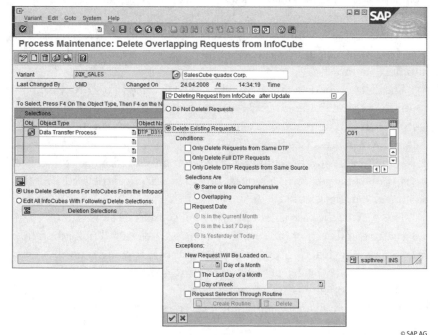

The available options for the selection of the requests to be deleted are enough to even make complex deletion selections. However, should the selection of the requests to be deleted be more comprehensive, then the respective requests can be identified with the use of an individual ABAP routine.

The selective deletion of requests only works if BasisCubes and aggregates were not compressed yet (see section 7.1.2). If this is the case, the selective deletion will not be possible.

If an open hub destination is directly posted to from the PSA, then the DataSource in the extraction layer absolutely needs to be able to provide delta information. Other than with BasisCubes, data that was supplied to an open hub destination cannot be deleted from that location since the supplied systems might already have picked up the data.

…with open hub destinations

Basically, it needs to be mentioned that the supply of an open hub destination from a DataSource is questionable since, in this case, BW would only be a continuous flow controller and the transferred data could not be reviewed subsequently

30.9 Repair of Cube Indexes

As soon as the posting of transactional data in the BasisCube is terminated, the cube indexes that were possibly deleted earlier need to be rebuilt.

Since the availability of indexes is a performance-critical point for the analysis operation of BW, the generation should be made for each Basis-Cube as early as possible. This means that the index generation of a Basis-Cube should not wait until all transactional data is posted, but only until the transactional data for the specific BasisCube was posted.

Posting into and generation of indexes can thus overlap for different BasisCubes; i.e., indexes can already be generated for a cube with FI data while a cube with SD data is still being filled with data.

The generation of cube indexes (also referred to as index repair) is defined in the process chain controlling by the process type *generate index* (see figure 30–11).

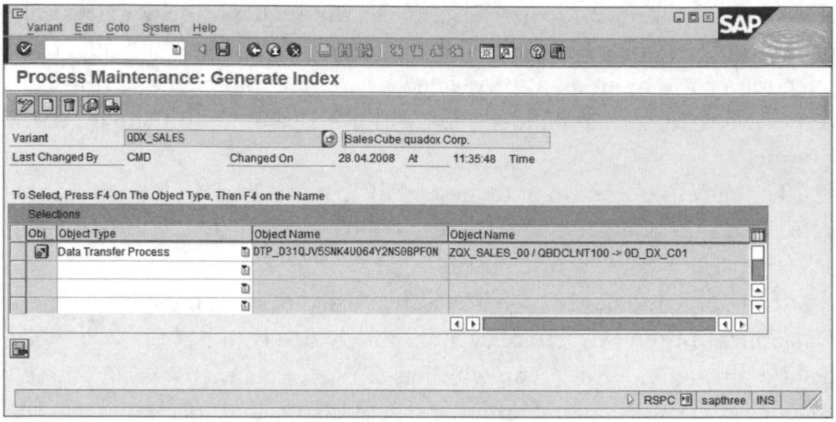

Figure 30–11

Process type: generate index

© SAP AG

30.10 Update of Database Statistics

The cost-based optimizers for all database systems rely on the current database statistics to enable well-performing accesses for the data analysis (see section 7.2.4).

The database statistics update for a single BasisCube can be made directly after the posting of new transactional data and thus needs to be integrated into standard operations accordingly.

If the changes to a BasisCube after the posting of new data are not significant enough to require an update of the database statistics after each posting, then the update is not applied at this stage and will be executed with an independent update of statistics.

The statistics need to be updated at regular intervals for all tables of the database system anyway. If statistics are to be recalculated specifically for all BasisCubes, then the program SAP_ANALYZE_ALL_INFOCUBES can be used.[207]

In the process chain controlling, the process type *construct database statistics* is available to purposefully generate statistics for a BasisCube. With the parameterization, the BasisCubes can be addressed in a fixed or relative way from the provided data transfer processes (see figure 30–12).

---

207. The program updates the statistics of the fact and dimension tables as well as the statistics of the master data tables of all BasisCubes.

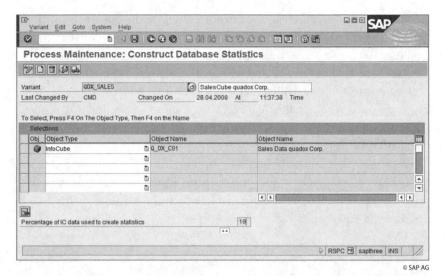

Figure 30–12
*Process type: construct
database statistics*

© SAP AG

When updating database statistics in process chains, you need to consider that the database tables of the respective BasisCubes are locked for the duration of the update.

Especially when the database statistics do not necessarily need to be updated right after the termination of a load process, since there is little change, the periodic update outside standard operations should be favored. These would typically be made with database tools (e.g., BRCON-NECT for Oracle).

30.11 Rollup of Filled Aggregates/BIA Indexes

If aggregates are defined for a BasisCube or the BasisCube is indexed in the BI accelerator, then the data of the posted requests is provided by the OLAP processor only when it is completely transferred in aggregates or BIA indexes, and the aggregates or the BIA indexes and the BasisCubes are consistently connected.

At the time of the rollup, requests can be deleted from a BasisCube only if they are defined as being request receiving (see section 7.1) or if all aggregates of the cube are deactivated.

From a quality assurance perspective, the rollup is an important level of automation. If a request is updated with the wrong content, then the correction can no longer be made through a simple deletion of the request.

In any case, the rollup is to be executed before the compression since with the compression of a BasisCube, all information in a BasisCube that would enable a selective transfer of request data into aggregates is lost.[208]

With the process chain controlling, the process type *rollup of filled aggregates* rolls up all filled aggregates of the addressed BasisCube. Depending on whether the aggregates of a cube are defined as request receiving or not, the compression of the aggregate fact table will be executed after the rollup.

It makes sense in special cases to not immediately rollup posted requests from a BasisCube. For this purpose, in the process type variant a sort of "waiting period" can be defined in which the requests are not rolled up (see figure 30–13).

Figure 30–13
Process type: rollup of filled aggregates

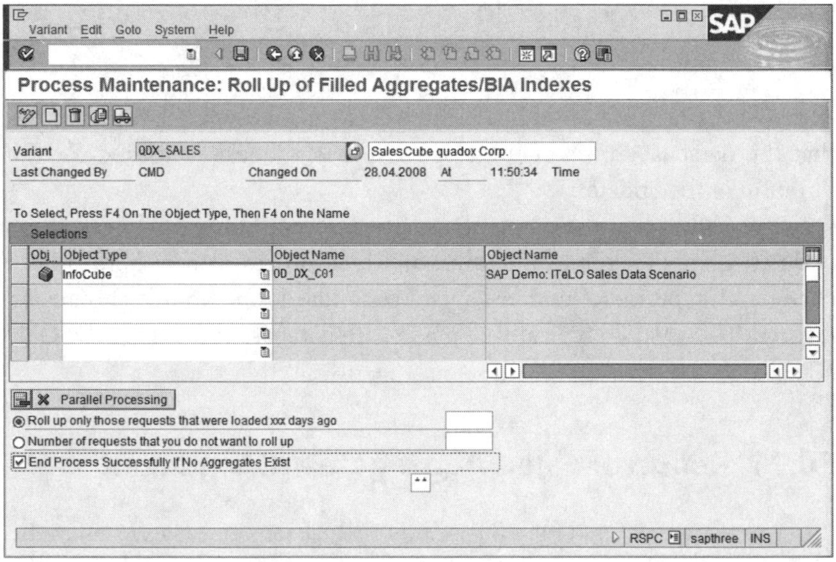

© SAP AG

The time delay of the rollup can make sense to review data in terms of quality before it is filled into aggregates. As long as a request was not rolled up into the aggregates of the cubes, it is not available for data analysis and is only considered in special queries that work in the request mode.

Initial fill of new aggregates

Any unactivated aggregate as well as any activated but not filled aggregate is not considered by the rollup, so new aggregates are not filled

---

208. Strictly speaking, the request ID that identifies the data of a load process is irrevocably lost with the compression.

initially. If active but not filled aggregates are to be initially filled from the process chain controlling, the process type *initial fill of new aggregates* can be used (see figure 30–14).

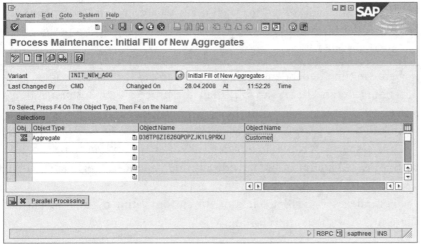

Figure 30–14
Process type: initial fill of new aggregates

For indexes in the BI accelerator, the initial fill of new aggregates has no special meaning.

The different options for parameterization enable the different usages of this process type. In practice, the following forms of parameterization have proven helpful:

■ *Fixed Parameterization of an Aggregate:* The indication of a specific aggregate is especially suited if a new aggregate made it into the BW system through the transport route and if this aggregate is to be given its own process chain for the initial fill. If the respective process chain is also provided with the start condition Immediate Start, then the aggregate is immediately filled after the execution of the transport.

■ *Fixed Parameterization of a Cube:* The indication of a specific cube results in the initial fill of all new aggregates of this cube (already filled aggregates remain untouched). Such a process is especially suited to create a tool that helps to initially fill all aggregates of a cube. Process chains with such a process are usually not included in the standard operation but started manually.

■ *Relative Parameterization via InfoPackages:* As with the indication of a specific cube, with the relative parameterization of an InfoPackage, all new aggregates that the cubes referenced in the InfoPackage are initially filled. With the use of the InfoPackage, this form of parameterization is especially suited for such cases where in standard operations (e.g., after the rollup) generally all newly added aggregates of the cubes are to be filled.

Customization of time-dependent aggregates   If there are time-dependent aggregates whose call date is to be identified depending on an OLAP variable, then the process type *customize time-dependent aggregates* will adjust these aggregates through a new calculation of the call date.

The respective process in BW does not offer any options to parameterize but instead it adjusts systemwide all time-dependent aggregates to the new value of the respective OLAP variables.

For indexes in the BI accelerator, the customization of time-dependent aggregates is without any meaning.

30.12 Compression

As a continuation of the rollup, the compression is the final condensation of the cube data. If a request was compressed in a BasisCube, it can never again be removed from a BasisCube by administrative means!

Should an erroneous request still make its way into the compressed fact table, then the data can be corrected only through a complete rebuilding of the cube or through individually developed mechanisms in the staging.

Still, especially with the use of Oracle and DB2/UDB databases, a compression of error-free requests should be executed to make use of the particular performance advantages that come with the partitioning, the multidimensional clustering, and the bitmapped indexes (see sections 7.2 and 7.3).

Other than the rollup, the compression of requests in a BasisCube has no impact on the availability of the requests for the data analysis (see section 7.1.2). Even uncompressed requests are used for analyses by the analytical engine, but they then originate from the normal fact tables that are unfavorably partitioned and indexed for the data analysis.

Thus, the compression could basically be made at regular intervals outside standard operations to faster terminate standard operations.

After a request is compressed, it can no longer be deleted from a Basis-Cube through the cube administration. Thus, the time of compression is especially relevant from a quality assurance perspective. Especially in the introductory phase of your BW system, you should carefully consider if an automation of the compression makes sense.

In the process chain controlling, the compression of a BasisCube is defined similarly to the rollup of filled aggregates. A sort of wait period can be defined for the requests here too (see figure 30–15).

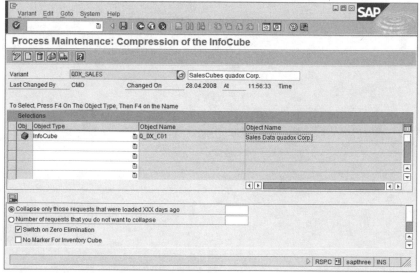

Figure 30–15

Process type: compression

© SAP AG

If the aggregates of a BasisCube are not defined as request receiving, then the aggregates will be compressed after the compression of the cube since the request information in the aggregates does not add any additional value from this point in time onward.

The functioning of the zero elimination as well as the suppression of the marker update corresponds in process chains with the procedure described in section 6.4.1.

31 Monitoring

The term *monitoring* describes the periodically repeated (manual) maintenance tasks that should be part of system administration. These are tasks to detect and eliminate unexpectedly occurring problems in running operations.

A range of monitoring functions have been created, partially from old BW releases and partially from the ERP basis technology. Due to the established structure, the functions often duplicate.

With release 7, BW itself combines a multitude of monitoring functions in the administration area of the Data Warehousing Workbench. It can be called via transaction RSMON (see figure 31–1).

In this chapter, we'll describe a selection of tasks that have proven helpful in most BW systems from an application maintenance perspective. The tasks that are additionally relevant for a specific BW system (e.g., validation of data content) will be defined individually in each case.

Fundamental for the *general monitoring* is the **application log,** the **data target administration,** and the **monitoring of process chains** (see sections 31.1–31.3).

General monitoring

Besides the general monitoring, there is a range of *specific monitoring areas* in BW where the **monitoring of load processes** and the monitoring of real-time data acquisition play a particular role. These are explicitly explained in sections 31.4 and 31.5.

Specific monitoring

The explanations on monitoring thus do not follow the structure given in the administration area of the Data Warehousing Workbench. If possible, reference to the Data Warehousing Workbench is made.

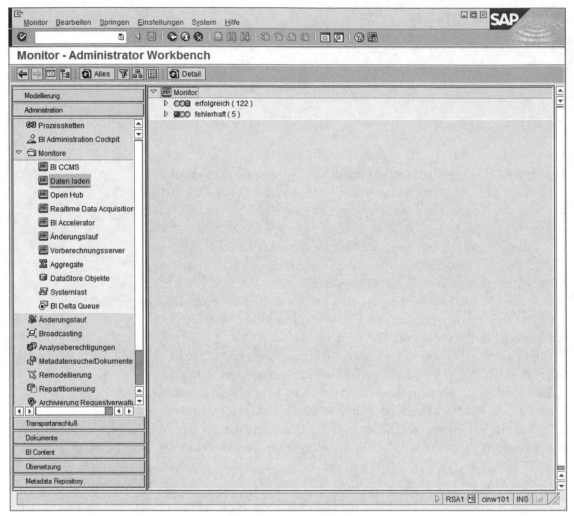

© SAP AG

Figure 31–1
Monitoring in the administration area of the DWWB

31.1 Application Log

As basic technology for the monitoring, BW provides the application log. The application log stores a range of information that spans from the definition of metadata via the data target administration to the staging processes. Numerous log entries are made repeatedly (e.g., rollup log from the respective BasisCube's and the corresponding requests' perspective).

The application log can be reached via transaction SLG1 and it is arranged in a hierarchical structure of **objects** and **subobjects** (see figure 31–2).

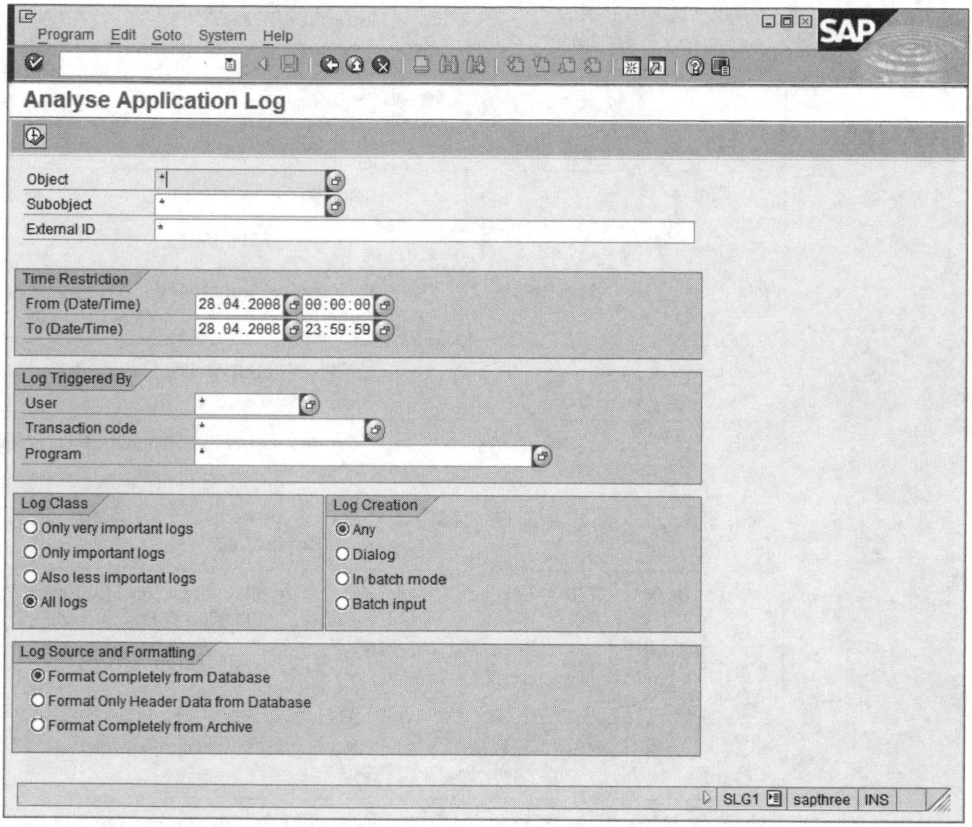

© SAP AG

Log entries that belong together from a time or content perspective are basically linked by an **external identification** and they allow for an exact categorization—e.g., all rollup processes for a BasisCube within the log subobject monitor.

For logging, over 900 objects and even more diverse external identifications are available where identical information is often stored several times or is irrelevant for the monitoring of staging processes. A rather small selection of log entries are relevant, especially entries under the object RSSM and the subobject MON (monitor).

With scheduler and monitor, more detailed information on the type of log is provided only by the external identification. The following table shows the entries relevant for monitoring.

Figure 31–2

Display of the application log

External identification of the log objects scheduler and monitor

Log Object RSSM (Scheduler, Monitor, Tree Callback)	
Log Subobject MON (Monitor)	
-DELET-<DATATARGET>	Deletion of a request in the data target *<DATATARGET>*
<REQUEST-ID>-DELETE_FROM_PSA	Deletion of the request *<REQUEST-ID>* from the PSA
BI_PROCESS_ATTRIBCHAIN	Change run through process chain
BI_STRU _EXT	Change run in the dialog
BI_STRU*<JOBNAME>*_EXT	Change run in the batch
MON:LOG_ACTION-AGGR1-*<CUBE>*	Rollup of aggregates to the Basis-Cube *<CUBE>*
MON:LOG_ACTION-AGGR2-*<CUBE>*	Rebuild of aggregates to the Basis-Cube *<CUBE>*
MON:LOG_ACTION-COMPR-*<CUBE>*	Compression of the BasisCube *<CUBE>*
MON:PROTOCOLL_ACTION-DELET-*<CUBE>*	Selective deletion of data in the BasisCube *<CUBE>*
MON:PROTOCOLL_ACTION-NULLELIM-	Zero value elimination through the program RSCDS_NULLELIM
MON:PROTOCOLL_ACTION-ODSAC-*<DATASTORE>*	Activation of new data in the Data-Store Object *<DATASTORE>*
REBU_<id>-BUILD-*<DATATARGET>*	Rebuild of the data target *<DATA-TARGET>*
RSMDATASTATE_*<DATATARGET>*	Adjustment of the read pointer in the data target *<DATATARGET>*

The general monitoring is especially suited to closer examine staging processes if errors occur and to obtain a historic view on BW processes, if required. For a general review of load processes or process chains, however, BW offers better options.

31.2 Data Target Administration

To receive a current status on the processing of the data transfer processes, the checking of data target administration is easy and often as helpful as the application log (at least if no errors occur). The data target administration can be reached via the standard functions when the respective DataStore Object of the BasisCube (see figure 31–3) is called.

Figure 31–3

Data target administration

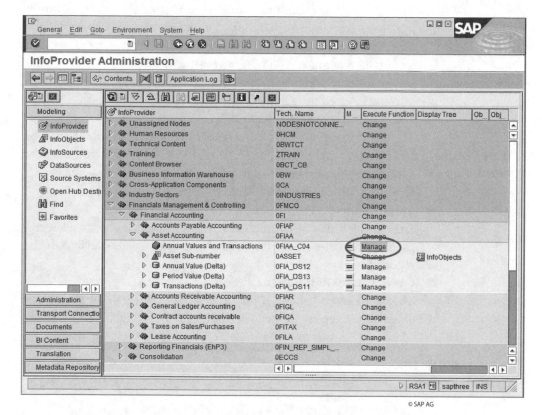

© SAP AG

In the data target administration, under the *Requests* tab, all *requests* posted into this data target are displayed. Depending on whether it is a DataStore Object or a BasisCube, further statuses are displayed.

For the data target administration of BasisCubes (see figure 31–4), these are the following statuses:

▪ **Request for Reporting Available:**
A request for reporting is available if it meets the criteria of the status *qualok;* that is, if it and all its requests are error free and rolled up into aggregates (see section 10.1.1).

▪ **Compression Status of the InfoCube:**
The compression status indicates whether the request is just being compressed (equal sign in the status field) or whether it is already compressed (check mark in the status field).

■ **Compression Status of Aggregates:**
The compression status of aggregates shows whether the request is also
compressed in the fact tables of the aggregate. The compression of
aggregates can either be made after a rollup or with the cube compression (see section 7.1). The situation displayed in figure 31–4 that
request 85 is compressed in the aggregates but request 91 is not is not
very realistic in practice since after the rollup, requests are either basically compressed in aggregates or not at all.

■ **Data Mart Status of the Request:**
The data mart status indicates whether the request from a BasisCube
was extracted and posted into further data targets. The symbol in the
data mart status is then also a button to call an overview of data targets
to which the request was transferred.

■ **Rollup Status (in the InfoCube and in the Aggregates):**
If the rollup is placed, the respective request is rolled up into all aggregates of the cube where the request is usually also available to the
reporting.

■ **Overall Status of the Request:**
This is the overall status of the DTP request. Here, the status field is
also a button through which the status can be maintained or manually
set.

Figure 31–4
Data target administration of
BasisCubes

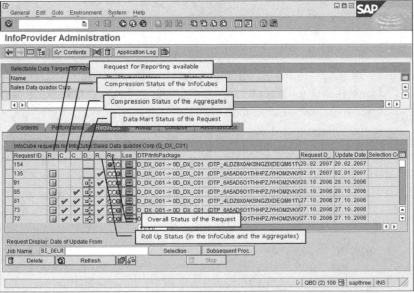

© SAP AG

For the data target administration of DataStore Objects (see figure 31–5), there are the following statuses:

■ **Request Available to Reporting:**
The check mark in this field primarily shows that the request was completely entered and activated and is thus available for further processing (or was further processed already). If the DataStore Object is also used as a basis for the data analysis, this status will also show the availability of the request for the data analysis.

■ **Request ID in the Change Log:**
If the respective request was completely posted and activated, the ID shows the request that was generated with the activation of new data in the change log of the DataStore Object.

The functions regarding the data mart status and the overall status are similar to the functions for cube administration.

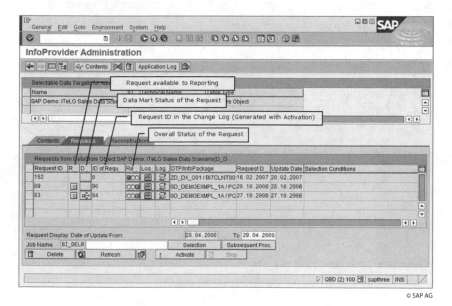

Figure 31–5
Data target administration of DataStore Objects

31.3 Monitoring Process Chains

There are special tools for the monitoring of process chains that help to monitor standard operations on three levels:

■ On the level of the overall status, an overview on selected process chains is given.

■ On the level of process steps, the processing of process steps of a selected process chain is displayed.

■ On detailed level, detailed information on a selected process step is given.

The levels of monitoring are explained in the following sections.

31.3.1 Overview of Selected Process Chains

Figure 31–6

Monitor daily process chains

An overview of the overall status for several process chains is provided with the transaction RSPCM or the program RSPC_MONITOR. Within the transaction, these process chains are defined (systemwide) where the last execution status is to be displayed in the overview (see figure 31–6).

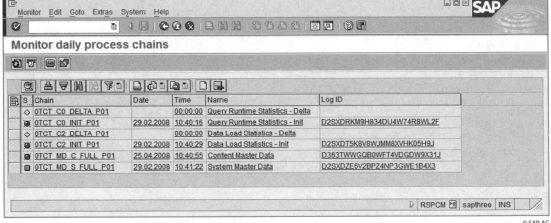

© SAP AG

When you click on a process chain, it can be branched from the overview into the monitoring of the selected process chain.

The monitoring of daily process chains is not designed for this purpose, but unfortunately, it is the only option to get an overview on the execution status of several process chains. Without the use of the transaction RSPCM, the monitoring can only be done in the log view of a selected process chain (see section 31.3.2).

Alert monitoring

The basic task of the monitoring of daily process chains is to periodically inform selected news recipients with an alert monitor about erroneously executed process chains.

The news recipients can be stored in the transaction RSPCM. The periodic review of the process chain status is not made by calling the program RSPC_MONITOR through the transaction RSPCM but by a background job. Thus, the program works in a different way, either as a status overview and customizing tool or as an alert monitor, depending on whether the program is started in the dialog or in the batch.

With the execution of the alert monitor, all erroneous process chains that are provided for the monitoring are reported. Here, the status of the most recent execution of a process chain is considered. If the alert monitor is executed more often than the process chain, the same error status of this process chain will be reported more often, i.e., with each execution of the alert monitor.

The intended use of the alert monitor is thus to monitor daily running process chains on a daily basis. This is the reason the alert monitor is referred to as "the monitor of daily process chains" even though it is not necessary from a technical perspective that the alert monitor or process chains are executed synchronously or even daily.

However, in practice, the transaction RSPCM is rather unsuitable as an alert monitor since the process chains to be monitored can be defined systemwide but not specifically by user or role. If several applications share one BW system, then the process chains of these applications can only be monitored as a whole.

31.3.2 Monitoring a Selected Process Chain

Ideally, the monitoring of a selected process chain is accessed via transaction RSPCM as long as it has been configured (see the previous section). If the RSPCM is not used, the monitoring can also be reached by calling the log view of the process chain. For this purpose, in the administration area of the Data Warehousing Workbench, the respective process chain can be selected and the log view of the chain can be called afterward (see figure 31–7).

In the log view, all process steps are shown in the same way as they were defined in the process chain maintenance. In addition, depending on the error status, the executed process steps will be shown in either green or red. Process steps that have not been executed yet are shown in gray. The connections between process steps are shown in dotted lines if the respective events have not been activated yet.

Figure 31–7

Log view of a process chain

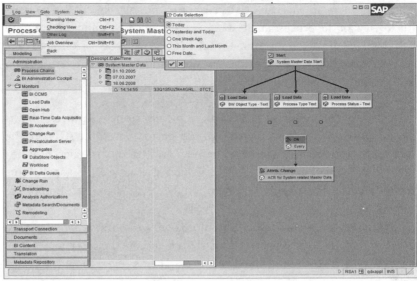

Figure 31–7

Log view of a process chain

© SAP AG

If a process step was executed with errors, it can be restarted with most process types. In such a case, the log view of the process chain will list the erroneous as well as the renewed execution (see figure 31–8).

Figure 31–8

Log view for repetition of process steps

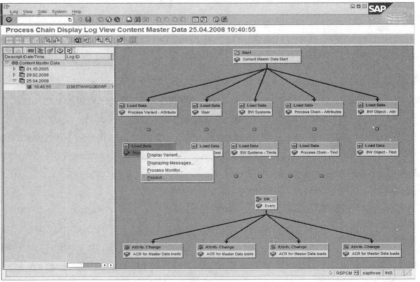

© SAP AG

If changes are made to the definition of the process chains that are already in use, a range of peculiarities needs to be considered.

Unknown jobs

If process steps are removed from a process chain, the respective jobs that were already scheduled might not be deleted correctly. Such jobs that react to events of the process chain but are no longer part of the process chain definition will be searched with the call of the process chain maintenance and the log view.

If such a "zombie job" is found, it will be displayed as a process step of the chain under the process type *unknown job*. Since this is not always noticed when process chains are developed, it is the task of the monitoring to remove such jobs from the job administration. Here, it is best to move from the context menu of the respective process step into the job overview and delete it from there. With the next call of the log view, the "zombie job" will no longer be displayed in the process chain.

Monitoring older logs

When a process chain is monitored, not only the current process chain run but also older runs can be selected and examined.

The log structure is derived from the current definition of the process chain. If a process chain is changed, all old logs will be deleted. If process chains are running at the time of the change, their logs will not be deleted but only process steps that are contained in the new definition of the process chain are executed. Thus, a change of running process chains should be avoided.

31.3.3 Detailed Information on a Selected Process Step

The monitoring of the process steps for a selected process chain gives a good overview of the current status of a process chain, and it might be used to reconstruct errors from the past.

In specific situations, especially if single process steps were executed erroneously, the combined information of the process chain log is not enough to better investigate the error.

Thus, for closer examination of a process step, detailed information can be obtained in the context menu of the respective process. The details on the process step are arranged in the *Chain, Backg,* and *Process* tabs.

Detailed information on the chain and on the background

The *Chain* tab contains information on the start and the end of the process as well as on the generated instance (see figure 31–9).

Information that can be obtained from the job log of the respective process is combined under the *Backg* tab (see figure 31–10).

Figure 31–9
Process chain log: Chain tab

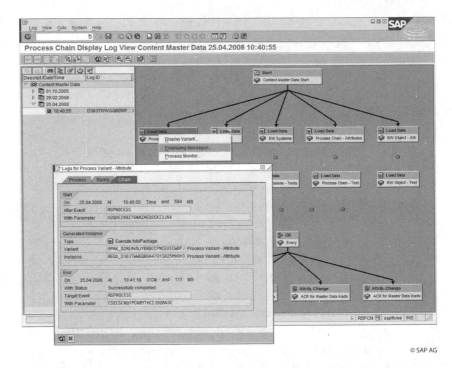

© SAP AG

Figure 31–10
Process chain log: Backg tab

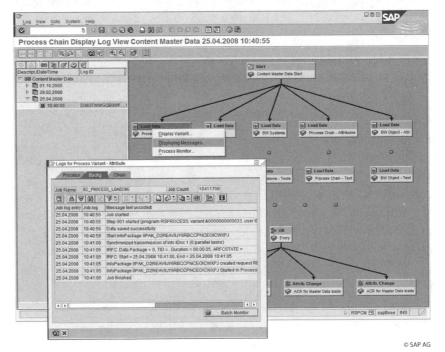

© SAP AG

With the display of the batch information, the job administration does not need to be called manually since the tab offers all logs for this job.

For some processes, BW offers a specific process monitor (e.g., load processes). In these cases, the respective process writes its own log, which can be viewed in the *Process* tab (see figure 31–11).

Detailed information on the process

Figure 31–11

Process chain log: Process tab

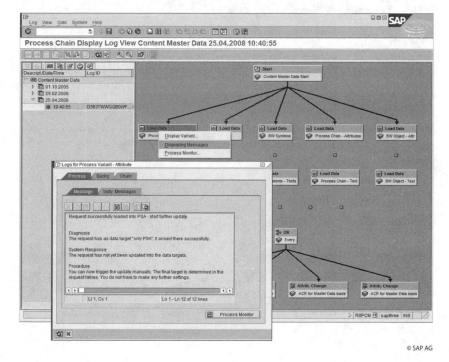

© SAP AG

Further, from the *Process* tab, the specific monitoring can be accessed via the *Process Monitor* button.

31.4 Monitoring Load Processes

Extraction and data transfer processes especially can be very complex and runtime intensive in BW. For monitoring the progress of the single load processes and checking whether they are error free, BW provides a respective monitoring tool.

This is the load process monitor in the administration area of the Data Warehousing Workbench (see figure 31–1), and it can be directly accessed via transaction RSMO. In this monitor, the extraction and data transfer processes are jointly shown in a tree display (consisting of date, status, DataSource, etc.) that can be customized individually (see figure 31–12).

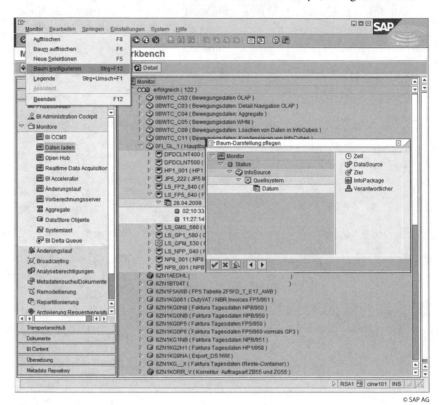

© SAP AG

The load process monitor of the Data Warehousing Workbench provides an overview on the executed load processes and thus primarily shows the status of the load processes as follows:

- Red = The request is erroneous.
- Yellow = The request is still in progress.
- Green = The request is error free.
- Deleted = The request was deleted from the PSA; however, monitor logs are available.

In addition, extraction processes and data transfer processes use detailed monitoring functions that can be called via the selection of a load process. Whether the monitoring is to be called for the extraction and data transfer processes is decided independently by BW.

We'll explain monitoring of extraction and data transfer processes in detail in the following two sections (31.4.1 and 31.4.2). Additionally, in section 31.4.3, we'll show you options for the error search in load processes.

31.4.1 Monitoring Extraction Processes

The monitoring of extraction processes arranges the log information of an extraction into *header, status information,* and *detailed information.*

The header of a request contains the information that defines the request:

Request header

- **The request ID:** With the start of a load process, the request ID is identified and it is clear systemwide. Thus, the request can be found with exactly this ID. From the request ID, the SID is identified too,[209] and it will be stored in the package dimension of BasisCubes.
- **Start time and runtime:** The start time is always the start time of the respective InfoPackage in BW. The runtime is calculated from the time at which the request was completely posted into the PSA. For direct staging, the time at which the data was posted into the master data of the InfoObject is applied.
- **Classification data:** Information that is defined by a request (DataSource, source system, InfoPackage, etc.) is also stored in the header. Most of this information could also be taken from the tree display in the monitor.
- **Processing status:** In the processing status, simplified information on the current processing status of the request is displayed. This comprises the current processing target[210] and the extraction mode.

Figure 31–13 shows the header of a request.

The status information provides an overview on the error status of a request that is displayed as a signal light (see figure 31–14). It has the following meanings:

Status information on the request

- Red = The request is erroneous.
- Yellow = The request is still in progress.
- Green = The request is error free.

---

209. The allocation is stored in the SID table /BIO/SREQUID of the InfoObject OREQUID.
210. With the new staging in BW 7 always "PSA"; with direct staging also "PSA and data targets in parallel", "PSA and data targets serialized", "only data targets" and "from PSA into data targets".

Figure 31–13
Request header in the monitor

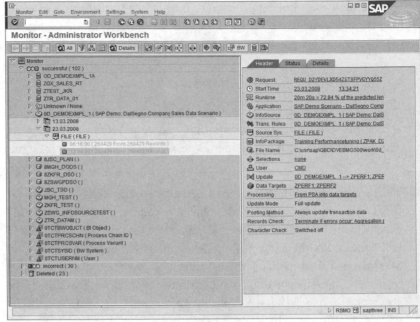

© SAP AG

Figure 31–14
Request status information in the monitor

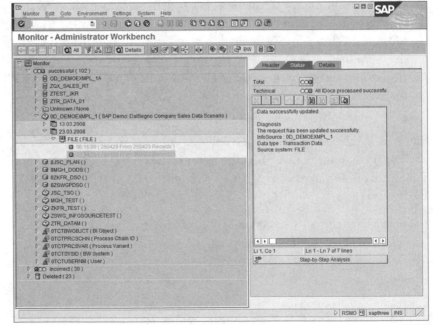

© SAP AG

Even if a request is considered erroneous in the status information, you may want to manually classify the status as being error free. This may be the case if a data supply does not contain any data and is thus considered to be erroneous (see section 23.1) even though there is actually no data and the request is thus error free from a content perspective.

The display of the overall status includes a button to manually change the status. Together with the change, information can be stored on why the status was manually changed (see figure 31–15).

Figure 31–15

Manual setting of the request status in the monitor

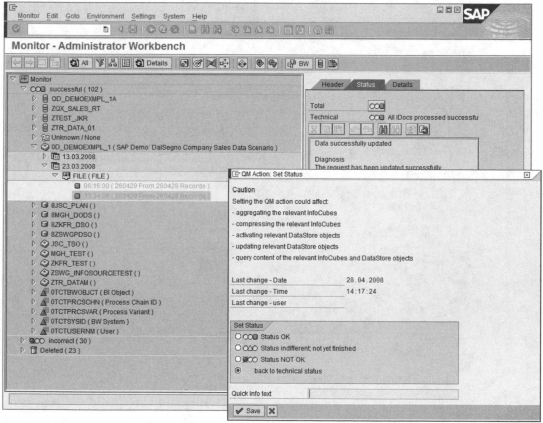

© SAP AG

To overrule the overall status of a request, the log entries of the request need to be completely available. This is not the case if request administration information was archived (see section 33.4). Thus, please take care that all status information maintenance activities are executed without delay or at least within the archiving time frames.

The original status of a request is not completely overwritten by the manual setting. Instead, it remains stored as *technical status* and cannot be changed.

Detailed information on the request

The detailed information on a request provides exact information on the processing steps (see figure 31–16).

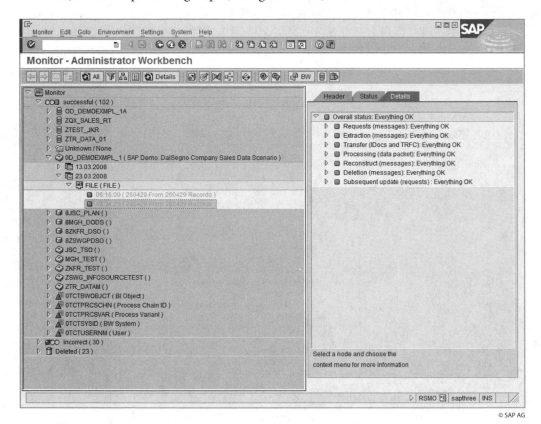

Figure 31–16

Request – detailed information in the monitor

The processing steps are separated into the following categories:

- Requests
- Extraction
- Transfer
- Processing
- Reconstruct
- Process chains

Within the processing steps, certain activities are further detailed and described by the *caller* (e.g., the compilation of data requests).

Each processing step and each caller is displayed in the monitoring with at least one specific time and one error code. In the following explanations, we'll list the relevant callers for the respective processing steps.[211]

The processing step ***request*** classifies actions that are executed with the compilation of the extraction requirements for the source system and the receipt of the request from the source system.

Request

The callers in this request are combined in the following table.

Caller	Meaning
01	Start of the data request
02	End of the data request/receipt of the request from the source system
09	Info IDoc (RQSTATE)

The processing step ***extraction*** comprises the notifications from the source system that describe the status of the extraction or receipt of the BW requests. These notifications are sent via IDoc from the source system to the BW system[212] (see figure 31–17).

Extraction

The type of message is described by the IDoc status that is stored with each notification. The following table shows all IDoc statuses.

IDoc Status	Meaning
0	Data request received
1	Data selection started
2	Data selection running
5	Error with data selection
6	Old transfer structure, transfer rules need to be regenerated
8	No data available, data selection completed
9	Data selection completed

211. A complete overview on all callers can be found in the value table of the domain RSCALLER.
212. Even if the extraction of data is made via TRFC.

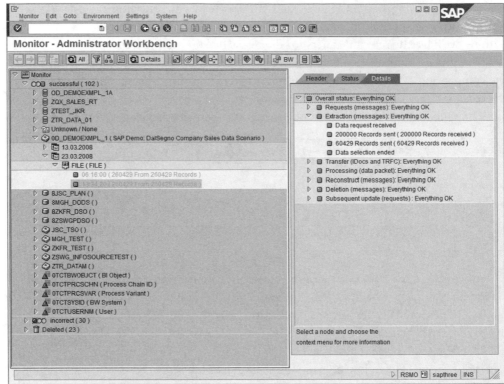

Figure 31–17

Processing step: extraction

Especially interesting are the messages that are sent with the IDoc status 2. These messages describe the number of data records that the source system extracts and sends to BW. This information is used to compare the data records actually received from BW and gives an indication on the approximate runtime of the request.

Depending on the selected package size (see section 24.1.1), the data is distributed into packages and several IDocs with status 2 are sent to BW.

Transfer

The processing step **transfer** is the counterpart of the processing step extraction. Here, similar to the information from the source system, all information IDocs that BW sends to the respective source system are listed.

In addition to the IDocs that are sent to request data from the source system, the transfer step lists all other IDocs with which BW confirms the receipt of data packages to the source system.

Processing

If data packages have arrived error free in BW, the **processing** of the data packages by the staging engine starts. With the new DataSources in

BW 7, the processing comprises only the storing of data packages in the PSA.

For the direct staging of master data, the extraction is connected to the entry of data into the master data tables of the respective InfoObject. How the posting in the PSA and in the master data tables is connected timewise is defined by the processing options in the respective InfoPackage. So, the processing might start if the extraction is still running but the first data packages have correctly arrived in BW already (see section 15.4.3).

With direct staging, the processing is the most complex (and usually most runtime-intensive) part of an extraction process. Therefore, the processing is further separated into the following steps:

- Update PSA
- Transfer rules
- Update
- End of processing

These steps arrange a series of callers that are combined in the following table.

Caller	Meaning	Use In
30	Writing into PSA started	Update PSA
32	Writing into PSA terminated	Update PSA
36	Reading from PSA started	Update PSA
39	Reading from PSA terminated	Update PSA
20	Start of processing in BW	Transfer rules
29	Data was written into the communication structure	Transfer rules
60	Insert/update in the database for transactional data	Update
61	Insert/update in the database for texts	Update
62	Insert/update in the database for master data	Update
63	Insert/update in the database for hierarchies	Update
66	Error with insert/update of database for transactional data	Update
70	Processing terminated	End of processing

Each processing step refers to a single data package within the logged request; i.e., each processing step is executed per data package (see figure 31–18).

Figure 31–18
Processing step: processing

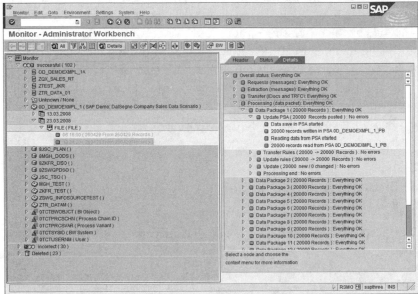

© SAP AG

Postprocessing   With the direct staging of master data, texts, and external hierarchies, the staging process is not completely terminated with the step *processing*:

- External hierarchies are first stored as an inactive version that needs to be activated by the change run. If external hierarchies are loaded with this option of automatic activation, then the activation will be made in the processing step *postprocessing*.
- When master data and texts are loading, a posting lock is placed that is removed in the processing step *postprocessing*.

The respective activities are logged by different callers in the processing step **postprocessing.** These are listed in the following table.

Caller	Meaning
80	Start second step for master data, texts, hierarchies
84	End interim step for hierarchies
89	End second step for master data, texts, hierarchies

> If errors occur when master data is loaded before the posting lock is removed by the postprocessing, no further load processes can be executed. This means the change run cannot be executed either. In such a situation, the posting lock needs to be released manually using transaction RS12.

If an InfoPackage is executed with the process chain controlling, then the processing step *process chains* will give information on the respective process chain and its status.

Process chains

31.4.2 Monitoring Data Transfer Processes

The monitoring of data transfer processes arranges the log information in *headers* and *details.*

The headers of a data transfer process contain information that defines the request. On the one hand, this is static information that describes the data source and data target as well as the transformation to be executed. On the other hand, information regarding the runtime is placed into the header; however, for delta extraction, the selection that shows the selected requests is especially relevant.

Figure 31–19 shows the header of a data transfer process.

DTP headers

Figure 31–19
DTP header information in the monitor

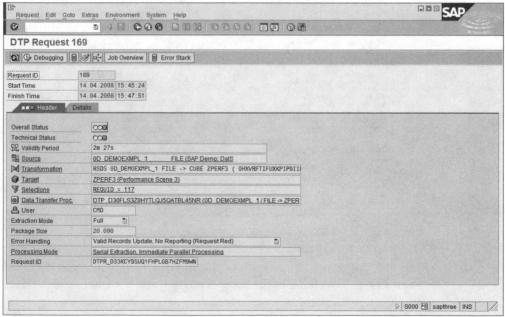

© SAP AG

The request status is integrated into the header. As with the status maintenance of extraction processes, the status display includes a button to manually set the status of the request. However, this is only possible if no subsequent activities that relied on a certain status have been executed; e.g.,
activation of new data in a DataStore Object, rollup into aggregates, and
compression, among others.

Further, you can directly switch from the monitor of the DTP request
to the error stack of the data transfer process (see section 23.5.3).

Detailed DTP information

The detailed information of a monitor log shows the processing steps
within a data transfer process (see figure 31–20).

Figure 31–20
Detailed DTP information in
the monitor

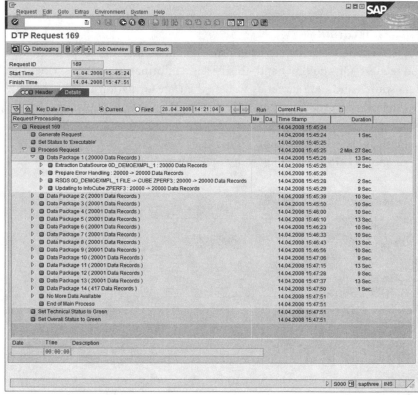

© SAP AG

The core of the detailed information is the logging of the request processing that comprises the extraction, the filtering of new records with the
same key, the execution of the transformation, and the entry of result data
into the target structure.

If an InfoSource is part of the transformation, the data transfer process comprises both transformations that surround the InfoSource. Thus, the request processing log might include several transformations.

To identify, with parallel processing of individual data packages (see section 24.1.2), which data package was terminated when or when it was executed in parallel, the log can be displayed for a fixed point in time. For this purpose, you can select a freely chosen processing step that was executed at the given time, and that is selected in the context menu under *Set Call Date/Time Stamp*.

31.4.3 Error Search in Data Transfer Processes

Especially with the use of ABAP routines or rule groups, "homemade" content errors may occur that need to be investigated.

Part of the troubleshooting is usually the ***review of temporary results*** of a data transfer process as well as ***debugging the transformation.***

Contrary to the old staging up to release 3.x, the staging with transformation and data transfer processes no longer provides an option to simulate a staging process. Instead, a data transfer process absolutely needs to be executed in BW 7 to further investigate the results. However, the data transfer process provides an option to log several temporary results during the request processing. The processing steps that are to be logged during the request processing need to be defined in the respective data transfer process (see figure 31–21).

Review of temporary results

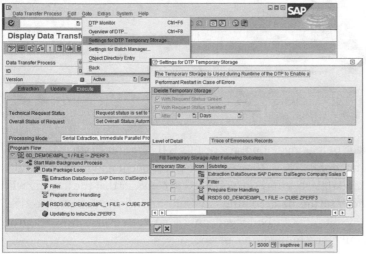

Figure 31–21
Logging temporary results of data transfer processes

© SAP AG

The detailing level for the generation of temporary results is very important. Temporary results can be logged for technically erroneous data records only or for all data records of the transformation. If the troubleshooting is about content errors, the temporary results definitely need to be stored for all records.

The temporary results of the transformation can be found in the detailed DTP information (see figure 31–22).

Figure 31–22

Display of results in the temporary DTP storage

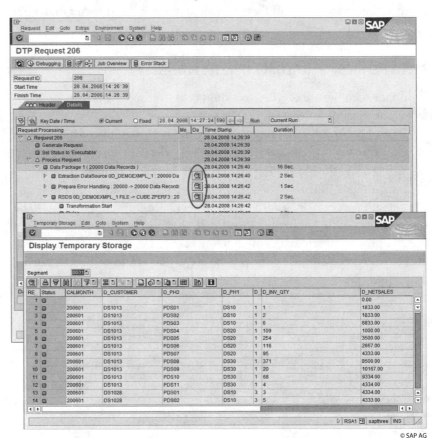

© SAP AG

An advantage of logging temporary results is the option to stock information in the temporary DTP storage in case errors occur and need to be subsequently investigated. However, you need to consider that the logging will strongly increase the data volume, so from a performance perspective, temporary results should be logged only for selected data transfer processes and only for a limited time period.

The analysis of temporary results might show that the data flow has been defined erroneously and also for which key figures/characteristics the data flow is incorrect. In many cases, this information is enough to find errors after the transformation review.

Debugging the transformation

If the cause of the error lies in self-developed routines for the transformation, only the debugging of these routines might help. Options are provided in different places, but they are mostly options that the SAP developers have given themselves to better investigate possible bugs.

From our perspective, the most efficient option for debugging is to search for the error with individual coding in the program generated from the transformation. The program generated from a transformation can be displayed via the menu item *Extras→Display Generated Program* (see figure 31–23).

Figure 31–23

Display program generated from a transformation

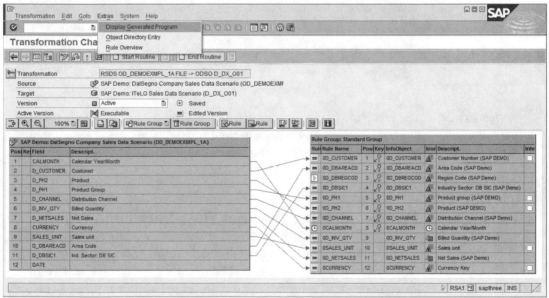

© SAP AG

This place needs to be marked with a breakpoint.[213] Subsequently, the transformation needs to be run in a dialog process (with the use of background processes, the breakpoint would be ignored). This is achieved by selecting the processing mode *serially in the dialog process* in the definition of the data transfer process (see figure 31–24).

---

213. As an alternative, the routine can also be called to branch into the debugger with the command BREAK-POINT.

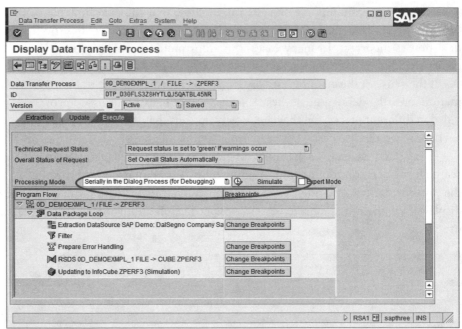

Figure 31–24
Simulation of data transfer
processes

The execution of the data transfer process can the be started via the *Simulate* button. Here, all routines of the transformation are executed, but the result sets of the transformation are not written into the respective data targets.

31.5 Monitoring the Real-Time Data Acquisition

The monitoring of the real-time data acquisition (RDA) is done outside the mechanisms for regular staging. Thus, neither the comprehensive monitoring of process chains nor the monitoring of load processes can be used to monitor the real-time data acquisition.

Instead, BW provides self-contained monitoring to check the workflow of the daemon processes. This can be found in the administration area of the Data Warehousing Workbench or via the transaction RSRDA (see figure 31–25).

In the monitoring of the real-time data acquisition, the status of the daemon processes as well as their assigned InfoPackages and data transfer processes are displayed. In addition, the open requests for extraction and further processing are displayed.

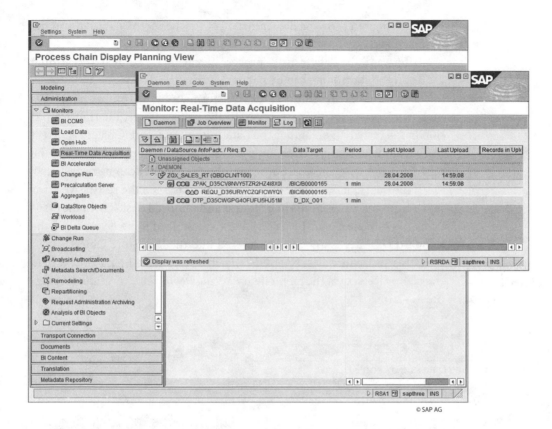

© SAP AG

Figure 31–25

Monitoring the real-time data acquisition

Particularly interesting is the behavior of the RDA on errors and their troubleshooting. Basically, a daemon will abort the RDA processes with all DataSources that generate an error and continue the processing of all other DataSources. The daemon process will stop only if all DataSources of a daemon process are aborted.

Depending on whether the extraction or the transformation has caused an error, the troubleshooting is different.

Errors during extraction

If an error during the extraction was responsible for the abort of the real-time data acquisition, then the request in question needs to be repeated and entered into the DataStore Object outside the controlling daemon Afterward, the daemon can resume the controlling of the extraction and the staging.

To manually load the request in question, the erroneous request first needs to be deleted from the PSA and a standard InfoPackage needs to be activated that starts a repeat of the delta extraction. Subsequently, the behavior of the used data transfer process needs to be defined as standard

DTP (see figure 22–6), the data transfer process needs to be started and the new data needs to be activated in the DataStore Object.

Afterward, the data transfer process can again be defined as real-time DTP and the controlling can be handed over to the daemon.

Errors during transformation

If an error occurred during the transformation, the troubleshooting is much easier than for the extraction. In the simplest case, the transformation has signaled an error, but the data in the DataStore Object is correct (e.g., from a warning). Then, only the status of the request needs to be overruled and set error free. Subsequently, the daemon can be restarted.

If the data in a DataStore Object is erroneous, then the respective error in the transformation needs to be found and removed first. Then, the erroneous DTP request and the change log request need to be deleted and the standard DTP needs to be newly entered into the DataStore Object. However, this procedure is supported only in the context menu of the data transfer processes via the menu item *Execute Repair Process Chain* (see figure 31–26).

Figure 31–26
Repair of a data transfer
process for RDA

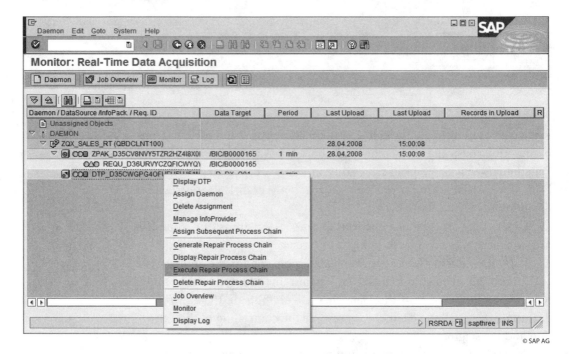

Only the subsequent activation of the request in the DataStore Object and the restart of the daemon process need to be executed manually.

32 Model Trimming

The data model design of BasisCubes and DataStore Objects is a very complex task, and in practice, it will rarely lead to the theoretically optimal model.

The causes for the deficiencies of a model come from the complexity of the basic conditions to be considered as well as from the dynamics of the model that may negatively impact (or degenerate) the combination of data for a long period of time.

Often, such errors can be detected only in live system operations. Also, the resulting problems often only become gradually obvious so that troubleshooting is usually done at a time when data has already been loaded and can no longer be deleted.[214]

However, even if a model could be considered optimal for a given data volume and a given combination of content, the quality of the data model is not a constant. With system operations, the data model "is alive" and moves away from the static structure that the modeling was initially based on.

To ensure long-term BW system performance, the BW data structures need to be reviewed and modified regularly but existing data should not be deleted. Such modifications are combined under the term *model trimming.* Model trimming needs to be executed in the following areas:

- Range partitioning
- Dimension tables
- Delta indexes of the BI accelerator
- Fact tables in the BI accelerator
- Index linking in the BI accelerator

These areas of model trimming are explained in the following sections.

---

214. This may be the case if data is no longer available in the source system or in preceding staging layers or if the runtime for the re-creation of data would be too long.

Similar to these topics are remodeling, reclustering, and subsequent zero value elimination. However, these are not the focus of the regular maintenance but come with the changes to the data model and are as such described with data modeling (see section 9.2).

32.1 Trimming the Range Partitioning

If the fact table of a BasisCube is provided with a range partitioning (see section 7.3.1), then the range partitioning schema will always be set for a certain time period that is to be mapped in the fact table. There should be enough partitions to map the data stored in a BasisCube. If the upper and lower limits of the partitioning are measured too narrow, the data that is not mapped will be collected in the upper and lower partitions and this will result in poorly performing database accesses.

If the partitioning is designed too generously, this will also result in performance disadvantages since the administration effort for the database system will increase with the accesses to the partitioned fact table.

An inappropriate selection of the partitioning can be detected in the overview on partition sizes in transaction DB02. There, all partitions of a fact table should roughly have a similar size—apart from some empty partitions for future periods. However, if the fact table shows very large partitions for the upper and lower limits of the partitioning schema, there is a lack of respective partitions. A number of empty partitions signals that some partitions at the lower and upper limits of the partitioning schema are redundant (see figure 32–1).

Since the stored time lines change with the deletion/archiving of old data and the entry of new data in a BasisCube, any partitioning schema of a BasisCube will eventually become unsuitable and needs to be modified, even though it might have been optimal at some point in time.

For this purpose, there is repartitioning, which helps to change the partitioning schema of a BasisCube without having to delete data from the cube. The repartitioning is integrated into the Data Warehousing Workbench and can be reached via the administration of the context menu of the respective BasisCube (see figure 32–2).

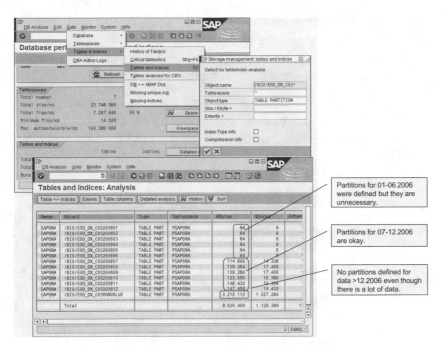

Figure 32–1

*Analysis of the partitioning
schema of a fact table*

Figure 32–1

*Analysis of the partitioning
schema of a fact table*

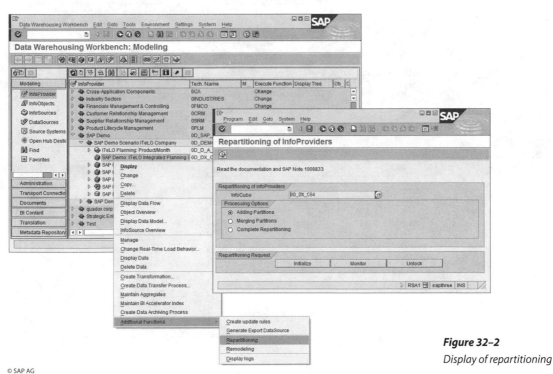

Figure 32–2

Display of repartitioning

The repartitioning comprises the **complete repartitioning** and the two options of **adding** and **merging partitions.**

Complete repartitioning

With complete repartitioning, the partitioning schema of a filled fact table can be completely modified. Complete repartitioning is used if the following apply:

■ The partitioning is to be switched on/off for a filled cube.
■ The partitioning characteristic is to be exchanged (0CALMONTH instead of 0FISCPER or vice versa).
■ The number of months/booking periods per partition is to be modified (deduced from the maximum number of partitions, see section 7.3.1).
■ The lower limit of the partitioning schema is to be expanded.
■ The upper limit of the partitioning schema is to be reduced.

Figure 32–3
Complete repartitioning

With a complete repartitioning, all settings of the partitioning can be modified in the same way as with the creation of a new BasisCube (see figure 32–3).

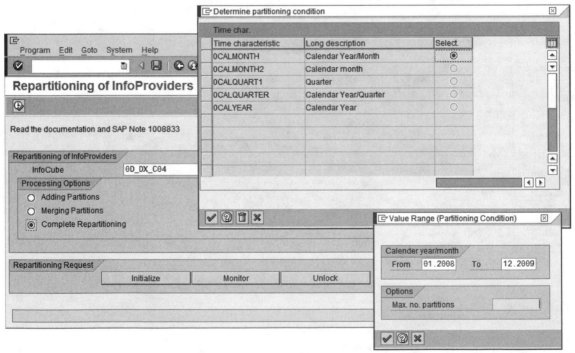

© SAP AG

The new partitioning schema of a cube can be predefined after the start of the repartitioning by initializing a partitioning request (with the *Initialize* button). The repartitioning request can be scheduled as a background job too.

> The repartitioning changes the metadata of a BasisCube without enforcing the adherence to defined transport routes (see appendix C). Thus, inconsistencies in the definition of a BasisCube between the different systems in a transport landscape may occur, and they may result in the fact that Basis-Cubes can no longer be transported. When using the repartitioning, please ensure that it is used on all systems within a transport landscape.

With the execution of the repartitioning, the F and the E fact tables of the respective cubes are re-created in the form of shadow tables where the (initially empty) shadow table is created and indexed similar to the existing F and E fact table; however, it will already be provided with the new partitioning schema.[215]

Afterward, the data of the existing fact tables will be copied into the shadow tables and they will as such be a true copy[216] of the existing fact tables—the only difference being that they have the desired partitioning schema.

From this starting point, the existing fact tables of the cubes are exchanged with the shadow tables; i.e., the fact and the shadow tables in the ABAP Dictionary remain the same but the link to the respective tables in the database system will be changed. Given this quick exchange, the data will not need to be copied back.

The fact that such an exchange of the database tables has taken place can be seen in the partitions that can be displayed via transaction SE14→*Edit Tables*→*Storage Parameters*. Figure 32–4 shows the partitions of the fact table /BIO/EOD_DX_C03 for the cube 0D_DX_C03. After the repartitioning, their names no longer follow the prefix /BIO/EOD_DX_C03* of the fact table but instead follow the prefix /BIO/4EOD_DX_CO* of the shadow table.

---

215. Only the E fact table comes with a user-defined partitioning schema that needs to be dealt with during repartitioning. The F fact table is always partitioned according to the request ID. However, when this book went to press, the repartitioning still handled both fact tables of a cube.

216. For the execution of a complete repartitioning, it is necessary to have sufficient memory space available to store a true copy of the old fact table.

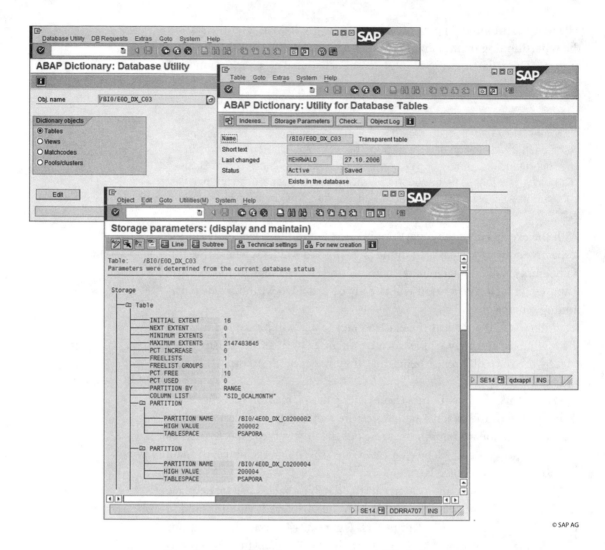

© SAP AG

Figure 32–4

Partitions of the fact table/BI0/E0D_DX_C03 after repartitioning

The shadow tables that are stored and filled during the repartitioning are not automatically deleted after the termination of the repartitioning. Only with another repartitioning will the shadow tables be deleted, so they can be used for the upcoming partitioning.

To free the memory space earlier, you need to delete the shadow table manually in the ABAP Dictionary in the transaction SE11. The right table can be found in the monitor logs (see figure 32–7 later in this chapter).

Depending of the type and scale of the repartitioning, the shadow tables that are created during the repartitioning may have a significant data volume. The shadow tables are not automatically deleted by BW; however, they lose in value if after successful repartitioning data is again entered into the respective BasisCube. Thus, after each repartitioning, you should manually delete the shadow tables in the ABAP Dictionary.

A complete repartitioning is not always necessary to modify the partitioning schema of a BasisCube in order to match changed basic conditions. Especially if the one of the following is true, the respective partitions only need to be copied into the shadow table:

Adding and merging partitions

- Partitions are to be merged at the lower end of the partitioning schema, e.g., since they no longer contain old data after an archiving or;
- The upper end of the partitioning schema is to be expanded by new partitions, i.e., since it is expected that respective data will be created.

If new partitions are to be added, then only the highest partition needs to be copied into the shadow table since it contains all data that exceeds the upper limit of the existing partitioning schema. If partitions are to be merged at the lower end of the partitioning schema, then all partitions that are to be merged are copied into the shadow table.

For inventory InfoCubes, depending on the BW release, the highest and lowest partition will also be used to store markers. The addition (new BW releases) or the merging (old BW releases) of partitions is thus not supported for inventory cubes. Instead, the complete repartitioning needs to be included.

After the copy process, the old partitions are dropped and the partitioning schema of the old cube is changed. Then, the partitions of the shadow table and the existing cube are exchanged on a database level so that it is also unnecessary to copy data back to existing cubes.

Ideally, no data needs to be copied with merging and adding partitions since the data in the merging partitions were deleted earlier during the archiving, or no data has been created for the added partitions yet. Thus, it should be defined with the cube development at what points in time and under what conditions a modification of the partitioning schema should be made and the appropriate timeslots should be defined, even if this is years in advance.

If a maximum number of partitions are defined for a cube (see section 7.3.1), then this number will be changed with the repartitioning so that after the merge/addition of partitions there will be as many months/booking periods combined in a partition as there were earlier. So, say you have a maximum number of five partitions for the period 01.2006–12.2006. If in each case three months will be combined in a partition (first partition for all values until 03.2006, last partition for all values >12.2006), then the maximum number of partitions after the addition of partitions until 12.2007 will be increased to nine.

Merging and adding a partition is started with the *Initialize* button in the repartitioning. As a precondition, you need to define only the new timeline that is to map the new partitioning schema (see figure 32–5).

Repartitioning and aggregates   The repartitioning of a fact table is a database-specific setting that BW no longer has to deal with after the partitioning schema is defined. Accordingly, it is irrelevant whether the fact tables of the aggregates of a cube are partitioned like the cube.

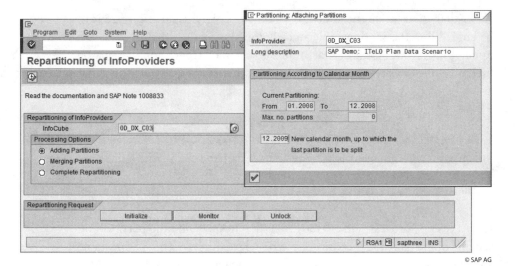

© SAP AG

Figure 32–5
Merging and adding partitions

Instead, the aggregates can have a completely different partitioning schema than the BasisCube without any impact on the functionalities of BW (apart from the performance impact).

For this reason, aggregates are basically kept unchanged after the partitioning but they keep their existing partitioning schema. If aggregates are to be provided with a modified partitioning schema too, this can only be done by a reactivation of the aggregates. As an alternative, with the creation of the initialization request for the repartitioning it can be defined that aggregates are to be re-created automatically after the repartitioning.

32.1.1 Monitoring and Troubleshooting

For each repartitioning, log information is stored that describes the repartitioning workflow and that can be displayed in the monitoring. Beyond its function as information supplier, the monitoring also serves to handle errors that occurred during the repartitioning.

Causes for these errors are mostly unexpected aborts by one or more of the maximum six dialog processes that are by default started with the main process of the partitioning. Troubleshooting options are to *reset the repartitioning request* or single process steps, to *restart the repartitioning request,* or to *delete the repartitioning request* (see figure 32–6).

The resetting of the repartitioning requests brings the BasisCube back into its original state; it deletes the created shadow tables and removes all locks that were set with the repartitioning.

Reset repartitioning requests

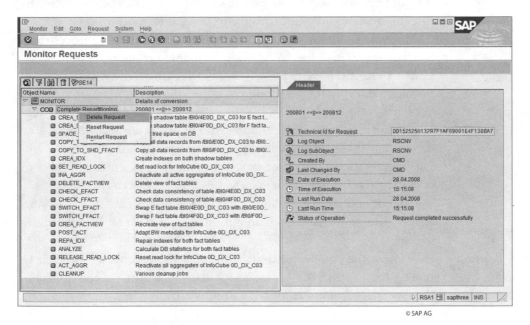

© SAP AG

Basically, a repartitioning request can be reset at any time; however, this should only be done with error-free repartitioning and definitely before new data is loaded into the respective cube.

Figure 32–6
Troubleshooting repartitioning

Reset processing steps

As for the complete repartitioning request, single processing steps can also be reset if they are aborted.

The targeted resetting of single processing steps is preferred over complete repartitioning if the repartitioning has terminated the runtime-intensive steps of copying data into the shadow tables and you want to maintain this processing status.

After you reset a request step, the partitioning request will restart.

Restart repartitioning requests

The single processing steps of an erroneous repartitioning request can basically be repeated[217] since each step uses a COMMIT controlling in all dialog processes and thus each processing steps is always executed completely or not at all.

Resetting an erroneous processing step is not absolutely necessary. However, since the repartitioning is both a new and a far-reaching tool, this option should be chosen if there is no chance to review the current status of the repartitioning.

If the repartitioning aborts because parallel dialog processes exceed the time-out period, the time-out period should be adjusted before the repartitioning resumes in order to avoid another abort.

Delete repartitioning requests

To avoid confusion over a large number of repartitioning processes on a cube, there is an option to delete repartitioning requests. With the deletion of a repartitioning request, its log entries are deleted and the request no longer shows in the monitoring.

Further troubleshooting cannot be done after the deletion of the repartitioning request. Despite the successful or erroneous repartitioning, all data remain in the current state. So to ensure data consistency, repartitioning requests should be deleted only after they were executed error free or after they have been reset completely.

The deletion of repartitioning requests does not have any functional significance, so the deletion is an optional component of the repartitioning.

Display of shadow tables

Besides the options for troubleshooting, the information on repartitioning has further significance. Particularly interesting is the display of shadow tables that are created with the repartitioning but not automatically deleted (see figure 32–7).

---

217. The repartitioning request definitely needs to be marked as erroneous (status red). If the respective background job is still running or if it is not marked aborted in the job administration, then the repartitioning request cannot be restarted.

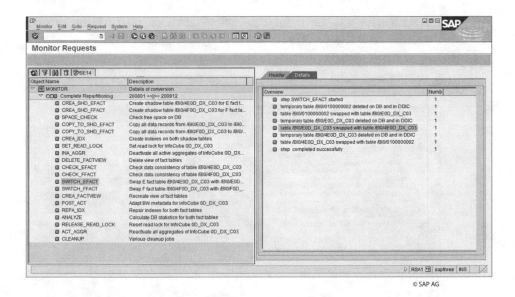

© SAP AG

The shadow tables displayed in the monitoring (in Figure 410 this is table /BIO/4E0D_DX_C03) should be deleted manually in the transaction SE11 in order to avoid the blocking of unnecessary memory space.

The deletion of shadow tables can be neglected if repartitioning is mostly used to merge or add partitions for which no data exists in the fact table yet or where data no longer exists.

Figure 32–7
Display of shadow tables from repartitioning

32.2 Trimming Dimensions

With the entry of new data into BasisCubes, entries into the fact tables as well as respective entries in the dimension tables are made. If data records are subsequently deleted, the dimension tables will not be deleted in return.

The deletion of data records in the fact table is made as follows:

- Deletion of the request in the cube administration (see section 31.2).
- Deletion of data records during archiving or with selective deletion of data (see section 33.1).
- Elimination of zero values during compression (see section 6.4.1).

There may also be orphaned entries in the dimension tables that no record refers to in the fact table. Significant performance losses may occur from the unnecessarily high data volume in the dimension tables.

Such data records in the dimension tables of a BasisCube can be detected and deleted via transaction RSRV (see figure 32–8).

Figure 32–8

Delete entries not used in the dimension tables

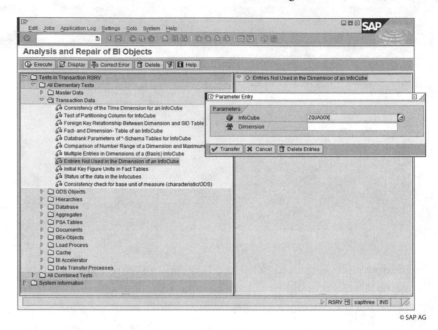

© SAP AG

The manual search and removal of unused entries in dimension tables is helpful for some BasisCubes and it can be done if orphaned entries in dimension tables are a rare exception.

Especially if the deletion of requests in the cube administration is used often to selectively delete data from BasisCubes and in specific cases for zero value elimination, it can be necessary to make this "trimming" of the dimension tables part of the standard operations.

In this case, the dimension trimming via transaction RSRV would require too much effort. It is better to use a program that can both be scheduled as a job and called via the process chain. A suitable program is shown here.

```
REPORT ZQX_RUNDIMID.

TYPE-POOLS: rsd.
DATA:  l_cube TYPE rsd_infocube.
SELECT-OPTIONS s_cube FOR l_cube NO INTERVALS.
PARAMETERS: p_check Default RS_C_FALSE Type BOOLEAN.
```

```
LOOP AT s_cube.
  l_cube = s_cube-low.
  CALL FUNCTION 'RSDRD_DIM_REMOVE_UNUSED'
  EXPORTING
      I_INFOCUBE                 = l_cube
*     I_T_DIME                   =
      I_CHECK_ONLY               = p_check
*     I_COMMIT_AFTER_N           = 50000
*     I_REPORT_ONLY_N            = 5
*     IMPORTING
*     E_REPAIR_POSSIBLE          =
*     CHANGING
*     C_T_MSG                    =
*     EXCEPTIONS
*     X_MESSAGE                  = 1
*     OTHERS                     = 2
              .
  IF SY-SUBRC <> 0.
*     MESSAGE ID SY-MSGID TYPE SY-MSGTY NUMBER SY-MSGNO
*          WITH SY-MSGV1 SY-MSGV2 SY-MSGV3 SY-MSGV4.
  ENDIF.
ENDLOOP.
```

32.3 Trimming Delta Indexes in the BIA

In section 24.7, we showed you how to accelerate the transfer of new requests from BasisCubes to the BI accelerator with the use of a delta index. The basic idea with this tuning measure is that the rollup process increases if the delta index is significantly smaller than the main index of a fact table in the BI accelerator.

However, the acceleration of the rollup will come to an end if the delta index grows to a size that corresponds with (or even surpasses) the size of the main index. Then, not only will the speed advantage of the delta index be lost, the analyses will run even slower on the BIA since two large indexes will have to be merged continuously.

Thus, in order to stay small, the delta index needs to be regularly merged with the main index. Merging the delta index of one or several BasisCubes can be executed or scheduled via the program RSDDTREX_DELTAINDEX_MERGE in the transaction SE38 (see figure 32–9).

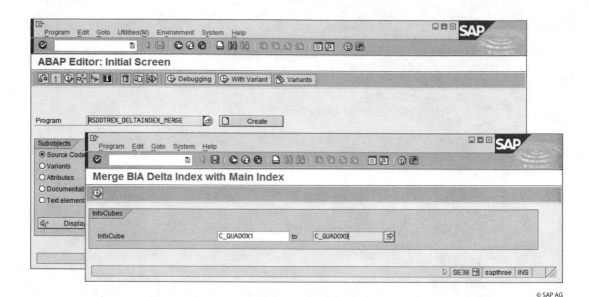

© SAP AG

Figure 32–9

Merging the BIA delta index with the main index

To get a feel for the delta indexes to be merged with the respective main index, in the transaction RSRV you can access the check *BI Accelerator→BI Accelerator Performance Check→Size of Delta Index* (see figure 32–10). Indexes are listed whose delta index size is at least 10 percent of the main index size. This is the recommendation on when to merge and it can be executed in the transaction RSRV via the *Debugging* button.

You should not use the transaction RSRV for the automated merge of delta indexes but to get a feel for the scheduling of the merges. You should keep in mind that in the current releases of BW and BIA, the merge can cause a substantial system strain and should be done only in times when few analyses are made.

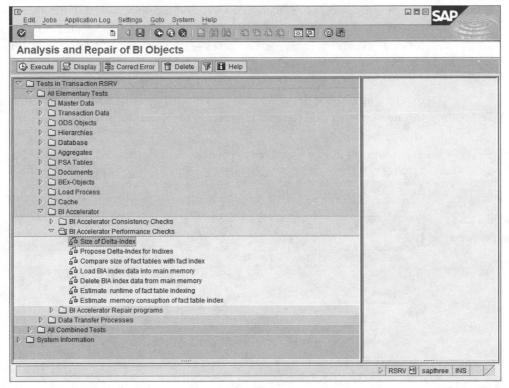

© SAP AG

Figure 32–10
Checking delta indexes

32.4 Trimming Fact Tables in the BIA

The transfer of data into the BIA indexes only serves to bring new data into the indexes. An update of existing data records or a compression as in BW is not possible in the BI accelerator.

This may (and will) soon lead to the fact that the BIA indexes contain more data records than the mapped tables in SAP BW. The number of data records is further increased if with the cube administration requests from the fact table are deleted in BW that were already rolled up into the BI accelerator. Then, the BI accelerator deletes the referencing entry in the index of the package dimension,[218] but it will not delete the respective data record in the fact table.

---

218. Technically, the entry is not deleted from the index. Rather, this index will be completely re-created for the package dimension.

How the sizes of the fact table in BW and the respective index in the BI accelerator differ can be found in the RSRV using the check *BI Accelerator→BI Accelerator Performance Checks→Compare Size of Fact Tables with Fact Index* (see figure 32–10).

To reduce indexes for fact tables that have grown too large for the required size, the indexes need to be rebuilt regularly. This can be done through targeted deletion and re-creation of an index using the index wizard (see section 7.4.5).

A more comprehensive approach is offered by the program RSDDTREX_ALL_INDEX_REBUILD, which rebuilds all indexes in the BIA (see figure 32–11).

Figure 32–11

Rebuilding all BIA indexes

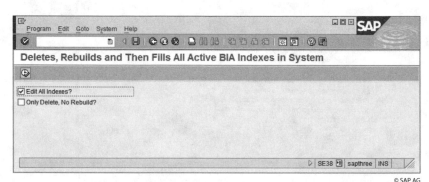

© SAP AG

From an administrative point of view, the use of this program is the most comprehensive and also the simplest option to reorganize the indexes in the BI accelerator. At the same time, this method requires the most effort from a resource perspective and should thus be executed only if no data analyses are made at the time of the index building and if the duration of this activity is known in advance.

32.5 Trimming Index Distribution in the BIA

The splitting of an index into several parts and the distribution of these partitions to different blades is one of the major tuning measures of the BI accelerator.

The creation of the index parts is determined by the resources of the blade server (see section 7.4.3). The distribution of these partitions to the blades depends on the selected algorithm, which can consider a number of basic conditions from the simple distribution up to the optimal design of join paths or the memory usage of the blades.

The splitting and the distribution are selected statically, and therefore, they will be ideal only as long as the basic conditions remain unchanged. As soon as indexes are removed from the main memory of the BIA (e.g., by an expulsion) or modified (e.g., by a rollup), the distribution of the partitions may no longer be ideal.

To completely rebuild all indexes would overreach the goal and require too many resources and too much time. It is more suitable to use the program RSDDTREX_REORGANIZE_LANDSCAPE, which can be executed or scheduled via transaction SE38.

The program redistributes the index partitions to the single index servers of the BIA if the given distribution is suboptimal. Since this is only an operation in the main memory of the blades, the reorganization takes only a few seconds.

It is different if the number of index servers in the BIA server was increased or decreased. Then, the adjustment of the physical index files becomes necessary. This can also be done using the program if the BI accelerator was configured accordingly. Otherwise, only the rebuilding of indexes will provide a suitable splitting option.

33 Information Lifecycle Management

In SAP BW operations, a very large data volume might evolve and spread over the data targets as well as the staging and even the administration areas. A large data volume might cause the following problems:

- Increased cost for storing data volume
- Poor performance during data analysis
- Poor performance during staging (data transfer processes, rollup, compression, change run, etc.)
- Poor performance of system administration
- Increased requirements for the backup infrastructure or longer runtimes for the backup

Thus, it makes sense to limit the data volume, and BW supports this through functions to delete and archive data as well as the option to shift data to other storage media. This falls under the scope of information lifecycle management (ILM).

Information lifecycle management

The approach of information lifecycle management is to evaluate data using the criteria of time and content. The evaluation of information based on the criteria of time follows the assumption that the value of data decreases with age until it is completely worthless and no longer required.

Evaluating data based on content takes it a step further. Under certain conditions, data might lose its value rapidly—e.g., after the sale of shares or the phasing out of a product.

One of the key challenges with the use of ILM is thus the classification of data or the preceding determination of classification criteria. These criteria always need to be adjusted as basic organizational and infrastructure conditions change.

Storage layer of the ILM

Depending on the "class" that data belongs to according to its age and content, it is stored in different storage layers in the ILM. Each storage layer represents a certain physical form of storing and therefore comes with individual access periods and storage costs.

Usually with increasing age (= decreasing value = rare access), data is shifted to cheaper storage layers. Access is slower or not even available. The differences in the storage layers are as follows:

- **Online:** Data is available and ready to be used in the database system.
- **Near-line:** Data is available in a storage that is organized outside the database system. Access to near-line storage needs to be executed explicitly and is thus slower than the online storage.
- **Offline:** Data has been archived. Access is possible only if the data is copied into the online storage during a restore.

It goes without saying that the deletion of data is another option to reduce data volume. Deletion differs from archiving in that no administration information is stored that would enable a re-creation of deleted data.

Storage layers of SAP BW   SAP picks up the term *ILM* and offers traditional archiving functions as well as an option to connect to near-line storage. However, the latter is only supported insofar as class interfaces are provided that SAP BW can use to communicate with systems for the near-line storing of data. SAP leaves the implementation of classes (and the provision of near-line storage) to certified third-party suppliers.

Depending on the data type, the ILM design is implemented differently in SAP BW, as shown in the following table.

BW Object	Archiving	Near-line Archiving	Deletion without Archiving
BasisCubes	✓	✓	✓
DataStore Objects	✓	✓	✓
Master Data	✗	✗	✓[1]
PSA and Change Log	✗	✗	✓
Request Administration Data[2]	✓	✗	✗
Application Logs	✗	✗	✓
BW Statistics	✗	✗	✓
Aggregates	✗	✗	✓

1. Only master data that BasisCubes no longer refer to.
2. Only request administration data on the execution of InfoPackages from SAP BW 7 and earlier. The archiving of request administration data on data transfer processes has not been enabled with SAP BW 7, support package 18.

The core archiving component is the ***archiving development kit*** (ADK), *Archiving* which forms the basis for archiving BasisCubes, DataStore Objects, and request administration data.

The ADK is a runtime environment that is part of the BW basis system. The task of this runtime environment is to provide mechanisms to read and write data in a platform- and release-independent way without having to explicitly consider the handling of different codepages or alphanumeric formats, structural changes to the data structure, compression during filing, archive administration, etc.

Each ADK archiving system is based on ***archiving objects.*** The archiving objects define the following:

- Which database tables are the basis for the archiving; i.e., which objects need to be bundled to obtain a self-contained object in terms of content.
- Which content criteria are used to select the database to be archived (if not all data is archived). This is not about the specific definition of a selection but rather about the specification of possible selection criteria to characterize, for example, the age of the data.
- Which file structure is used to build archive data.
- Where the archives are to be stored. This includes the storing of files on file servers as well as the use of file systems (e.g., StorHouse by FileTek, CBW by PBS Software, or DiskXtender for BW by Legato).
- Which programs can be used to write archive data or to delete the database tables.
- When the deletion of data from the database tables is to be made (e.g., right after the creation of archive data or scheduled manually).

Archiving objects can be defined via the transaction AOBJ.

Archiving objects are required to write as well as read archived data. Since an archiving object is always linked to a BasisCube/DataStore Object, this object is not to be deleted because the related archiving object would be deleted too. It is not possible to restore archived data via the archive administration.

To facilitate this job for standard situations, for numerous applications there are archiving objects or options to define these objects more easily; this is the case for BasisCubes, DataStore Objects, and request administration data.

Near-line archiving   However, the administration of near-line storage is the responsibility of third-party suppliers of such solutions. The guidelines from the file archiving process describe only rough basic data for this form of archiving—e.g., sorting sequences and selection criteria to access the data.

The core component of near-line archiving is the definition of a connection to the near-line storage system. The connection to the near-line storage system is stored via the transaction SM30 in the table RSDANLCON.

Figure 33–1   Here, a three-digit ID for the connection, the name of the class implemented by the third-party supplier, and the RFC destination of the storage system are stored (see figure 33–1).

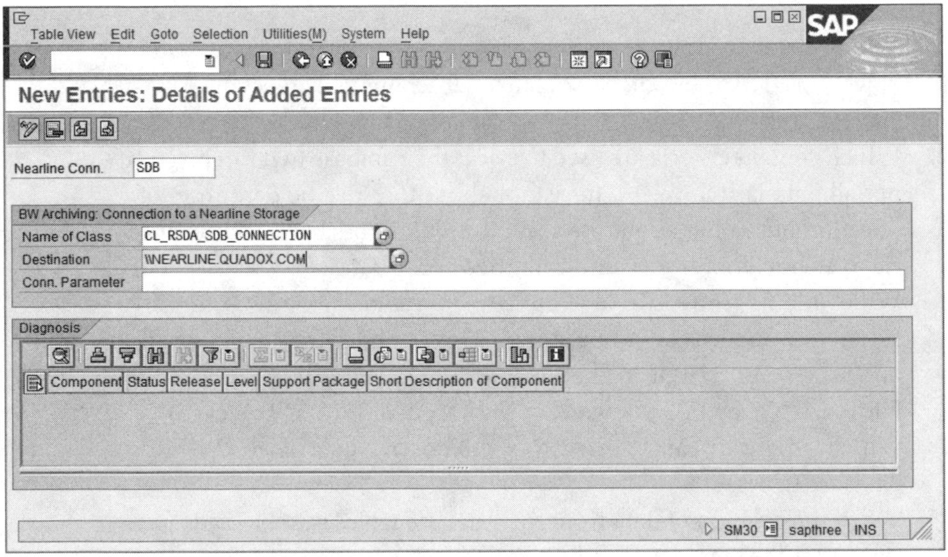

Maintain near-line connection

© SAP AG

If data is moved to a near-line storage system, it is *not* accessed at first for reasons of performance. Only if, in the query properties the option *Near-Line Storage to Be Read* is activated, will access to the near-line storage be made.

We'll explain how data is archived or can be moved to a near-line storage and how a possible restore can be made, or simply how data can be deleted for the respective BW objects, in the following sections:

- ILM for BasisCubes and DataStore Objects (section 33.1)
- ILM for master data (section 33.2)
- ILM for PSA and change log (section 33.3)
- ILM for monitor information (section 33.4)

- ILM for application logs (section 33.5)
- ILM for BW statistics data (section 33.6)

33.1 ILM for BasisCubes and DataStore Objects

As important objects for data storage and data analysis, BasisCubes and DataStore Objects offer a universal support for all options of the information lifecycle management; i.e., data can be archived, moved to a near-line archive, and deleted. The data can be deleted with the archiving as well as independently from the archiving.

The basis for the archiving of BasisCubes and DataStore Objects is a data archiving process that can be created via the transaction RSDAP. This data archiving process is for regular archiving as well as the near-line archiving.

Data archiving process

To configure a data archiving process, first you need to indicate the respective BasisCube or DataStore Object and select the *Edit* menu item. The data archiving process is given the technical name of the respective objects. In the general settings of the data archiving process, you select whether only ADK-based archiving is used or whether the archiving is also to be done in near-line storage (see figure 33–2).

Figure 33–2

General settings of the data archiving process

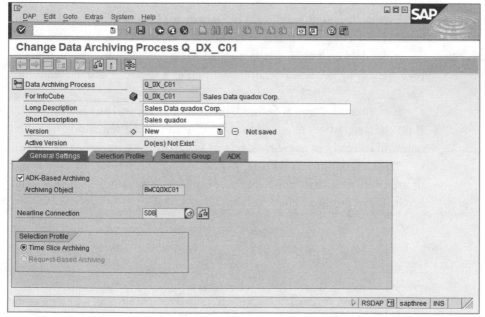

© SAP AG

ADK-based archiving

For the ADK-based archiving, an archiving object is generated from the definition of the data archiving.[219] The definition of the data archiving process thus replaces the definition of archiving objects for BasisCubes and DataStore Objects as they were required up to release 3.x.

> The definition of archiving objects during the modeling is completely replaced by the definition of data archiving processes. However, for compatibility reasons the old functionalities from BW releases 3.x still exist. You should not use them since the archiving objects generated from the data archiving process are defined differently.

Selection schema for ADK-based archiving

The *selection schema* of a data archiving process defines the criteria for limiting the data during the execution of ADK-based archiving (if not all data of the InfoProvider is to be archived).

In most cases, this will be one of the time characteristics of the BasisCube that characterizes the age of the data. If the archiving is to be controlled not by timely but by other organizational criteria, other characteristics can be used as selection criteria if they are added to the selection schema (see figure 33–3). Such a selection can be important in specific cases when products are to be phased out or company divisions are to be sold and where the data is to be archived prematurely and outside the regular archiving cycle.

Especially with the archiving of DataStore Objects, you need to keep in mind that only key fields can be chosen as selection criteria.

Semantic group for ADK-based archiving

If the data is to be sorted as it's filed, then the grouping characteristics that the sorting is based on can be defined as a semantic group (see figure 33–4).

If a semantic group is defined, the read process will already be sorted. If no characteristics are added to the definition of the semantic group, the data will be read but not sorted, or sorted according to technical criteria.

The sorted filing of archive files is advantageous if restoring of data out of archived files shall not happen completely but rather selectively and according to grouping characteristics.

---

219. The name of the generated archiving object is composed of the prefix BWC for Basis-Cubes or BWO for DataStore Objects, and the technical name of the BasisCube or the DataStore Object is reduced to seven characters.

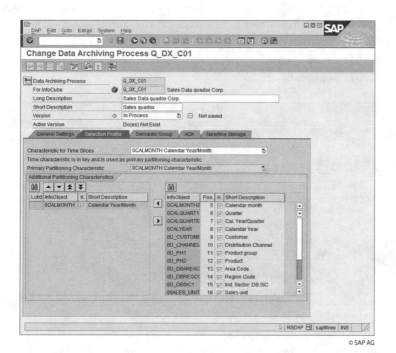

Figure 33–3
Selection schema for ADK-based archiving

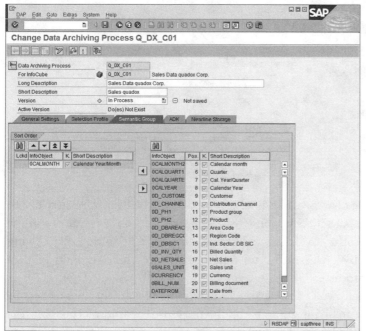

Figure 33–4
Semantic group for ADK-based archiving

File storage for ADK-based archiving

Finally, the archive system is determined with the definition of the ADK-based archiving. Generally, you indicate a logical filename that describes the data on a file server from which, in a separate process, data is collected by an archive system (see figure 33–5).

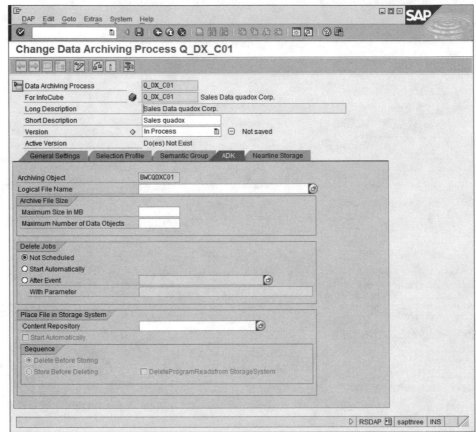

© SAP AG

Figure 33–5
File storage for ADK-based archiving

The creation of archive files is determined by the fields of the BasisCube to be archived, and it corresponds with the structure /BIC/V<Cube>I in the ABAP Dictionary. A default field selection for the definition of archiving objects in BW releases 3.x no longer exists for the definition of data archiving processes.

Optionally, you can determine a maximum file size for the archive file. To keep the archiving administration effort for BW as low as possible, the file size should be small enough to at least fit twice into the main memory of the application server.

33.1.1 Archiving

If the data archiving process for a BasisCube is defined, the archiving can be controlled via the *Archiving* tab in the cube administration. The tab is only visible for BasisCubes for which archiving is defined (see figure 33–6).

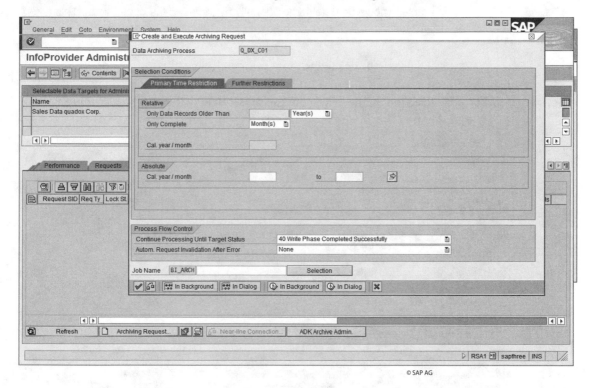

© SAP AG

You can define and start new archiving sessions in the archive administration of a BasisCube. With the definition of the restrictions, the age of the data records can be defined as a criterion. Here, the age is deduced from the characteristic that was defined as a time slice characteristic in the selection schema of the archiving process (see figure 33–3).

Figure 33–6
Definition and execution of archiving

Alternatively, the selection criteria defined in the archiving process can be used in the *Further Restrictions* tab to limit the archiving session.

33.1.2 Deletion

The deletion of archived data from BasisCubes and DataStore Objects is not done automatically after the archiving. Rather, the deletion needs to be started manually in the transaction SARA. You need to indicate the

archiving object that is to be generated with the data archiving process for
the respective BasisCube or the DataStore Object.

> With the deletion of data from a BasisCube, data from the fact table but not
> from the dimension tables is deleted. Unused data records in dimension
> tables should be deleted additionally by trimming the dimensions. This is to
> achieve the performance that you expected for the archiving.

Figure 33-7

Selective deletion of cube content

If data is to be deleted without prior archiving, this can be done in the Content tab of the cube administration with the *Selective Deletion* button. The
selection can be reached in the subsequent dialog via the *Deletion Selection*
button (see figure 33-7).

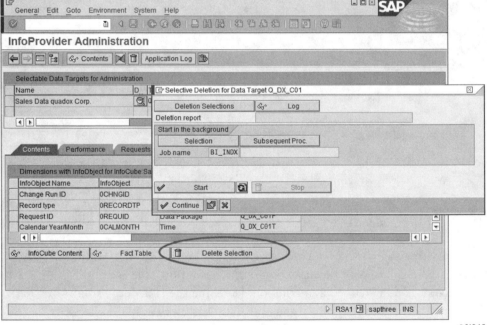

© SAP AG

With the administration of cube content and load processes, data can per
request be deleted from a BasisCube. The deletion of a request from a
BasisCube is possible only if these requests were compressed neither in the
BasisCube nor in its aggregates. You can prevent a request in aggregates
from being compressed after the rollup by deactivating the *Compress After
Rollup* option in the cube administration (see figure 7-6).

Besides the deletion of data from a BasisCube, it's important to consider the handling of storage areas that redundantly hold the data of a BasisCube—i.e., aggregates and indexes of the BI accelerator.

Aggregates and BIA indexes

The data of all aggregates is automatically adjusted for the deletion after the archiving and the selective deletion. If an aggregate contains all characteristics that were defined as deletion criteria for the deletion of the BasisCube, then the aggregates will also be selectively deleted. Otherwise, the respective aggregates are completely rebuilt. It is different with the indexes of the BI accelerator. They are not automatically adjusted but need to be rebuilt manually.

The deletion of requests is different. For aggregates, the deletion of requests is similar to the deletion of requests from a BasisCube. If data was already compressed in an aggregate, the respective request can no longer be deleted from the BasisCube (even if it is not compressed yet).

For BIA indexes, the index for the package dimension of a BasisCube is automatically rebuilt after the deletion of a request from the BasisCube. The data in the index for the fact table remains unchanged, but for the deleted request, the references in the package dimension are gone, so the data is no longer read.

33.1.3 Restore

A restore of archived data from a BasisCube and from DataStore Objects is not a restore in the common sense since the archived data is not re-created in the same way they were before the archiving.

The restore process is rather an extraction from the archive to enter data with help from the staging engine into the original but also into new data targets. The basis is always the BasisCube or the DataStore Object from which the data to be restored was deleted. The restore is made based on a transformation that uses the archived cube or the archived DataStore Object as the source structure for the transformation.

The definition of the data archiving processes and the archiving objects is inseparably related to the respective BasisCubes or DataStore Objects. A restore of data from a BasisCube or a DataStore Object can be made only if the BasisCube or the DataStore Object exists in the system. Thus, you should never delete archived BasisCubes or DataStore Objects if you still want to access the archives.

Contrary to the other functions, the transformation can be kept very simple, and it is basically a mapping of identical fields from the data source to the data target; after all, the transformation has been done already.

The restore is done with a data transfer process. If this is defined with the extraction mode *full,* then additional options for extraction from the archive are available. Figure 33–8 shows the definition of a data transfer process that uses an archived BasisCube as source structure.

Figure 33–8
Restore of archived data

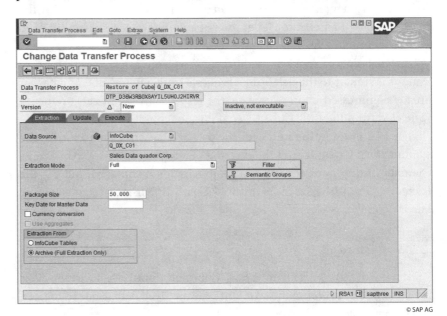

© SAP AG

Usually, the data to be restored is only used to meet special short-term requirements and it can again be deleted after the analysis (without another archiving). Data should thus be restored into a separate data target that is created only for this purpose and can be deleted together with the data once the data is no longer required. The merge of restored data with existing data can be made with a MultiProvider if required.

33.2 ILM for Master Data

In BW, master data is always related to transactional data or other master data (e.g., as a navigation attribute of an InfoObject). Since master data can never be considered isolated from other data, archiving and deletion are much more complex. Thus, there is no archiving concept whatsoever.

However, the deletion of master data is possible even though it may seem to be very restricted.

External hierarchies can be deleted freely since no other objects of the data model refer to them.[220] However, the data records in the attribute and SID tables can be referred to by transactional data or other master data. BW permits the deletion of such data records only if there are no (longer any) references.

Whether there have ever been any references to a master data record shows the SID table of the respective InfoObject. The flag DATAFL provides information on whether the record was or is referenced by transactional data, other master data, or hierarchies. The flag is set with the creation of a corresponding reference but it is not deleted when there is no reference anymore.

The deletion of single master data records is made manually in the master data maintenance. Alternatively, in the context menu of the InfoObject in the Data Warehousing Workbench, you can delete all master data records to which there is no longer a reference (see figure 33–9).

Figure 33–9

Deletion of master data without references

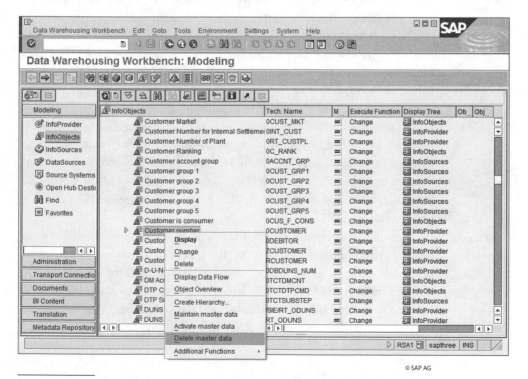

© SAP AG

220. References from query objects are not considered.

Depending on whether the SID table shows any references, a check of the references will be made prior to deletion and it can be very time consuming.

33.3 ILM for PSA and Change Log

The contents of the persistent staging area (PSA) and the change log are not automatically deleted after further processing. Since this data is usually stored on a very granular level, the capacity of the PSA and change log can soon claim a large part of the overall system capacity. Thus, it is strongly recommended that you leave data in the PSA and change log for only a short period of time and delete it as soon as the received data and its further processing have proven to be error free. So, from an ILM perspective, the use of the PSA is a limited "cost factor".

Here, the PSA and change log are considered to be temporary data areas that have a staging function but whose data has no further value in terms of content. Thus, BW does not provide an option to archive the PSA and change log.

You can manually delete certain requests in the administration of the PSA for a DataSource (see figure 15–26). The change logs are PSA tables too. The names of the respective DataSources are derived from the technical name of the respective DataStore Object with the prefix 8, e.g., 8QUADOX as the DataSource for the DataStore Object QUADOX.[221]

To automatically delete requests with the process chain controlling, there are the process types *deletion of requests from PSA* and *deletion of requests from the change log*. With an indication of the respective Data-Sources or an InfoPackage of the DataSource, requests can thus be deleted from the PSA. For change logs, the respective DataStore Objects are defined (see figure 33–10).

Deletion of partitioned PSA tables

Especially for database systems where PSA tables are provided with range partitioning (see section 24.2), a particular system behavior is observed for the deletion of requests from the PSA and the change log. To improve the deletion process for these database systems, data is not deleted selectively; rather, whole partitions are deleted. Since the data from requests and partitions do not match but a partition can contain data from

---

221. These DataSources are expert DataSources that were used to further process data in BW releases up to 3.x. These functions are no longer used with the staging in BW 7. However, the export DataSources are still the starting point for the ILM in BW 7.

several requests or a request can span over several partitions, the separate administration table RSTSODSPART stores information on which request is contained in which partition and which requests were already deleted from the PSA.

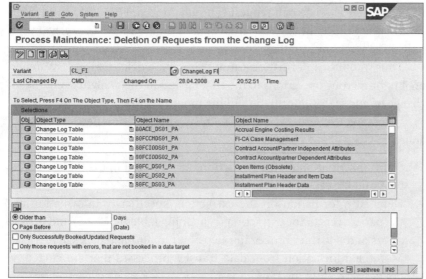

© SAP AG

Figure 33–10
Process type: deletion of requests from the change log

The deletion of a request from the PSA and the change log thus only leads to the fact that a respective flag is set in the table RSTSODSPART that marks this request as deleted. Only if all requests from a partition were deleted will this partition physically be deleted.[222] Thus, it may happen that the deletion of a request does not result in more free memory on the database system or (vice versa) the deletion of a request can free much more memory than the deleted request required per se.

33.4 ILM for Monitor Information

With the extraction as well as with the further processing of extracted data, monitor information that has a direct relation to the individual requests is stored in BW. With the extraction, this information is generated during the execution of InfoPackages and stored as request administration data. With

---

222. The deletion of a partition is made in a DROP PARTITION so that no reorganization is necessary to release memory space.

further processing, monitor information is generated from data transfer processes.

A characteristic of handling monitor information in the information lifecycle management is that the monitor information to a request needs to be archived or deleted independently from the corresponding data of the request—after all, data of a request can remain in the BW data targets for several years while the monitor information on the request is relevant for only some weeks or months.

Thus, monitor information cannot simply be deleted since BW relies on it in numerous operations in the staging and in the analytical engine to change or add status information in the monitor entries.

In relation to the archiving, the following information needs to be separated:

- Status information on the extraction that is stored in the tables RSREQ-DONE and RSSELDONE
- Detailed information on the extraction, specifically information on the parameters of the extraction (remaining tables RS*DONE) and on the status of the further processing steps[223] (remaining tables RSMON*)
- Monitor information from data transfer processes that are currently not considered in the ILM

Archiving request administration data

The archiving of monitor information is thus mostly about the archiving of detailed information from extraction processes (referred to as request administration data) from which especially BW systems where a large number of logs from old staging processes exist benefit.

The archiving handles the entries in the tables RS*DONE and RSMON*, but not all data records in these tables are subject to deletion after the archiving. In the tables RSREQDONE and RSSELDONE, one data record will remain for each that describes the status of the requests. In the table RSREQDONE, the status of the archiving is stored, too.

Requests whose monitor information was archived can thus only be processed in operations that add to or change the detailed information of the monitoring information if the respective data was previously restored

---

223. For staging via transformation and data transfer processes, the extraction of a request with a data transfer process from the PSA is logged as a further processing step. For staging prior to BW release 7, the further processing was also logged with rollup, compression, activation in DataStore Objects, further processing from DataStore Objects in a delta procedure, rebuilding of a data target from DataStore Objects in the delta procedure, and when the QM status in the extraction monitor was changed.

from the archive. The information on an extraction should therefore be archived only if the respective request was finally processed. SAP recommends waiting for at least three months before archiving the administration data of a request. This seems to be a very general recommendation and should be adjusted to meet your needs.

For the archiving of request administration data, the archiving object BWREQARCH is predefined. Besides several other predefined settings, it mostly contains references to other predefined programs to write/delete/restore monitor information.

Archiving objects for request administration data

Crucial for the execution of the archiving is the logical file path that is stored in the archiving object and that defines the storage location for the archived data. This is the default file path ARCHIVE_DATA_FILE (see figure 33–11).

Figure 33–11
Customizing settings for the archiving object RSREQARCH

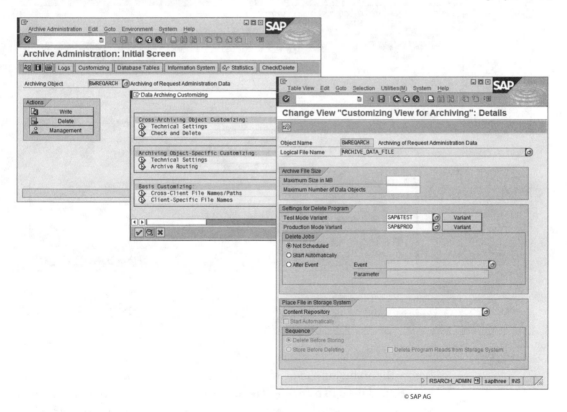

© SAP AG

The definition of the archiving object can be modified, if required, for example, to store a different logical file path. Information on handling logical files and file paths can be found in appendix B.

33.4.1   Archiving

The central entry point for the archiving of request administration data is the archive administration that can be reached via the transaction SARA. After the indication of the archiving object BWREQARCH, it enables you to write archiving data, to delete database tables, to manage archives, and to control the restore.

Specifically for the archiving of request administration data, the archive administration can be called from the administration area of the Data Warehousing Workbench or from the transaction RSREQARCH (see figure 33–12).

Figure 33–12
Calling the archive administration

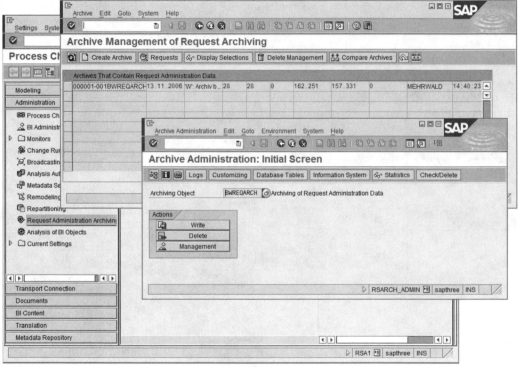

© SAP AG

Before the archiving can be started, the settings on the archiving session to be executed need to be made. These settings need to be stored as a variant. With the *Write* button, the archive administration automatically branches into the variant maintenance. Settings for the archiving session are the requests or the period that describe the age of the request to be archived (see figure 33–13).

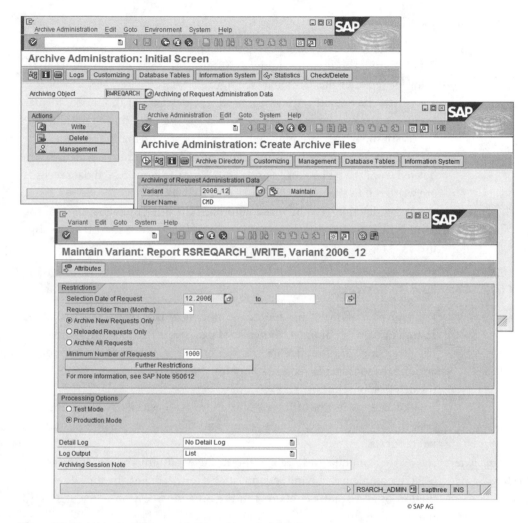

© SAP AG

Figure 33–13 Variant maintenance in the archive administration

After the variant maintenance, the start data and the spool parameters for the archiving can be set and the archiving can be scheduled.

For each request that is archived in an archiving session, SAP BW sets a lock entry. A large number of such lock entries can significantly impact the performance of system administration and the extraction processes. Thus, you should choose the selection for an archiving session so that approximately 1,000 up to 10,000 requests are handled per archiving session. It can be identified via the field SELDAT in the table RSSELDONE how many requests were created over a defined time period.

33.4.2 Deletion

The archiving object BWREQARCH for the archiving of request administration data is defined so that the archived monitor information is not automatically deleted after the archiving (see figure 33–11).

When the default settings are used, the deletion of monitor information thus needs to be manually started in the archive administration with the use of the ABAP program RSREQARCH_DELETE. During the deletion, first the written archive file is verified, and subsequently, the data records are deleted from the tables RSMON* and RS*DONE or the compressed data records are written into the tables RSREQDONE and RSSELDONE.

If the deletion is to be made automatically after the generation of the archive files, then the archiving object BWREQARCH can be modified (see figure 33–11).

33.4.3 Restore

For a number of operations for the old staging of BW releases up to 3.x, the restore of request administration data is necessary. For the new staging that uses transformation and data transfer processes, the restore of request administration data is required only for the extraction from the PSA and the deletion of requests.

For the execution of the restore, there are basically two options: the restore of complete archiving sessions and the targeted restore of individual requests.

Restore of a complete archiving session

With a manual restore, in the archive administration (transaction SARA) a complete archiving session can be restored; i.e., the monitor information of all requests contained in the archiving session is reloaded into the system.

Restore of selected requests

Since the restore of a complete archiving session might cost too much effort to work on only a handful of requests, there is the alternative option to reload monitor information of single requests from the archive in a targeted way. This can be made in the archive administration for the request administration data (see figure 33–14), but it is not mandatory since BW automatically reloads the respective information from the archive for operations that rely on the request administration data.

At first glance, the targeted reload of single requests thus seems to be significantly easier than the restore of a complete archiving session. However, the automatic reload has consequences for the archiving sessions insofar as they remain unchanged but the requests are deleted from these sessions in the archive administration (to possibly be stored again in a different archive file).

Figure 33–14
Administration of single requests in the archive

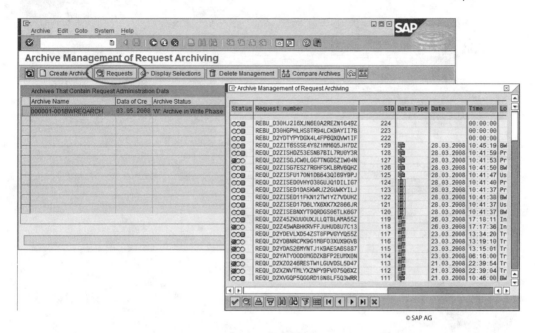

© SAP AG

So, it can happen that an archiving session contains only few or no requests at all. Such archiving sessions can be deleted in the archiving administration via the menu item *Archive→Delete* if they do not contain any requests that were not restored.

Deletion of archiving sessions

If there is a large number of archiving sessions that only partially contain the original archived requests, the archiving sessions can (and should) be reorganized. In this case, the respective archiving sessions are marked and merged via the menu item *Archive→Reorganize Archive*.

Reorganization of archiving sessions

33.5 ILM for Application Logs

In addition to the monitor information (see section 31.1), the log information is stored in the application log. Regarding request-related data, the information is not as detailed as information in the BW monitor, but it also contains additional information, for example, on the maintenance of metadata. More detailed information on the application log can be found in section 31.1.

For the log information in the application log, there is only the option to delete it. This is made via transaction SLG2 (see figure 33–15).

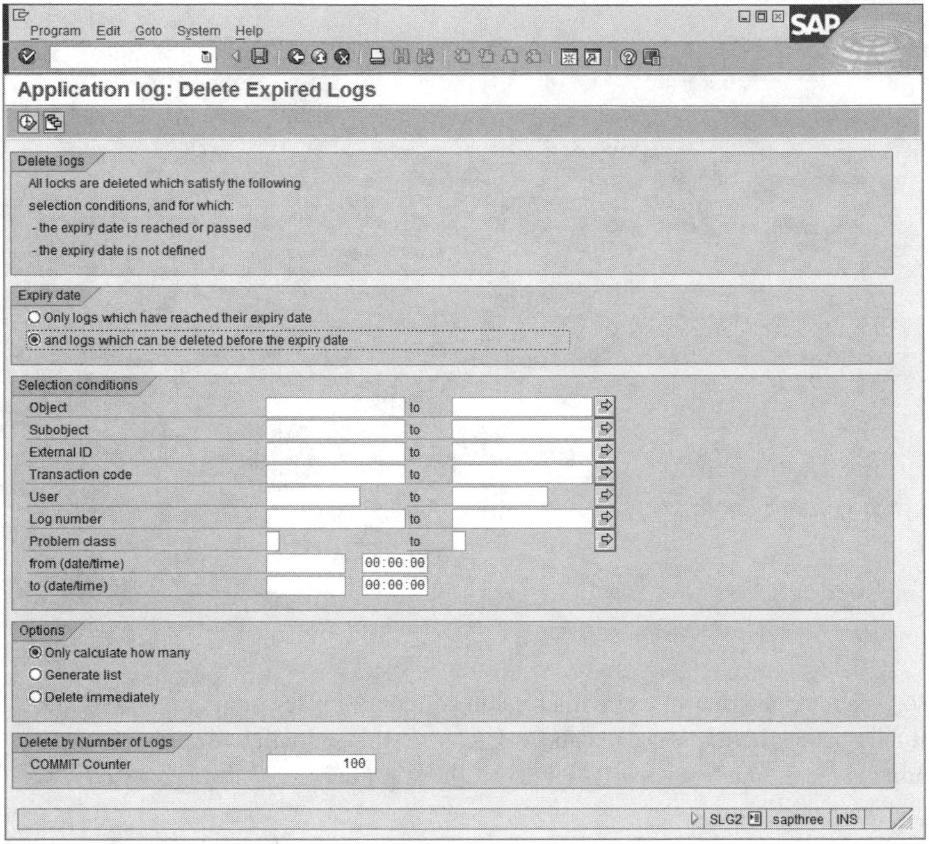

© SAP AG

Figure 33–15
Deletion of application logs

The deletion removes entries from the tables BALHDR, BAL_INDX and BATDAT. To automate the deletion of application logs in the process chain controlling, as an alternative to the transaction SLG2, the ABAP program SBAL_DELETE can be included in a process chain; it corresponds with transaction SLG2.

33.6 ILM for BW Statistics Data

For the review of system usage and as a basis for performance tuning, the staging and the analytical engine create statistics data and store it in BW (see section 13.2).

The tables in which statistics data is stored can be very large and should thus be deleted regularly. An archiving of statistics data is not provided in BW, and it is not necessary if technical content (see appendix D.2.2) that transfers the statistics data into predefined BasisCubes (that can be archived) is used.

Consequently, there are two options for the deletion: the automatic deletion via the data transfer of technical content or the manual deletion of statistics data.

If the technical content is used, then with each data transfer from the statistics data by the DataSources OTCT_DS01, OTCT_DS02, and OTCT_DS03, all data of the underlying tables that are older than 14 days is deleted.

Deletion of statistics data from the technical content

The default retention time of 14 days can be overruled, if required, by entering in the table RSADMIN the requested retention period in the parameter TCT_KEEP_OLAP_DM_DATA_N_DAYS. For the maintenance of the table RSADMIN, you can use the program SAP_RSADMIN_MAINTAIN.

Apart from the automism in the technical content, the statistics data can be deleted via the transaction RSDDSTAT (see figure 33–16).

Manual deletion of statistics data

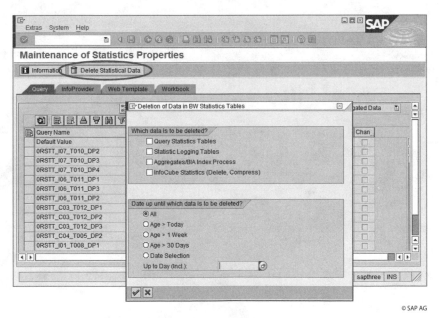

Figure 33–16
Deletion of statistics data from the analytical and staging engines

© SAP AG

If the deletion is to be automated in the process chain controlling, the ABAP program RSDDSTAT_DATA_DELETE can be included into the process chain for this purpose.

VII   Appendix

A   Currency Conversion

Amounts might be extracted in different currencies from the source systems and they might need to be further converted into different currencies in the staging or the data analysis.[224] Each currency conversion is based on the same principles.[225]

The preconditions for the conversion of currencies are as follows:

- Definition of exchange rates or translation ratios
- Definition of conversion types

A.1   Exchange Rates/Translation Ratios

For the conversion of currencies, it is necessary to store exchange rates or translation ratios (e.g., the translation ratio 1.95583 for the conversion of DEM in EUR).

Exchange rates or translation ratios refer to rate types; i.e., each conversion is stored for one or several rate types in order to thus enable the conversion at bank buying rates, at bank selling rates, or at average rates (see figure A–1).

Exchange rate types are stored in the table TCURV and can be maintained via the transaction OB07. Based on the exchange rate types, the exchange rates can be stored as follows:

- As exchange rates
- As translation ratios (alternative rates)

---

224. Currency conversion is not possible with the analysis of InfoSets.
225. The currency conversion in BW was taken from SAP R/3; however, given the BW-specific modifications, it is not identical to the currency conversion in R/3.

Figure A–1
*Maintenance of exchange
rate types*

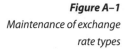

ExRt	Usage	Ref.crcy	Buy.rt.at	Sell.rt.at	Inv	E	Fixed	
100*	Reference value = group value				☐	☐	☐	
1001	Current exchange rate				☐	☐	☐	
1002	Average exchange rate				☐	☐	☐	
1003	Historical exchange rate				☐	☐	☐	
1004	Current exch. rate prior year				☐	☐	☐	
200*	Reference value = group value				☐	☐	☐	
2001	Current exchange rate				☐	☐	☐	
2002	Average exchange rate				☐	☐	☐	
2003	Historical exchange rate				☐	☐	☐	
2004	Current exch. rate prior year				☐	☐	☐	
B	Standard translation at bk.selling				☐	☐	☐	
EURO	EMU regulation, fixed exchange r	EUR			☐	☑	☑	
EURX	EMU regulation, variable exchang	EUR			☐	☑	☐	
G	Standard translation at bank buyi				☐	☐	☐	
I	Intrastat exchange rate type				☐	☐	☐	
M	Standard translation at average r				☐	☐	☐	
P	Standard translation for cost plar				☐	☐	☐	

Position...   Entry 1 of 17

OB07   sapthree   INS

© SAP AG

A.1.1   Definition of Exchange Rates

Exchange rates can be stored as *volume quotation* (indirect quotation) or as price *quotation* (direct quotation).

Volume quotation

With the volume quotation, the number of foreign currency units per unit of the local currency is shown. If the local currency is shown in EUR and the foreign currency in USD, the exchange rate in the volume quotation would, for example, be shown as 1.2965; i.e., for 1.0000 EUR, one receives 1.2965 USD.

Price quotation

The price quotation is the counterpart of the volume quotation. Here, the volume of local currency units is shown per unit of the foreign currency. For the previous example, the quotation would be shown as 0.77131; i.e., for 1.0000 USD, one receives, 0.77131 EUR.

The maintenance of exchange rates is made via transaction 0B08 (see figure A–2).

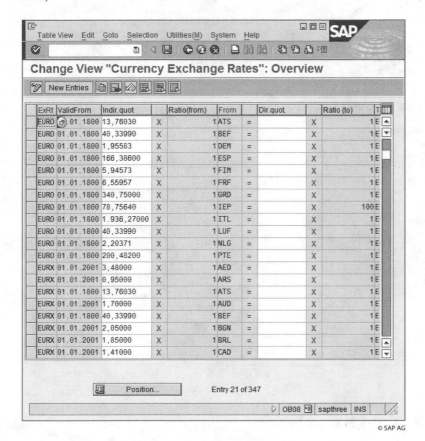

© SAP AG

Figure A–2

Maintenance of exchange rates

A.1.2 Maintenance of Translation Ratios

Translation ratios are used to deduce currency conversions for a certain currency combination from other currency combinations (e.g., conversion of DEM to USD is deduced from DEM → EUR → USD).

The use of translation ratios assumes that a joint alternative currency (e.g., EUR) is given and can be used (as an interim step) for all other currency conversions.

Translation ratios can thus be used to reduce the number of maintained currency combinations.

The maintenance of translation ratios is made via the transaction 0BBS (see figure A–3).

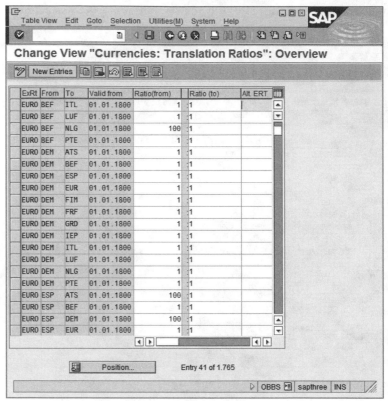

Figure A–3
Maintenance of translation ratios

A.2   Conversion Types

Depending on the situation, it might be required to use a certain exchange rate for the currency conversion. The exchange rate to be used for the conversion depends on the *source currency,* the *target currency,* the *exchange rate type,* and the *time reference.*

How these parameters are to be identified is determined in the definition of the *conversion types* that can be created via the transaction RSCUR.

Each defined conversion type determines for the conversion of currencies a combination of the following properties:

- Exchange rate type
- Source currency
- Target currency
- Time reference

A.2.1 Exchange Rate Type

The settings on an exchange rate type determine at what exchange rate type the conversion is to be made. The exchange rate type can either be fixed (e.g., use of the bank selling rate) or it can be taken from the content of an InfoObject (see figure A–4).

```
┌─────────────────────────────────────────────────────────────────────┐
│ ☞                                                        _ □ ☒  SAP   │
│   Currency Conversion Key  Edit  Goto  Extras  System  Help          │
│  ⊘ ▢              ◁ ▯ | ◐ ◎ ◎ | □ ⊞ ⊞ | ⊠ ⊠ ⊠ ⊠ | ▨ ▨ | ⊘ ▣        │
│                                                                       │
│  Edit Currency Conversion Type                                        │
│  ▨ ▨ ▨ ▨ | ⓘ Obj. directory entry                                    │
│                                                                       │
│  Conversion Type  │TESTCONV │                                        │
│  Description       │TestConversion             │                     │
│                                                                       │
│   ╱ Properties ╲ Exchange Rate ╲ Currncy ╲ Time Ref. ╲                │
│  ┌──────────────────────────────────────────────────────────────┐   │
│  │                                                                │   │
│  │  ◉ Exchange Rate Type        B  ⟦⟧    Standard translation at bk.selling rate │
│  │  ○ Ex. Rate Type from Var.          ⟦⟧                         │   │
│  │                                                                │   │
│  │  ○ Dyn. Ex. Rate Determination                                 │   │
│  │  ◉ Exchange Rate from InfoObj.  IO_W_CU    ⟦⟧ InfoObject with currency │
│  │                                                                │   │
│  │  ☐ Inverse Ex.Rate                                             │   │
│  │                                                                │   │
│  └──────────────────────────────────────────────────────────────┘   │
│                                            ▷ │ RSCUR ▣ │ sapthree │ INS │
└─────────────────────────────────────────────────────────────────────┘
                              © SAP AG
```

The identification of the exchange rate type from an InfoObject assumes that the InfoObject uses the attribute ORATE_TYPE. The content of this attribute is used as the exchange rate type for the conversion. With the conversion in transformations, the InfoObject needs to be available in the structure of the data source.

  Figure A–5 shows the definition of an InfoObject that is suited for the exchange rate type identification.

Figure A–4

Creation of exchange rate types: exchange rate from InfoObject

> Any InfoObject that a definition of conversion types refers to needs to be available at the time of the conversion. With the conversion at the time of the analysis, not only the key figures but also the InfoObject that contains the exchange rate type needs to be available.

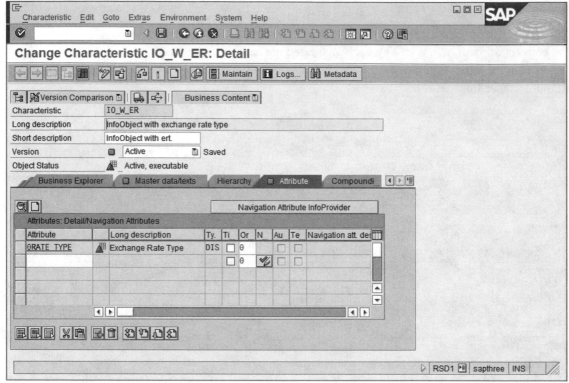

Figure A–5
InfoObject with exchange rate type

A.2.2 Source Currency

In the source currency of a conversion type, you define the currency on which the conversion is to be based. The source currency can be derived from either the data records of the amount key figure or a specified InfoObject.

Source currency of the data record

For an extraction with BI content, all key figures are transferred to BW together with the correctly filled unit field. This should also be the case when generic DataSources in SAP ERP or other source systems are used.

Then, the currency is stored for each key figure in a respective currency field and is available to the data record for the conversion. The option *Source Currency from Data Record* means that exactly this procedure can be used.

Source currency of an InfoObject

Sometimes, BW is provided with key figures without an indication of the currency. On this basis, a conversion of amounts is not possible, so you need to refer to other ways to identify the respective units.

One possibility is to try to deduce the source currency from a certain characteristics value. If it is possible to gather the source currency based on a certain value of a characteristics value, then this source currency can be used for the conversion. Such a derivation could be based on the fact that in the country DE the currency is always provided in EUR.

Figure A–6 shows the determination of the source currency depending on the InfoObject IO_M_WB.

Figure A–6

Creation of conversion types: currency determination from InfoObject

© SAP AG

As a prerequisite for such a derivation, the InfoObject needs to contain information on the source currency to be identified in its master data. For this purpose, in the attributes of the InfoObject, a unit InfoObject of the type Currency needs to be added (e.g., OCURRENCY).

Further, this attribute needs to be defined as a currency attribute of the InfoObject (see figure A–7). Each InfoObject can have a maximum of one currency attribute.

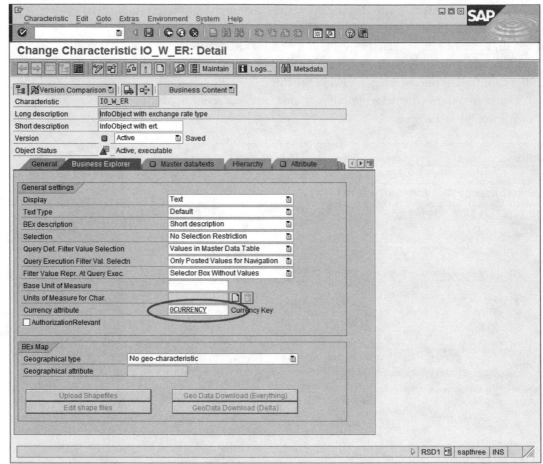

© SAP AG

Figure A–7

Creation of conversion types: InfoObject with currency attribute

A.2.3   Target Currency

There are three options for the definition of the target currency (see figure A–6):

- Selection of target currency during conversion
- Fixed target currency
- InfoObject to determine the target currency

Selection of target currency during conversion

The selection of the target currency at the time of the conversion makes sense especially for the currency conversion in the data analysis. Here, a respective target currency can be selected at the time of the conversion.

A fixed target currency cannot be changed with the use of this conversion type. This conversion type makes sense for conversions in the staging if no interaction with a user is possible.

Fixed target currency

As for the determination of a source currency from an InfoObject, the target currency can also be identified from an InfoObject. The same basic conditions apply as for the determination of the source currency (see appendix A.2.2); i.e., the respective InfoObject needs to have a currency attribute and accordingly maintained master data.

InfoObject to determine the target currency

A.2.4 Time Reference

Exchange rates are not constant but change over time. Each rate is thus stored related to a validity period (see figure A–2). For the currency conversion, you need to determine for which period in time the exchange rate is to be applied.

To identify the time, you can define either a fixed or a variable point in time (see figure A–8).

Figure A–8

Creation of conversion types: time reference

© SAP AG

Fixed time reference For the definition of a fixed time, the time of the exchange rate finding is independent from the data to be converted. For the time, either a current system date at the time of the conversion or a fixed date defined in the conversion type is used.

Variable time reference For the variable time reference, the time of the conversion depends on the data specifications that are stored in the data to be converted. These date specifications can be taken from a standard DataStore Object or from a specific InfoObject. Based on the content of the indicated InfoObject, the following times are available as a basis for the currency conversion and they are deduced from the indicated InfoObject:

- End of fiscal year
- Beginning of fiscal year
- End of period
- Beginning of period
- End of calendar year
- Beginning of calendar year
- End of month
- Beginning of month
- End of week
- Daily

A.3 Global Settings

Often, part of the transformation is the conversion of exchange rates in different currencies, the handling of measurements, and the time conversion (see section 19.3.7). The preconditions are the global settings. These are stored currencies, measurements, fiscal year variants, and the calendar.

A.3.1 Currencies

A prerequisite for the conversion of currencies is the definition of the respective currency. In BW, all currencies are already stored with their respective ISO codes.

If other codes are used in the source systems (and not changed during the staging), then they need to be maintained in BW. The transaction SPRO can be used to review the activity *Check Currency Codes* in the implementation guide of BW (see figure A–9).

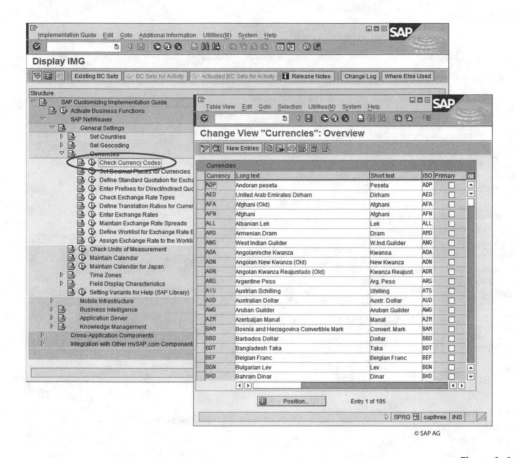

© SAP AG

Figure A–9
Maintenance of currencies

A.3.2   Measurements

As with currencies, all measurements need to be maintained in BW so that BW can convert units, if required (e.g., grams into kilograms).

In BW, units are defined according to the international system of units. If required, adjustments can be made via the transaction CUNI.

A.3.3   Fiscal Year Variants

For the use of booking periods in the BW data model, it is necessary to maintain respective fiscal year variants. These describe how many booking periods and special periods a year has as well as the preconditions for a respective time conversion.

The fiscal year variants can be maintained in the transaction SPRO (see figure A–10).

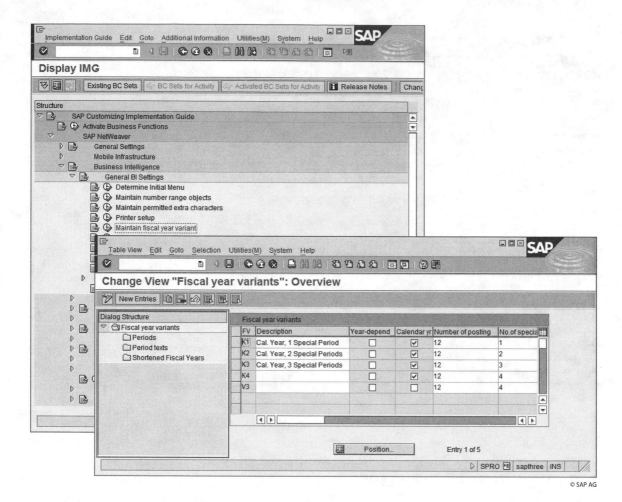

Figure A–10
Maintenance of fiscal year variants

A.3.4   Calendar

The calendar is maintained to define holidays and workdays and it is used with calendar days in the data model. The calendar is already maintained with the delivery of BW, but it can be modified via the transaction SCAL.

A.3.5   Transfer from SAP ERP

To facilitate the maintenance and modification of the global settings to match company-specific requirements, BW offers the option to directly take the respective settings from SAP ERP systems. For this purpose, the menu item *Transfer Global Settings* is available in the context menu of the

ERP source systems in the source system tree of the Data Warehousing Workbench. Via this menu item, all (or only certain) settings can be transferred (see figure A–11).

© SAP AG

A transfer of global settings from source systems other than SAP ERP is not possible.

Figure A–11
Transfer of global Settings from SAP ERP systems

A.4   Exchange Rates

As a prerequisite for the execution of currency conversions, you need the exchange rates with the respective conversion types that are stored in BW. The settings can be found in transaction SPRO (see figure A–12).

The maintenance of the exchange rates as well as the required settings (exchange rate types, etc.) can be very complex, especially if the exchange rate information is to be updated several times during a month. For this reason, there is the option to take the information from a connected source system.

The following source systems can be used:

- SAP ERP systems
- Flat files

Figure A–12

Settings on currency conversion

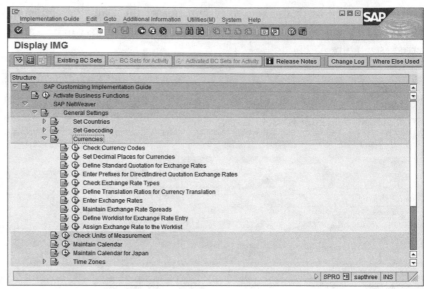

A.4.1   Transfer from SAP ERP Systems

The transfer of exchange rates from SAP ERP systems is made in the Data Warehousing Workbench in the menu item *Transfer Exchange Rates* in the context menu of the selected source system. Exchange rates and conversion types are transferred and they can be selected prior to the transfer (see figure A–13).

Figure A–13

Selection of exchange rates with the transfer from SAP ERP

A.4.2 Transfer from Flat Files

Similar to SAP ERP systems, it is possible to transfer exchange rates from flat files. Here, the program RSIMPCURFILE is available. The flat file needs to exactly match the format of the table TCURR.

Unlike with SAP ERP systems, only exchange rates but no conversion types are transferred. In this case, the conversion types need to be maintained manually (see appendix A.2).

B   Logical Files and Paths

In order to design file names and path indications as independently as possible from the infrastructure and file systems in use, the BW basis system uses logical files and logical file paths, a concept that originally stems from the SAP ERP basis system and was (and is) provided for manifold tasks.

In connection with data warehousing in SAP BW, the concept of logical files and file paths is especially visible with the definition of InfoPackages and the information lifecycle management to archive data.

In this chapter, we'll briefly explain the concept of logical files and path indications. The focus is to provide a procedure for the definition of logical file names that is suitable for the definition of load processes in BW.

The definition of logical files is made in the transaction FILE,[226] where the following settings need to be made (in the indicated order):

1. Definition of variables
2. Creation of logical file paths
3. Creation of logical file names

Figure B–1 gives an overview of the connections among the settings.

---

226. The definition is made cross-client. The use of the transaction SF01 to define client-independent logical files does not make any sense since BW is not client enabled.

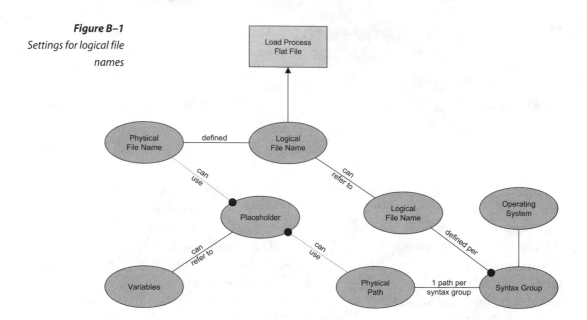

Figure B–1
Settings for logical file names

Definition of variables

Figure B–2
Definition of variables for path indications

System-related settings can be stored with the definition of variables. These include, for example, IP addresses or path indications that are specific to the respective system. Figure B–2 shows the definition of a variable with the name Q_FILESERV that is to describe a system-specific path definition.

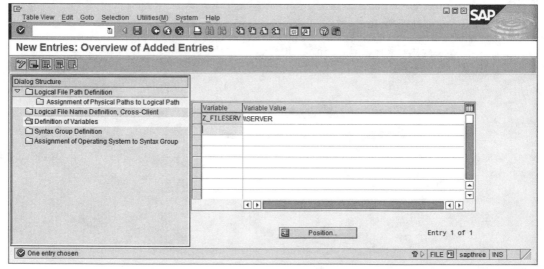

© SAP AG

The logical file path defines part of the logical file name that describes the path of a file and can be derived from the physical path. First, the logical file path is defined clearly as well as a key across the system and it is named (see figure B–3).

Creation of logical file paths

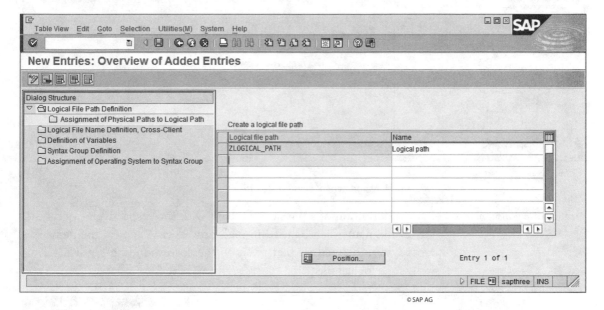

© SAP AG

After you define a logical file path, you need to assign the corresponding physical file path. The following properties are determined with the indication of the physical file path:

Figure B–3
Definition of logical file paths

- Parts of the path or the complete path can be defined by fixed strings.
- Parts of the path or the complete path can be defined by placeholders[227] and/or variables.
- The location in the path where the file name is to be inserted needs to be marked by <FILENAME>.

Figure B–4 shows the description of the physical file path \\SERVER\BW\DATA\INPUT\.

In the physical path indicated in the figure, the path name would be composed of the content of the variables Z_FS and the string \BW\DATA\INPUT\ as well as the name of the physical file.

---

227. A complete listing of possible placeholders can be found in the appendix (see appendix E.2).

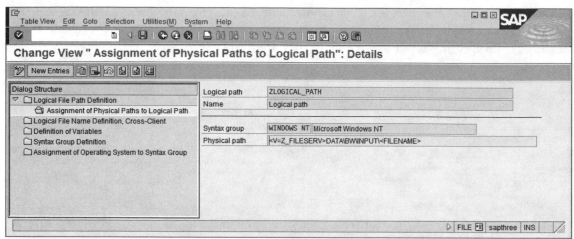

Figure B–4 *Assignment of physical file paths*

Creation of logical file names

For the definition of a physical file path with the respective physical file, logical file names can be used in load processes. A logical file name is a cross-system defined ID that refers to the corresponding physical file as well as the logical file path.

Figure B–5
Creation of logical file names

In figure B–5, the logical file is defined by the placeholder <SYEAR>, <MONTH>, <DAY> as well as the file extension .DAT. The file name is thus dynamically defined depending on the system date, and, for example, for the date Jan 18, 2007, the file name would be 20070118.DAT.

With the definition of a logical file paths, it is possible with the execution of a load process to identify the complete physical file path and the file name.

If the file name `ZLOGICAL_FILE` is indicated, the name `\\SERVER\BW\DATA\INPUT\20070218.DAT` would thus be defined on 02/18/2007.

The definition of the physical file name and the file path based on the logical file name is made in BW via the function module `FILE_GET_NAME`. This can also be used to test the correct definition (transaction `SE37`).

C   Transport System

A typical BW system in live operation ideally consists of the following components:

■ Development system, where the modeling and the program development are made and tested. The development system usually has no or few test data.

■ Test system, whose environment is similar to the live system (source systems, data marts, data content, etc.) and which can thus be used for quality assurance of new developments before developments are handed over to live operation.

■ Live or production system (also referred to as productive system), into which developments are transported only if they were tested for accuracy in the test system.

In SAP terminology, all systems together are referred to as the *transport landscape*. The creation of a complete transport landscape with all three named systems is recommended[228] to make and test developments without impacting the live operation.

Content development

The transport system that is also known from SAP ERP is specifically supplemented with content systems in SAP BW. Content systems provide predefined metadata for BW objects for the development system that can be transferred and modified from the metadata content if required. Thus, they do not need to be redeveloped completely (for the transfer of BW objects from the metadata content, see appendix D).

The use of the content systems is ideal and is especially suited for developers who want to supply their customers with developments in content form and also for companies with decentralized BW systems that are to be provided with standard development templates. For "regular" BW transport landscapes, the use of content systems is usually not recommended.

---

228. Technically, the creation of a complete transport landscape is not mandatory.

The BI content supplied by SAP also mostly originates from an SAP content system even though this is not completely correct from a technical perspective.

Figure C–1

Transport landscape of

SAP BW

Figure C–1 shows the transport landscape in the SAP BW environment, and besides the business content system of SAP, it also considers further optional content development systems.

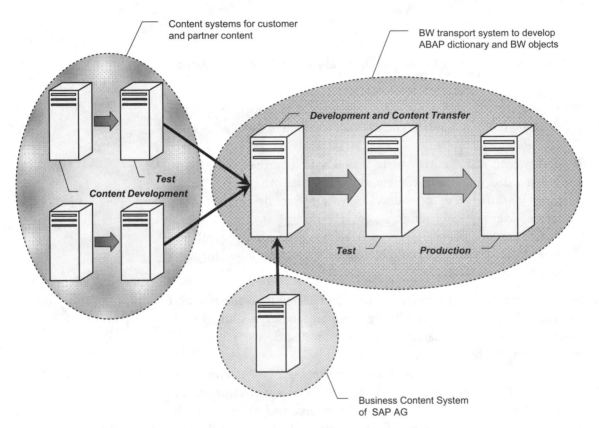

We'll explain the following topics in this chapter:

■ The BW transport system to develop and provide ABAP Dictionary and BW objects

■ The content transport system to develop and provide individual metadata content

■ The exchange of metadata on BW objects via the XML format

C.1   BW Transport System

The basis of the transport system is the *change and transport organizer* (CTO) that is responsible for the logging of developments and their transportation.

From an application development perspective, the basic job of the CTO is to **transport objects, transport packages,** and **transport requests.**

Transport objects

All developments are composed of one or several objects. An object in the CTO sense can be an ABAP Dictionary element (e.g., data elements, table definitions), programs, table content, documents from the business document store, or a BW object.[229]

While ABAP Dictionary elements and BW objects were still considered separately in chapter 4, the transport system considers all developments to be **transport objects.** The definition of a table structure passes for an object like a complex BasisCube.[230]

Especially the metadata of BW objects includes complex definitions from which programs and ABAP Dictionary elements might be generated. For BW objects, only the respective metadata is stored and transported as transport objects. During the transport process, all derived elements are generated in the target system from the metadata.

This can be, for example, the generation of programs from the definition of the transformation or the generation of SID or master data tables from the definition of an InfoObject. For all BW objects, after the transport to the target system, a respective generation procedure is executed that can be compared to the activation of the respective BW objects.

Transport packages

For better coordination of complex developments, certain development parts (i.e., transport objects) can be assigned to **transport packages** in order to categorize them.

With the use of transport packages, it is thus very easy to oversee all objects of a certain transport package and to transport them jointly.

> Transport packages are very useful for the separation of developments from different projects or of independent subareas of complex projects. For BW projects that do not offer this complexity, it makes sense to use only one single transport package.

---

229. In this context, objects have nothing to do with object orientation in the programming.
230. For the content transport systems (see appendix C.2) and the metadata exchange via XML (see appendix C.3), this is different. They are limited to metadata from BW objects and are not suited to transport objects from the ABAP Dictionary.

Each object has an ***object directory entry*** where exactly one transport package can be entered. From this categorization of objects, the function of the transport packages for the transport system is derived. The transport package defines which objects are to be transported (it defines transport-relevant and local transport packages) and which target systems are provided for a transport package (if a development system provides several other systems with transports).

Transport requests

Figure C–2

Object list of a transport request

All newly developed or changed objects that a transportable transport package is assigned to are combined in ***transport requests,*** where several tasks can be assigned to one transport request that can take the transport objects from a certain developer (see figure C–2).

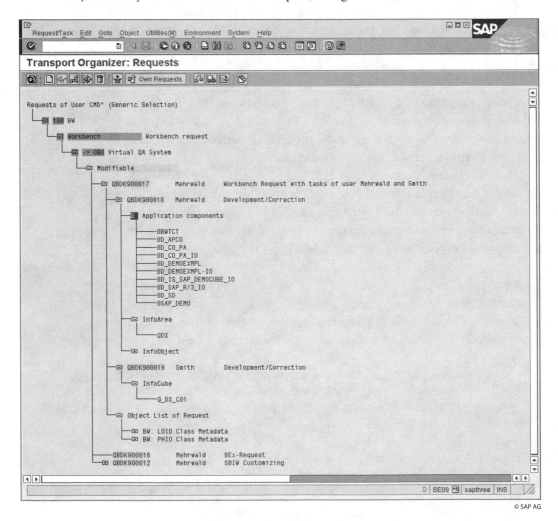

© SAP AG

With the release[231] of a transport request, the content of the request is exported into a file and it can be reimported by the target system.[232] For the import of a request, the CTO considers the dependencies of herein contained objects; i.e., it first creates domains and data elements and the tables that are based on the data elements. Thus, the sequence at which the objects were added to the transport request is irrelevant.

How the transport objects make their way into the transport request or how the objects first receive the necessary entry of a transportable transport package in the object directory catalog is explained in detail in section 36.1.1.

Further, there is a range of peculiarities for the BW transport system that need to be considered:

- Realization of source system references in the staging
- Transport of process chains
- Transports in large-scale architectures
- Developments in the production system
- Creation of source systems

The peculiarities are explained after the general description of the transport connection in the appendices C.1.2 to C.1.6.

C.1.1 Transport Connection

As already explained, the addition of transport objects to transport requests requires the assignment of a transport package to the respective object.

With the creation of **ABAP Dictionary elements** (e.g., tables, structures, programs), for each element the system requires the indication of a transport package for the object directory entry and a subsequent transport request.

Assignment of transport packages to ABAP Dictionary elements

As soon as an object is assigned to a transport package, no further transport package is requested when the object is changed. Instead, with each change a transport request to which the object is to be added is immediately requested. All objects with a transportation package are subject to the **automatic change recording,** also referred to as **engineering change management.**

---

231. The release is made via the transactions SE01, SE09 and SE10.
232. The import is executed via transaction STMS.

As long as an object is contained in a transport request and has not been released for transporting, any development on the respective object is automatically integrated into the corresponding transport request. This ensures that older developments of an object cannot be released for transport after the newer ones.[233]

If a development is not to be transported, you can assign the transport package $TMP, which is a standard transport package for objects that are not transportable (local). This can make sense if developments in the ABAP directory are created only for test purposes and are to be deleted or assigned to a transportable transport package together with other objects at a later time.

Assignment of transport packages to BW objects

With the creation of **BW objects,** the assignment of the object directory entry to a transport package is different. There is a choice of two very different procedures:

- Standard transport system
- BW transport system

Standard Transport System

In the standard transport system, BW behaves with the creation of BW objects in the same way it behaves with the creation of ABAP Dictionary objects; i.e., for each BW object, an object directory entry is requested right after the creation of a transport package and the object is immediately stored in a transport request.

This procedure is suitable for objects of the ABAP Dictionary since the respective developments usually consist of fewer objects that can mostly be handled isolated from each other in the transport system.

However, BW objects show significantly more dependencies—InfoObjects are attributes of other InfoObjects, and all are contained in one or several InfoObject directories that are again categorized in an InfoArea. The definition of cubes is based on these InfoObjects in addition to InfoObject directories and InfoAreas and also shows transformations, queries, and much more.

These dependencies could be freely continued and expanded in complexity. In fact, when objects are combined in transport requests, the dependencies between the entered objects need to be considered in particular.

---

233. Then, current developments in the test and production system would be overwritten by old developments.

Otherwise, a transport could be executed erroneously because, besides the dozens of contained objects, one single attribute is missing.

SAP BW accounts for the disadvantages of the standard transport connection by *not* using this transport connection as a default setting. Instead, the BW transport connection is used.

Whether the standard transport connection is to be used is defined as a cross-system setting in the transport connection of the Data Warehousing Workbench (see figure C–3).

Figure C–3

Switching between standard transport system and BW transport system

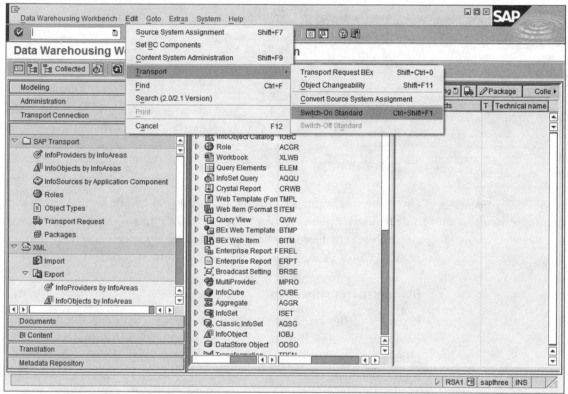

© SAP AG

This cross-system setting of the used transport connection can be overruled in the user parameters of each single user. For this purpose, in the user maintenance in the transaction SU01, the parameter RSOSTANDARD-CTOACTIVE can be set. With an X as parameter, the standard transport connection is activated; with a blank space, the BW transport connection is activated. Figure C–4 shows the activation of the standard transport connection for the user MEHRWALD.

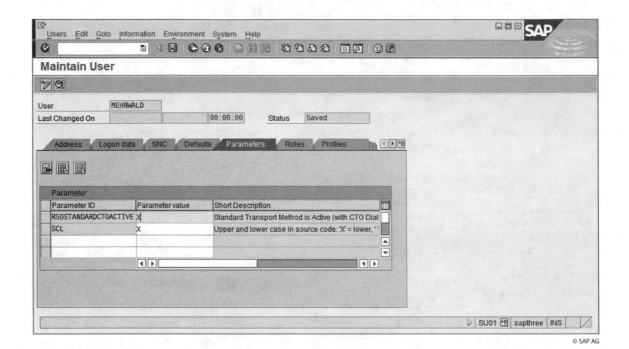

Figure C–4

User-specific selection of the transport connection

Given the disadvantages of the standard transport connection, it should only be used if there are very good reasons to do so—e.g., since for each single object an object directory entry is explicitly selected, which is hardly possible with an automated collection of objects.

BW Transport Connection

Contrary to the standard transport connection, with the BW transport connection for new BW objects, no transport package/transport request is required. Instead, SAP BW quietly assigns the transport package $TMP to each new object.

This enables you to first create new scenarios without dealing with the transport. The objects need to be assigned to a transportable transport object only if all corresponding objects (BasisCubes with InfoObjects, transformations, InfoSources, etc.) are completely defined and are to be transported for the first time.

Transport connection

Specifically for the compilation of corresponding BW objects and the assignment of transportable *transport packages,* SAP BW offers the so-called transport connection that is part of the Data Warehousing Workbench (see figure C–5).

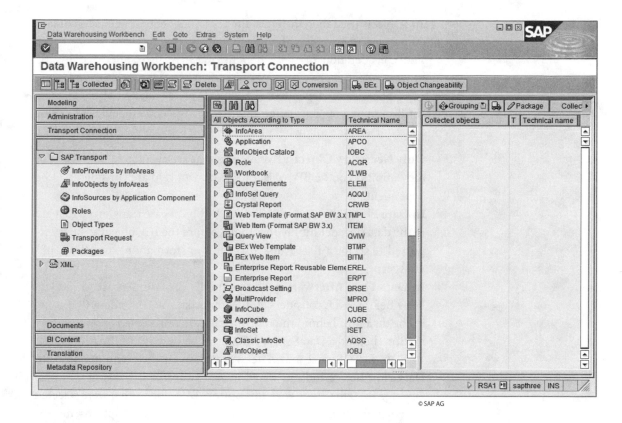

© SAP AG

In the transport connection, the selection of BW objects can be made according to different aspects and can be combined by drag and drop (e.g., based on InfoSources, InfoObjects, InfoAreas, or transport packages).

If BW objects that are assigned to the transport package $TMP are compiled in the transport connection, a transport package for these objects is requested when the transport request is created. This request is made only once per transport request so that all BW objects of a transport request receive the same transport package (unless they were previously assigned to another transport package).

As soon as a BW object is assigned to a transport package, the engineering change management for the object is activated; i.e., with each further change to the BW object, a transport request is automatically made for the object.

With the compilation of BW objects in the transport connection, the consideration of dependencies is especially important. For example, if a cube is transported, then its definition at least depends on the existence of

Figure C–5

Object types of the transport connection

Consideration of dependencies

the InfoObjects used therein. Thus, the transport request needs to contain both the BasisCube and its InfoObjects.

The consideration of these dependencies is also supported by the transport connection; i.e., if a BW object is taken over, by drag and drop, for transport, then all dependent BW objects are also taken over. With the help of grouping, you can define to what degree dependencies are to be considered. Here, the following options can be selected (see figure C–6):

- **Only Necessary Objects:** BW objects that are absolutely necessary for the definition of the BW object to be transported are considered to be dependent.
- **In Data Flow Before:** Additionally, BW objects are transferred that are in the data flow definition positioned before the BW object to be transported (e.g., for a BasisCube also the transformations and the DataSources).
- **In Data Flow Afterwards:** This option is the counterpart to In Data Flow Before and it considers all BW objects to be dependent that come in the data flow behind the BW object to be transferred (e.g., transformations behind a DataSource or queries behind an InfoProvider).
- **In Data Flow Before and Afterwards:** This is the combination of In Data Flow Before and In Data Flow Afterwards.
- **Save for System Copy:** With this option, BW objects that were selected are entered into a transport request. Contrary to other options, dependent requests can thus be used to save in a targeted way single objects that are to be restored after a system copy.

After the compilation, individual objects can be manually marked or unmarked for transport before the transport request is created via the respective button (that looks like a truck).

As soon as an object is assigned to a transport package, the engineering change management for the object is activated so that each change to the BW object is recorded and stored in a transport request.

The transport connection considers the dependencies of all BW objects. Excluded from this treatment are ABAP Dictionary elements, programs or includes, and other developments even if they are related to the transported BW objects. Such objects need to be assigned to a transport package via the transport connection for ABAP Dictionary objects and a corresponding transport request needs to be created.

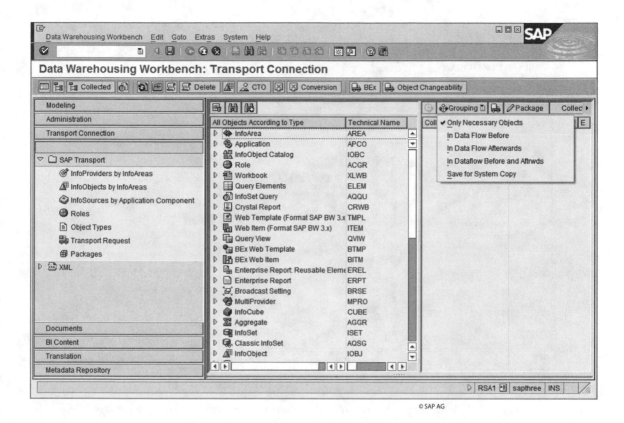

© SAP AG

Figure C–6

Grouping of BW objects for the transport

In particular, with the compilation of transport requests, the following need to be considered:

■ Objects related to source systems
■ BEx objects

If BW objects are compiled in the transport connection that (or whose dependent BW objects) are related to source systems (e.g., through the definition of transfer rules from a source system DataSource), it is often desired that only certain source systems are considered (e.g., since the compilation of BW objects would otherwise be very runtime intense or since some source systems are not created in the target system yet).

Objects related to source systems

For this reason, it needs to be explicitly defined for each source system whether it is to be considered for source system references. For this purpose, there is a specific dialog in the transport connection where the consideration of source system references can be activated (see figure C–7).

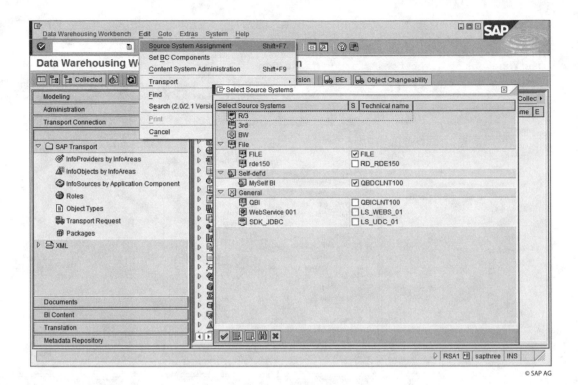

© SAP AG

Figure C–7
Assignment of source systems

For each newly created source system, the source system assignment is deactivated at first and it needs to be activated manually when transports are made.

The activation or deactivation of source system assignments is made via the user settings. Thus, you can make your own settings without having to discuss them with other developers.

Transport of BEx objects

If BW objects with a transportable transport package are changed, the engineering change management is applied and it requires the transport request to which the changed object is to be added.

This mechanism makes sense for BW objects that are changed by developers within the Data Warehousing Workbench. However, this service causes problems with the modification of BEx objects that are often also changed in the development systems by users. Usually, these users do not have any knowledge of the transport system.

Due to this problem, there is a particular enhancement to the engineering change management for BEx objects. Within a transport connection, a central transport request can be created for BEx objects (BEx request). All BEx objects are automatically written into this BEx request where usually a transport request would be required. The user is not made aware of this procedure.

> If several users can change BEx objects, the agreement on the execution of transports is usually very difficult. You should thus define fixed transport intervals (e.g., daily) where you release and transport the BEx request. Immediately after the release, a new BEx request needs to be created.

Figure C–8

Creation of a transport request for BEx objects

The creation of a BEx request can be made in the transport connection via the menu item *Edit→Transport→Transport Request BEx* (see figure C–8).

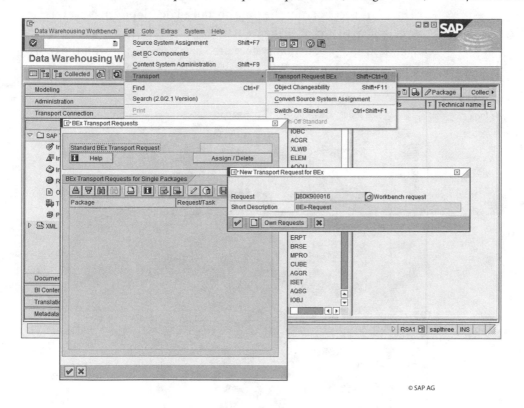

© SAP AG

Transport packages are used to structure objects. This often serves the purpose to compile objects with their different transport packages in separate transport requests.

If only one transport request was created for all BEx objects as described earlier, all objects (i.e., also objects with different transport packages) would

BEx requests for different transport packages

be compiled in the same transport request. If this is not to happen, for certain transport packages an individual BEx request can be created.

C.1.2   Changeability of Source System Assignments in the Staging

The majority of all settings that describe the staging in a BW system refer to the metadata of a certain source system (metadata on the transfer structure and DataSources).

It needs to be assumed that the source systems also use a transport landscape and that it is similar to the transport landscape of BW.[234] This means that other logical source systems are connected to the BW development system instead of to the productive BW system.

Thus, it is necessary for the transport of all developments that refer to a source system to exchange the source system so that the respective development, test, and production system are always converted with the transport. Figure C–9 shows the necessity of this changeability.

Figure C–9

Changeability of logical system names with transport

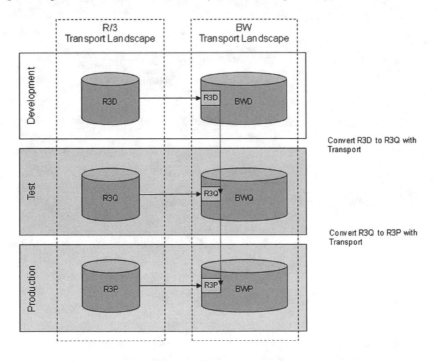

---

234. Source systems of the type flat file are an exception since their data source (the file name) is only determined with the definition of the load processes.

The logical system name is always changed after the transport to the target system.[235] It needs to be stored in this system how the source systems are to be called after the transport. The required setting needs to be made manually in the respective BW system via the transaction RSLGMP or in the transport connection via the menu item *Edit→Transport→Convert Source System Assignment* (see figure C–10).

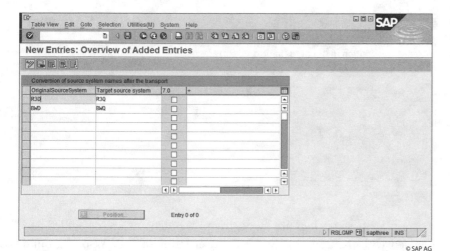

Figure C–10

Definition of changeability of logical system names

© SAP AG

The figure shows a test system that uses the source systems R3Q and BWQ. In the development system, these source systems are called R3D or BWD, respectively, and they are correspondingly changed with the transport to the test system.

The change in source system assignments is made only for references that are obvious from the staging. Systems that are named in process chains (e.g., to call a remote process chain or to asynchronously call ABAP programs) are not considered with this change. Such assignments to other systems need to be manually adjusted in the test and production system.

C.1.3   Transport of Process Chains

As BW objects themselves, process chains are not peculiarities in the BW transport system. However, we should mention that with the transport of a process chain, not only the chain itself is transported and activated in the target system. Instead, the process chain is scheduled and released accord-

---

235. The target system is the system into which a development is transported.

ing to the start options defined in the process chain starter. Process chains that are defined with an immediate start are immediately started after the transport.

A precondition for the scheduling and release of the respective job is the setting that needs to be *made in the target system* in the transaction RSTPRFC (see figure C–11).

Figure C–11
Import settings for the
transport of process chains

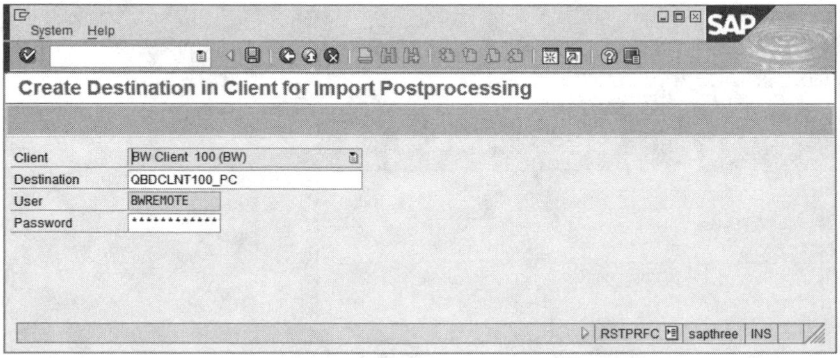

© SAP AG

As soon as these settings are made, the process chains are scheduled and released with the transport under the user name of the BW background user (see section 15.1.1). What scheduling options make sense is explained in section 28.3.1.

If this setting is not made, the start option is not completely transported and the process chain can only be scheduled in the target system by a redefinition of the start conditions and a reactivation of the process chain. This does not make much sense, but it can be done if the system changeability of process chains is enabled (see appendix C.1.5).

C.1.4   Transports in Large-Scale Architectures

A closer consideration of the transport landscape is relevant for large-scale architectures. In this specific connection, this applies to each architecture that has more than one production BW system.

With the use of several production BW systems, you'll often see a request to "share" the respective development systems and possibly even the test systems in order to save the cost of further development systems. A central development system is used to create developments for several production systems. Developments are either transported to all production systems or to the respective systems for which they were made.

However, apart from the advantage of reduced hardware cost, a range of disadvantages need to be considered:

- The operation of a joint development system needs to fit into the organizational structure of the company. If the production systems are run by different business divisions, then the joint development system will soon cause political quarrels.
- The sharing of the development system also results in the fact that more project teams than usual develop on a system. There is a danger that project teams will obstruct each other or even destroy each other's work.
- It requires effort to identify joint developments that are to be implemented in all production systems. And developments that are specifically created for certain production systems need to be separated. This is a problem especially if the joint developments are subject to specific modifications.

These aspects result in significant organizational disadvantages from the use of a joint development system; they are clear arguments against mere cost considerations. A general recommendation cannot be given.

Specifically in the BW transport landscape, there is another difficulty besides the organizational disadvantages.

In the most cases where BW systems are used, data is exchanged between systems (e.g., in a hub-and-spoke architecture). This includes master data as well as transactional data.

Communication between live systems

The data exchange requires that one BW system is defined as a source system in a production system. In order to enable a system to refer to another system, a corresponding definition needs to be made in the other source system. Figure C–12 clarifies this connection.

To enable a data exchange between production systems, it is necessary that a data exchange between the corresponding development systems can be defined. However, it is not enough to define the data exchange; the respective source system needs to physically available!

> The sharing of a joint development system means for the BW system architecture that no data can be exchanged between production systems. This can be avoided only if the communication between these systems is enabled with flat files; however, this requires more development effort.

Figure C–12

Transport landscape in large-scale architectures

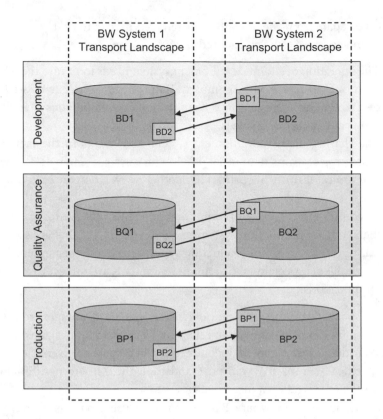

C.1.5   Developments in the Production System

Once a system is defined as a production or live system, it can no longer be changed; i.e., no new objects can be created and no objects can be changed. This applies both to objects of the ABAP dictionary as well as to BW objects.

However, specifically in BW it can make sense for some object types to directly create and maintain the respective objects in the production system. Typical examples are aggregates; the functions of aggregates can only be tested in a very limited way in the development and the test system if no corresponding data volume is given.

Target systems that are stored in process chains to call remote process chains and asynchronous ABAP programs unfortunately need to be adjusted manually in the test and the live system since the transport system does not support such a change yet.

At this point, arguments are given that might support the development on the production system. However, this does not mean that we support the development of objects in a production system. Quite the contrary! Be aware that the development and maintenance of objects in the production system might at first seem tempting due to the shorter development cycles; however, experience shows that this always results in chaotic conditions and unstable system behavior.

Apart from aggregates, there are other object types where arguments for the direct maintenance in the production system could be made. The changeability of these object types in the production system can be set in the transport connection via the menu item *Edit→Transport→Object Changeability* (see figure C–13).

Figure C–13

Changeability of object types in the production system

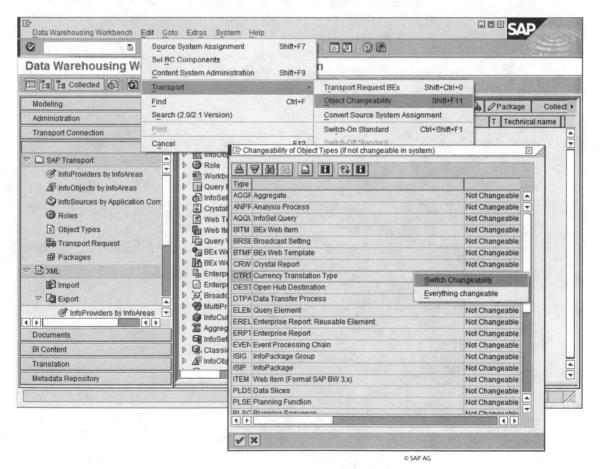

© SAP AG

There are three options:

- **Everything Changeable:** All objects of the respective type are changeable.
- **Not Changeable:** No object is changeable.
- **Originals Changeable:** New objects can be created and changed. Objects that originate from the development system cannot be changed.

C.1.6   Creation of Source Systems

In BW, the creation of source systems corresponds with a repository change that cannot be transported and that is to be made in the respective BW system directly. This also applies to the production system where with each creation of a source system some settings need to be enabled in the system change options. The starting point for setting the system options is the program *Administration→Set System Change Option* of the transport organizer tools that can be called via the transaction SE03. Figure C–14 shows the start of this program.

Figure C–14

Set system changeability

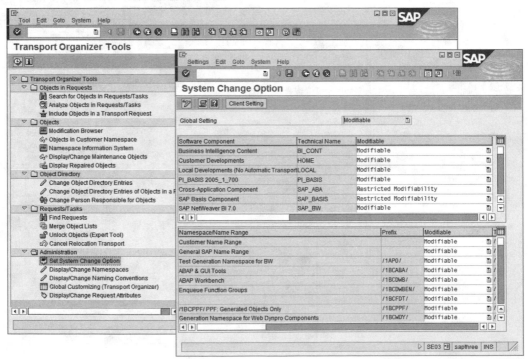

© SAP AG

To create new source systems, the following needs to be permitted:

- Changes to software components and name ranges
- Customer-independent customizing
- Repository changes

The following changes are to be permitted in the system changeability for software components and name ranges:

Changes to software components and name ranges

- Local developments
- Business information warehouse
- Changes to customer name ranges
- Changes in the BW name ranges /BIO/
- Changes in the BW name ranges /BIC/

In addition, changes to cross-client objects are to be permitted by selecting the individual client and making the respective settings via the *Client Settings* button. Figure C–15 clarifies this procedure.

Customer-independent customizing and repository changes

Figure C–15
Allow customizing of cross-client objects

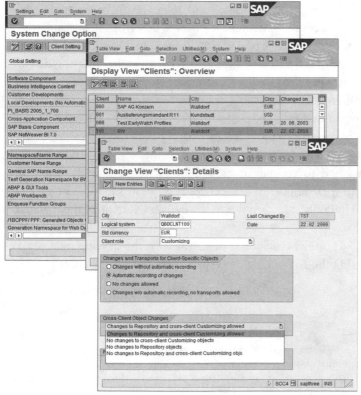

© SAP AG

C.2   Content Transport System

With the explanation of namespaces for objects of the ABAP Dictionary as well as for BW objects, we showed you how the preparation of central developments for decentralized BW systems can make sense (see sections 4.2.4 and 4.3.1, respectively). Examples are companies where developments from one central BW system are to be migrated to several decentrally organized BW development systems. It is also interesting for SAP system vendors to prepare proprietary developments for their customers.

Regarding the "regular" BW transport system, this would mean that transport requests are prepared by central development systems and imported into decentralized BW system or customer systems. Basically, this procedure is technically possible, but even SAP takes another route with the BI content (see appendix D), which gives the decentralized systems more freedom.

The BI content provided by SAP is available in the metadata in a so-called delivery version and can be (but does not need to be) transferred into the active version of metadata, and it can even be customized, if required. The procedure for content transfer is described in appendix D.

In the same way that SAP provides its content in a specific delivery version, it is possible for SAP customers and system vendors to provide content in delivery releases for their decentralized business units or customers. The main difference to the usual transport is that this content can be optionally transferred into and customized in the target system.

For this purpose, BW provides an option to also copy developed BW objects with the saving/activation of metadata into the delivery version of the metadata and to compile it as a delivery version in the transport requests. With their import into a transport request, such BW objects are not activated but only transferred into the delivery version of the metadata at first.[236]

Figure C–16 shows the system behavior with the development of BW objects by using the BW transport system versus using the content transport system.

---

236. Technically, the installation of BI content represents the import of a respective transport request into the delivery version of the metadata. Thus, SAP needed to provide the respective functionality to import delivery versions and not to activate them yet in order to be able to deliver its own BI content.

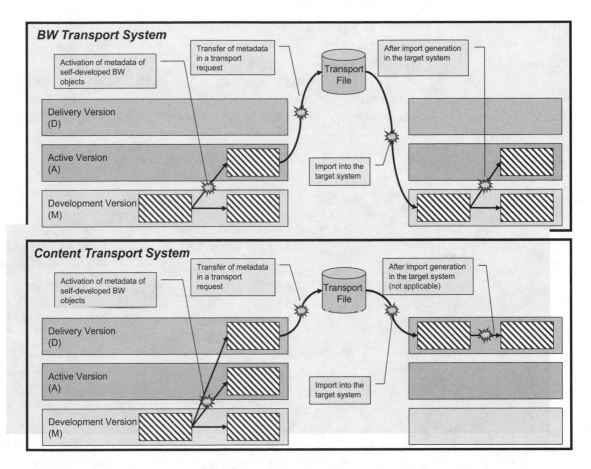

After the import into the target system, the content objects created in the delivery version can be activated and even customized by transfer of the metadata content.

Figure C–16

BW transport system versus the content transport system

We'll explain following topics in the next sections:

- Content development
- Content delivery

The use of the metadata content in the respective target system is explained in appendix D in detail.

C.2.1   Content Development

To develop BW objects in the delivery version and to make them available in transport requests, the respective BW development system needs to be defined as a ***content development system.*** Thus, the use of the content transport system is not subject to the use of certain functions but to a certain status in the overall system.

The respective system status can be defined in the Data Warehousing Workbench in the area of the BI content via the menu item *Edit→Content System Administration* or via the transaction RSOCONTENT (see figure C–17).

Figure C–17

Selection of the system status

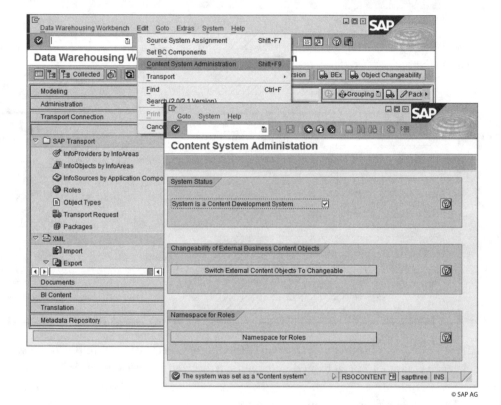

© SAP AG

As soon as a system receives the status of content development system, it reacts differently than a "regular" BW system in terms of metadata maintenance and with the creation of transport requests (see figure C–16).

Accordingly, the status of a BW system that has received content status should never again be revised. Otherwise, self-developed BW objects would in part be contained in the delivery version (and thus also be offered in the BI content) and in part be contained in the active metadata version. Also, transport requests of the system would in part receive the delivery version status of BW objects and in part the active version.

> With the creation of a BW system, you should bindingly and unchangeably
> define whether it is only a regular development system or a content devel-
> opment system. Do not change the status from content to noncontent sys-
> tem and do not play around with the status. The consequence would be
> chaos in the metadata that could only be removed with a lot of effort.

If required, the system status can be overruled by user-specific parameters.
For this purpose, the parameter RSOISCONTENTSYSTEM in the user maintenance should have the value X if the system is to behave for this developer
like a content development system. (see figure C–18).

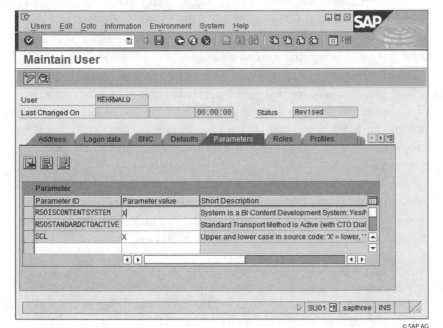

Figure C–18
User-specific selection of the
system status

© SAP AG

For the same reasons that the system status should not be switched from a
content to a noncontent system, you should also avoid making a noncontent development system behave for some developers like a content development system. Here, chaos in the metadata would be asked for, too.

With the development of proprietary metadata content, the question of
how external content (i.e., BW objects in an external name range) can be
dealt with often arises. Often, this question is limited to the SAP BI content; however, it also applies to the metadata content that was supplied by
system vendors.

Use of external content
objects

Basically, external content can be used in the proprietary content development without being changed. For example, the InfoObject OPOSTAL_CD (postal code) can be used as an attribute in proprietary content InfoObjects or the InfoObject OCUSTOMER (customer number) can be used as a reference characteristic for the self-defined partner role.

By the way, these examples also explain why all metadata content is stored in the same delivery version—whether it is self-developed or supplied as SAP BI content; after all, there is no clear separation of different content objects since objects from different content deliveries may refer to each other.

Customizing external content objects

The situation is different if external content is not only used but also needs to be customized. For example, if the InfoObject OCUSTOMER (customer number) from the SAP BI content may need to be reduced by some attributes while some others are to be added.

While the customizing of BW objects from metadata content in "regular" BW development systems comes naturally (after all, it is not the metadata content but only the derived development version or the active version of the BW objects that is being customized), this would result in irrevocable[237] modification of the metadata content in content development systems.

For system vendors that want to transfer proprietary metadata content to their customers, SAP basically bans the modification of content objects. However, SAP customers that want to customize only the delivery version of the BI content for their internal use can do so freely.

Modifications to external content objects can be overwritten with a patch or an upgrade. After you run the patch or the upgrade, these objects need to be manually repaired and resupplied to the decentralized systems. Even if the customizing of external content objects is possible, it results in an immense additional administrative effort.

To enable the customizing of external content objects, the content objects need to be defined in the transaction RSOCONTENT via the *Switch External Content Objects to Changeable* button (see figure C–17).

For this purpose, you name single object types that are changeable. The following properties need to be defined:

237. The change is not completely irrevocable because the delivery transports of the respective content (e.g., BI content from SAP) can be reimported into the system. However, all other changes to the respective metadata content are then revoked.

- External content objects are changeable but are not to be transported with the delivery version of the objects (the "Object Can Be Changed, No CTO Connection" option).
- Changes to external content objects are to be transferred into the transport requests with the transport (the "Object Can Be Changed, Has CTO Connection" option).

By default, the object types that were not named are not changeable. The object types can be defined generically (i.e., with the signs * and ?—see figure C–19).

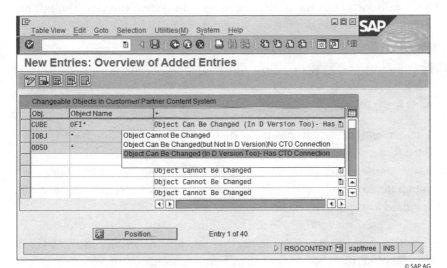

Figure C–19
Change options of external objects in content systems

© SAP AG

Content development systems do not provide any option to transfer objects from the metadata content (see appendix D) since the same objects that are taken over from the content would be rewritten directly into the content. For this reason, the transfer of all required objects from the metadata content should be made before the BW system receives its content development status.

If a subsequent transfer of single content objects becomes necessary in a content development system, then a single user that is to execute the transfer from the metadata content can be provided with user parameters that overrule and deactivate the system status (and possibly the standard transport connection). Similar to the user parameters in figure C–18, for this purpose the parameters RSOISCONTENTSYSTEM and RSOSTANDARDCTO-ACTIVE need to be provided with a blank space as parameter.

C.2.2   Content Delivery

For the creation of transport requests with the delivery version of self-developed BW objects, the content development system as described in the previous section will meet all requirements.

However, the limitation to the content development system can be a problem since transports can be compiled incompletely or with inconsistent development status. In this case, the transfer of metadata content would lead to activation errors in the target system.

To avoid this situation, a separate content test system that is supplied with transports from the content development system can (and should) be used for content development. The content test system has the following purpose:

- To test whether the transfer and activation of objects from the metadata content is error free
- To build delivery transports

Transfer test

The content test system has the status of a content development system; thus, in a sense the content transfer would not be possible. To enable the testing of the content transfer, you need to create a specific user whose user parameters overrule and deactivate the system status (and possibly the standard transport system).

As described in the previous sections this user can be provided as shown in figure C–18 with the user parameters RSOISCONTENTSYSTEM and RSOSTANDARDCTOACTIVE where a blank space is used as parameter.

Building delivery transports

If the transfer of self-developed metadata content was executed successfully, then one or more delivery transports that contain the metadata content can be compiled in the content test system (this time with a regular user whose parameters do not overrule the system status).

Thus, the consolidated metadata content can be transferred into delivery transports. Repeatedly created delivery transports from the content development system can thus be combined in one delivery transport. BW objects that were taken over erroneously in the test transports are not transferred into the delivery transports.

C.3   Metadata in XMI Format

In addition to the exchange mechanisms of the transport system, BW offers an option since release 3.0 to exchange metadata via XML. The XML interface is more an alternative to than a supplement of the transport system, and it has a completely different design. Given its low relevance in practice, the XML interface still needs to be considered as an interesting but unimportant "appendix" to the transport system.

Here, BW uses an XML model that is deduced from the CWM standard,[238] which is the XML metadata interchange (XMI).

Due to the numerous peculiarities of BW, this model does not exactly meet the CWM standard, but it was enhanced with numerous BW-specific elements. In the following, an excerpt of an XMI model that describes the metadata of a BasisCube is shown.

```
<?xml version="1.0" encoding="utf-8"?>
<BWMetadataRepository BWXMLVersion-"1.0">
<com.sap.bw.cwm.olap.InfoCube
ID="ZFIGL_C01">"Metadata for InfoCube ZFIGL_C01
<BWStatistics>
false    "No logging of BW statistics (OLAP)
</BWStatistics>
<BWStatisticsWHM>
false    " No logging of BW statistics (WHM)
</BWStatisticsWHM>
<DBStatisticsOnDeltaLoad>
false    "Database statistics not updated after delta
</DBStatisticsOnDeltaLoad>
<DBStatisticsPercentage>
010      "Database statistics from 10% of the data volume
</DBStatisticsPercentage>
<DBStatisticsRebuild>
false    "Database statistics not updated
</DBStatisticsRebuild>
<aggrDimDataType/>"Standard datatype f. dim-tables of aggregates
<aggrDimSizeCategory/>"Standard size cat. for dim-tables of aggr.
<aggrFactDataType/>"Standard data type for fact tables of aggr.
<aggrFactTableSizeCategory/>"Stnd.size cat. for fact tab. of aggr.
<componentBCT/>"No component of BI content
<compressionNullRemove>
```

---

238. The common warehouse metamodel (CWM) describes a generally applicable model for metadata in a data warehouse. Detailed information on the CWM can be found on the home page of the Object Management Group (OMG) at www.omg.org.

```
true       "Eliminate zero values with compression
</compressionNullRemove>
<contentRelease/>"No version in BI content
<contentTimeStamp>
0          "Time stamp of the BI content version
</contentTimeStamp>
<dimensionDataType/>"Standard data type for dimension tables
<dimensionSizeCategory/>"Standard size cat. for dimension tables
<factTable>
/BIC/FZFIGL_C01"Name of the fact table: /BIC/FZFIGL_C01
</factTable>
<factTableCompressed>
/BIC/EZFIGL_C01"Name of the compressed fact table: /BIC/EZFIGL_C01
</factTableCompressed>
(...)
```

The use of the XMI model instead of the conventional transport system makes sense if no transport routes are defined between the BW systems but metadata still needs to be exchanged. This can especially be the case in large-scale architectures where different test systems are partially to be provided with identical metadata without creating a transport dependency between the developments.

With the standardization of the XMI model for the metadata of data warehouse systems, it is theoretically possible to exchange metadata with other data warehouse systems. However, since the XMI model in BW does not exactly match the OMG model, such an exchange is still unrealistic in practice.

Exporting metadata　　The import or export of metadata in XMI format can be made via the transport connection (see figure C–20).

For the export, the metadata can be stored in file format to subsequently be imported into the target system.

For the export of the complete BW model without the transport connection, the ABAP program RSO_REPOSITORY_EXCHANGE_XML can also be used.

Importing metadata　　Like the export, the import of metadata can be made via a file. In addition, each BW system provides an HTTP service that provides metadata as XML. This HTTP service can be used to import metadata in the same way as via the file (see figure C–21).

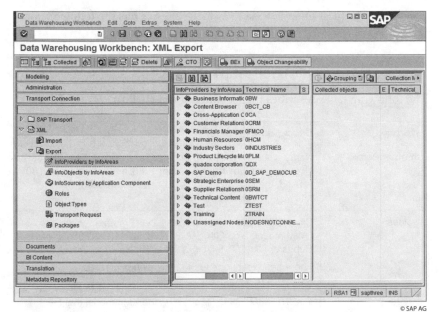

Figure C–20

Metadata exchange as XMI model

Figure C–21

Import of metadata via HTTP service

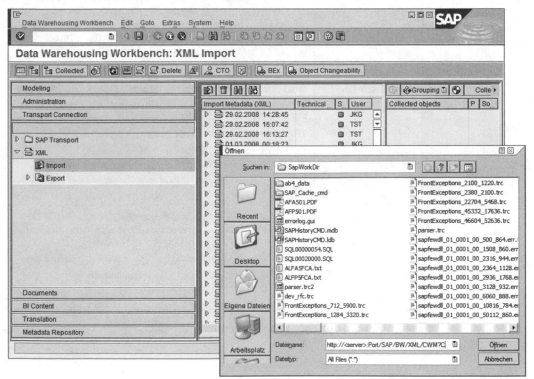

The URL to request metadata via the HTTP service has the following syntax:

```
http://<Server:Port>/SAP/BW/XML/CWM?CLASSID=
<Class>&ID=<Name>&DETAIL=<Detailinfo>&OBJECTVERSION=<Version>
```

The following table describes the wording of the URL.

Wording	Description
<Server:Port>	Name of the server (or IP address) and port of the HTTP service, e.g., http://qx4.quadox.com:1080. If the standard port 80 is used, the indication of the port can be dropped: http://qx4.quadox.com.
<Class>	Class of the BW object that classifies the object within the CWM model, e.g., COM.SAP.BW.CWM.OLAP.INFOCUBE for InfoCubes or COM.SAP.BW.CWM.CORE.INFOOBJECT for InfoObjects. There are exceptions to the indication of classes: CLASSID=LIST: Requesting all BW objects (cross-class). CLASSID=METAMODEL: Requesting the XML model that the metadata are based on.
<Name>	Technical name of the requested BW object within the class that specifies the object type, e.g. 0FIGL_C01 for the InfoCube 0FIGL_C01 within the class COM.SAP.BW.CWM.OLAP.INFOCUBE or 0CUSTOMER for the InfoObject 0CUSTOMER within the class COM.SAP.BW.CWM.CORE.INFOOBJECT.
<Detailed Info>	Indication on whether only the header of the object (class of the BW object, technical name, and date of last change) or the metadata of the InfoObject is requested. The request of metadata (DETAIL=X) is a precondition for the exchange with other systems. The request of the header (DETAIL=) makes sense only if (e.g., for test purposes) an overview on several BW objects is to be given.
<Version>	Version of the metadata in the repository (see section 4.3). Usually, the active versions of the BW objects in the metadata repository are of interest (OBJECTVERSION=A). Objects of the BI content (OBJECTVERSION=D) or updated versions (OBJECTVERSION=M) can be requested too.

For example, to request the metadata of the InfoObject 0CUSTOMER from the server qx4.quadox.com in a targeted way, the URL

```
http://qx4.quadox.com/sap/bw/xml/cwm?classid=
COM.SAP.BW.CWM.CORE.INFOOBJECT&id=0CUSTOMER&detail=
X&objectversion=A((ZENTRIERT))
```

can be used (see figure C–22).

Figure C–22

XMI model for InfoObjects

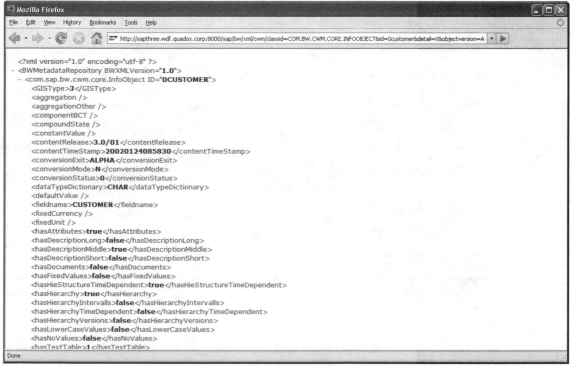

© SAP AG

To get an overview on active metadata of all BW objects, the URL

```
http://qx4.quadox.com/sap/bw/xml/cwm?classid=
LIST&id=&detail=&objectversion=A
```

can be used (see figure C–23).

Figure C–23

XMI model for all BW objects

D   Use of Metadata Content

In the metadata repository of SAP BW, BW objects can be stored in a so-called delivery version (see section 4.3). Here, the respective BW objects are available in the BW metadata repository; however, at first they do not show any active version and thus they form no objects in the ABAP Dictionary or in the database system.

Such BW objects can be provided by system vendors in the metadata repository and they can map predefined scenarios for business processes. Such objects are usually called **metadata content.** How the content development is made is described in appendix C.2.

SAP itself provides very comprehensive metadata content for very different business processes and applications and calls it BI content. It contains the definition of all BW objects that are relevant for a business process from the extraction via InfoObjects and staging definitions up to predefined analysis applications.

Thus, the BI content is split into two areas:

- BI content of SAP ERP source systems
- BI content of BW

The following two sections focus on the BI content of SAP and describe how the delivery versions of the metadata in a SAP ERP system or in the BW system can be transferred into the active data.

In addition, the appendices D.2.1 and D.2.2 describe two areas of the BW content that might be particularly interesting, the **demo content** and the **technical content.**

D.1   BI Content of the SAP ERP Source Systems

The BI content for SAP ERP source systems is part of the plug-ins that provide the technical basis for the extraction. In BW systems (they can be connected to another BW system as a source system too), the BI content is a fixed component of the system and does not need to be subsequently installed via plug-ins. For other source systems (e.g., SAP R/3 prior to version 3.0D, other OLTP systems), there is no BI content to support the extraction.

Before the use of the BI content, the individual components of the BI content need to be activated. For new DataSources of BW 7, the activation is made with the content transfer into BW (see appendix D.2); i.e., with the transfer of staging processes from the BI content, the respective DataSources are implicitly activated in the source systems[239] if the staging is based on new DataSources.

With the use of 3.x DataSources, the activation needs to be made explicitly in the source system. This is done via the implementation guide (IMG) for the extractor, which can be reached both in BW and in SAP ERP via the transaction SBIW (see figure D–1).

Figure D–1
Transfer of BI content
(source systems)

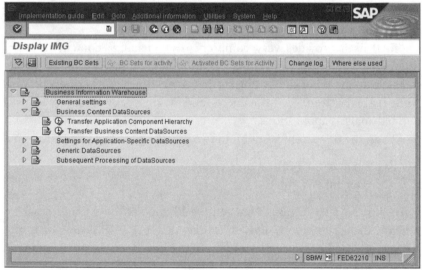

© SAP AG

With the transfer from the metadata that defines the BI content, structures, tables, and programs are generated and used for the extraction of the respective process data.

The transfer of BI content is separated into the transfer of the application component hierarchy and the transfer of DataSources.

---

239. This process is also called remote activation.

The application component hierarchy arranges all DataSources offered by the BI content in a hierarchic tree that is similar to the application component hierarchy in BW. This hierarchy needs to be transferred from the BI content so that the DataSources can later be arranged in the hierarchy with their later transfer.

Transfer of the application component hierarchy

The application component hierarchy can only be transferred from the content as a whole. A transfer of parts is not possible; however, the hierarchy can be modified subsequently (see section 14.2.2).

The transfer of DataSources can be made selectively (see figure D–2).

Transfer of DataSources

Figure D–2

Transfer of DataSources from the BI content (source systems)

© SAP AG

From a business perspective, the transfer of the *complete* BI content has no disadvantages. However, the less BI content transferred, the faster the metadata is transferred into BW and the clearer the administration of the provided DataSources.

After the replication of the metadata of the source system, the transferred DataSources are available in the DataSource tree of the Data Warehousing Workbench and can even be modified and activated (see section 15.2).

D.2   BI Content of BW

The transfer of BI content in BW is made in the same way as the compilation of transport requests. The only difference is that instead of the already active BW objects being compiled in a transport, BW objects are first transferred from the metadata of the BI content and only subsequently compiled in a transport request to transport the content into the target systems.

If objects are transferred from content that is based on the definition of DataSources,[240] then these objects are created for the DataSources of all source systems that are to be considered (see figure C–7). For the new DataSources of BW release 7, this can even contain a remote activation of DataSources in the respective source system. Thus, you need to review at this point whether only a certain source system should be considered specifically for the transfer of BI content.

> It is basically possible to transfer the complete BI content. However, this results in the fact that the navigation in the systems can become very confusing (also for the user) since a large number of unnecessary BW objects exist. Also, the performance might be impacted by the navigation in BW and all administration functions due to the comprehensive metadata. Thus, only transfer parts of the BI content that you are using in the project.

With the transfer of objects from the BI content, a merge with existing objects is made.

Merge with existing BW objects

BW objects that are transferred from the BI content can be customized without any problems. After all, it is not the content version of the metadata that is being changed but the derived active version.

This procedure can cause conflicts with the renewed transfer of BI content if the active version of a content object is not identical to the content version (e.g., since it was customized or a newer version of content is given).

To handle such conflicts, with the transfer of BI content, a merge of the objects to be transferred can be required in some cases[241] (see figure D–3).

---

240. E.g., transformation or transfer rules.
241. A merge is only possible for DataStore Objects, InfoCubes, InfoObjects, InfoObject directories, MultiProviders, DataSources (7.0), process chains, transfer rules, jump target definitions (cube/query), data mining models, and data mining data sources.

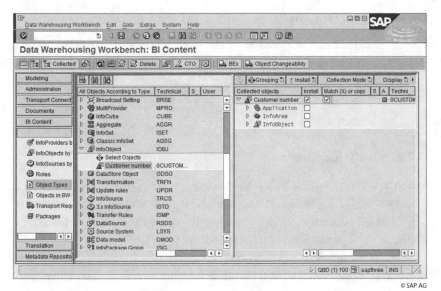

Figure D–3

Merge of objects during transfer (1)

If a merge is required, you need to decide what properties of the content object are to be transferred and what properties of the active object are to remain (see figure D–4).

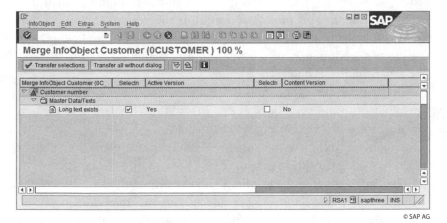

Figure D–4

Merge of objects during transfer (2)

Both the transfer of BI content and the update of content do not necessarily need to result in changes to existing developments.

A peculiarity in the BI content is the InfoObject 0MATERIAL (material number). Before the transfer of the material number, the settings for the material number conversion[242] need to be made via the transaction 0MSL.

InfoObject 0MATERIAL

---

242. Technically, this is the conversion routine MATN1.

D.2.1   Demo Content

For test and training purposes, the *demo content* is provided as part of the BI content. It contains predefined queries and data models and describes the staging from flat files. The required flat files are part of the demo content and can be generated on the application server with the program RSO_BC_FILES_IN_BDS.

D.2.2   Technical Content

When we described the analytical engine, we explained how times and data volume of processes in the analytical and staging engines can be logged in the runtime statistics. Based on these logs, it is possible to deduce bottlenecks or possible problems (see section 13.2).

For a clear analysis of the logged data, BW provides technical content that extracts the raw data from runtime statistics of one or several BW systems, transfers them into InfoProviders, and provides them as web templates and in predefined analyses.

The analyses provided by the queries or the web templates can be used and enhanced with individual analyses. In addition, BW offers a predefined solution that merges web templates of the technical content in a portal application. This portal application is the administration cockpit, which is supplied with the workset BI administration 1.0 (see figure D–5). The use of the administration cockpit is optional and not required to analyze data from the technical content.

The analysis of runtime statistics enables a long-term view on the system behavior over several days/weeks. In addition, the technical content contains analyses of the current system status.

Parts of the technical content are DataSources for extraction, objects within BW, and elements in the portal.

Extraction of runtime statistics
The DataSources in the technical content extract the log tables of the analytical engine and the staging engine and provide them for extraction. Further, the technical content comprises content master data DataSources for the metadata of the system (mostly texts, e.g., names of InfoProviders, InfoSources, users, etc.)

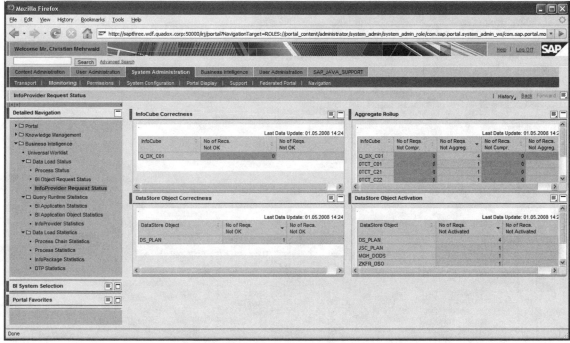

At first, it might seem strange that BW needs to extract data from itself—after all, the required data exists already. The reason is that the data is treated in the same way as all other data in BW. However, it is particularly charming that the runtime statistics and metadata are not to be processed in the same BW system but that they can be transferred to another BW system that centrally prepares the technical content for all available BW systems.

Figure D–5
Administration cockpit

The DataSources of the technical content can be recognized from their prefix 0TCT (see figure D–6). The DataSources with the prefix 0BWTC are part of the technical content up to release 3.x and they are no longer used in BW 7.

Within BW, the technical content is created with BW objects that map the job of the extracted runtime statistics from the extraction up to the storage and analysis. Inconsequently, these objects of the (new) technical content are completely developed based on the old staging of release 3.x. Instead of transformation and data transfer processes, transfer roles, 3.x InfoSources, and update rules are used. InfoPackages for transactional data not only extract data from the PSA, they also enter it directly into the data targets. The web templates are provided in old object structures too.

BW objects of the technical content

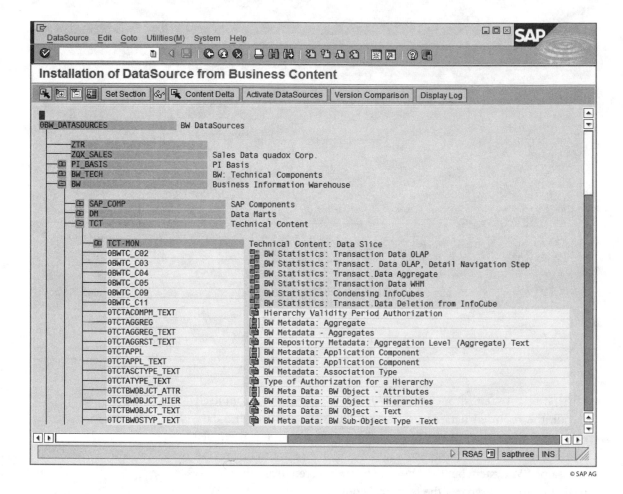

Figure D–6
DataSources of the technical content

From the data analysis perspective, a range of MultiProviders forms the core component of the technical content (see figure D–7).

Each MultiProvider of the technical content accesses, depending on the definition of a query, one of two InfoCubes each. One of these Info-Cubes is a BasisCube into which the runtime statistics are transferred. The other InfoCube is a virtual InfoCube that reads the data of the DataSources via direct access. Additionally, the queries and web templates of the technical content receive their data from the BasisCubes. The following table shows these web templates (in BW 3.x format).

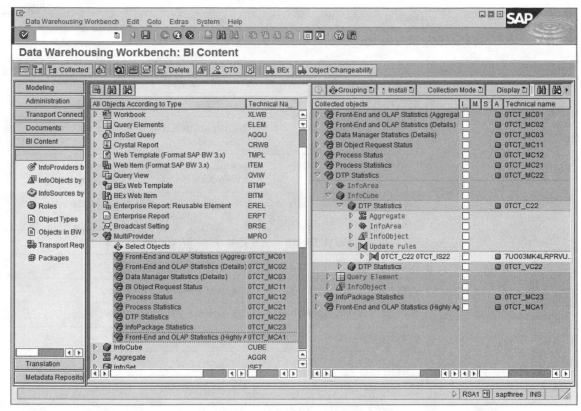

© SAP AG

Figure D–7

BW objects of the technical content

Web Template (BW 3.x)	Description
Higher aggregated query runtime statistics	
0TPLI_0TCT_MC01_Q0111	Runtimes of BI applications
0TPLI_0TCT_MC01_Q0112	Deviations in runtimes of BI applications
0TPLI_0TCT_MC01_Q0113	Short-term trends in overall runtimes of BI applications
0TPLI_0TCT_MC01_Q0114	Long-term trends in overall runtimes of BI applications
0TPLI_0TCT_MC01_Q0121	Runtimes of BI application objects
0TPLI_0TCT_MC01_Q0122	Deviations in runtimes of BI application objects
0TPLI_0TCT_MC01_Q0123	Short-term trends in overall runtimes of BI application objects

Web Template (BW 3.x)	Description
0TPLI_0TCT_MC01_Q0124	Long-term trends in overall runtimes of BI application objects
0TPLI_0TCT_MC01_Q0131	Runtimes of InfoProviders
0TPLI_0TCT_MC01_Q0132	Deviations in runtimes of InfoProviders
0TPLI_0TCT_MC01_Q0133	Short-term trends in overall runtimes of InfoProviders
0TPLI_0TCT_MC01_Q0134	Long-term trends in overall runtimes of InfoProviders
Status of loaded requests in InfoProviders, flexible update of InfoObjects and PSA tables	
0TPLI_0TCT_MC11_Q0110	Status of PSA tables
0TPLI_0TCT_MC11_Q0120	Status of master data
0TPLI_0TCT_MC11_Q0130	Status of the DataStore Object
0TPLI_0TCT_MC11_Q0131	Correctness of the DataStore Object
0TPLI_0TCT_MC11_Q0132	Activation of the DataStore Object
0TPLI_0TCT_MC11_Q0140	InfoCube status
0TPLI_0TCT_MC11_Q0141	InfoCube correctness
0TPLI_0TCT_MC11_Q0142	Aggregate rollup
Current data load status of process chains and processes	
0TPLI_0TCT_MC12_Q0100	Status of process chains
0TPLI_0TCT_MC12_Q0110	Process status
Data load statistics of process chains and processes	
0TPLI_0TCT_MC21_Q0101	Overall runtimes of process chains
0TPLI_0TCT_MC21_Q0102	Deviations in overall runtimes of process chains
0TPLI_0TCT_MC21_Q0103	Short-term trends in overall runtimes of process chains
0TPLI_0TCT_MC21_Q0104	Long-term trends in overall runtimes of process chains
0TPLI_0TCT_MC21_Q0111	Overall runtimes of processes
0TPLI_0TCT_MC21_Q0112	Deviations in overall runtimes of processes

Web Template (BW 3.x)	Description
0TPLI_0TCT_MC21_Q0113	Short-term trends in overall runtimes of processes
0TPLI_0TCT_MC21_Q0114	Long-term trends in overall runtimes of processes
Data load statistics of data transfer processes	
0TPLI_0TCT_MC22_Q0101	Overall runtime of DTPs
0TPLI_0TCT_MC22_Q0102	Deviations in overall runtimes of DTPs
0TPLI_0TCT_MC22_Q0103	Short-term trends in overall runtimes of DTPs
0TPLI_0TCT_MC22_Q0104	Long-term trends in overall runtimes of DTPs
Data load statistics of InfoPackages	
0TPLI_0TCT_MC23_Q0101	Overall runtime of InfoPackages
0TPLI_0TCT_MC23_Q0102	Deviations in overall runtimes of InfoPackages
0TPLI_0TCT_MC23_Q0103	Short-term trends in overall runtimes of Info-Packages
0TPLI_0TCT_MC23_Q0104	Long-term trends in overall runtimes of Info-Packages

The InfoCubes for the direct access to the DataSources are mostly used in the expert mode in the transaction ST03, where current analyses on runtime statistics of the analytical engine can be executed.[243]

Content transfer

Part of the technical content are several hundred BW objects whose transfer is difficult and error prone even if collection mechanisms are used for the content transfer. To simplify the transfer, there is the transaction RSTCC_INST_BIAC, which can also be called from the BW implementation guide in the transaction SPRO (see figure D–8).

With the activation of the technical content, DataSources on one hand and BW objects on the other hand are activated. Here, the source system reference to the Myself system is automatically activated, DataSources are replicated, etc.

---

243. The runtime statistics are regularly deleted from the log tables with the use of the technical content. By default, only the logs of the last 14 days are available via direct access (see section 33.6).

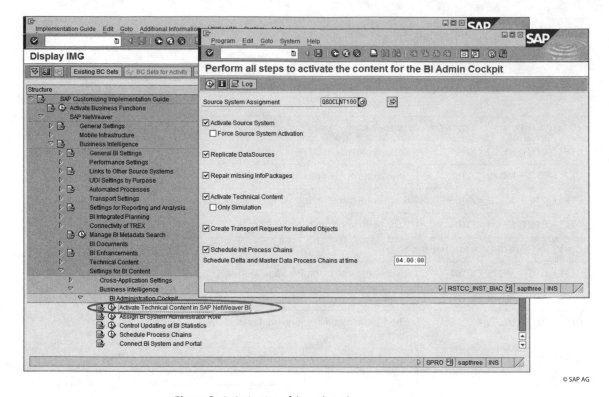

© SAP AG

Figure D–8 *Activation of the technical content*

Direct access

In addition to the automated processes for the activation, the direct access for the virtual InfoProviders of the technical content needs to be activated, and it can be defined whether only the Myself system or even the data from another BW system is to be read in direct access (see figure 22–12 on the activation of the direct access).

Rolling

Further, the role SAP_BW_BI_ADMINISTRATOR (SAP NetWeaver BI Administrator) is to be assigned to all users that are to work directly with the activated web templates.

Controlling

To control the data transfer from the DataSources into the cubes of the technical content, process chains are supplied with the technical content. They can be found in the transaction RSPC under the node RSTCC (Admin Cockpit, see figure D–9).

The process chain 0TCT_MD_S_FULL_P01 (system master data) should be started once. It loads the general master data of the technical content (e.g., texts on procedure types). This master data is unchangeable (subject to new functions in later patch levels) and does not need to be updated.

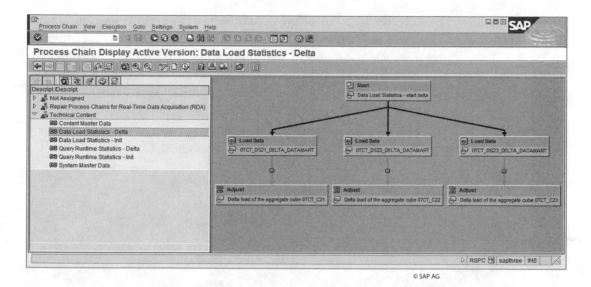

© SAP AG

Also, the process chains OTCT_C2_INIT_P01, OBWTCT_STA_INIT_P01, and OTCT_C0_INIT_P01 are to be started once. They initialize the delta procedure for the extraction of ***data load statistics, Front-end/OLAP Statistics,*** and ***Query Runtimes.***

Figure D–9

Process chains of the technical content

Similarly, for the regular update of delta information, the process chains OTCT_C2_DELTA_P01, OBWTCT_DELTA_INIT_P01, and OTCT_C0_DELTA_P01 need to be scheduled periodically.

Further, the process chain TCT_MD_C_FULL_P01 is to be executed regularly. It transfers master data of the technical content via full extraction. With this process chain, currently[244] only master data attributes and texts or BW objects, process chain variants, and process chains are considered. To load further master data of the technical content (e.g., master data on the users), proprietary controlling mechanisms need to be developed.

Similar to the new structure of runtime statistics, the technical content has been remodeled compared to the technical content of the BW releases up to 3.x. A migration of data from the old model of the technical content is not enabled and not provided.

Migration

The following basically needs to be considered:

■ The BasisCube 0BWTC_C02 (BW statistics—OLAP) does not contain any new data. Instead, all data is transferred into the new cubes OTCT_C01, OTCT_C02, and OTCT_C03.

---

244. Content release 703 (support pack SAPKIBIIP4)

- ■ The BasisCubes 0BWTC_C03 (BW statistics—detailed navigation) and 0BWTC_C05 (BW statistics—WHM) still contain data; however, they do not make use of the full possibilities provided with the new content. It is better to access the new BasisCubes 0TCT_C02 and 0TCT_C23.
- ■ The BasisCubes 0BWTC_C04 (BW statistics—aggregates), 0BWTC_C09 (BW statistics—deletion of data from InfoCube) and 0BWTC_C11 (BW statistics—condensation of InfoCubes) are also fully used in the new technical content.

E Tables

E.1 Lock Logic for Processes

	Archiving	Selective Deletion	Compression	Rollup Aggregates	Build Aggregates	Build Statistics	Delete/Create Indexes	Entry into Cubes	Change Run	Extraction from BasisCubes
Data Analysis	✓	✗	✗	✓	✓	✗	✗	✓	✓	✓
Extraction from BasisCubes	✓	✗	✗	✓	✓	✗	✗	✓	✓	
Change Run	✓	✓	✗	✗	✗	✗	✗	✓		
Entry into Cubes	✗	✗	✗	✓	✓	✗	✗			
Create/Delete Indexes	✗	✗	✗	✗	✗	✗				
Build Statistics	✗	✗	✗	✗	✗					
Build Aggregates	✓	✗[1]	✗	✗						
Rollup Aggregates	✓	✗[2]	✗							
Compression	✗	✗[3]								
Selective Deletion	✓									

1. Request can be deleted that have not been released for reporting, yet (e.g., due to the request status or since the request has not been rolled up into existing aggregates).
2. Requests can be deleted that are not included in the rollup since not all requests are rolled up.
3. Requests that are not included in the compression can be deleted since not all requests are compressed.

E.2   Placeholders

The following table gives an overview on placeholders that can be used for the definition of logical files (see section 15.1.3).

Reserved Word	Replacing Value
<OPSYS>	Operating system as per requirements
<INSTANCE>	Instance of the ERP application
<SYSID>	Name of the ERP system as per SY-SYSID
<DBSYS>	Database system as per SY-DBSYS
<SAPRL>	ERP release as per SY-SAPRL
<HOST>	Host name as per SY-HOST
<CLIENT>	Client as per SY-MANDT
<LANGUAGE>	Sign-on language as per SY-LANGU
<DATE>	Date as per SY-DATUM
<YEAR>	Year as per SY-DATUM, four-digit
<SYEAR>	Year as per SY-DATUM, two-digit
<MONTH>	Month as per SY-DATUM
<DAY>	Day as per SY-DATUM
<WEEKDAY>	Weekday as per SY-FDAYW
<TIME>	Time as per SY-UZEIT
<STIME>	Hour and minute as per SY-UZEIT
<HOUR>	Hour as per SY-UZEIT
<MINUTE>	Minute as per SY-UZEIT
<SECOND>	Second as per SY-UZEIT
<PARAM_1>	External parameter 1
<PARAM_2>	External parameter 2
<PARAM_3>	External parameter 3
<P=name>	Name of the profile parameter (To request all profile parameters, the report RSPARAM can be used.)
<V=name>	Name of a variable

Reserved Word	Replacing Value
<F=name>	Return value of a function module (The function module needs to have an export parameter with the name OUTPUT that is used to transfer the return value to the variable.) Naming convention for this function module: FILENAME_EXIT_*name*

E.3 Properties of Adapters

Source System Type	Adapter	Parser required[1]	No Packaging[2]	Multi-segment-enabled[3]	Extractor splits[4]	Transfer fields only[5]	Direct access only[6]	Real-time only[7]	For push only[8]
ERP and BW	SAPI	✓		✓	✓	✓			
	SAPICRT	✓				✓		✓	
	SAPIDIRECT		✓	✓	✓	✓	✓		
File	BIN_GUI_EX								
	BIN_OPE_EX								
	GUI_UPLOAD	✓		✓					
	OPEN_DS	✓		✓					
DB connect	DBEXTRACT								
UD connect	UDCGEN								
Web Service	WEBS_PUSH			✓		✓			✓

1. Typing of data with the definition of the DataSources required for the task of the data format parser.
2. Method does not allow for packaging during loading.
3. Access method is multisegment enabled.
4. Extractor splits the segments by itself.
5. Extractor only provides fields of the transfer structure.
6. Adapter allowed only for direct access.
7. Adapter provided only for real-time extraction via pull.
8. Adapter provided only for push.

F   Table of Abbreviations

ABAP/4	Advanced Business Application Programming 4GL
ABAP-OO	Advanced Business Application Programming Object Oriented
ABR	After/Before/Reverse
ADD	Additive
ADK	Archiving Development Kit
AIM	After-Image
AIM/AIMD	After-Image/After-Image Delete
ALE	Application Link Enabling
API	Application Programming Interface
APO	Advanced Planner and Optimizer
ASCII	American Standard Code for Information Interchange
BAPI	Business Application Programming Interface
BEx	Business Explorer
BIA	Business Intelligence Accelerator
BLOB	Binary Large Object
BPS	Business Planning and Simulation
BSC	Balanced Scorecard
BSP	Business Server Page
BW	Business Information Warehouse
CATT	Computer Aided Test Tool
CR	Carriage Return
CRM	Customer Relationship Management
CSV	Comma Separated Variables
CTO	Change and Transport Organizer

CWM	Common Warehouse Metamodel
DDIC	Data Dictionary
DIM ID	Dimension Identification
DSS	Decision Support Systems
DWWB	Data Warehousing Workbench
ERP	Enterprise Resource Planning
ETL	Extraction Transformation Loading
GUI	Graphical User Interface
HTTP	HyperText Transfer Protocol
ICF	Internet Communication Framework
ICM	Internet Communication Manager
IDOC	Intermediate Document
ILM	Information Lifecycle Management
I/O	Input/Output
IP	Internet Protocol
ISO	International Standards Organization
JCo	Java Connector
JRA	Java Resource Adapter
LIS	Logistics Information System
MDC	Multidimensional Clustering
MDX	Multidimensional Expression
MOLAP	Multidimensional OLAP
ODBC	Open Database Connection
ODBO	OLE DB (Object Linking and Embedding Database) for OLAP
ODS	Operational Data Store (Predecessor of DataStore Objects)
OLAP	Online Analytical Processing
OLTP	Online Transaction Processing
OMG	Object Management Group
PSA	Persistent Staging Area

PTS	Pivot Table Service
RDA	Real-Time Data Acquisition
RFC	Remote Function Call
ROLAP	Relational OLAP
RRI	Report-Report-Interface (= BBS)
SCM	Supply Chain Management
SEM	Strategic Enterprise Management
SID	Masterdata Identification
SNC	Secure Network Communication
SOAP	Simple Object Access Protocol
SQL	Structured Query Language
TCP	Transport Control Protocol
TRFC	Transactional Remote Function Call
UDC	Universal Data Connect
UDI	Universal Data Interchange
URL	Uniform Resource Locator
VBA	Visual Basic
WAN	Wide Area Network
XI	eXchange Infrastructure
XMI	XML Metadata Interchange
XML	Extensible Markup Language
XML/A	XML for Analysis

Index

Klaus Hoermann
Markus Mueller
Lars Dittmann
Joerg Zimmer

Automotive SPICE in Practice

Surviving Interpretation and Assessment

Automotive SPICE is a framework for designing and assessing software development processes. Today, Automotive SPICE has become a standard in the international automotive industry.

This book is written as a guide to help the reader understand and interpret the requirements of this standard and to implement Automotive SPICE in a real world application environment. It is written for engineers, practitioners, managers, and project managers who need practical guidance in applying or implementing the Automotive SPICE framework in their company, and for any assessor looking for clear, consistent, and constructive rating guidelines. Important topics, such as traceability, functional safety (IEC 61508), and the relationship between Automotive SPICE and CMMI are given particular attention.

1st edition, 2008
312 pages
Price: US $ 54.95, CAN $ 54.95
ISBN 978-1-933952-29-1

rockynook

26 West Mission Street, Suite 3
Santa Barbara, CA 93101

phone 1-805-687-8727
www.rockynook.com

Judy McKay

Managing the Test People

A Guide to Practical Technical Management

Managing the Test People was written for managers, leads, and those who may soon find themselves in a technical leadership position. It focuses on some of the unique problems in the software quality assurance profession, yet the bulk of the book is applicable to any technical management job. In this book you will find practical advice for the novice and affirmation for the expert. Written from a practitioner's viewpoint, it contains real world stories illustrating the concepts discussed in the text.

Author Judy McKay has been in software management for over 20 years, working in a variety of companies. Managing the Test People is real – it's about the real world where there are real problems and real people, and it provides viable solutions that can actually be implemented.

1st edition, 2007
200 pages
Price: US $ 39.95, CAN $ 51.95
ISBN 978-1-933952-12-3

rockynook

26 West Mission Street, Suite 3
Santa Barbara, CA 93101

phone 1-805-687-8727
www.rockynook.com

2nd edition, 2007
288 pages
Price: US $ 44.95, CAN $ 58.95
ISBN 978-1-933952-08-6

Andreas Spillner · Tilo Linz ·
Hans Schaefer

Software Testing Foundations

A Study Guide for the Certified
Tester Exam

Professional testing of software has
become an increasingly important task,
which requires a profound knowledge
of testing techniques. Recently, an
internationally recognized certification
program has been developed.

This book covers the "Foundations Level" (i.e., entry level), and teaches the
most important methods of software
testing. It is designed for self-study
and provides the necessary knowledge
to pass the "Certified Tester: Foundations Level" exam as defined by the
universally recognized ISTQB.

It also covers more recent topics, such
as test-first approach and risk-based
testing.

rockynook

26 West Mission Street, Suite 3
Santa Barbara, CA 93101

phone 1-805-687-8727
www.rockynook.com

1st edition, 2009
570 pages
Price: US $ 54.95, CAN $ 54.95
ISBN 978-1-933952-36-9

Rex Black
Advanced Software Testing— Vol. 2

Guide to the ISTQB Advanced Certification as an Advanced Test Manager

This book teaches test managers what they need to know to achieve advanced skills in test estimation, test planning, test monitoring, and test control. Readers will learn how to define the overall testing goals and strategies for the systems being tested.

This hands-on, exercise-rich book provides experience with planning, scheduling, and tracking these tasks. You'll be able to describe and organize the necessary activities as well as learn to select, acquire, and assign adequate resources for testing tasks. Learn how to form, organize, and lead testing teams. Master the organizing of communication among the members of the testing teams, and between the testing teams and all the other stakeholders. Additionally, you'll learn how to justify decisions and provide adequate reporting information where applicable.

This book will also help you prepare for the ISTQB Advanced Test Manager exam.

rockynook

26 West Mission Street, Suite 3
Santa Barbara, CA 93101

phone 1-805-687-8727
www.rockynook.com